For the women who made me

Contents

AMY KURZWEIL

FLYING COUCH

A GRAPHIC MEMOIR

Catapult/Black Balloon
New York

Published by Black Balloon, an imprint of Catapult
catapult.co

ISBN: 978-1-936787-28-9

Catapult titles are distributed to the trade by
Publishers Group West
Phone: 800-788-3123

Library of Congress Control Number: 2015955987

Printed in the United States of America

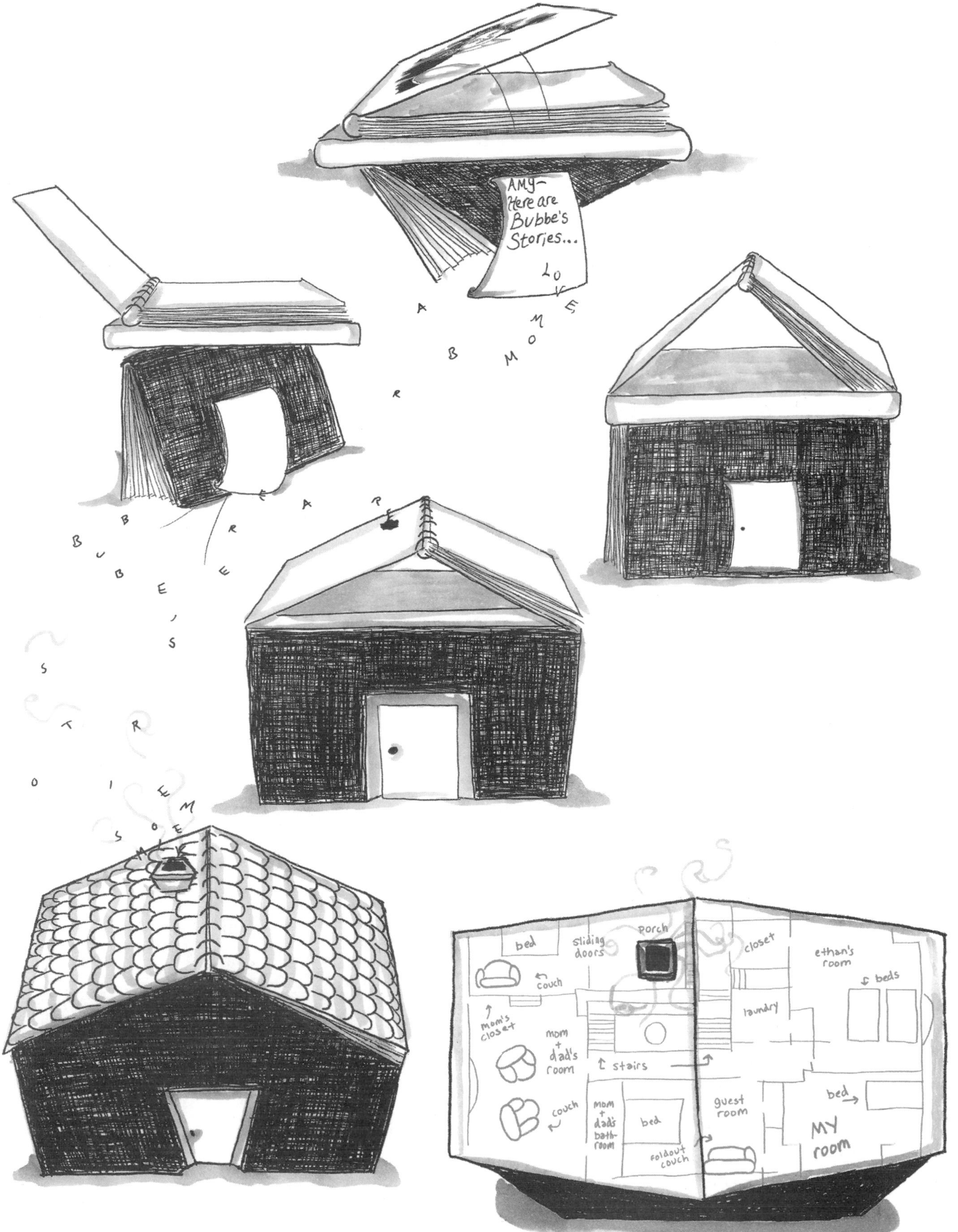
AMY—
Here are
Bubbe's
Stories...
LOVE
bed
sliding
doors
porch
closet
ethan's
room
couch
beds
mom's
closet
laundry
mom
+
dad's
room
stairs
couch
mom
+
dad's
bath-
room
bed
guest
room
bed
foldout
couch
MY
room

Chapter One:
Home Entertainment

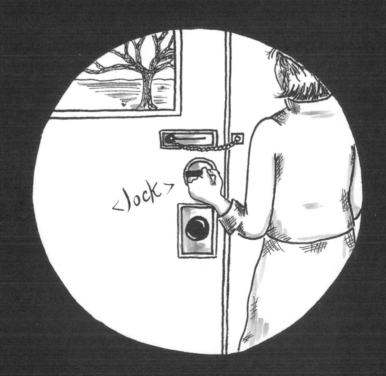

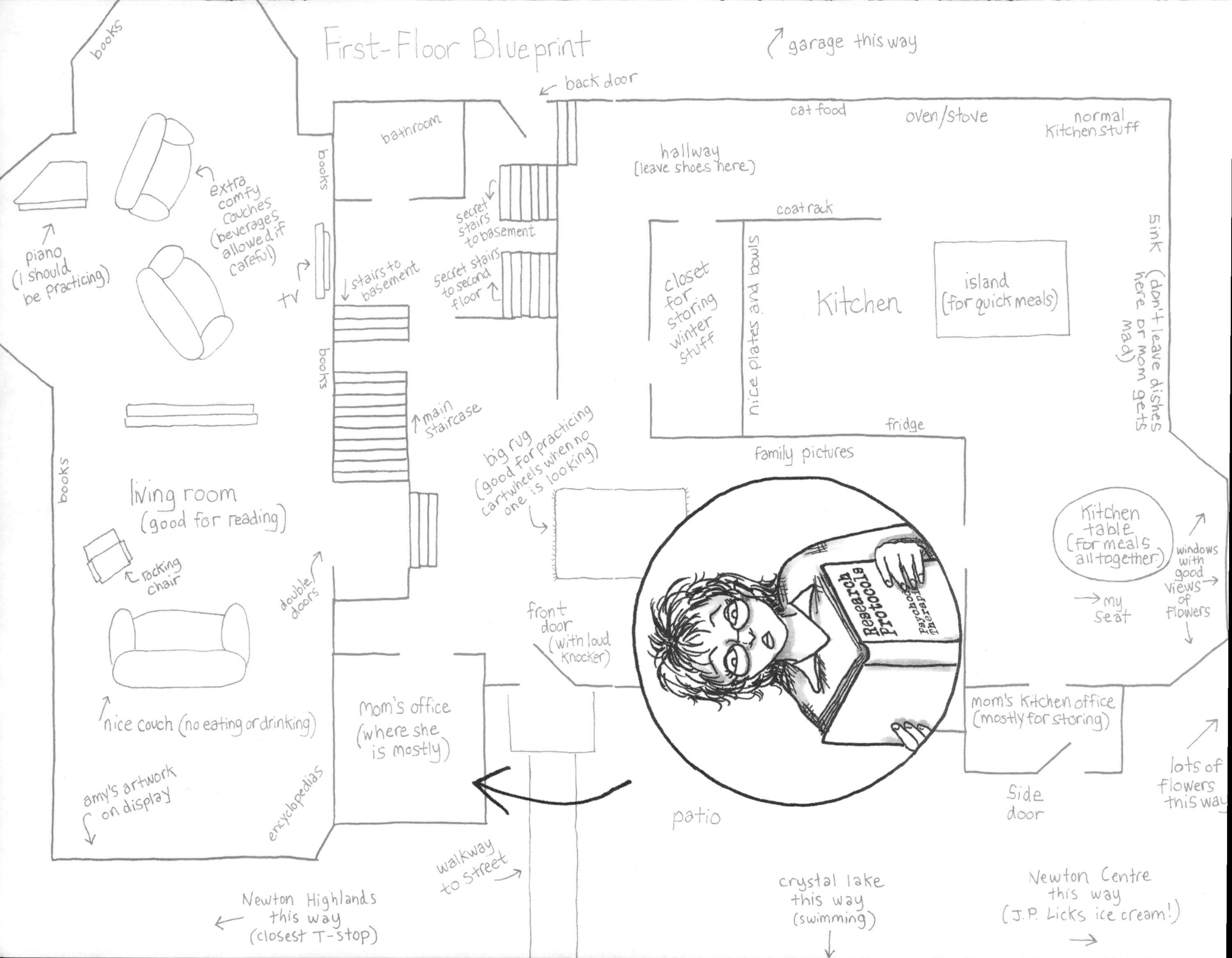
First-Floor Blueprint
garage this way
back door
books
piano (I should be practicing)
extra comfy couches (beverages allowed if careful)
books
tv
bathroom
secret stairs to basement
secret stairs to second floor
stairs to basement
books
main staircase
cat food
oven/stove
normal Kitchen stuff
hallway (leave shoes here)
coat rack
closet for storing winter stuff
nice plates and bowls
Kitchen
island (for quick meals)
sink (don't leave dishes here or mom gets mad)
fridge
family pictures
books
living room (good for reading)
rocking chair
big rug (good for practicing cartwheels when no one is looking)
Kitchen table (for meals all together)
windows with good views of flowers
my seat
double doors
front door (with loud knocker)
Research Protocols
Psychod
Therapi
nice couch (no eating or drinking)
mom's office (where she is mostly)
mom's Kitchen office (mostly for storing)
amy's artwork on display
encyclopedias
patio
side door
lots of flowers this way
walkway to street
Newton Highlands this way (closest T-stop)
crystal lake this way (swimming)
Newton Centre this way (J.P. Licks ice cream!)

Second-Floor Blueprint

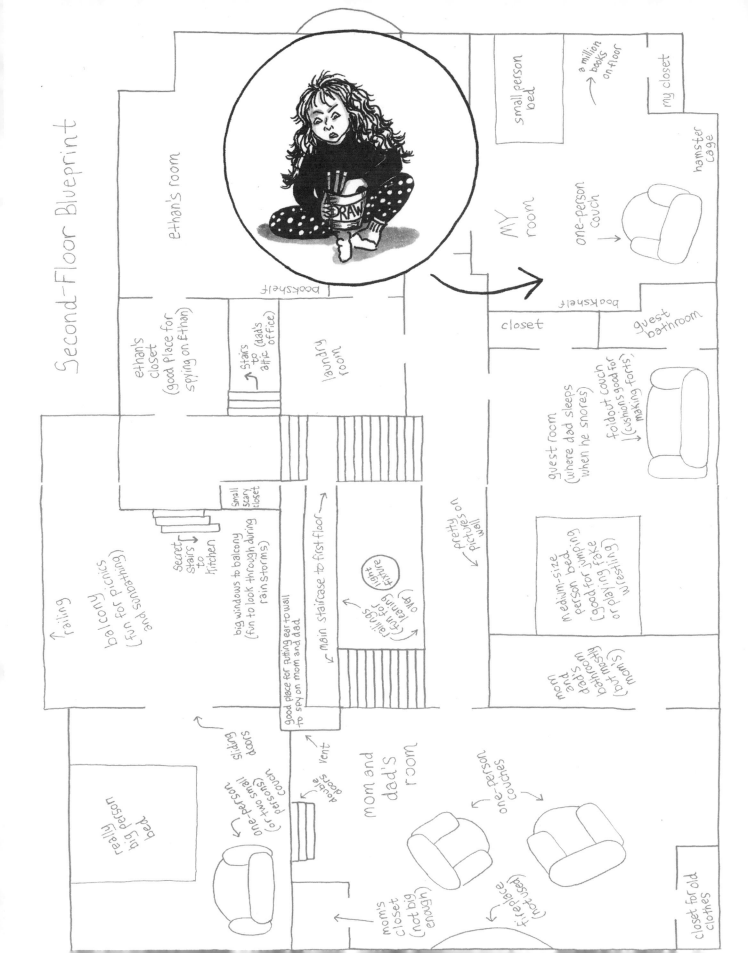

Ethan's room

ethan's closet (good place for spying on Ethan)

↑ Stairs to (dad's attic office)

laundry room

bookshelf

Secret Stairs ↑ to kitchen

Small scary closet

big windows to balcony (fun to look through during rainstorms)

Railing ↑

balcony (fun for picnics and sunbathing)

good place for putting ear to wall to spy on mom and dad

← main staircase to first floor

light fixture (falling or leaning over?)

← pretty pictures on wall

sliding doors ↗

really big person bed

one-person (or two small persons) couch

vent

double doors

mom and dad's room

one-person couches

mom's closet (not big enough)

fireplace (not used)

closet for old clothes

mom and dad's bathroom (mostly mom's)

medium-size person bed (good for jumping or playing fake wrestling)

guest room (where dad sleeps when he snores)

foldout couch (cushions good for making forts)

closet

guest bathroom

bookshelf

MY room

one-person couch

→ a million books on floor

small person bed

my closet

hamster cage

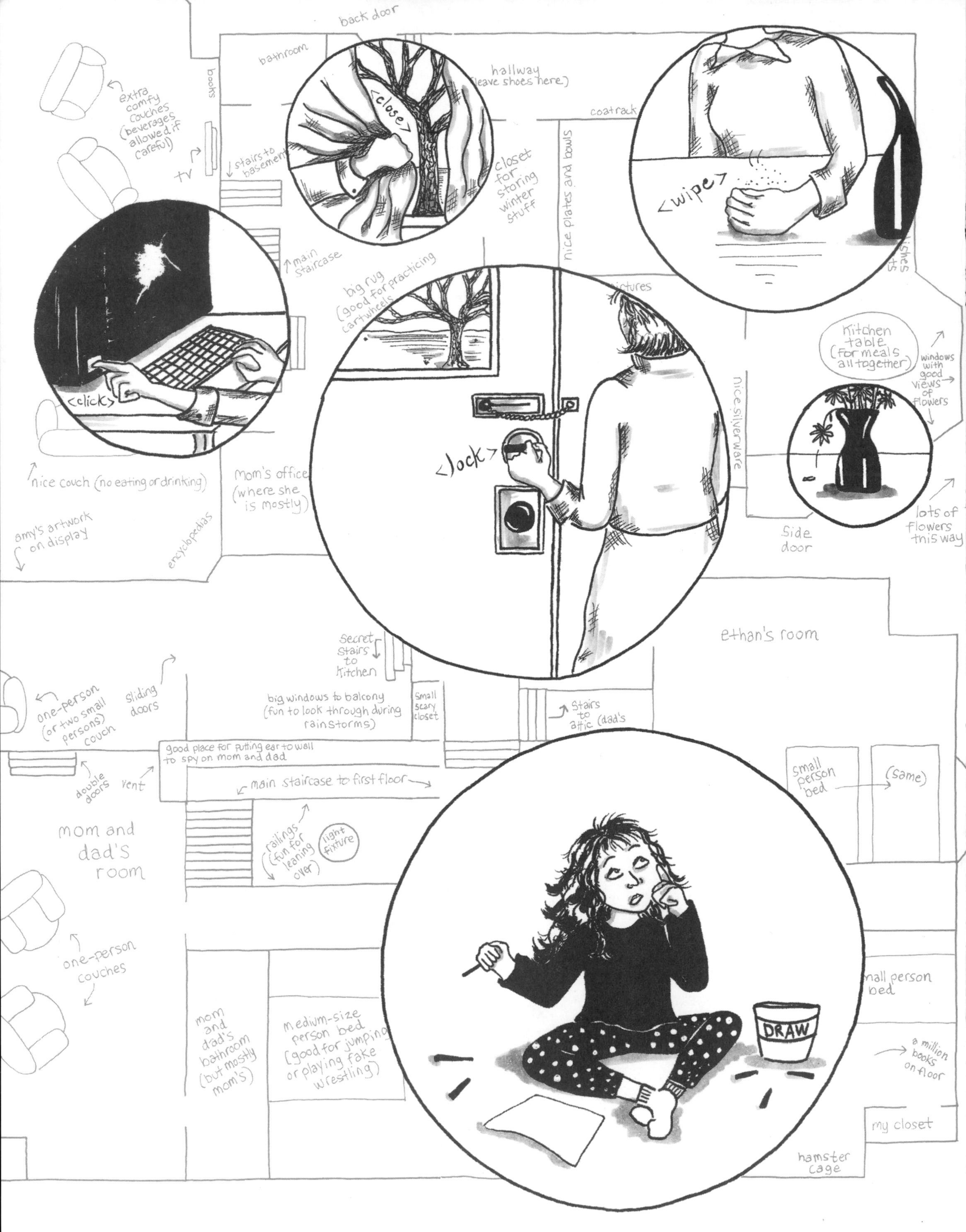
back door
bathroom
books
extra comfy couches (beverages allowed if careful)
tv
stairs to basement
<close>
hallway (leave shoes here)
coatrack
closet for storing winter stuff
nice plates and bowls
<wipe>
main staircase
big rug (good for practicing cartwheels
pictures
<click>
<lock>
Kitchen table (for meals all together)
windows with good views of flowers
nice silverware
nice couch (no eating or drinking)
Mom's office (where she is mostly)
amy's artwork on display
encyclopedias
Side door
lots of flowers this way
ethan's room
secret stairs to kitchen
one-person (or two small persons) couch
sliding doors
big windows to balcony (fun to look through during rainstorms)
small scary closet
stairs to attic (dad's
good place for putting ear to wall to spy on mom and dad
double doors
vent
main staircase to first floor
small person bed
(same)
mom and dad's room
railings (fun for leaning over)
light fixture
one-person couches
mom and dad's bathroom (but mostly mom's)
medium-size person bed (good for jumping or playing fake wrestling)
DRAW
mall person bed
a million books on floor
my closet
hamster cage

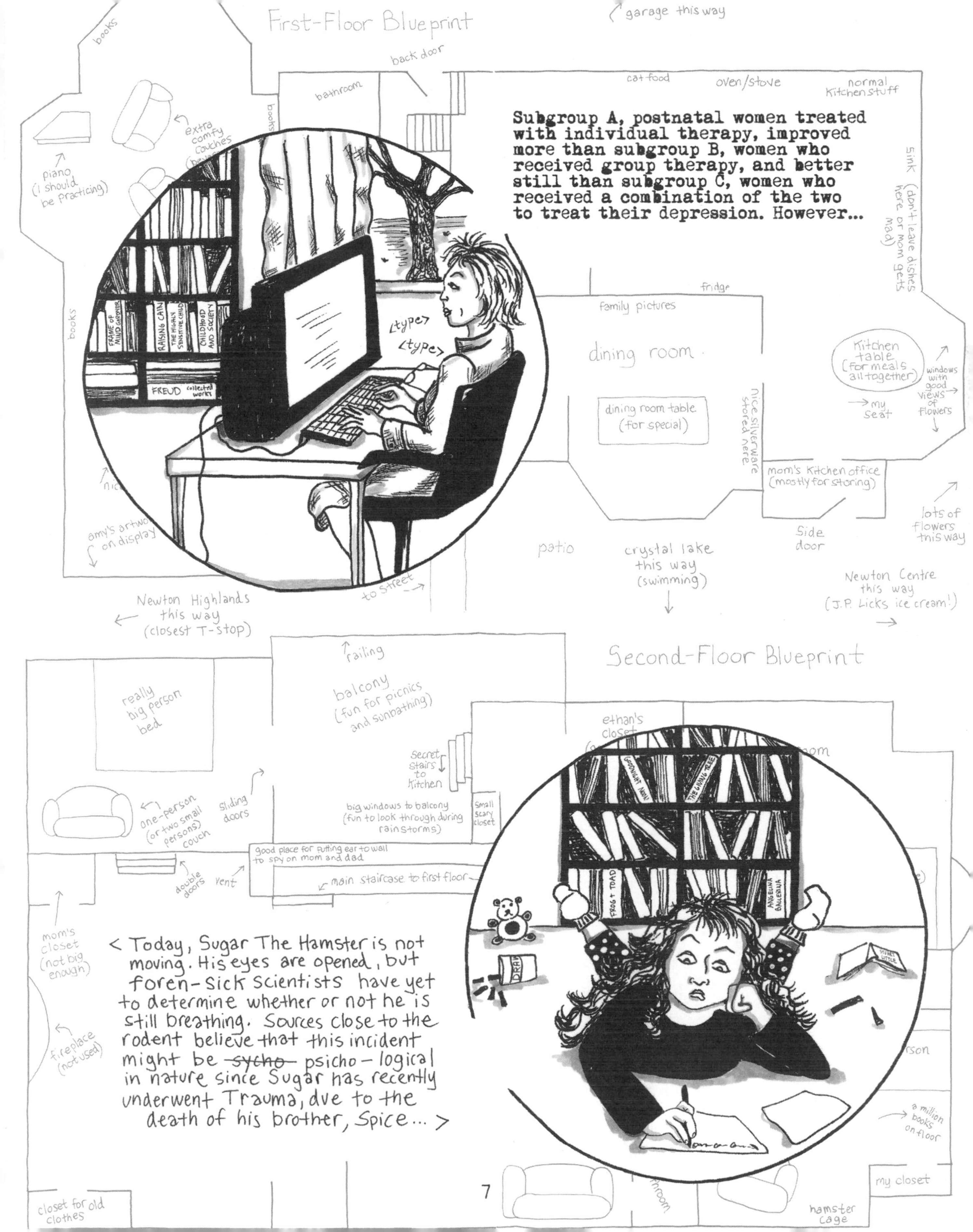

First-Floor Blueprint
garage this way
books
back door
bathroom
books
cat food
oven/stove
normal Kitchen stuff
extra comfy couches
piano (I should be practicing)
Subgroup A, postnatal women treated with individual therapy, improved more than subgroup B, women who received group therapy, and better still than subgroup C, women who received a combination of the two to treat their depression. However...
sink (don't leave dishes here or mom gets mad)
books
FRAME OF MIND GARDNER
RAISING CAIN
THE HIGHLY SENSITIVE CHILD
CHILDHOOD AND SOCIETY
FREUD collected works
<type>
<type>
fridge
family pictures
dining room
Kitchen table (for meals all together)
windows with good views of flowers
my seat
dining room table (for special)
nice silverware stored here
mom's Kitchen office (mostly for storing)
amy's artwork on display
patio
crystal lake this way (swimming)
Side door
lots of flowers this way
to street
Newton Highlands this way (closest T-stop)
Newton Centre this way (J.P. Licks ice cream!)
Second-Floor Blueprint
railing
really big person bed
balcony (fun for picnics and sunbathing)
ethan's closet
Secret stairs to Kitchen
GOODNIGHT MOON
THE GIVING TREE
one-person (or two small persons) couch
sliding doors
big windows to balcony (fun to look through during rainstorms)
Small scary closet
good place for putting ear to wall to spy on mom and dad
double doors
vent
main staircase to first floor
FROG + TOAD
ANGELINA BALLERINA
mom's closet (not big enough)
< Today, Sugar The Hamster is not moving. His eyes are opened, but foren-sick scientists have yet to determine whether or not he is still breathing. Sources close to the rodent believe that this incident might be ~~sycho~~ psicho-logical in nature since Sugar has recently underwent Trauma, dve to the death of his brother, Spice... >
DRAW
STUART LITTLE
fireplace (not used)
a million books on floor
my closet
closet for old clothes
hamster cage

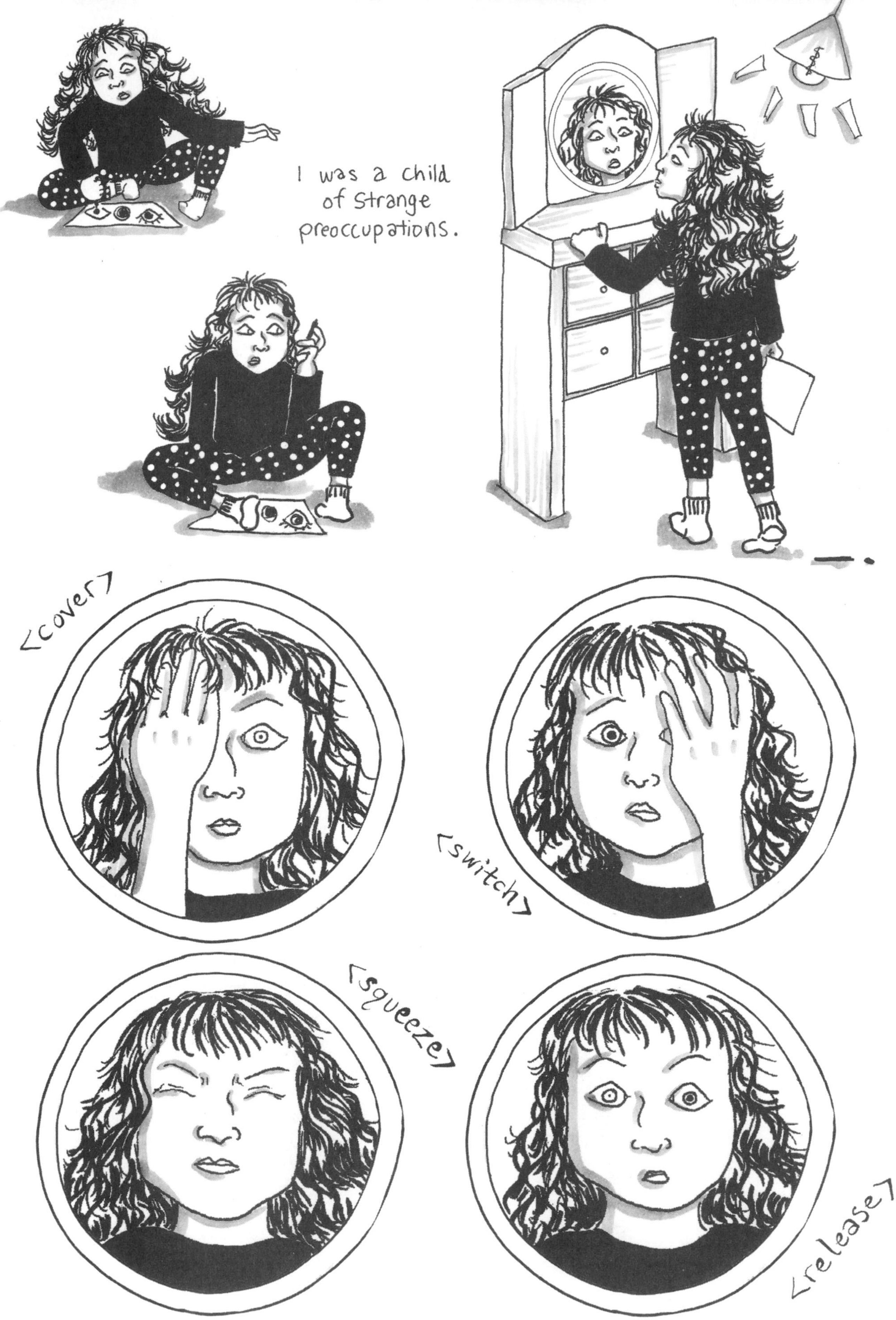
I was a child of strange preoccupations.
<cover>
<switch>
<squeeze>
<release>

This pulsing, oozing blackness at the source of all sight, it terrified me.

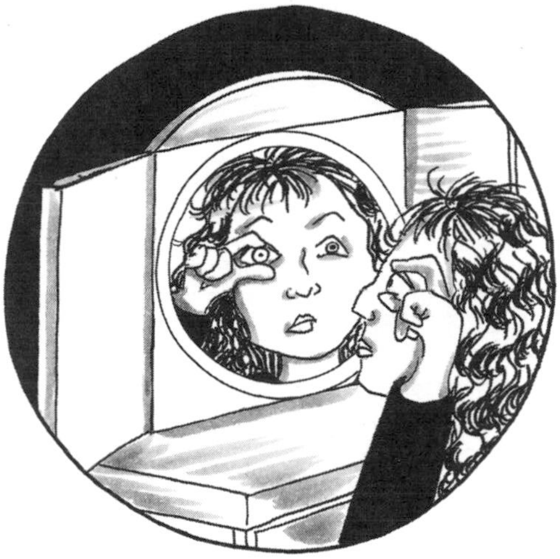

My mother had a respectable amount of patience for my hypochondriacal obsessions, although I suspect she could not relate.

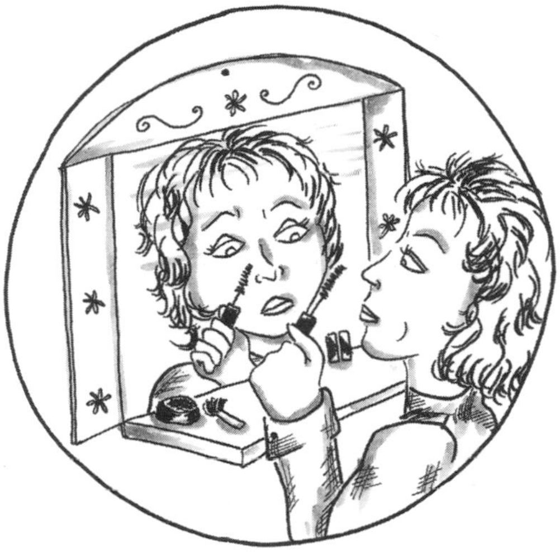

Her preoccupations were different from mine.

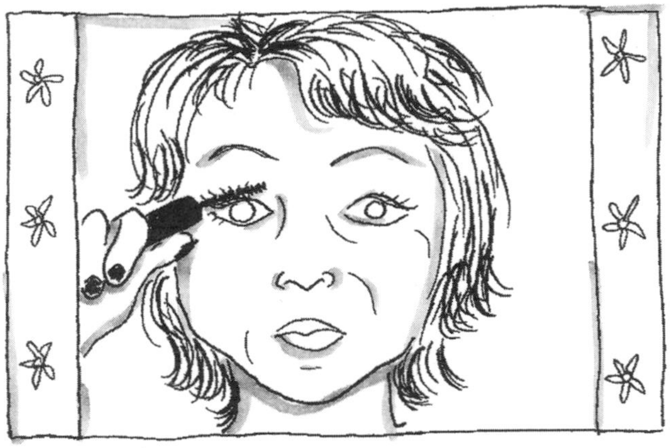

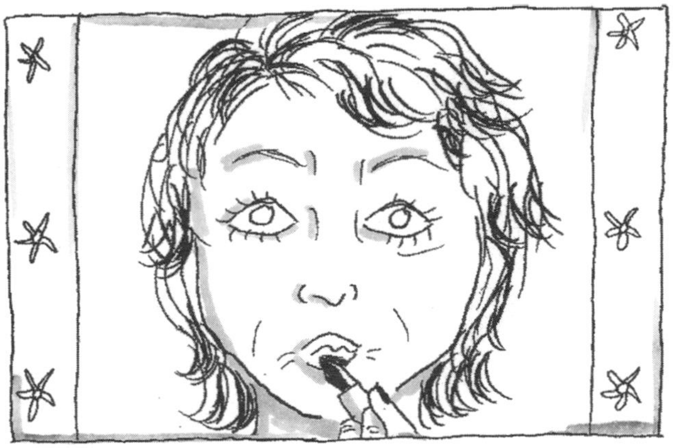

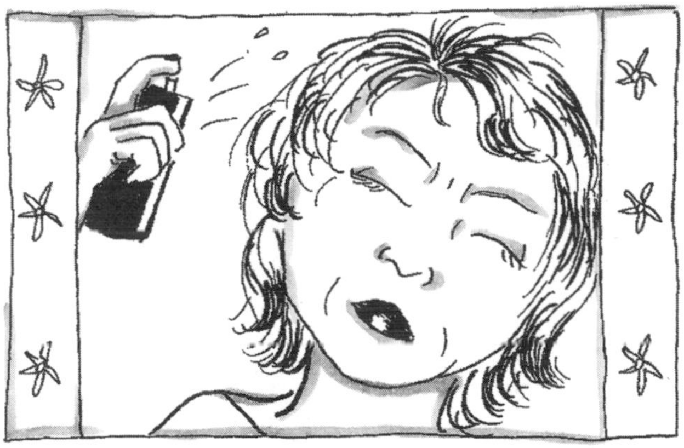

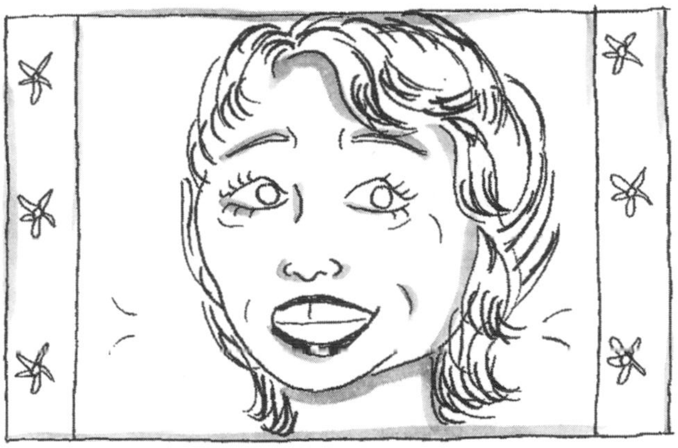

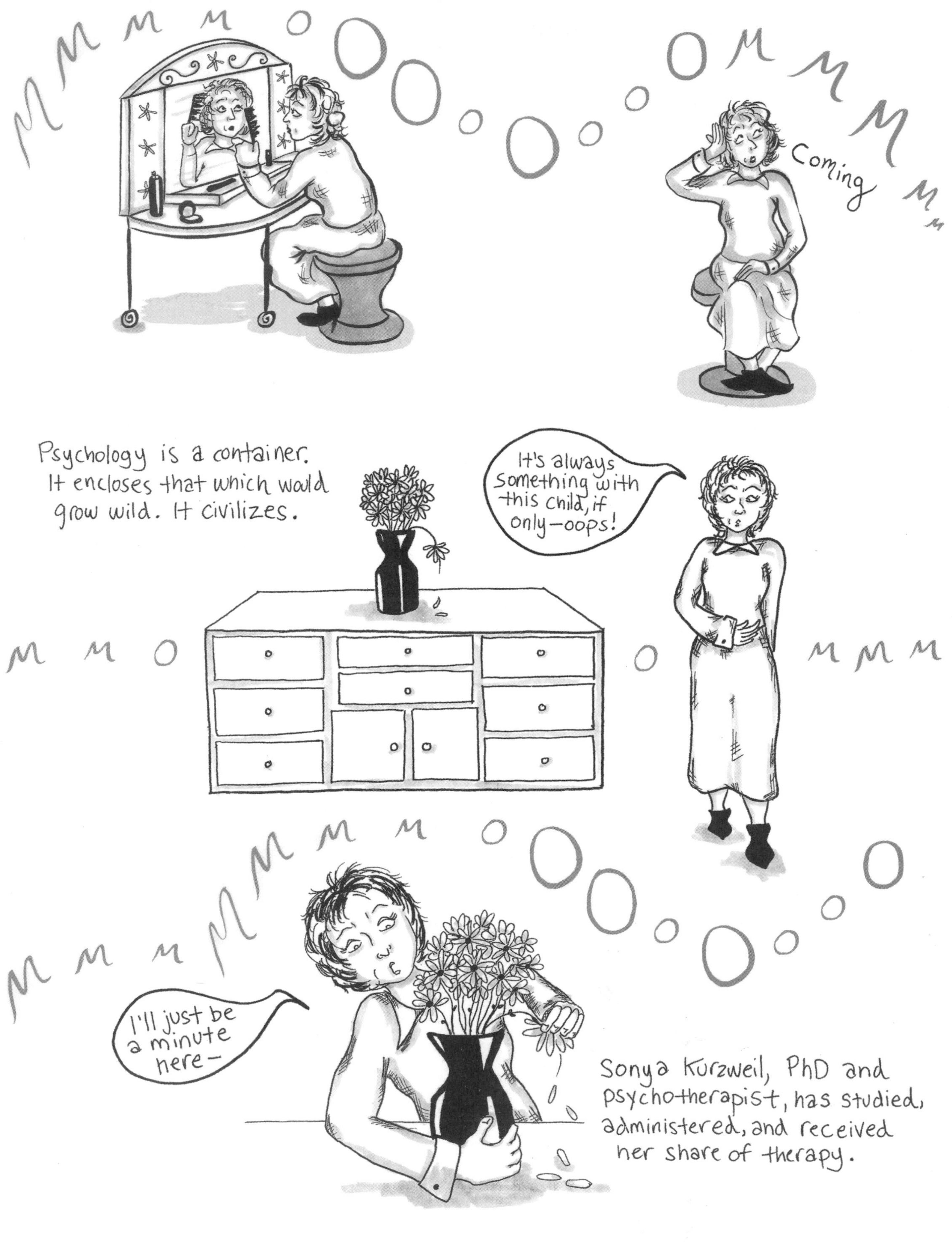
Coming
Psychology is a container. It encloses that which would grow wild. It civilizes.
It's always something with this child, if only—oops!
I'll just be a minute here—
Sonya Kurzweil, PhD and psychotherapist, has studied, administered, and received her share of therapy.

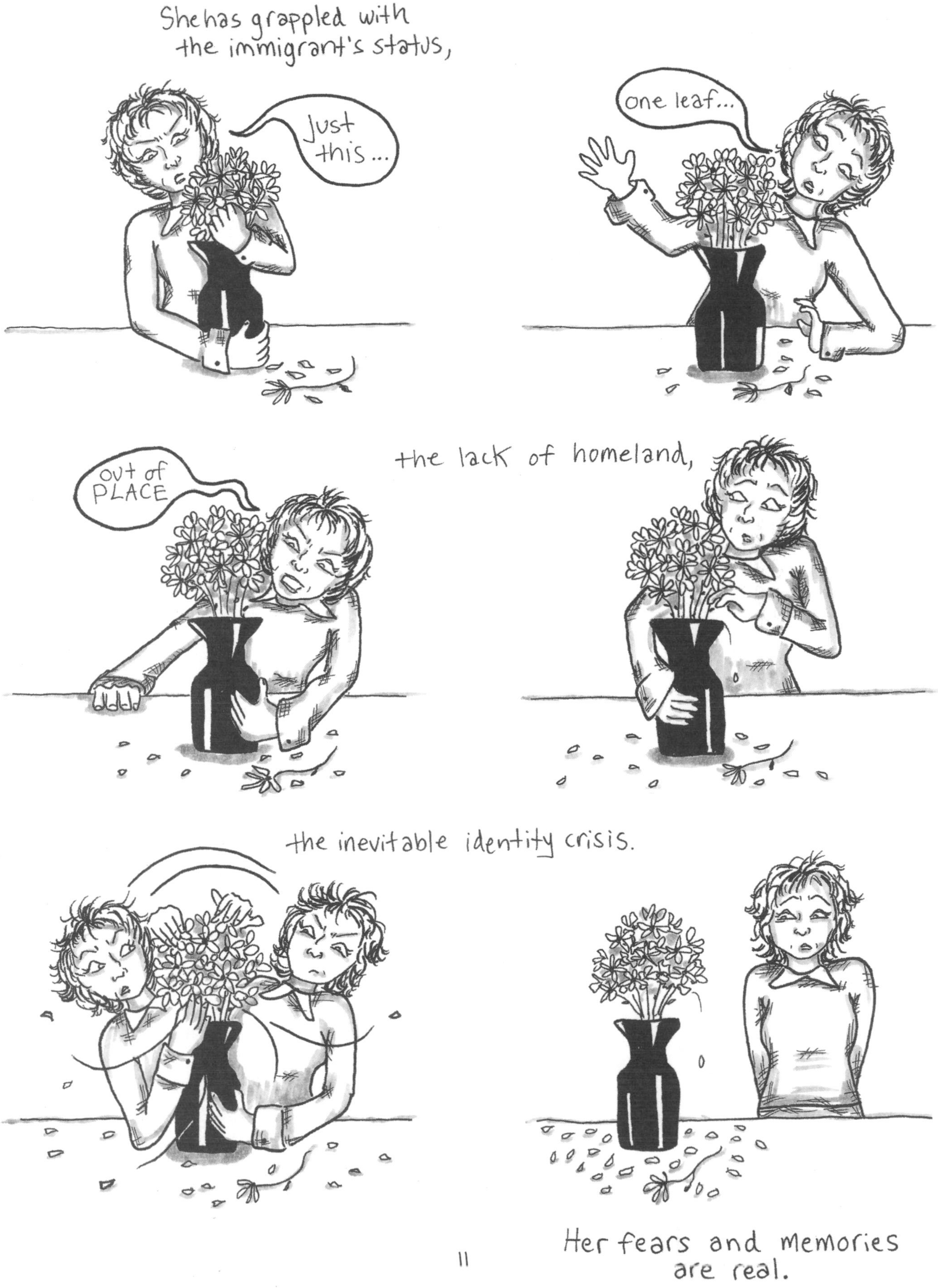
She has grappled with the immigrant's status,
Just this...
one leaf...
the lack of homeland,
out of PLACE
the inevitable identity crisis.
Her fears and memories are real.

Mine are mostly imaginary.

Amy?

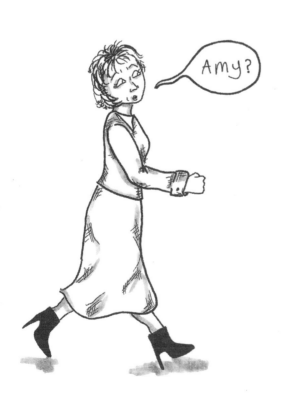

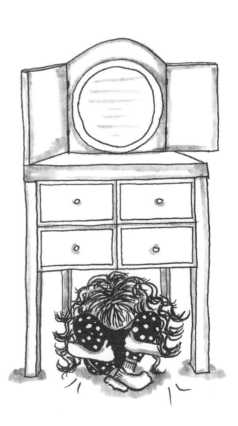

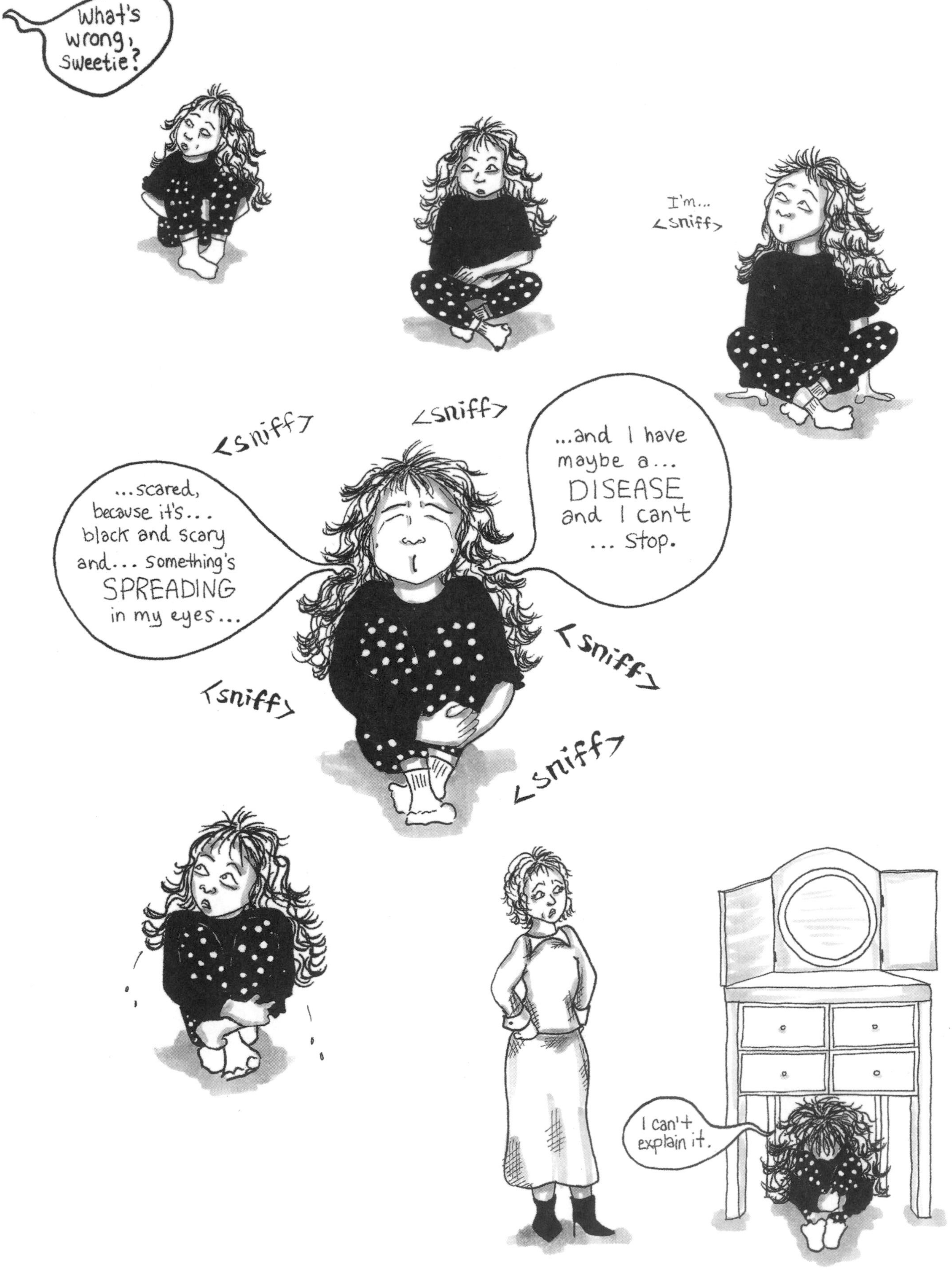
What's wrong, sweetie?
I'm... <sniff>
<sniff>
<sniff>
...scared, because it's... black and scary and... something's SPREADING in my eyes...
...and I have maybe a... DISEASE and I can't ... stop.
<sniff>
<sniff>
<sniff>
I can't explain it.

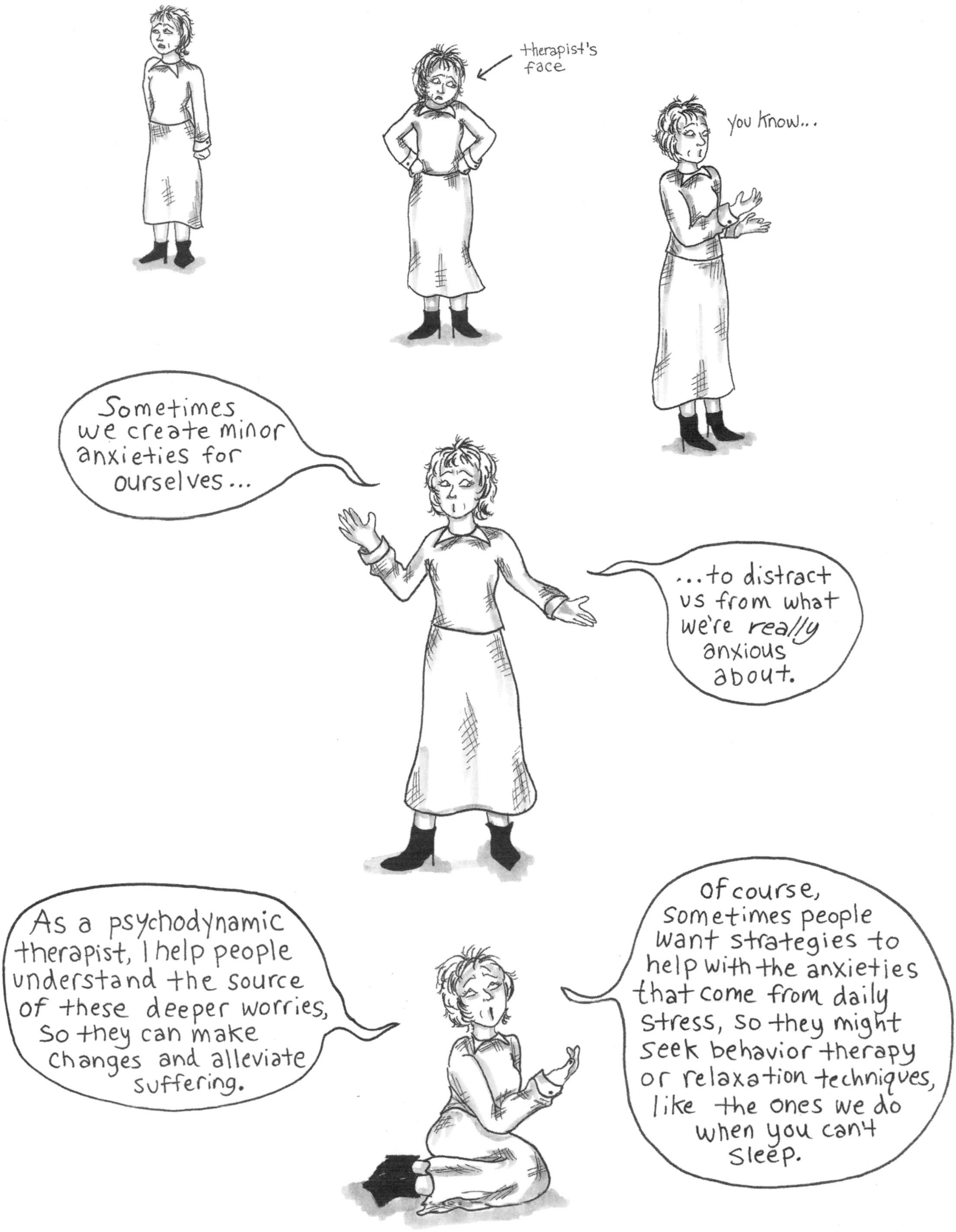
therapist's face
you know...
Sometimes we create minor anxieties for ourselves...
...to distract us from what we're *really* anxious about.
As a psychodynamic therapist, I help people understand the source of these deeper worries, so they can make changes and alleviate suffering.
Of course, sometimes people want strategies to help with the anxieties that come from daily stress, so they might seek behavior therapy or relaxation techniques, like the ones we do when you can't sleep.

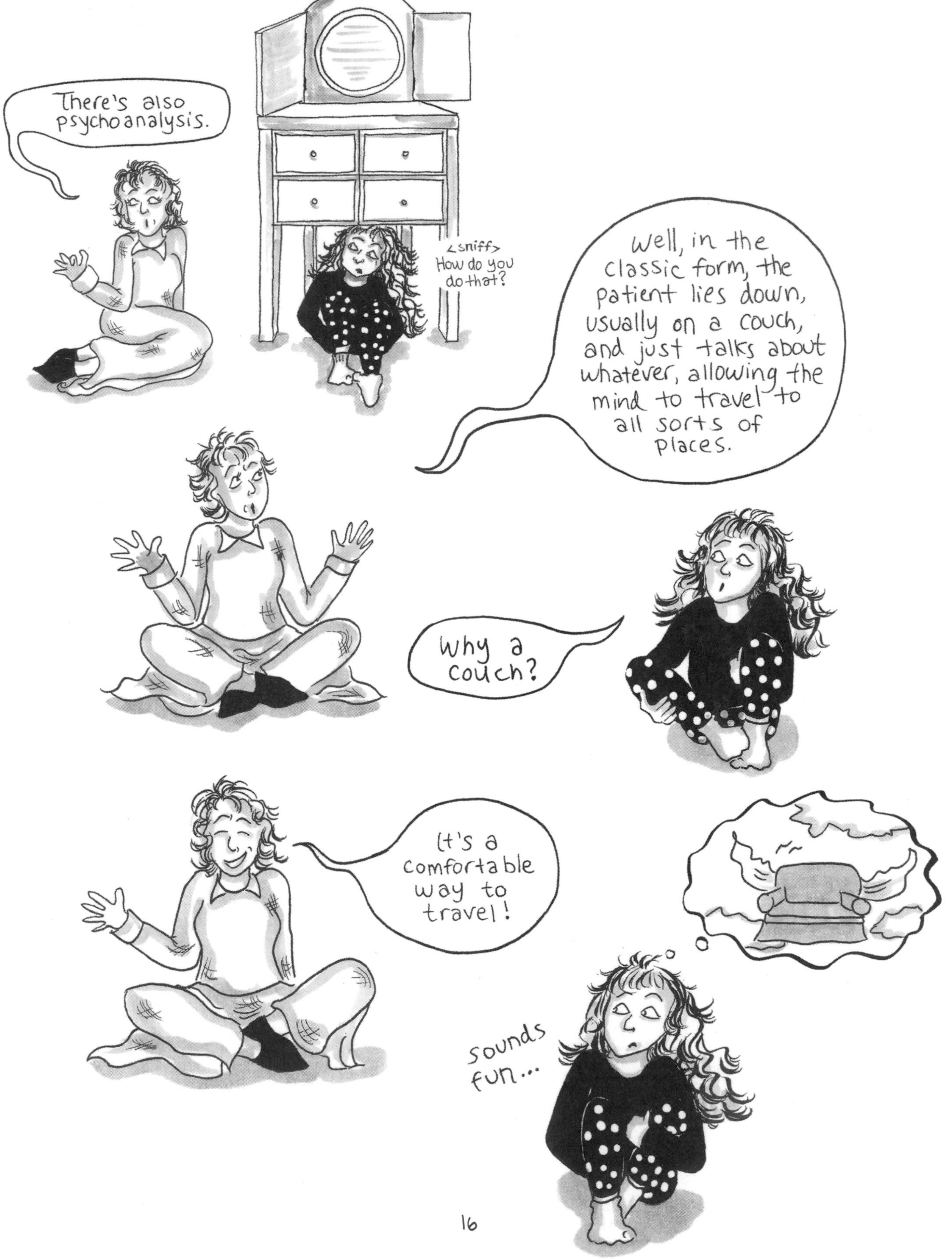
There's also psychoanalysis.
<sniff> How do you do that?
Well, in the classic form, the patient lies down, usually on a couch, and just talks about whatever, allowing the mind to travel to all sorts of places.
Why a couch?
It's a comfortable way to travel!
sounds fun...

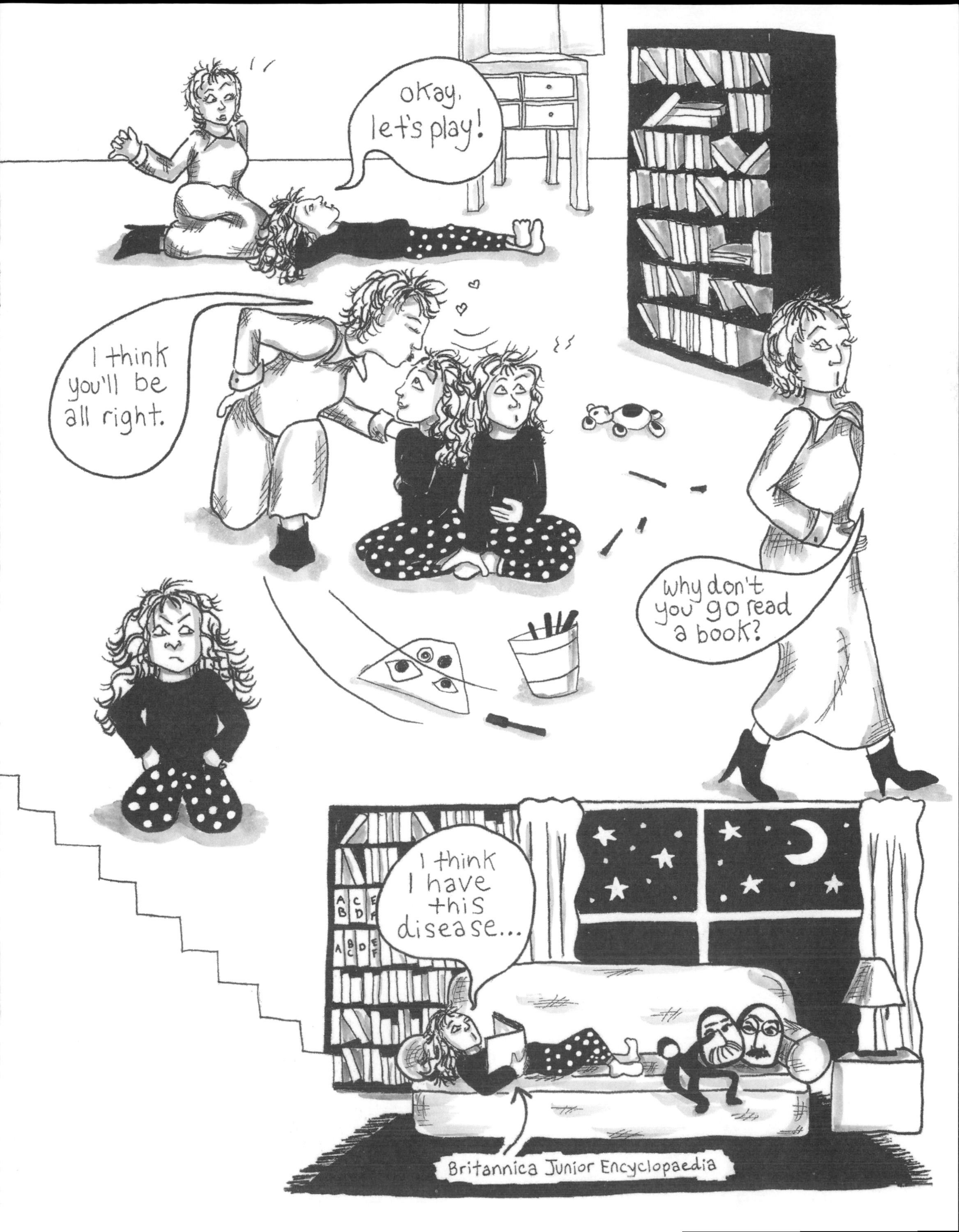
okay, let's play!
I think you'll be all right.
why don't you go read a book?
I think I have this disease...
Britannica Junior Encyclopaedia

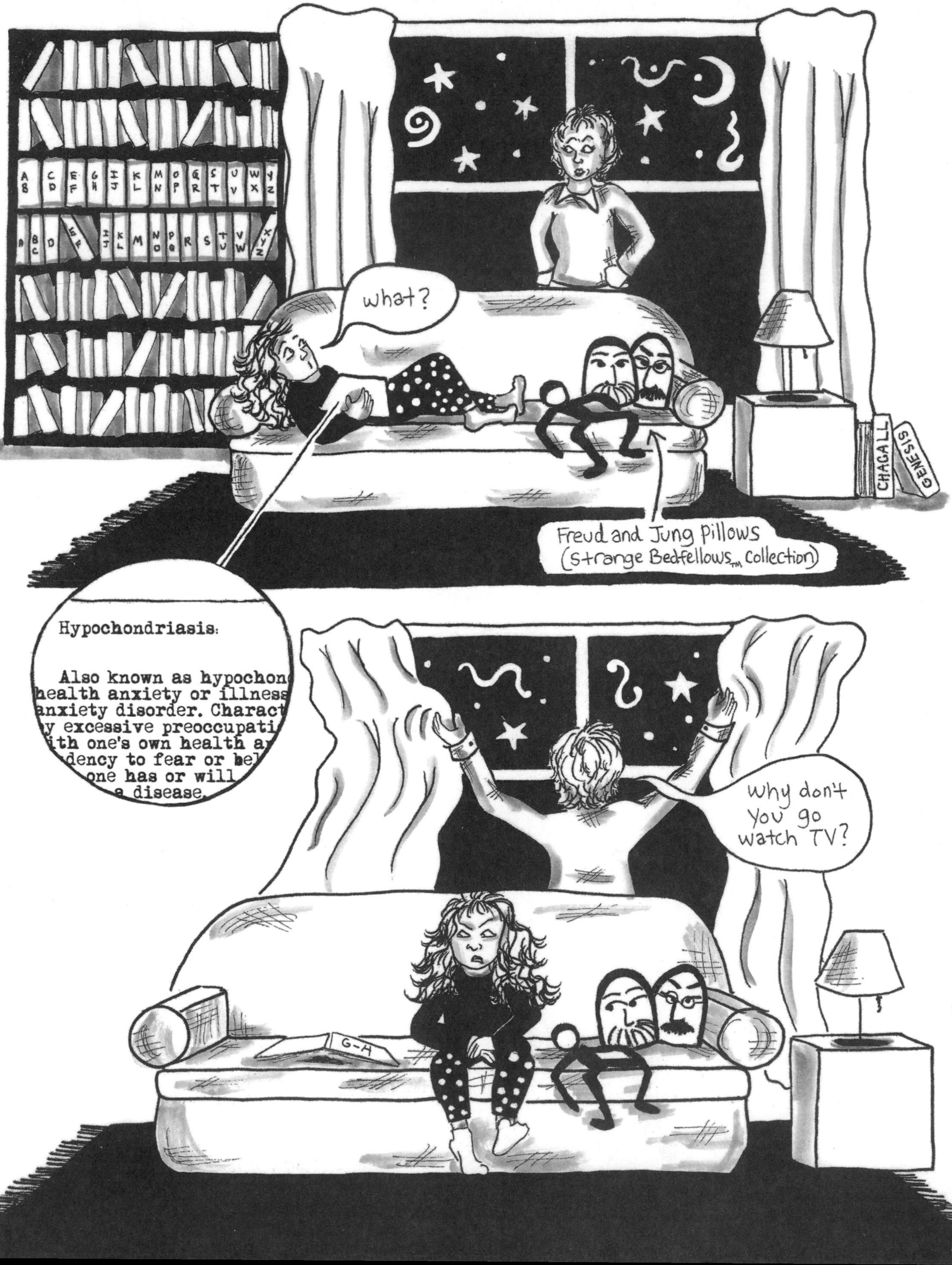
what?
Freud and Jung Pillows (Strange Bedfellows™ Collection)
CHAGALL
GENESIS
Hypochondriasis:
Also known as hypochond
health anxiety or illness
anxiety disorder. Charact
y excessive preoccupati
ith one's own health a
dency to fear or bel
one has or will
a disease.
Why don't you go watch TV?
G-H

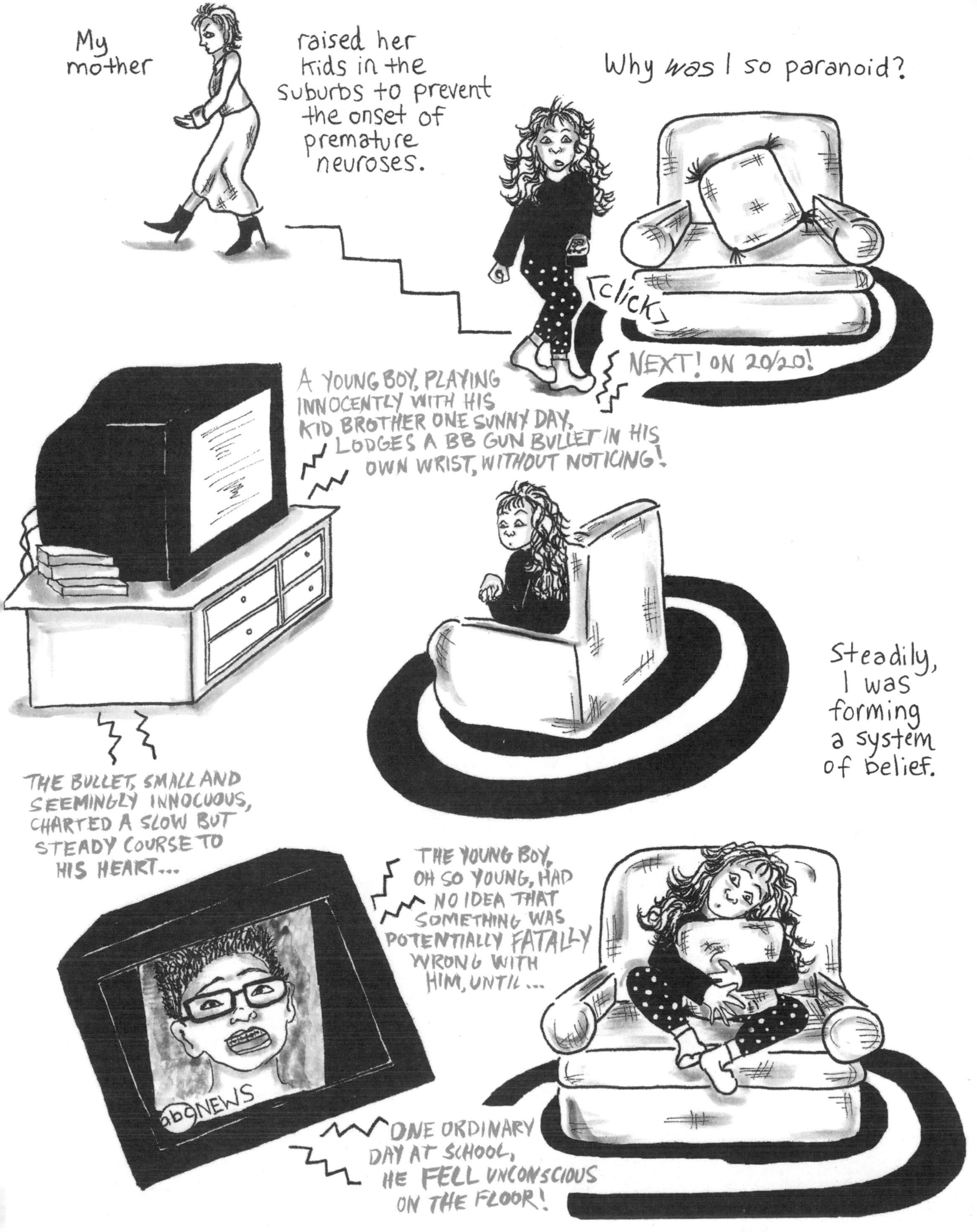
My mother
raised her kids in the suburbs to prevent the onset of premature neuroses.
Why *was* I so paranoid?
[click]
NEXT! ON 20/20!
A YOUNG BOY, PLAYING INNOCENTLY WITH HIS KID BROTHER ONE SUNNY DAY, LODGES A BB GUN BULLET IN HIS OWN WRIST, WITHOUT NOTICING!
Steadily, I was forming a system of belief.
THE BULLET, SMALL AND SEEMINGLY INNOCUOUS, CHARTED A SLOW BUT STEADY COURSE TO HIS HEART...
THE YOUNG BOY, OH SO YOUNG, HAD NO IDEA THAT SOMETHING WAS POTENTIALLY FATALLY WRONG WITH HIM, UNTIL ...
abc NEWS
ONE ORDINARY DAY AT SCHOOL, HE FELL UNCONSCIOUS ON THE FLOOR!

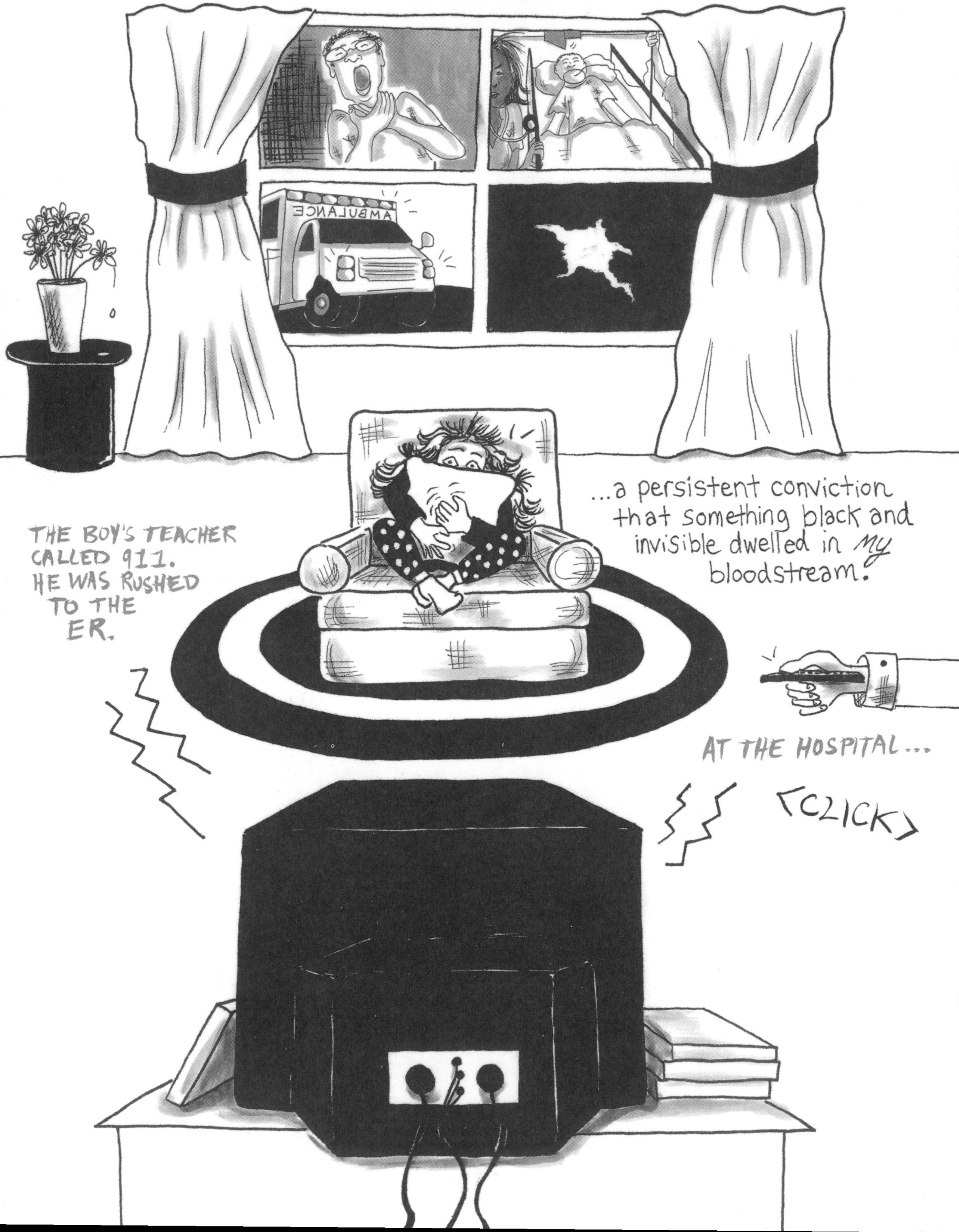
AMBULANCE
THE BOY'S TEACHER CALLED 911. HE WAS RUSHED TO THE ER.
...a persistent conviction that something black and invisible dwelled in *my* bloodstream.
AT THE HOSPITAL...
<CLICK>

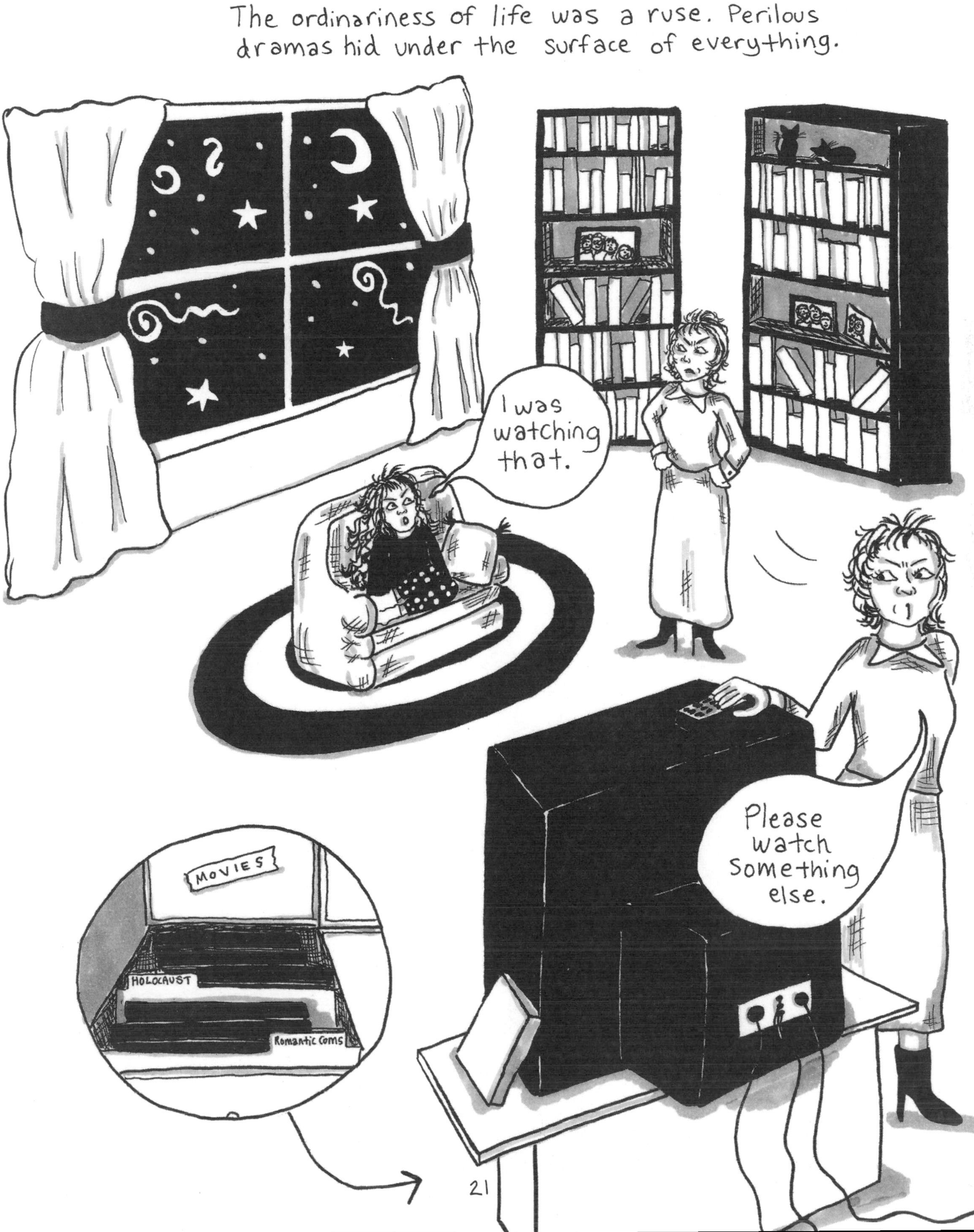
The ordinariness of life was a ruse. Perilous dramas hid under the surface of everything.
I was watching that.
Please watch something else.
MOVIES
HOLOCAUST
Romantic Coms

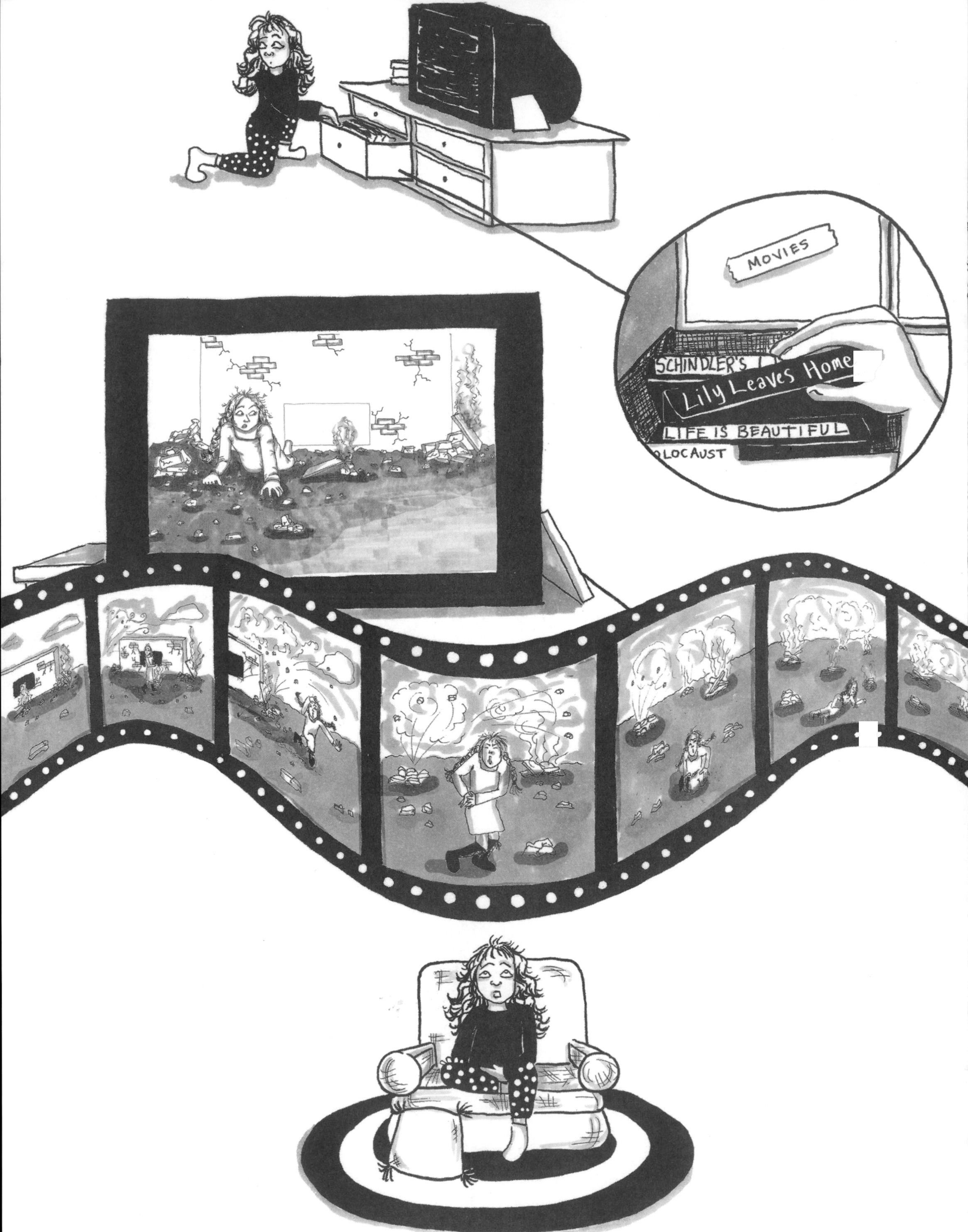
MOVIES
SCHINDLER'S
Lily Leaves Home
LIFE IS BEAUTIFUL

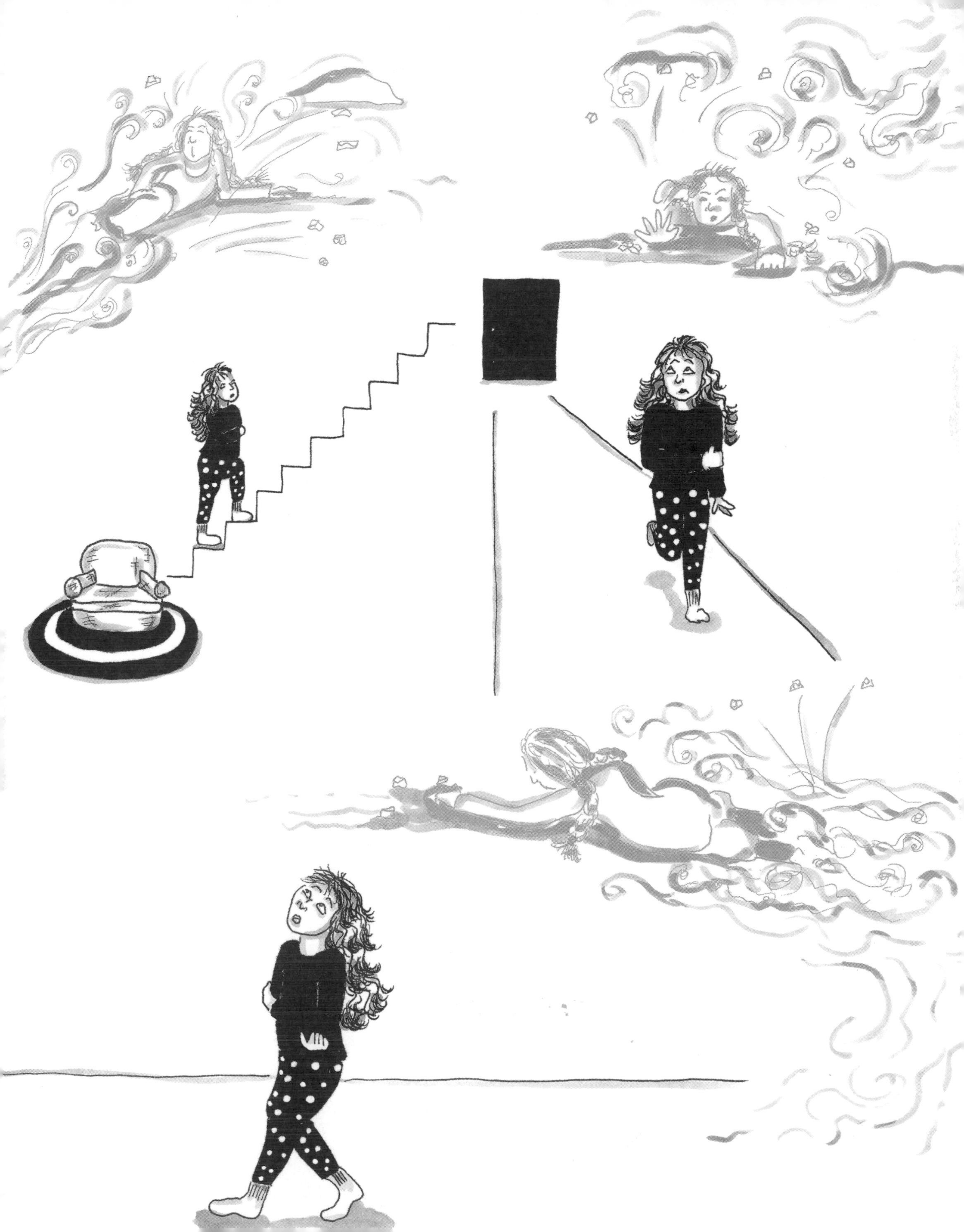

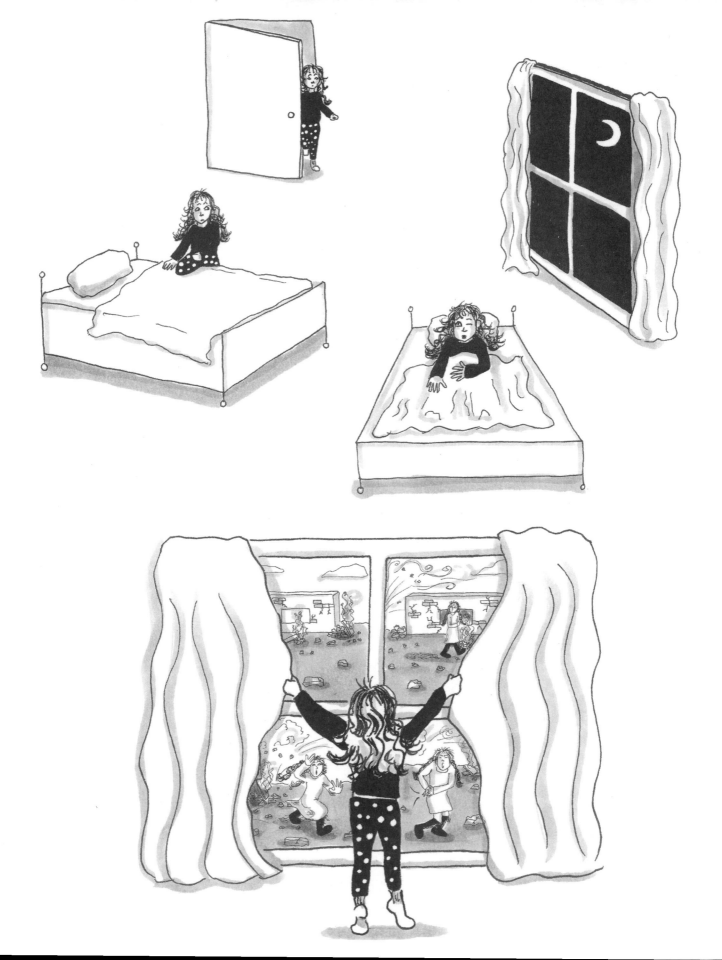

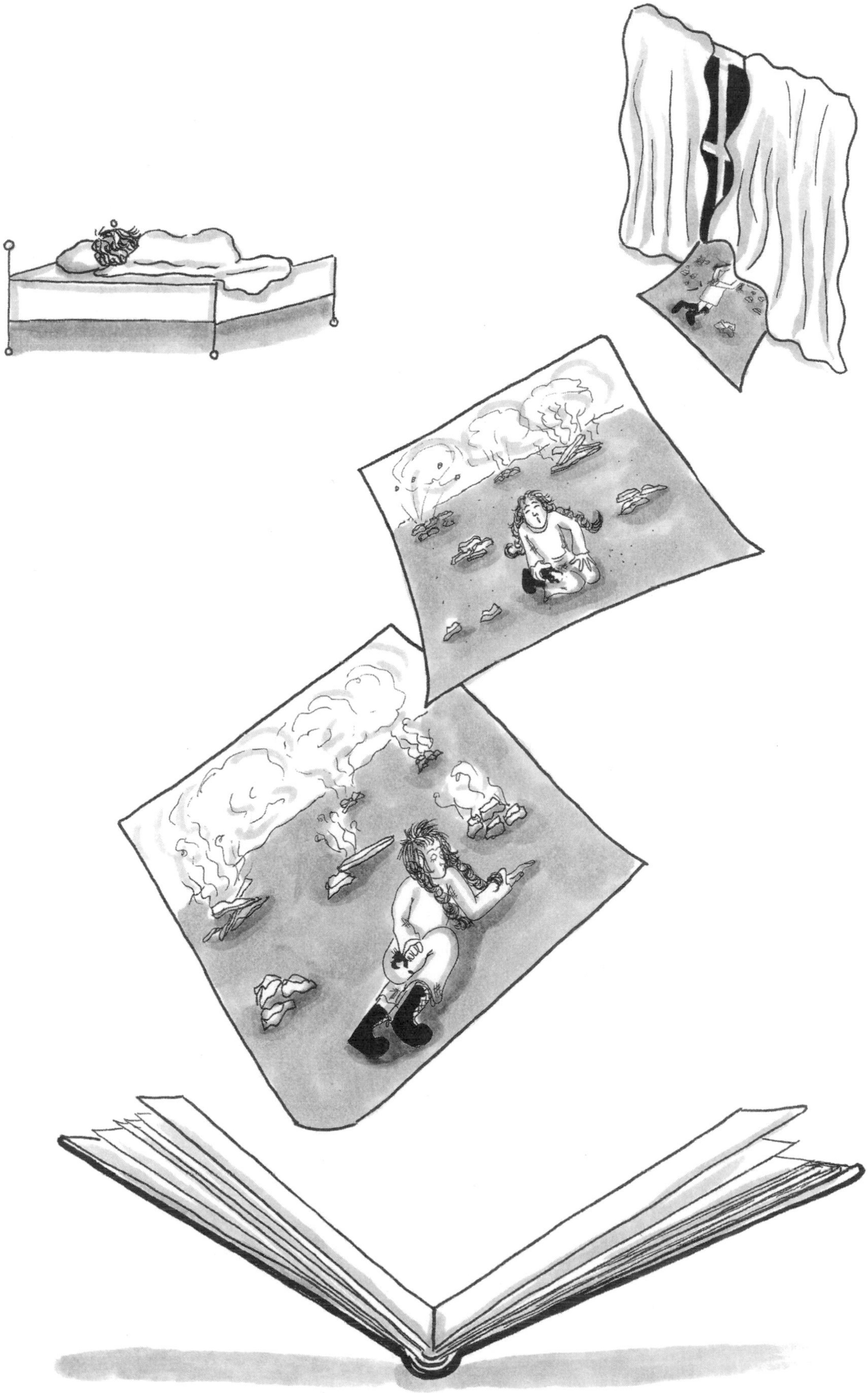

Chapter Two:
Bed Bath & Beyond

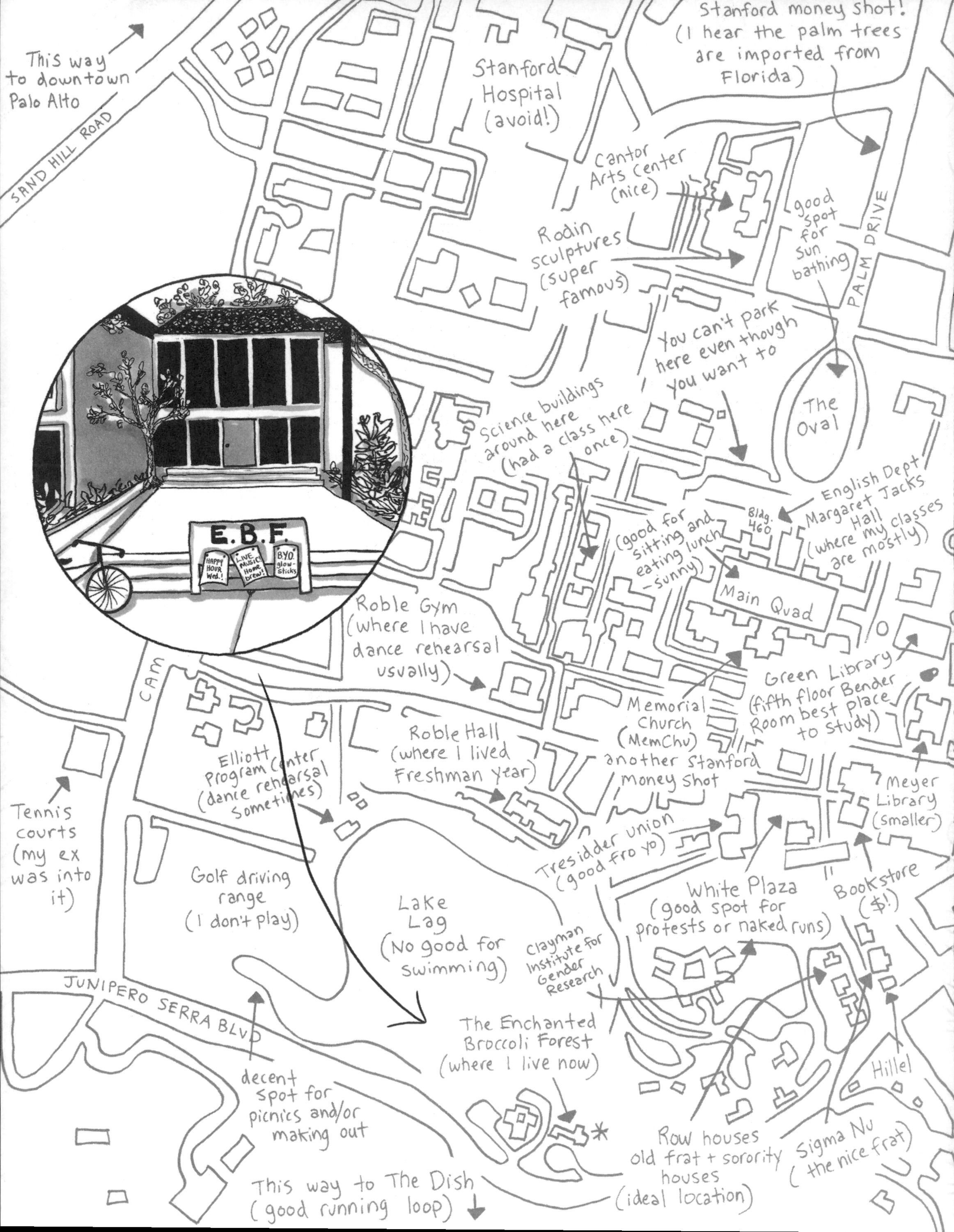
This way to downtown Palo Alto
SAND HILL ROAD
Stanford Hospital (avoid!)
Stanford money shot! (I hear the palm trees are imported from Florida)
Cantor Arts Center (nice)
Rodin sculptures (super famous)
good spot for sun bathing
PALM DRIVE
You can't park here even though you want to
The Oval
Science buildings around here (had a class here once)
English Dept Margaret Jacks Hall (where my classes are mostly)
Bldg. 460
(good for sitting and eating lunch - sunny)
Main Quad
E.B.F.
HAPPY HOUR Wed.!
LIVE MUSIC! Home brew!
B.Y.O. glow-sticks
Roble Gym (where I have dance rehearsal usually)
Green Library (fifth floor Bender Room best place to study)
Memorial Church (MemChu) another Stanford Money Shot
CAM
Roble Hall (where I lived Freshman year)
Elliott Program Center (dance rehearsal sometimes)
Meyer Library (smaller)
Tennis courts (my ex was into it)
Tresidder union (good fro yo)
Golf driving range (I don't play)
Lake Lag (No good for swimming)
White Plaza (good spot for protests or naked runs)
Bookstore ($!)
Clayman Institute for Gender Research
JUNIPERO SERRA BLVD
The Enchanted Broccoli Forest (where I live now)
Hillel
decent spot for picnics and/or making out
Row houses old frat + sorority houses (ideal location)
Sigma Nu (the nice frat)
This way to The Dish (good running loop)

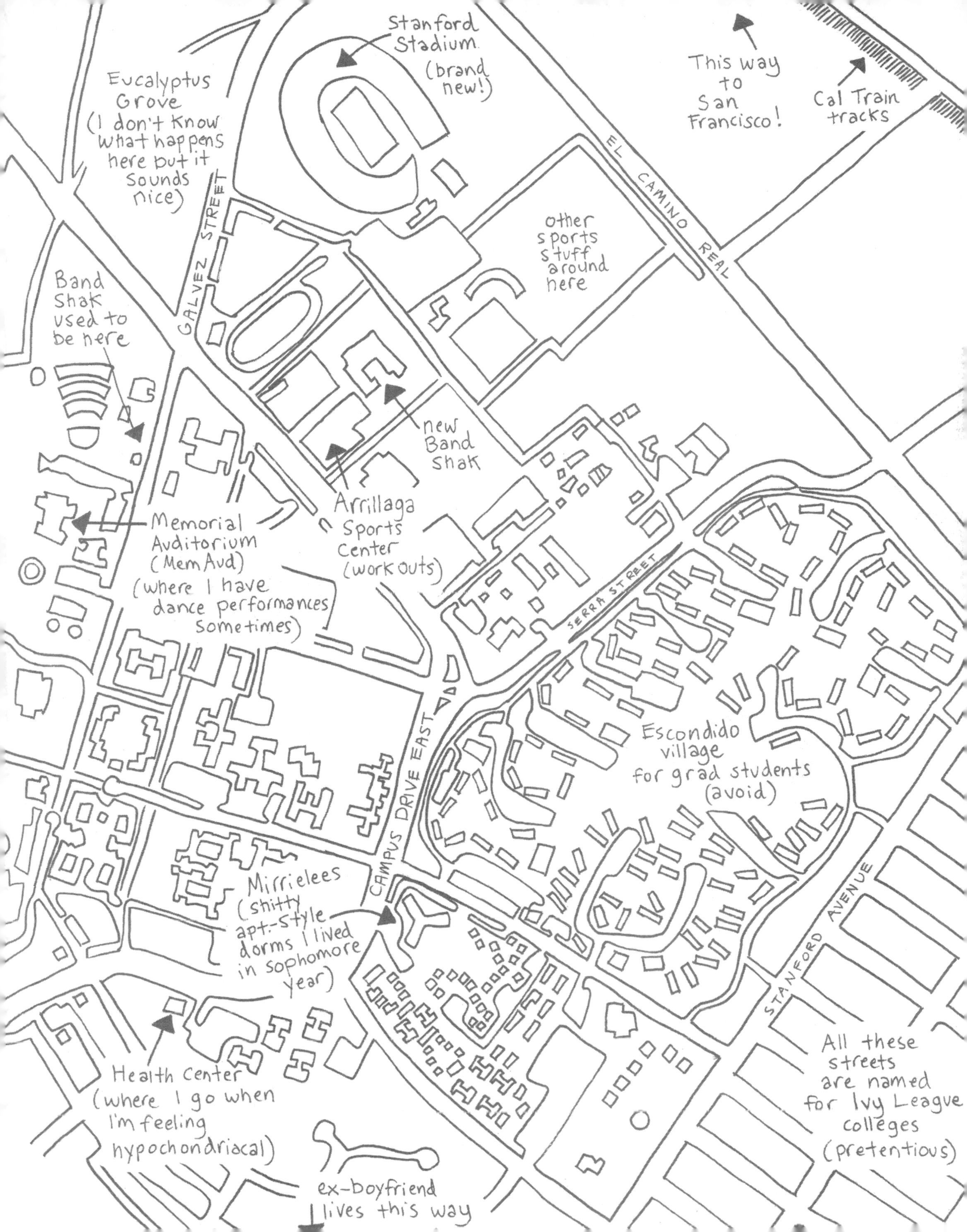
Stanford Stadium
(brand new!)
This way to San Francisco!
Cal Train tracks
Eucalyptus Grove (I don't know what happens here but it sounds nice)
GALVEZ STREET
EL CAMINO REAL
other sports stuff around here
Band Shak used to be here
new Band Shak
Arrillaga Sports Center (workouts)
Memorial Auditorium (MemAud) (where I have dance performances sometimes)
SERRA STREET
Escondido village for grad students (avoid)
CAMPUS DRIVE EAST
Mirrielees (shitty apt.-style dorms I lived in sophomore year)
STANFORD AVENUE
All these streets are named for Ivy League colleges (pretentious)
Health Center (where I go when I'm feeling hypochondriacal)
ex-boyfriend lives this way

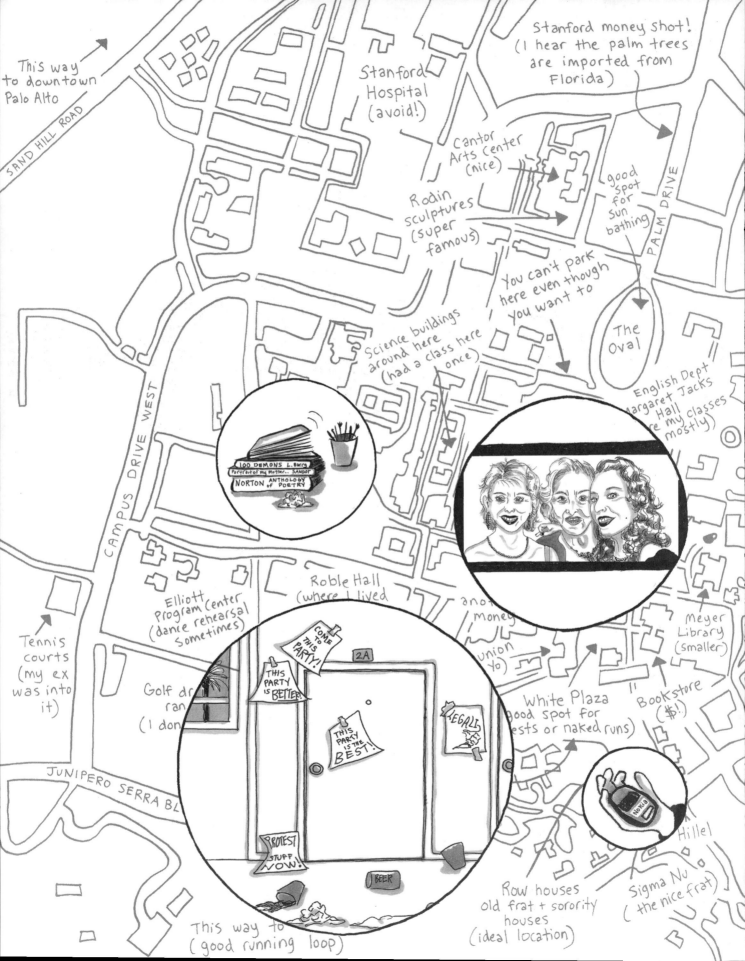

This way to downtown Palo Alto

SAND HILL ROAD

Stanford Hospital (avoid!)

Stanford money shot! (I hear the palm trees are imported from Florida)

Cantor Arts Center (nice)

Rodin sculptures (super famous)

good spot for sun bathing

PALM DRIVE

You can't park here even though you want to

The Oval

Science buildings around here (had a class here once)

English Dept Margaret Jacks Hall (where my classes are mostly)

100 DEMONS L. Barry
Portrait of my Mother... SANDOR
NORTON ANTHOLOGY of POETRY

CAMPUS DRIVE WEST

Elliott Program Center (dance rehearsal sometimes)

Roble Hall (where I lived

anot... money

union yo)

Meyer Library (smaller)

Tennis courts (my ex was into it)

Golf dr... ran... (I don...

COME TO THIS PARTY!

THIS PARTY is BETTER!

THIS PARTY IS THE BEST!

2A

ILEGAL!

PROTEST STUFF NOW!

BEER

White Plaza (good spot for protests or naked runs)

Bookstore ($!)

NOKIA

Hillel

JUNIPERO SERRA BL

This way to (good running loop)

Row houses old frat + sorority houses (ideal location)

Sigma Nu (the nice frat)

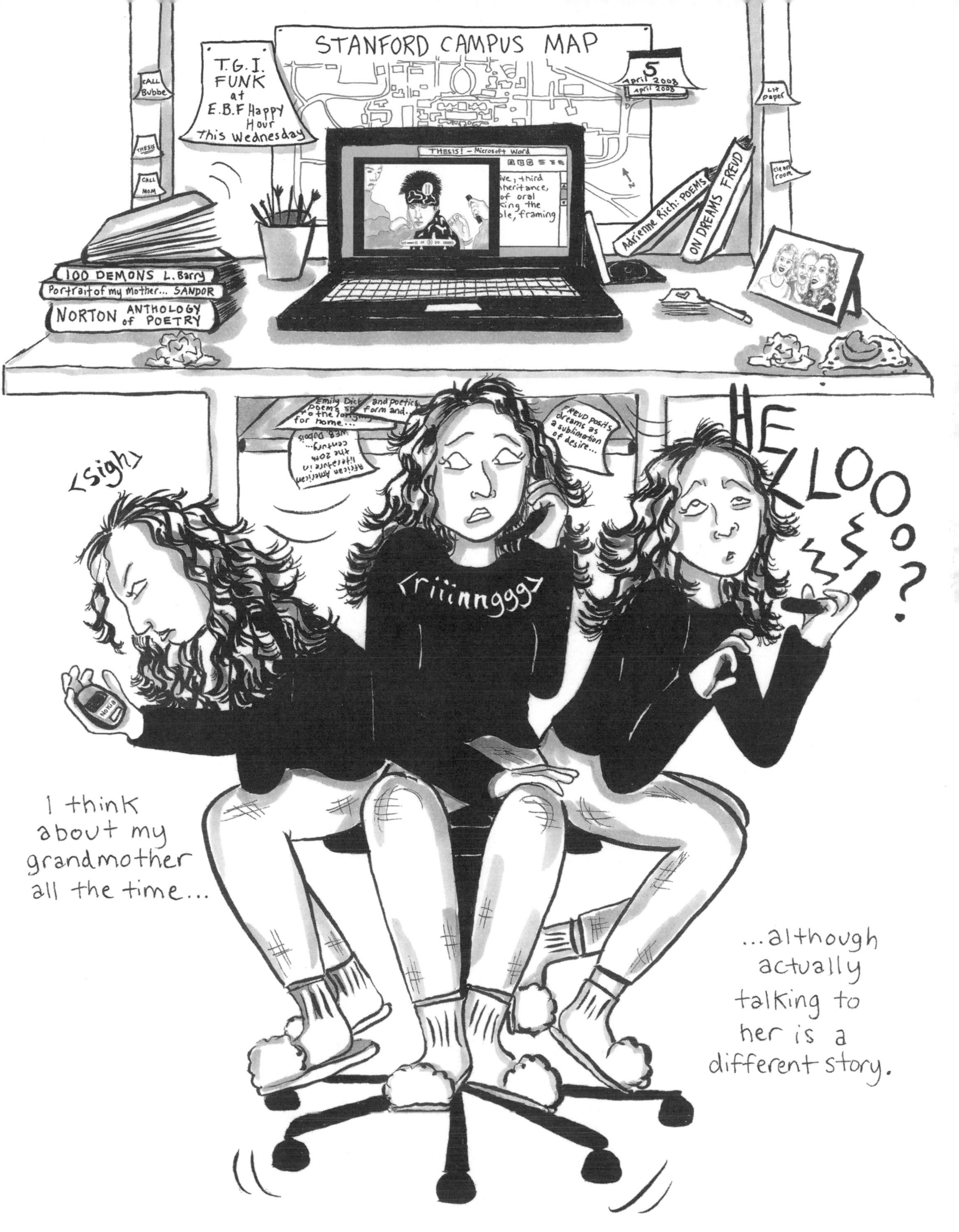

STANFORD CAMPUS MAP
T.G.I. FUNK at E.B.F Happy Hour This Wednesday
CALL Bubbe
THESIS
CALL MOM
5 April 2008
April 2008
Lit paper
clean room
THESIS! - Microsoft Word
100 DEMONS L. Barry
Portrait of my mother... SANDOR
NORTON ANTHOLOGY of POETRY
Adrienne Rich: POEMS
ON DREAMS FREUD
FREUD posits dreams as a sublimation of desire...
<sigh>
<riiinnggg>
HELLOOo?
Nokia
I think about my grandmother all the time...
...although actually talking to her is a different story.

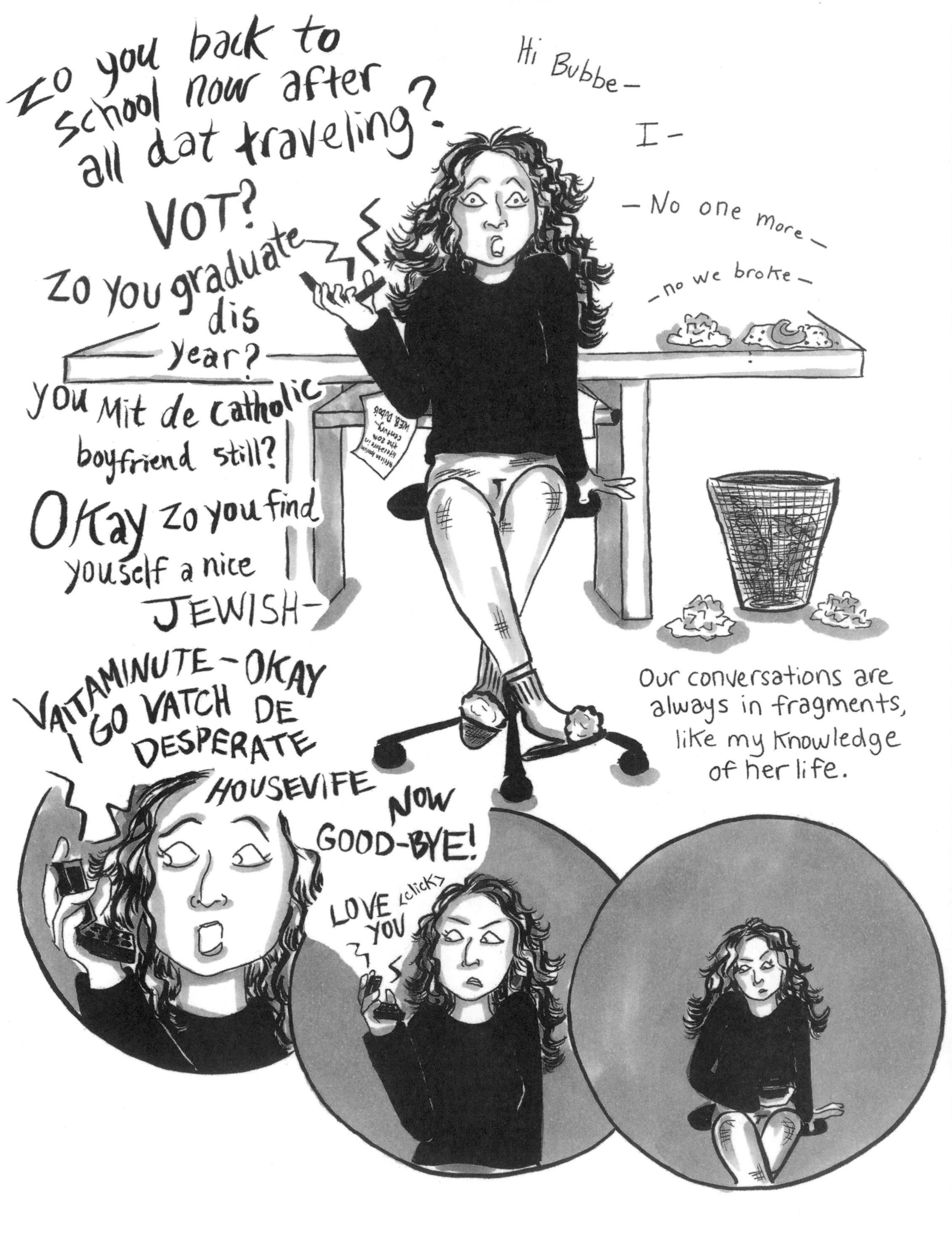
Zo you back to school now after all dat traveling?
Hi Bubbe—
I—
VOT?
—No one more—
Zo you graduate dis year?
—no we broke—
You mit de catholic boyfriend still?
Okay zo you find youself a nice JEWISH—
Our conversations are always in fragments, like my knowledge of her life.
VAITAMINUTE—OKAY I GO VATCH DE DESPERATE HOUSEVIFE NOW
GOOD-BYE!
LOVE YOU
<click>

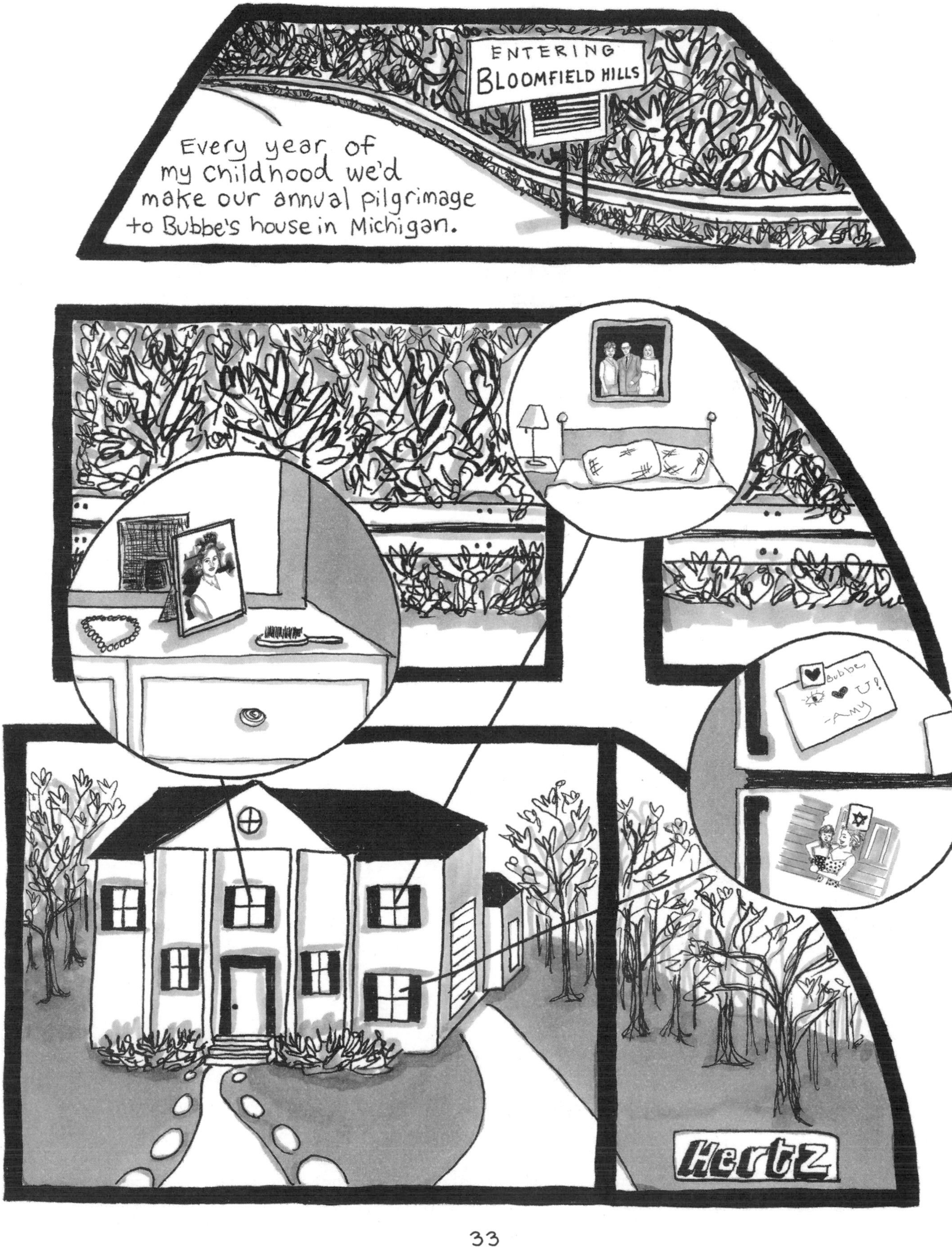
ENTERING
BLOOMFIELD HILLS
Every year of my childhood we'd make our annual pilgrimage to Bubbe's house in Michigan.
Bubbe, U! -Amy
Hertz

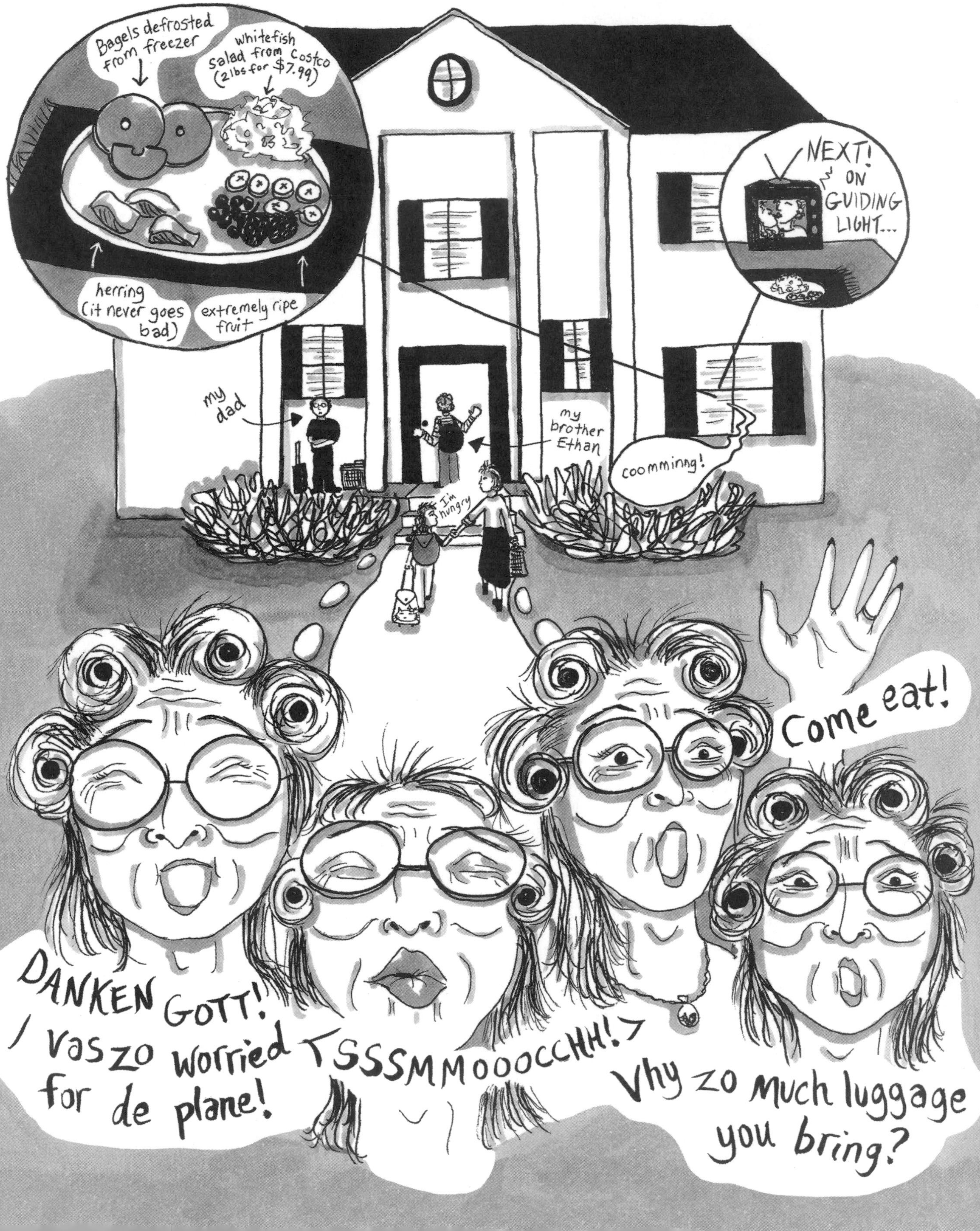
Bagels defrosted from freezer
whitefish salad from Costco (2 lbs for $7.99)
herring (it never goes bad)
extremely ripe fruit
NEXT! ON GUIDING LIGHT...
my dad
my brother Ethan
coomminng!
I'm hungry
DANKEN GOTT! I vas zo worried for de plane!
TSSSMMOOOCCHH!
Come eat!
Vhy zo much luggage you bring?

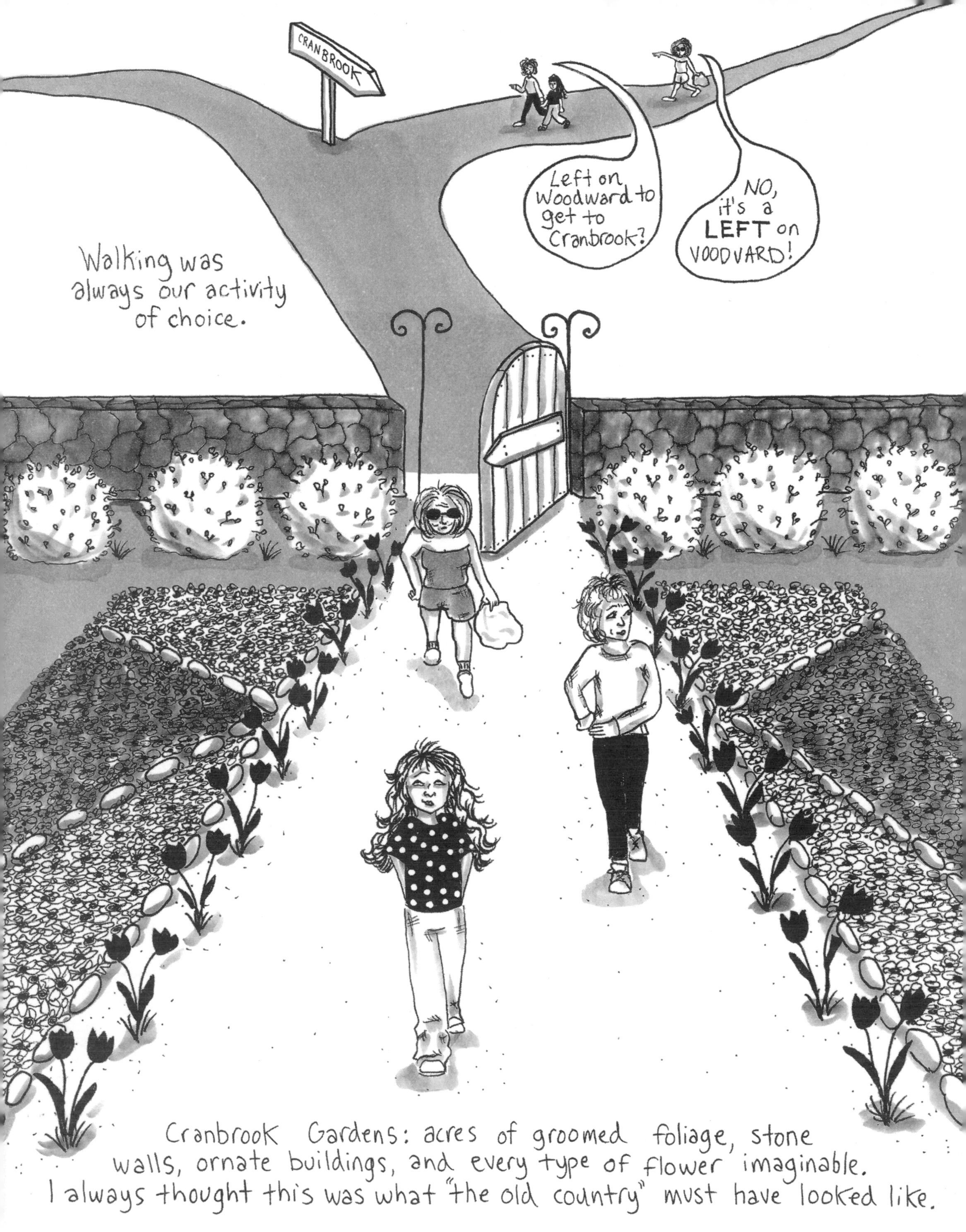
CRANBROOK
Walking was always our activity of choice.
Left on Woodward to get to Cranbrook?
NO, it's a LEFT on VOODVARD!
Cranbrook Gardens: acres of groomed foliage, stone walls, ornate buildings, and every type of flower imaginable. I always thought this was what "the old country" must have looked like.

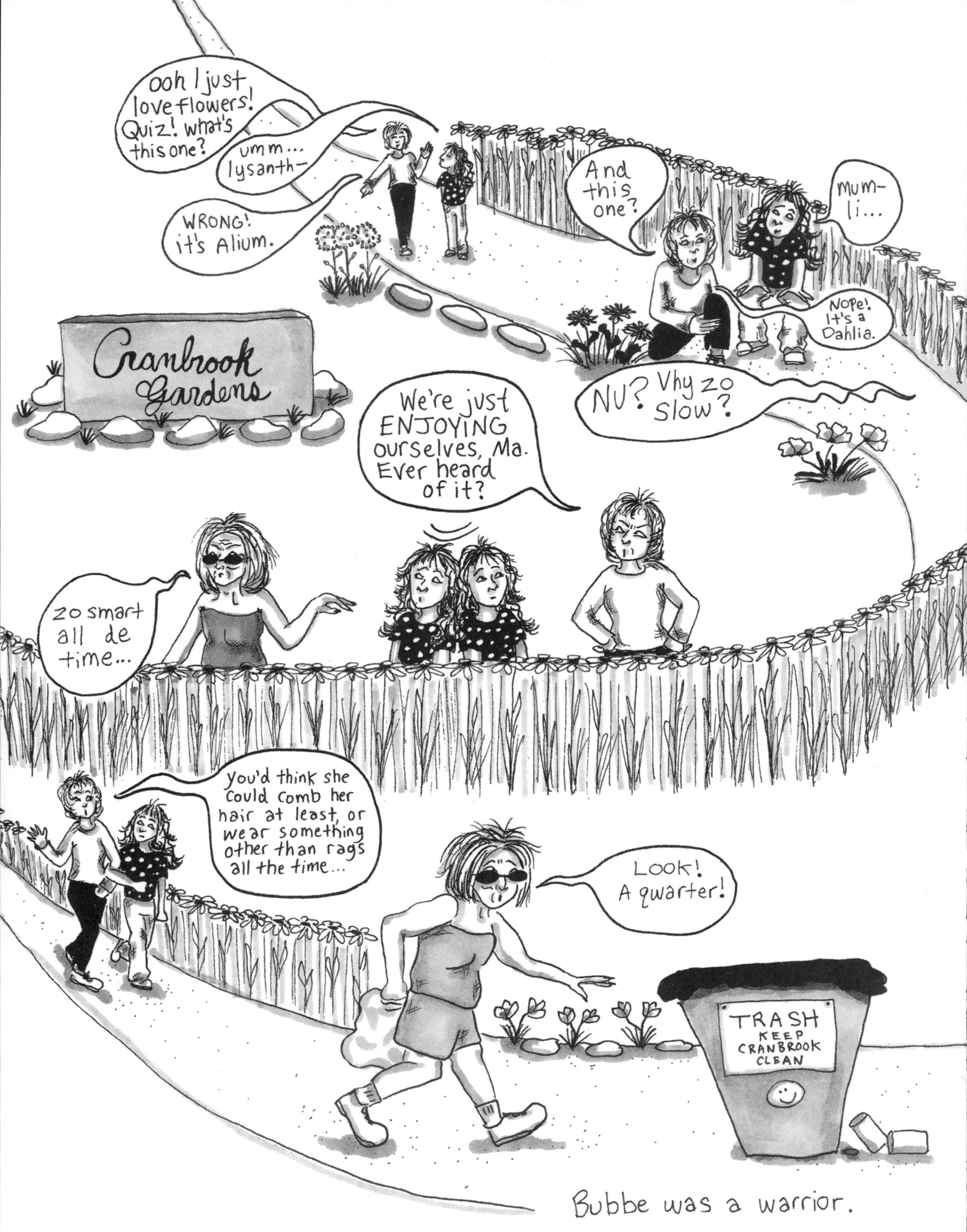

ooh I just love Flowers! Quiz! what's this one?
umm... lysanth—
WRONG! it's Alium.
And this one?
mum-li...
Nope! It's a Dahlia.
Cranbrook Gardens
NU? Vhy zo slow?
We're just ENJOYING ourselves, Ma. Ever heard of it?
zo smart all de time...
you'd think she could comb her hair at least, or wear something other than rags all the time...
LOOK! A qwarter!
TRASH KEEP CRANBROOK CLEAN
Bubbe was a warrior.

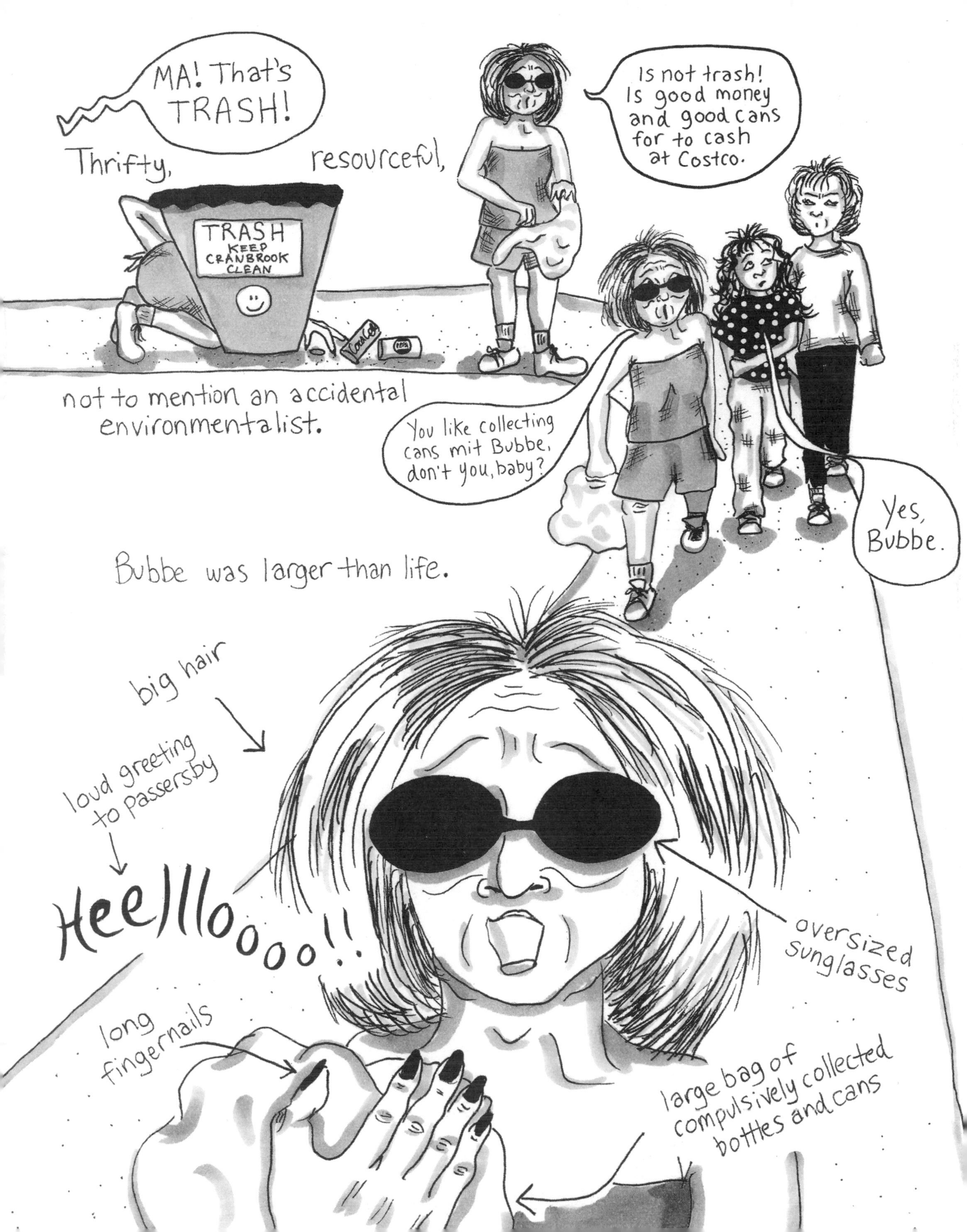
MA! That's TRASH!
Thrifty,
resourceful,
Is not trash! Is good money and good cans for to cash at Costco.
TRASH KEEP CRANBROOK CLEAN
not to mention an accidental environmentalist.
You like collecting cans mit Bubbe, don't you, baby?
Yes, Bubbe.
Bubbe was larger than life.
big hair
loud greeting to passersby
Heelllooooo!!
oversized sunglasses
long fingernails
large bag of compulsively collected bottles and cans

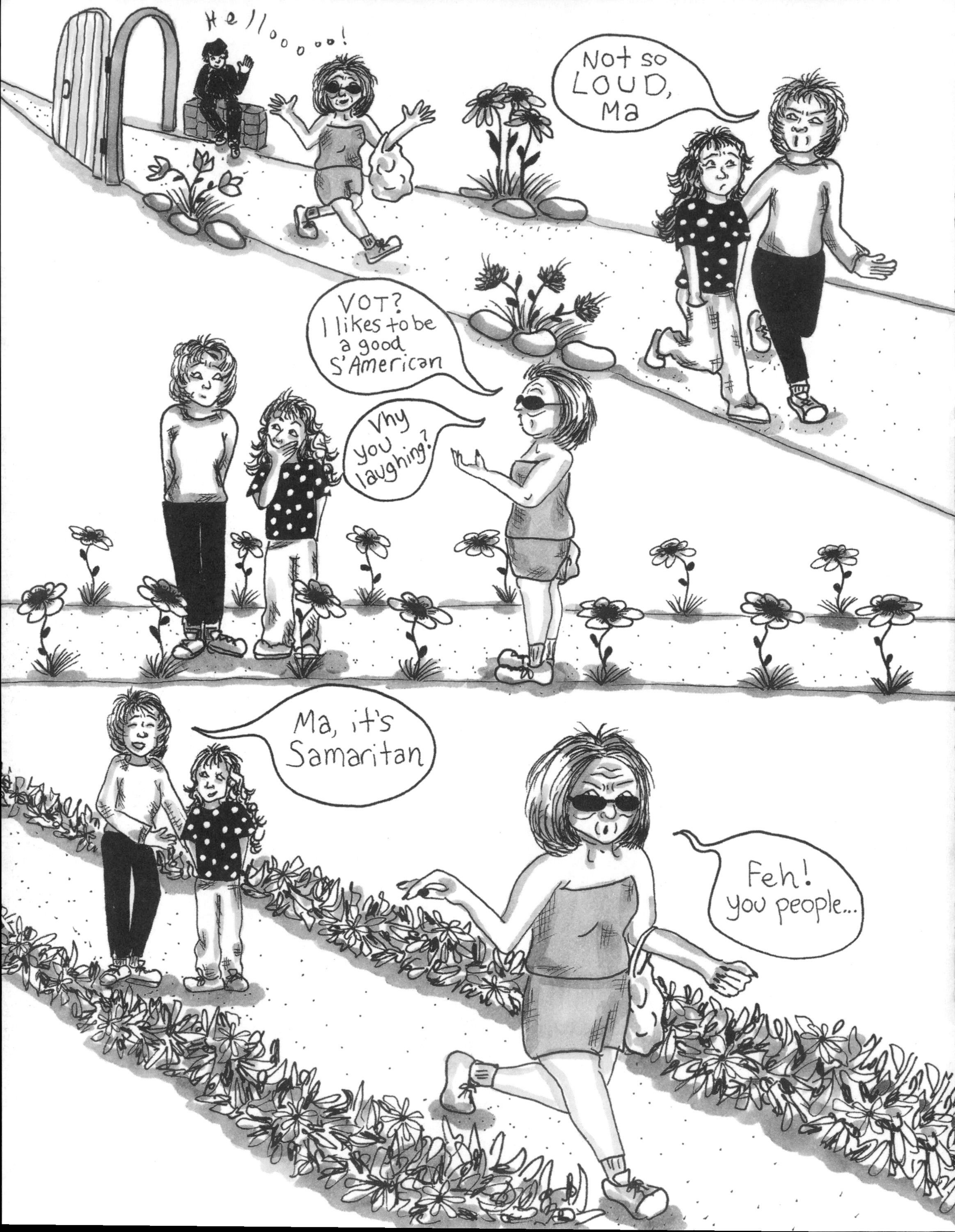
Helloooooo!
Not so LOUD, Ma
VOT? I likes to be a good S'American
Vhy you laughing?
Ma, it's Samaritan
Feh! you people...

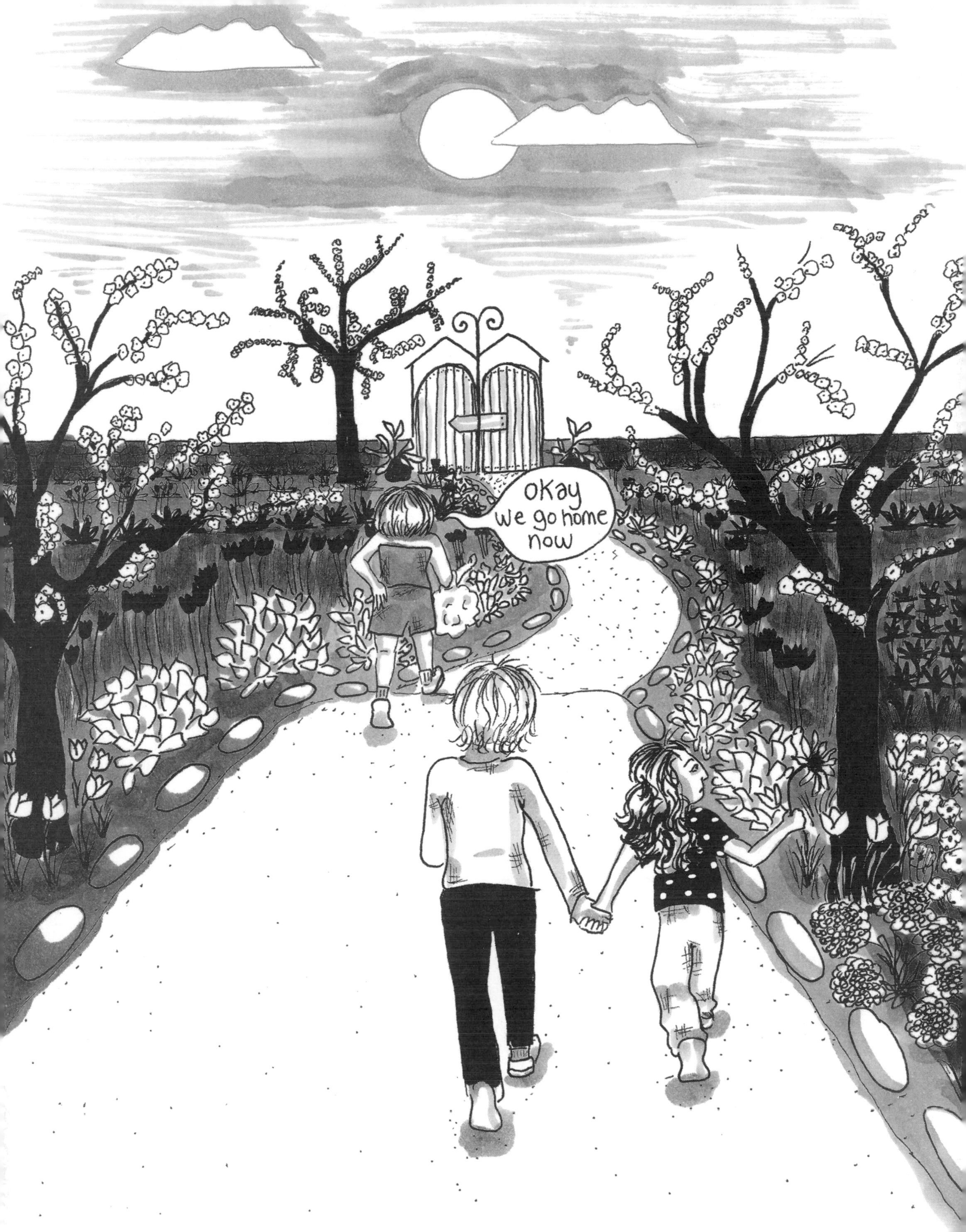
OKay we go home now

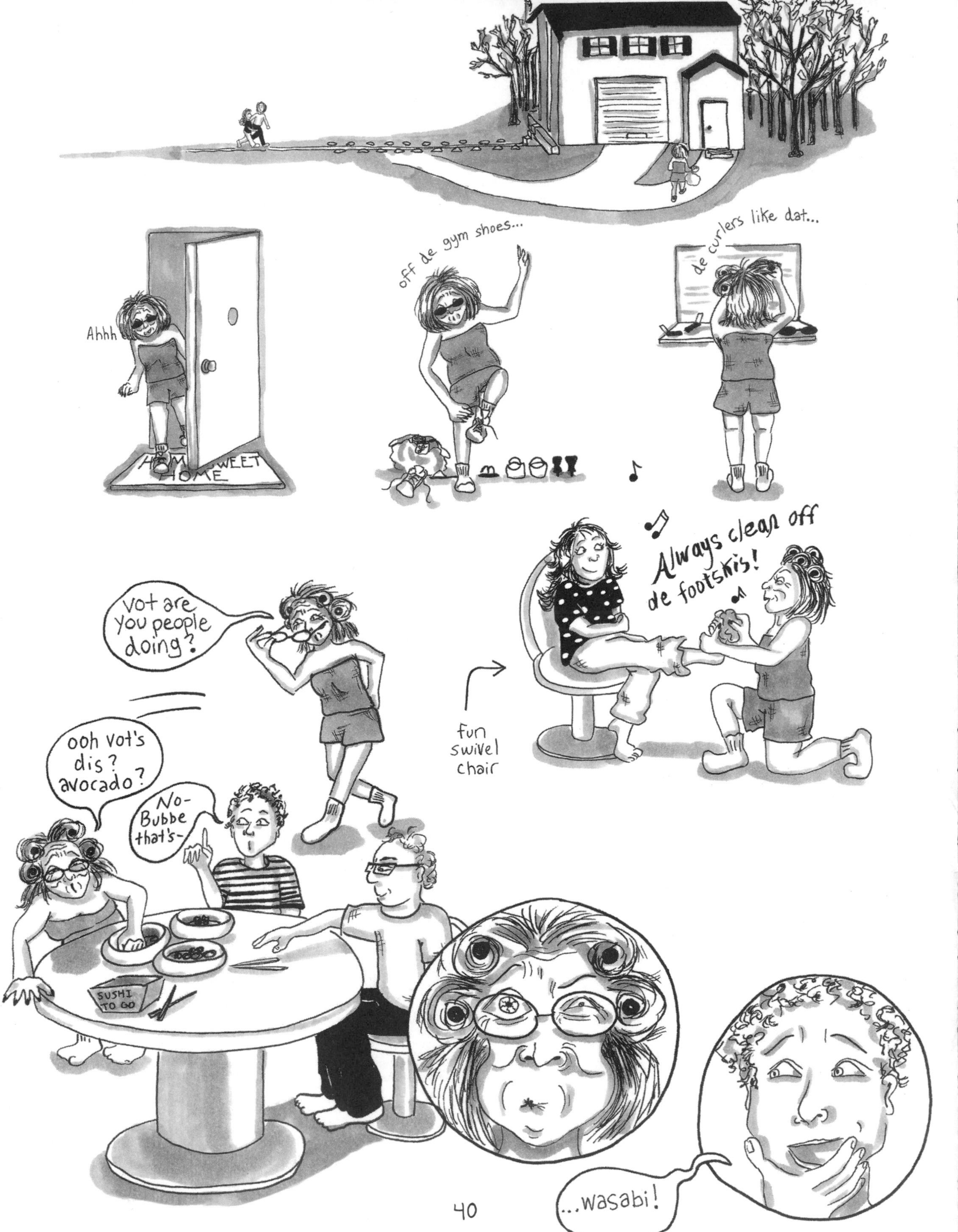
Ahhh
HOME SWEET HOME
off de gym shoes...
de curlers like dat...
Always clean off de footskis!
fun swivel chair
Vot are you people doing?
ooh vot's dis? avocado?
No- Bubbe that's-
SUSHI TO GO
...wasabi!

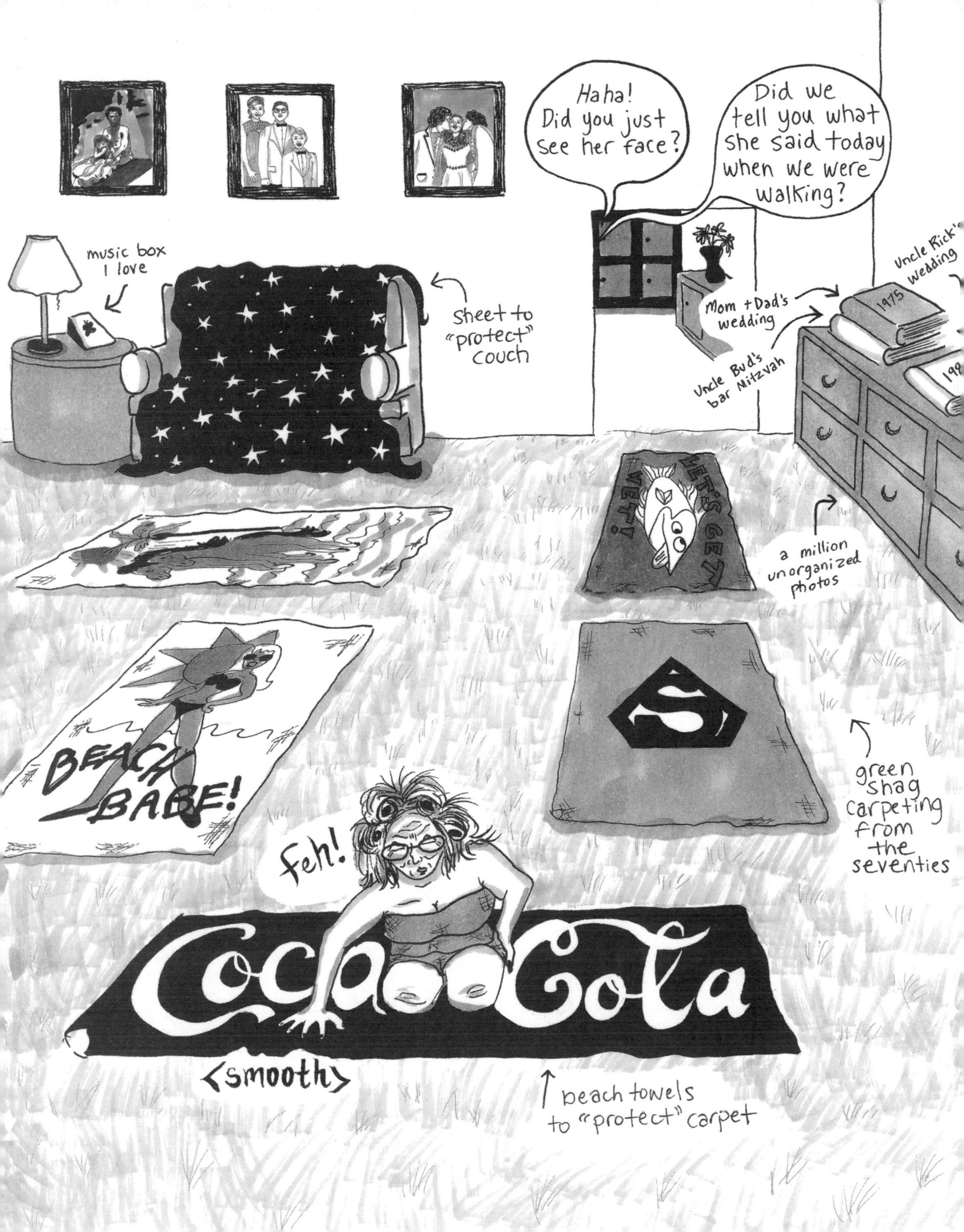
Haha! Did you just see her face?
Did we tell you what she said today when we were walking?
music box I love
sheet to "protect" couch
Uncle Rick's wedding
Mom + Dad's wedding
1975
Uncle Bud's bar Mitzvah
a million unorganized photos
BEACH BABE!
green shag carpeting from the seventies
Feh!
Coca-Cola
<smooth>
beach towels to "protect" carpet

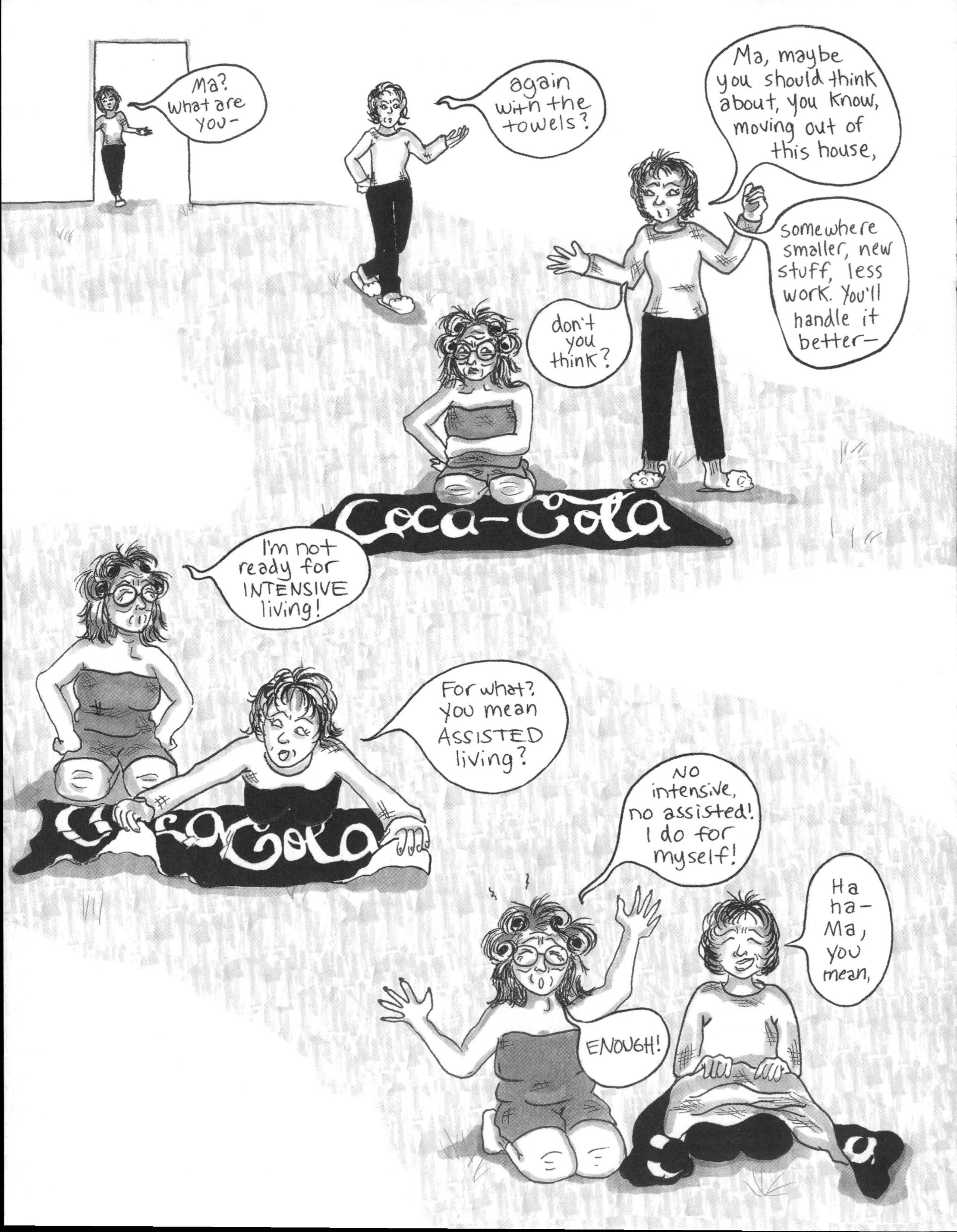
Ma? what are you-
again with the towels?
Ma, maybe you should think about, you know, moving out of this house,
somewhere smaller, new stuff, less work. You'll handle it better-
don't you think?
I'm not ready for INTENSIVE living!
For what? You mean ASSISTED living?
NO intensive, no assisted! I do for myself!
Ha ha- Ma, you mean,
ENOUGH!

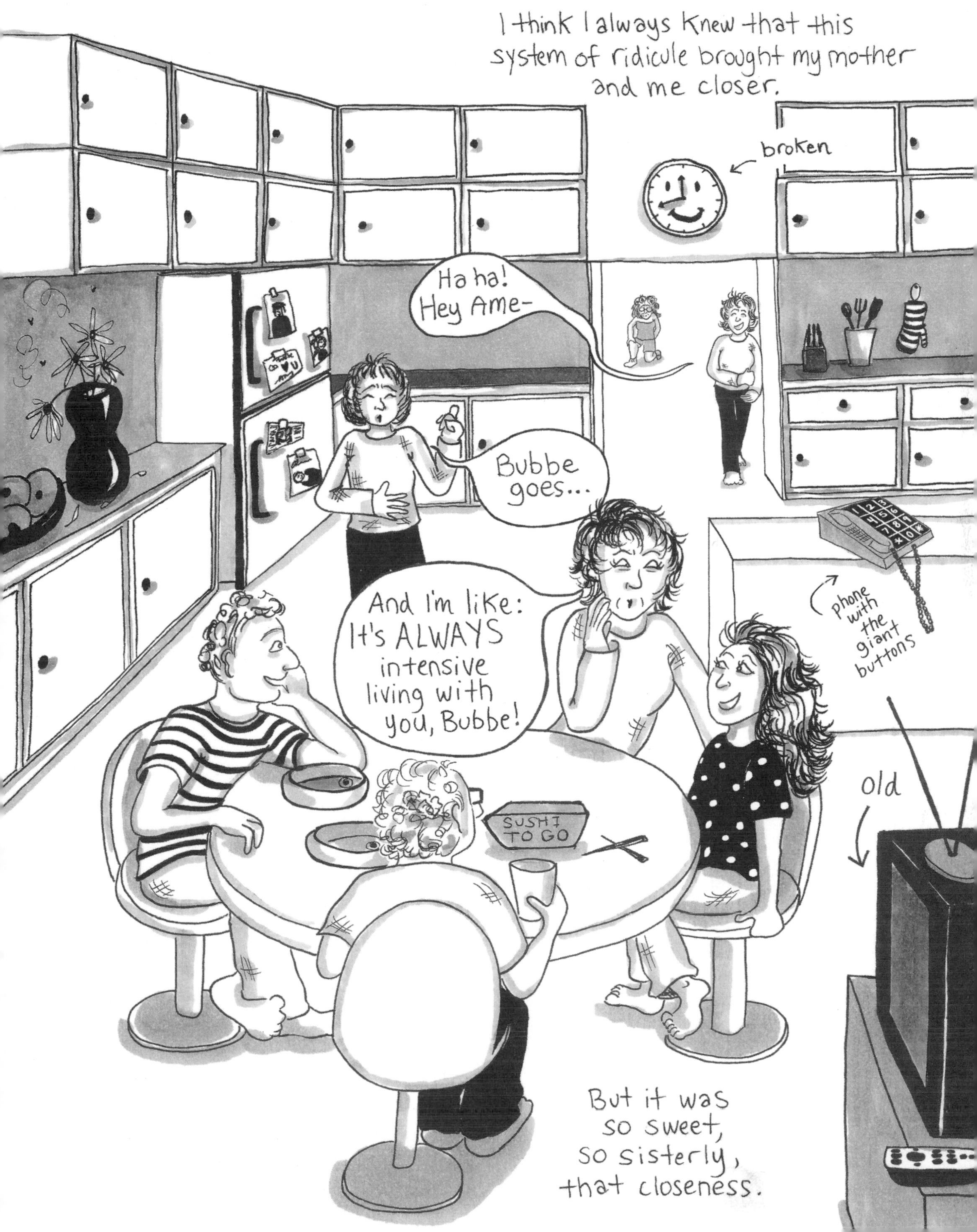

I think I always knew that this system of ridicule brought my mother and me closer.
broken
Ha ha! Hey Ame-
Bubbe goes...
And I'm like: It's ALWAYS intensive living with you, Bubbe!
phone with the giant buttons
SUSHI TO GO
Old
But it was so sweet, so sisterly, that closeness.

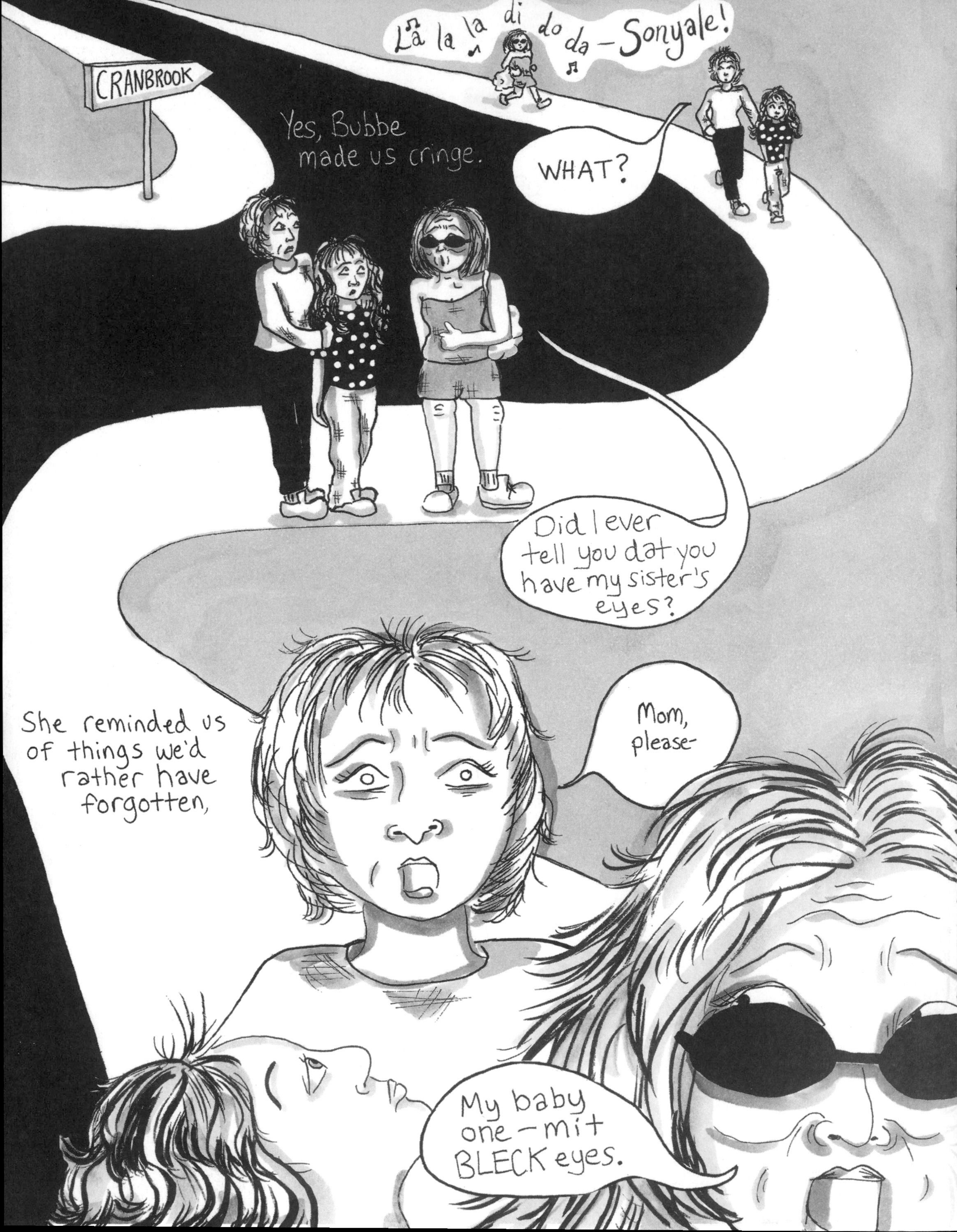
Là la la di do da - Sonyale!
CRANBROOK
Yes, Bubbe made us cringe.
WHAT?
Did I ever tell you dat you have my sister's eyes?
She reminded us of things we'd rather have forgotten,
Mom, please-
My baby one-mit BLECK eyes.

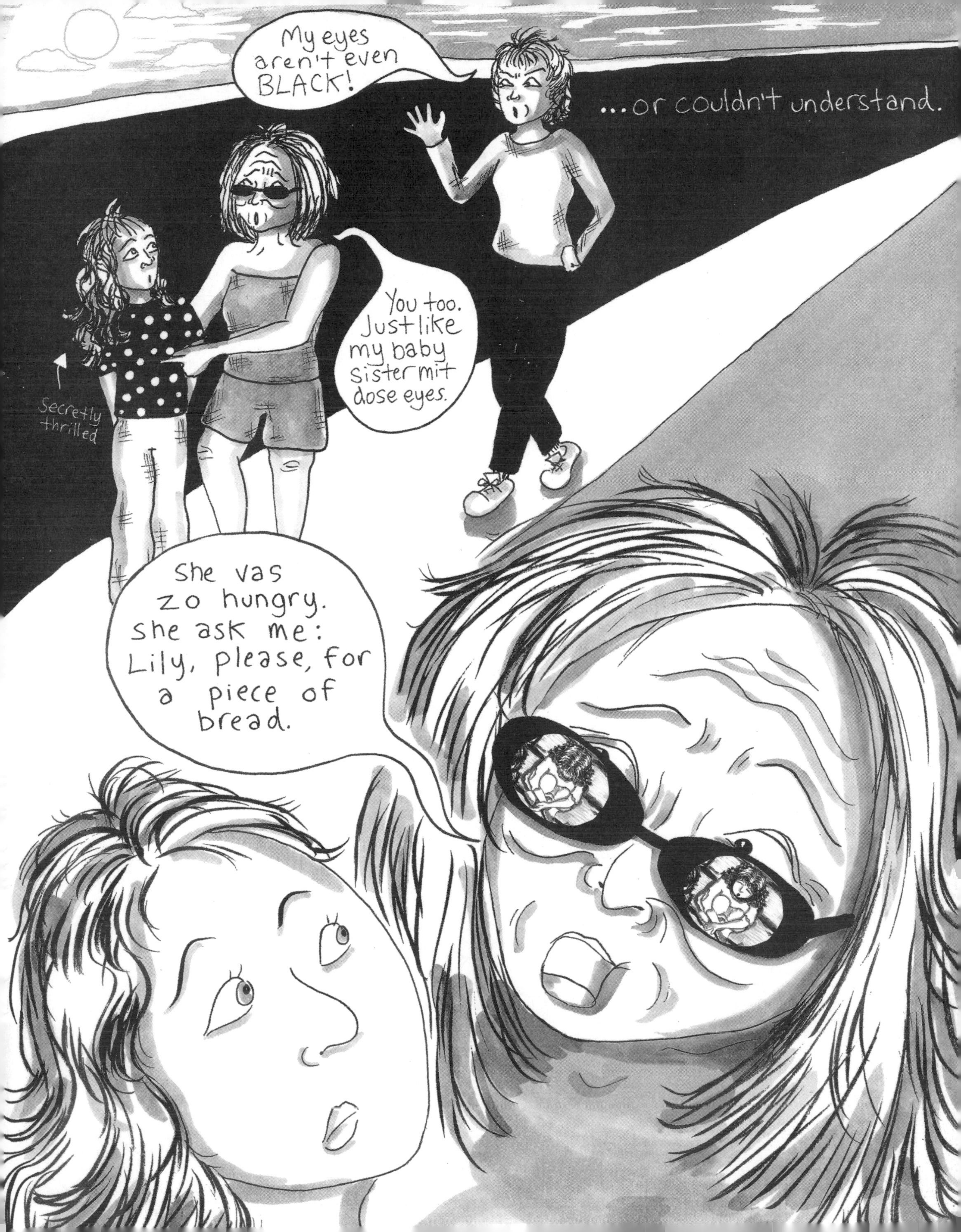
My eyes aren't even BLACK!
...or couldn't understand.
You too. Just like my baby sister mit dose eyes.
Secretly thrilled
She vas zo hungry. she ask me: Lily, please, for a piece of bread.

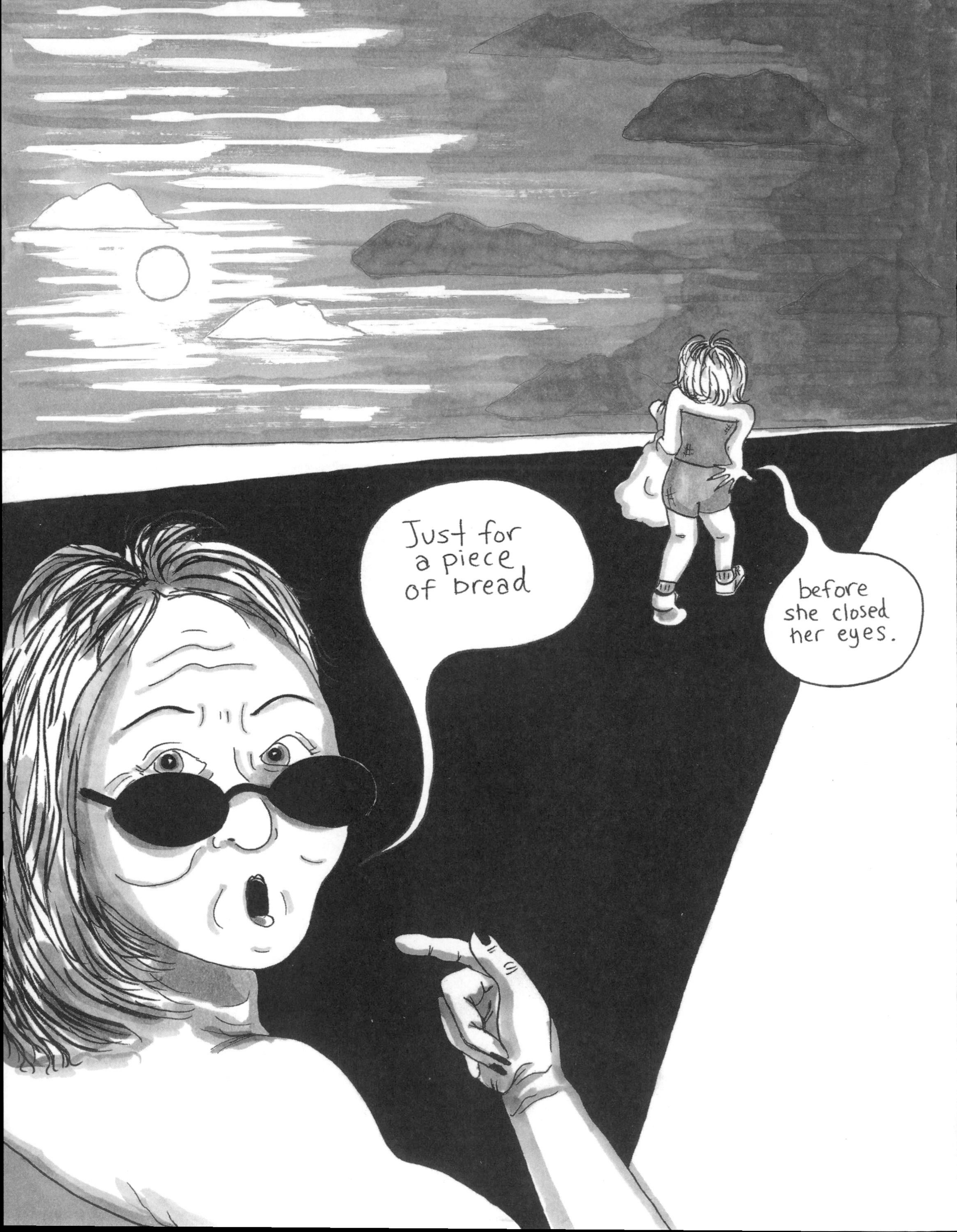
Just for a piece of bread
before she closed her eyes.

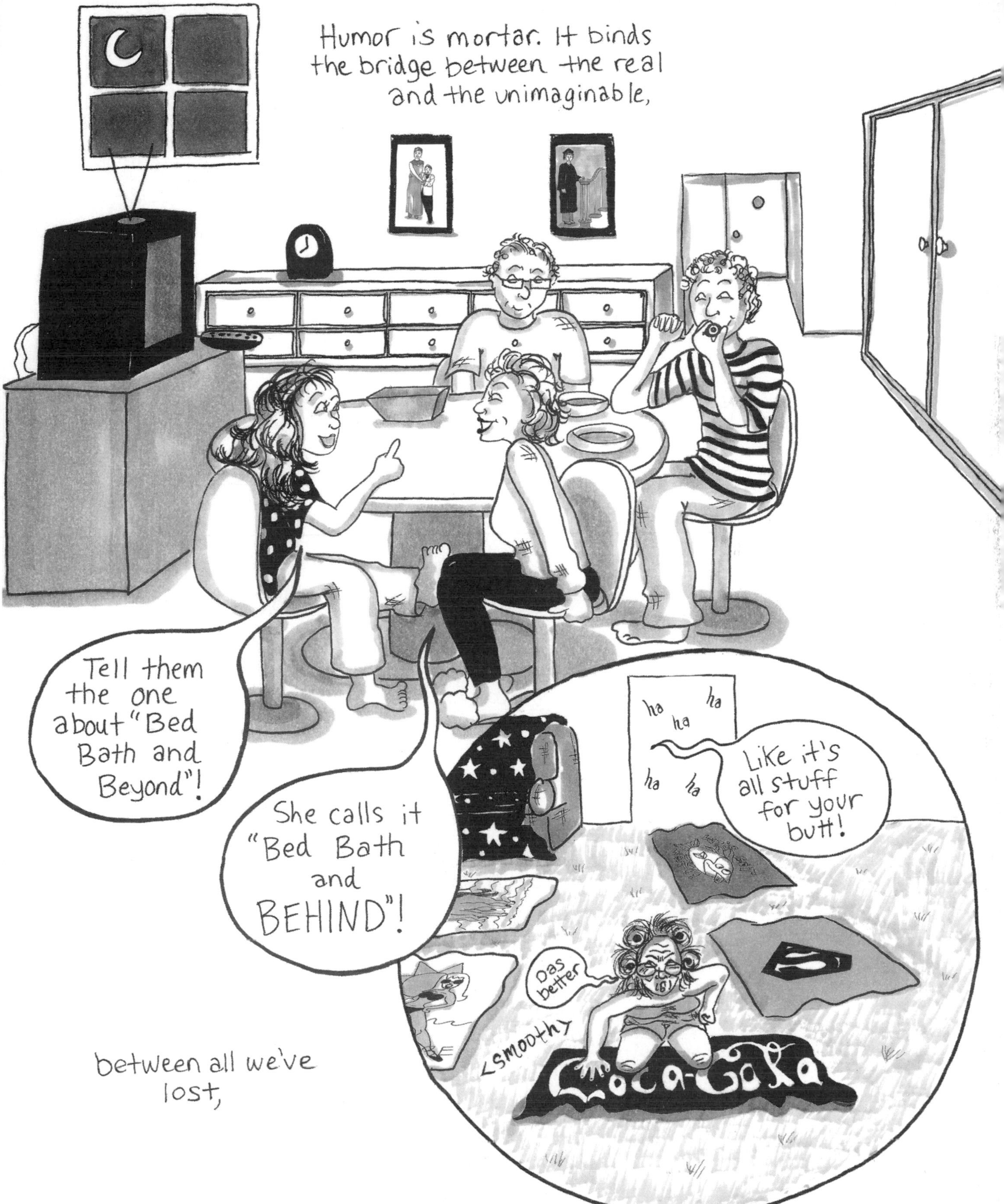

Humor is mortar. It binds the bridge between the real and the unimaginable,
Tell them the one about "Bed Bath and Beyond"!
She calls it "Bed Bath and BEHIND"!
ha ha ha ha ha
Like it's all stuff for your butt!
Das better
<smoothy>
Coca-Cola
between all we've lost,

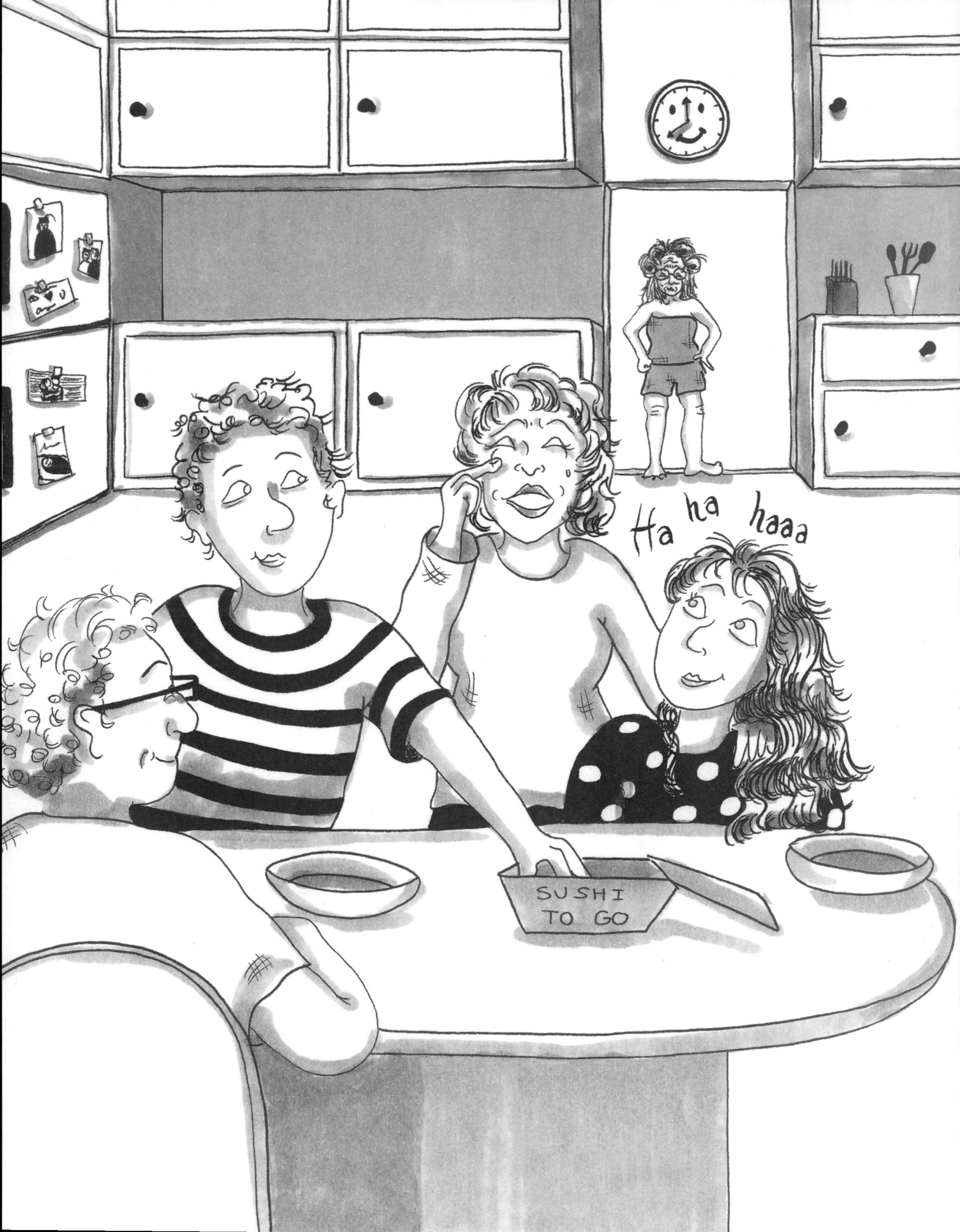
Ha ha haaa
SUSHI TO GO

... and what we can't get rid of.

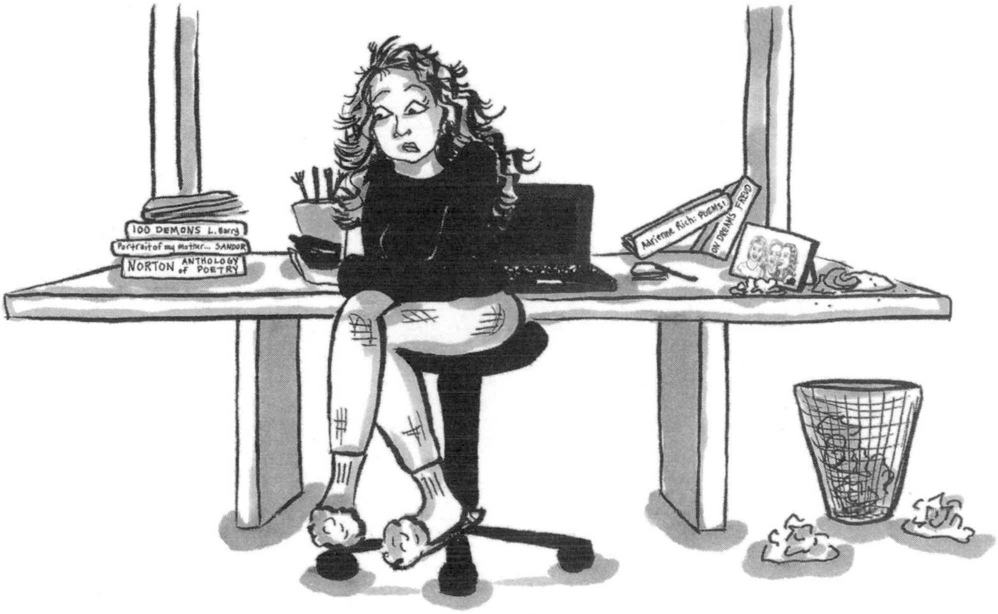
100 DEMONS L. Barry
Portrait of my mother... SANDOR
NORTON ANTHOLOGY of POETRY
Adrienne Rich: POEMS!
ON DREAMS FREUD

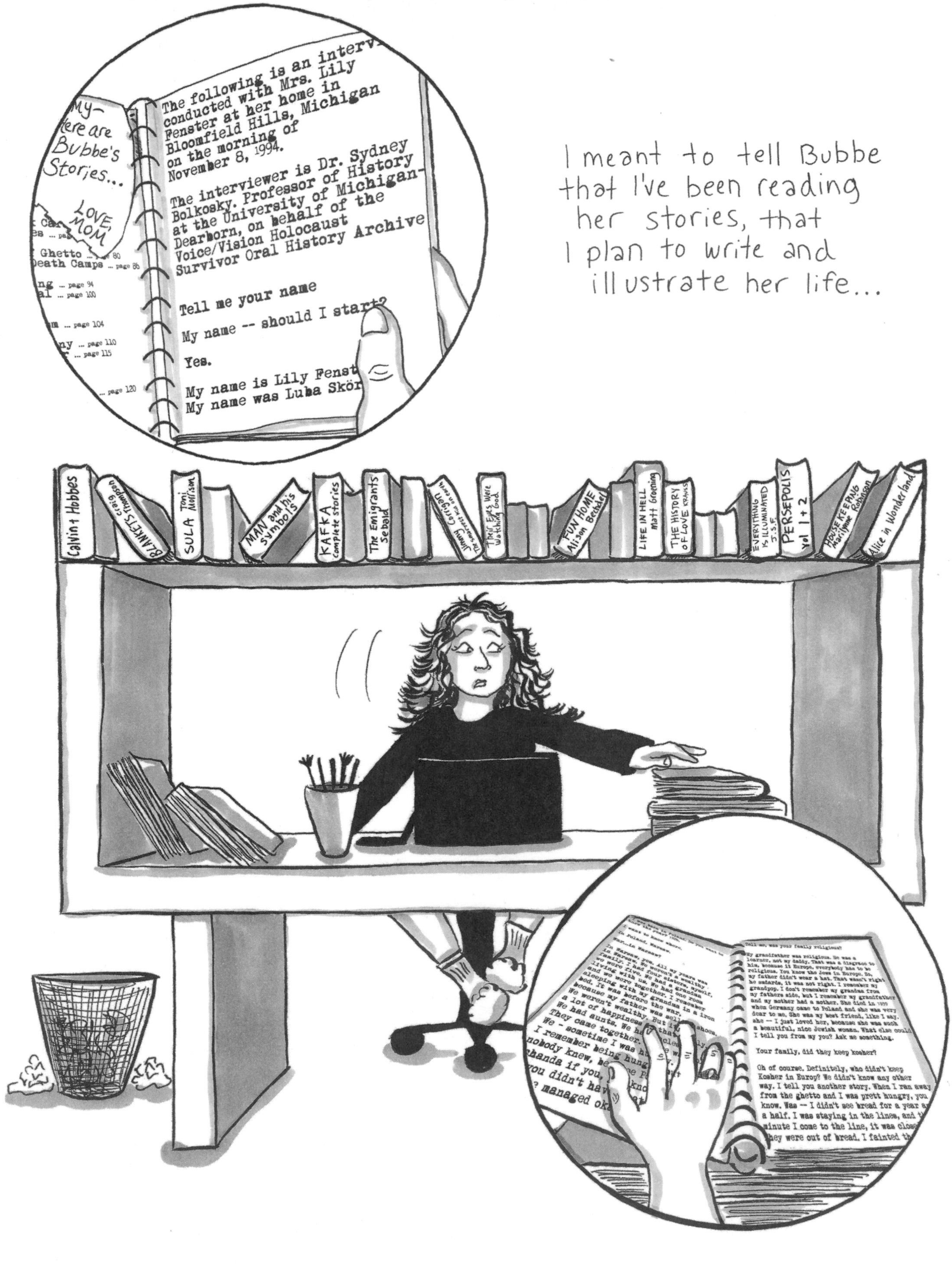

My—
Here are Bubbe's Stories...
LOVE, MOM
Ghetto ... page 80
Death Camps ... page 86
... page 94
... page 100
... page 104
... page 110
... page 115
... page 120
The following is an interv
conducted with Mrs. Lily
Fenster at her home in
Bloomfield Hills, Michigan
on the morning of
November 8, 1994.
The interviewer is Dr. Sydney
Bolkosky, Professor of History
at the University of Michigan-
Dearborn, on behalf of the
Voice/Vision Holocaust
Survivor Oral History Archive
Tell me your name
My name -- should I start?
Yes.
My name is Lily Fenst
My name was Luba Skör
I meant to tell Bubbe
that I've been reading
her stories, that
I plan to write and
illustrate her life...
Calvin + Hobbes
BLANKETS Craig Thompson
SULA Toni Morrison
MAN and his symbols
KAFKA complete stories
The Emigrants Sebald
Their Eyes Were Watching God
FUN HOME Alison Bechdel
LIFE IN HELL Matt Groening
THE HISTORY OF LOVE KRAUSS
EVERYTHING IS ILLUMINATED J.S.F.
PERSEPOLIS Vol 1 + 2
HOUSEKEEPING Marilynne Robinson
Alice in Wonderland
Tell me, was your family religious?
My grandfather was religious. He was a learner, not my daddy.
Your family, did they keep kosher?
Oh of course. Definitely, who didn't keep Kosher in Europ? We didn't know any other way. I tell you another story. When I ran away from the ghetto and I was prett hungry, you know.

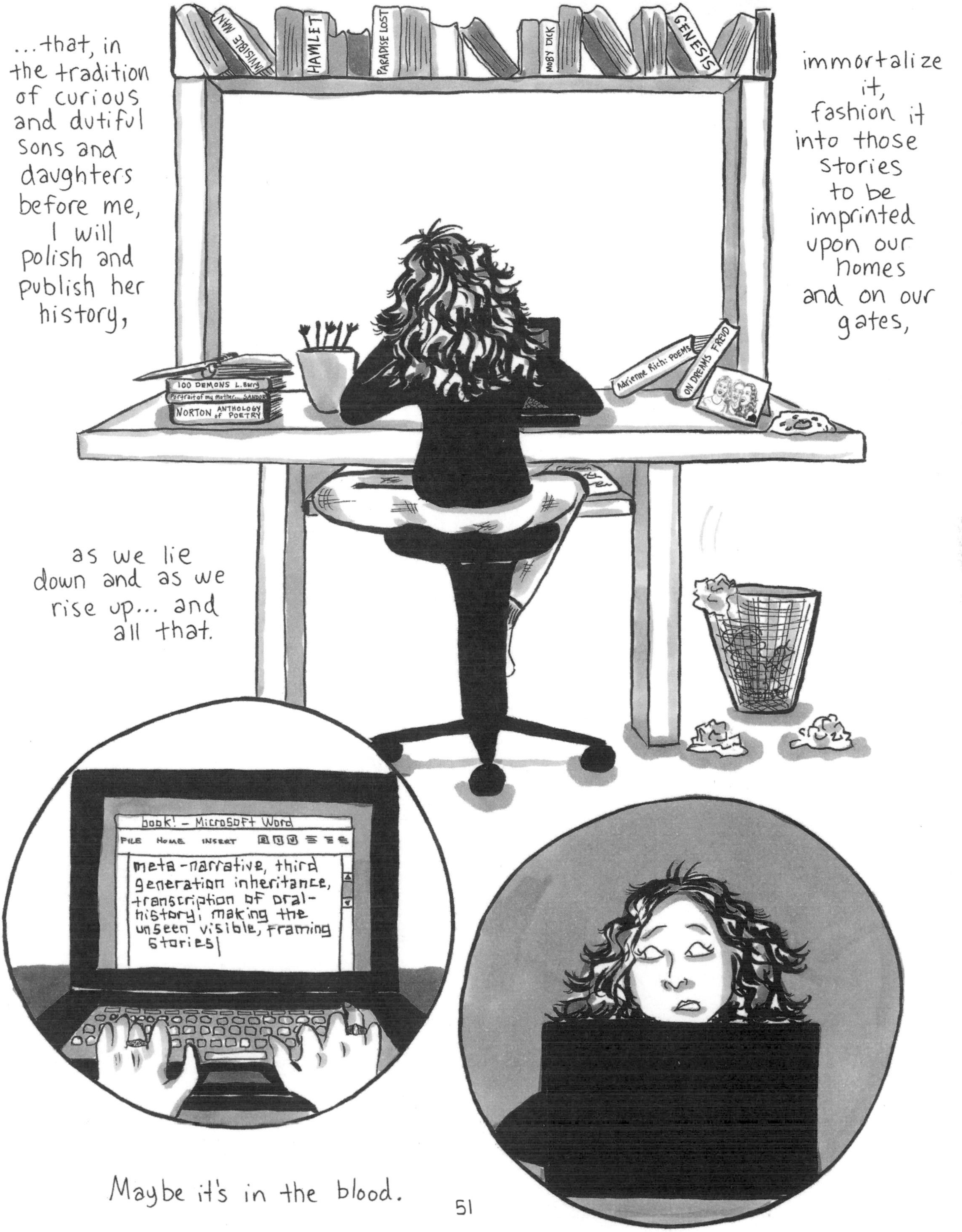
...that, in the tradition of curious and dutiful sons and daughters before me, I will polish and publish her history,
INVISIBLE MAN
HAMLET
PARADISE LOST
MOBY DICK
GENESIS
immortalize it, fashion it into those stories to be imprinted upon our homes and on our gates,
100 DEMONS L. Barry
NORTON ANTHOLOGY of POETRY
Adrienne Rich: POEMS
ON DREAMS FREUD
as we lie down and as we rise up... and all that.
book! – Microsoft Word
FILE HOME INSERT
meta-narrative, third generation inheritance, transcription of oral-history, making the unseen visible, framing stories|
Maybe it's in the blood.

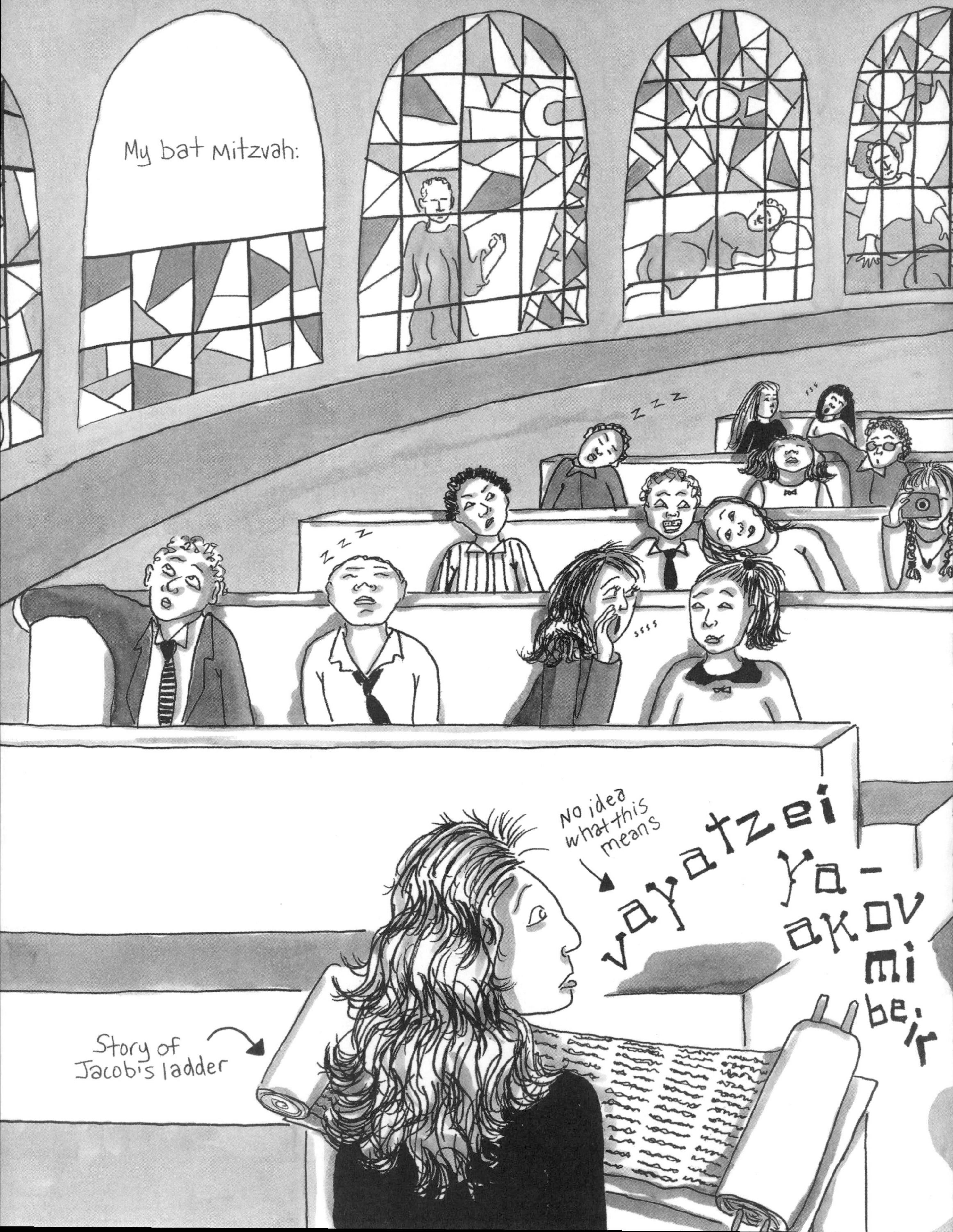
My bat Mitzvah:
No idea what this means
vayatzei ya-akov mi beir
Story of Jacob's ladder

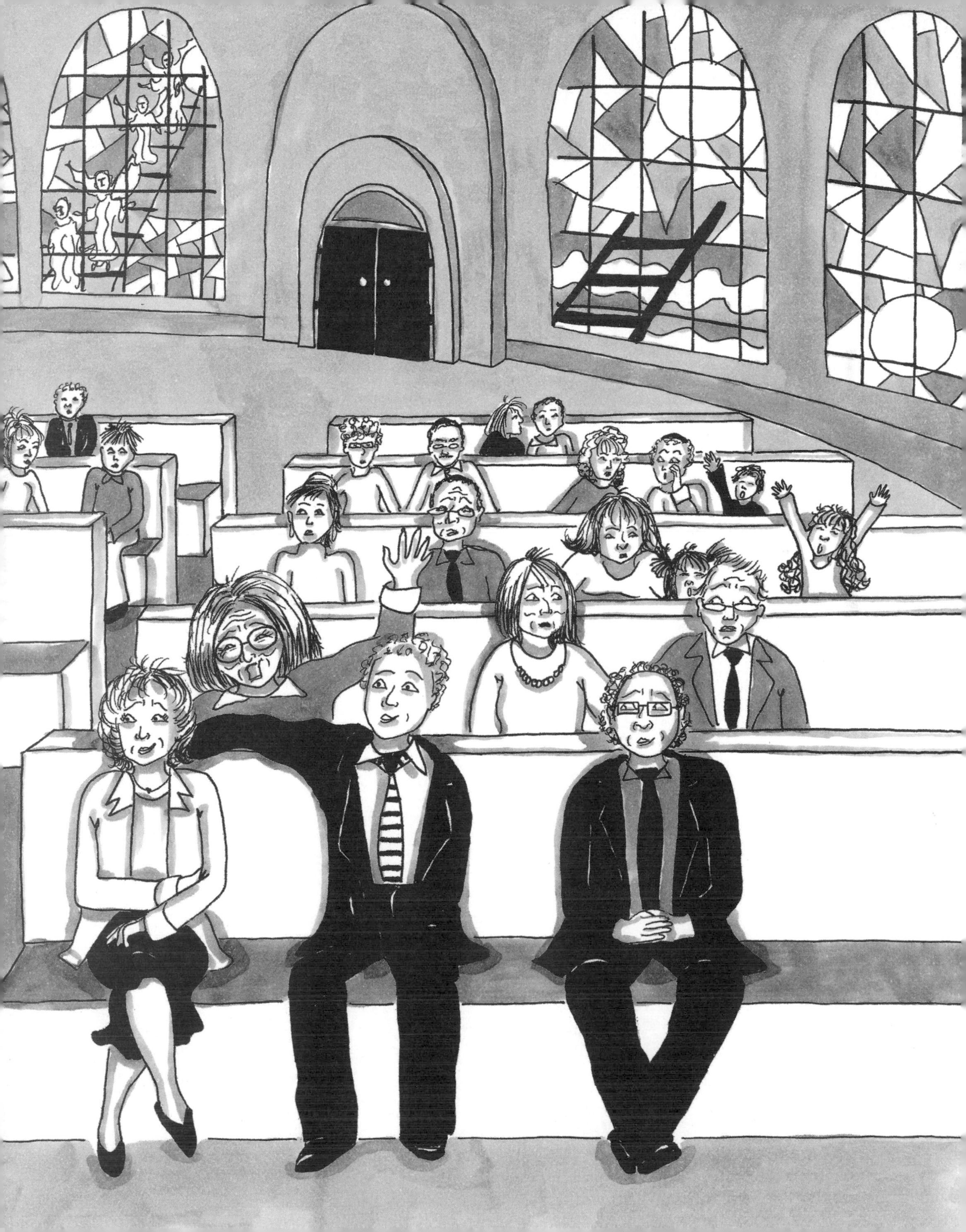

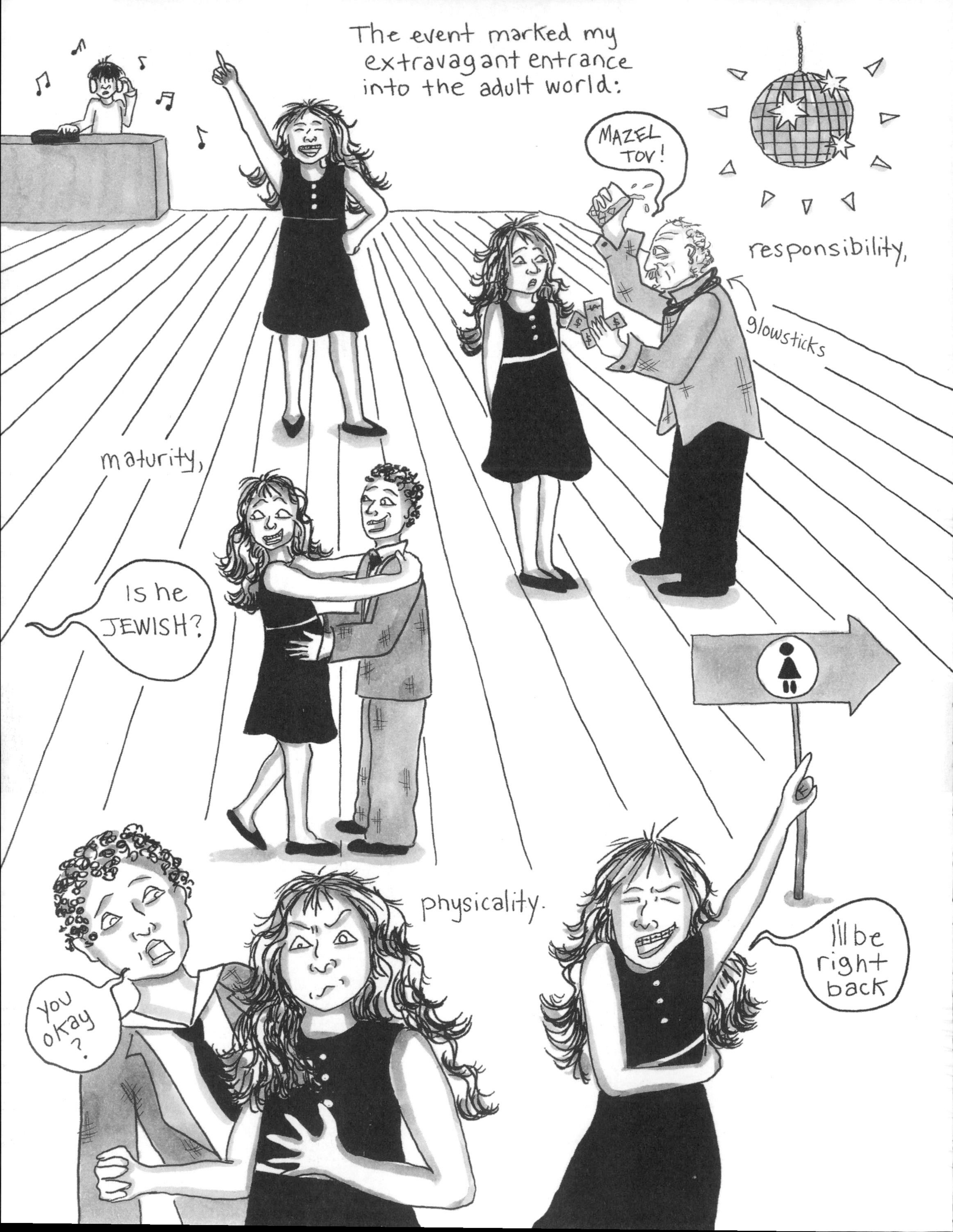
The event marked my extravagant entrance into the adult world:
MAZEL TOV!
responsibility,
glowsticks
maturity,
Is he JEWISH?
physicality.
you okay?
I'll be right back

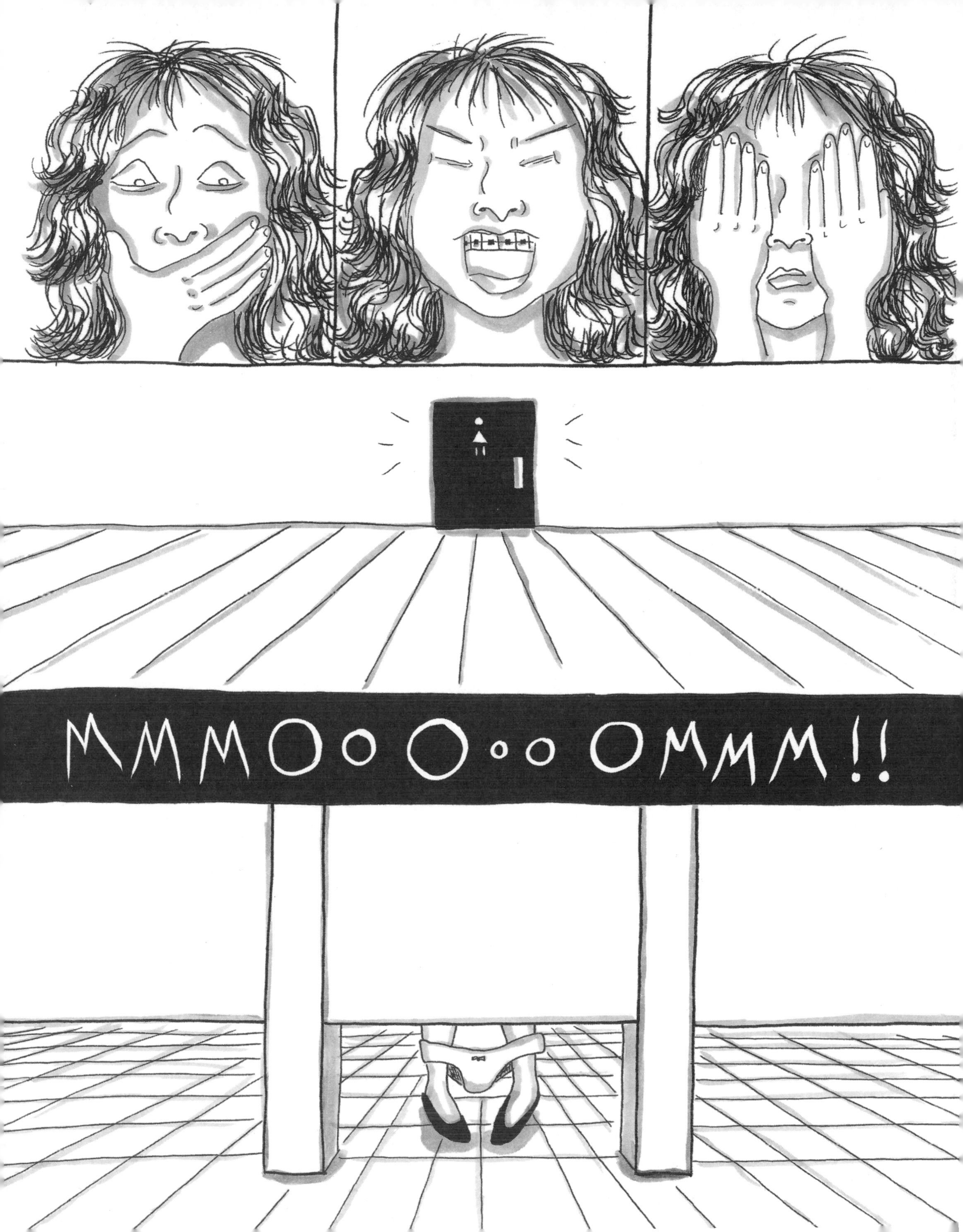
MMMOoOooOMMM!!

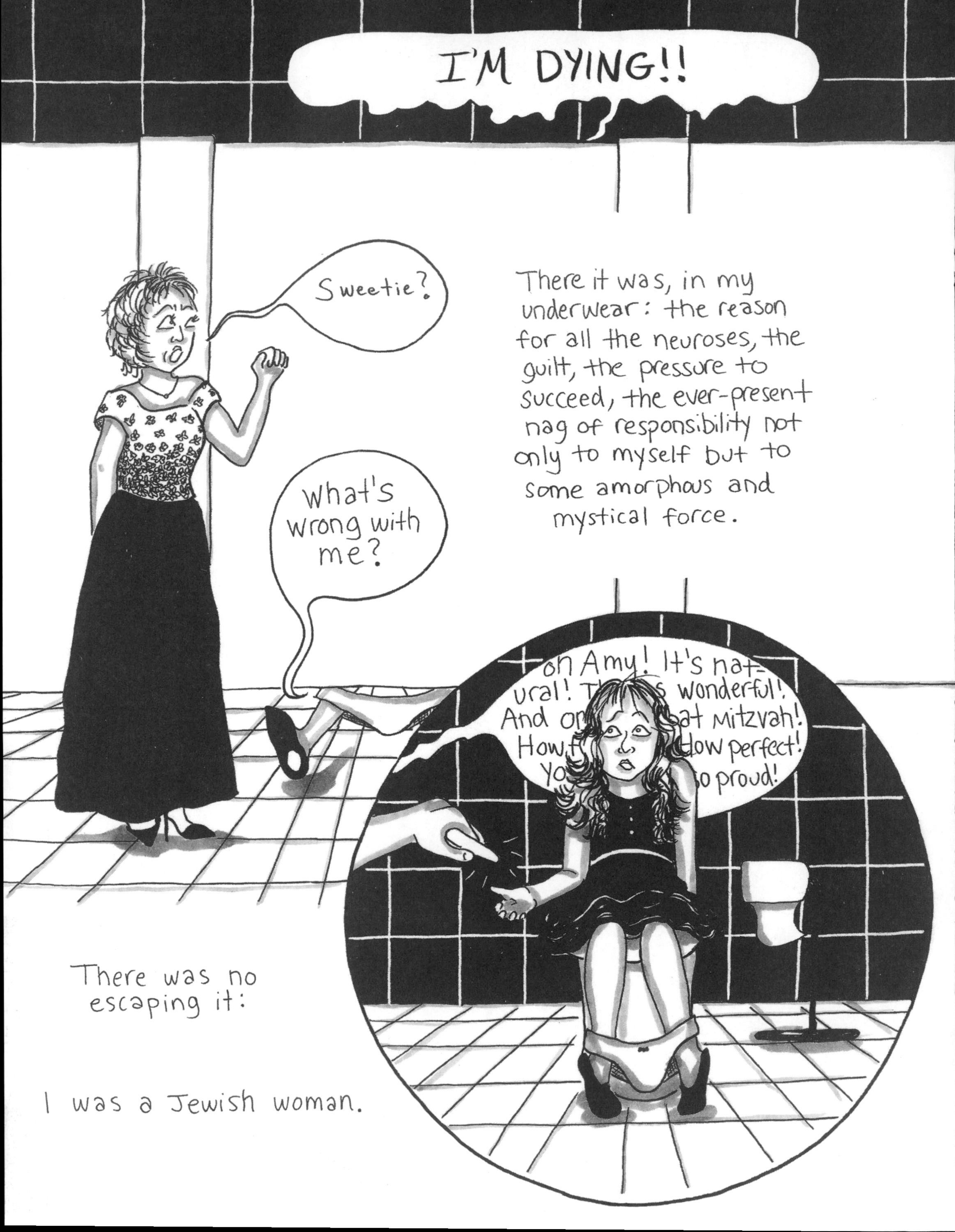
I'M DYING!!
Sweetie?
What's wrong with me?
There it was, in my underwear: the reason for all the neuroses, the guilt, the pressure to succeed, the ever-present nag of responsibility not only to myself but to some amorphous and mystical force.
Oh Amy! It's nat- ural! Th s wonderful! And on at Mitzvah! How How perfect! Yo so proud!
There was no escaping it:
I was a Jewish woman.

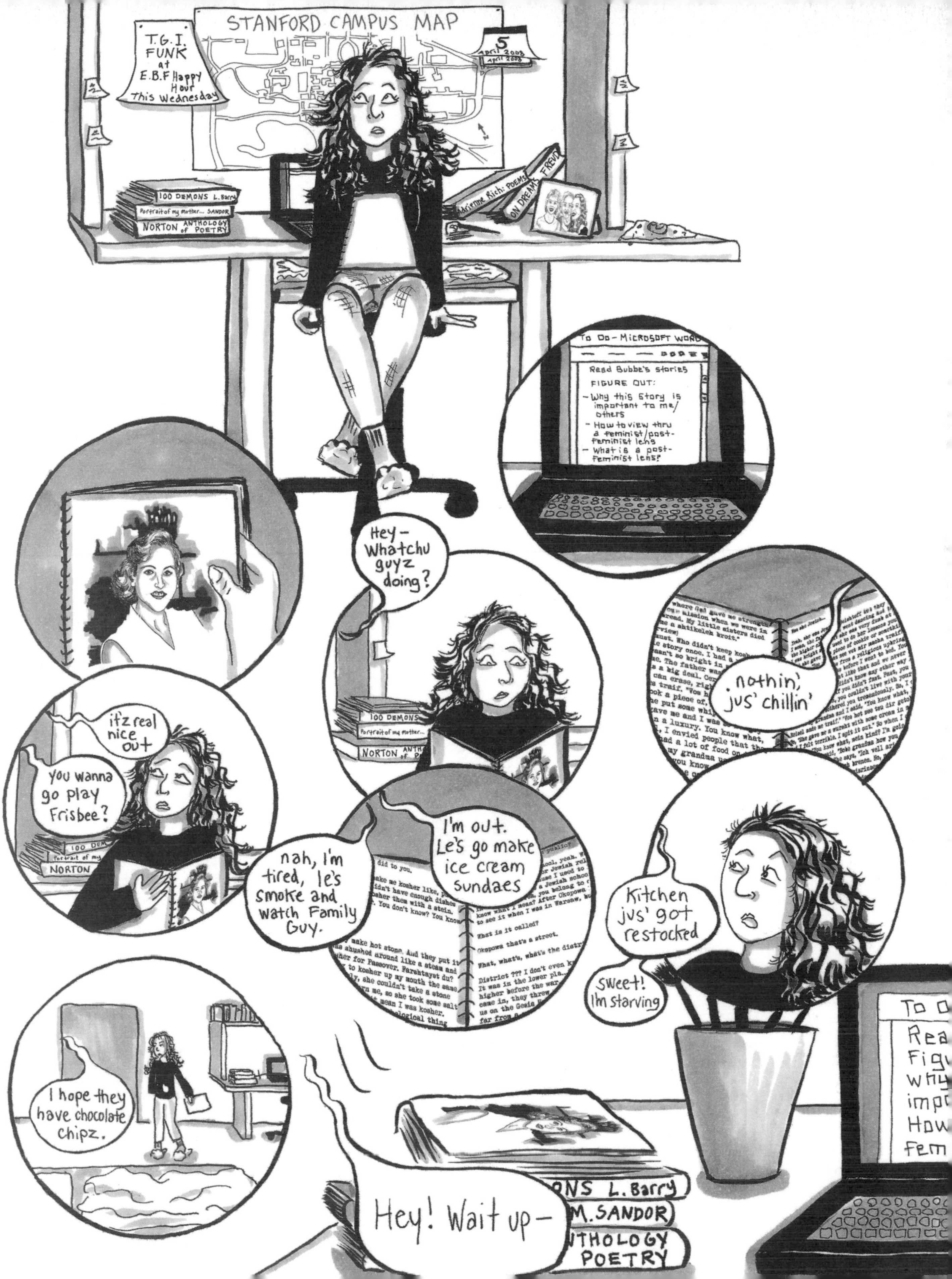
STANFORD CAMPUS MAP
T.G.I. FUNK at E.B.F Happy Hour This Wednesday
5 April 2008
100 DEMONS L.Barry
Portrait of my Mother... SANDOR
NORTON ANTHOLOGY of POETRY
Adrienne Rich: POEMS
ON DREAMS FREUD
To Do - MICROSOFT WORD
Read Bubbe's stories
FIGURE OUT:
- Why this story is important to me/others
- How to view thru a feminist/post-feminist lens
- What is a post-feminist lens?
Hey- Whatchu guyz doing?
.nothin; jus' chillin'
itz real nice out
you wanna go play Frisbee?
nah, I'm tired, le's smoke and watch Family Guy.
I'm out. Le's go make ice cream sundaes
Kitchen jus' got restocked
Sweet! I'm starving
I hope they have chocolate chipz.
Hey! Wait up-

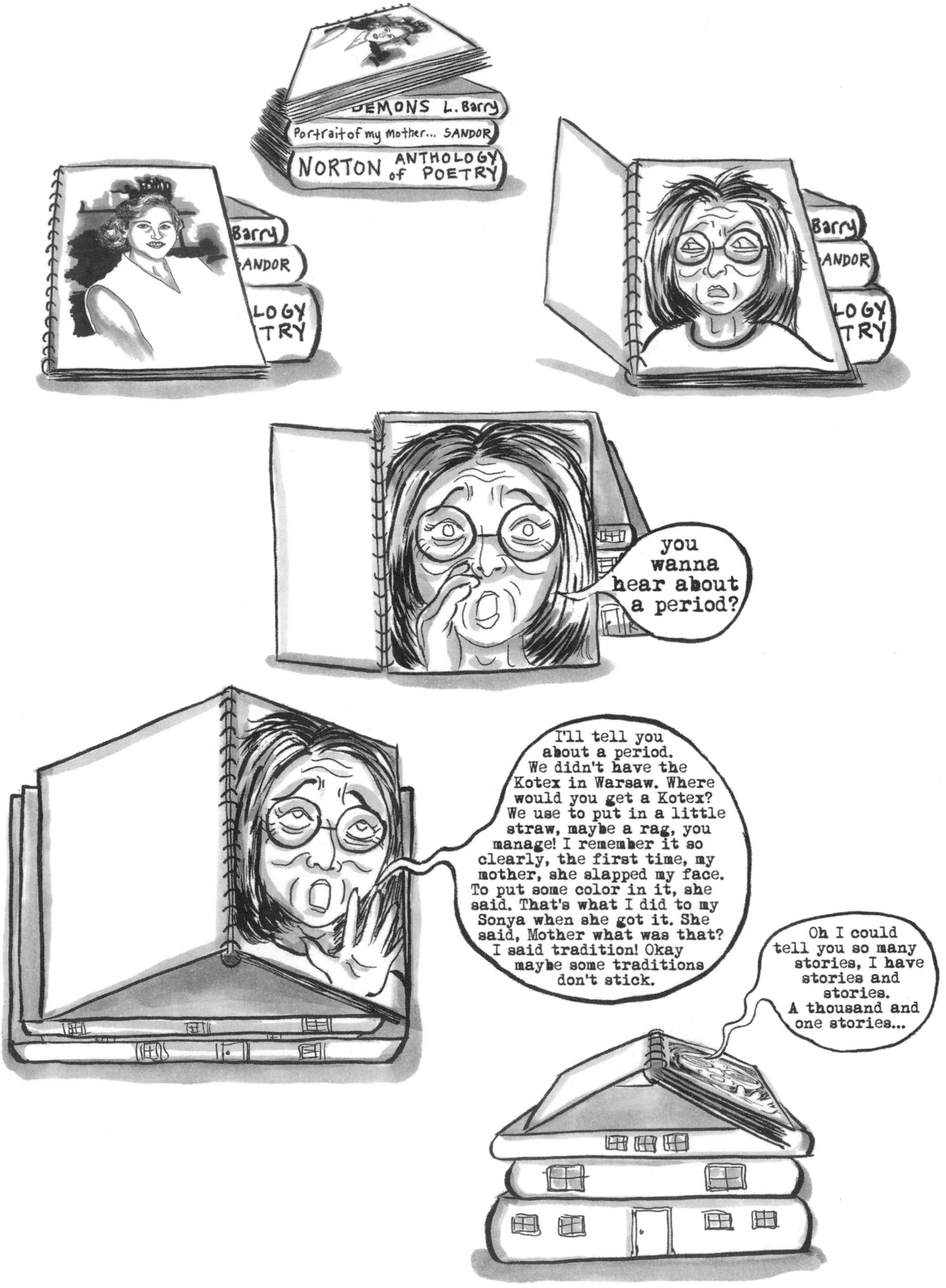
DEMONS L. Barry
Portrait of my mother... SANDOR
NORTON ANTHOLOGY of POETRY
you wanna hear about a period?
I'll tell you about a period. We didn't have the Kotex in Warsaw. Where would you get a Kotex? We use to put in a little straw, maybe a rag, you manage! I remember it so clearly, the first time, my mother, she slapped my face. To put some color in it, she said. That's what I did to my Sonya when she got it. She said, Mother what was that? I said tradition! Okay maybe some traditions don't stick.
Oh I could tell you so many stories, I have stories and stories. A thousand and one stories...

Before the war we manage okay. I was with my mother and my father.
I had four sisters, myself we were five. We had a Bubbe with us too.
We had one room, all together. I remember I was sleeping with my Bubbe
in the same little bed. She was my best friend, like you say. We were
not a wealthy family - sometimes I was hungry but I didn't tell nobody.
Not wealthy but close, close. Not like how you have today with everybody
in their different place. Crowded, okay, but never lonely.

Some in the family were religious. My father, no. He was
for the Jewish people. Religion he didn't care for, but he
sticked with the people who cared for him. All I remember
is Friday. Friday for us was when we could afford to have
a little soup, with a little challah, and there was festivity.
That was happiness. My grandma wore a beautiful little white
apron and she said the blessings. Traditions.

Here, in America, we don't have so much relatives. Okay,
I have three kids, six gorgeous grandchildren, but some
of them is far. It's more to be alone in this country.

There was anti-Semitism, of course. They used to take snow and put a rock in it and throw it at the Jew. But I had the blonde hair and the blue eyes. I looked like a shiksa, a gentile. I had beautiful long braids. I was scared for the men grabbing at me, but I managed.

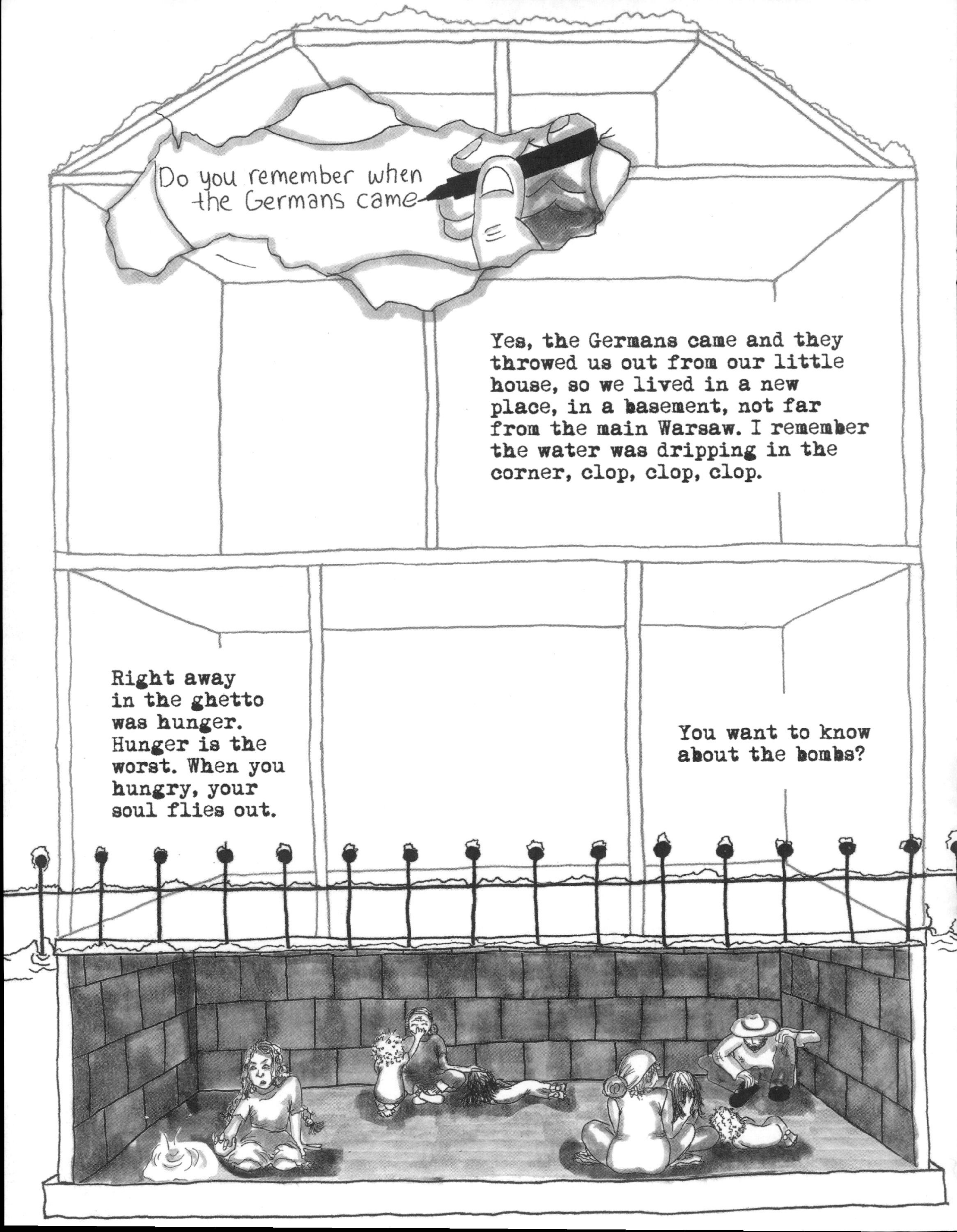

Do you remember when the Germans came
Yes, the Germans came and they throwed us out from our little house, so we lived in a new place, in a basement, not far from the main Warsaw. I remember the water was dripping in the corner, clop, clop, clop.
Right away in the ghetto was hunger. Hunger is the worst. When you hungry, your soul flies out.
You want to know about the bombs?

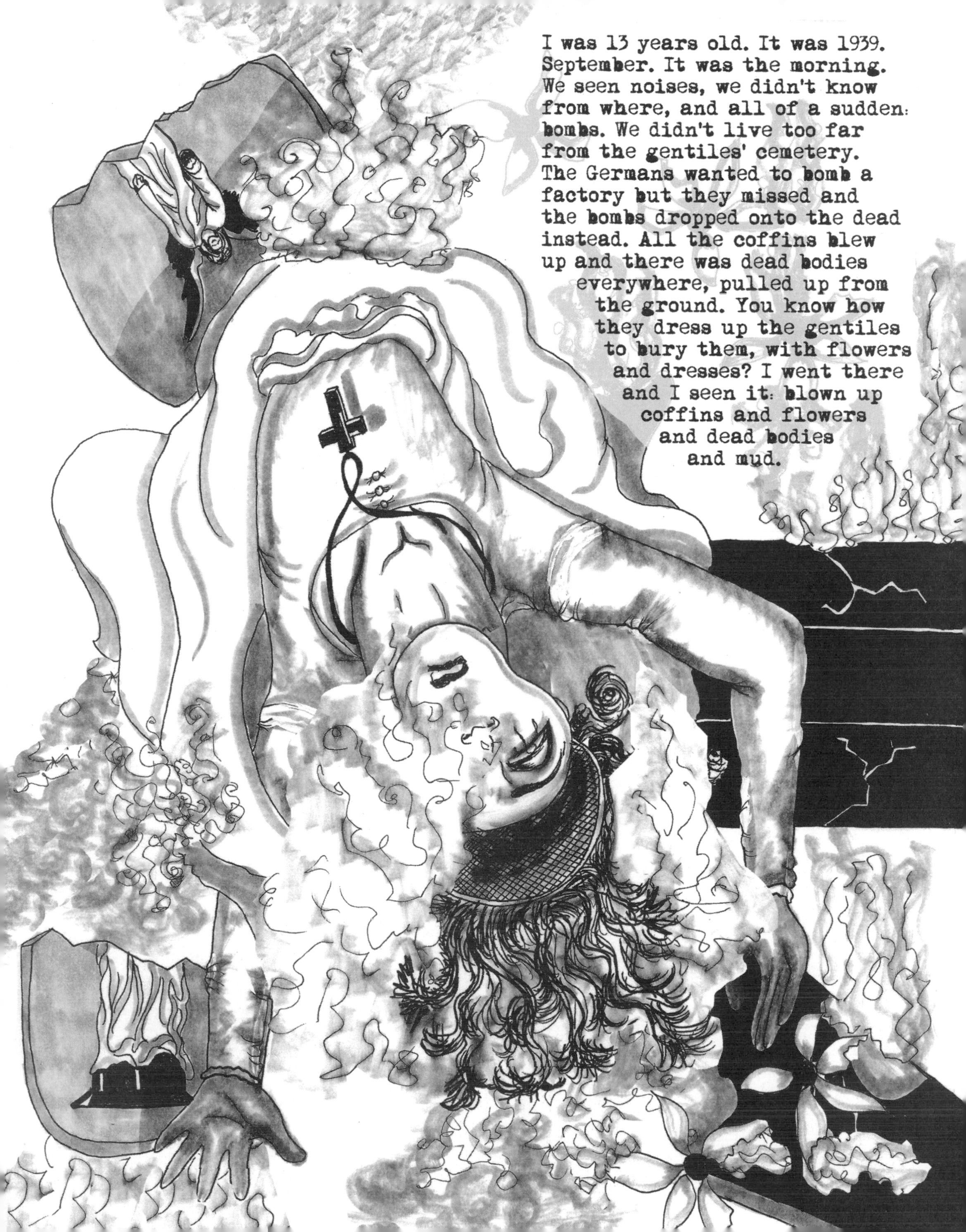
I was 13 years old. It was 1939. September. It was the morning. We seen noises, we didn't know from where, and all of a sudden: bombs. We didn't live too far from the gentiles' cemetery. The Germans wanted to bomb a factory but they missed and the bombs dropped onto the dead instead. All the coffins blew up and there was dead bodies everywhere, pulled up from the ground. You know how they dress up the gentiles to bury them, with flowers and dresses? I went there and I seen it: blown up coffins and flowers and dead bodies and mud.

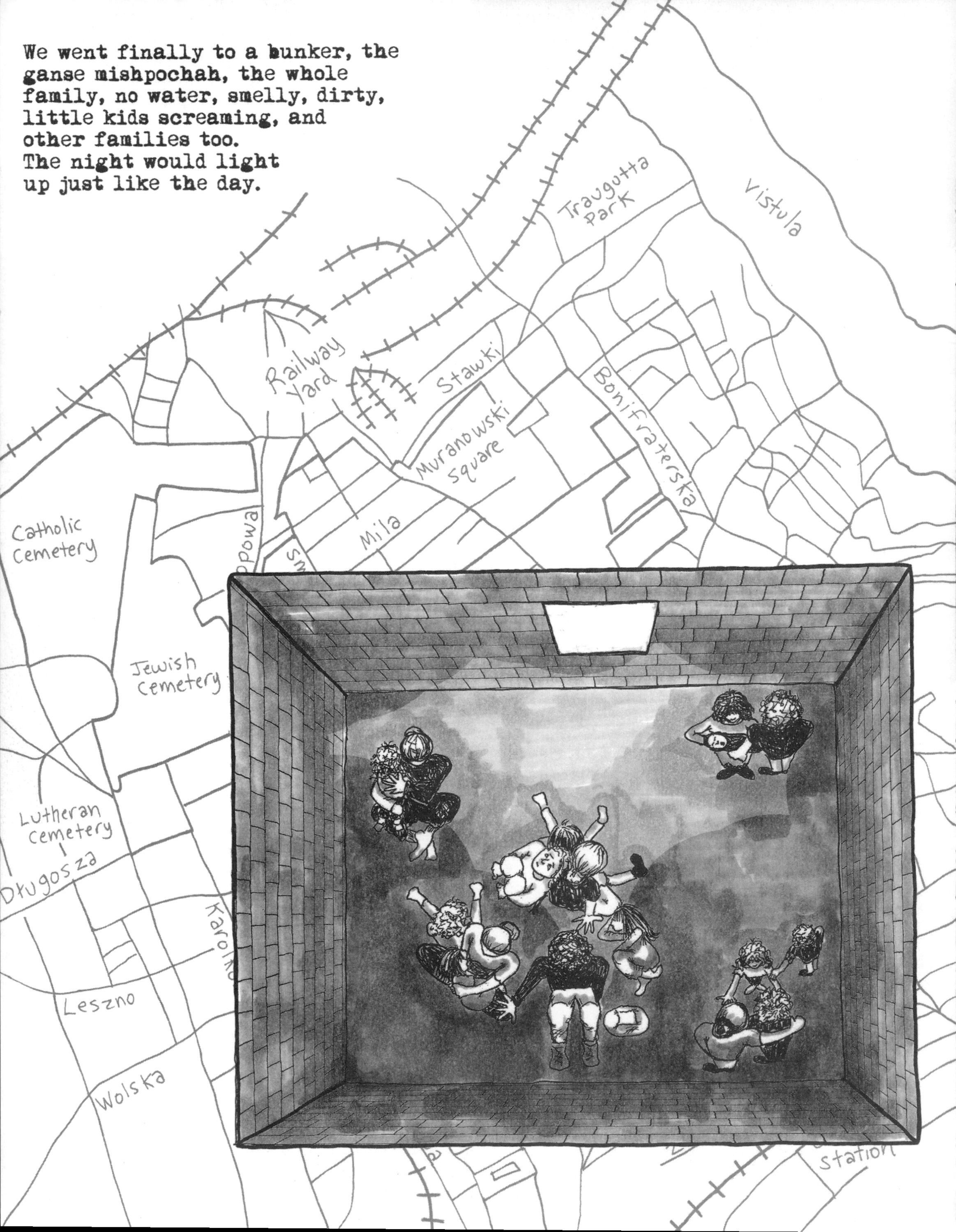
We went finally to a bunker, the ganse mishpochah, the whole family, no water, smelly, dirty, little kids screaming, and other families too.
The night would light up just like the day.
Traugutta Park
Vistula
Railway Yard
Stawki
Bonifraterska
Muranowski Square
Mila
Catholic Cemetery
Jewish Cemetery
Lutheran Cemetery
Długosza
Leszno
Wolska
station

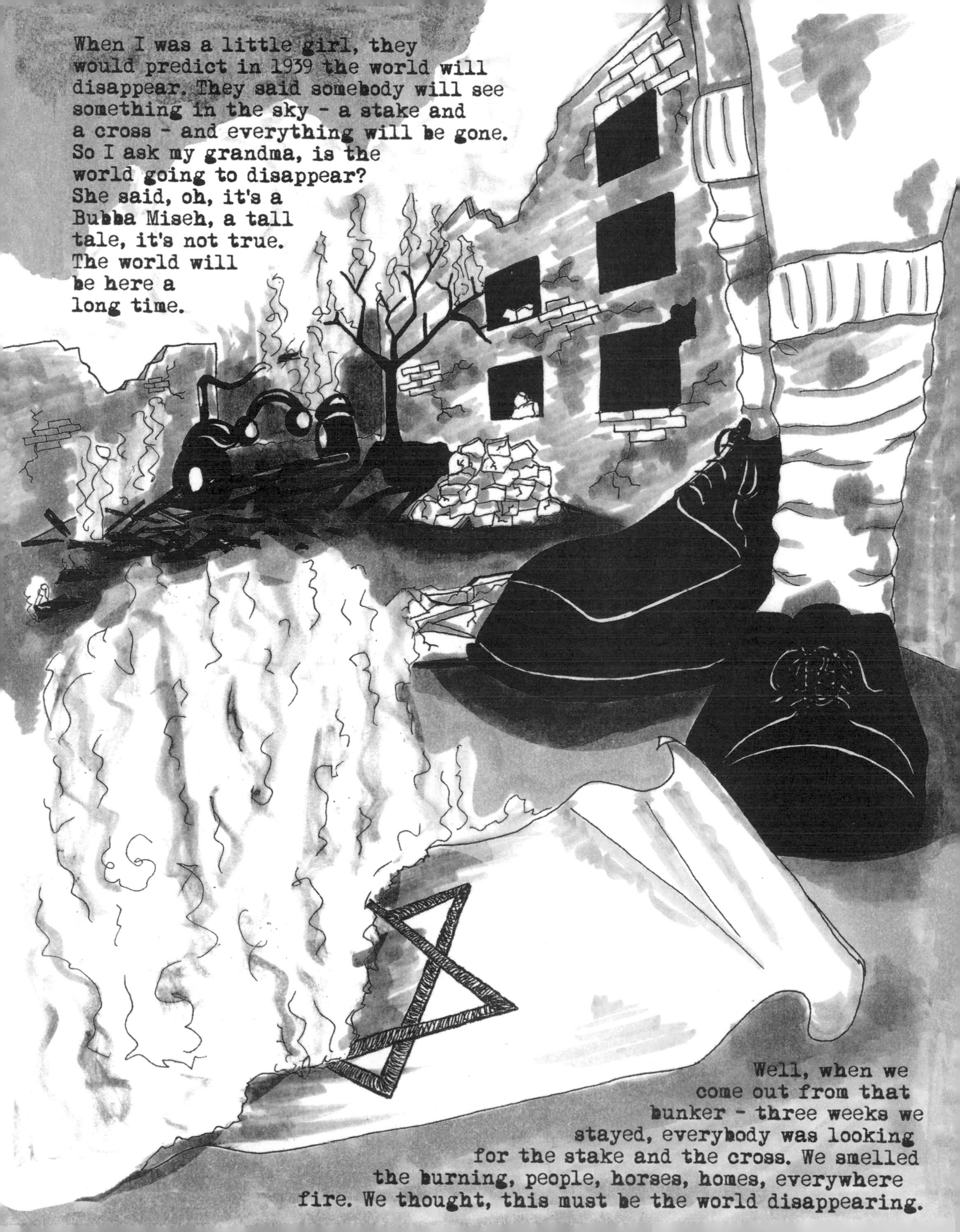
When I was a little girl, they would predict in 1939 the world will disappear. They said somebody will see something in the sky - a stake and a cross - and everything will be gone. So I ask my grandma, is the world going to disappear? She said, oh, it's a Bubba Miseh, a tall tale, it's not true. The world will be here a long time.
Well, when we come out from that bunker - three weeks we stayed, everybody was looking for the stake and the cross. We smelled the burning, people, horses, homes, everywhere fire. We thought, this must be the world disappearing.

Sometimes a whole world is one person.
My worlds were disappearing, one by one.

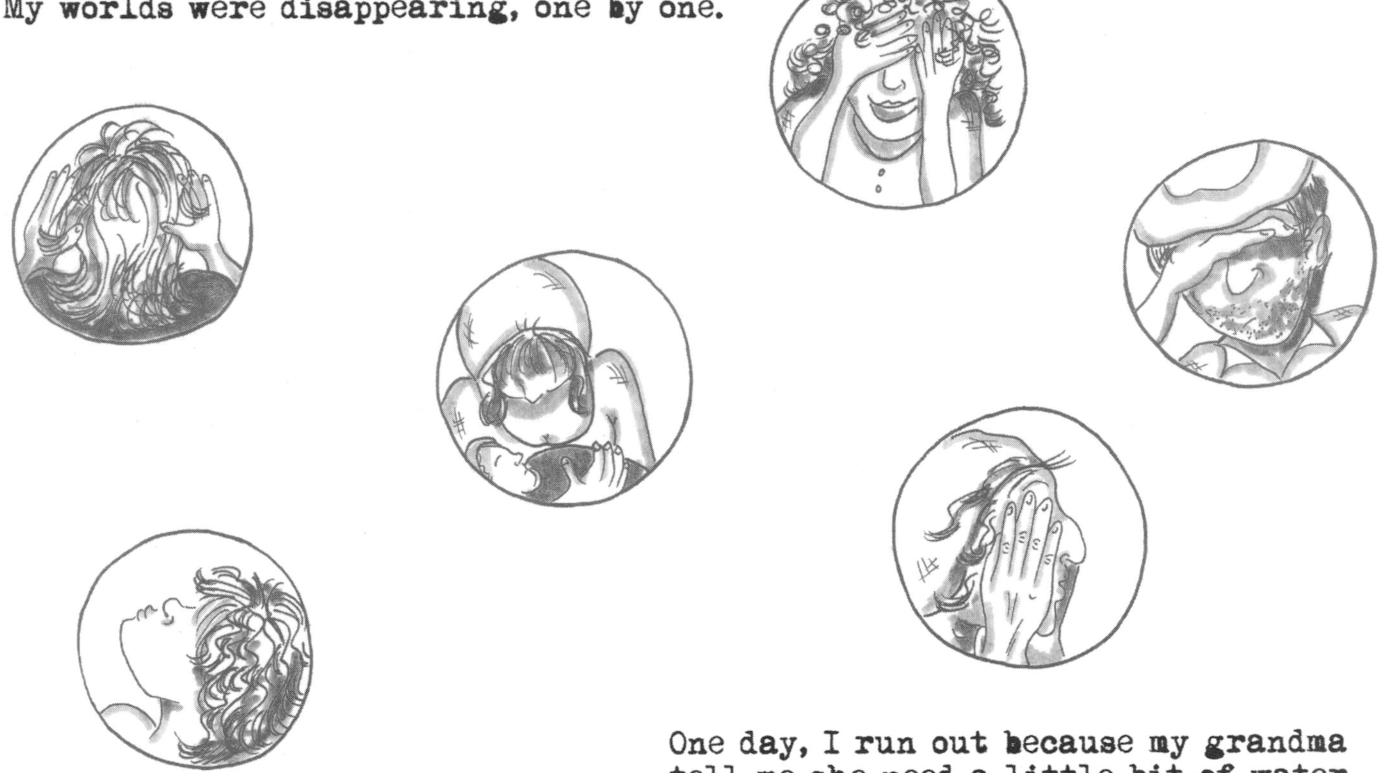

One day, I run out because my grandma
tell me she need a little bit of water.

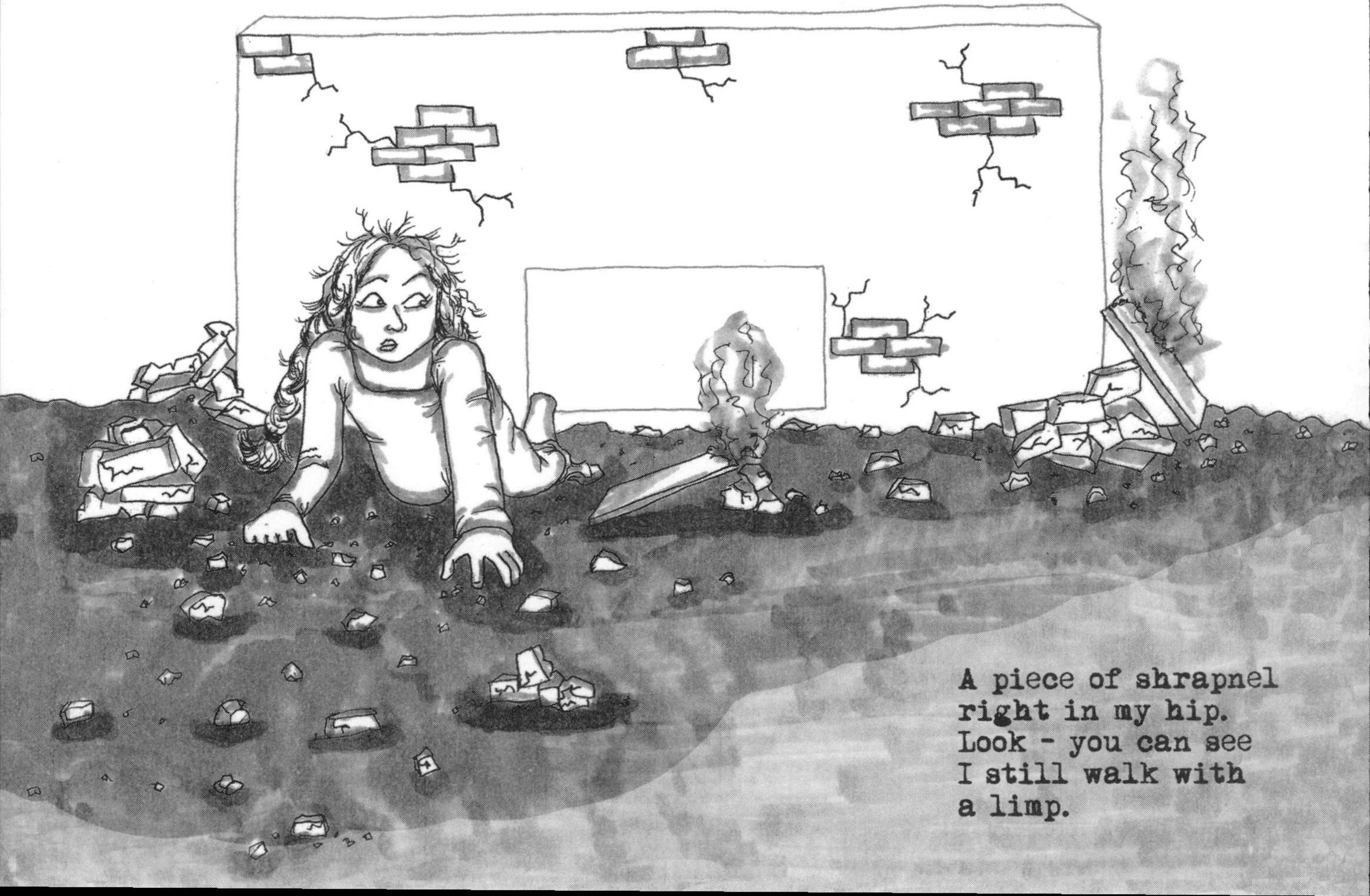
A piece of shrapnel
right in my hip.
Look - you can see
I still walk with
a limp.

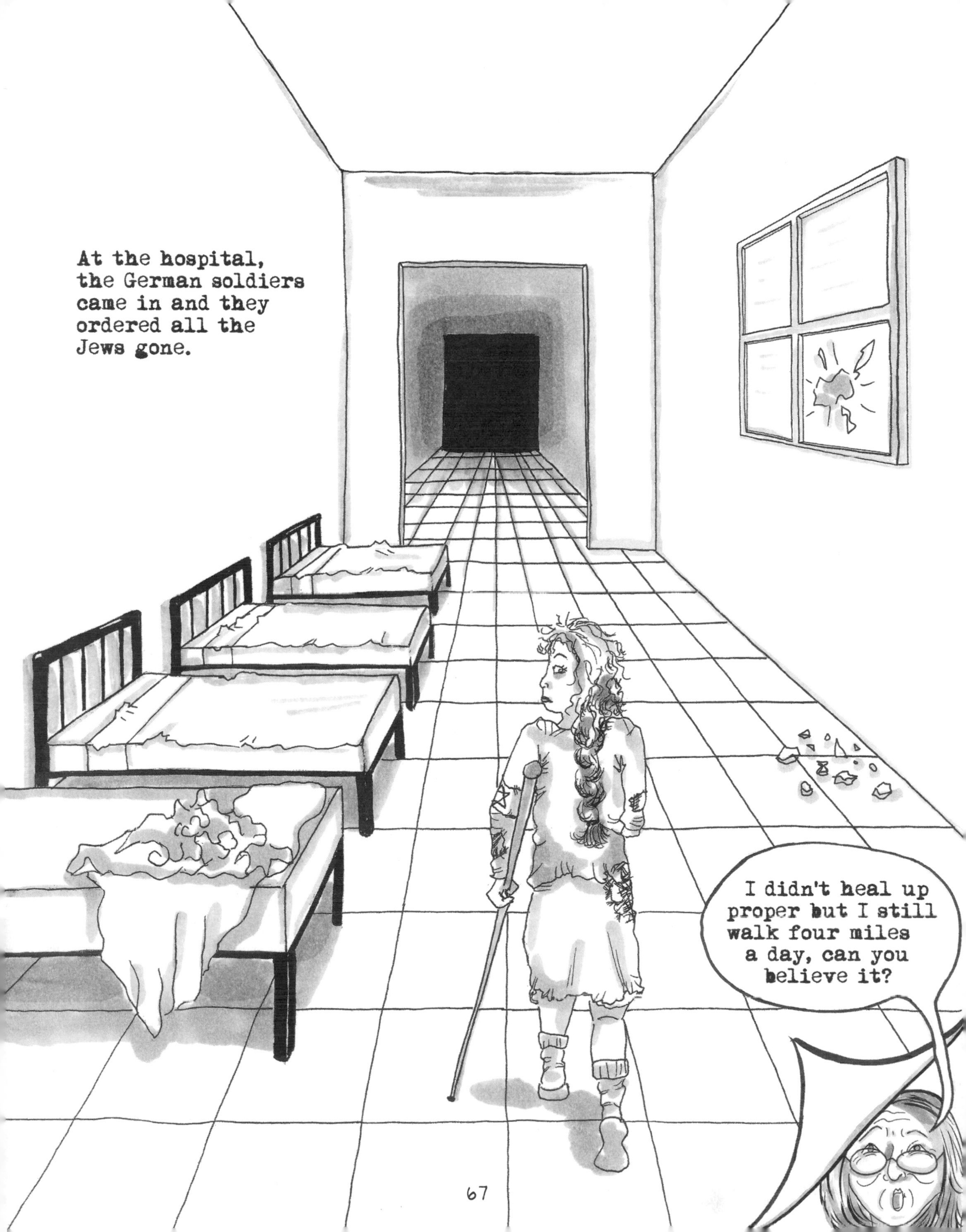
At the hospital, the German soldiers came in and they ordered all the Jews gone.
I didn't heal up proper but I still walk four miles a day, can you believe it?

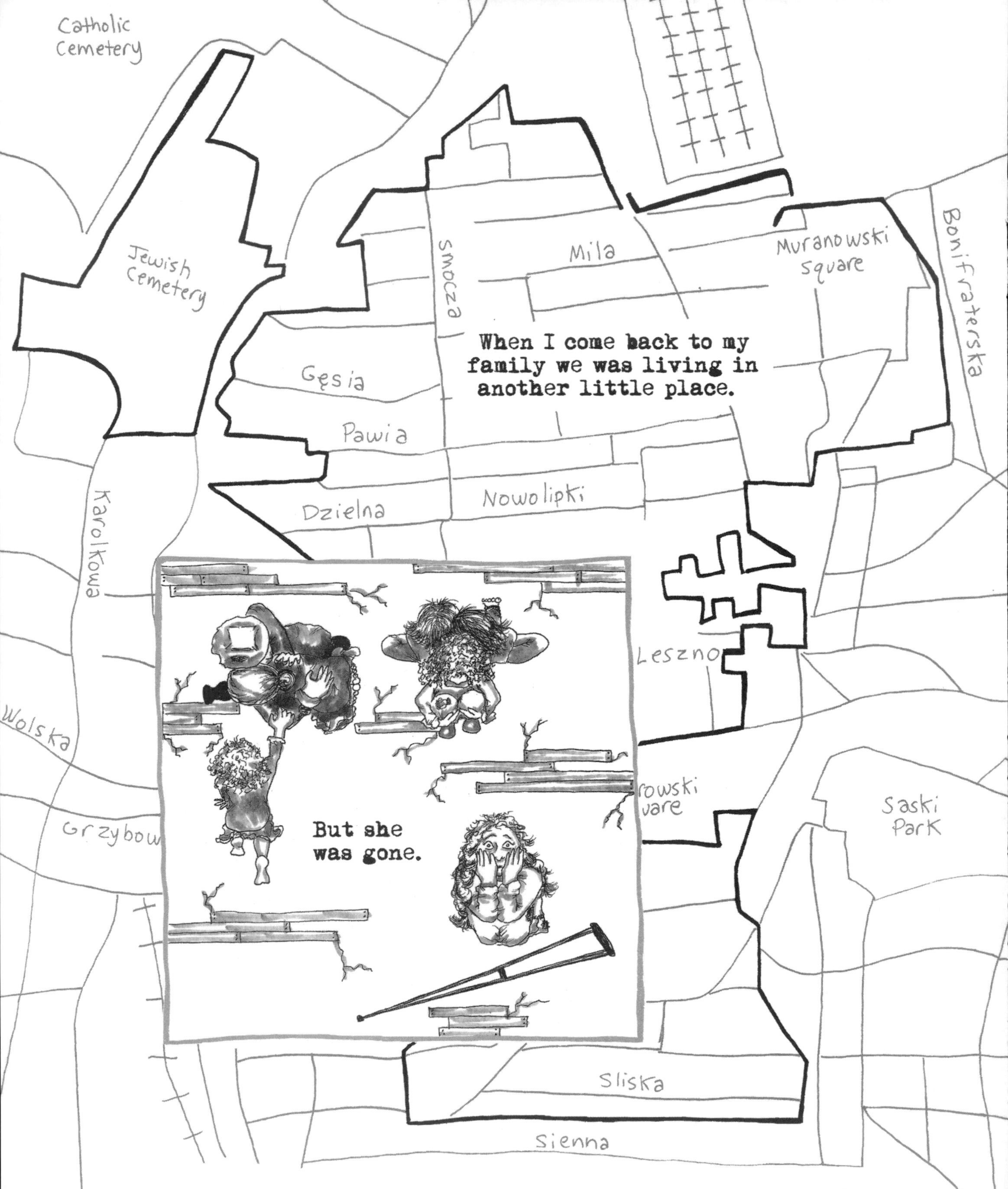
Catholic Cemetery
Jewish Cemetery
Smocza
Mila
Muranowski Square
Bonifraterska
When I come back to my family we was living in another little place.
Gęsia
Pawia
Karolkowa
Dzielna
Nowolipki
Leszno
Wolska
But she was gone.
Grzybow
Saski Park
Sliska
Sienna

My Bubbe. She had died. And I had black metal in my hip. Can you imagine? To come home...

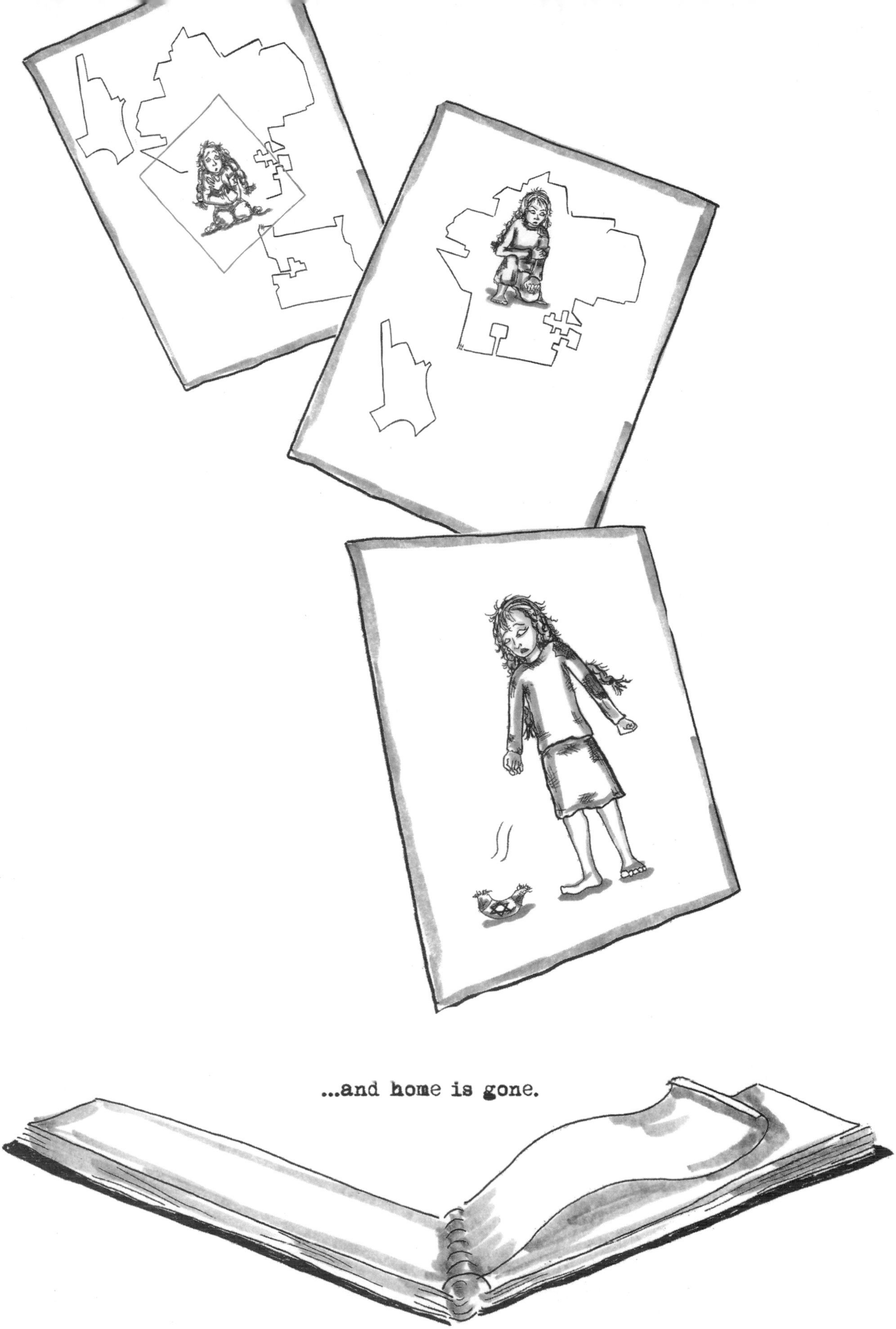
...and home is gone.

Chapter Three:

Home Schooling

TURKEY
CYPRUS
SYRIA
Mediterranean Sea
LEBANON
IRAN
IRAQ
ISRAEL
JORDAN
EGYPT
SAUDI ARABIA
KUWAIT

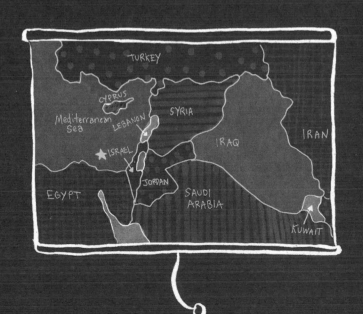

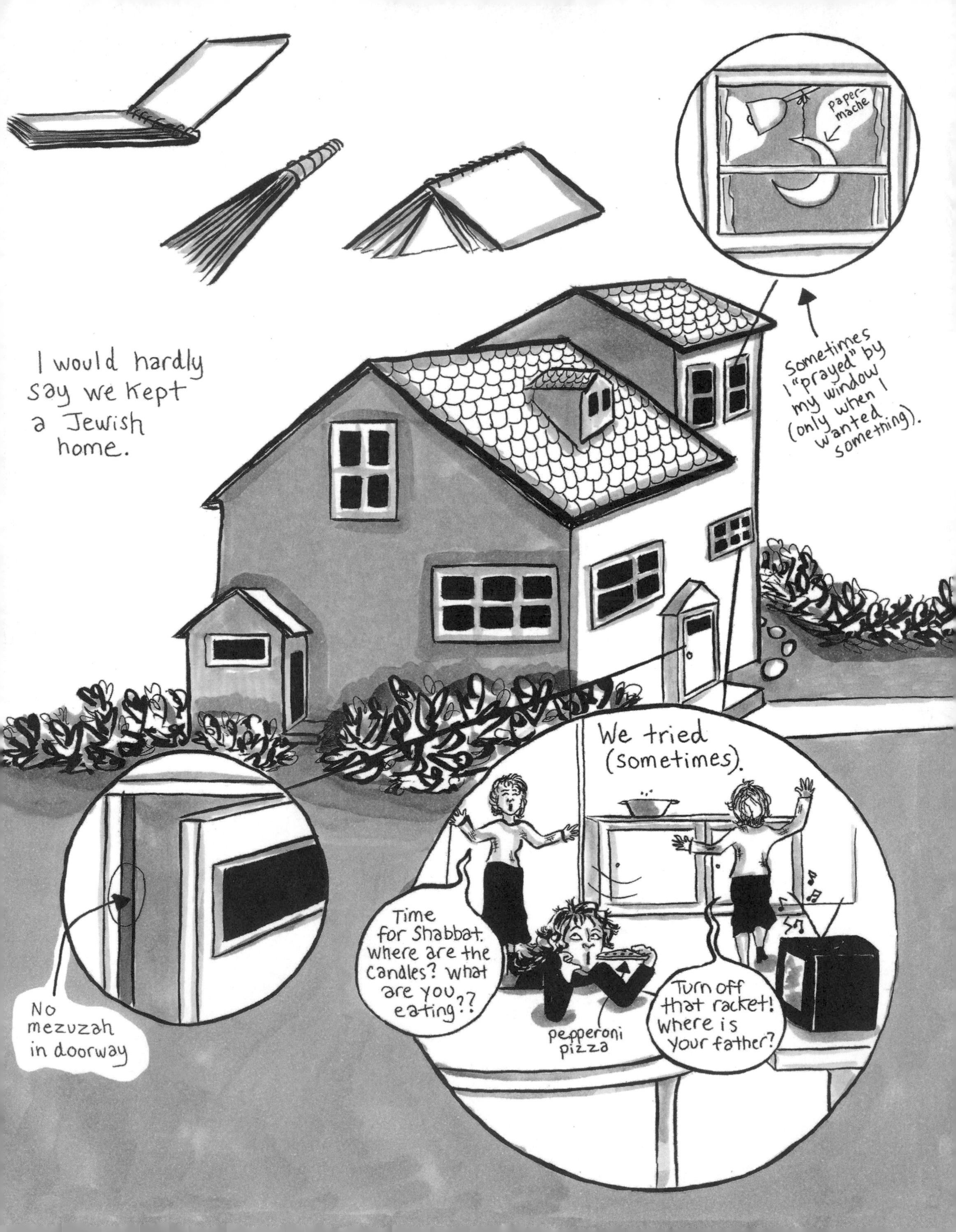
I would hardly say we kept a Jewish home.
paper-mache
Sometimes I "prayed" by my window (only when I wanted something).
We tried (sometimes).
Time for Shabbat. Where are the candles? What are you eating??
pepperoni pizza
Turn off that racket! Where is your father?
No mezuzah in doorway

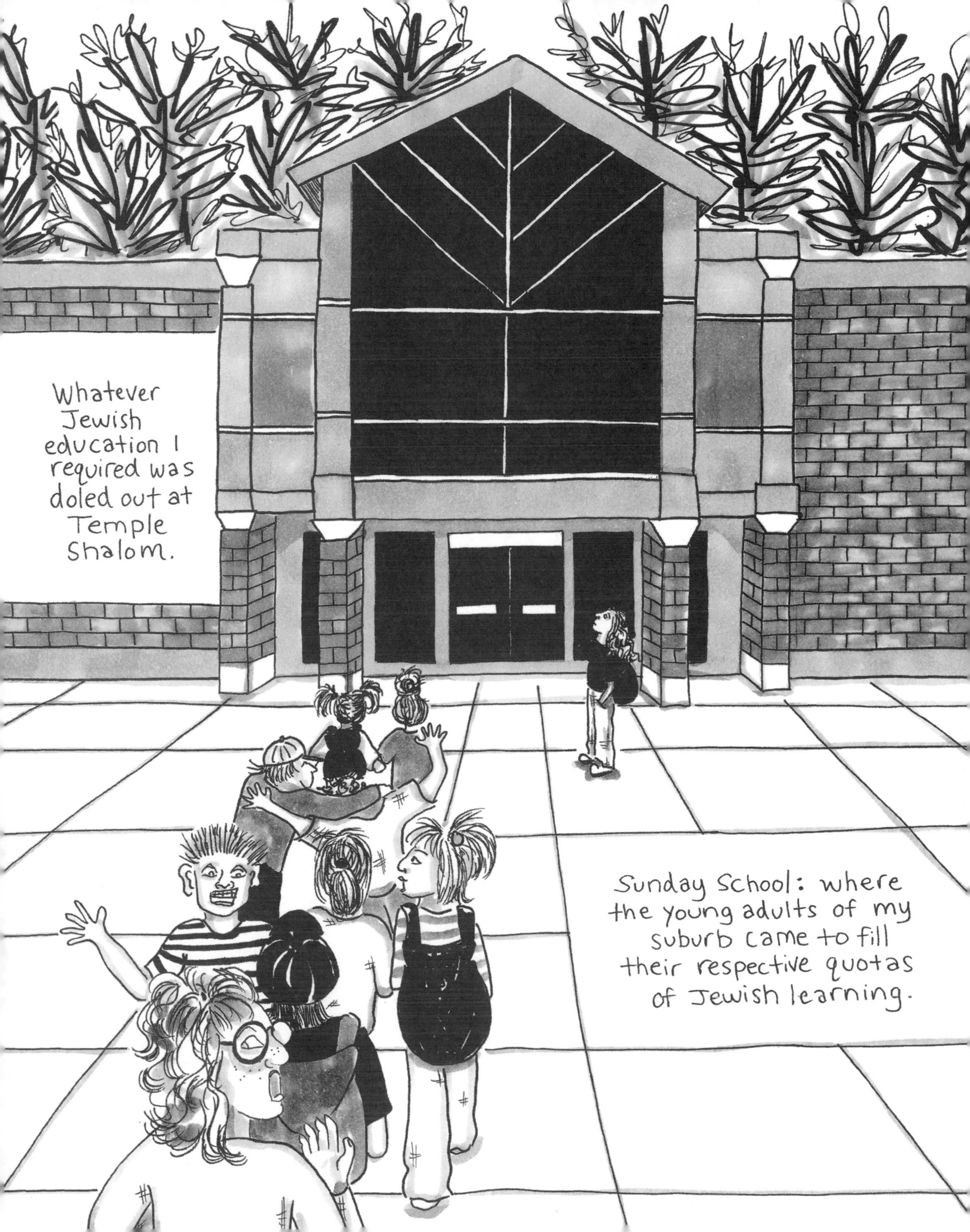
Whatever Jewish education I required was doled out at Temple Shalom.
Sunday School: where the young adults of my suburb came to fill their respective quotas of Jewish learning.

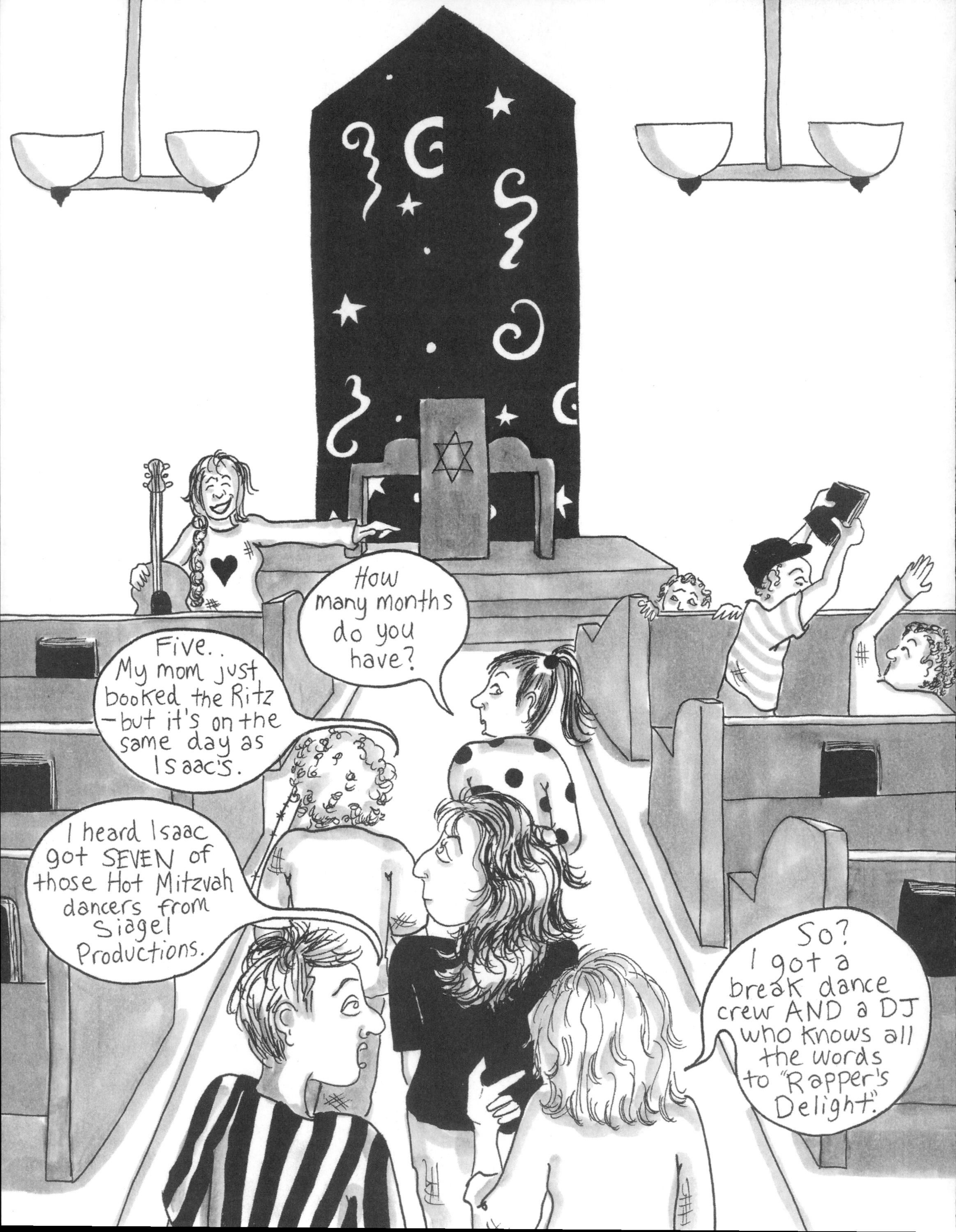
How many months do you have?
Five.. My mom just booked the Ritz—but it's on the same day as Isaac's.
I heard Isaac got SEVEN of those Hot Mitzvah dancers from Siagel Productions.
So? I got a break dance crew AND a DJ who knows all the words to "Rapper's Delight."

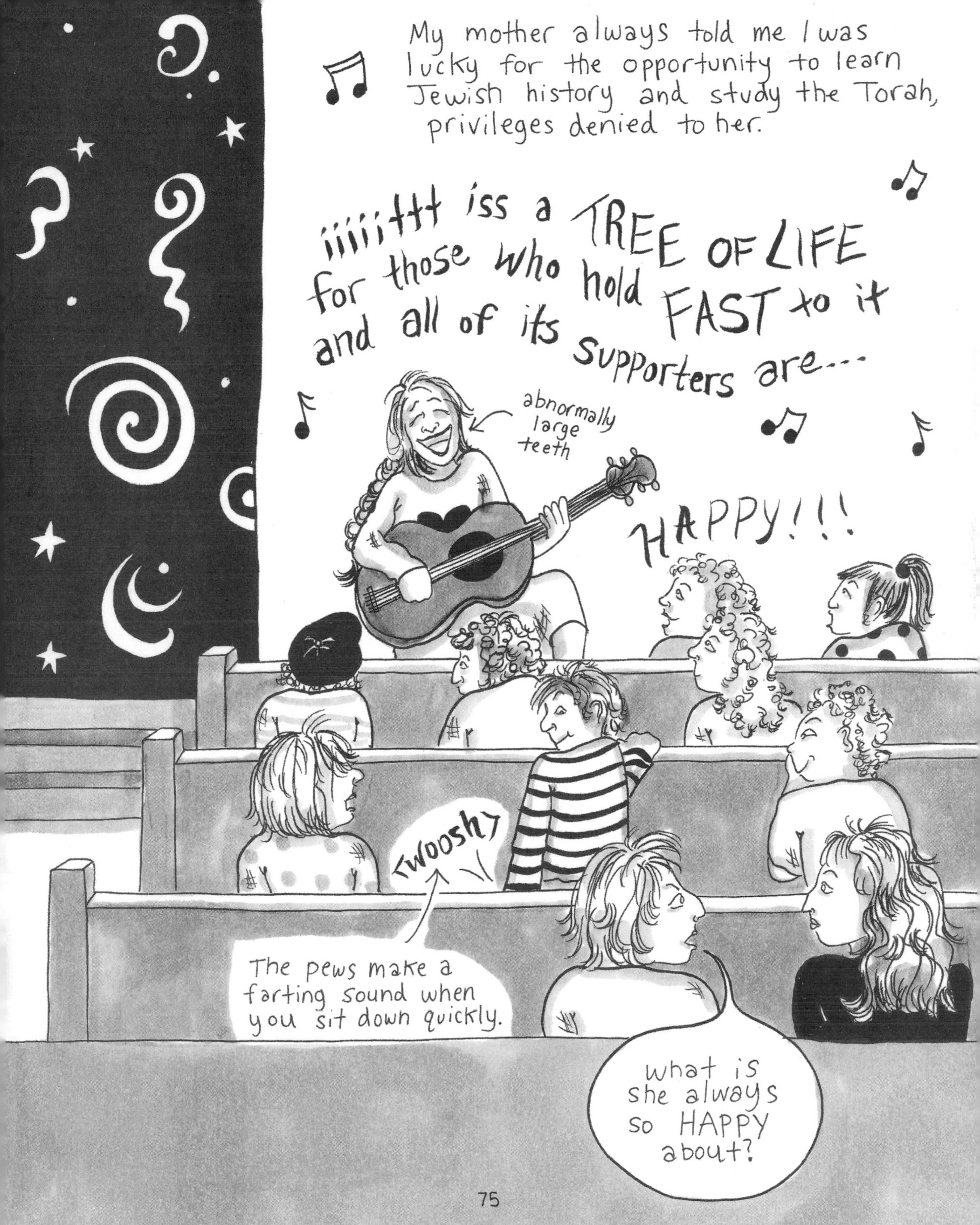

My mother always told me I was lucky for the opportunity to learn Jewish history and study the Torah, privileges denied to her.
iiiiittt iss a TREE OF LIFE for those who hold FAST to it and all of its supporters are...
abnormally large teeth
HAPPY!!!
<WOOSH>
The pews make a farting sound when you sit down quickly.
what is she always so HAPPY about?

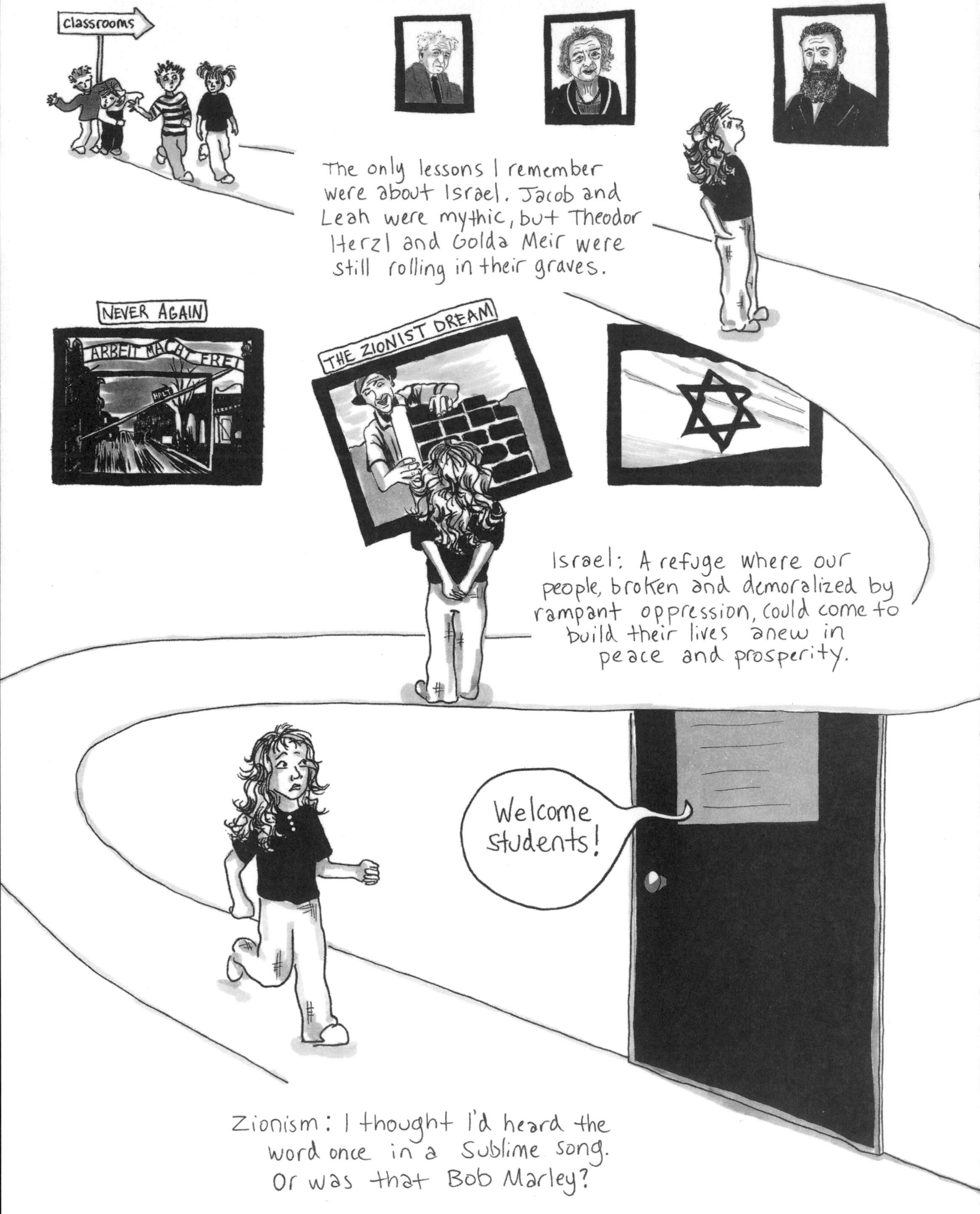
Classrooms
The only lessons I remember were about Israel. Jacob and Leah were mythic, but Theodor Herzl and Golda Meir were still rolling in their graves.
NEVER AGAIN
ARBEIT MACHT FREI
THE ZIONIST DREAM
Israel: A refuge where our people, broken and demoralized by rampant oppression, could come to build their lives anew in peace and prosperity.
Welcome students!
Zionism: I thought I'd heard the word once in a Sublime song. Or was that Bob Marley?

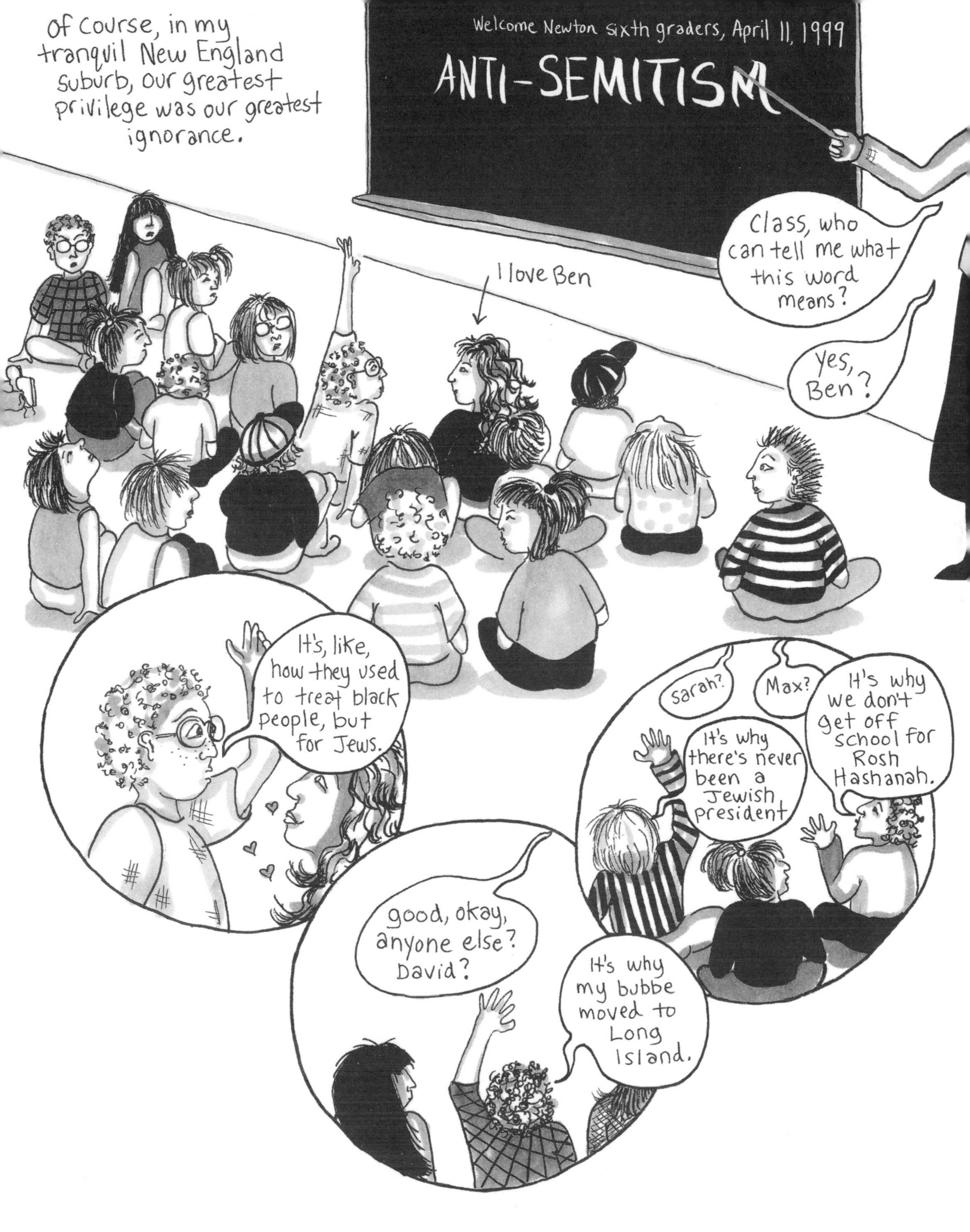
Of course, in my tranquil New England suburb, our greatest privilege was our greatest ignorance.
Welcome Newton sixth graders, April 11, 1999
ANTI-SEMITISM
Class, who can tell me what this word means?
Yes, Ben?
I love Ben
It's, like, how they used to treat black people, but for Jews.
Good, okay, anyone else? David?
It's why my bubbe moved to Long Island.
Sarah?
It's why there's never been a Jewish president
Max?
It's why we don't get off school for Rosh Hashanah.

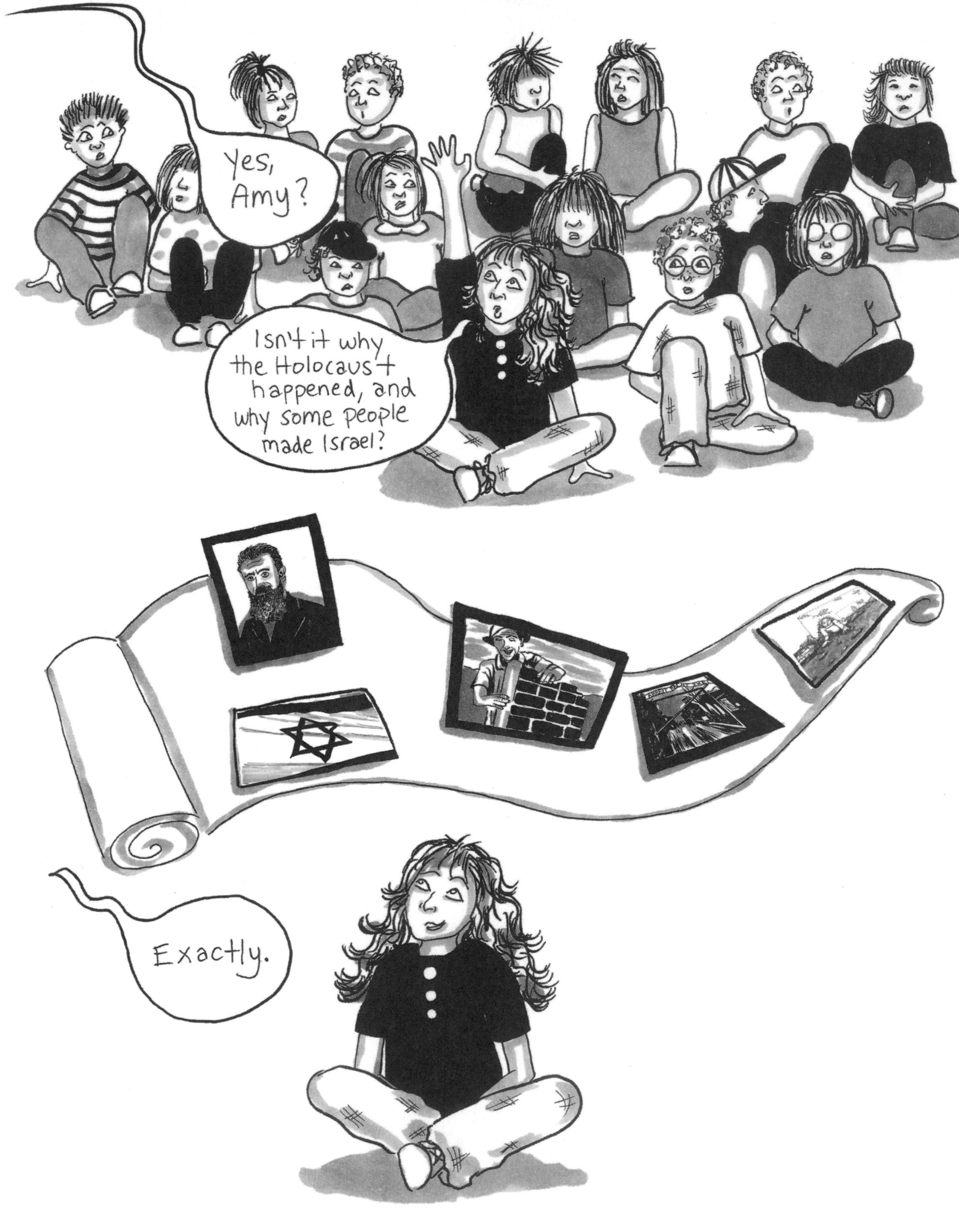
Yes, Amy?
Isn't it why the Holocaust happened, and why some people made Israel?
Exactly.

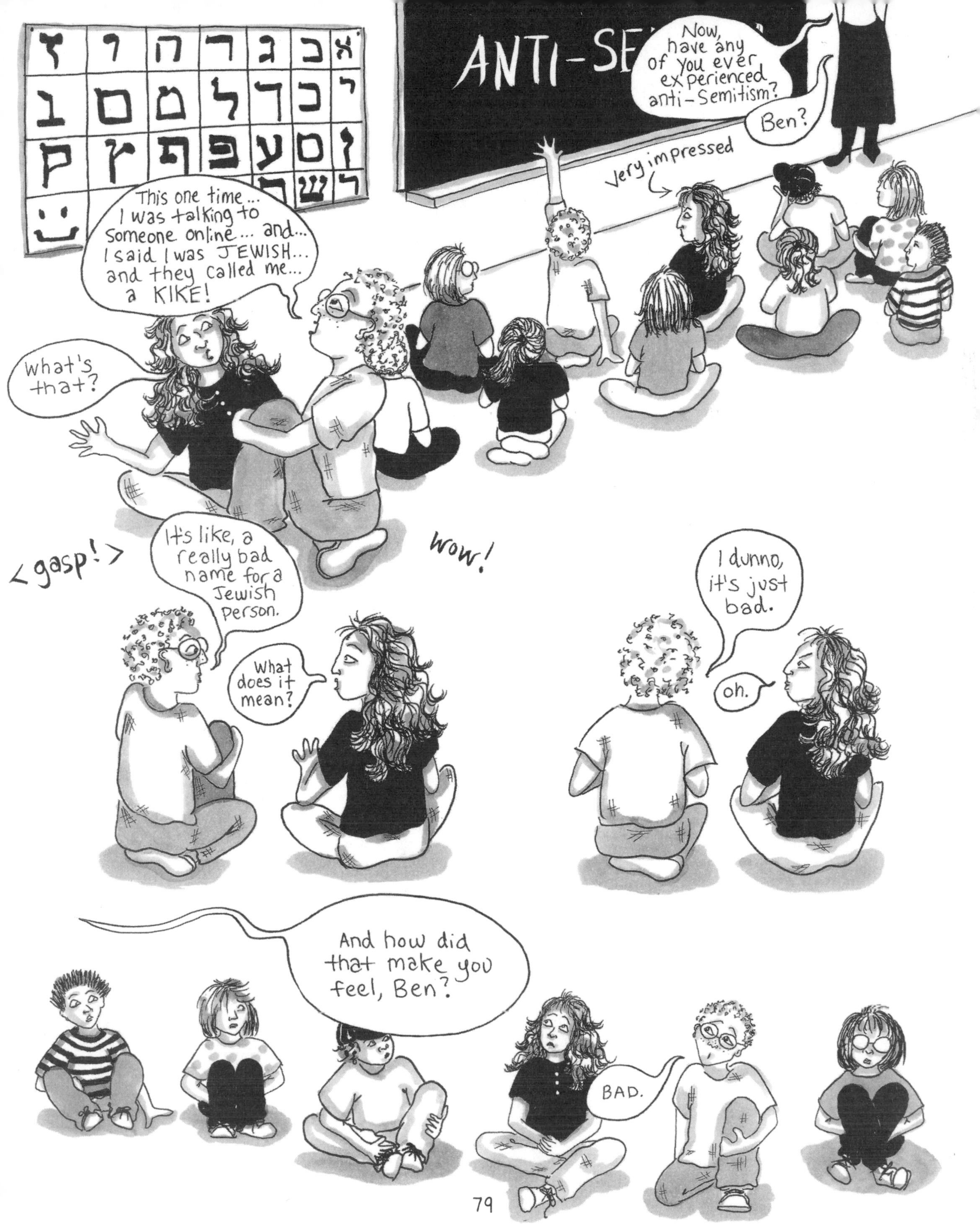
ANTI-SE
Now, have any of you ever experienced anti-Semitism?
Ben?
Very impressed
This one time... I was talking to someone online... and... I said I was JEWISH... and they called me... a KIKE!
What's that?
<gasp!>
It's like, a really bad name for a Jewish person.
wow!
What does it mean?
I dunno, it's just bad.
oh.
And how did that make you feel, Ben?
BAD.

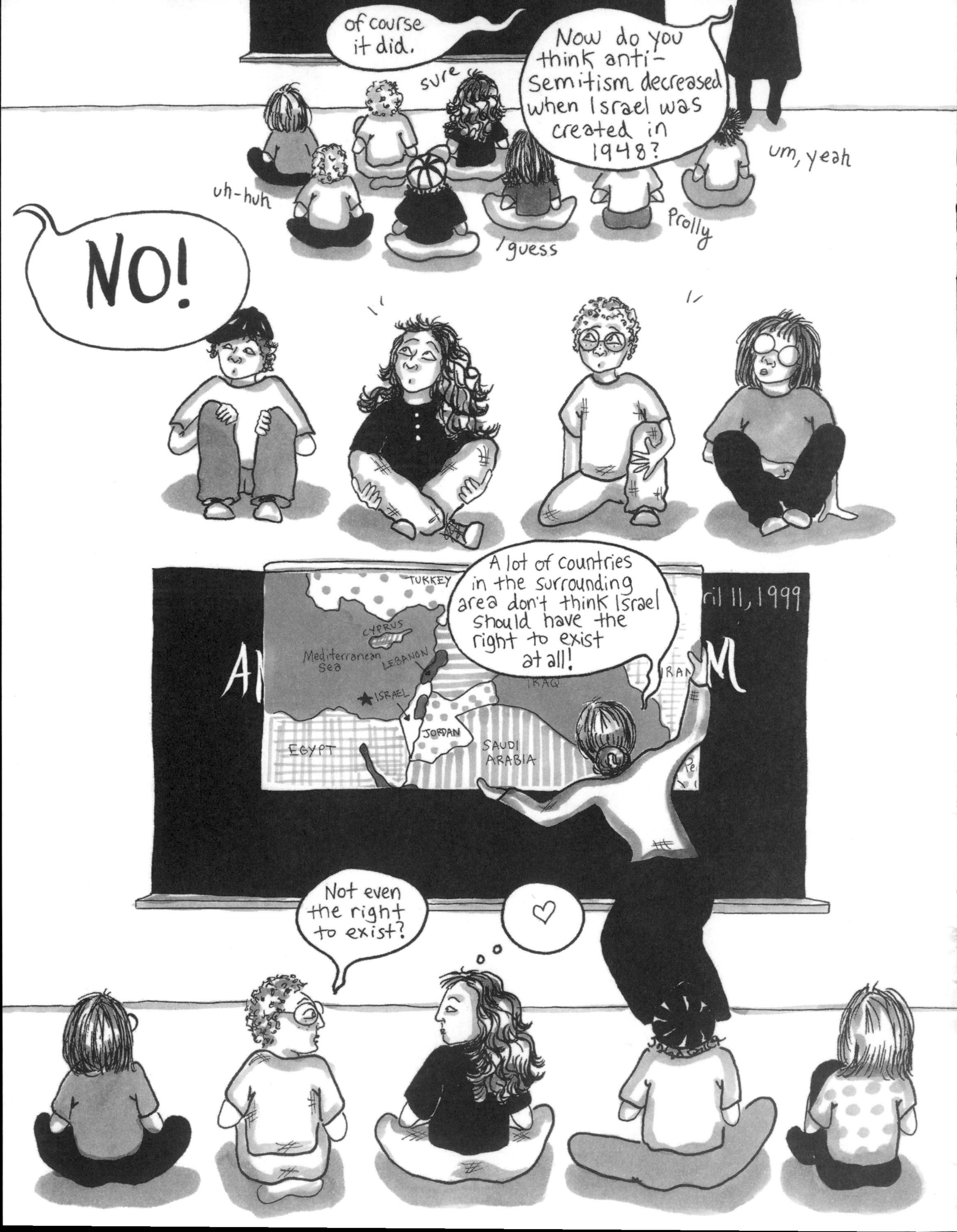
of course it did.
sure
Now do you think anti-Semitism decreased when Israel was created in 1948?
um, yeah
uh-huh
Prolly
I guess
NO!
TURKEY
CYPRUS
Mediterranean Sea
LEBANON
ISRAEL
JORDAN
EGYPT
SAUDI ARABIA
IRAQ
IRAN
A lot of countries in the surrounding area don't think Israel should have the right to exist at all!
ril 11, 1999
Not even the right to exist?

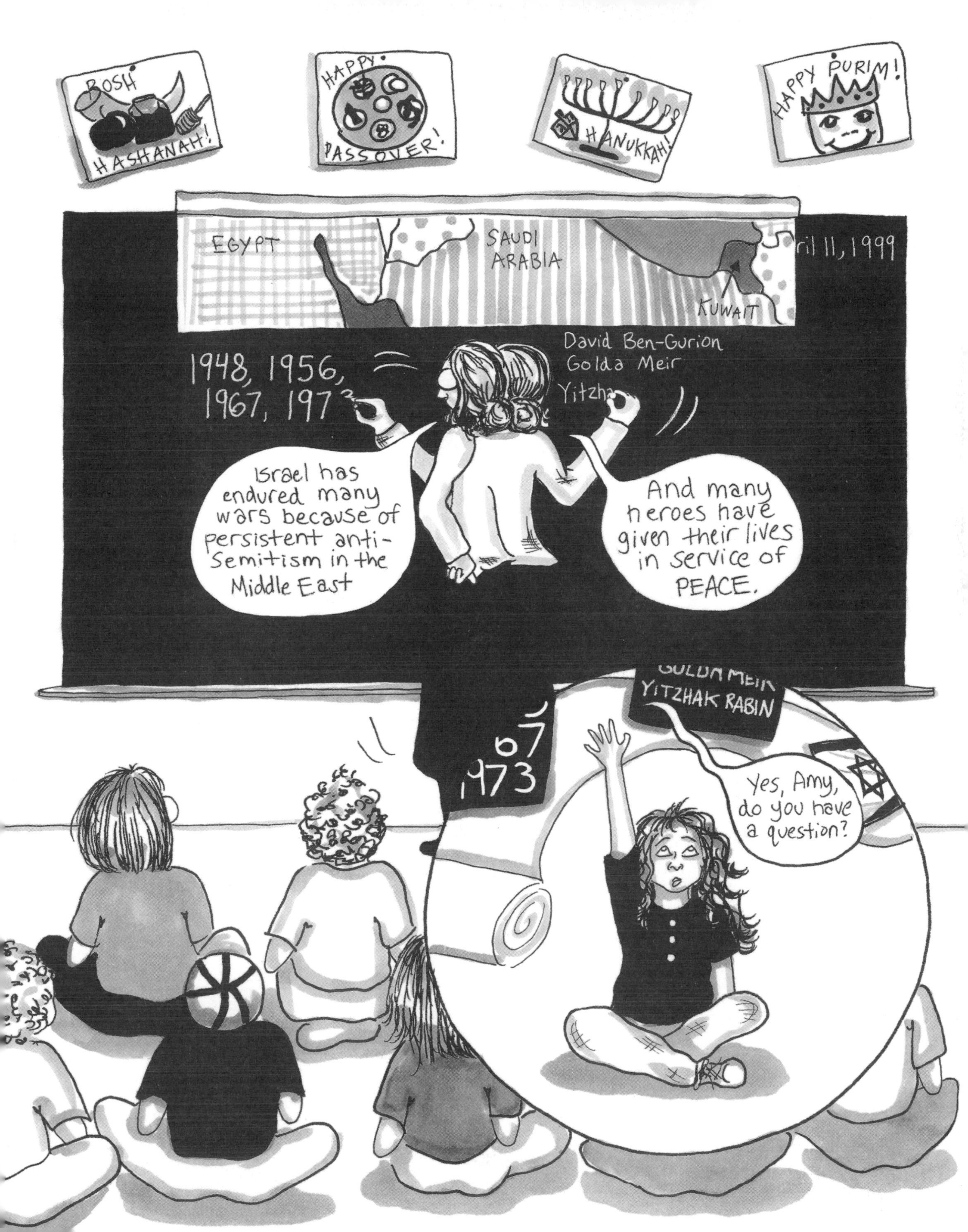
ROSH HASHANAH!
HAPPY PASSOVER!
HANUKKAH!
HAPPY PURIM!
EGYPT
SAUDI ARABIA
KUWAIT
ril 11, 1999
1948, 1956, 1967, 1973
David Ben-Gurion
Golda Meir
Yitzha
Israel has endured many wars because of persistent anti-Semitism in the Middle East
And many heroes have given their lives in service of PEACE.
GOLDA MEIR
YITZHAK RABIN
67
1973
Yes, Amy, do you have a question?

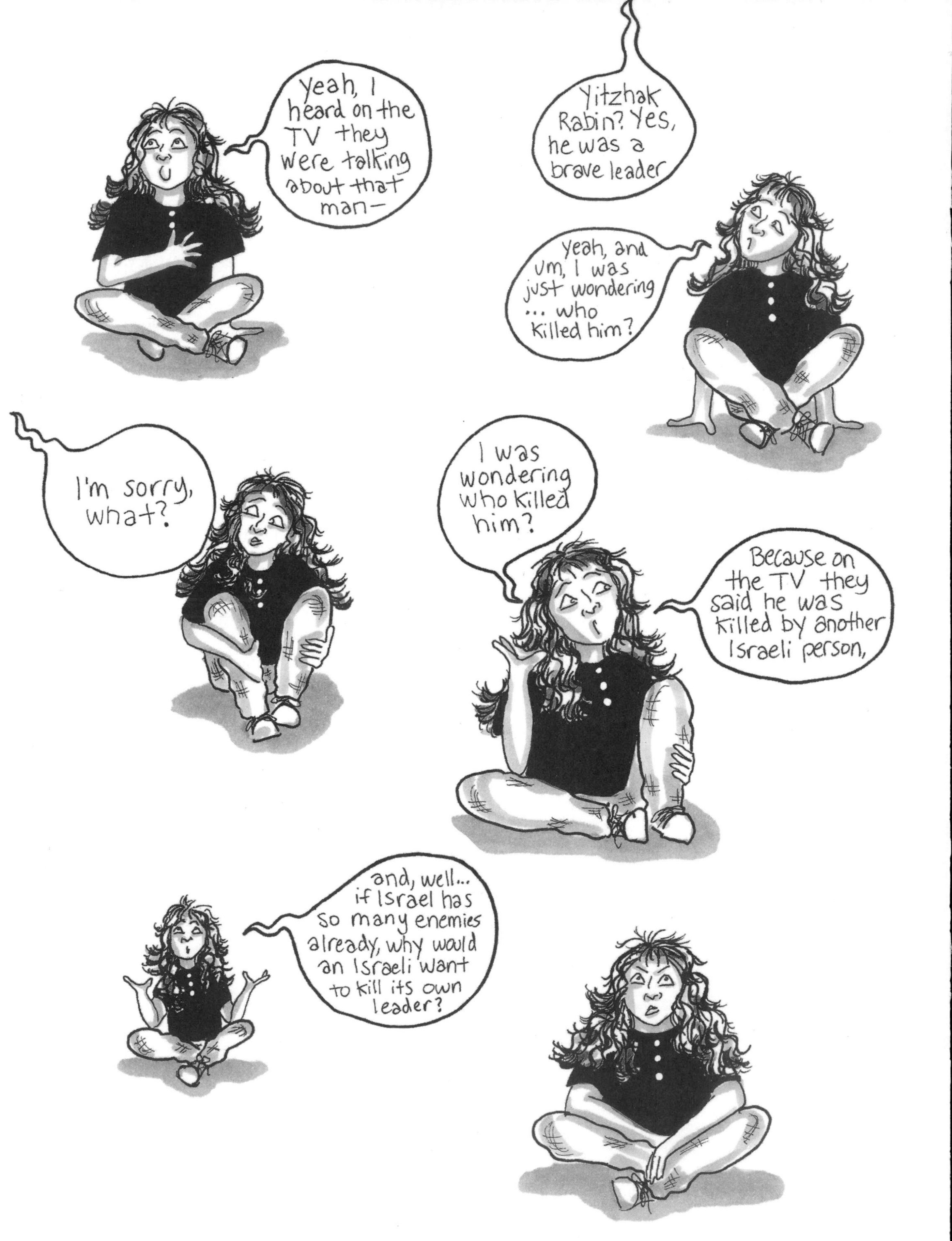
yeah, I heard on the TV they were talking about that man—
Yitzhak Rabin? Yes, he was a brave leader
yeah, and um, I was just wondering ... who killed him?
I'm sorry, what?
I was wondering who killed him?
Because on the TV they said he was killed by another Israeli person,
and, well... if Israel has so many enemies already, why would an Israeli want to kill its own leader?

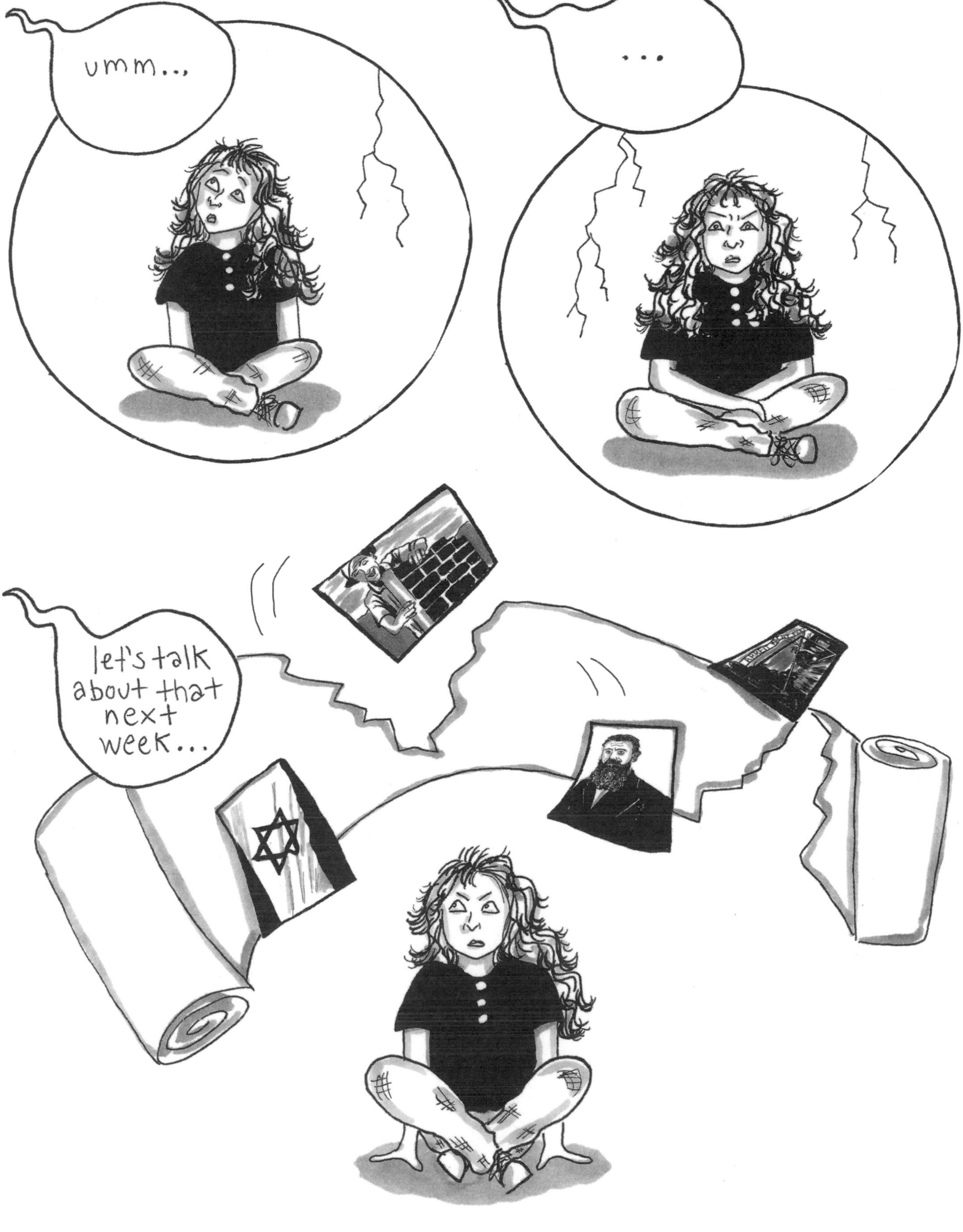
umm...
...
let's talk about that next week...

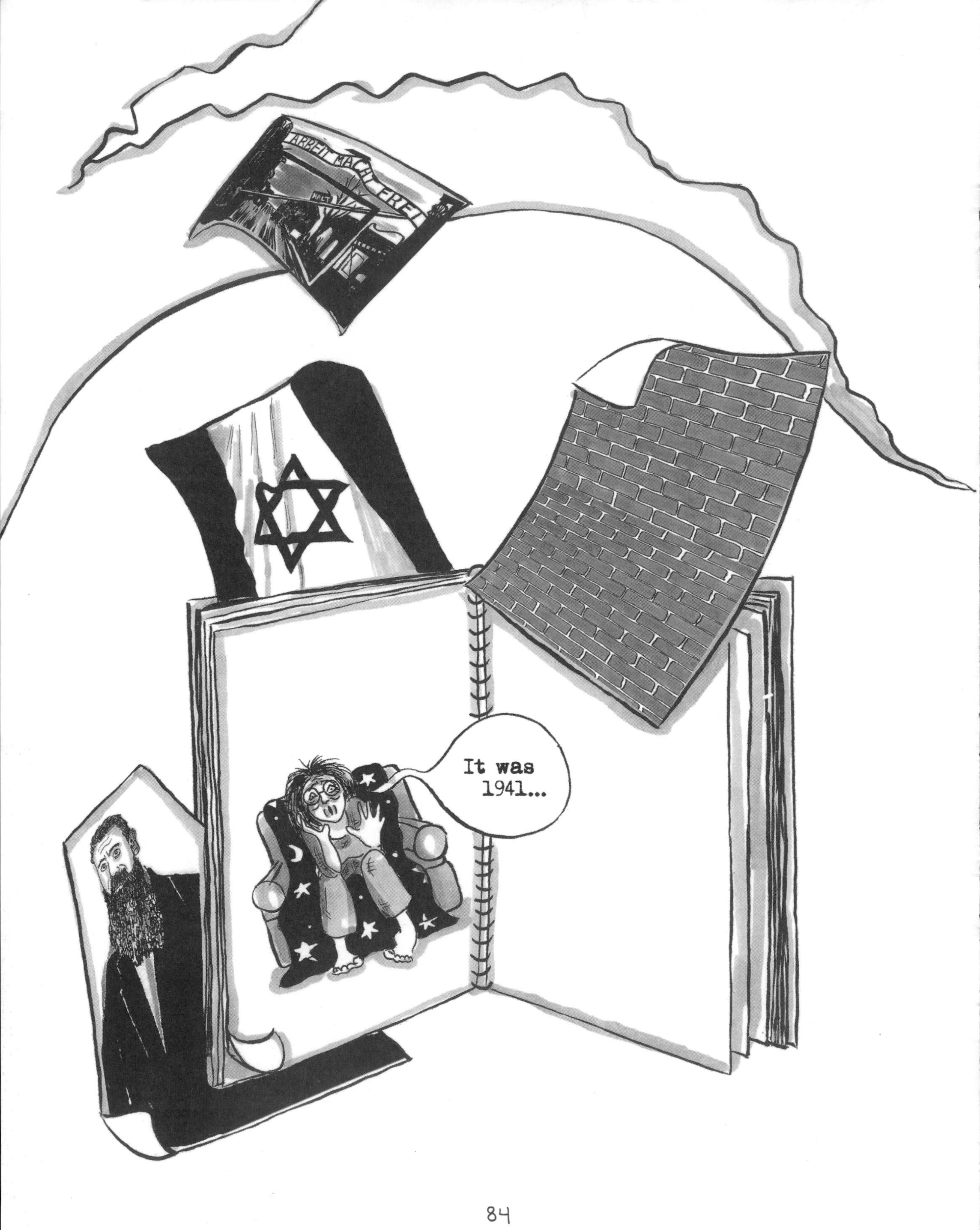
ARBEIT MACHT FREI
HALT
It was 1941...

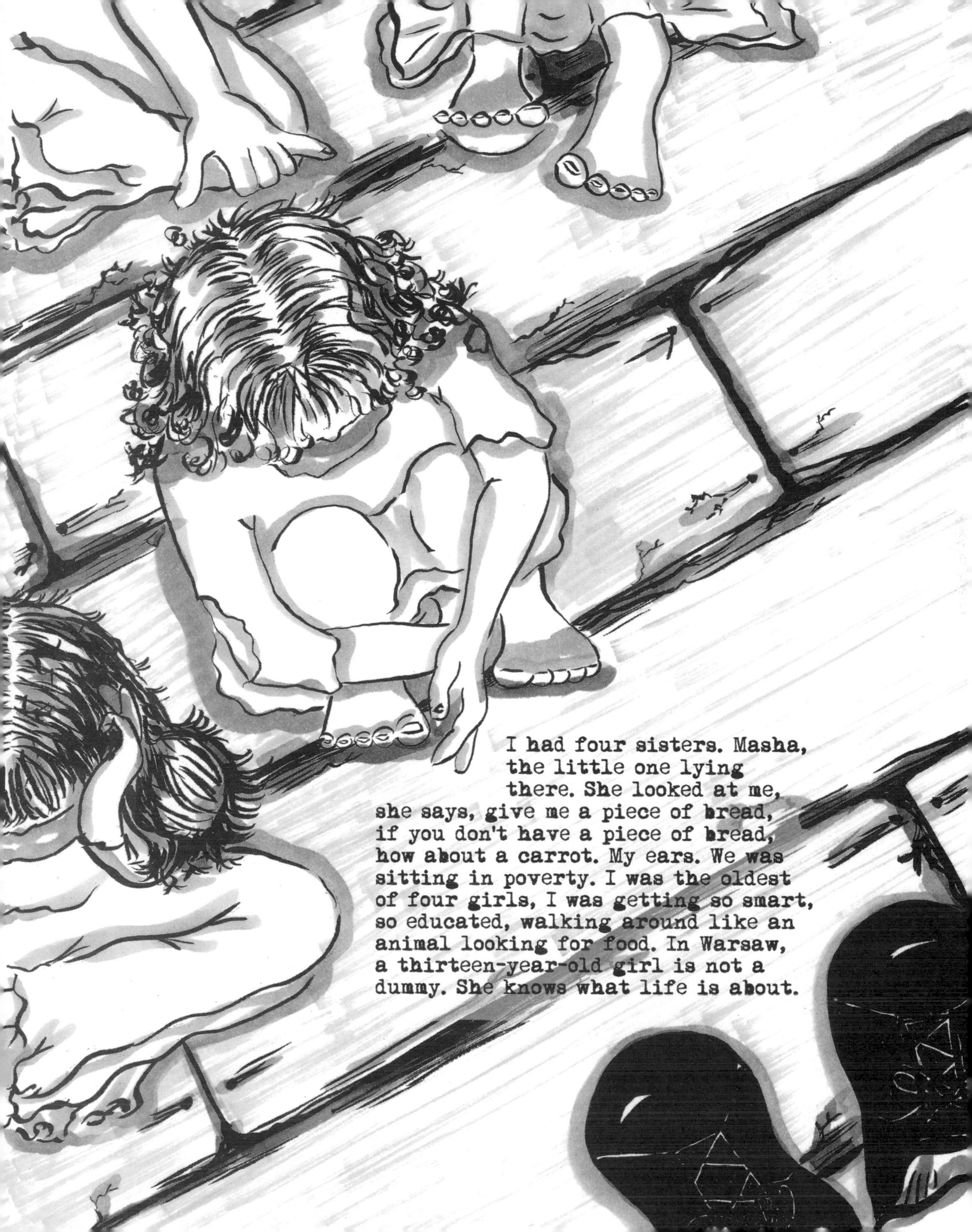
I had four sisters. Masha, the little one lying there. She looked at me, she says, give me a piece of bread, if you don't have a piece of bread, how about a carrot. My ears. We was sitting in poverty. I was the oldest of four girls, I was getting so smart, so educated, walking around like an animal looking for food. In Warsaw, a thirteen-year-old girl is not a dummy. She knows what life is about.

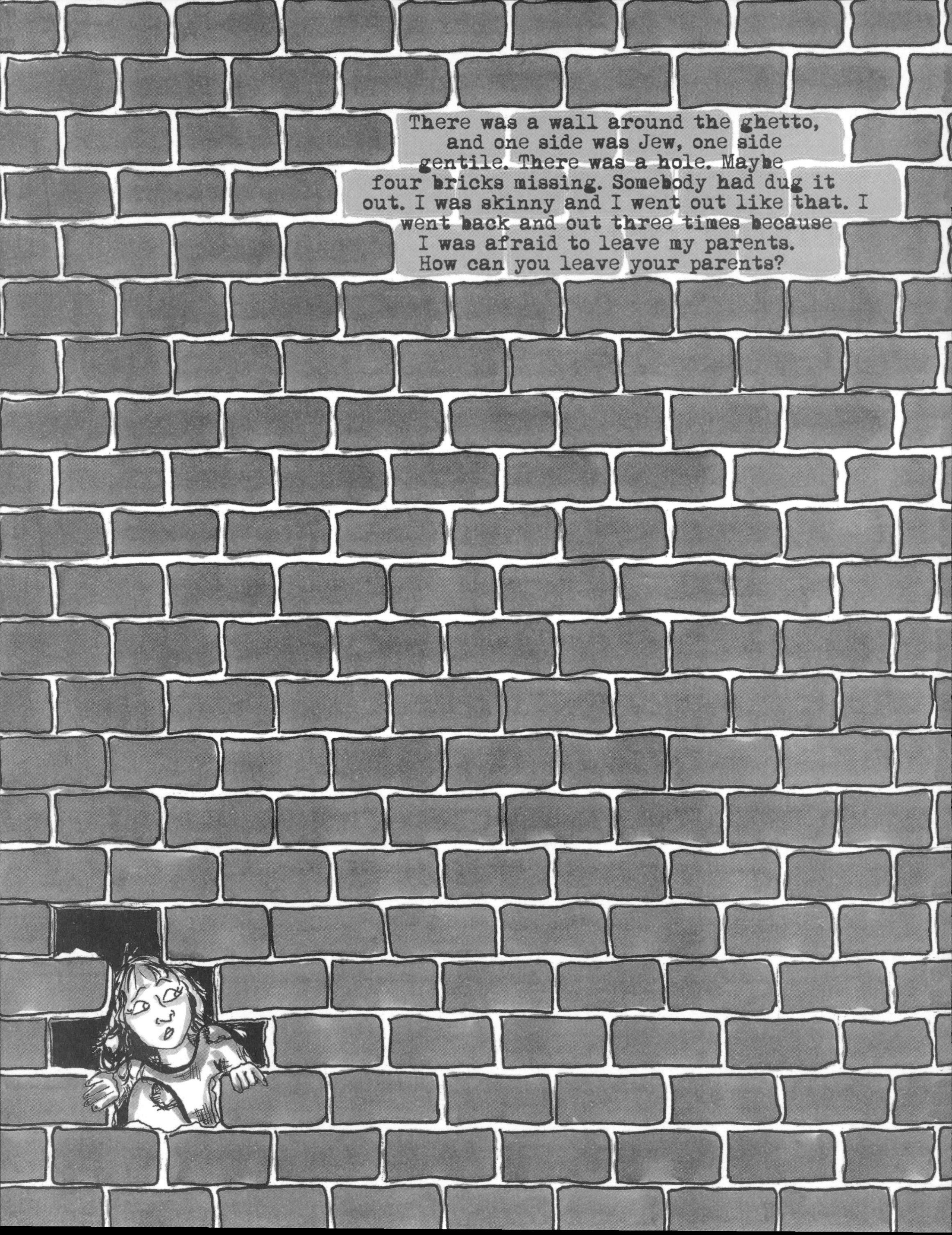
There was a wall around the ghetto, and one side was Jew, one side gentile. There was a hole. Maybe four bricks missing. Somebody had dug it out. I was skinny and I went out like that. I went back and out three times because I was afraid to leave my parents. How can you leave your parents?

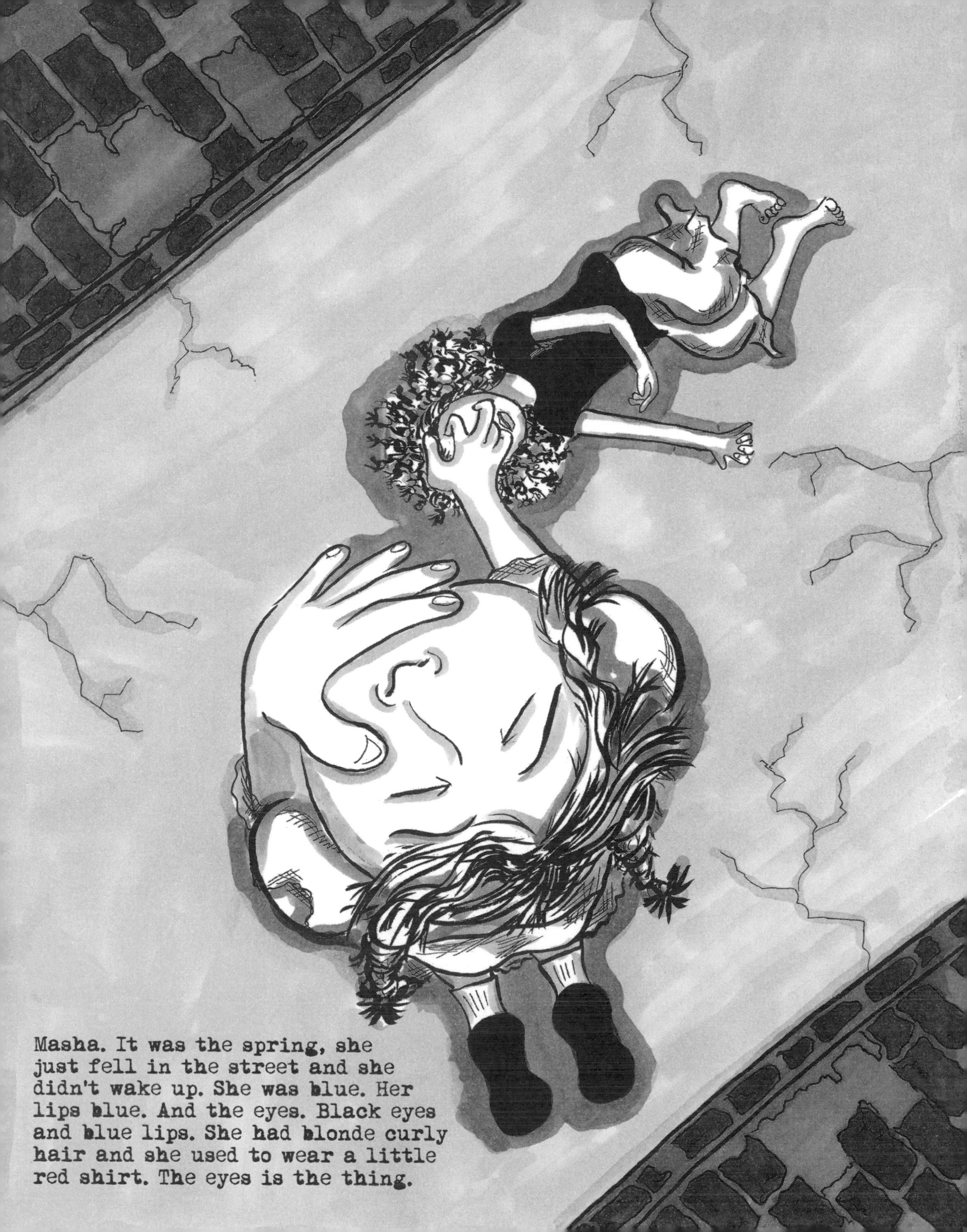
Masha. It was the spring, she just fell in the street and she didn't wake up. She was blue. Her lips blue. And the eyes. Black eyes and blue lips. She had blonde curly hair and she used to wear a little red shirt. The eyes is the thing.

My mother's face. Such a thing I have to
recollect. A lot of things you block out.

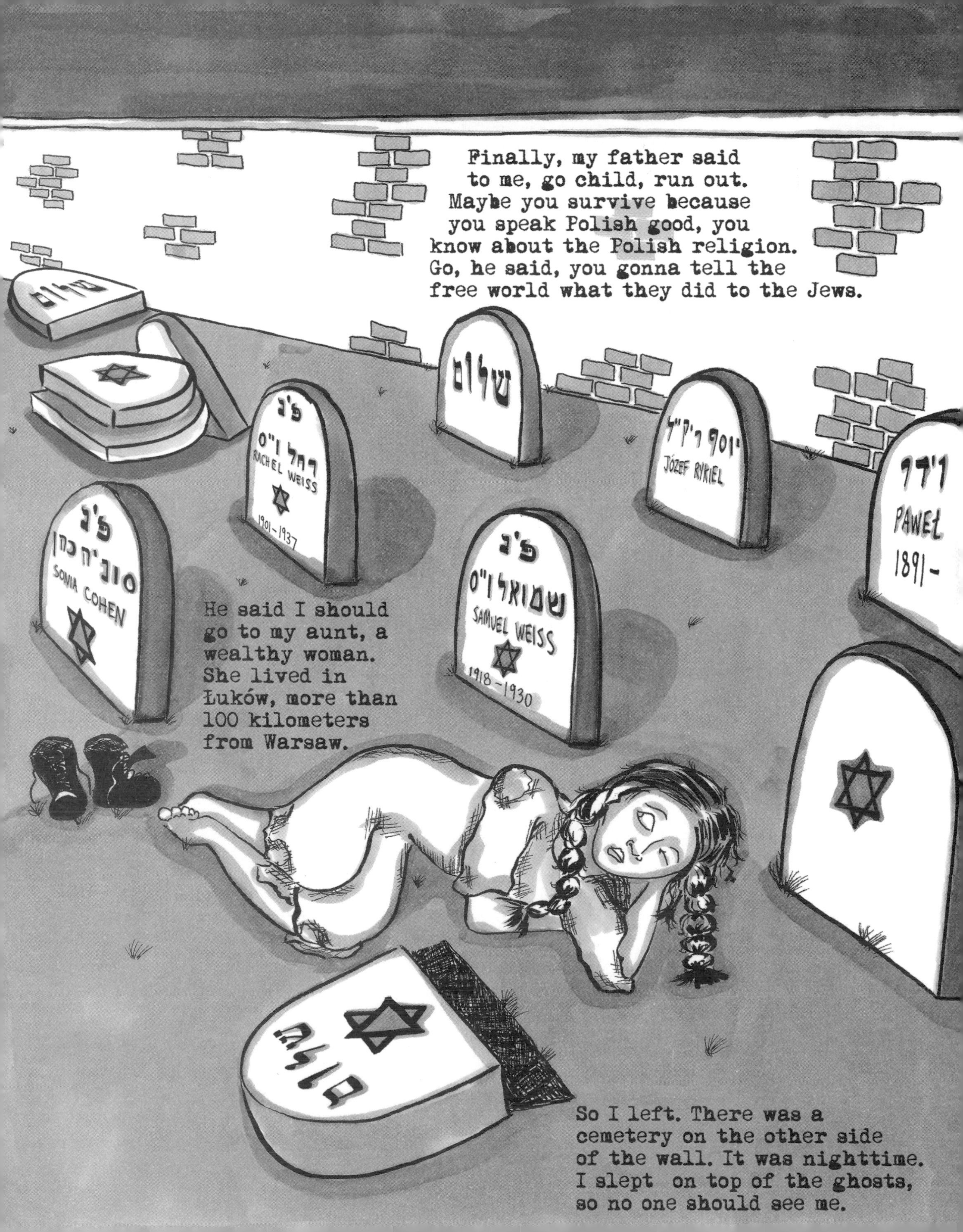
Finally, my father said to me, go child, run out. Maybe you survive because you speak Polish good, you know about the Polish religion. Go, he said, you gonna tell the free world what they did to the Jews.
שלום
RACHEL WEISS
1901-1937
JÓZEF RYKIEL
PAWEŁ
1891-
SONIA COHEN
SAMUEL WEISS
1918-1930
He said I should go to my aunt, a wealthy woman. She lived in Łuków, more than 100 kilometers from Warsaw.
So I left. There was a cemetery on the other side of the wall. It was nighttime. I slept on top of the ghosts, so no one should see me.

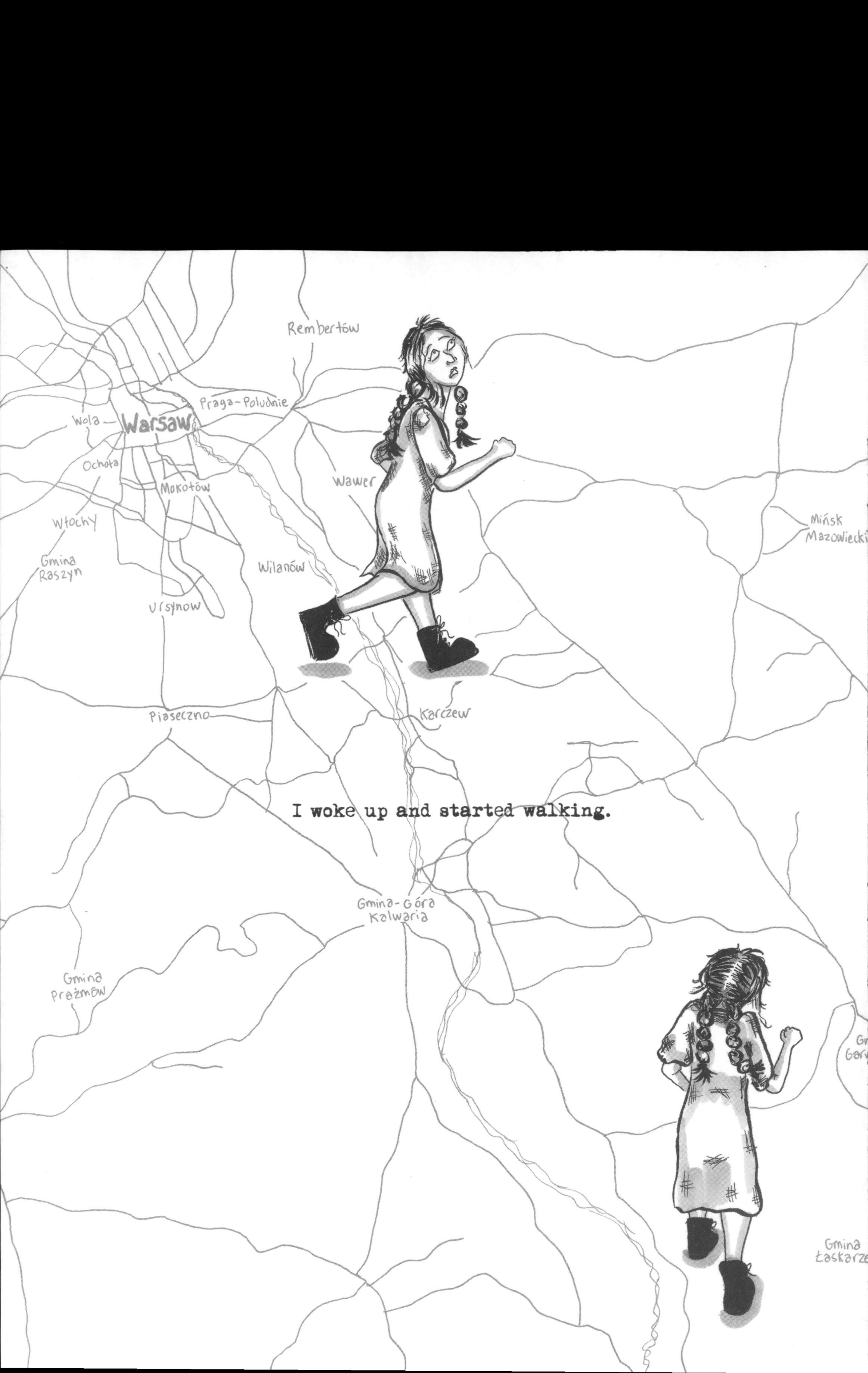
I woke up and started walking.
Rembertów
Praga-Poludnie
Wola
Warsaw
Ochota
Mokotów
Włochy
Gmina Raszyn
Wawer
Wilanów
Ursynow
Mińsk Mazowiecki
Piaseczno
Karczew
Gmina-Góra Kalwaria
Gmina Prażmów
Gmina

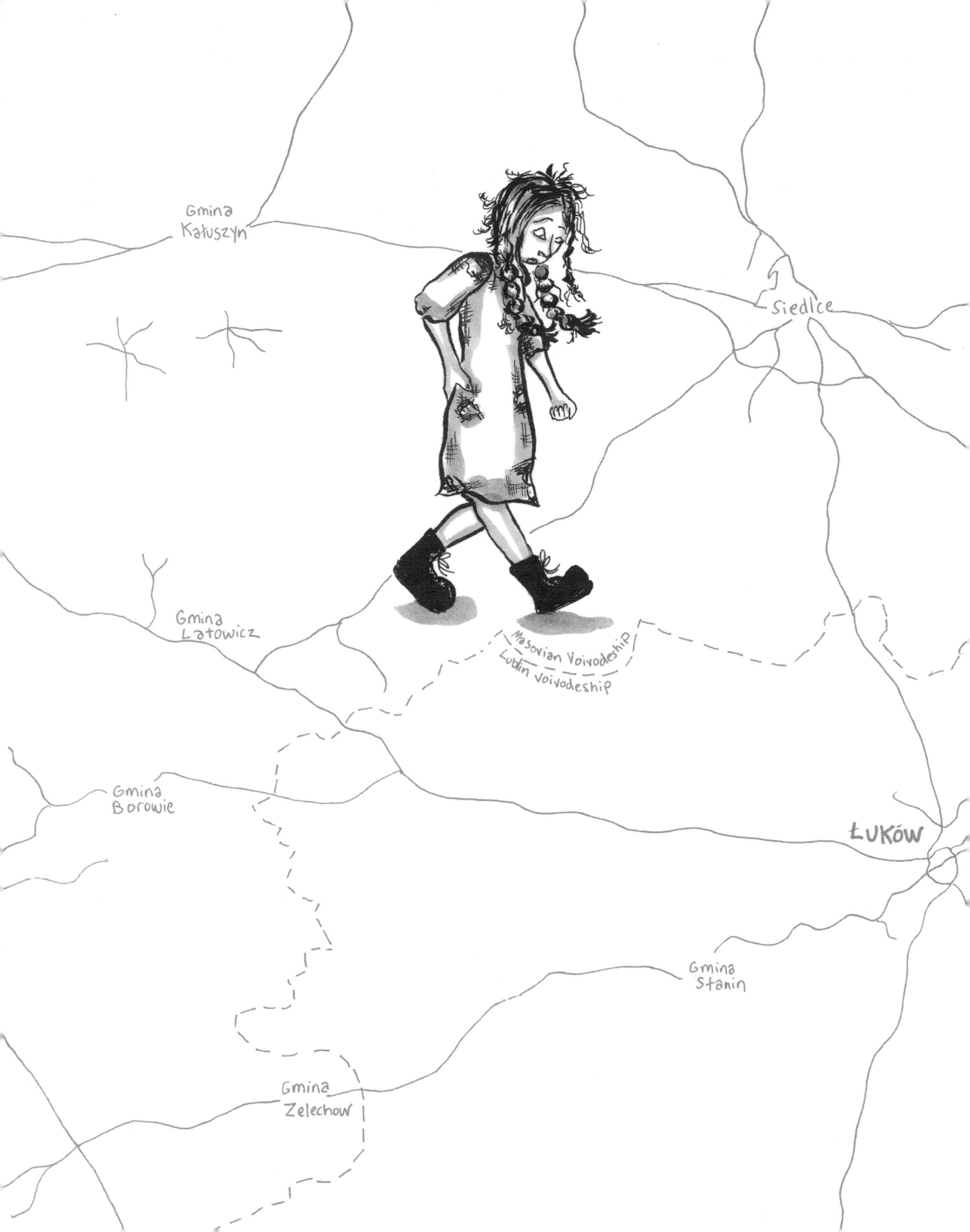
Gmina
Kałuszyn
Siedlce
Gmina
Latowicz
Masovian Voivodeship
Lublin Voivodeship
Gmina
Borowie
ŁUKÓW
Gmina
Stanin
Gmina
Zelechow

It took me ten days and nights to get where I was going. I would come to a little town and look around, maybe there are nice people. I would say, I'm just passing through, could you give me a place where I could sleep, and maybe they give me a little food. I think they would sort of pity me. I was a cute girl, quiet, and with the blue eyes and the blonde hair, I didn't look a Jew.

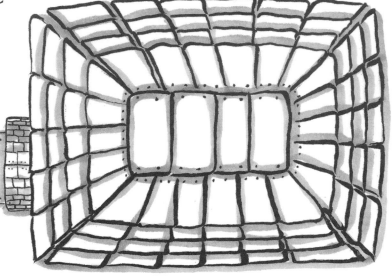

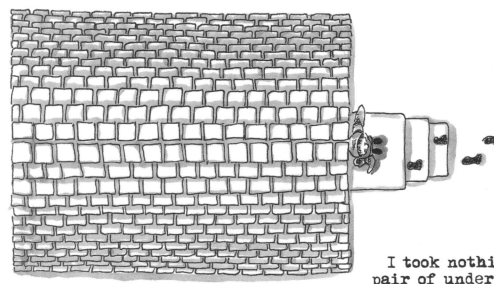

I took nothing with me, just one pair of underpants. I washed them every night. And I had shoes, but I didn't always want to wear them because I only had one pair. When I came finally to my aunt's house, my feet were so blistered. She was not very nice to me, my aunt. Maybe she was scared too.

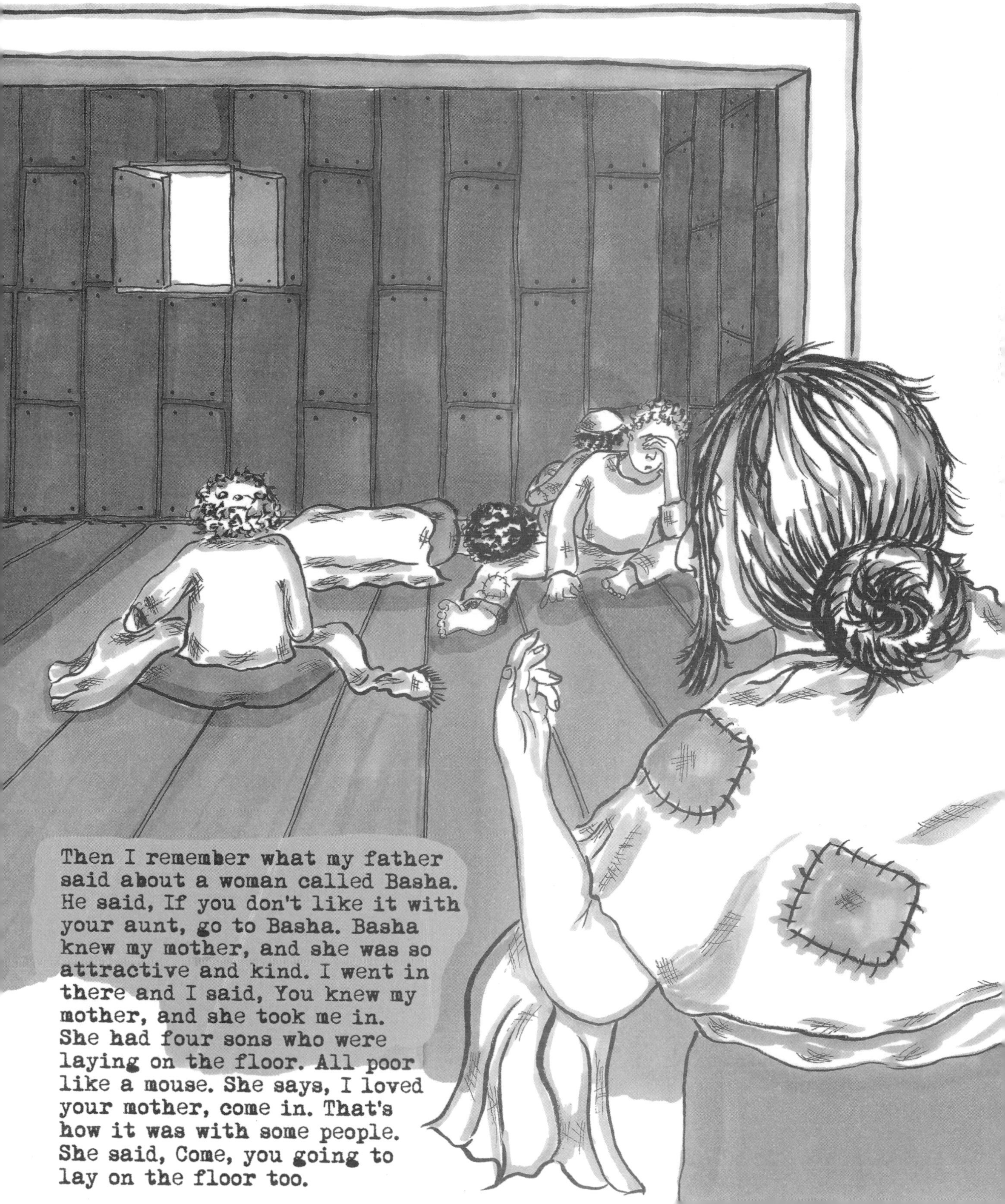
Then I remember what my father said about a woman called Basha. He said, If you don't like it with your aunt, go to Basha. Basha knew my mother, and she was so attractive and kind. I went in there and I said, You knew my mother, and she took me in. She had four sons who were laying on the floor. All poor like a mouse. She says, I loved your mother, come in. That's how it was with some people. She said, Come, you going to lay on the floor too.

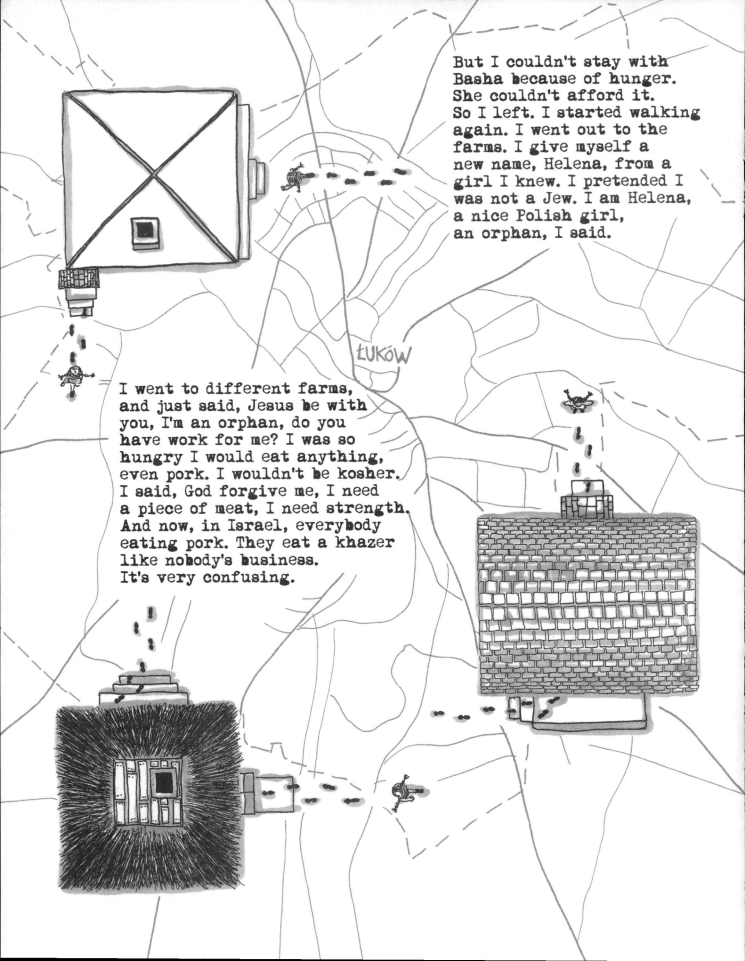

But I couldn't stay with
Basha because of hunger.
She couldn't afford it.
So I left. I started walking
again. I went out to the
farms. I give myself a
new name, Helena, from a
girl I knew. I pretended I
was not a Jew. I am Helena,
a nice Polish girl,
an orphan, I said.

ŁUKÓW

I went to different farms,
and just said, Jesus be with
you, I'm an orphan, do you
have work for me? I was so
hungry I would eat anything,
even pork. I wouldn't be kosher.
I said, God forgive me, I need
a piece of meat, I need strength.
And now, in Israel, everybody
eating pork. They eat a khazer
like nobody's business.
It's very confusing.

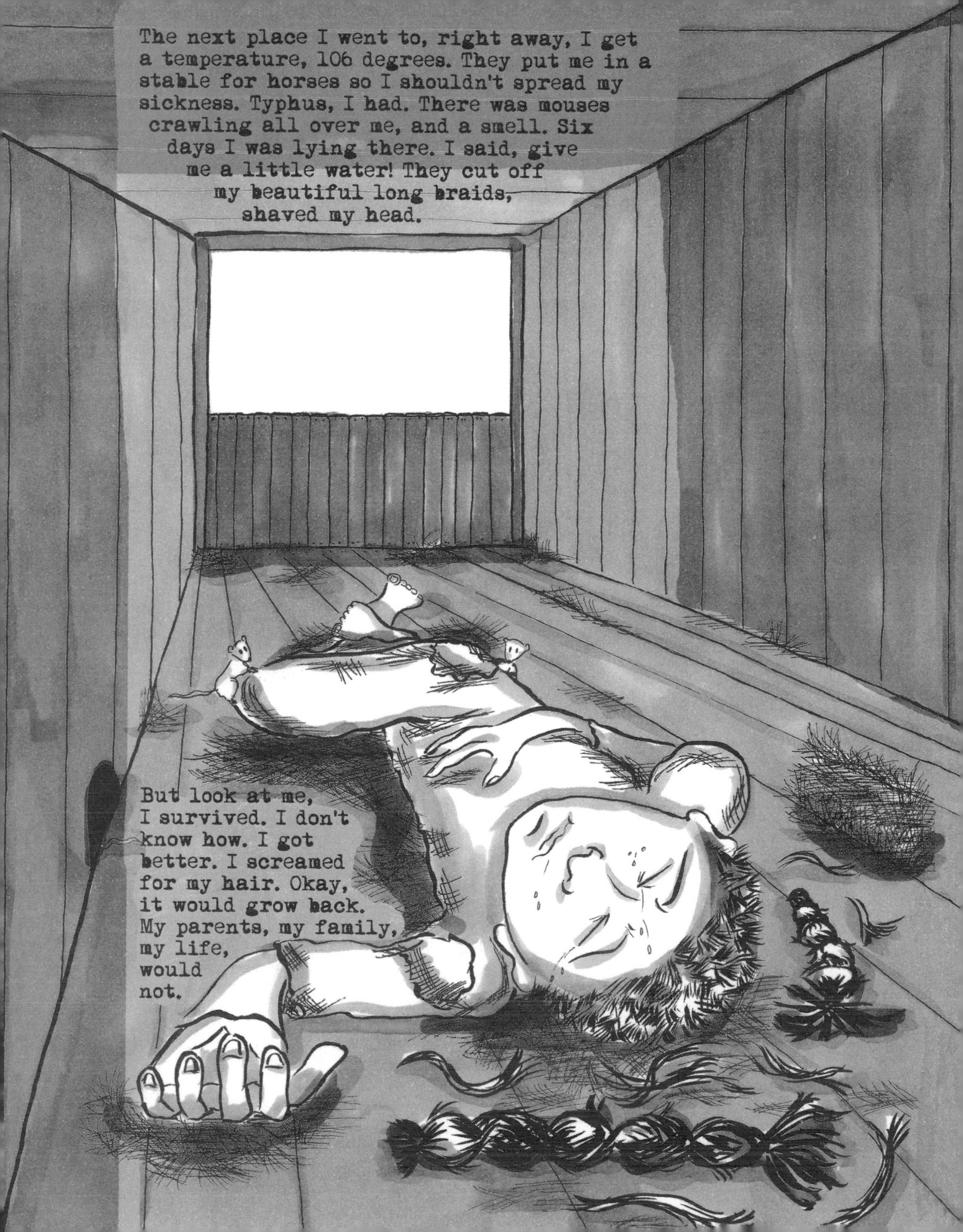
The next place I went to, right away, I get a temperature, 106 degrees. They put me in a stable for horses so I shouldn't spread my sickness. Typhus, I had. There was mouses crawling all over me, and a smell. Six days I was lying there. I said, give me a little water! They cut off my beautiful long braids, shaved my head.
But look at me, I survived. I don't know how. I got better. I screamed for my hair. Okay, it would grow back. My parents, my family, my life, would not.

I got up and kept on going.
One lady she said to me,
You can be my cowgirl.
I was afraid, but what
can you do? The milk was
dripping all down my
elbows, and it would
spray in my face.

I was with the animals mostly.
From the spring till late
October, I was cleaning up the
fields, the carrots, the potatoes.
The worst time for the farms
was the winters, because there
was nothing for a maid to do
but work on the loom, with the
spinning of the threads and the
wool, and I was so terrible,
I couldn't do it.

That lady she saved my life.
She taught me how to milk
the cow. She helped me with
the loom. Then she gave me
bread and fresh milk. I was
fourteen years old.

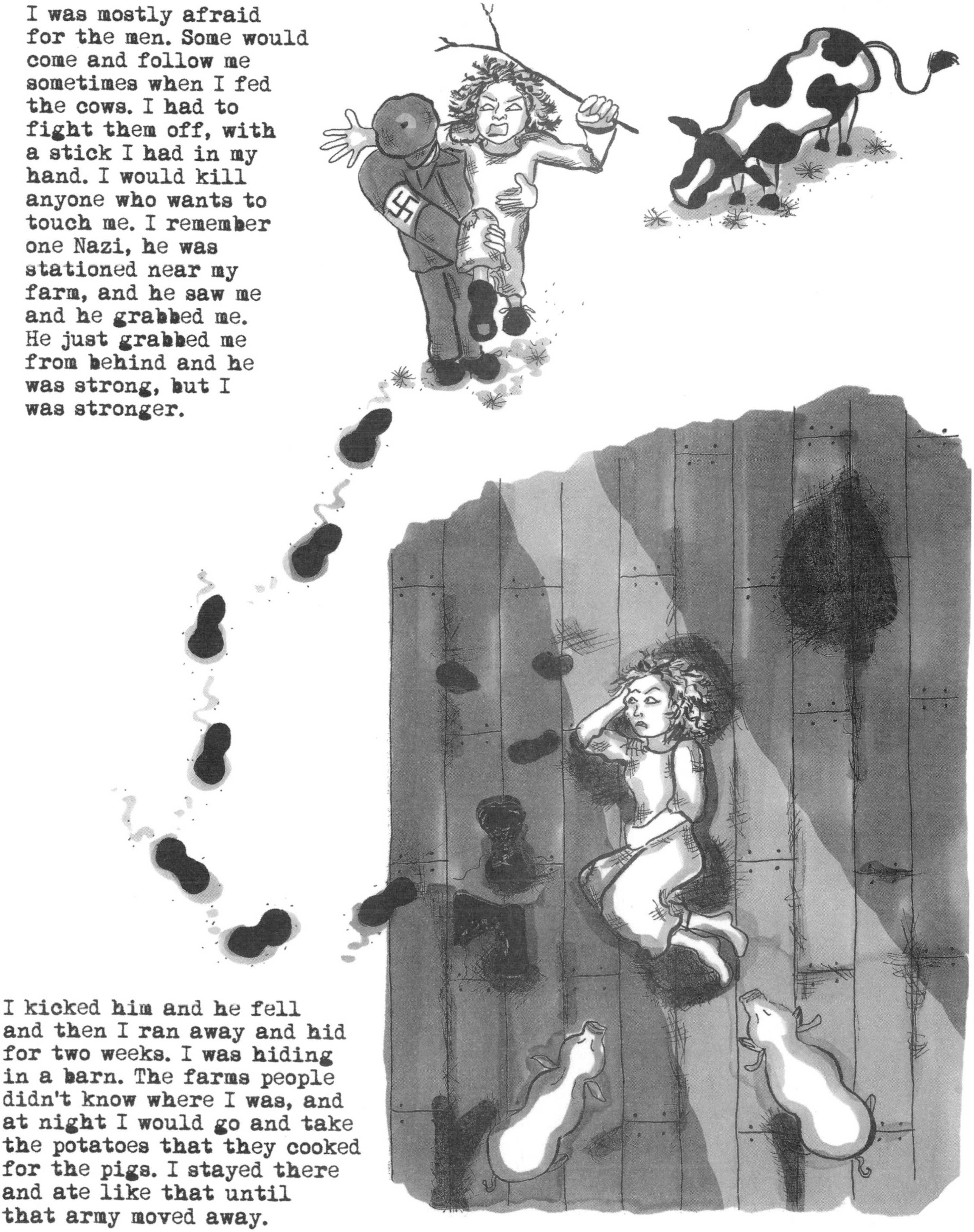
I was mostly afraid for the men. Some would come and follow me sometimes when I fed the cows. I had to fight them off, with a stick I had in my hand. I would kill anyone who wants to touch me. I remember one Nazi, he was stationed near my farm, and he saw me and he grabbed me. He just grabbed me from behind and he was strong, but I was stronger.
I kicked him and he fell and then I ran away and hid for two weeks. I was hiding in a barn. The farms people didn't know where I was, and at night I would go and take the potatoes that they cooked for the pigs. I stayed there and ate like that until that army moved away.

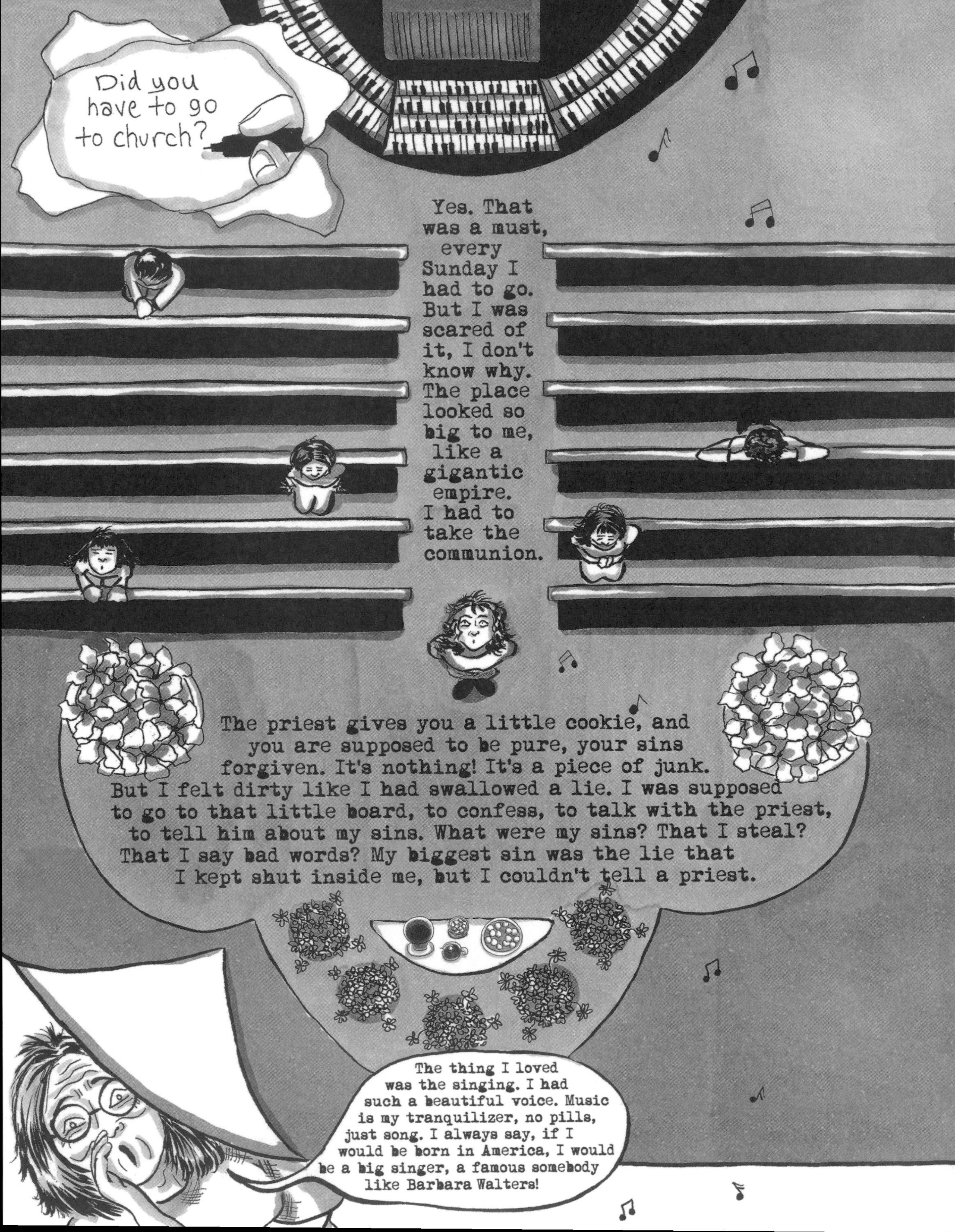
Did you have to go to church?
Yes. That was a must, every Sunday I had to go. But I was scared of it, I don't know why. The place looked so big to me, like a gigantic empire. I had to take the communion.
The priest gives you a little cookie, and you are supposed to be pure, your sins forgiven. It's nothing! It's a piece of junk. But I felt dirty like I had swallowed a lie. I was supposed to go to that little board, to confess, to talk with the priest, to tell him about my sins. What were my sins? That I steal? That I say bad words? My biggest sin was the lie that I kept shut inside me, but I couldn't tell a priest.
The thing I loved was the singing. I had such a beautiful voice. Music is my tranquilizer, no pills, just song. I always say, if I would be born in America, I would be a big singer, a famous somebody like Barbara Walters!

Even though I wasn't practicing Jewish, I was still a Jew in the heart. I remember one day a boy came to the farm and I could see that he was Jewish. The lady said only potatoes, don't let him take nothing else. But I had some bread I just baked, fresh.

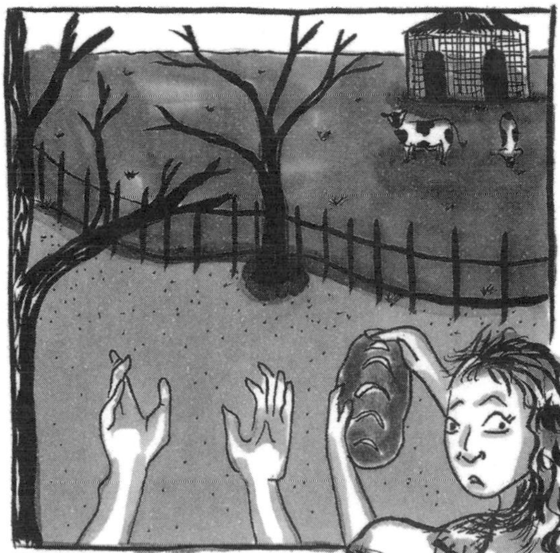

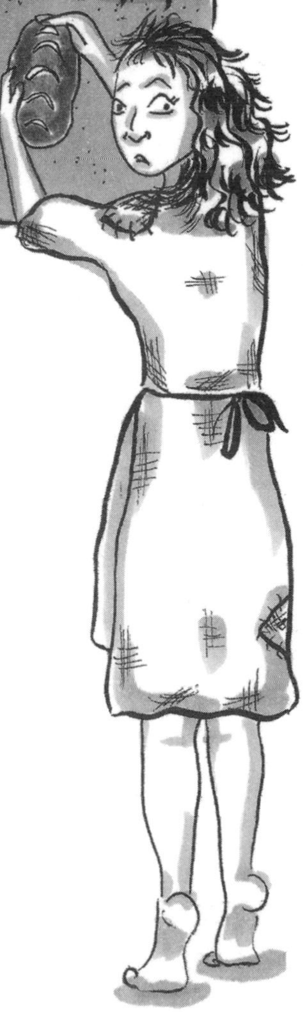

I gave that bread like a secret.

I was so scared,

but I gave it.

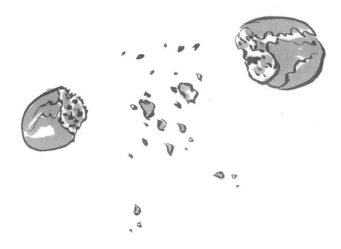

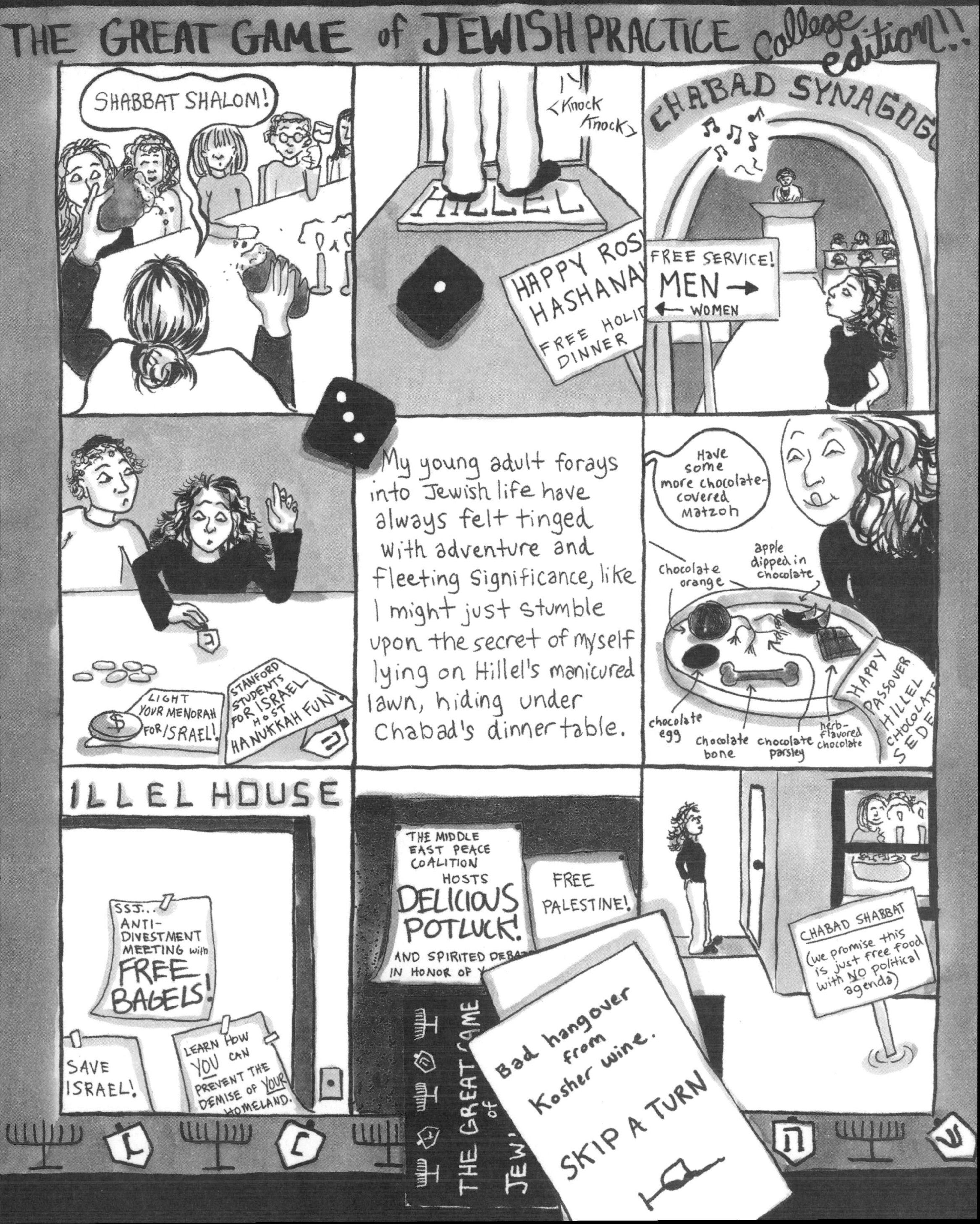
THE GREAT GAME of JEWISH PRACTICE College edition!!
SHABBAT SHALOM!
Knock Knock
HILLEL
HAPPY ROSH HASHANAH
FREE HOLIDAY DINNER
CHABAD SYNAGOGUE
FREE SERVICE!
MEN →
← WOMEN
LIGHT YOUR MENORAH FOR ISRAEL!
STANFORD STUDENTS FOR ISRAEL HOST HANUKKAH FUN!
My young adult forays into Jewish life have always felt tinged with adventure and fleeting significance, like I might just stumble upon the secret of myself lying on Hillel's manicured lawn, hiding under Chabad's dinner table.
Have some more chocolate-covered Matzoh
Chocolate orange
apple dipped in chocolate
chocolate egg
Chocolate bone
Chocolate parsley
herb-flavored chocolate
HAPPY PASSOVER HILLEL CHOCOLATE SEDER
HILLEL HOUSE
SSJ... ANTI-DIVESTMENT MEETING with FREE BAGELS!
SAVE ISRAEL!
LEARN HOW YOU CAN PREVENT THE DEMISE OF YOUR HOMELAND.
THE MIDDLE EAST PEACE COALITION HOSTS DELICIOUS POTLUCK! AND SPIRITED DEBATE IN HONOR OF Y
FREE PALESTINE!
CHABAD SHABBAT (we promise this is just free food with NO political agenda)
Bad hangover from Kosher wine.
SKIP A TURN
THE GREAT GAME of JEW

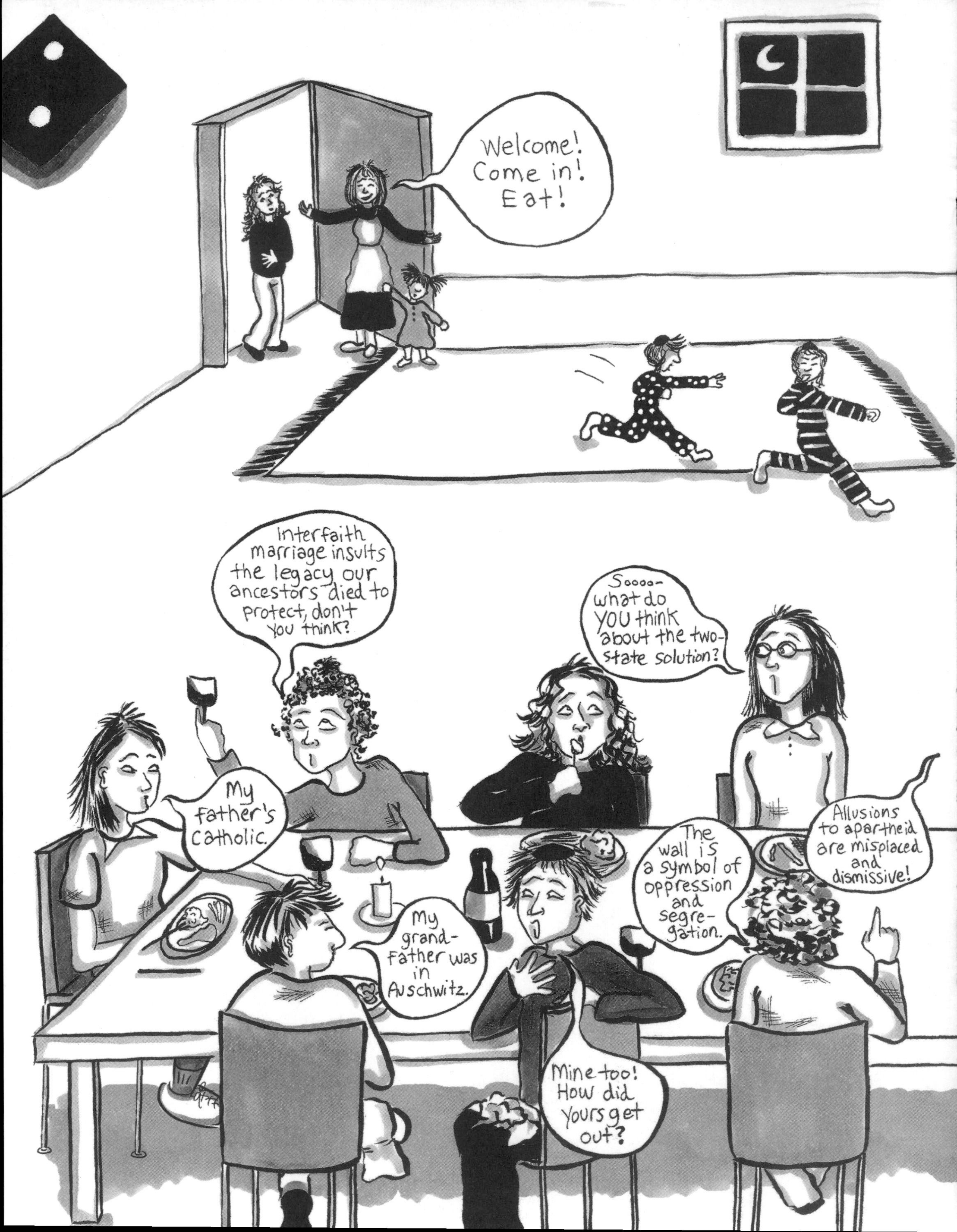
Welcome! Come in! Eat!
Interfaith marriage insults the legacy our ancestors died to protect, don't you think?
Soooo- what do YOU think about the two-state solution?
My father's catholic.
The wall is a symbol of oppression and segregation.
Allusions to apartheid are misplaced and dismissive!
My grand-father was in Auschwitz.
Mine too! How did yours get out?

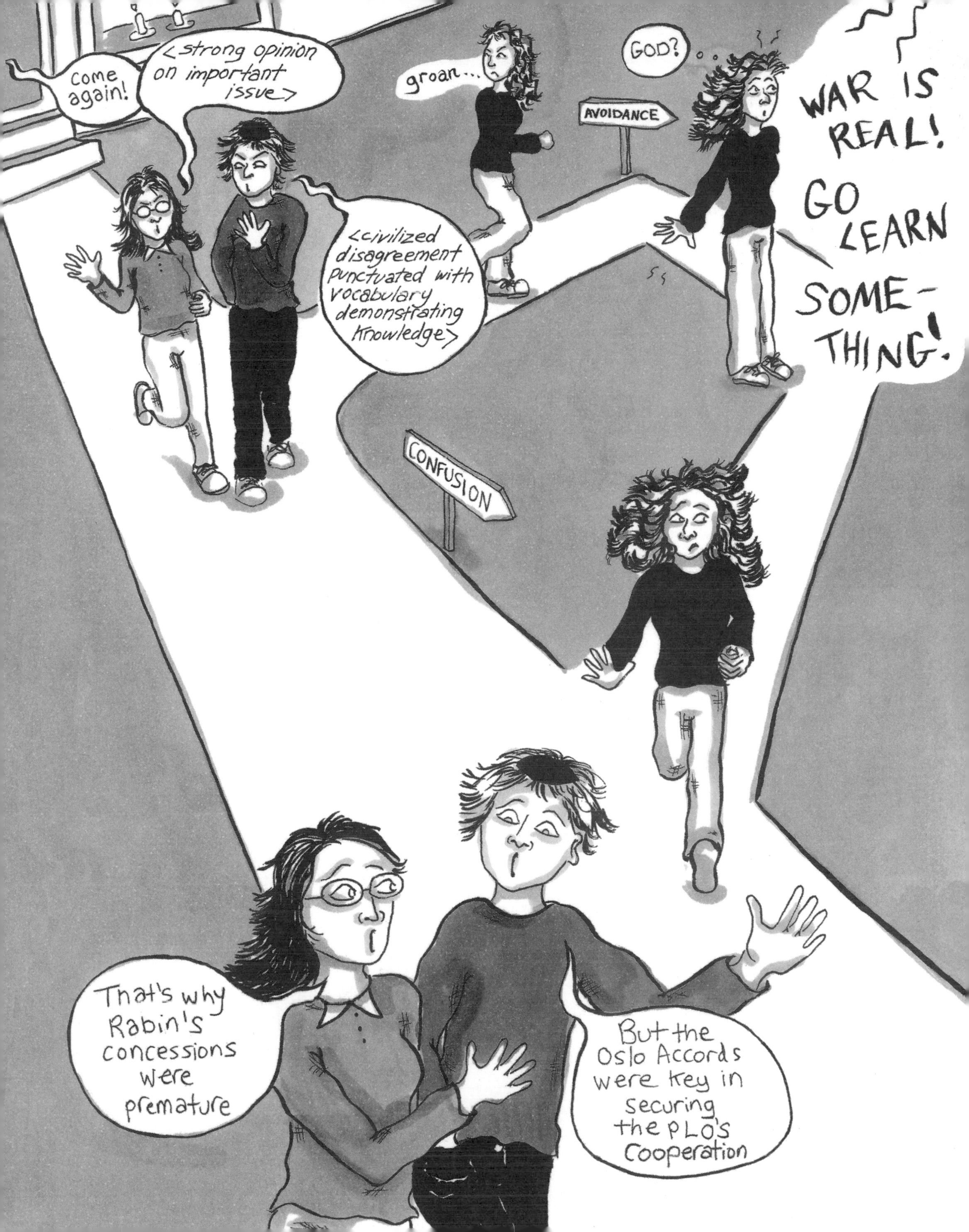
come again!
<strong opinion on important issue>
<civilized disagreement punctuated with vocabulary demonstrating knowledge>
groan...
AVOIDANCE
GOD?
WAR IS REAL! GO LEARN SOME-THING!
CONFUSION
That's why Rabin's concessions were premature
But the Oslo Accords were key in securing the PLO's cooperation

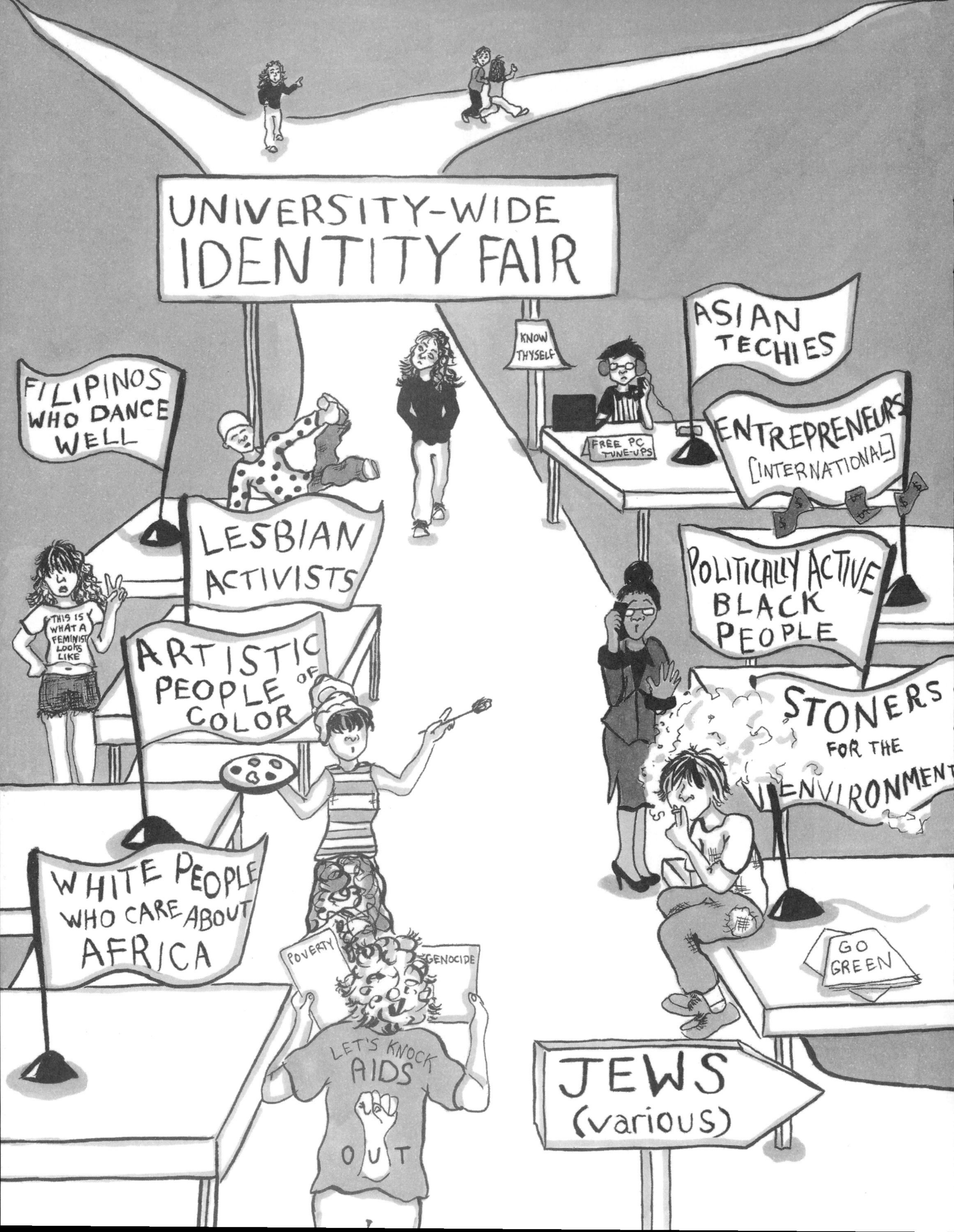
UNIVERSITY-WIDE
IDENTITY FAIR
KNOW THYSELF
FILIPINOS WHO DANCE WELL
ASIAN TECHIES
FREE PC TUNE-UPS
ENTREPRENEURS [INTERNATIONAL]
LESBIAN ACTIVISTS
POLITICALLY ACTIVE BLACK PEOPLE
THIS IS WHAT A FEMINIST LOOKS LIKE
ARTISTIC PEOPLE OF COLOR
STONERS FOR THE ENVIRONMENT
WHITE PEOPLE WHO CARE ABOUT AFRICA
POVERTY
GENOCIDE
GO GREEN
LET'S KNOCK AIDS OUT
JEWS (various)

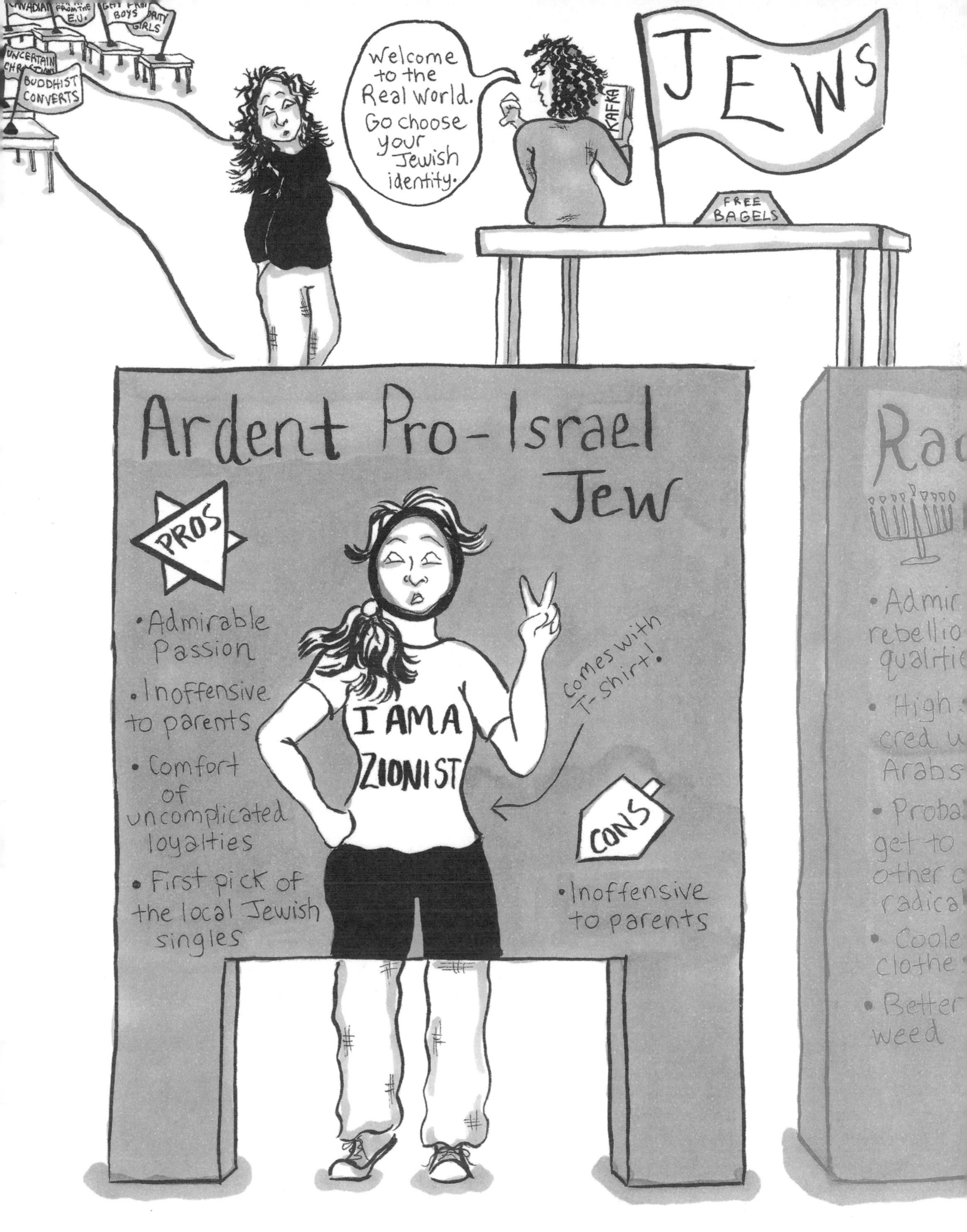

UNCERTAIN
BUDDHIST CONVERTS
Welcome to the Real World. Go choose your Jewish identity.
KAFKA
JEWS
FREE BAGELS
Ardent Pro-Israel Jew
PROS
• Admirable Passion
• Inoffensive to parents
• Comfort of uncomplicated loyalties
• First pick of the local Jewish singles
I AM A ZIONIST
comes with T-shirt!
CONS
• Inoffensive to parents

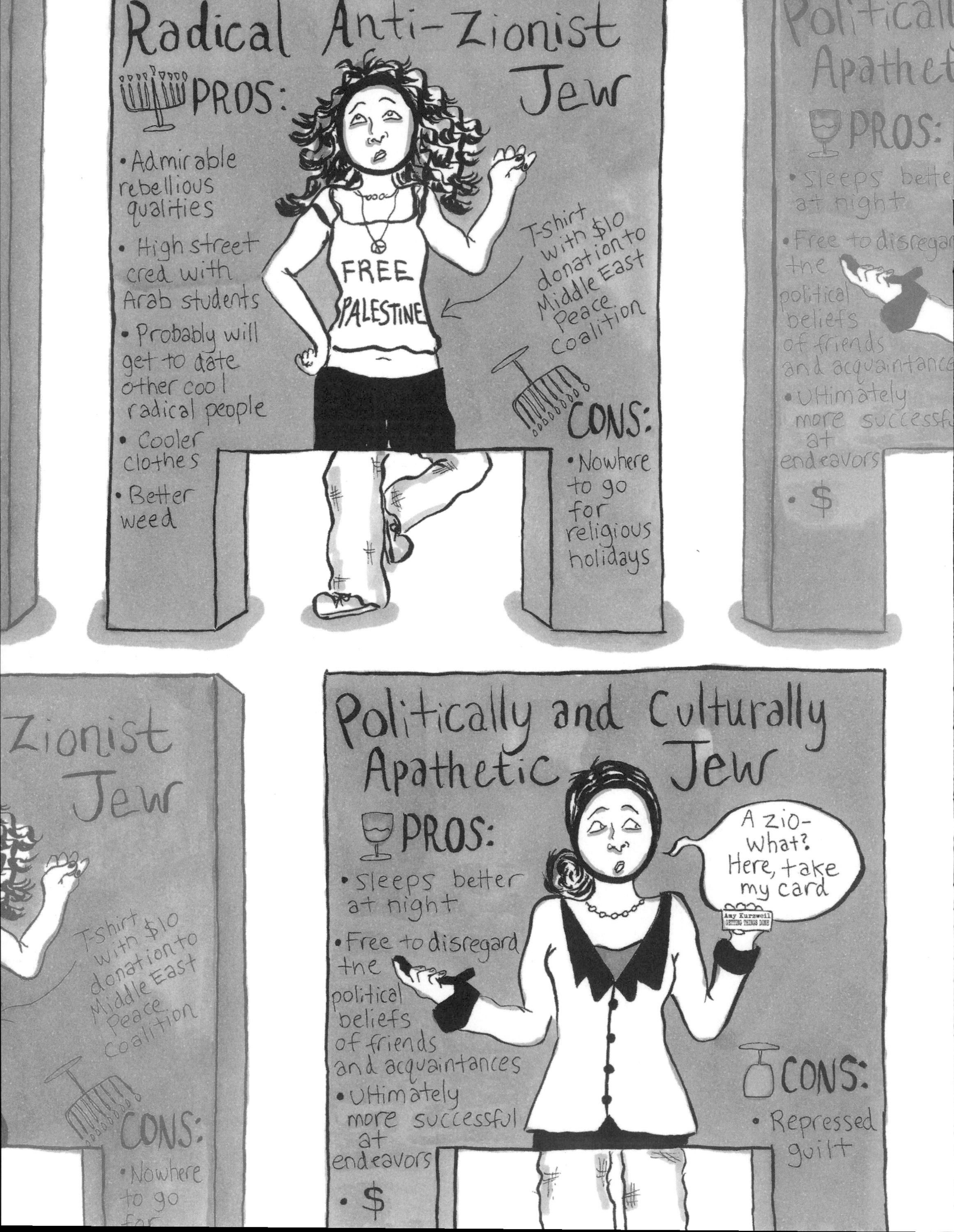
Radical Anti-Zionist Jew
PROS:
• Admirable rebellious qualities
• High street cred with Arab students
• Probably will get to date other cool radical people
• Cooler clothes
• Better weed
FREE PALESTINE
T-shirt with $10 donation to Middle East Peace coalition
CONS:
• Nowhere to go for religious holidays
Politically and Culturally Apathetic Jew
PROS:
• sleeps better at night
• Free to disregard the political beliefs of friends and acquaintances
• Ultimately more successful at endeavors
• $
A zio-what? Here, take my card
Amy Kurzweil
GETTING THINGS DONE
CONS:
• Repressed guilt

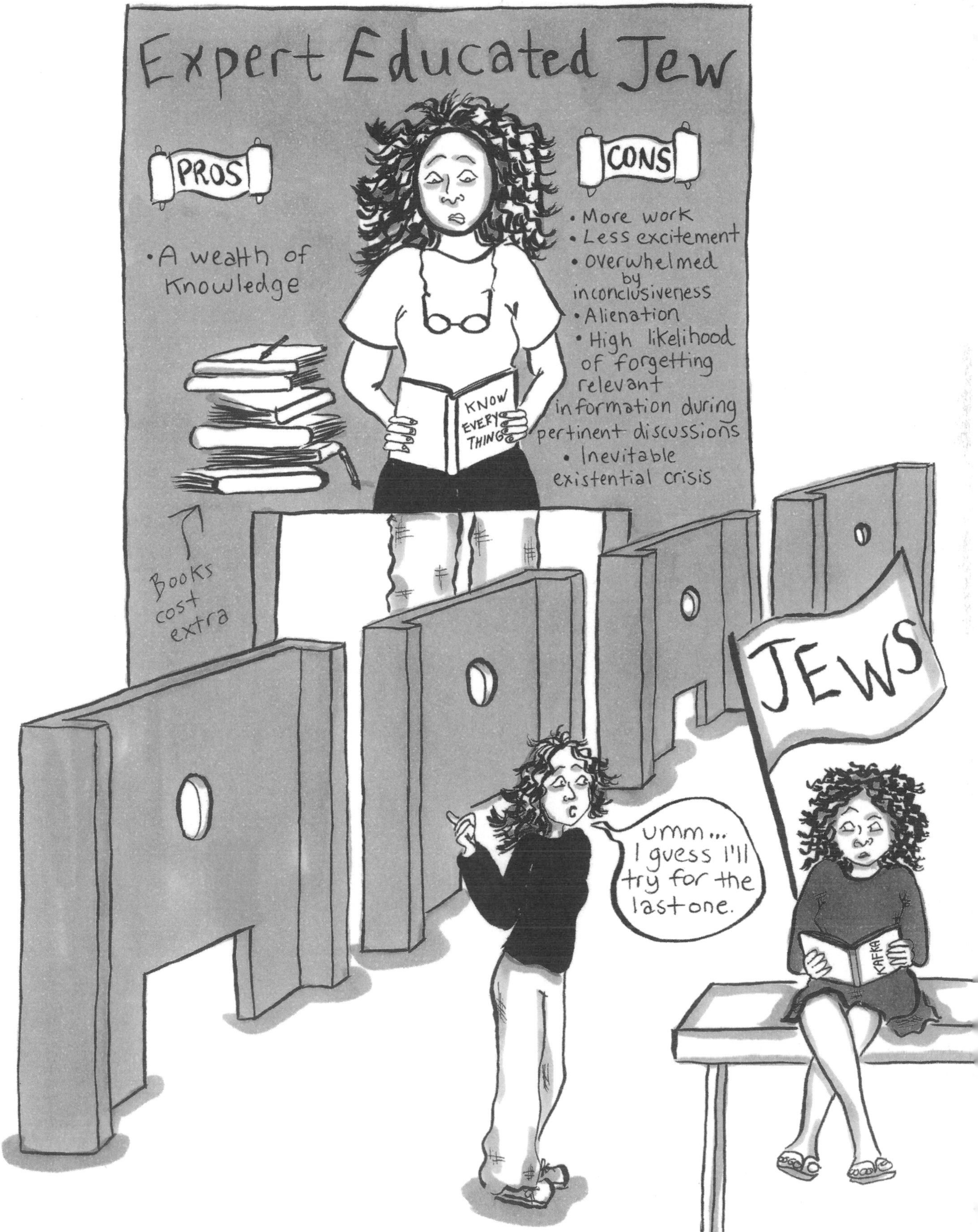
Expert Educated Jew
PROS
• A wealth of Knowledge
CONS
• More work
• Less excitement
• overwhelmed by inconclusiveness
• Alienation
• High likelihood of forgetting relevant information during pertinent discussions
• Inevitable existential crisis
KNOW EVERY THING
Books cost extra
JEWS
umm... I guess I'll try for the last one.
KAFKA

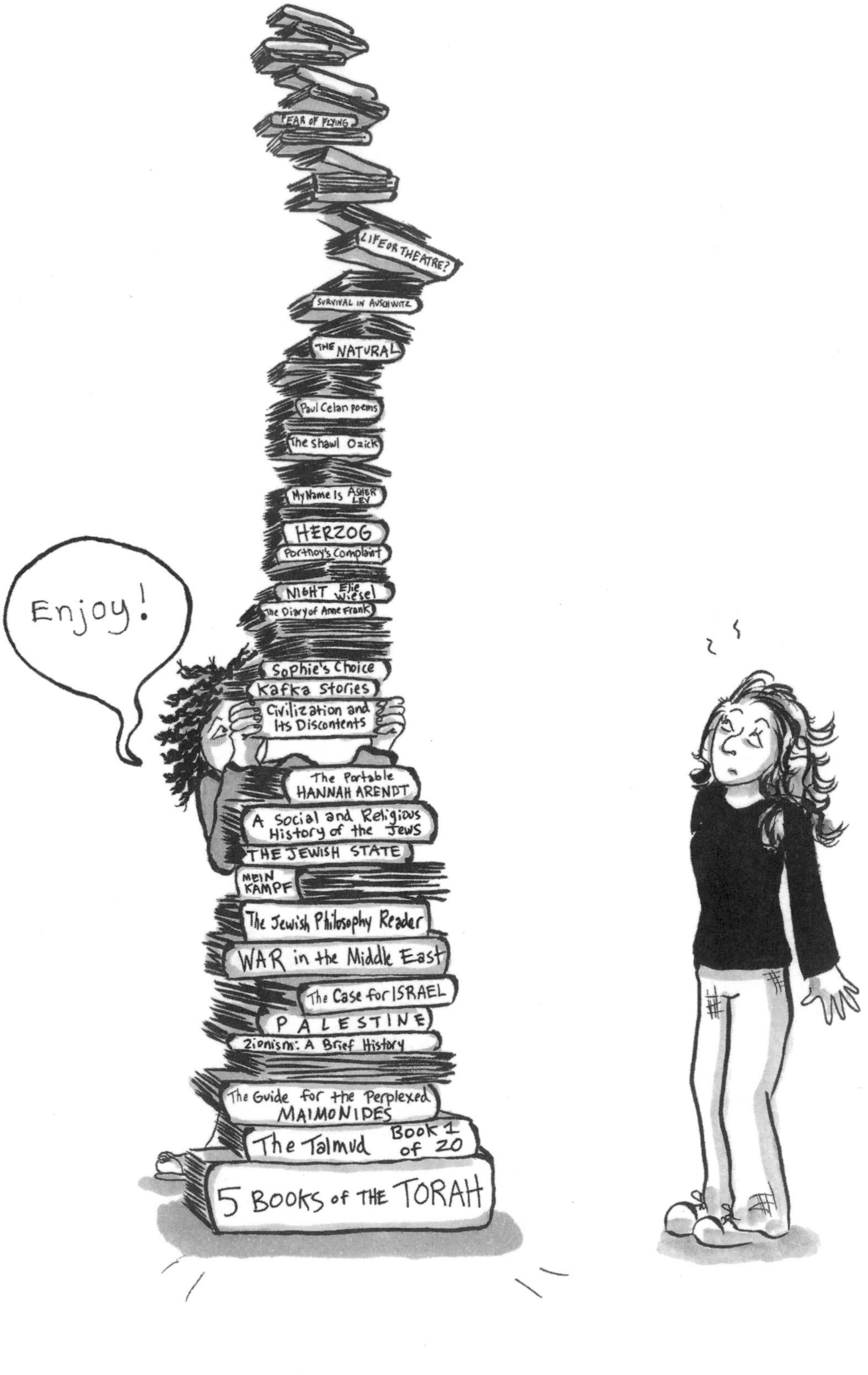
Enjoy!
FEAR OF FLYING
LIFE OR THEATRE?
SURVIVAL IN AUSCHWITZ
THE NATURAL
Paul Celan poems
The Shawl Ozick
My Name Is Asher Lev
HERZOG
Portnoy's Complaint
NIGHT Elie Wiesel
The Diary of Anne Frank
Sophie's Choice
Kafka Stories
Civilization and Its Discontents
The Portable HANNAH ARENDT
A Social and Religious History of the Jews
THE JEWISH STATE
MEIN KAMPF
The Jewish Philosophy Reader
WAR in the Middle East
The Case for ISRAEL
PALESTINE
Zionism: A Brief History
The Guide for the Perplexed MAIMONIDES
The Talmud Book 1 of 20
5 BOOKS of THE TORAH

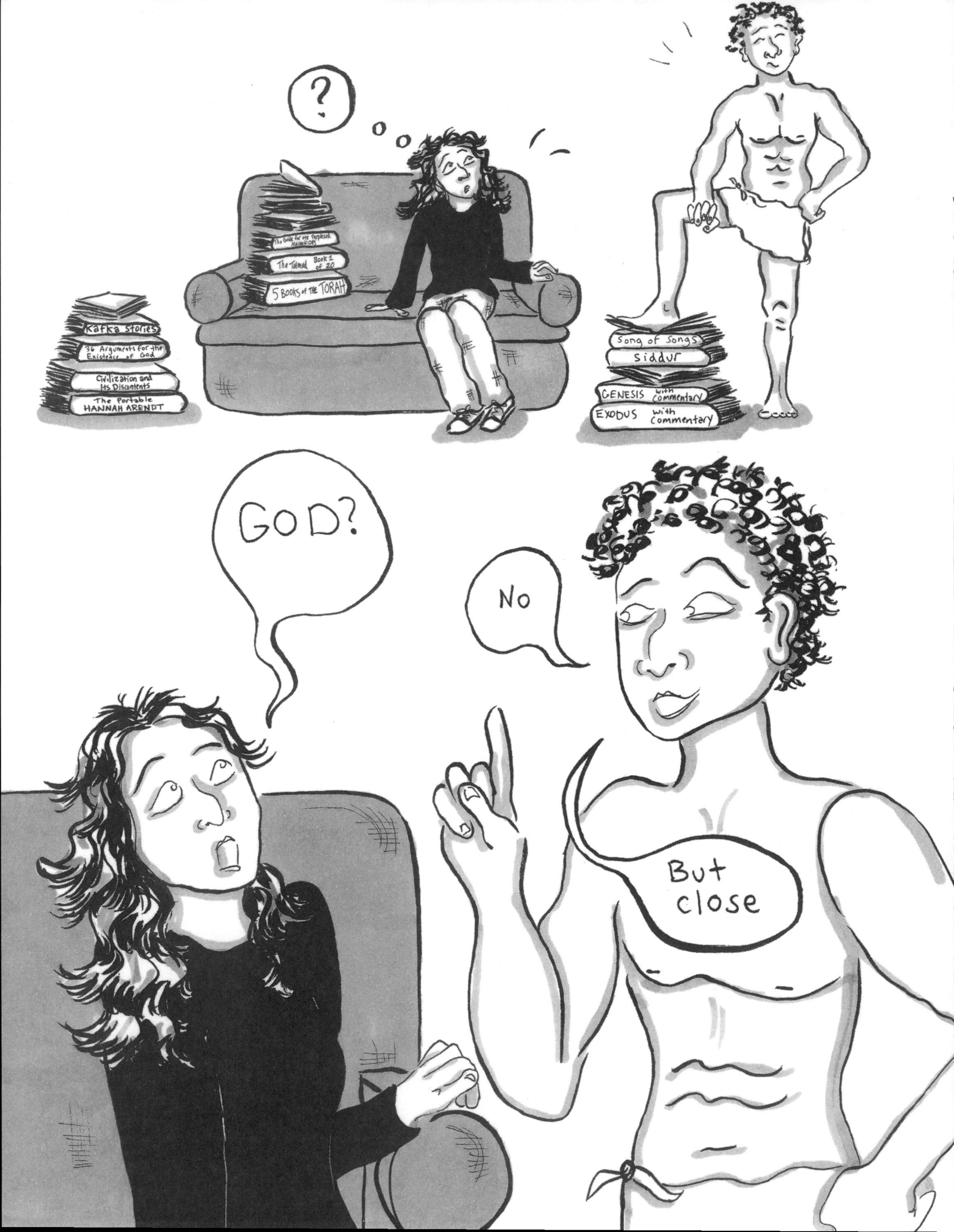
?
Kafka Stories
36 Arguments for the Existence of God
Civilization and Its Discontents
The Portable HANNAH ARENDT
The Guide for the Perplexed MAIMONIDES
The Talmud Book 1 of 20
5 BOOKS of THE TORAH
Song of Songs
siddur
GENESIS with commentary
EXODUS with commentary
GOD?
No
But close

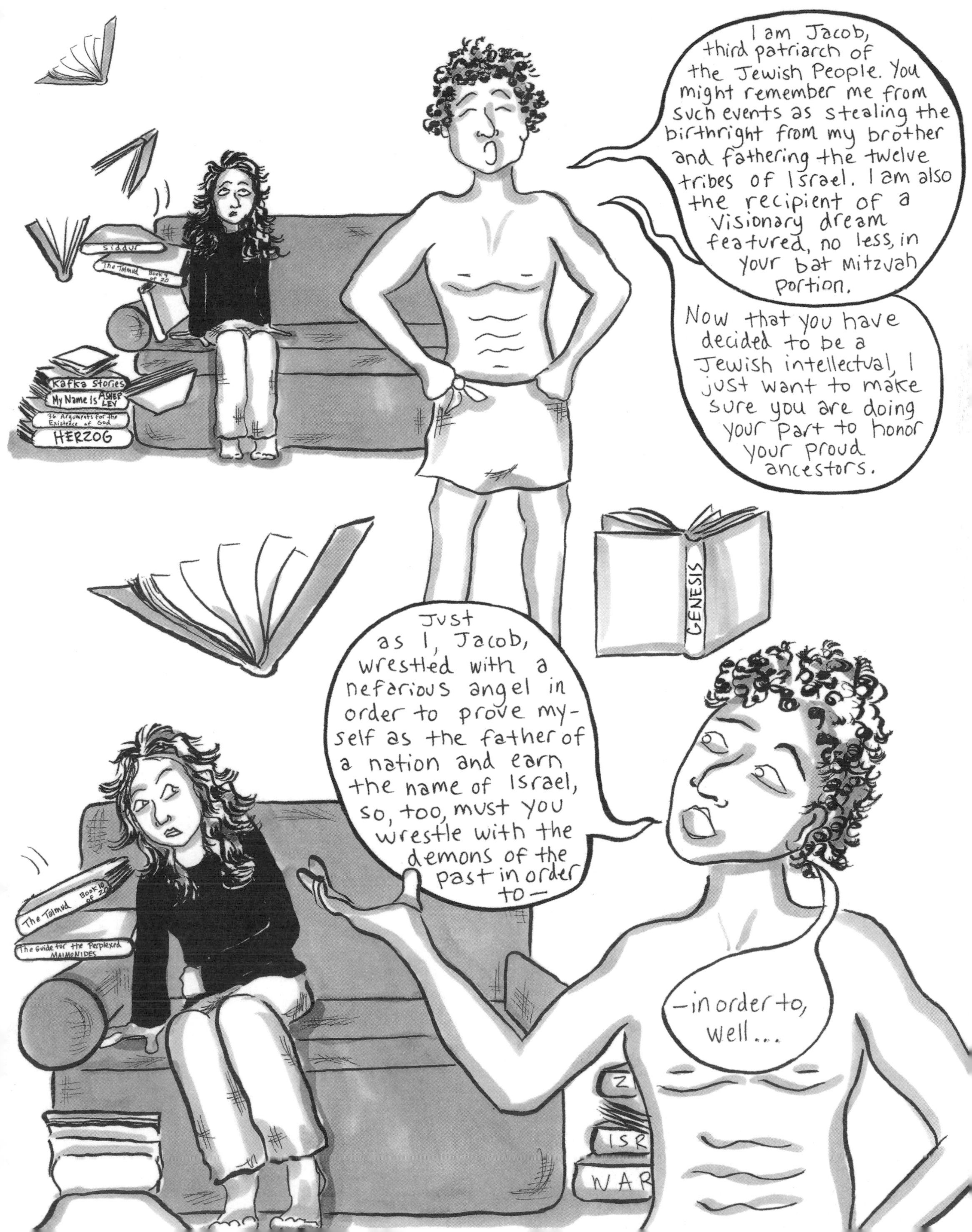
siddur
The Talmud Book 4 of 20
Kafka Stories
My Name Is Asher Lev
36 Arguments for the Existence of God
HERZOG
I am Jacob, third patriarch of the Jewish People. You might remember me from such events as stealing the birthright from my brother and fathering the twelve tribes of Israel. I am also the recipient of a visionary dream featured, no less, in your bat mitzvah portion.
Now that you have decided to be a Jewish intellectual, I just want to make sure you are doing your part to honor your proud ancestors.
GENESIS
Just as I, Jacob, wrestled with a nefarious angel in order to prove myself as the father of a nation and earn the name of Israel, so, too, must you wrestle with the demons of the past in order to—
The Talmud Book 10 of 20
The Guide for the Perplexed MAIMONIDES
—in order to, well...
Z
ISR
WAR

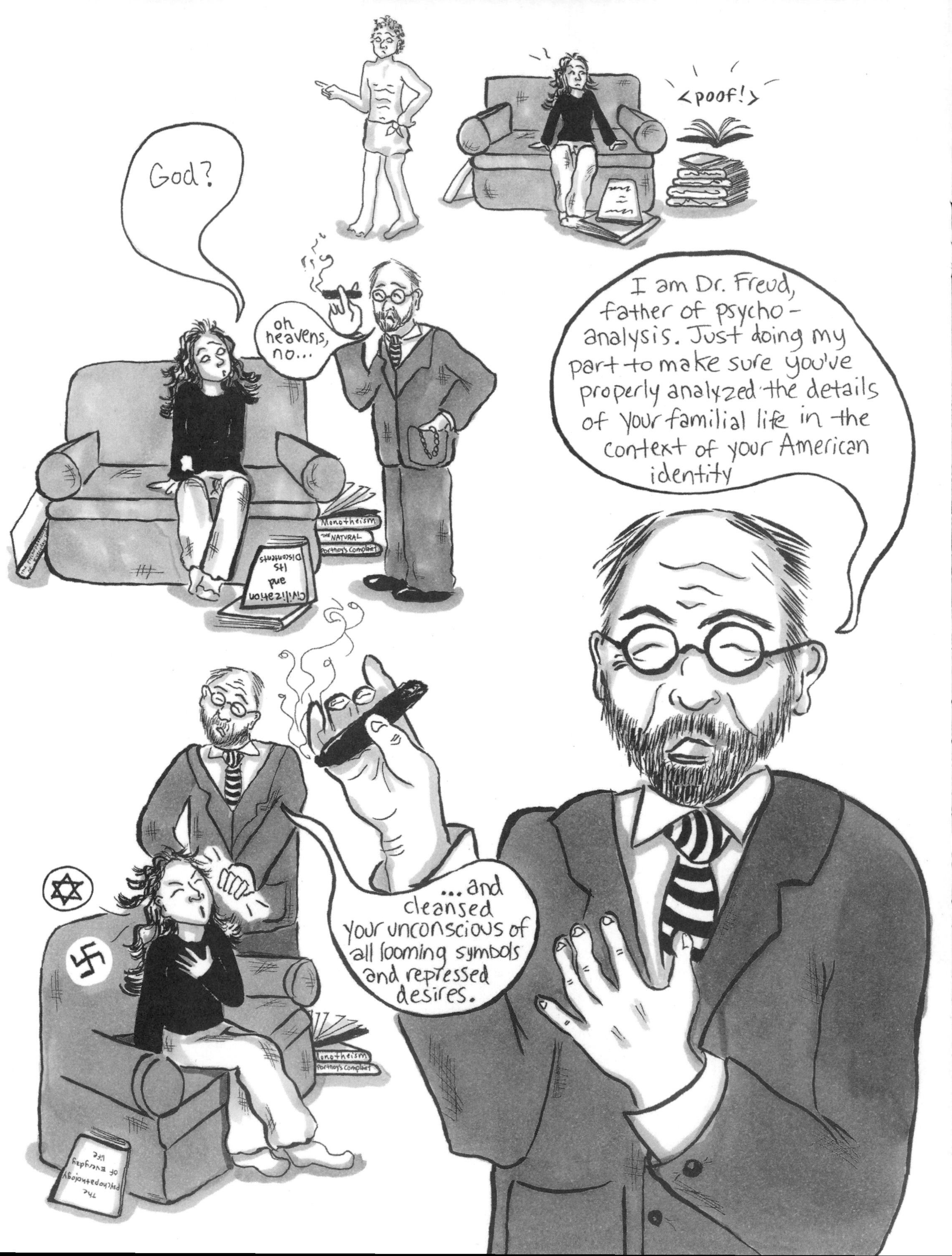
<poof!>
God?
oh heavens, no...
Monotheism
THE NATURAL
Portnoy's Complaint
Civilization and Its Discontents
I am Dr. Freud, father of psycho-analysis. Just doing my part to make sure you've properly analyzed the details of your familial life in the context of your American identity
...and cleansed your unconscious of all looming symbols and repressed desires.
Monotheism
Portnoy's Complaint
The Psychopathology of Everyday Life

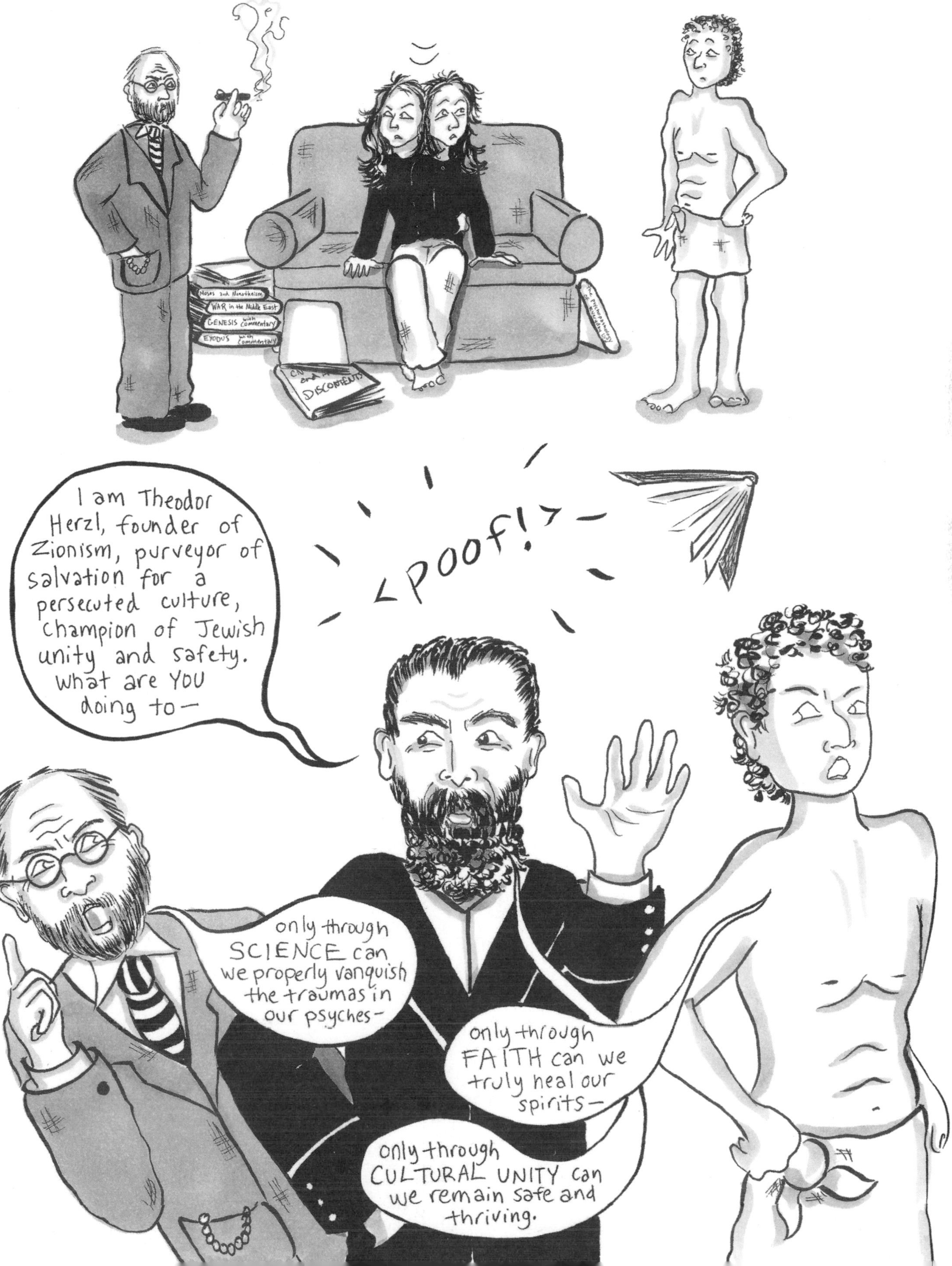

Moses and Monotheism
WAR in the Middle East
GENESIS with Commentary
EXODUS with Commentary
DISCONTENTS
The Psychopathology of Everyday Life
I am Theodor Herzl, founder of Zionism, purveyor of salvation for a persecuted culture, champion of Jewish unity and safety. What are YOU doing to—
<POOF!>
only through SCIENCE can we properly vanquish the traumas in our psyches-
only through FAITH can we truly heal our spirits—
only through CULTURAL UNITY can we remain safe and thriving.

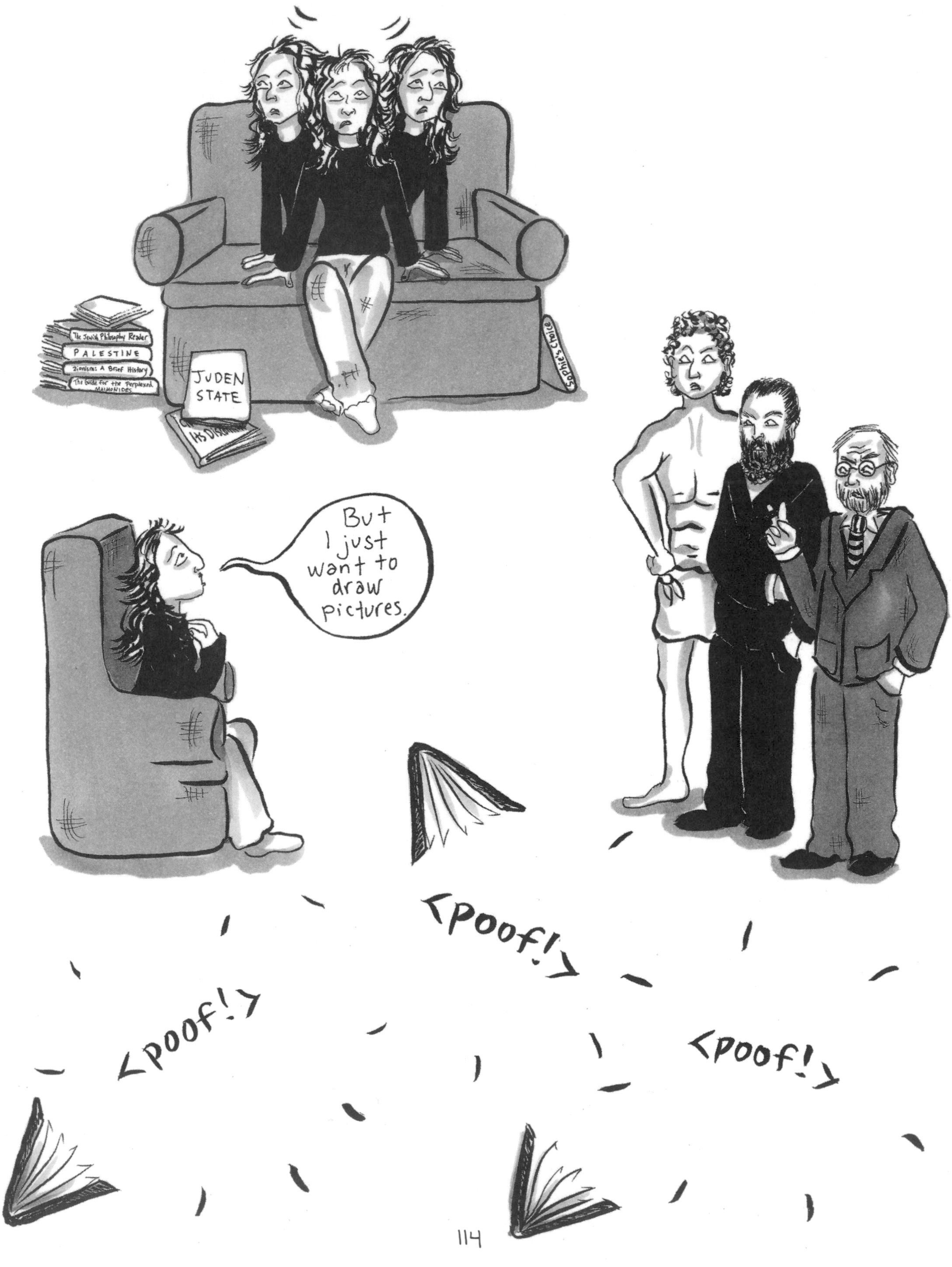
The Jewish Philosophy Reader
PALESTINE
Zionism: A Brief History
The Guide for the Perplexed MAIMONIDES
JUDEN STATE
Sophie's Choice
But I just want to draw pictures.
<poof!>
<poof!>
<poof!>

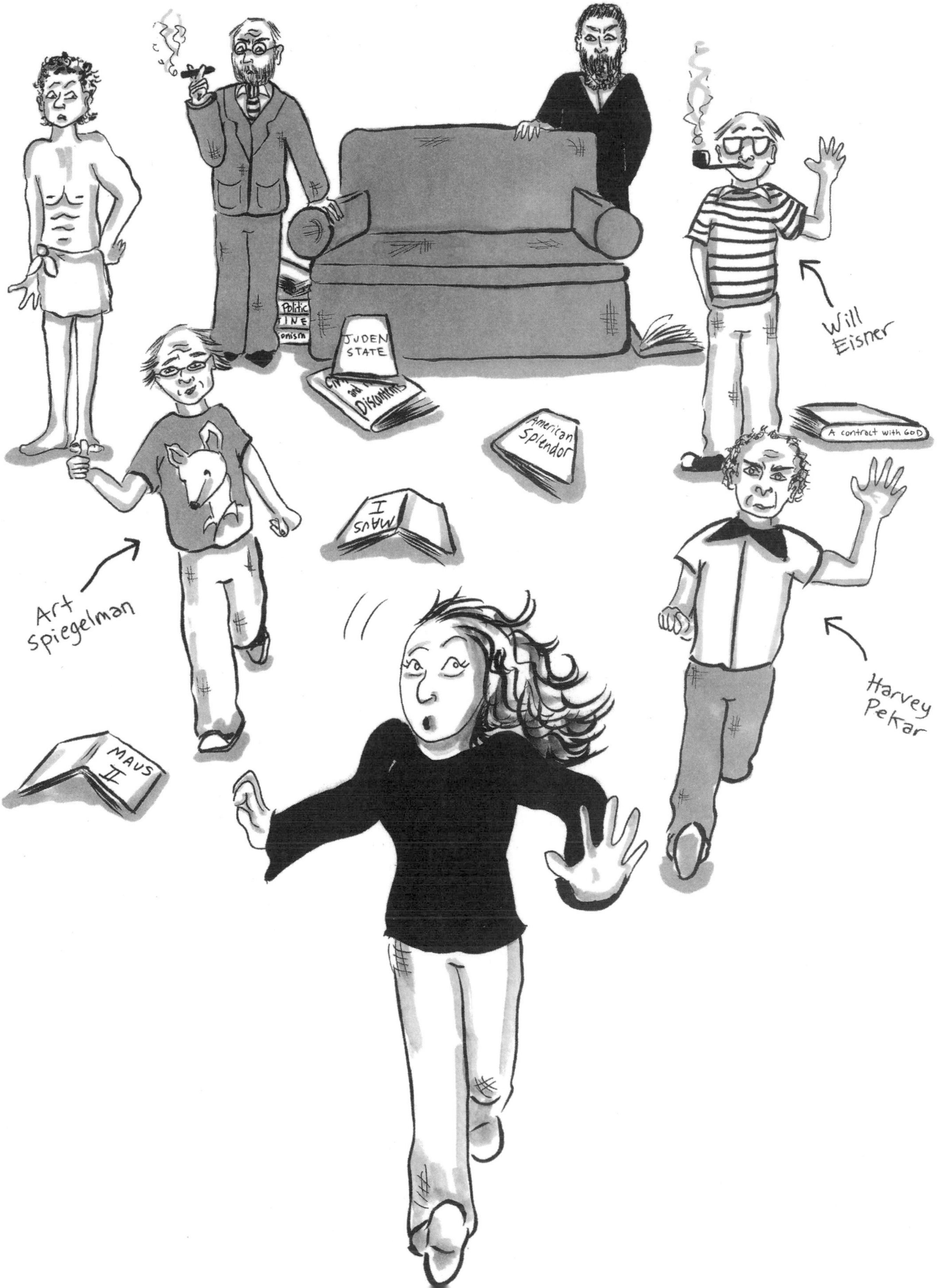
Politic
JUDEN STATE
and
Discontents
American Splendor
A contract with GOD
Will Eisner
MAUS I
Art Spiegelman
MAUS II
Harvey Pekar

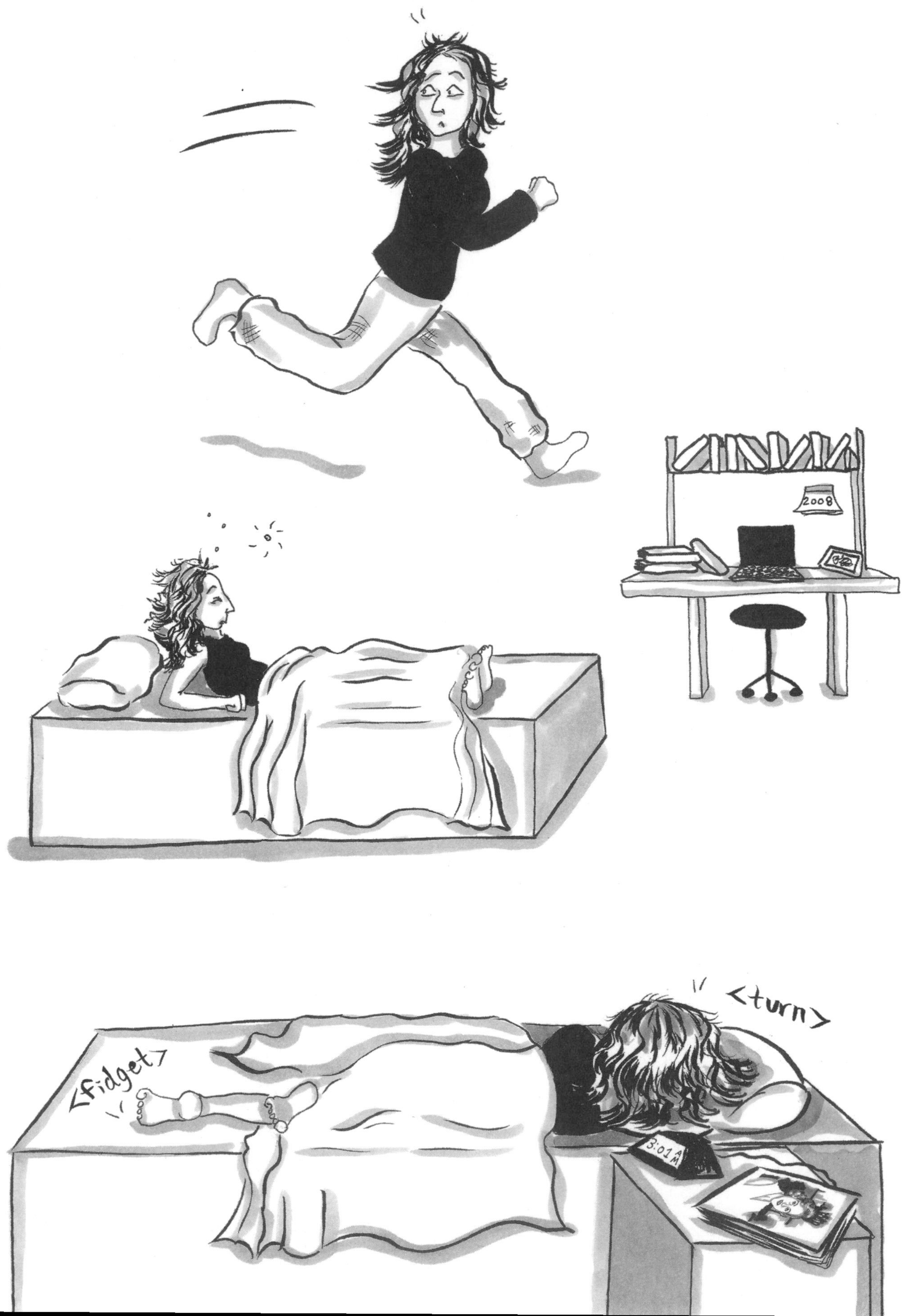
2008
<fidget>
<turn>
3:01A

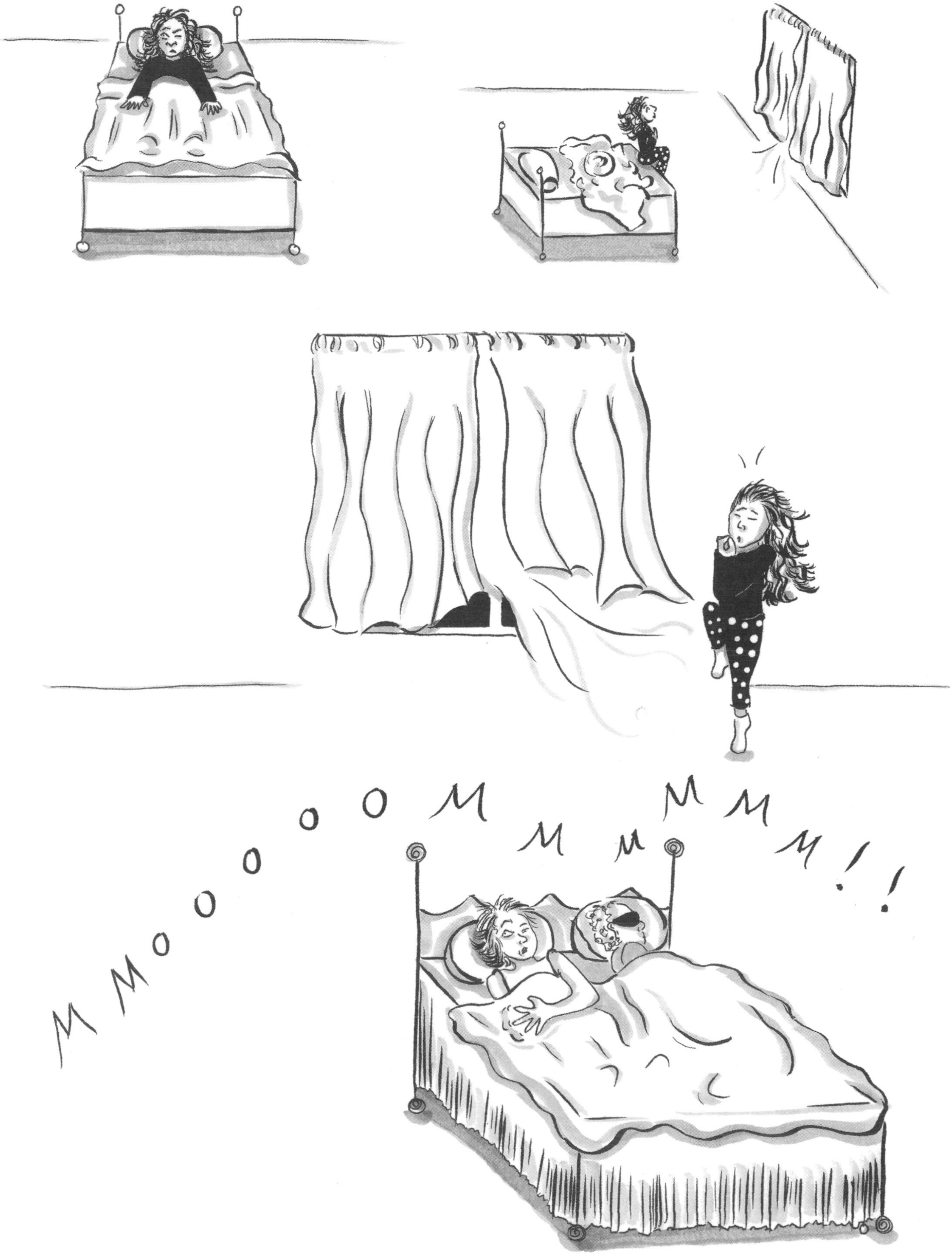
MMOOOOOMMMMMM!!

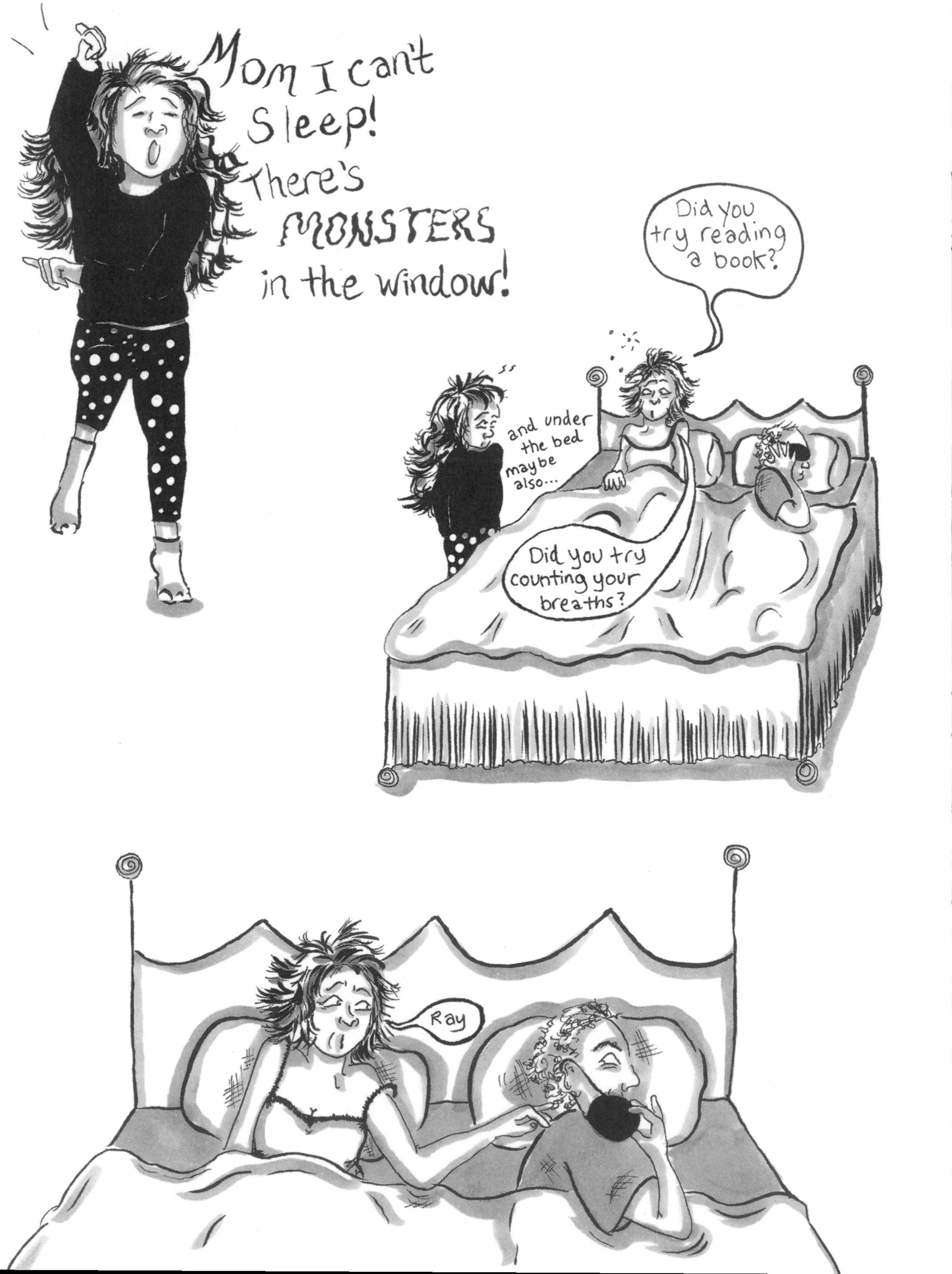

Mom I can't Sleep! There's MONSTERS in the window!
Did you try reading a book?
and under the bed maybe also...
Did you try counting your breaths?
Ray

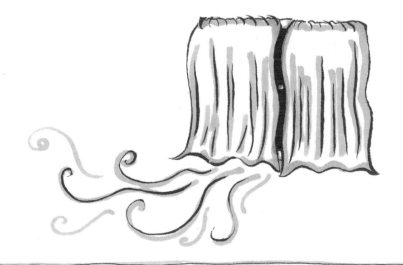

Chapter Four.
Homeland

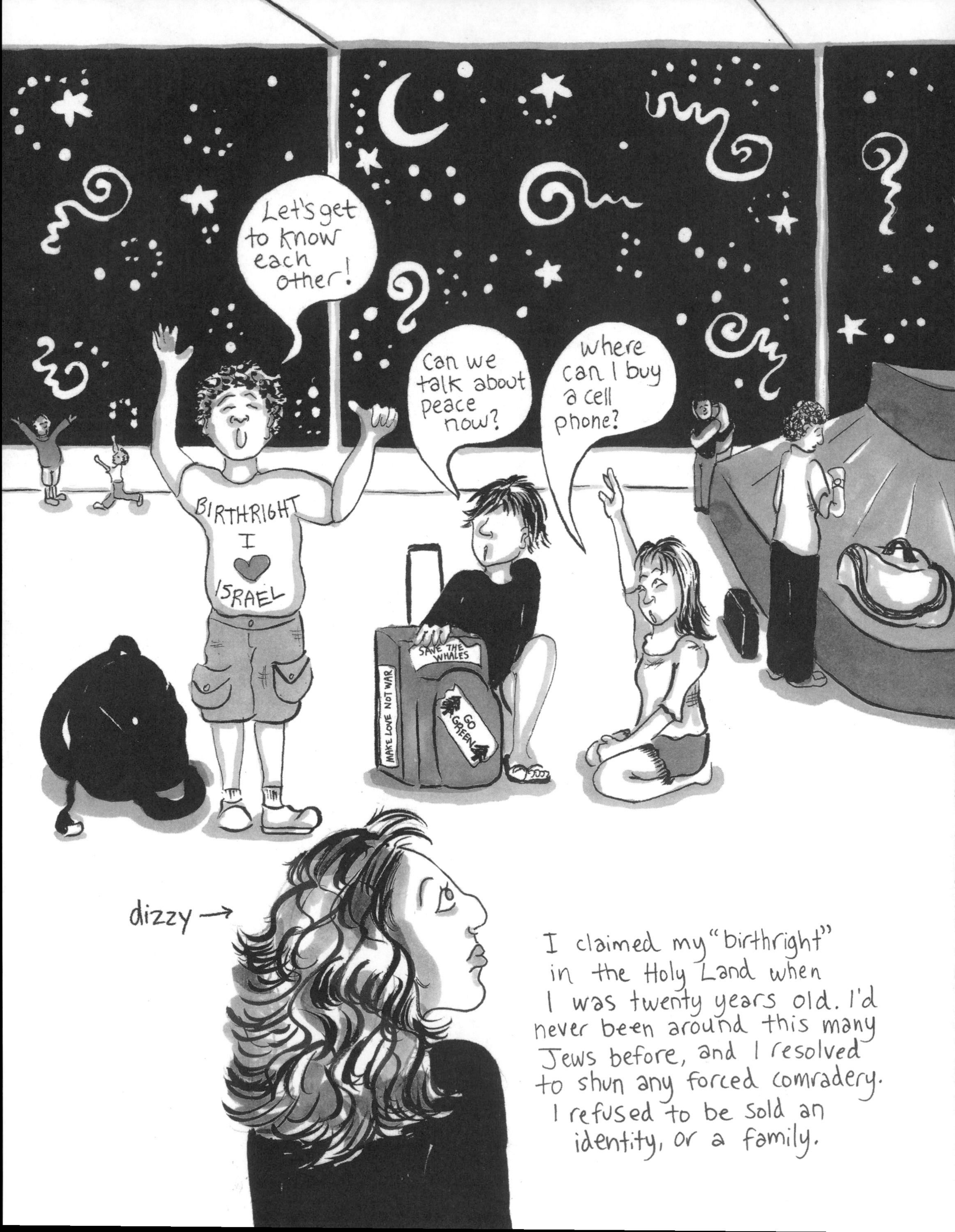
Let's get to know each other!
Can we talk about peace now?
where can I buy a cell phone?
BIRTHRIGHT I ♥ ISRAEL
SAVE THE WHALES
MAKE LOVE NOT WAR
GO GREEN
dizzy
I claimed my "birthright" in the Holy Land when I was twenty years old. I'd never been around this many Jews before, and I resolved to shun any forced comradery. I refused to be sold an identity, or a family.

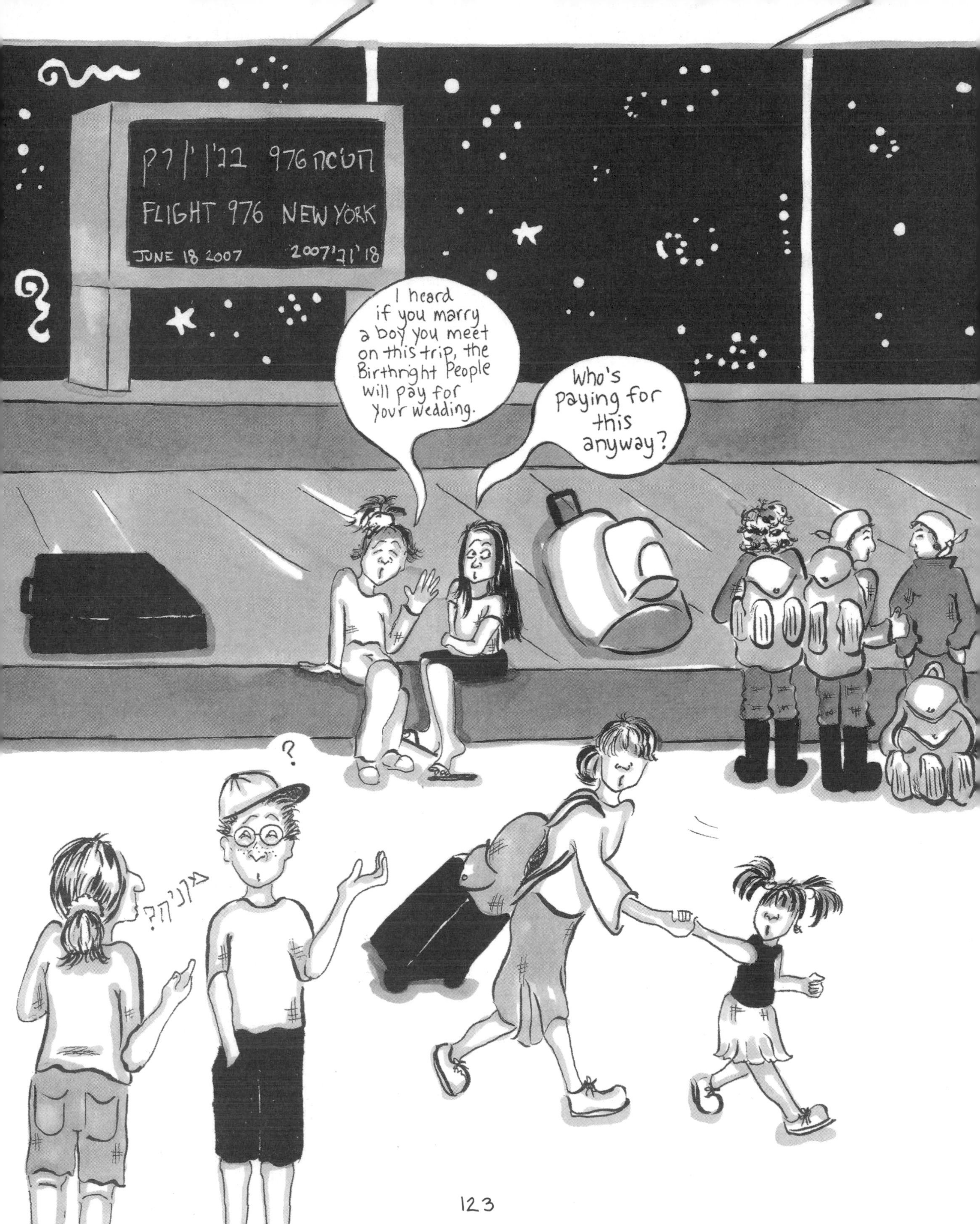
הטיסה 976 בניו יורק
FLIGHT 976 NEW YORK
JUNE 18 2007
18'וב'2007
I heard if you marry a boy you meet on this trip, the Birthright People will pay for your wedding.
Who's paying for this anyway?
?
אנ'ה?

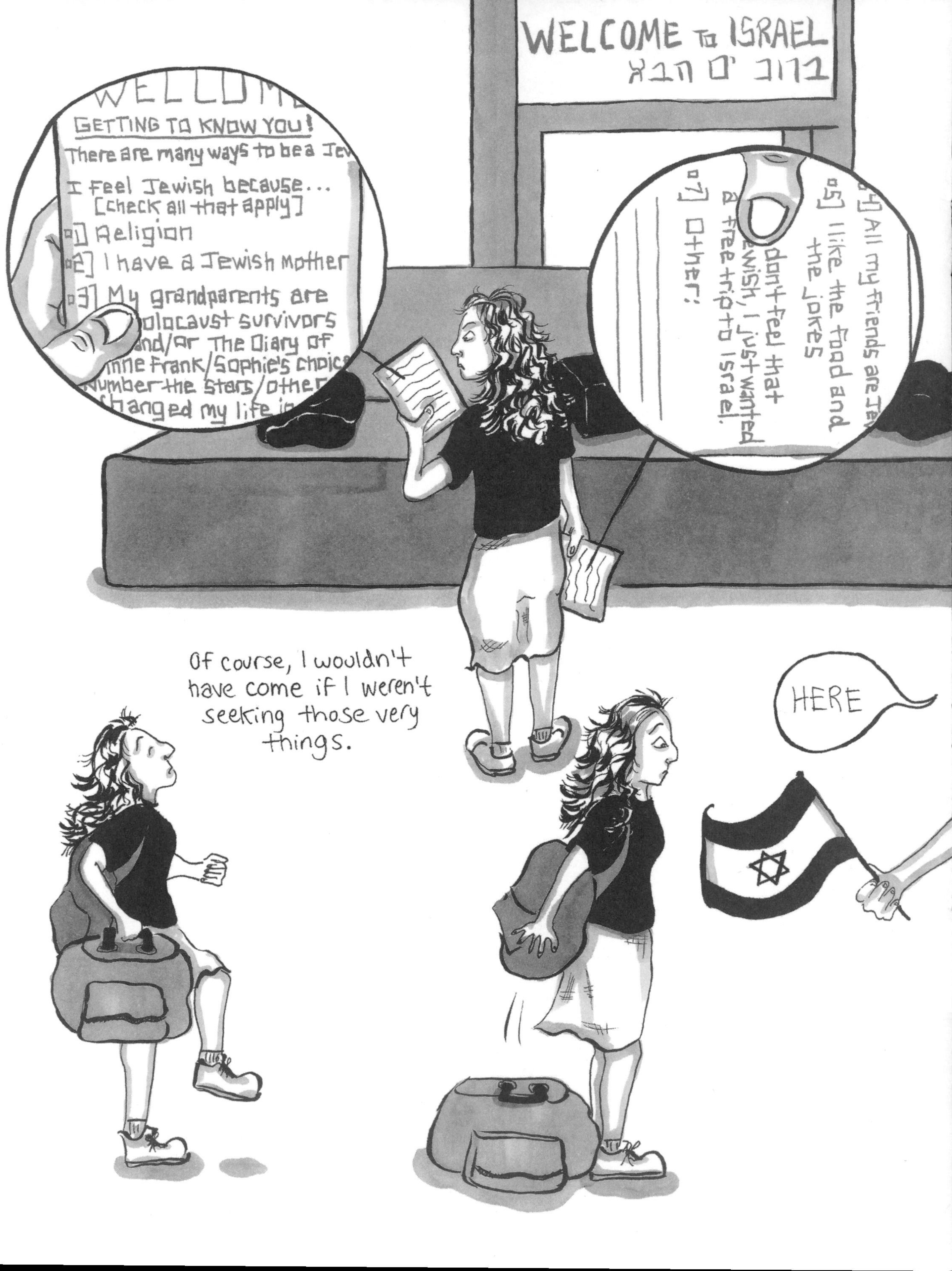
WELCOME TO ISRAEL
ברוך הבא
GETTING TO KNOW YOU!
There are many ways to be a Je
I feel Jewish because...
[check all that apply]
1] Religion
2] I have a Jewish mother
3] My grandparents are
olocaust survivors
and/or The Diary of
nne Frank/Sophie's choice
Number the Stars/other
hanged my life in
4] All my friends are Je
5] I like the food and the jokes
6] I don't feel that
ewish, I just wanted
a free trip to Israel.
7] Other:
Of course, I wouldn't have come if I weren't seeking those very things.
HERE

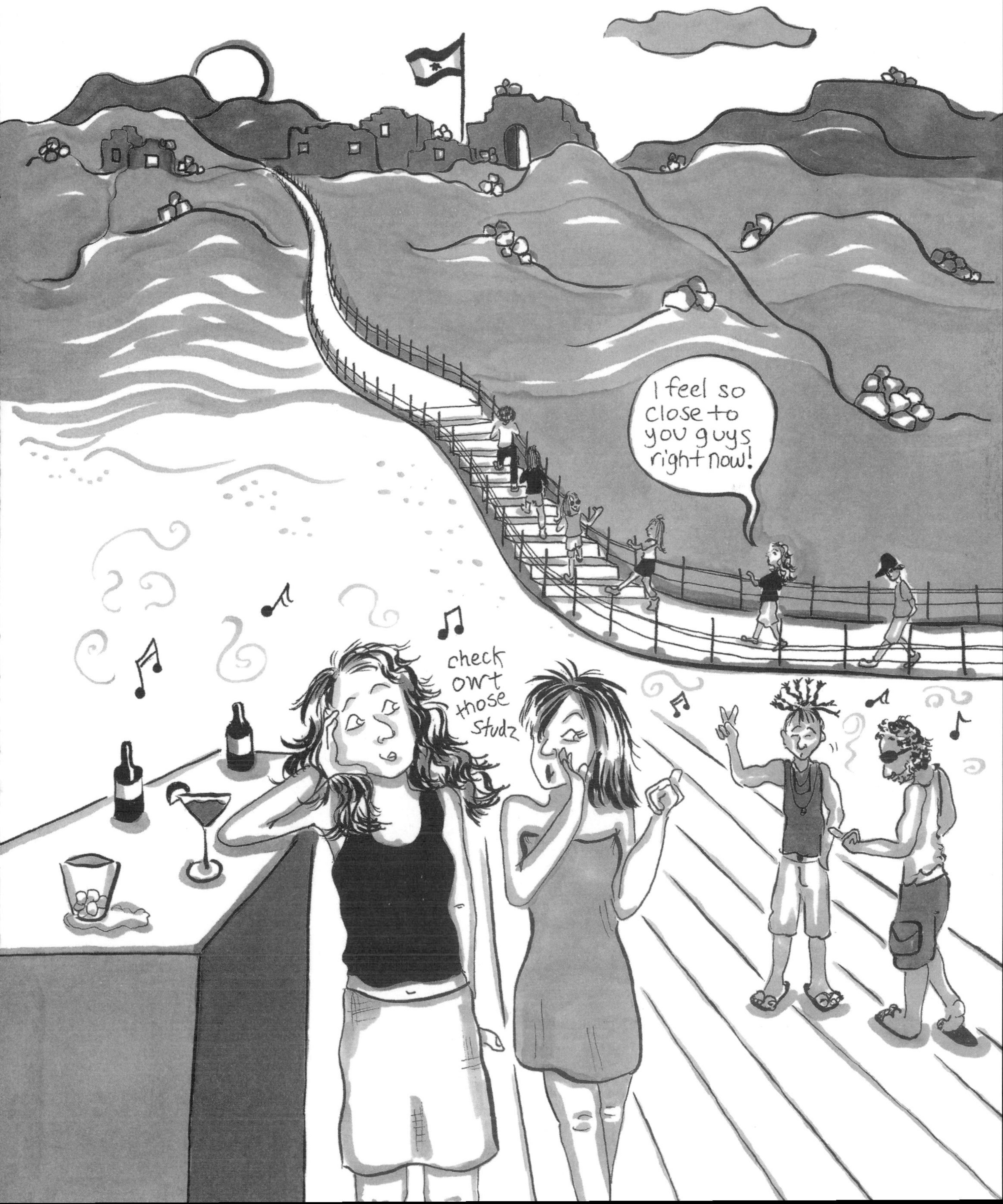
I feel so close to you guys right now!
check owt those studz

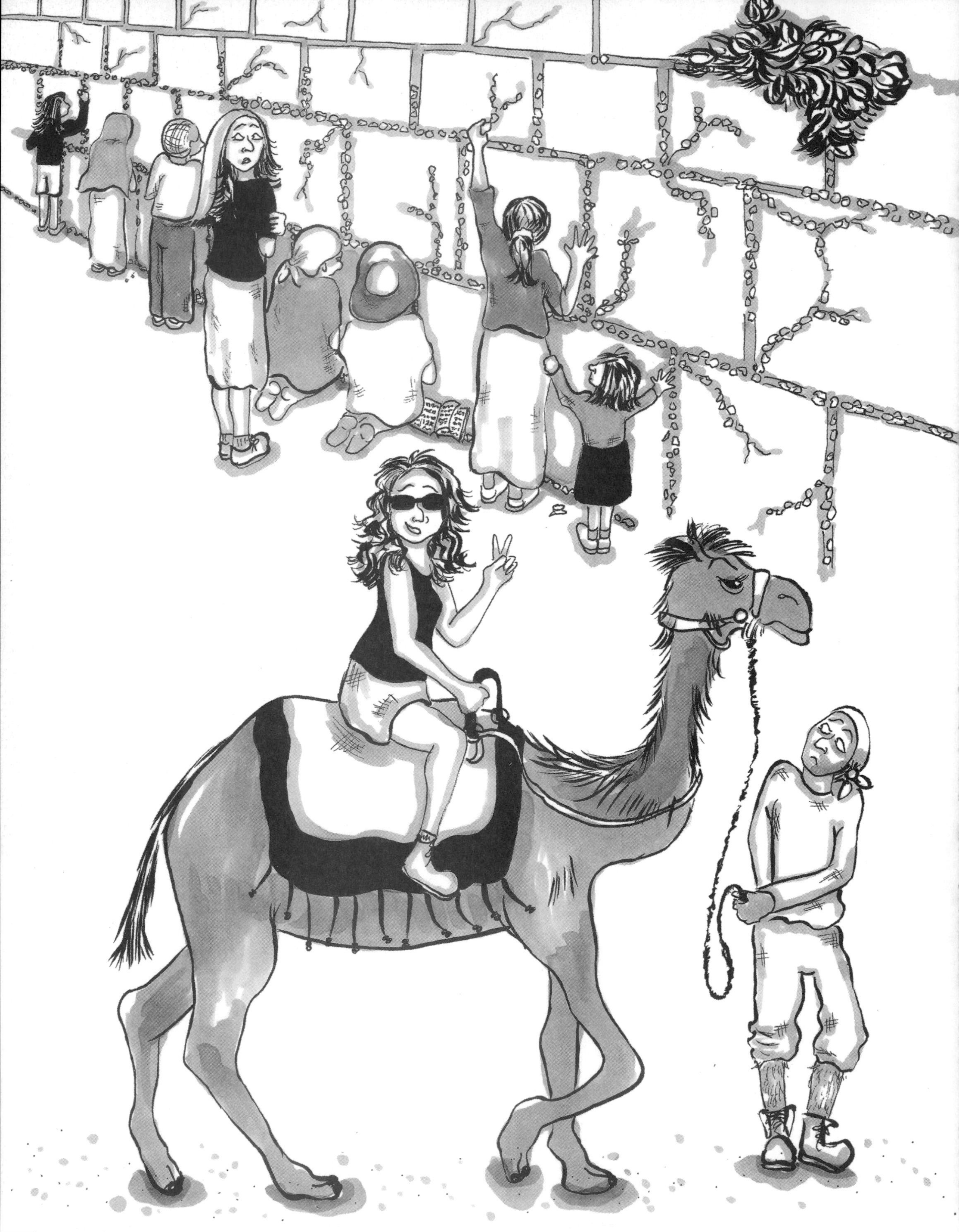

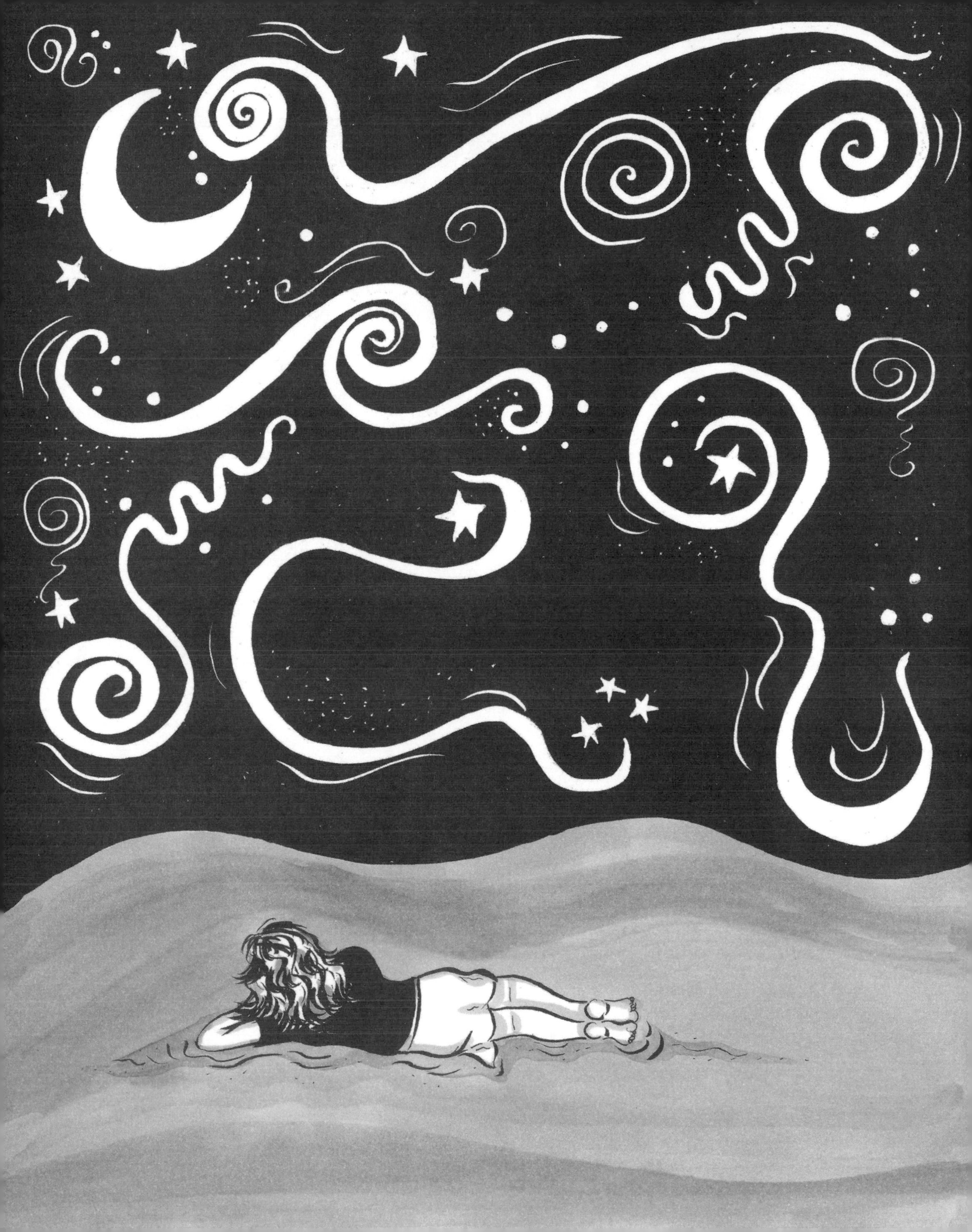

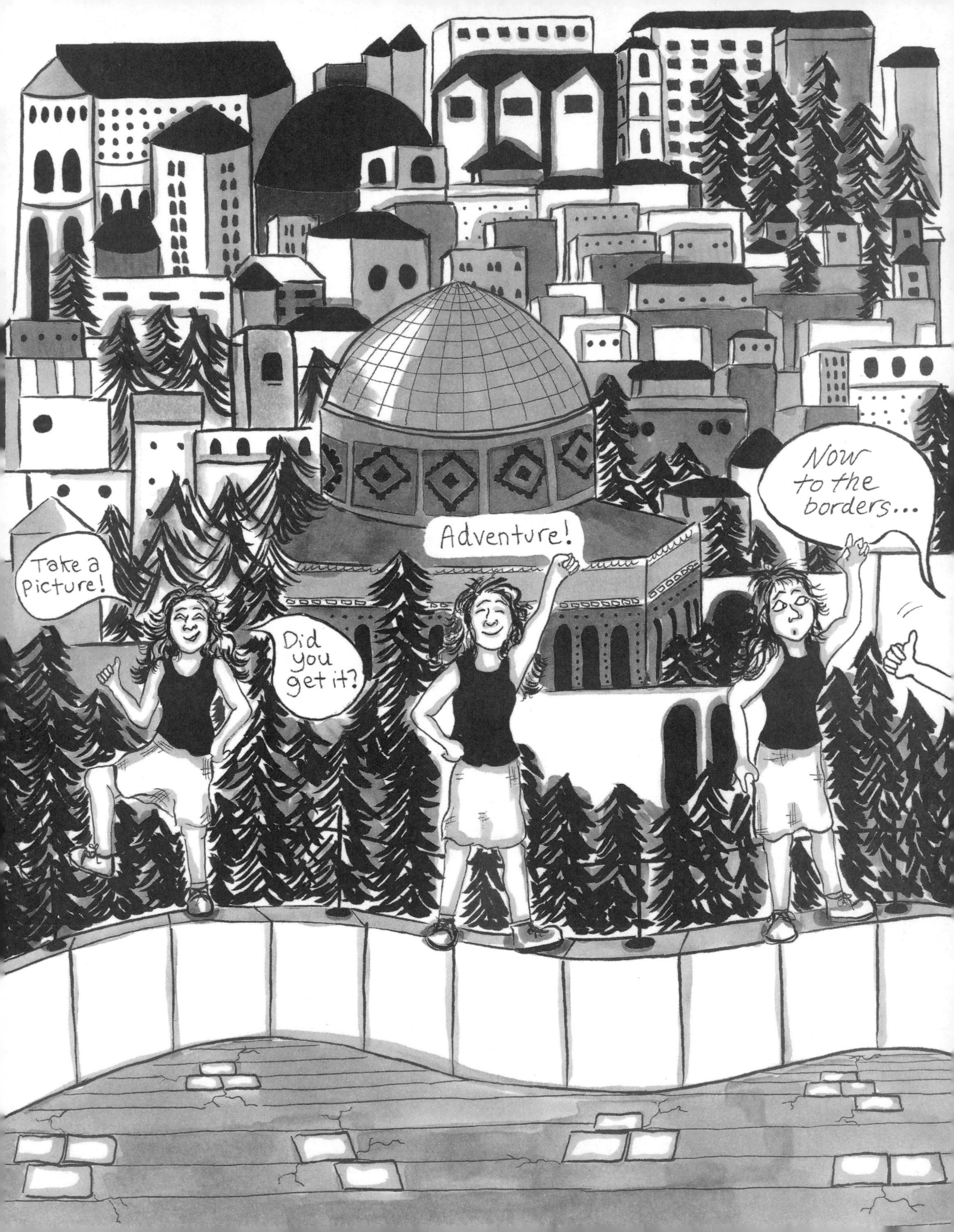
Take a picture!
Did you get it?
Adventure!
Now to the borders...

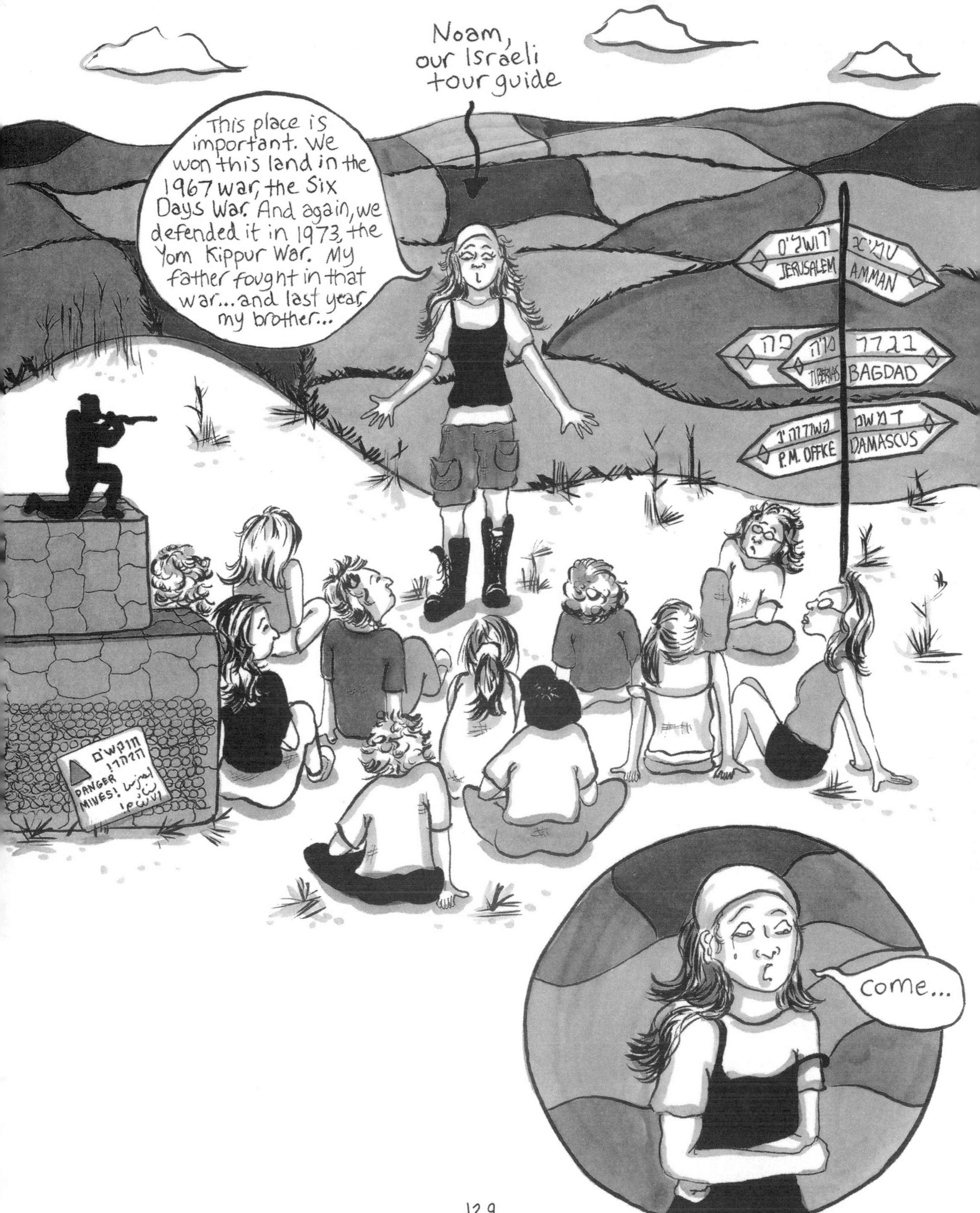
Noam, our Israeli tour guide
This place is important. We won this land in the 1967 war, the Six Days War. And again, we defended it in 1973, the Yom Kippur War. My father fought in that war... and last year, my brother...
JERUSALEM
AMMAN
TIBERIAS
BAGDAD
P.M. OFFICE
DAMASCUS
DANGER MINES!
come...

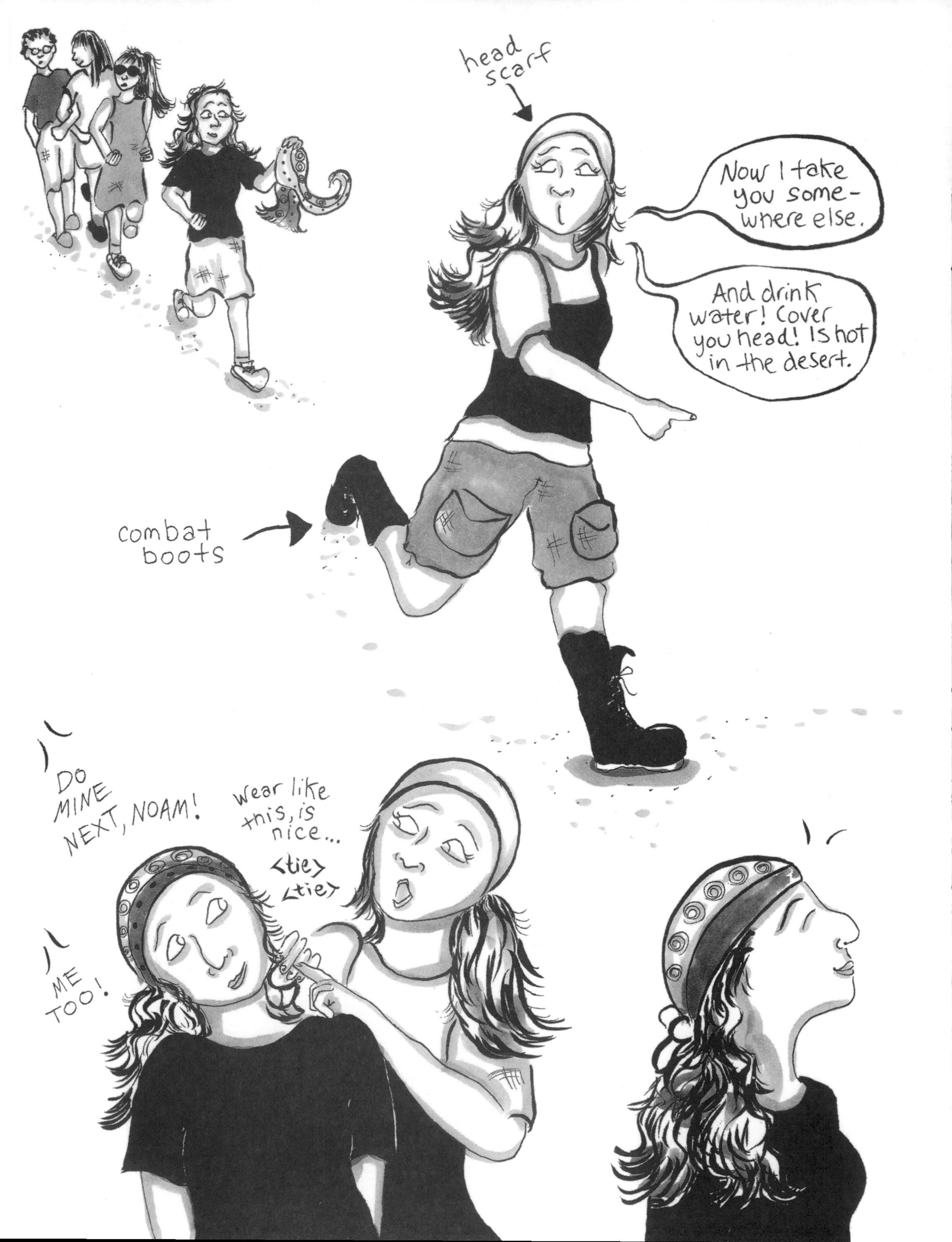
head scarf
Now I take you some-where else.
And drink water! Cover you head! Is hot in the desert.
combat boots
DO MINE NEXT, NOAM!
wear like this, is nice...
<tie> <tie>
ME TOO!

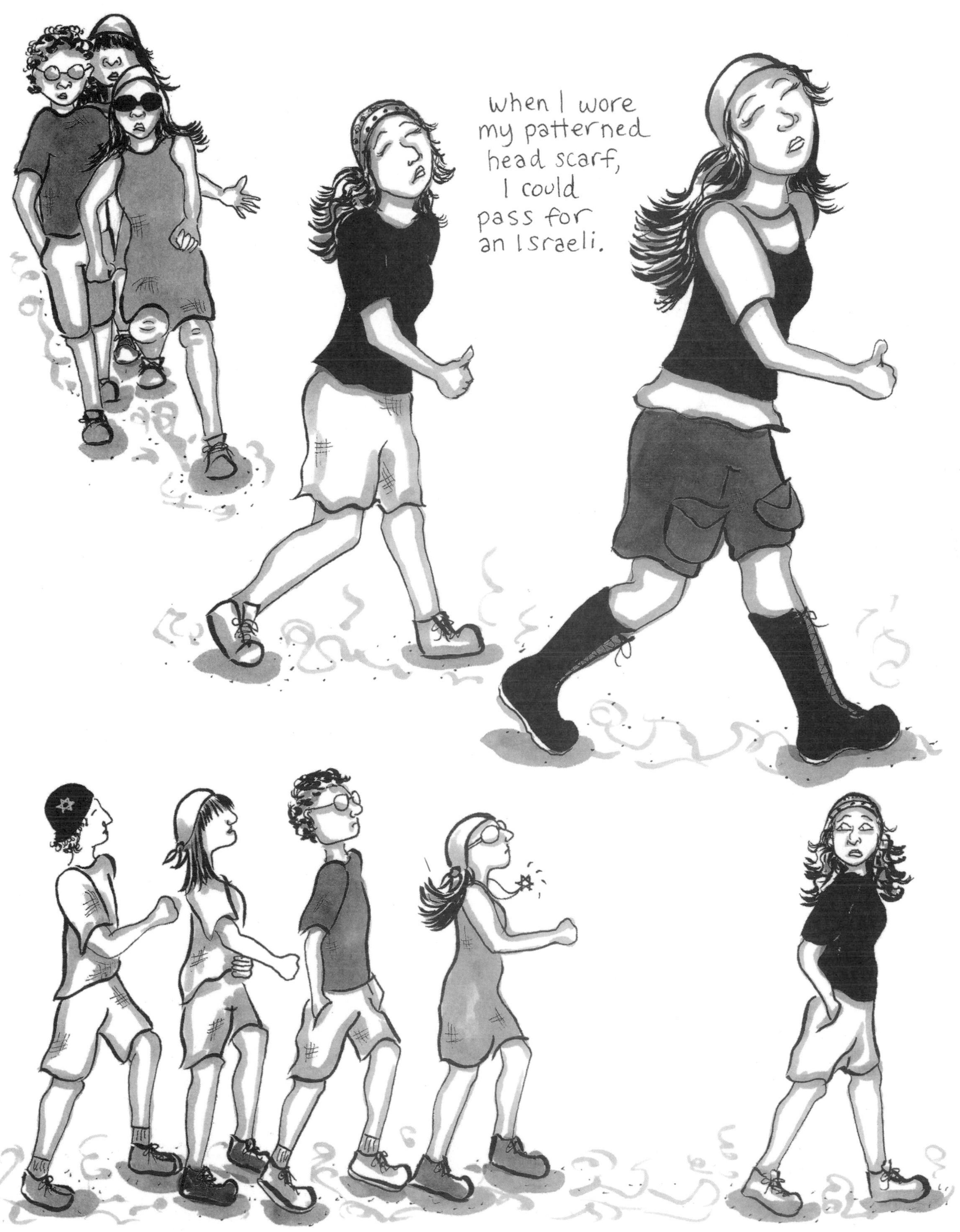
when I wore
my patterned
head scarf,
I could
pass for
an Israeli.

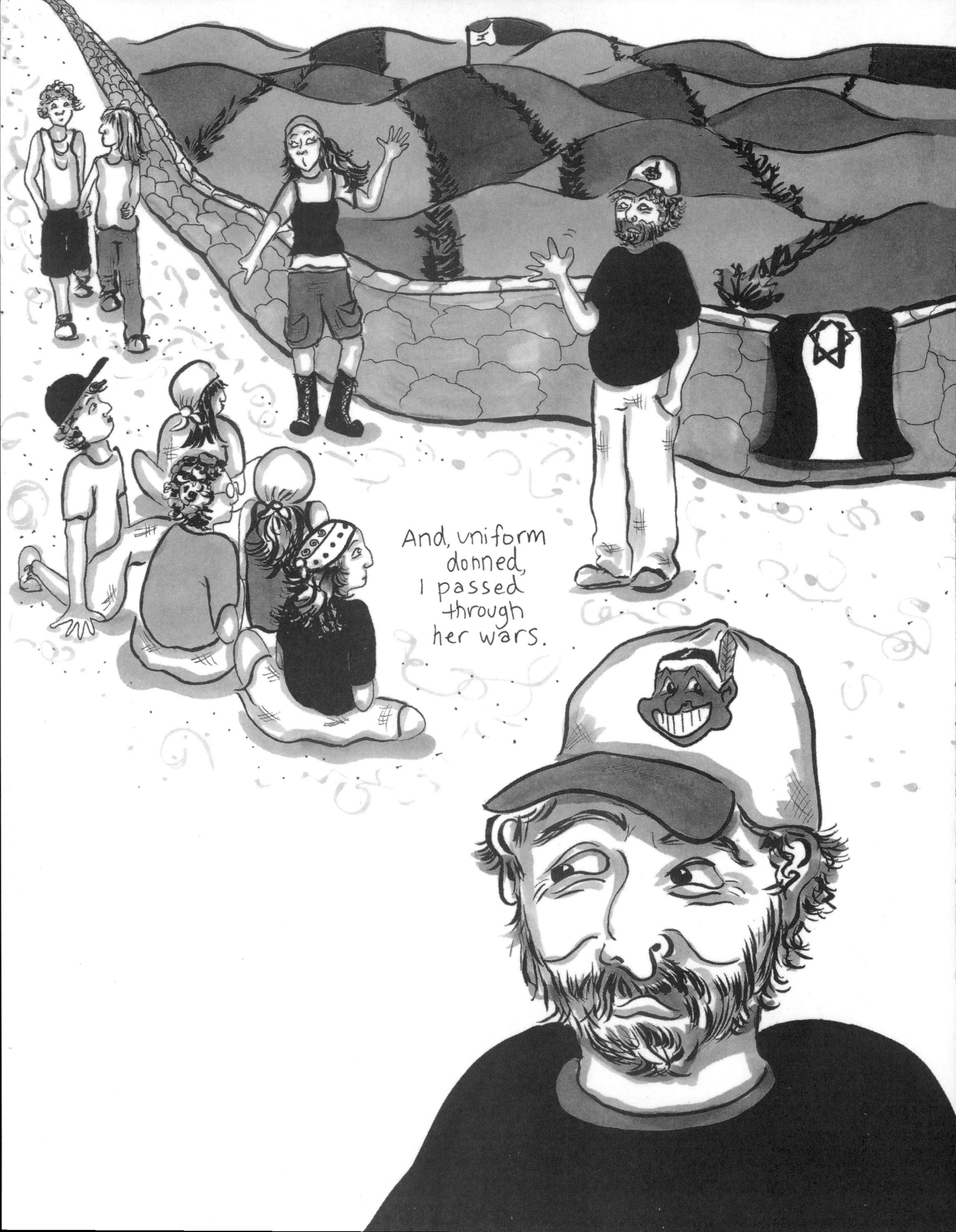
And, uniform donned, I passed through her wars.

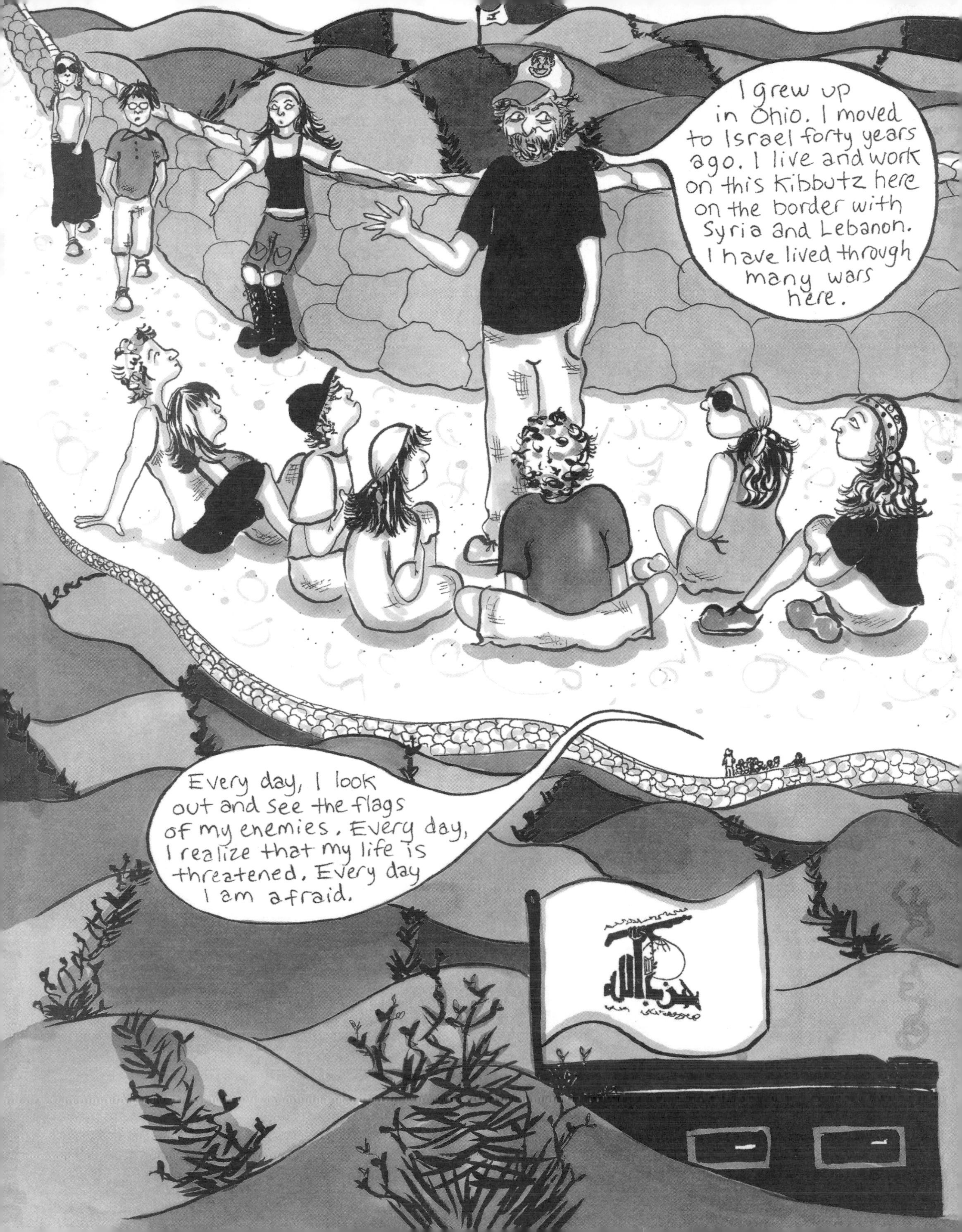
I grew up in Ohio. I moved to Israel forty years ago. I live and work on this Kibbutz here on the border with Syria and Lebanon. I have lived through many wars here.
Every day, I look out and see the flags of my enemies. Every day, I realize that my life is threatened. Every day I am afraid.

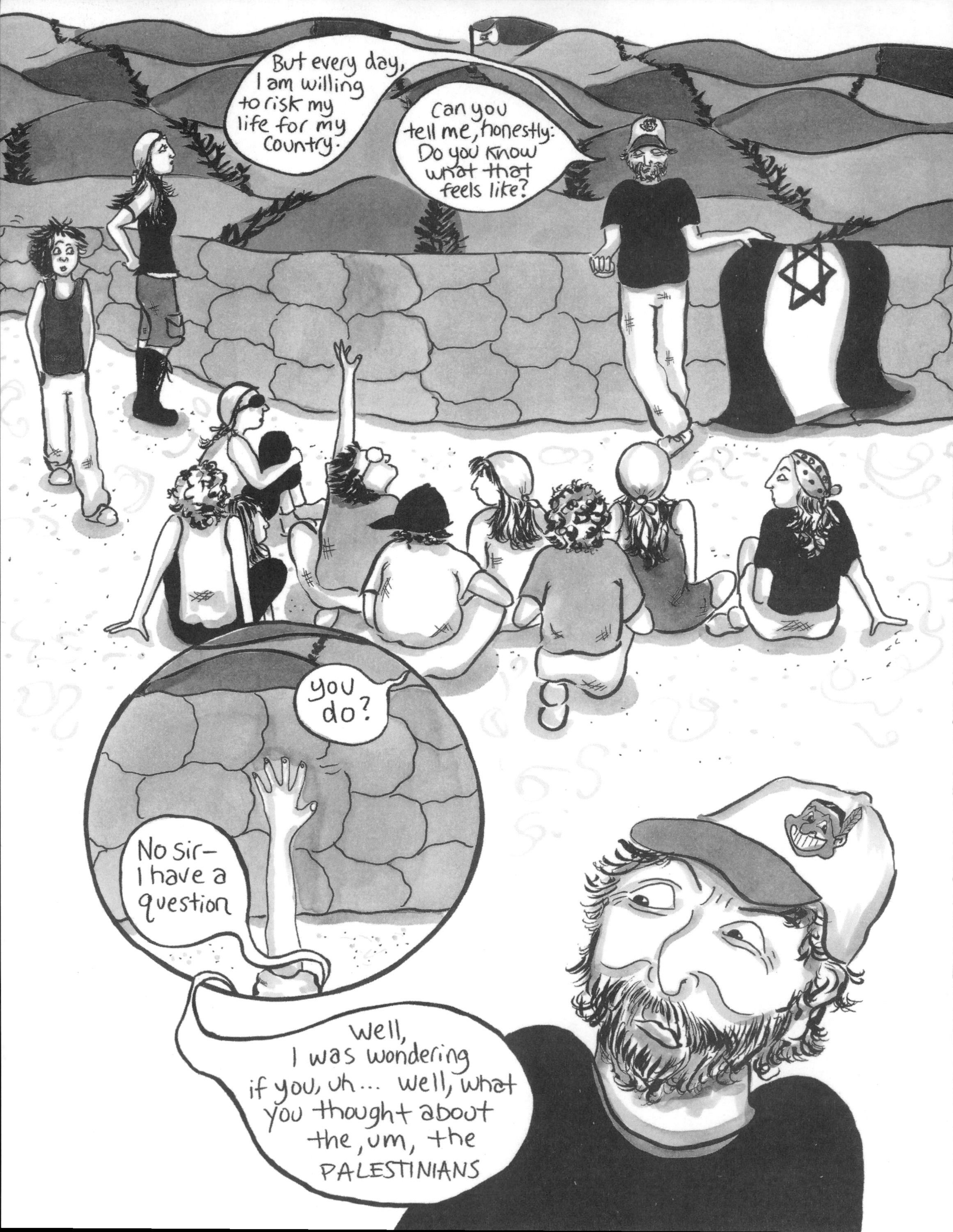
But every day, I am willing to risk my life for my country.
Can you tell me, honestly: Do you know what that feels like?
you do?
No sir– I have a question
Well, I was wondering if you, uh… well, what you thought about the, um, the PALESTINIANS

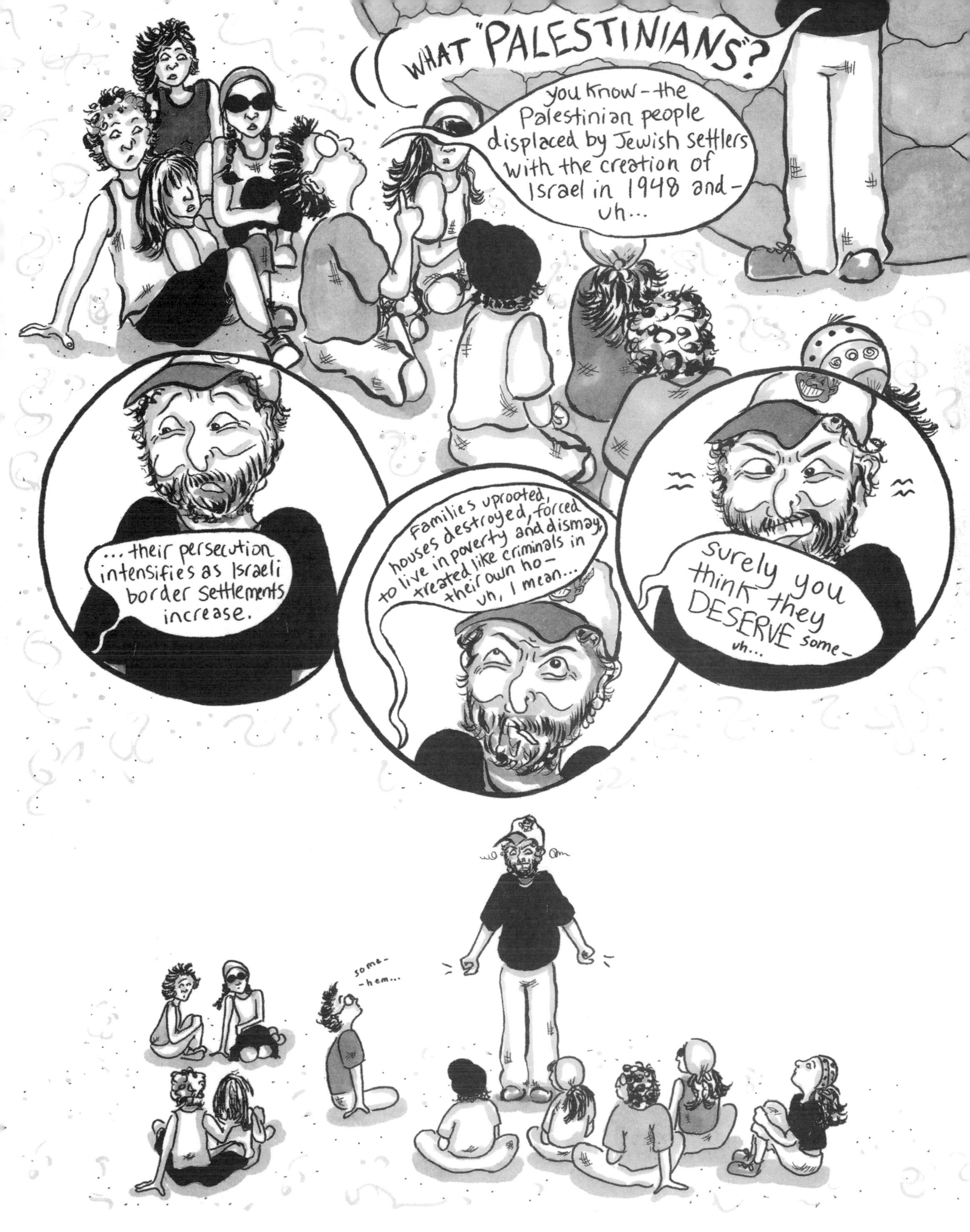
WHAT "PALESTINIANS"?
you know - the Palestinian people displaced by Jewish settlers with the creation of Israel in 1948 and - uh...
... their persecution intensifies as Israeli border settlements increase.
Families uprooted, houses destroyed, forced to live in poverty and dismay, treated like criminals in their own ho- uh, I mean...
Surely you think they DESERVE some- uh...
some- -hem...

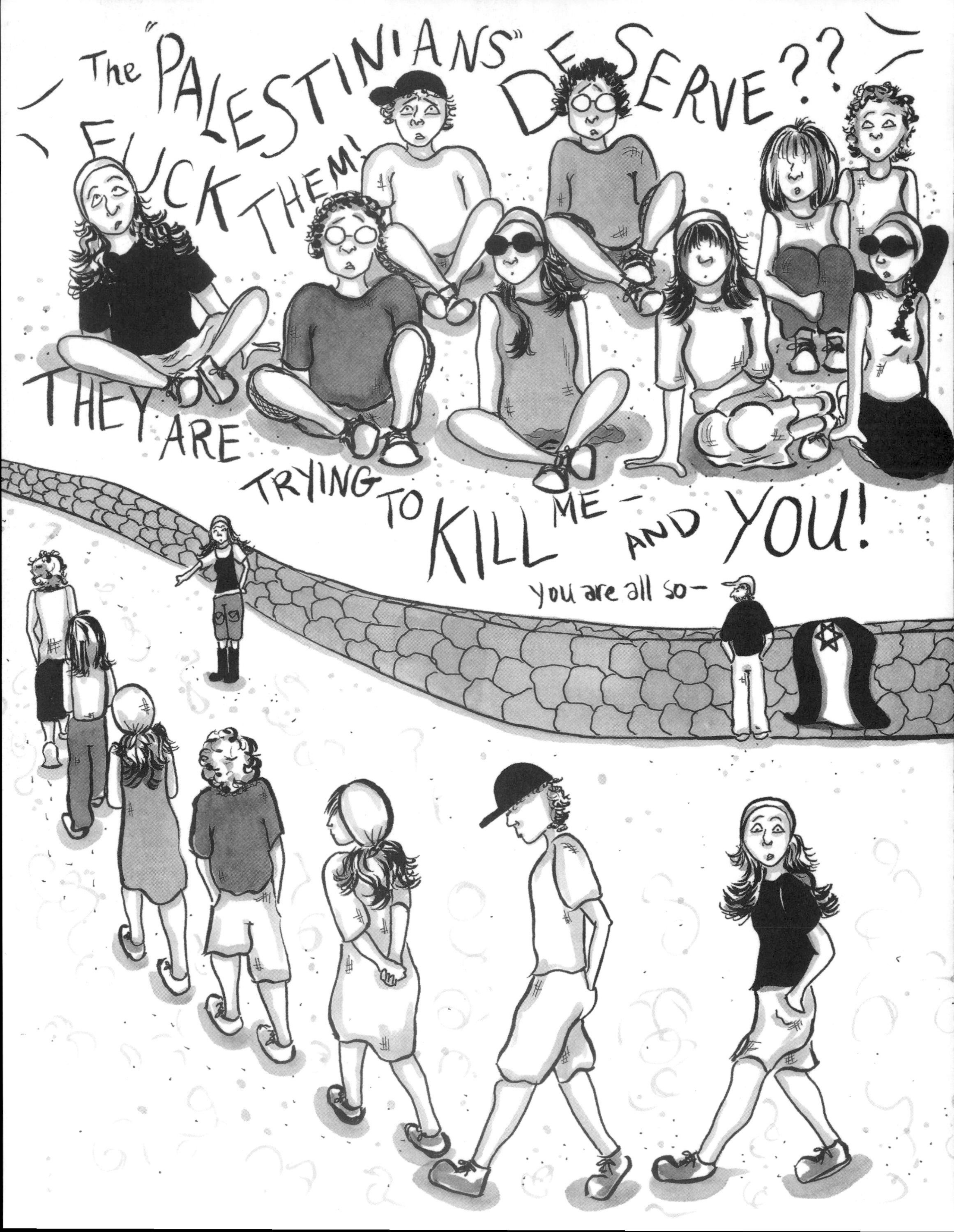

The "PALESTINIANS" DESERVE??
FUCK THEM!
THEY ARE TRYING TO KILL ME – AND YOU!
you are all so–

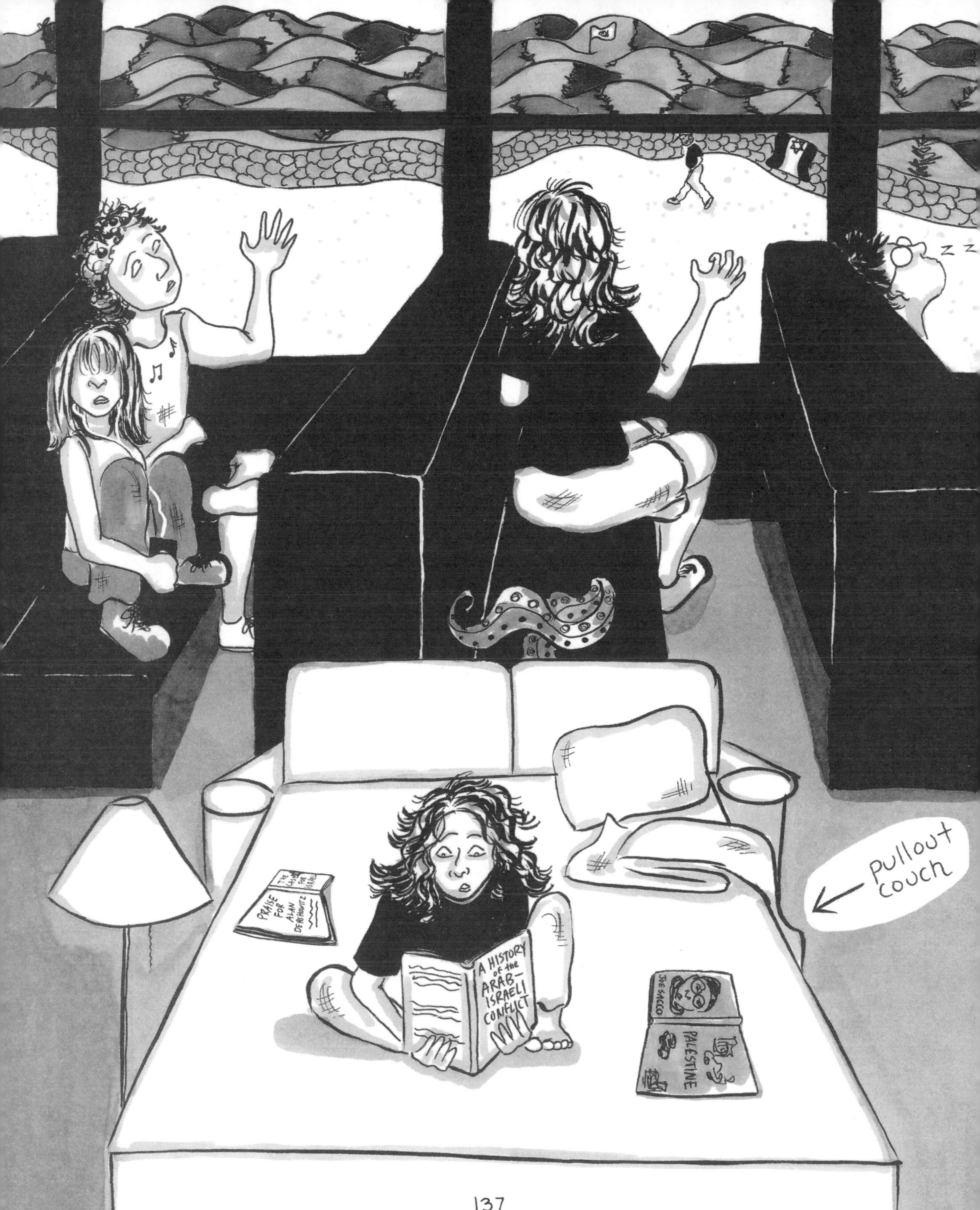
pullout couch
THE CASE FOR ISRAEL
PRAISE FOR ALAN DERSHOWITZ
A HISTORY of the ARAB-ISRAELI CONFLICT
JOE SACCO
PALESTINE

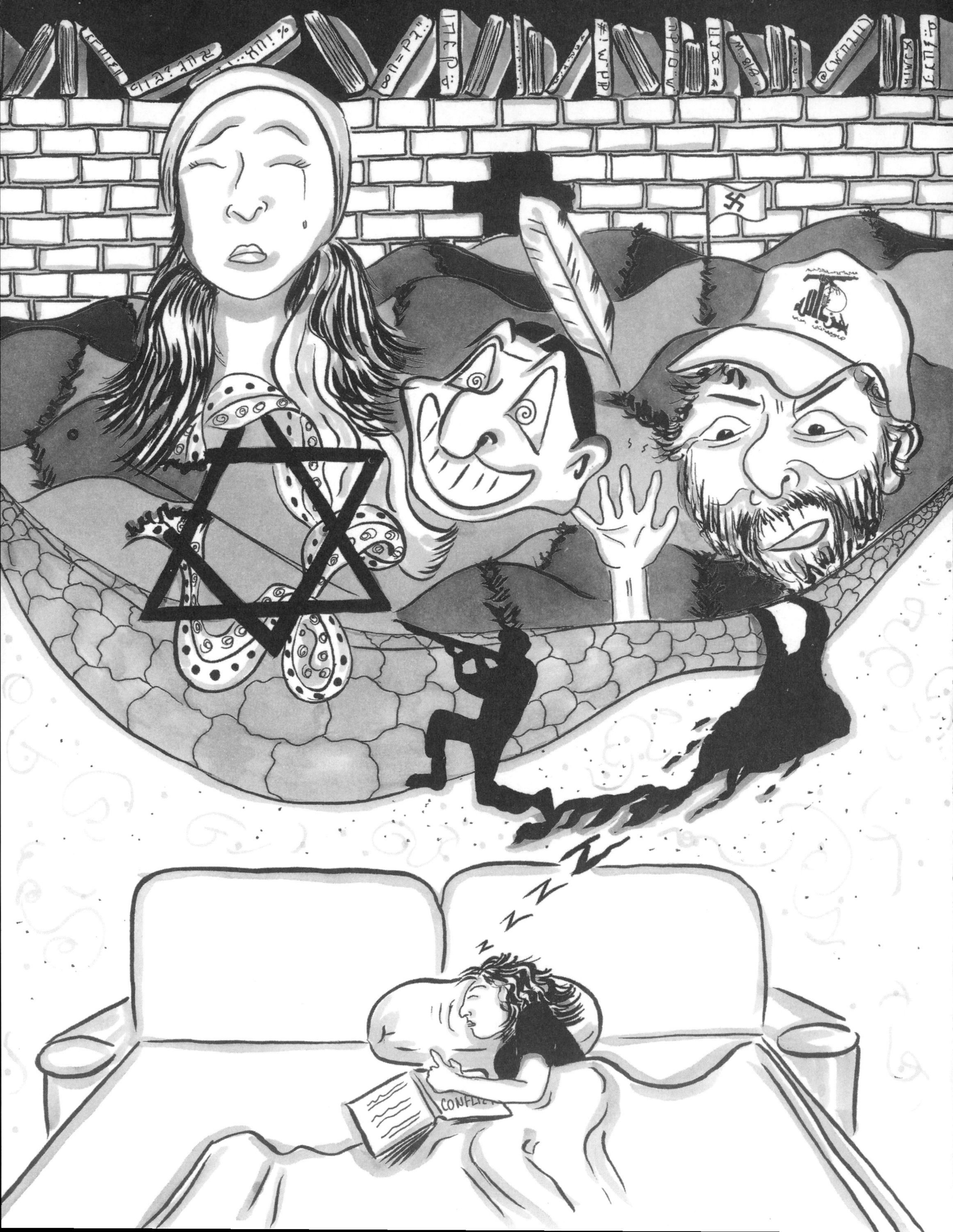
CONFLI

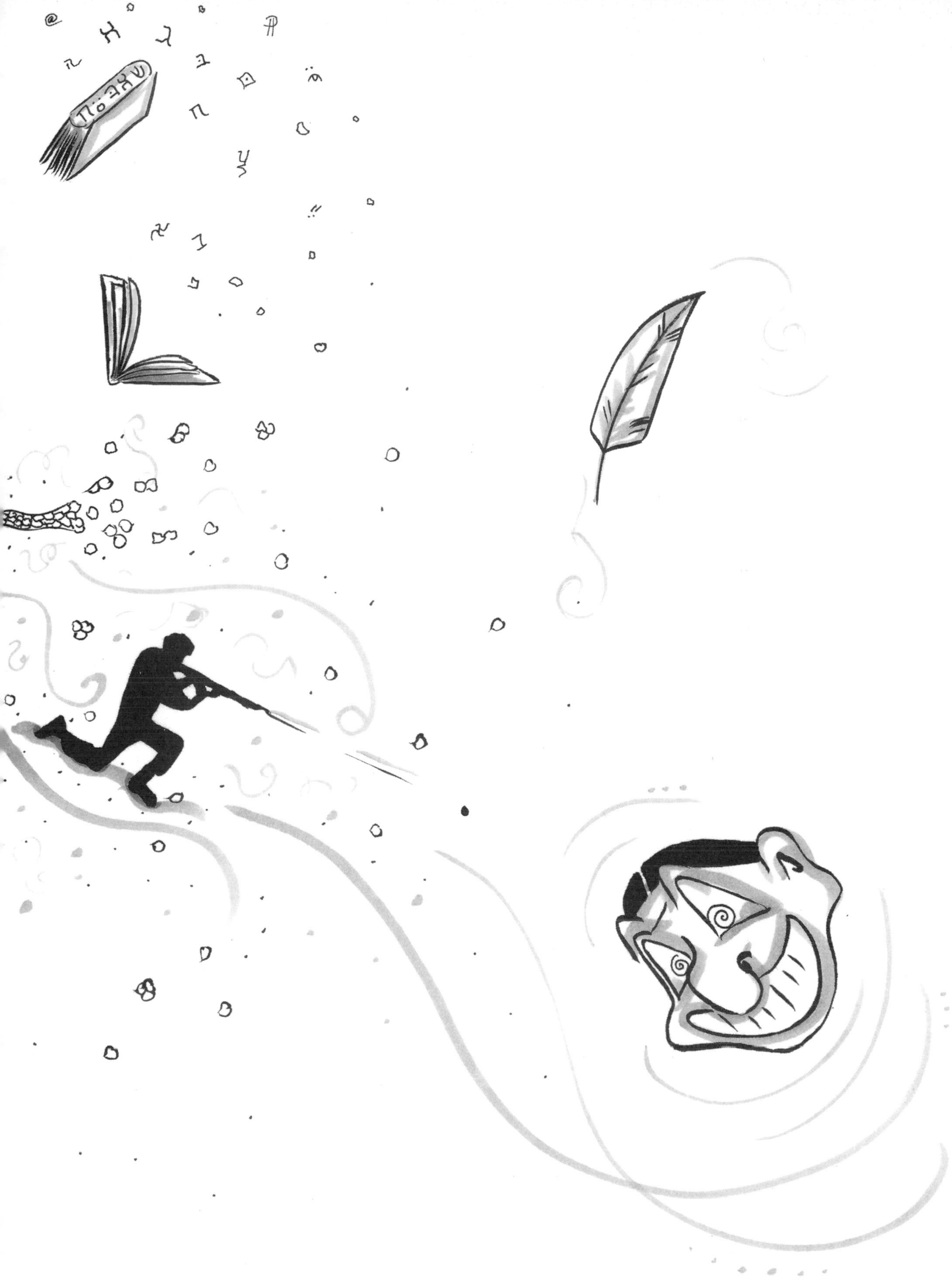

My roommate sophomore year was a Palestinian girl who had grown up in Kuwait. Her grandparents fled in the forties.

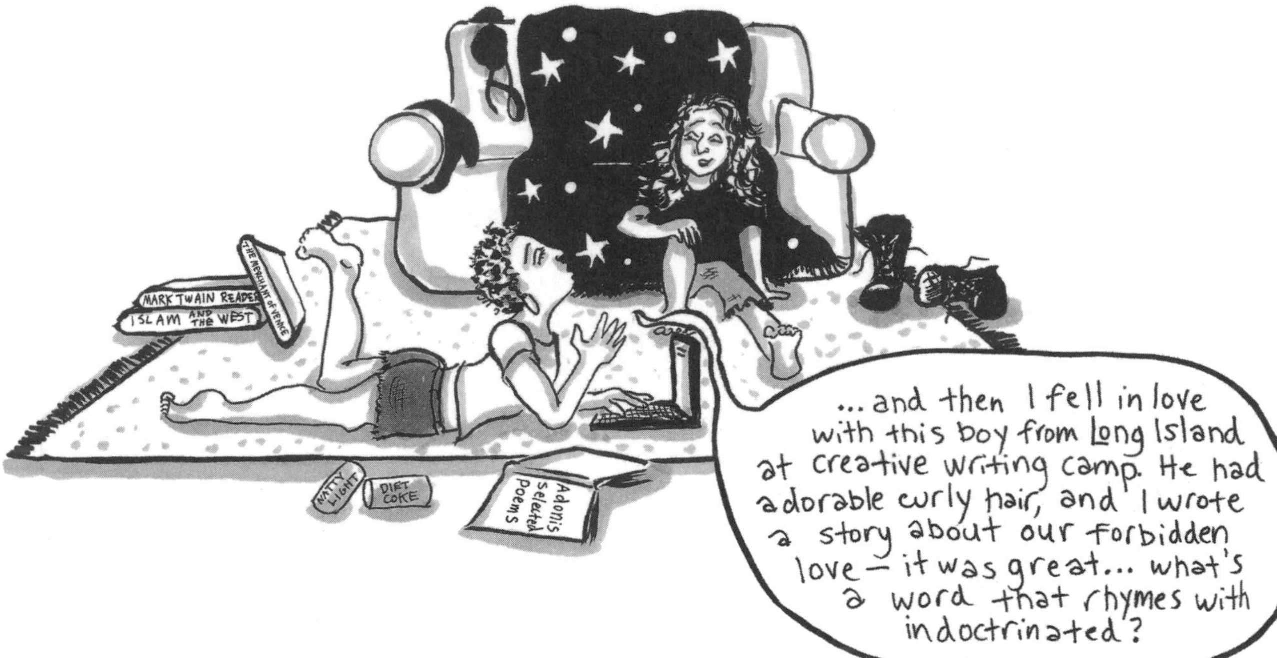
THE MERCHANT of VENICE
MARK TWAIN READER
ISLAM AND THE WEST
NATTY LIGHT
DIET COKE
Adonis selected Poems
...and then I fell in love with this boy from Long Island at creative writing camp. He had adorable curly hair, and I wrote a story about our forbidden love — it was great... what's a word that rhymes with indoctrinated?

We'd stay up late writing bad poetry, and she'd tell me about how she'd come to accept the Jews.

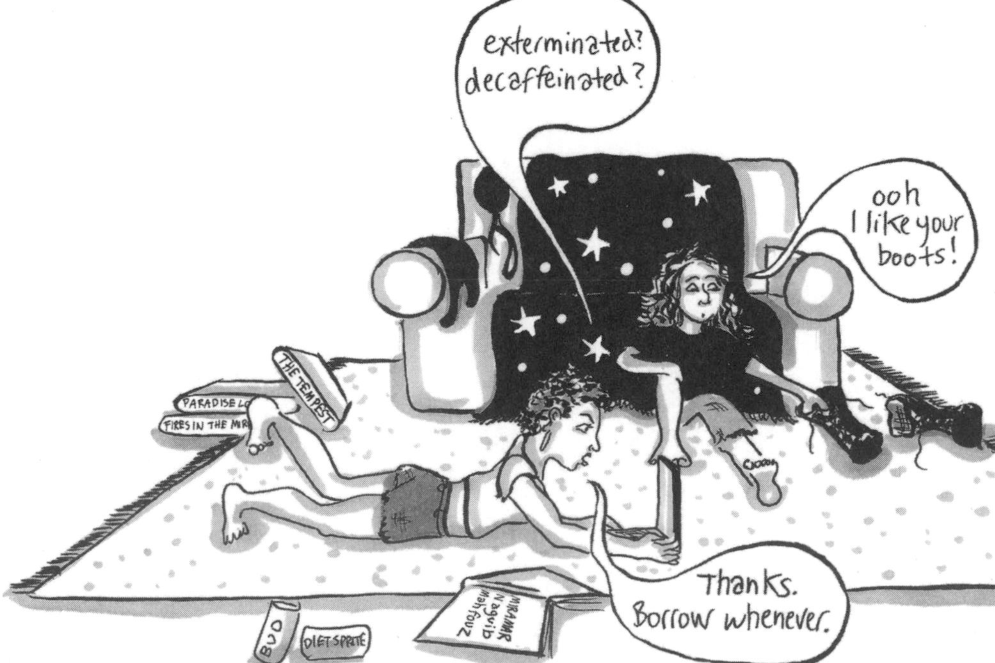
exterminated? decaffeinated?
ooh I like your boots!
THE TEMPEST
BUD
DIET SPRITE
MIRAMAR Naguib Mahfouz
Thanks. Borrow whenever.

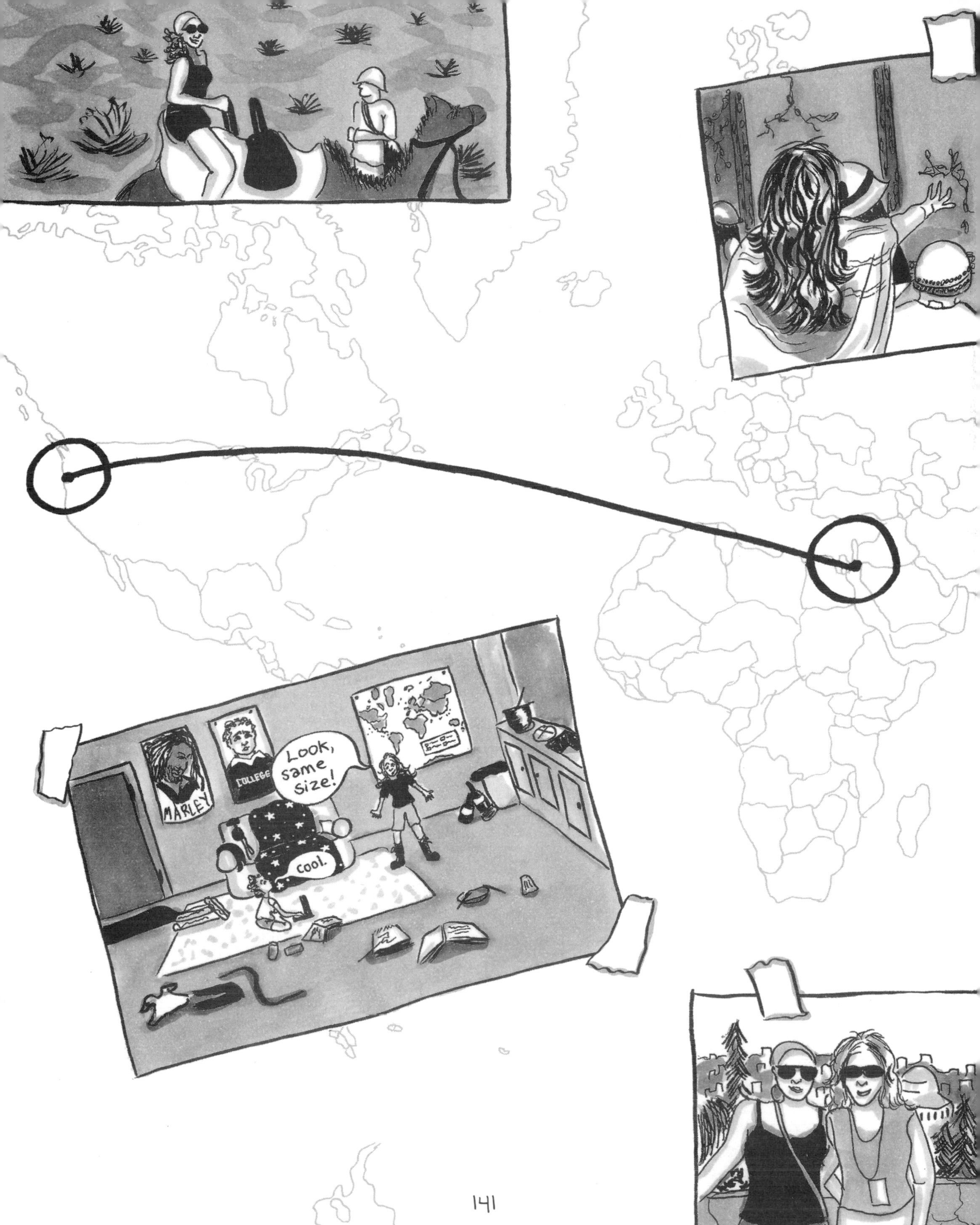
MARLEY
COLLEGE
Look, same size!
cool.

ONWARDS...
YAD VASHEM POLICY
מדיניות יד ושם
THE GHETTO
WARSAW
<click>
<flash>
Ey! Respect de history!
BETWEEN WALLS AND FENCES
THE WARSAW GHETTO
ONEG SHABBAT: UNDERGROUND ARCHIVES IN THE WARSAW GHETTO
DOCUMENTS
DRAWINGS

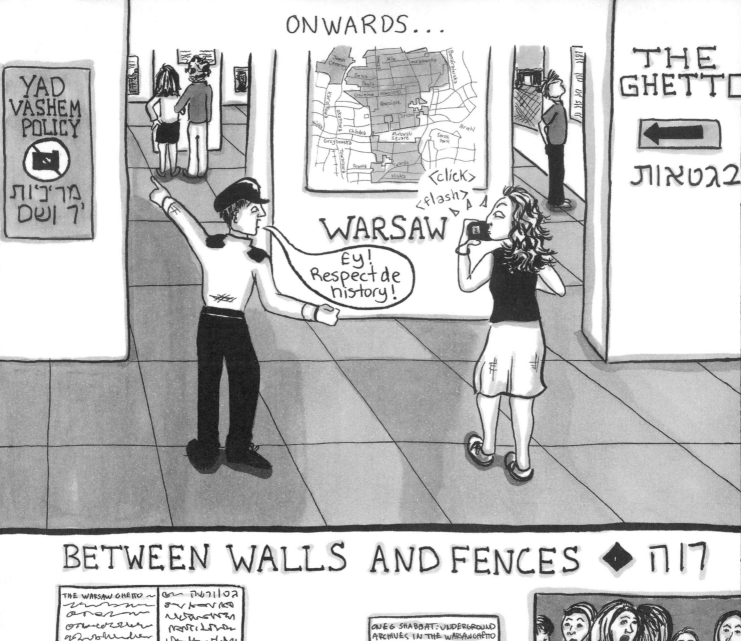

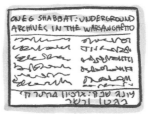

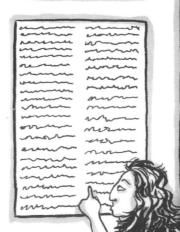

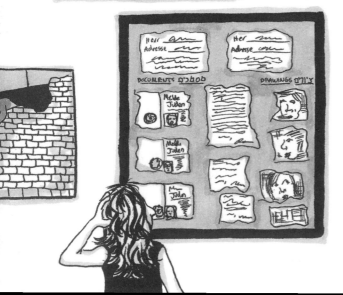

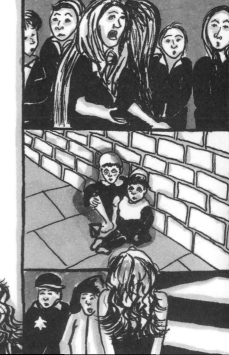

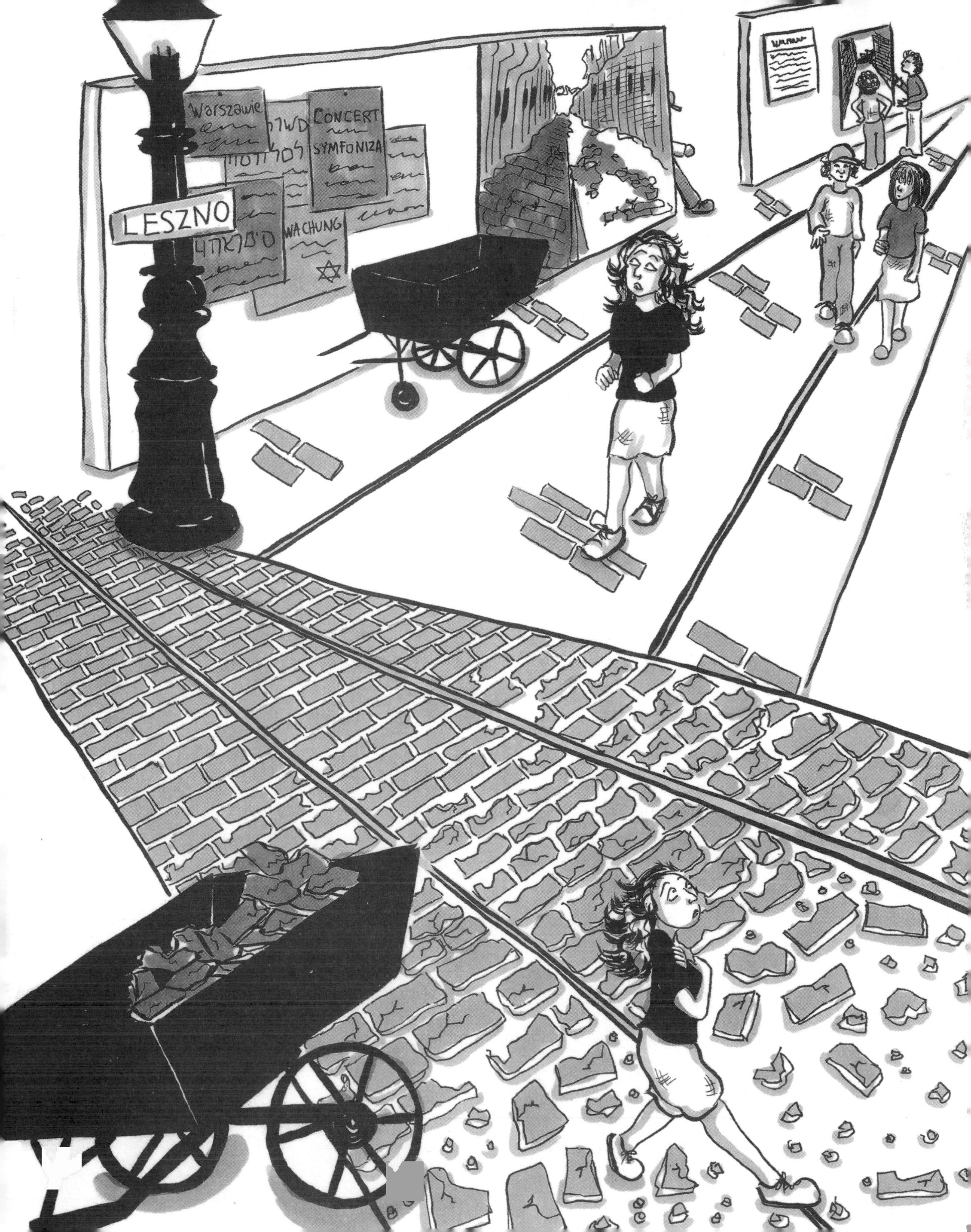
Warszawie
CONCERT
SYMFONIZA
LESZNO
WACHUNG

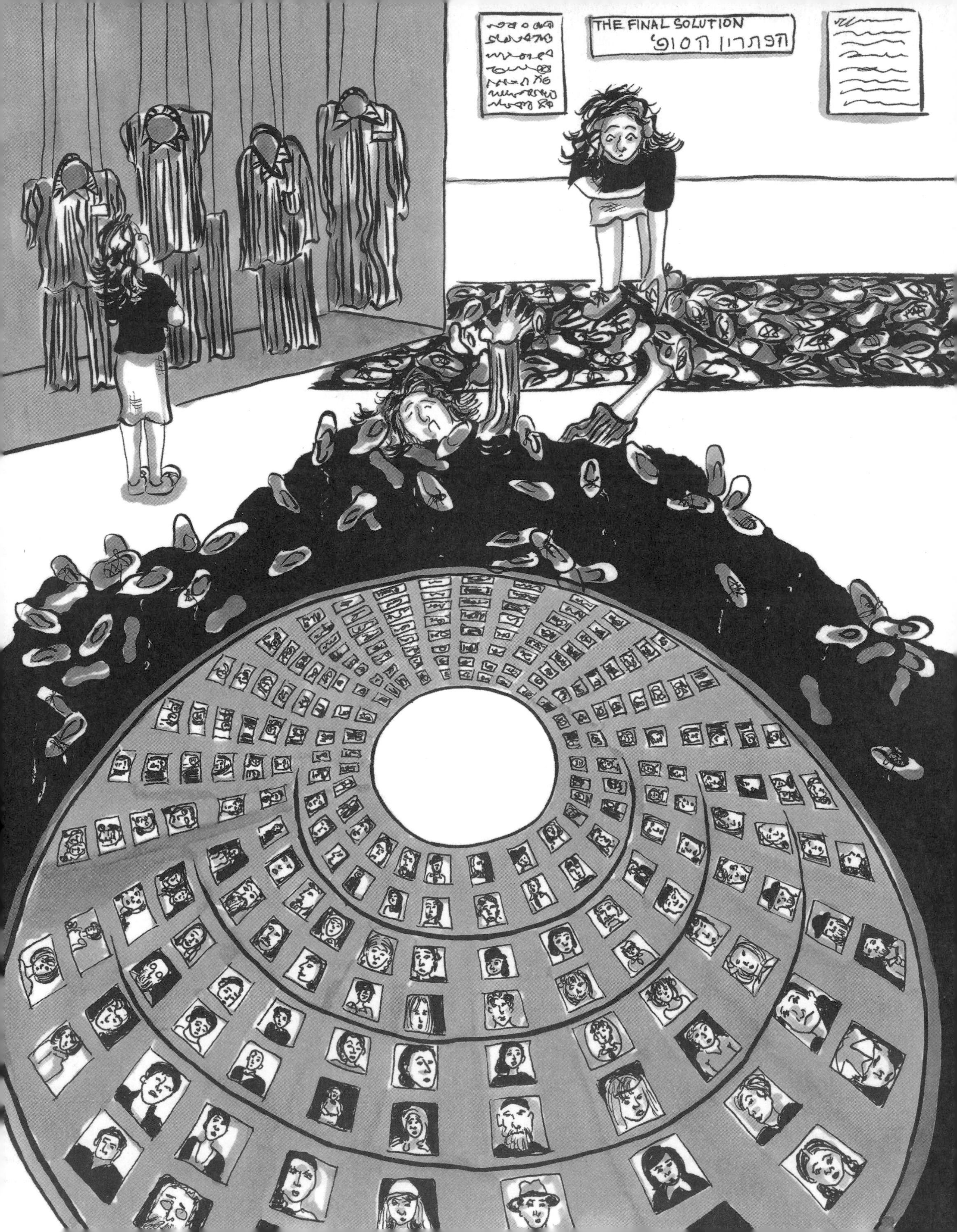
THE FINAL SOLUTION
הפתרון הסופי

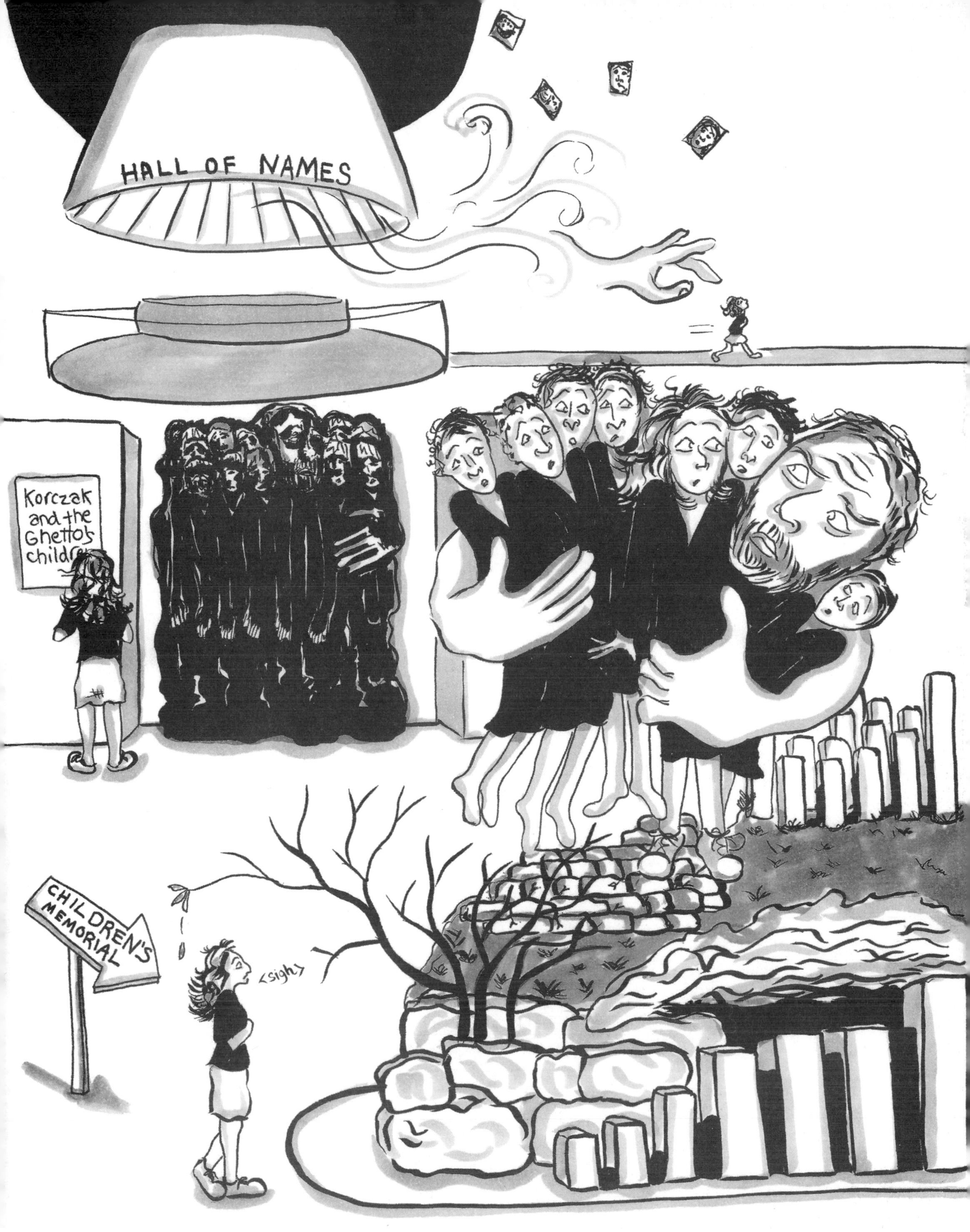
HALL OF NAMES
Korczak and the Ghetto's childr
CHILDREN'S MEMORIAL
<sigh>

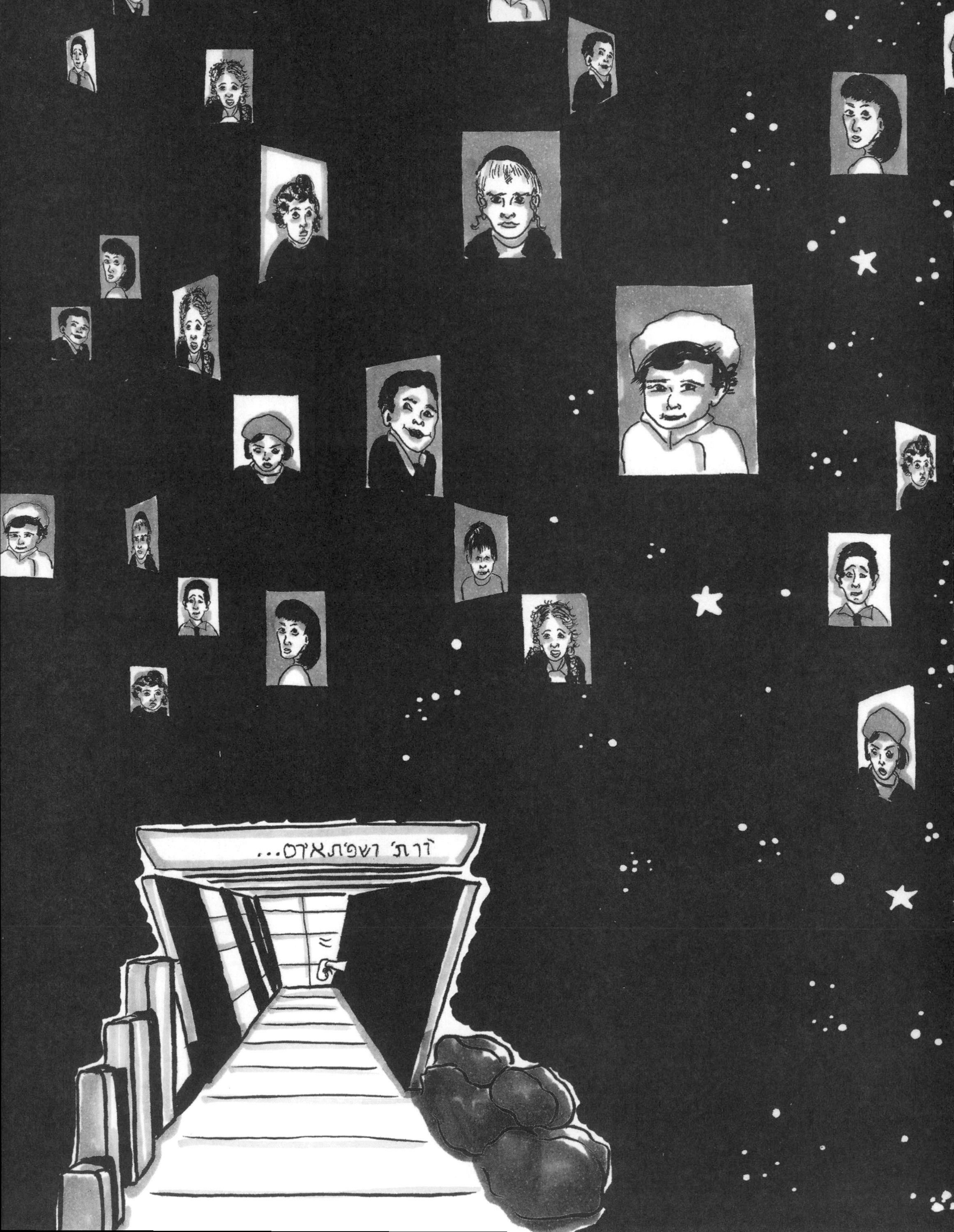

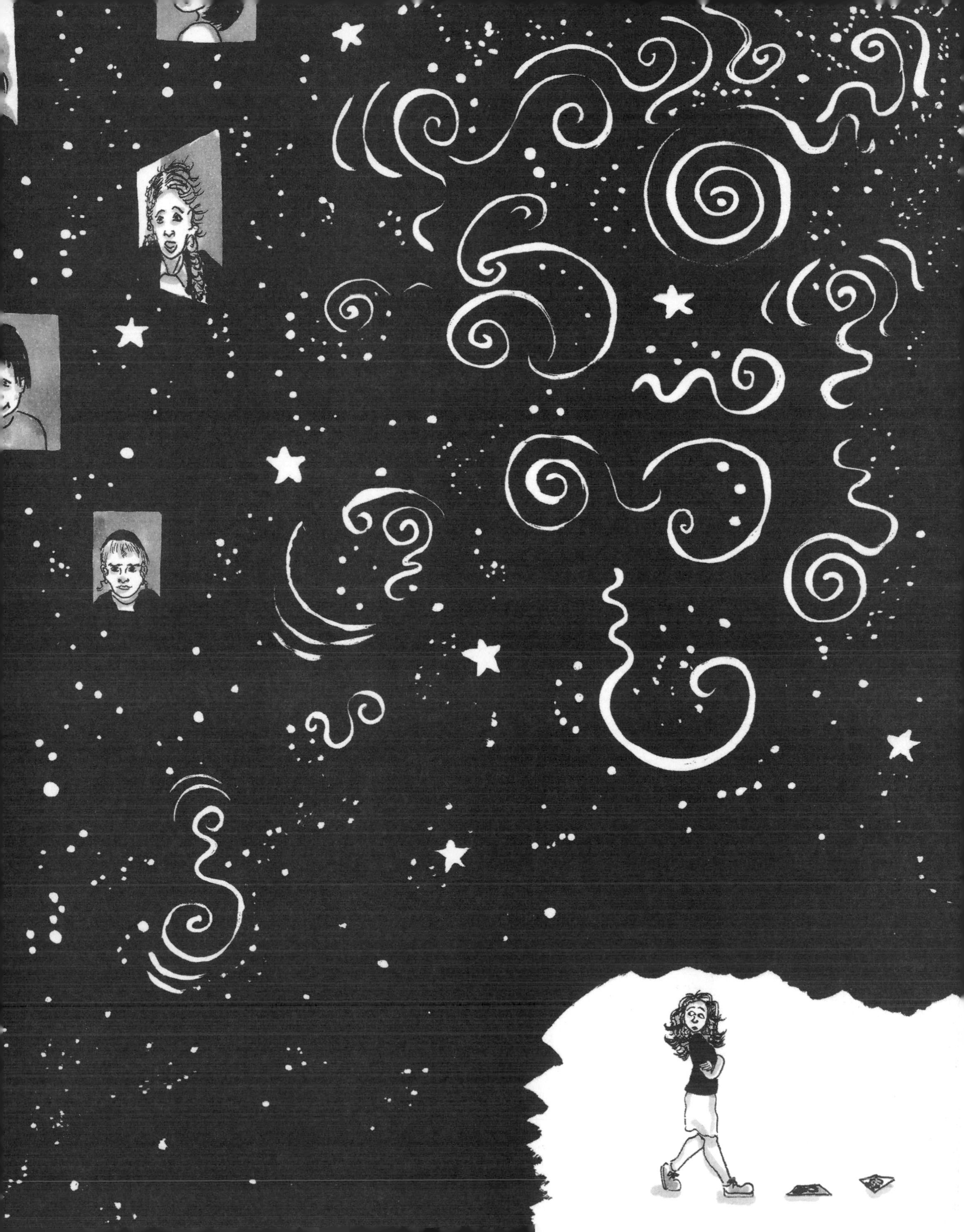

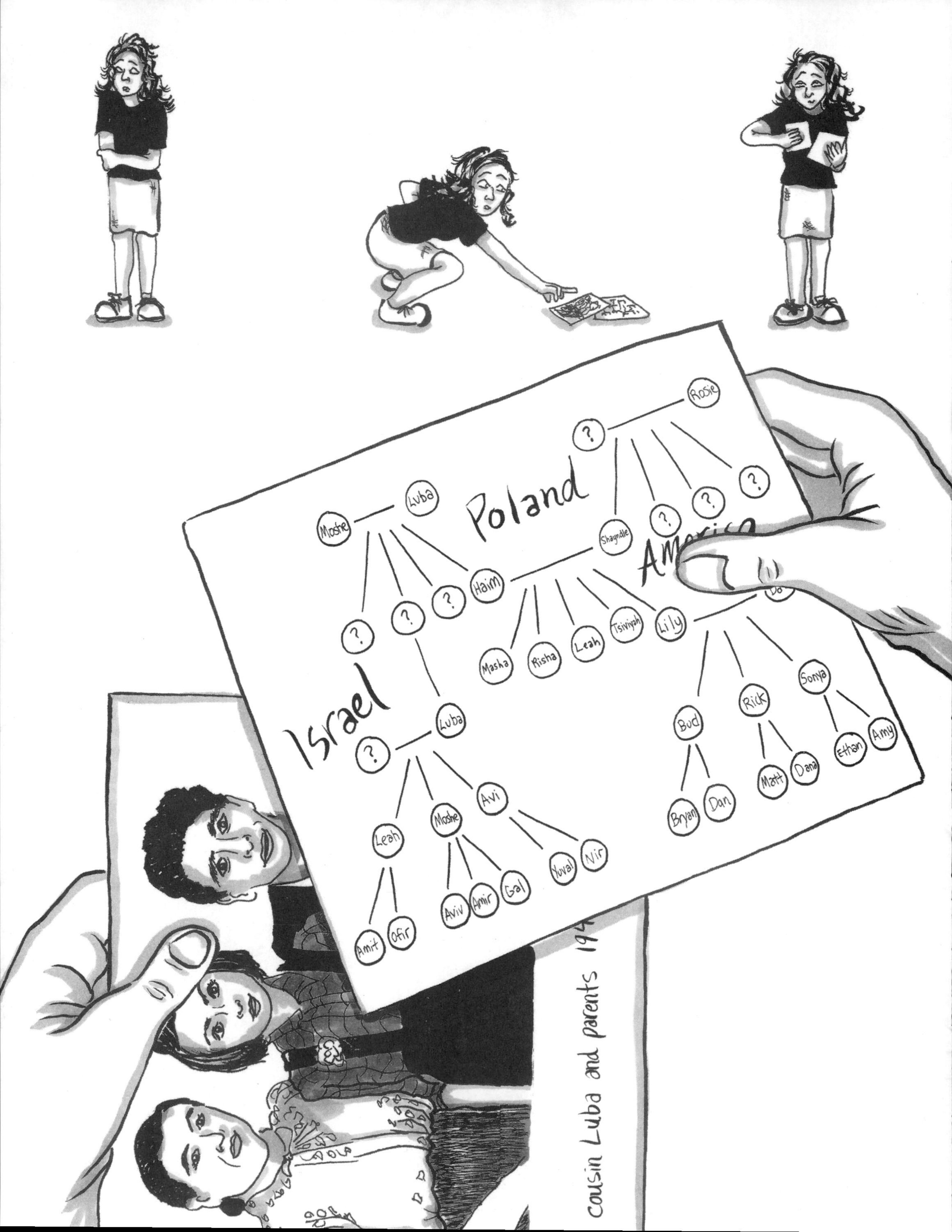
Poland
Israel
Rosie
?
Moshe
Luba
Shayndle
Haim
Lily
Masha
Risha
Leah
Tsiviyah
Bud
Rick
Sonya
Ethan
Amy
Matt
Dana
Bryan
Dan
Avi
Moshe
Yuval
Nir
Aviv
Amir
Gal
Amit
Ofir
cousin Luba and parents

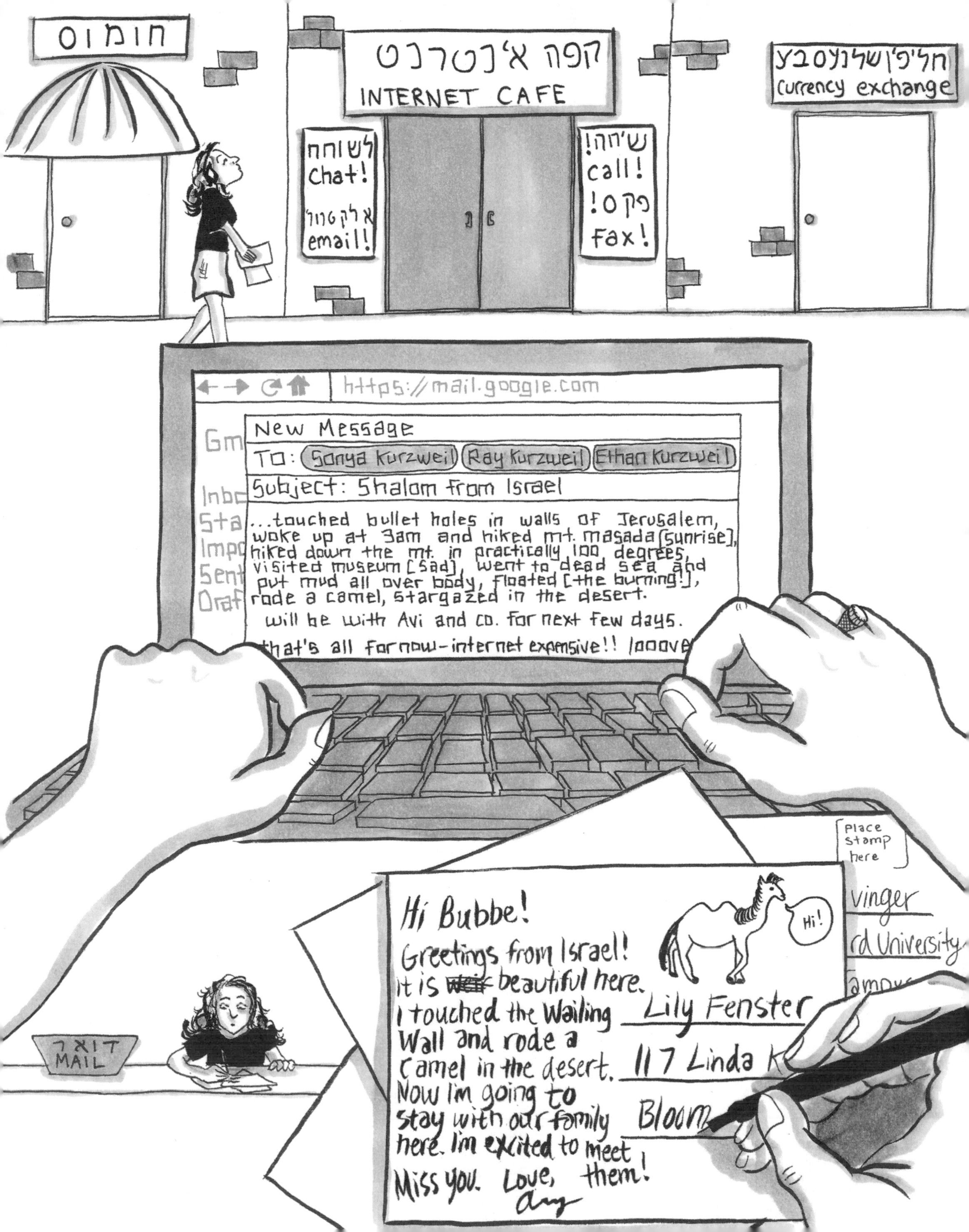
חומוס
קפה אינטרנט
INTERNET CAFE
Currency exchange
לשוחח
Chat!
email!
שיחה!
call!
פקס!
Fax!
https://mail.google.com
New Message
To: Sonya Kurzweil Ray Kurzweil Ethan Kurzweil
Subject: Shalom from Israel
...touched bullet holes in walls of Jerusalem, woke up at 3am and hiked mt. masada [sunrise], hiked down the mt. in practically 100 degrees, visited museum [sad], went to dead sea and put mud all over body, floated [+the burning!], rode a camel, stargazed in the desert.
will be with Avi and co. for next few days.
that's all for now - internet expensive!! looove
Place stamp here
Hi Bubbe!
Greetings from Israel!
It is ~~weir~~ beautiful here.
I touched the Wailing Wall and rode a camel in the desert.
Now I'm going to stay with our family here. I'm excited to meet them!
Miss you. Love,
Hi!
Lily Fenster
117 Linda K
Bloom
vinger
rd University
דואר
MAIL

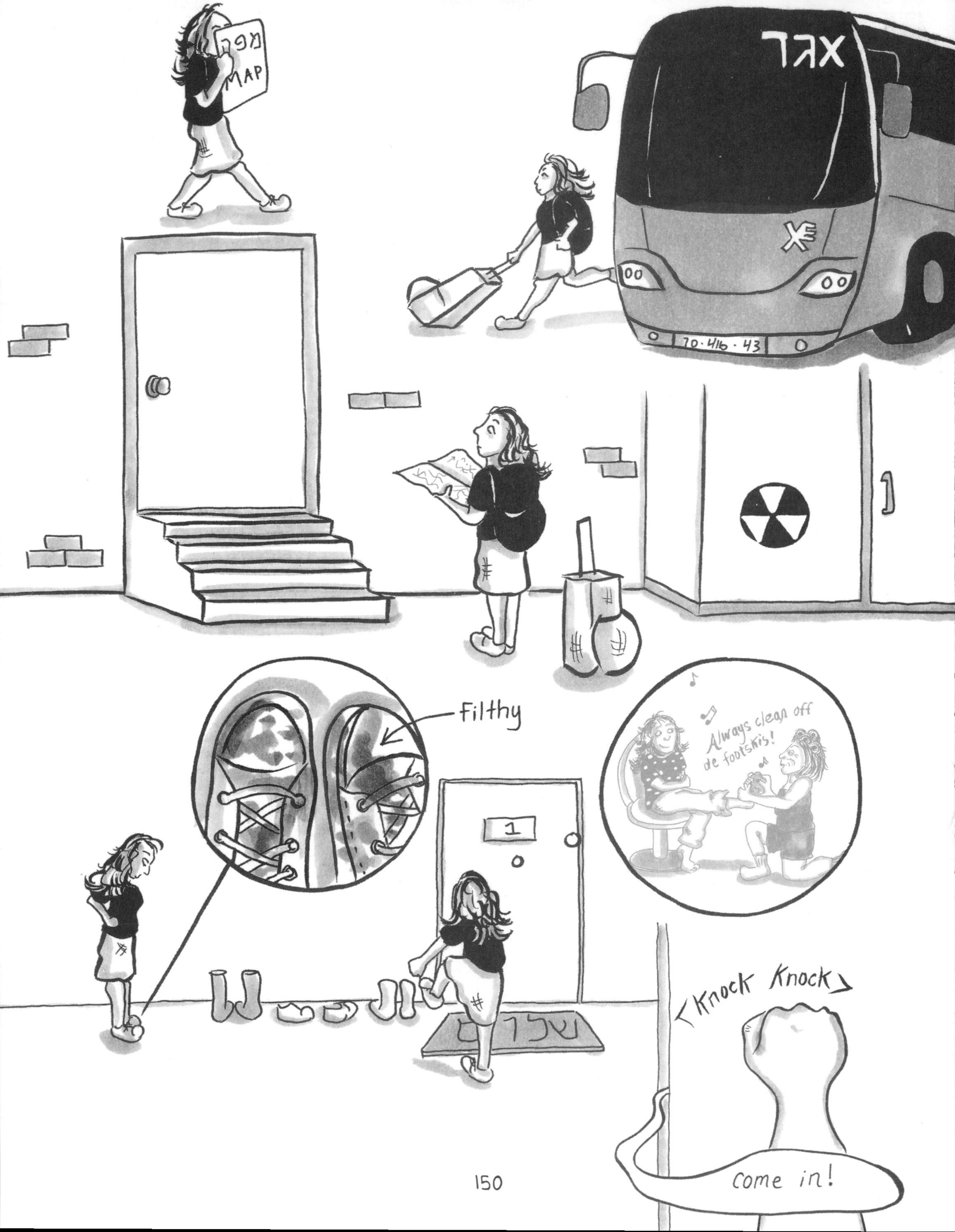
מפה
MAP
אגד
70·416·43
Filthy
1
שלום
Always clean off de footskis!
<Knock Knock>
come in!

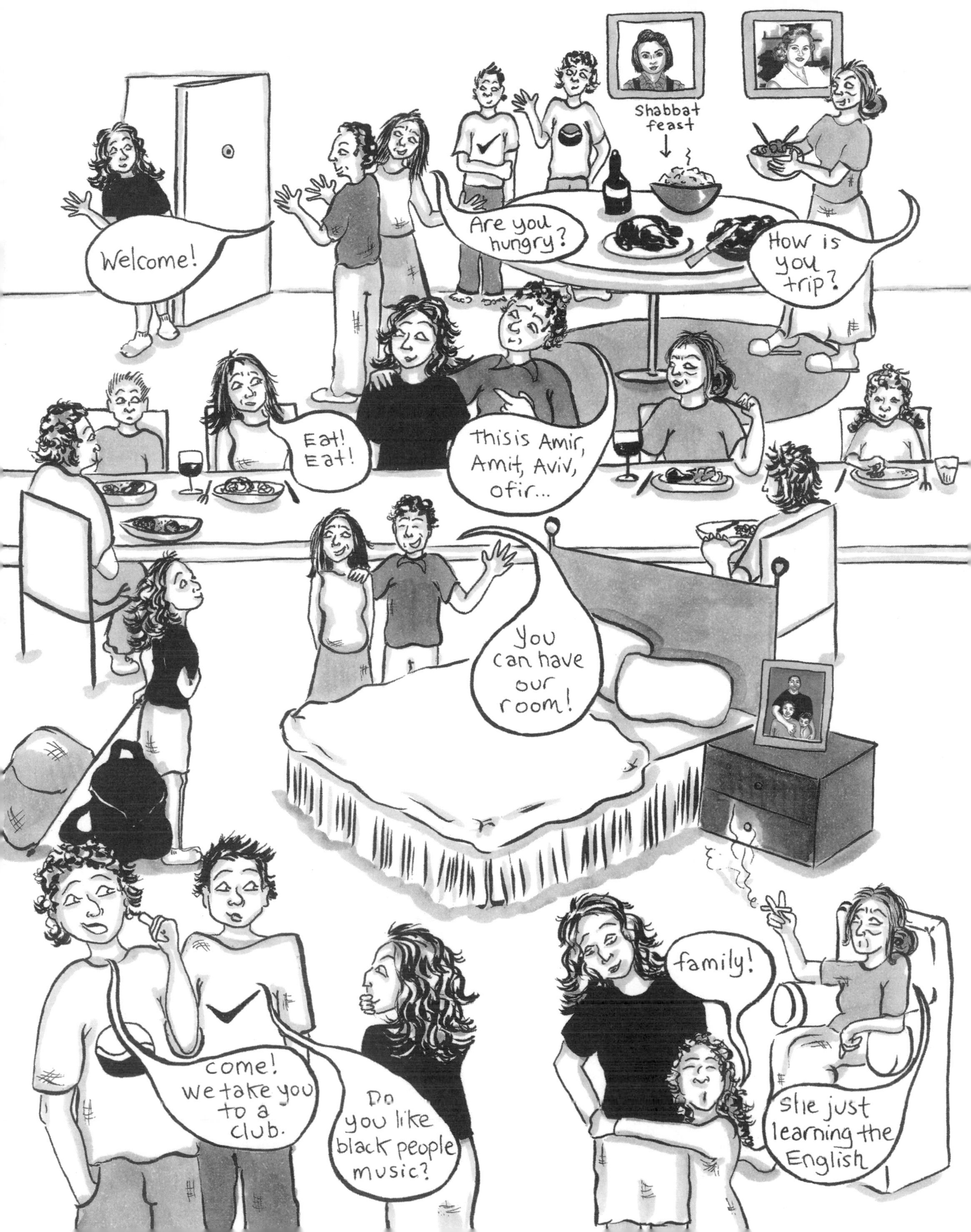
Welcome!
Are you hungry?
Shabbat feast
How is you trip?
Eat! Eat!
this is Amir, Amit, Aviv, ofir...
You can have our room!
come! we take you to a club.
Do you like black people music?
family!
She just learning the English

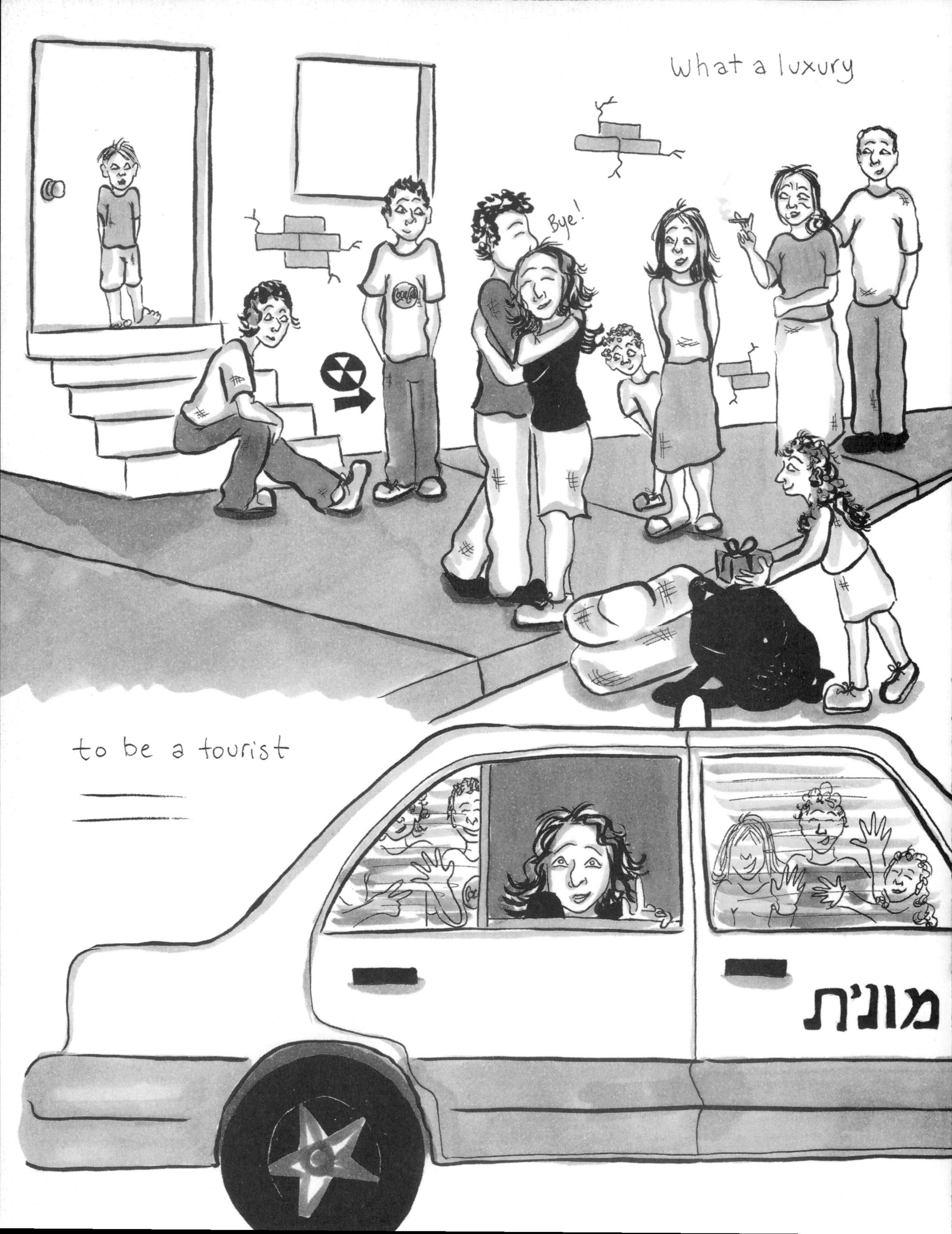
What a luxury
Bye!
to be a tourist
מונית

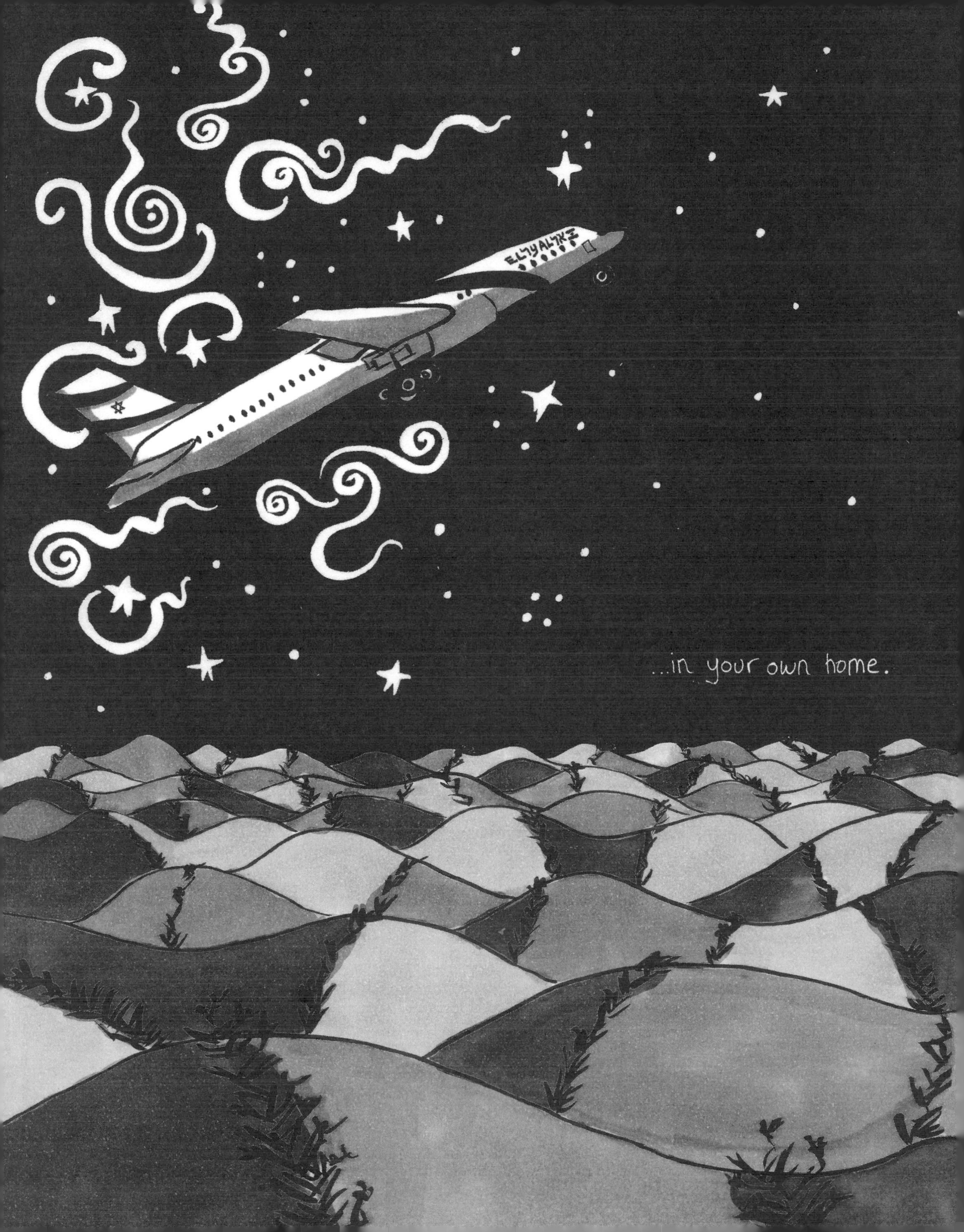
...in your own home.

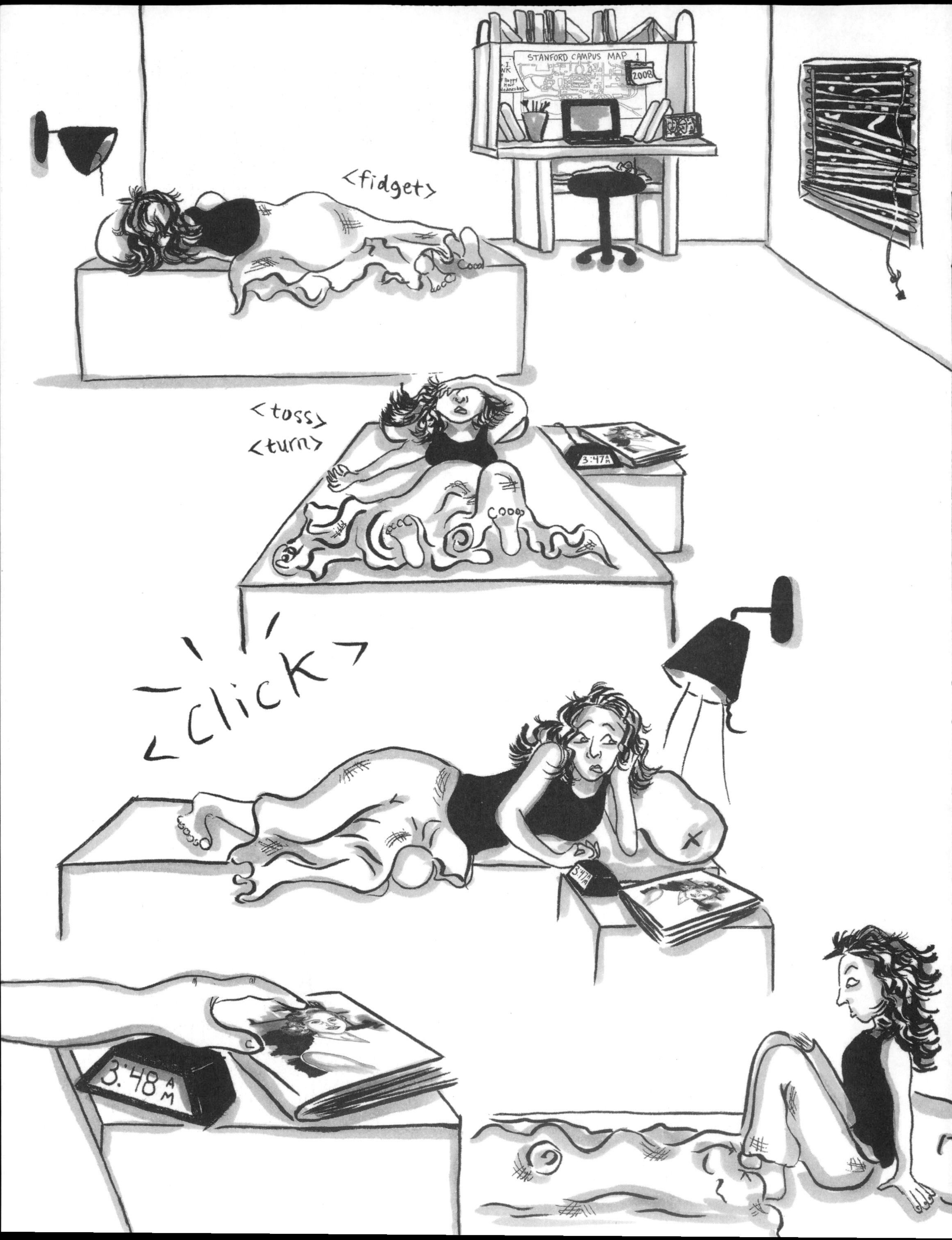
STANFORD CAMPUS MAP
2008
<fidget>
<toss>
<turn>
3:47 AM
<click>
3:47 AM
3:48 AM

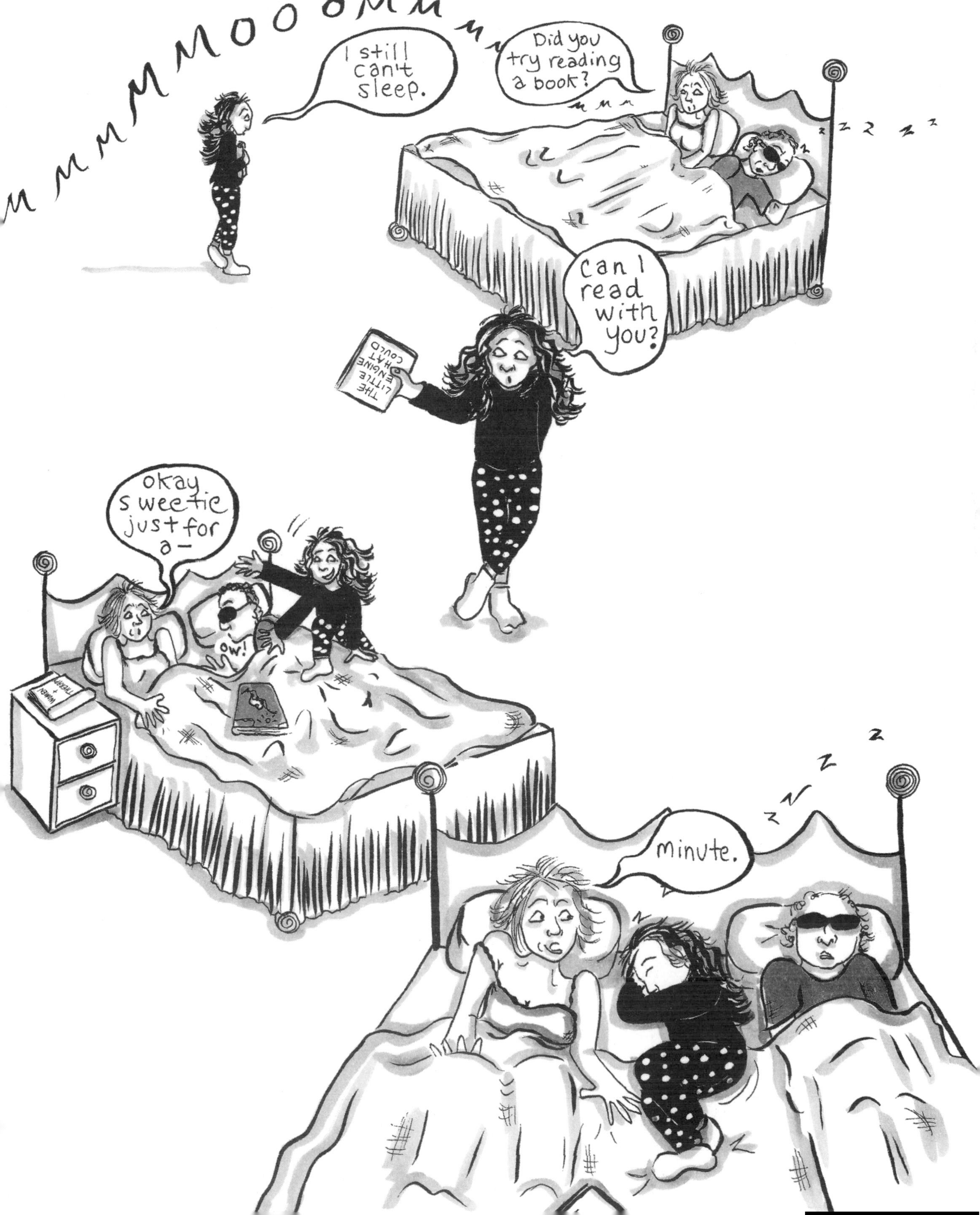
MMMMMMOOOOMMMMM
I still can't sleep.
Did you try reading a book?
Can I read with you?
THE LITTLE ENGINE THAT COULD
Okay sweetie just for a–
OW!
minute.

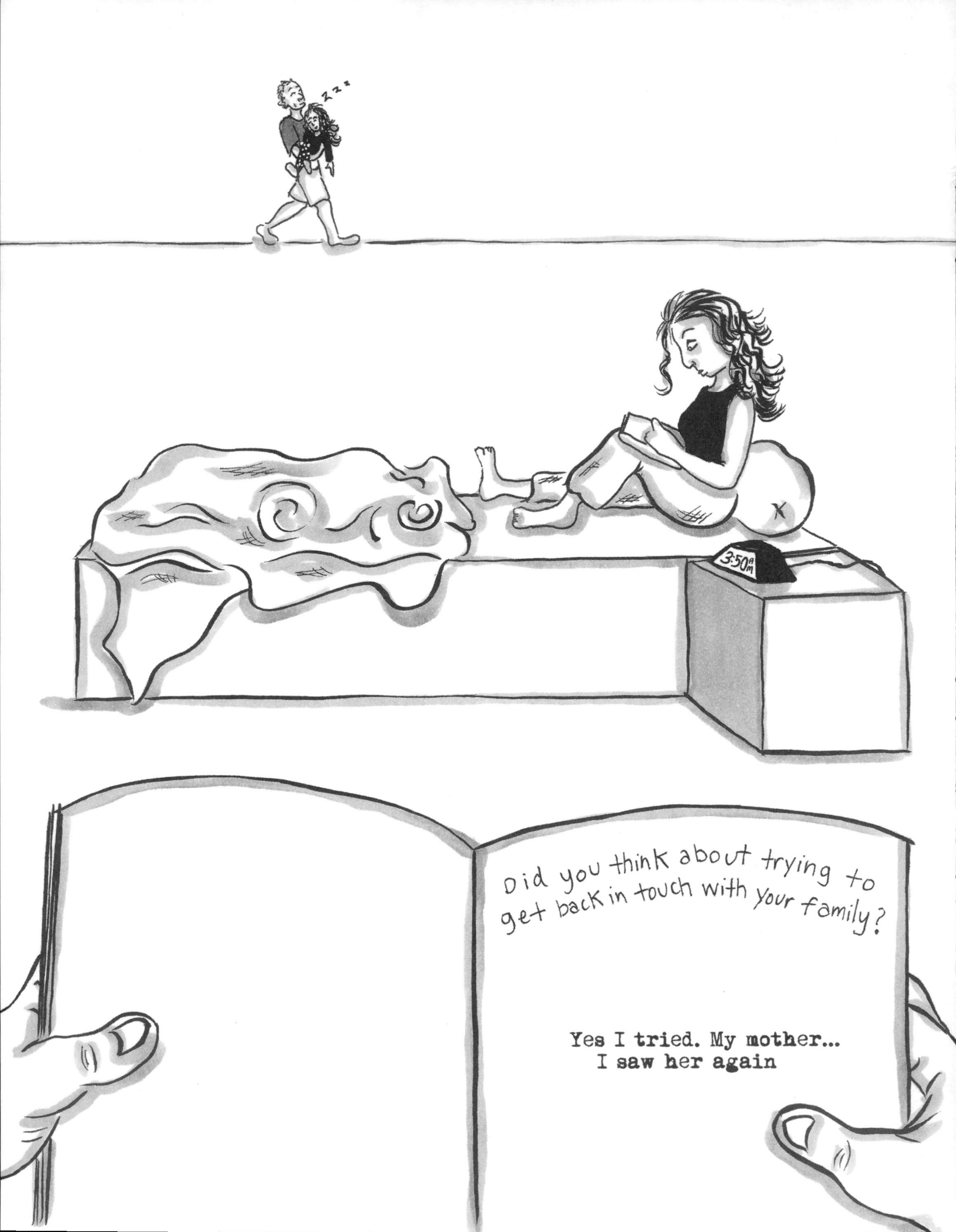
zzz
3:50am
Did you think about trying to get back in touch with your family?
Yes I tried. My mother...
I saw her again

I went and gave my saved up money with a big bread that I baked to a man and I say, bring my mother here. I knew how to get in touch because everybody in the little towns was talking. We didn't have no radio, no mail, no nothing, but you knew what was going on. There was a ghetto in Łuków, but not so like Warsaw. I could come and go.

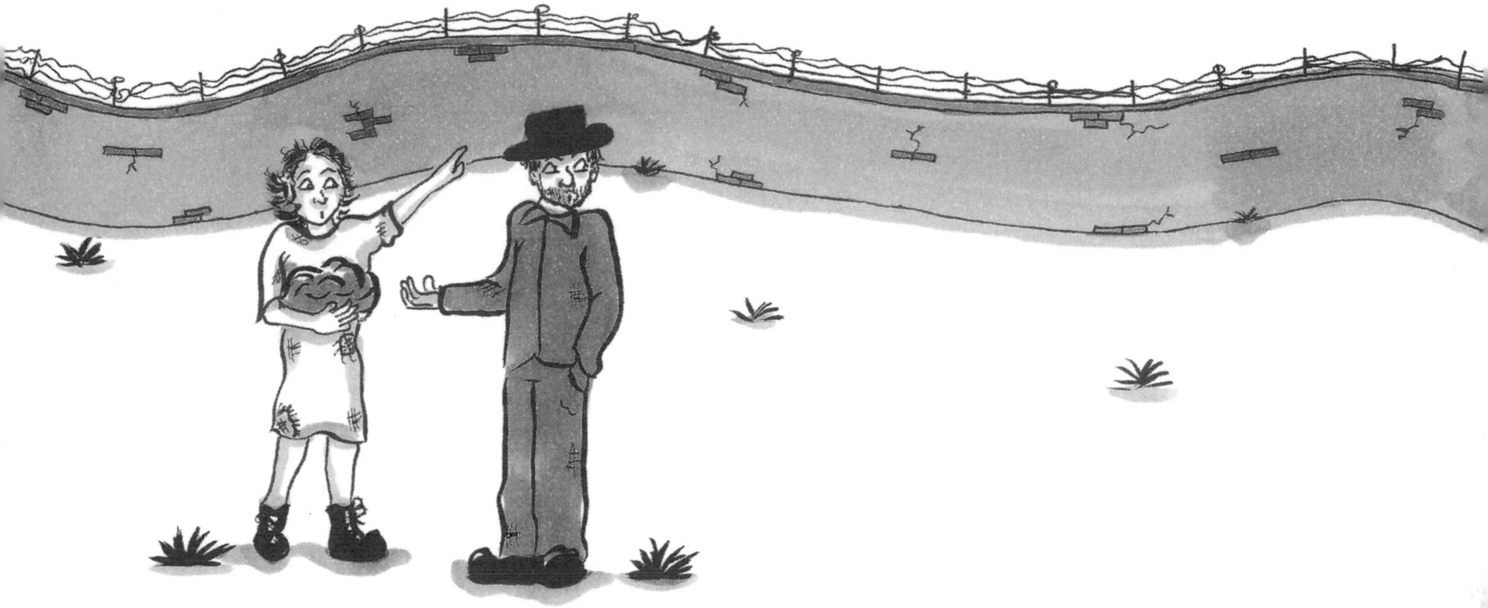

When I saw my mother, you don't know how I felt. My mother, so fashriveled, the way she was so hungry. She say, I don't have nobody but you, all the kids gone from hunger, father's underground in the ghetto, you my only thing. That's what she told me. From then on, I could go and see her sometimes. But it wasn't long.

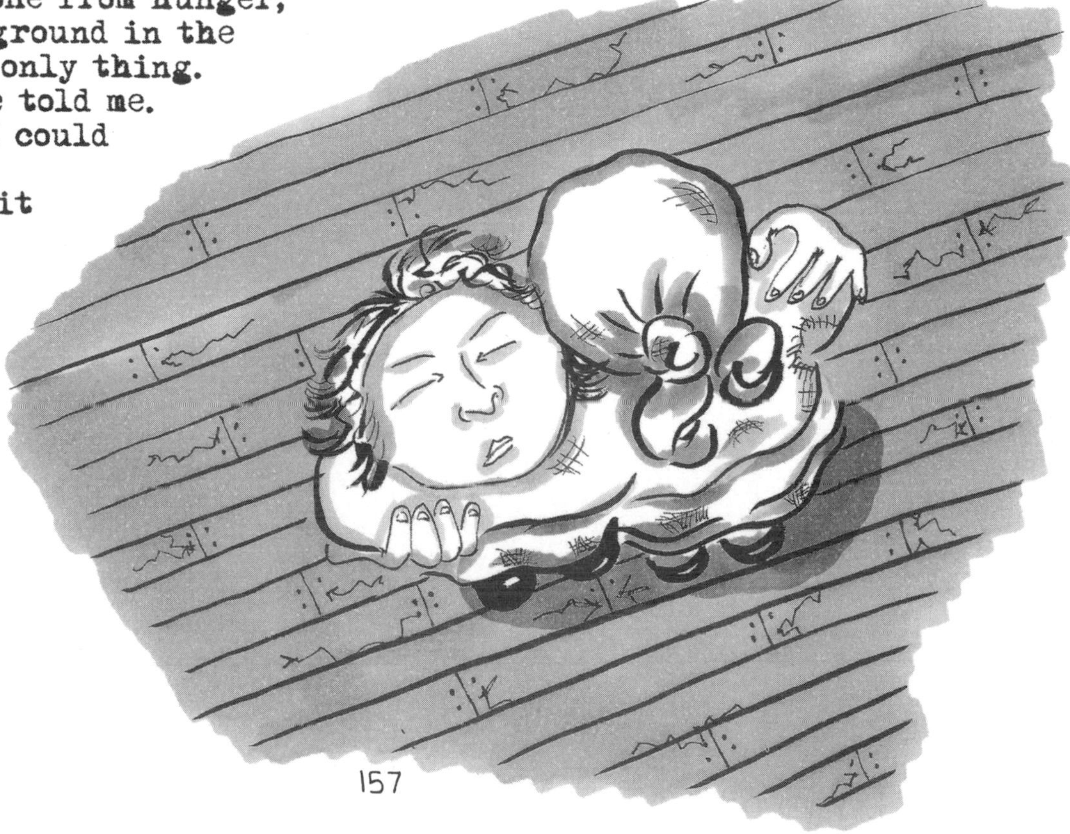

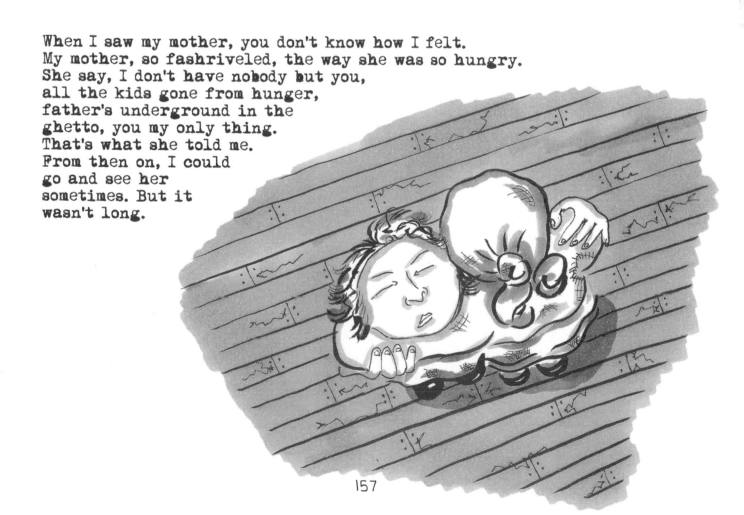

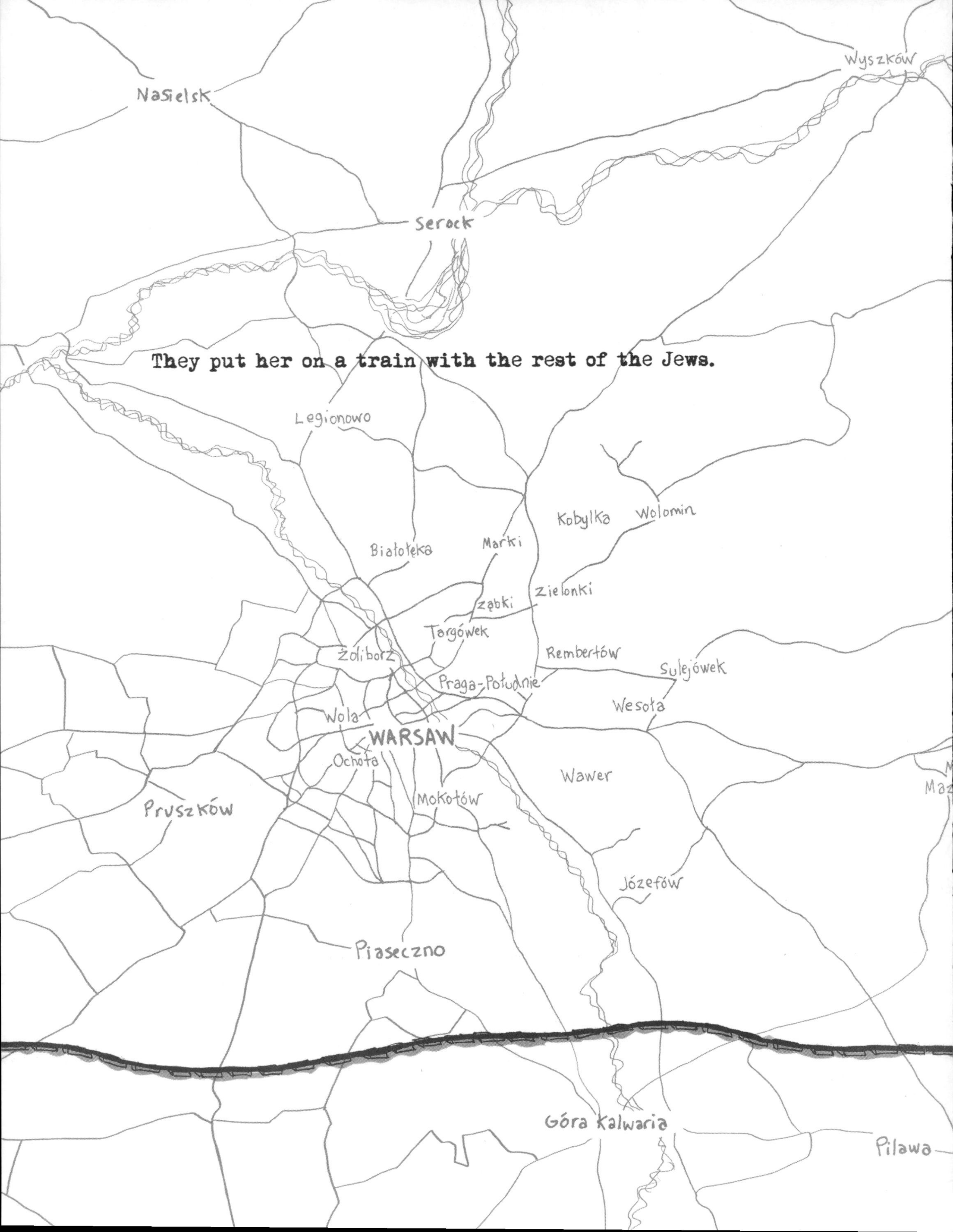
They put her on a train with the rest of the Jews.
Nasielsk
Wyszków
Serock
Legionowo
Kobylka
Wolomin
Białołęka
Marki
ząbki
Zielonki
Targówek
Żoliborz
Rembertów
Sulejówek
Praga-Południe
Wesoła
Wola
WARSAW
Ochota
Wawer
Mokotów
Pruszków
Józefów
Piaseczno
Góra Kalwaria
Pilawa

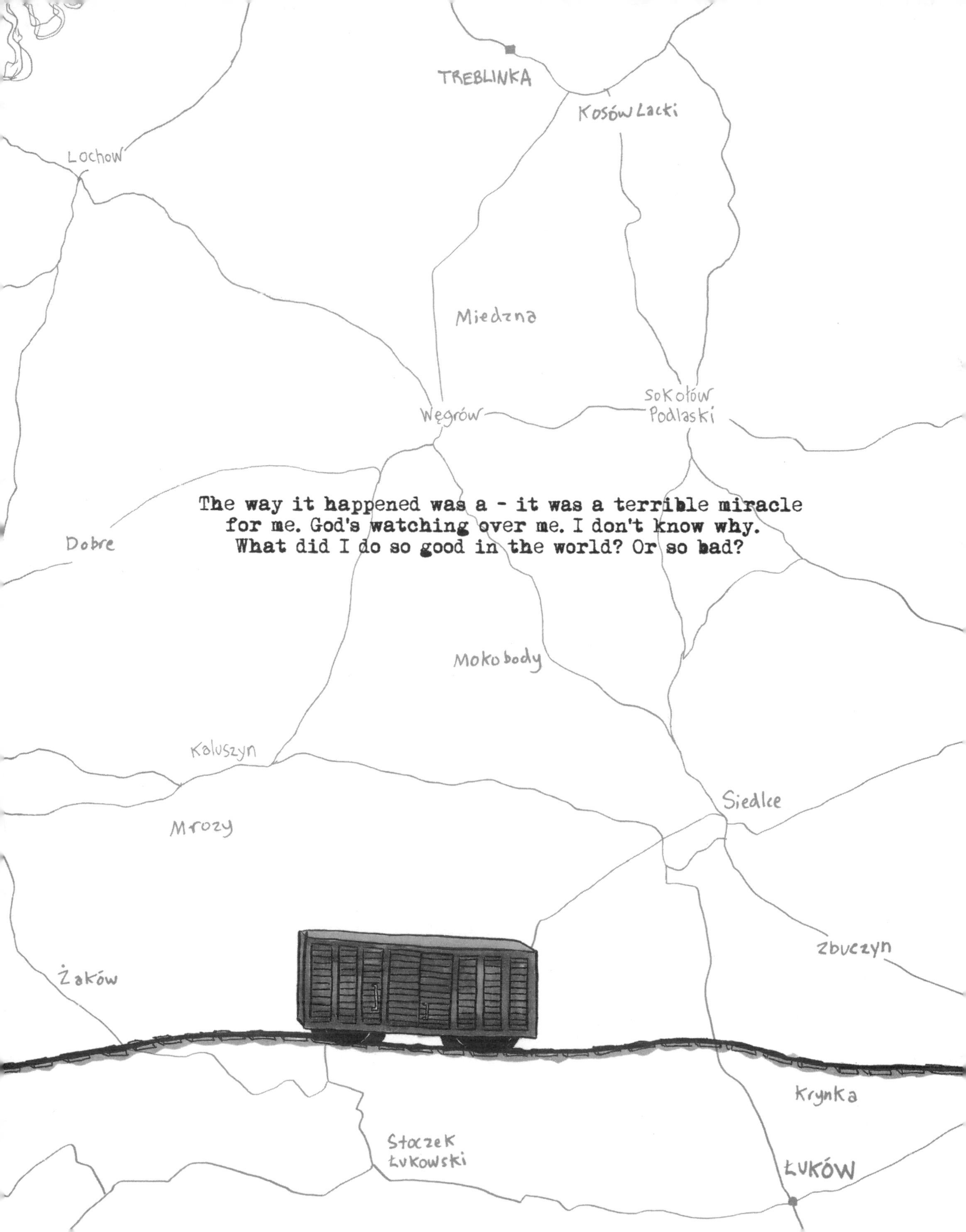
TREBLINKA
Kosów Lacki
Lochow
Miedzna
Węgrów
Sokołów Podlaski
The way it happened was a - it was a terrible miracle for me. God's watching over me. I don't know why. What did I do so good in the world? Or so bad?
Dobre
Mokobody
Kaluszyn
Siedlce
Mrozy
Zbuczyn
Żaków
Krynka
Stoczek Łukowski
ŁUKÓW

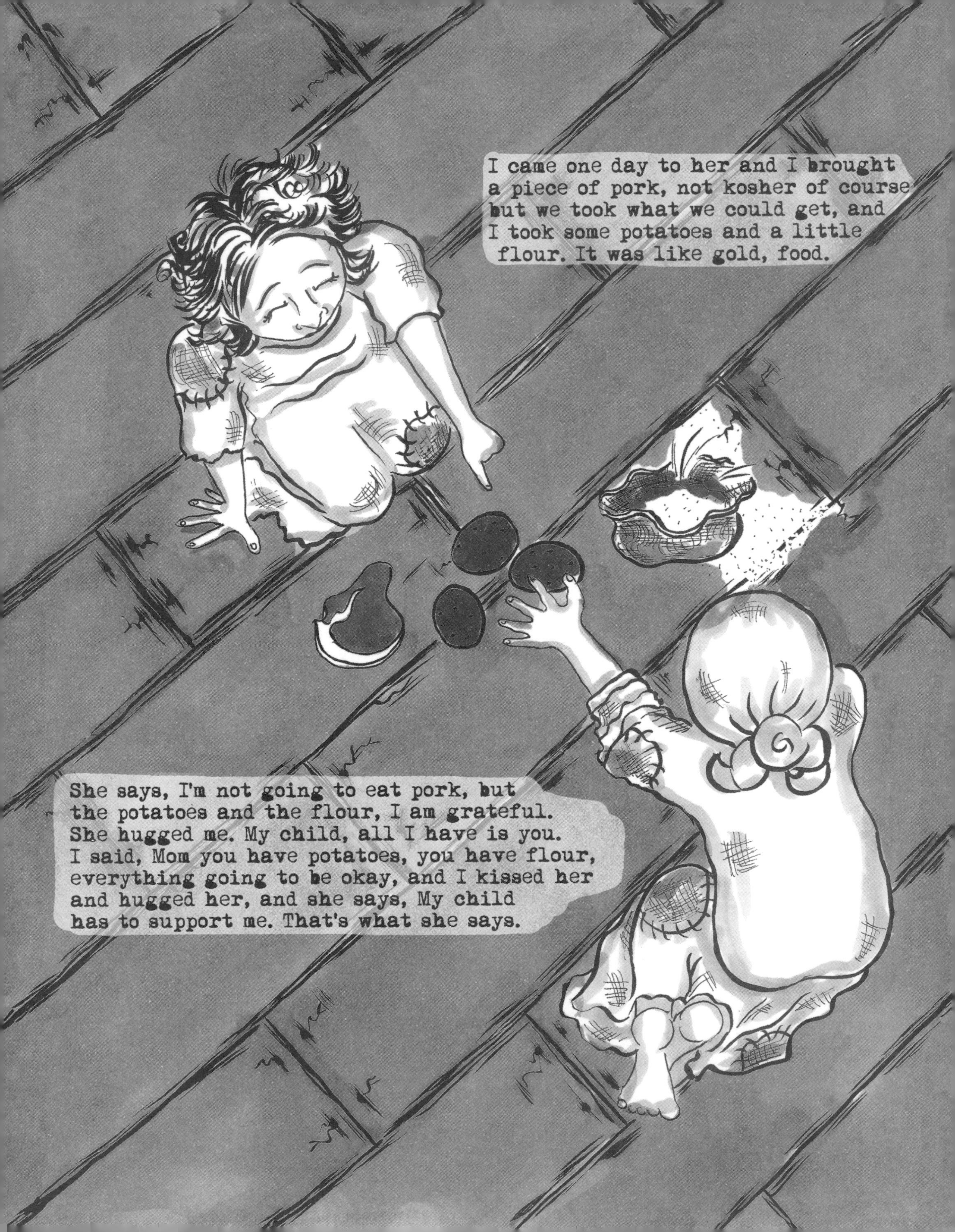
I came one day to her and I brought a piece of pork, not kosher of course but we took what we could get, and I took some potatoes and a little flour. It was like gold, food.
She says, I'm not going to eat pork, but the potatoes and the flour, I am grateful. She hugged me. My child, all I have is you. I said, Mom you have potatoes, you have flour, everything going to be okay, and I kissed her and hugged her, and she says, My child has to support me. That's what she says.

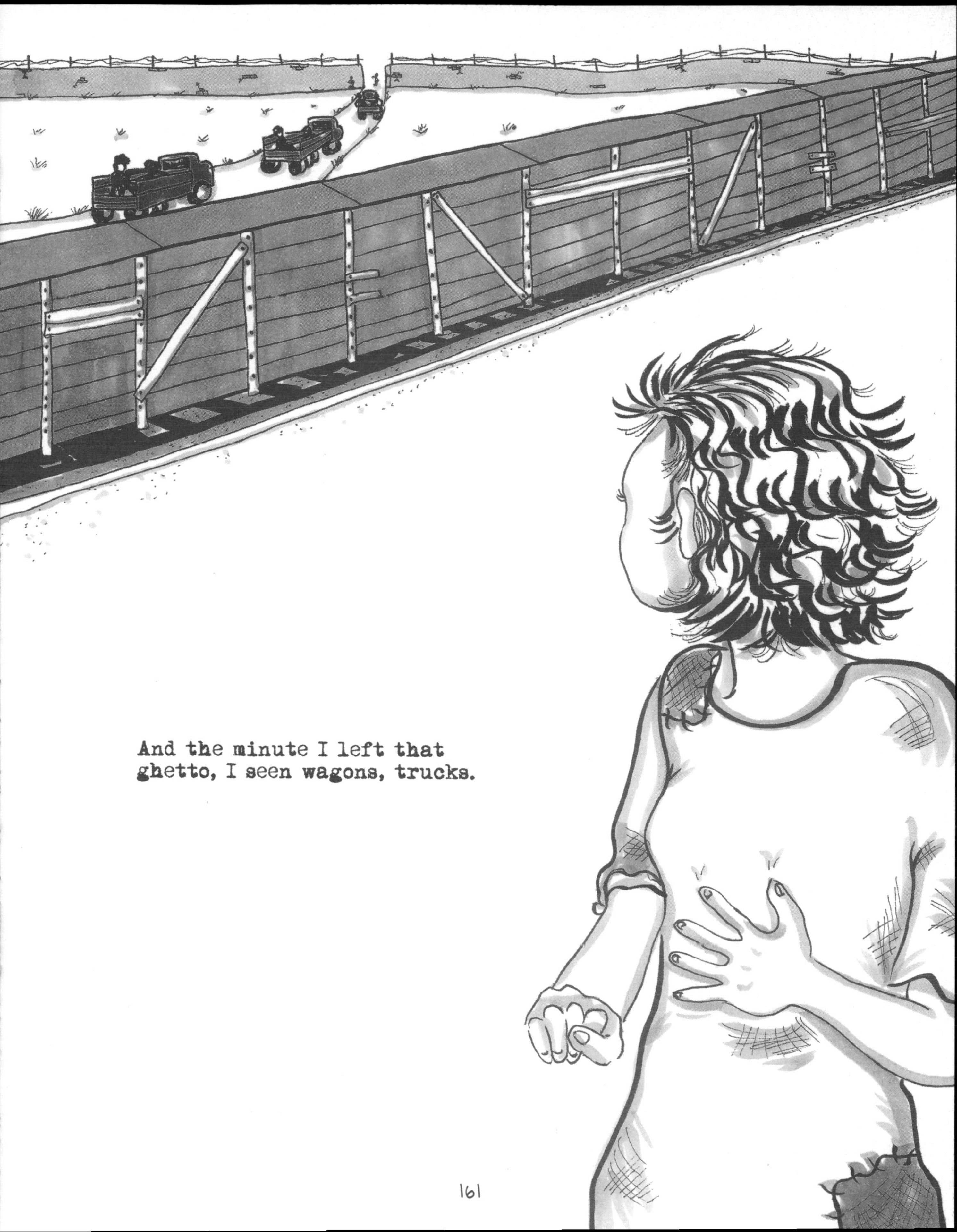
And the minute I left that ghetto, I seen wagons, trucks.

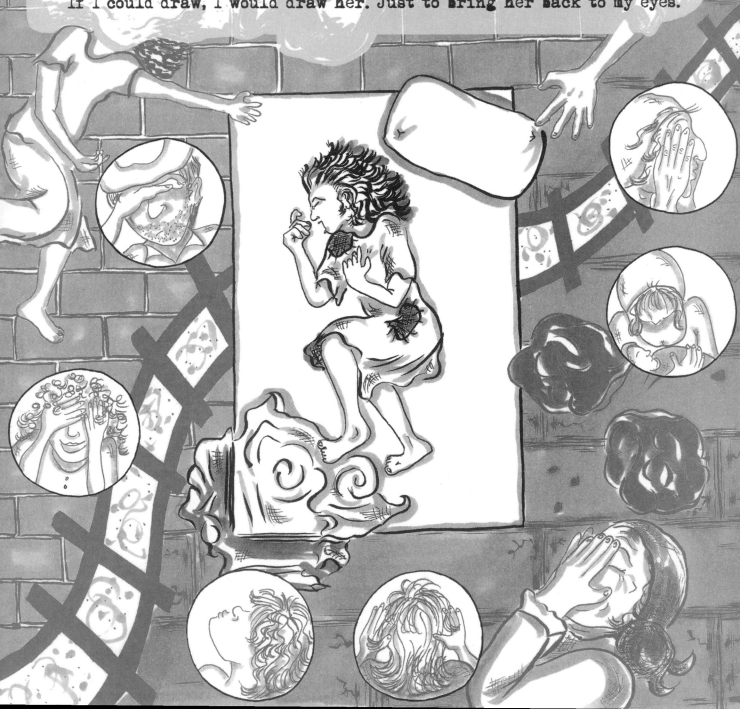

I came back to the gentiles I was living with and the man said, So many Nazis, I bet they are going to kill off those Jews. That was the day they were going to take the rest of them to Treblinka. I knew about this place. I went to my bed. I say to myself, I don't have a mother now. I didn't eat. The gentiles said, Helena what's the matter with you? I say, I don't feel good. I couldn't tell them that I had lost everything, my mother, all my family.

I ask myself, Was I born from a stone? Do I still speak Jewish? Does Jewish still exist? I try to say the words to myself. Maybe somebody should hear me. I try to picture a face. My mother's face. If I could draw, I would draw her. Just to bring her back to my eyes.

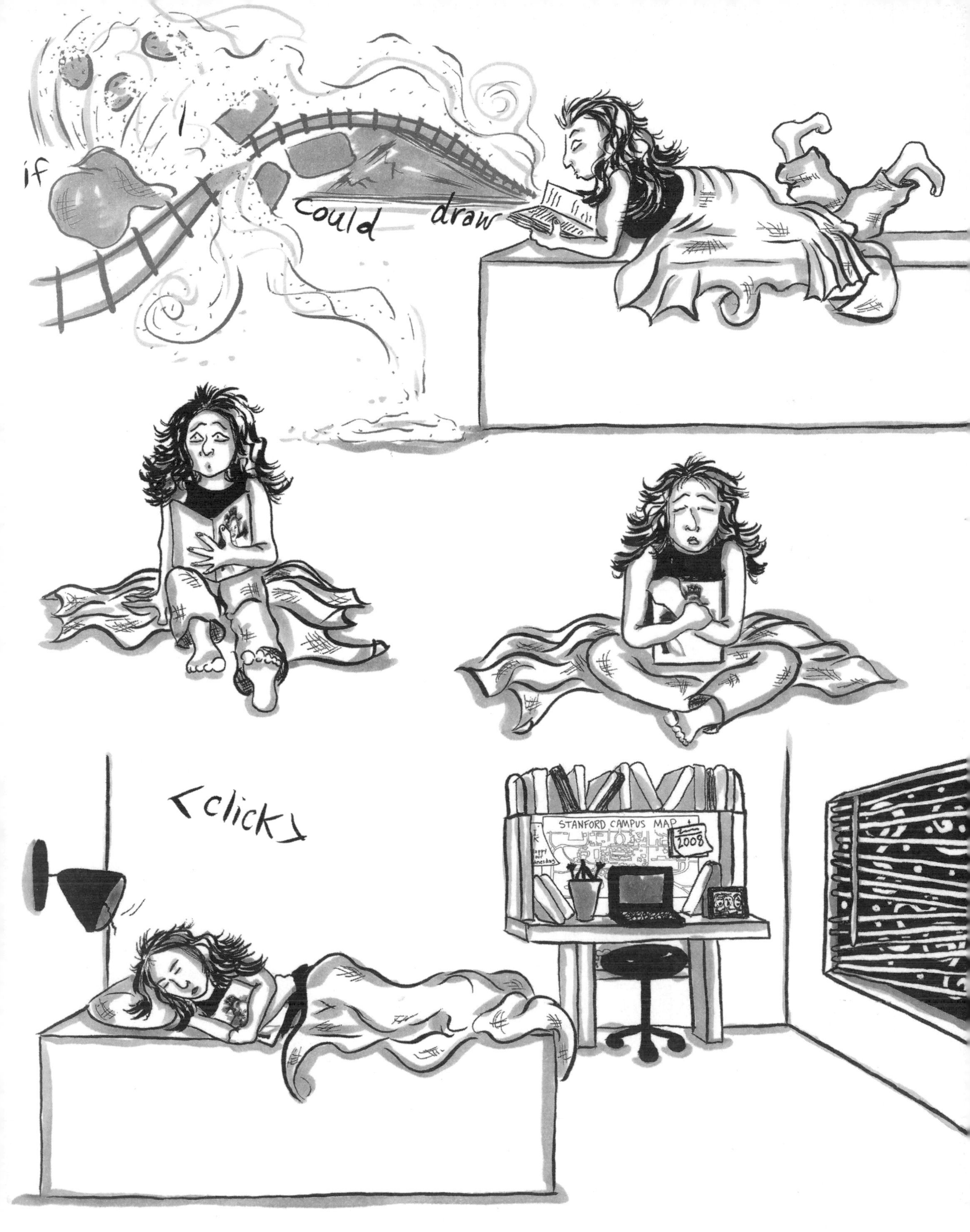
if
I
could
draw
[click]
STANFORD CAMPUS MAP
2008

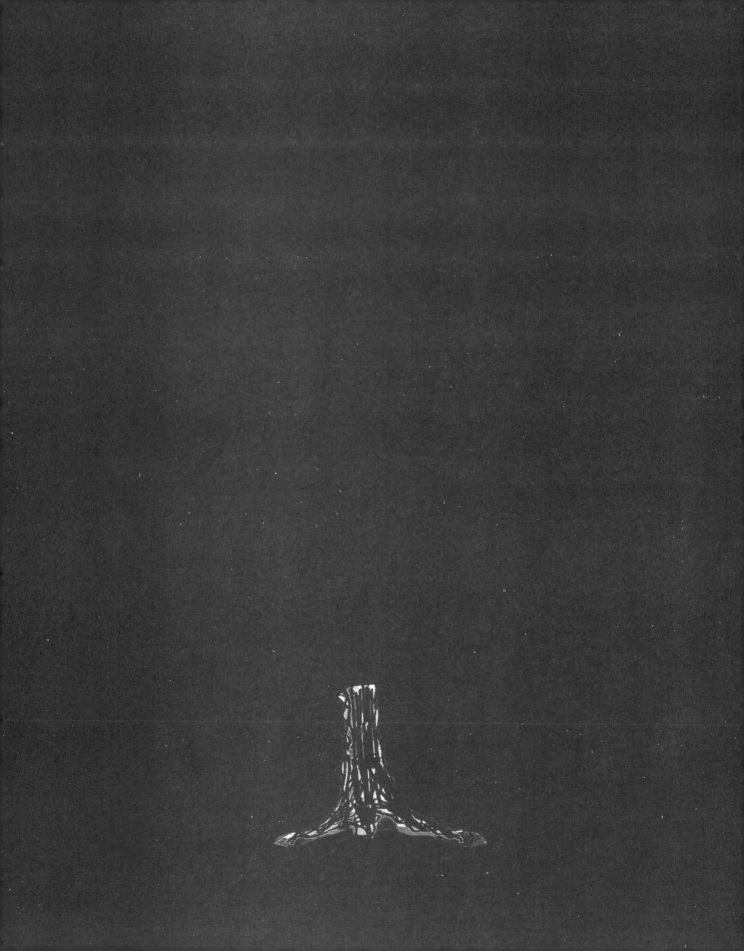

Chapter Five:
Homegrown

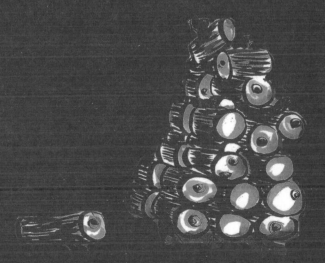

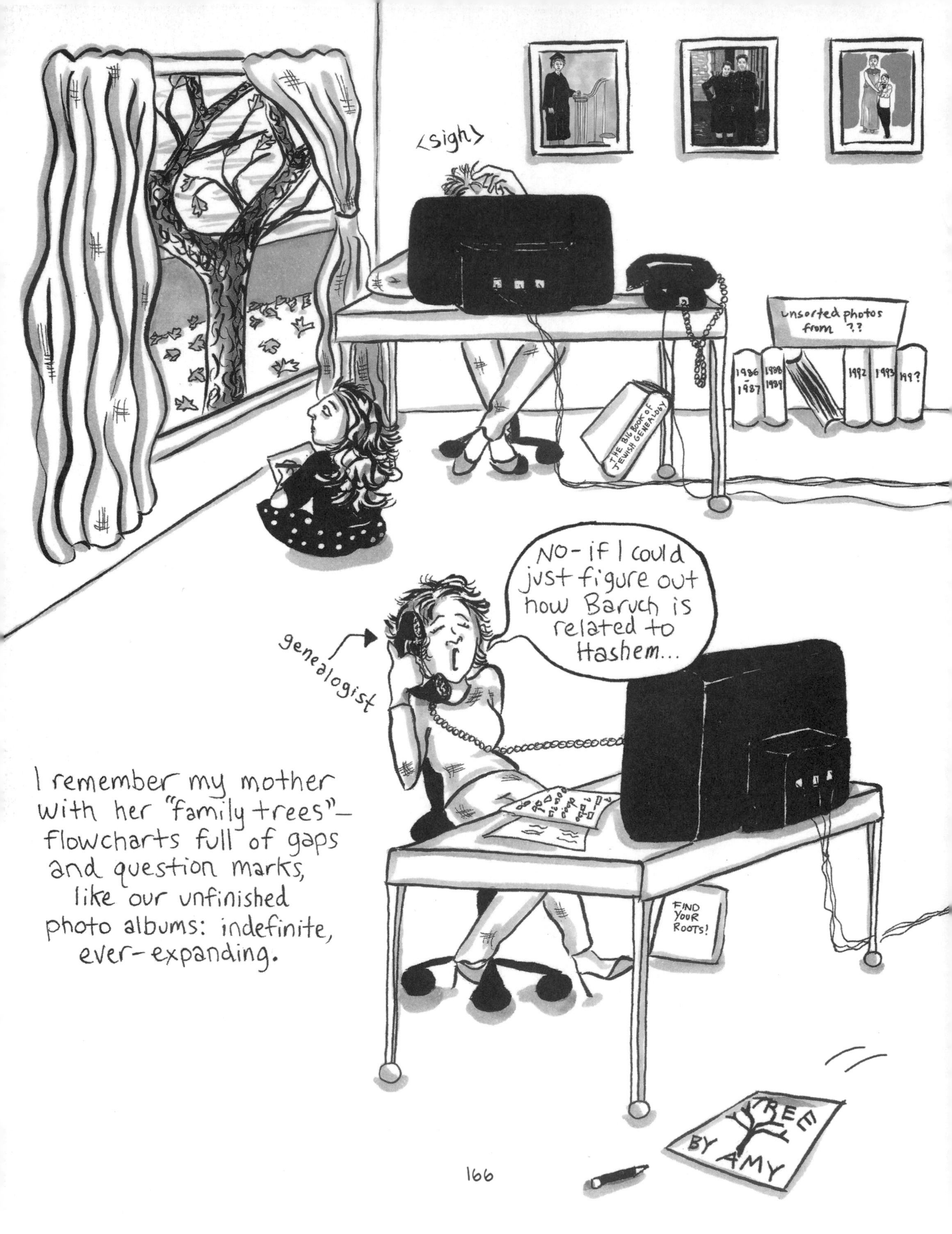
<sigh>
unsorted photos from ??
1986 1987
1988 1989
1992
1993
199?
THE BIG BOOK OF JEWISH GENEALOGY
NO- if I could just figure out how Baruch is related to Hashem...
genealogist
I remember my mother with her "family trees"— flowcharts full of gaps and question marks, like our unfinished photo albums: indefinite, ever-expanding.
FIND YOUR ROOTS!
TREE BY AMY

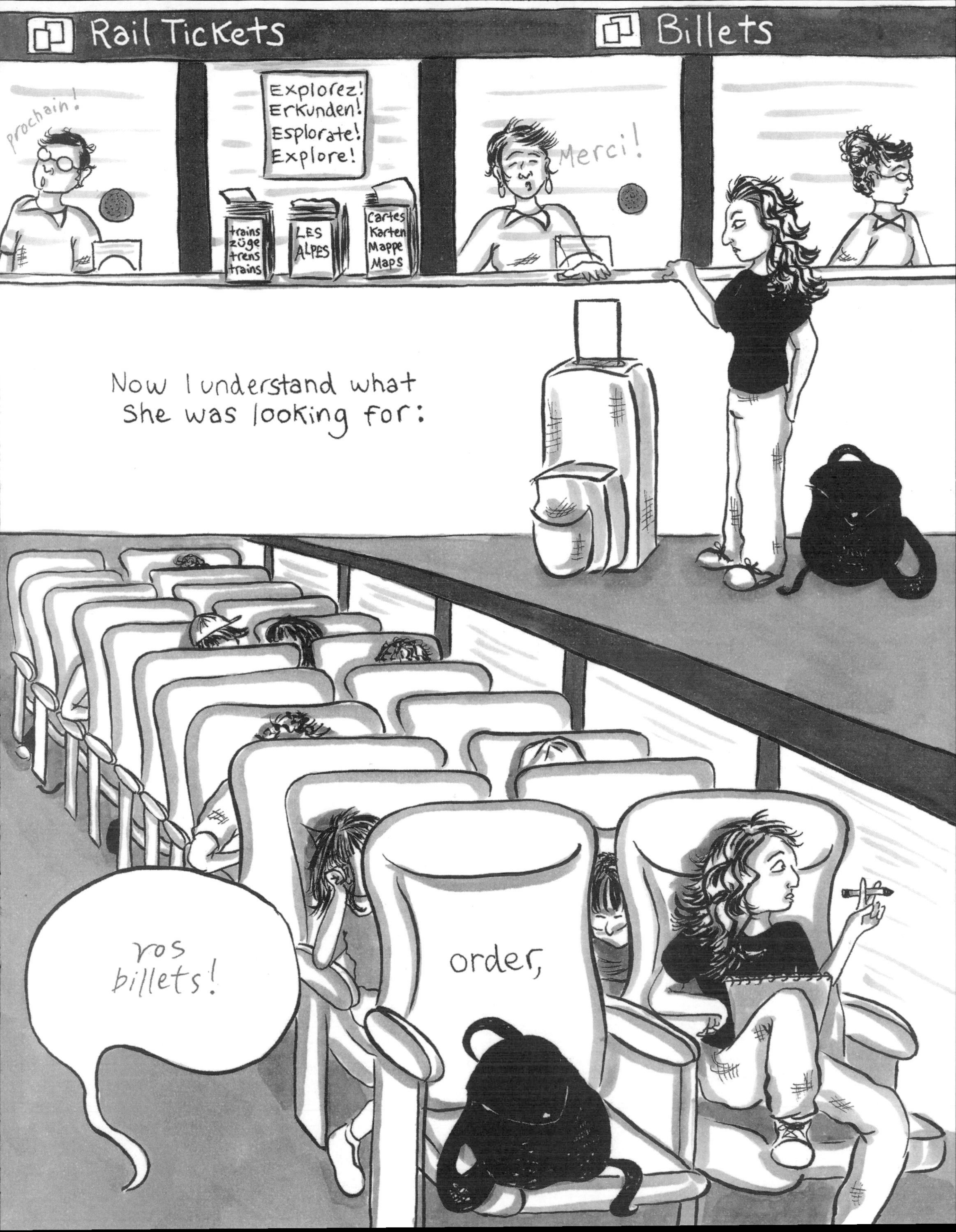

Rail Tickets
Billets
prochain!
Explorez! Erkunden! Esplorate! Explore!
trains züge trens trains
LES ALPES
Cartes Karten Mappe Maps
Merci!
Now I understand what she was looking for:
vos billets!
order,

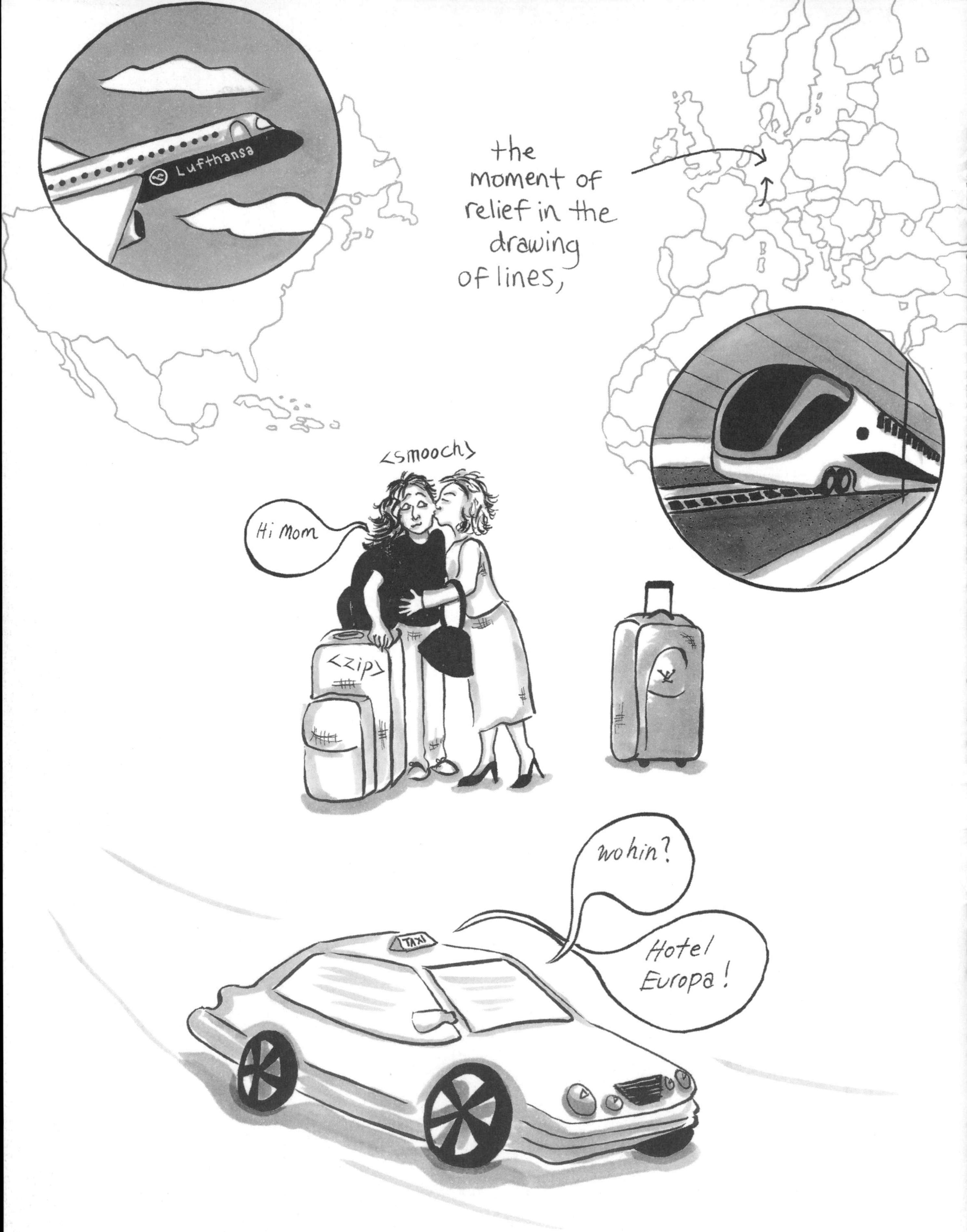
Lufthansa
the moment of relief in the drawing of lines,
<smooch>
Hi Mom
<zip>
TAXI
wohin?
Hotel Europa!

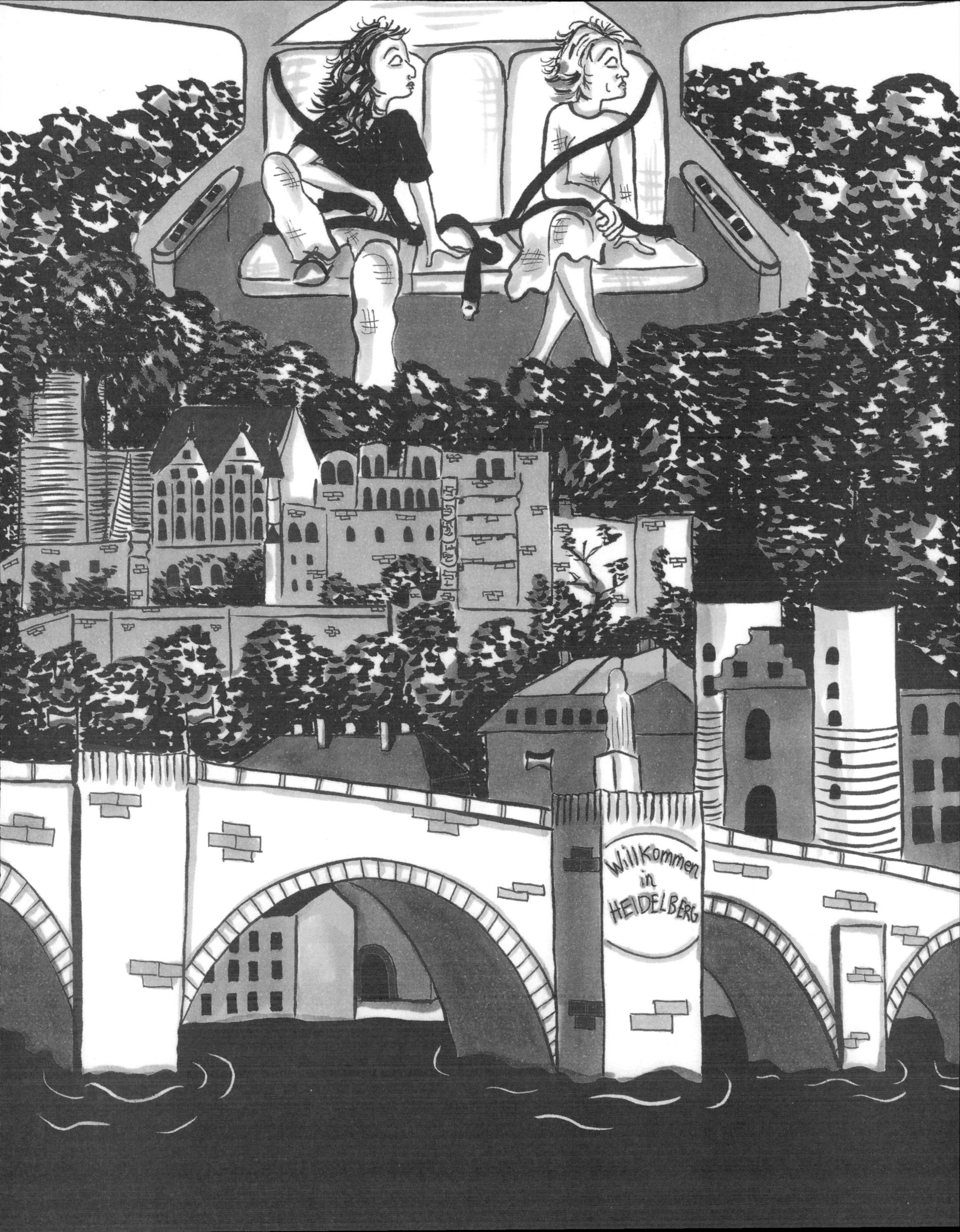
Willkommen
in
HEIDELBERG

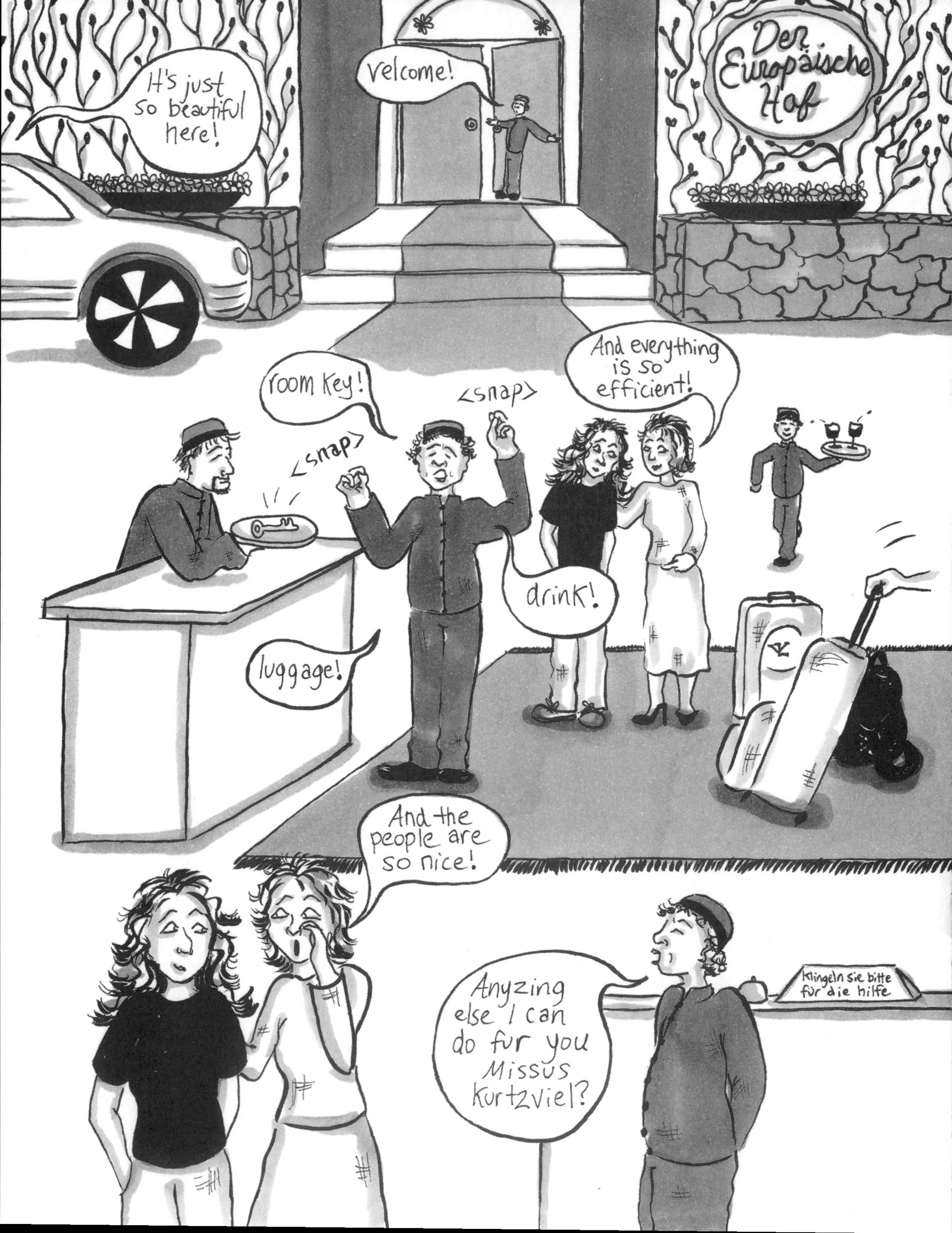
Den Europäische Hof
It's just so beautiful here!
Velcome!
room key!
<snap>
<snap>
And everything is so efficient!
drink!
luggage!
And the people are so nice!
Anyzing else I can do fur you Missus Kurtzviel?
Klingeln sie bitte für die hilfe

We'd decided to meet in Heidelberg before I headed to England for a semester abroad. I'd been traveling for just a week and a half.

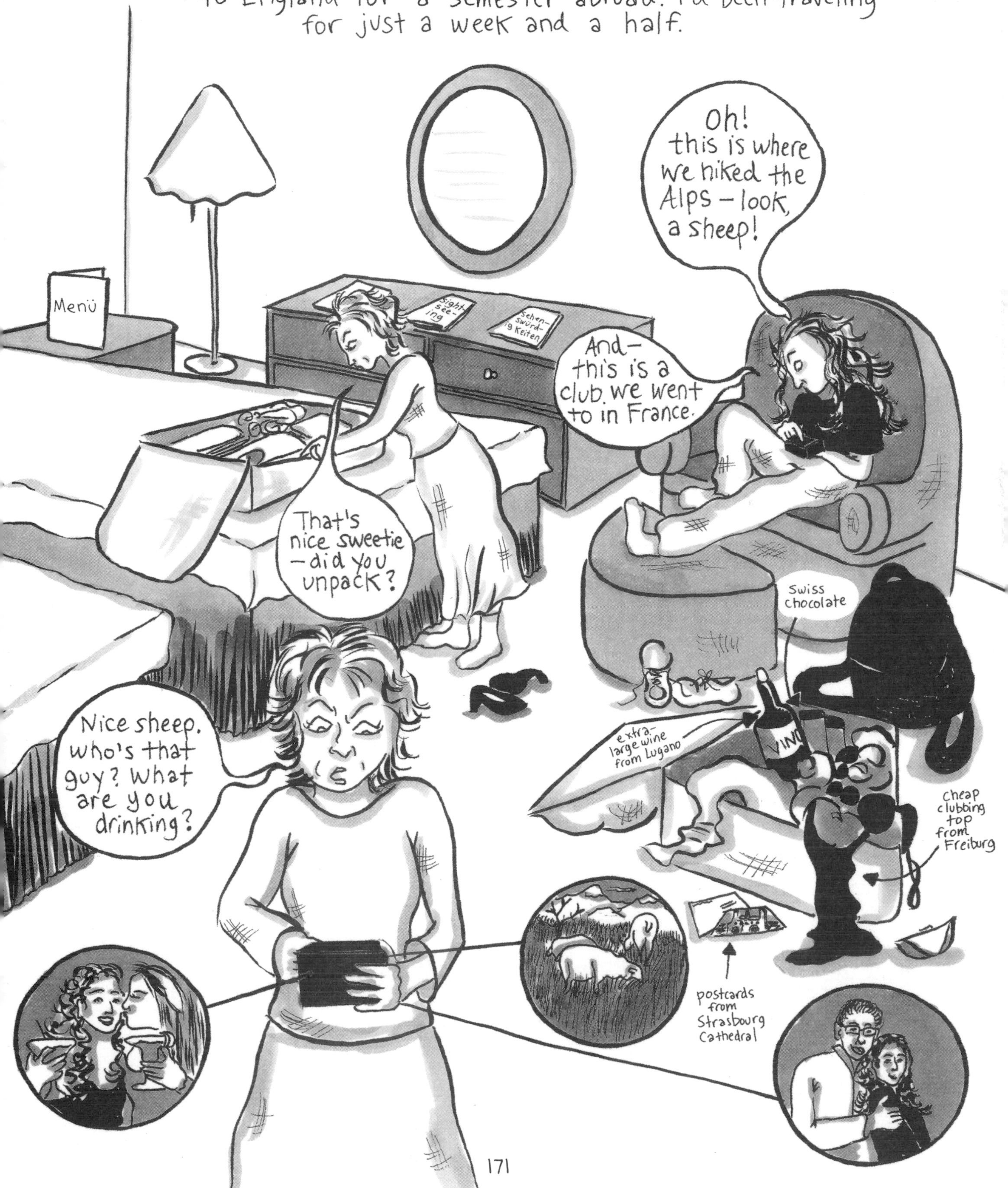
Oh! this is where we hiked the Alps – look, a sheep!
And– this is a club we went to in France.
That's nice sweetie – did you unpack?
Nice sheep. who's that guy? What are you drinking?
Menü
Sight-see-ing
Sehen-swürd-ig keiten
Swiss chocolate
extra-large wine from Lugano
VINO
Cheap clubbing top from Freiburg
postcards from Strasbourg Cathedral

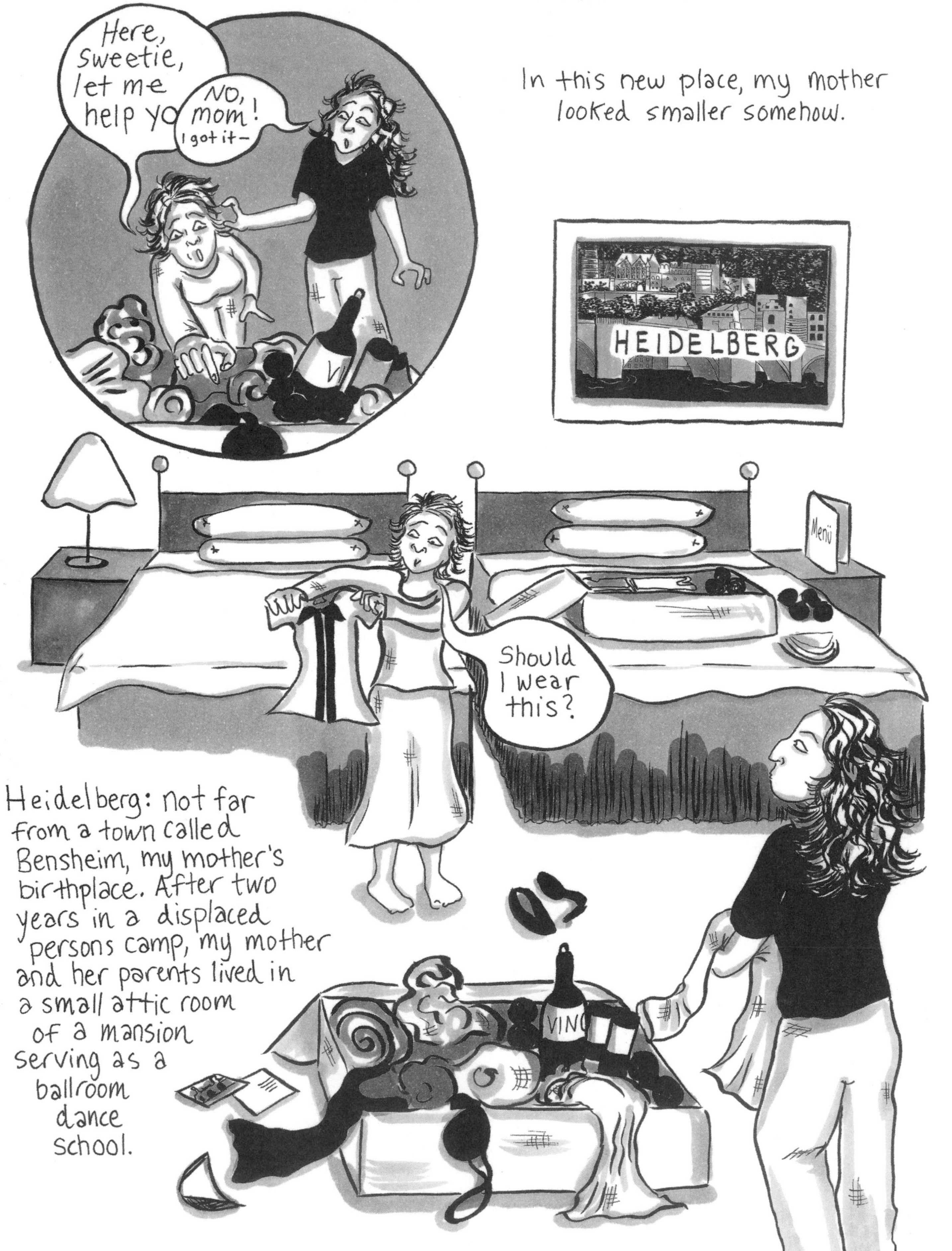
Here, sweetie, let me help yo
NO, mom! I got it–
In this new place, my mother looked smaller somehow.
HEIDELBERG
Menü
Should I wear this?
Heidelberg: not far from a town called Bensheim, my mother's birthplace. After two years in a displaced persons camp, my mother and her parents lived in a small attic room of a mansion serving as a ballroom dance school.
VINO

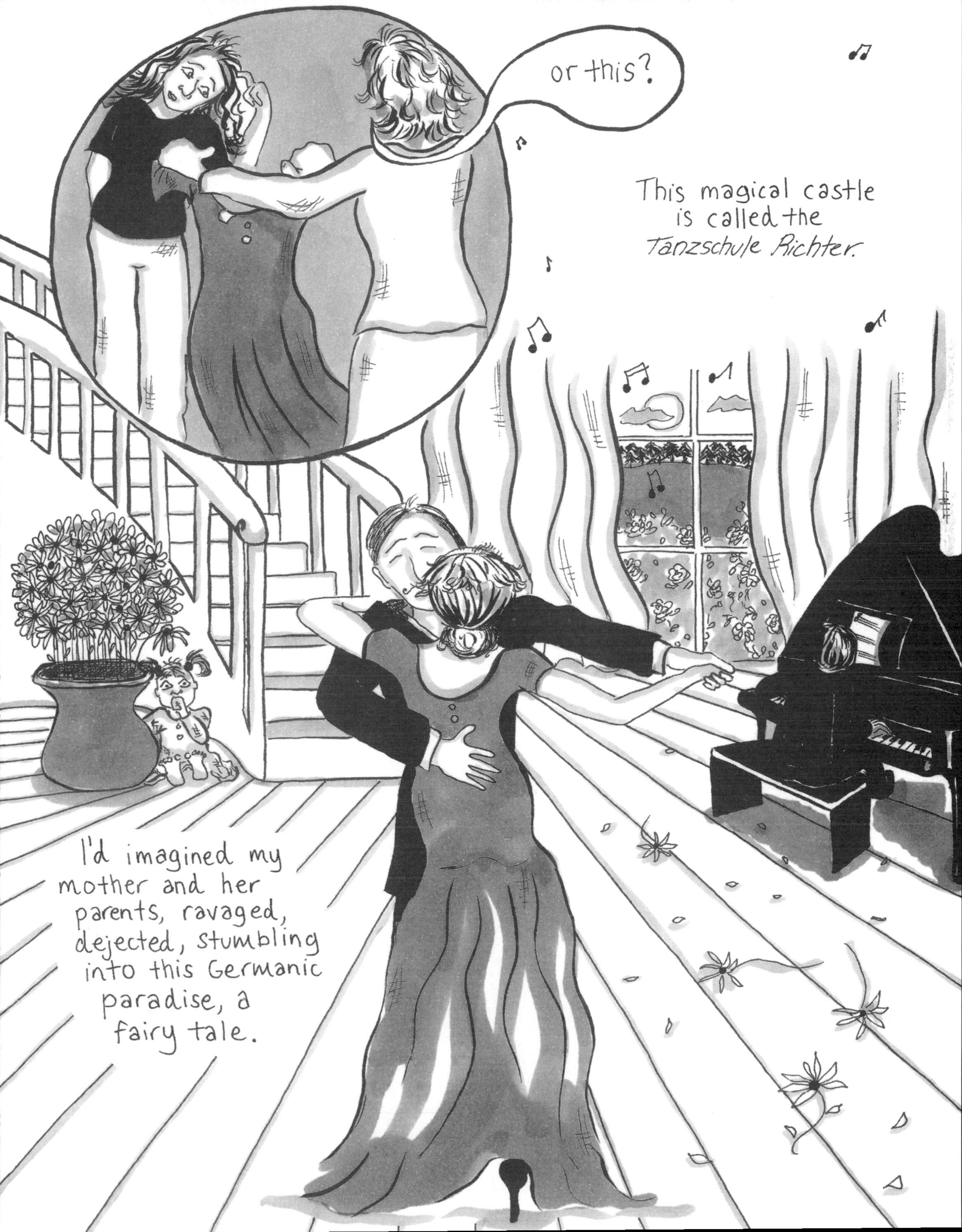
or this?
This magical castle is called the *Tanzschule Richter.*
I'd imagined my mother and her parents, ravaged, dejected, stumbling into this Germanic paradise, a fairy tale.

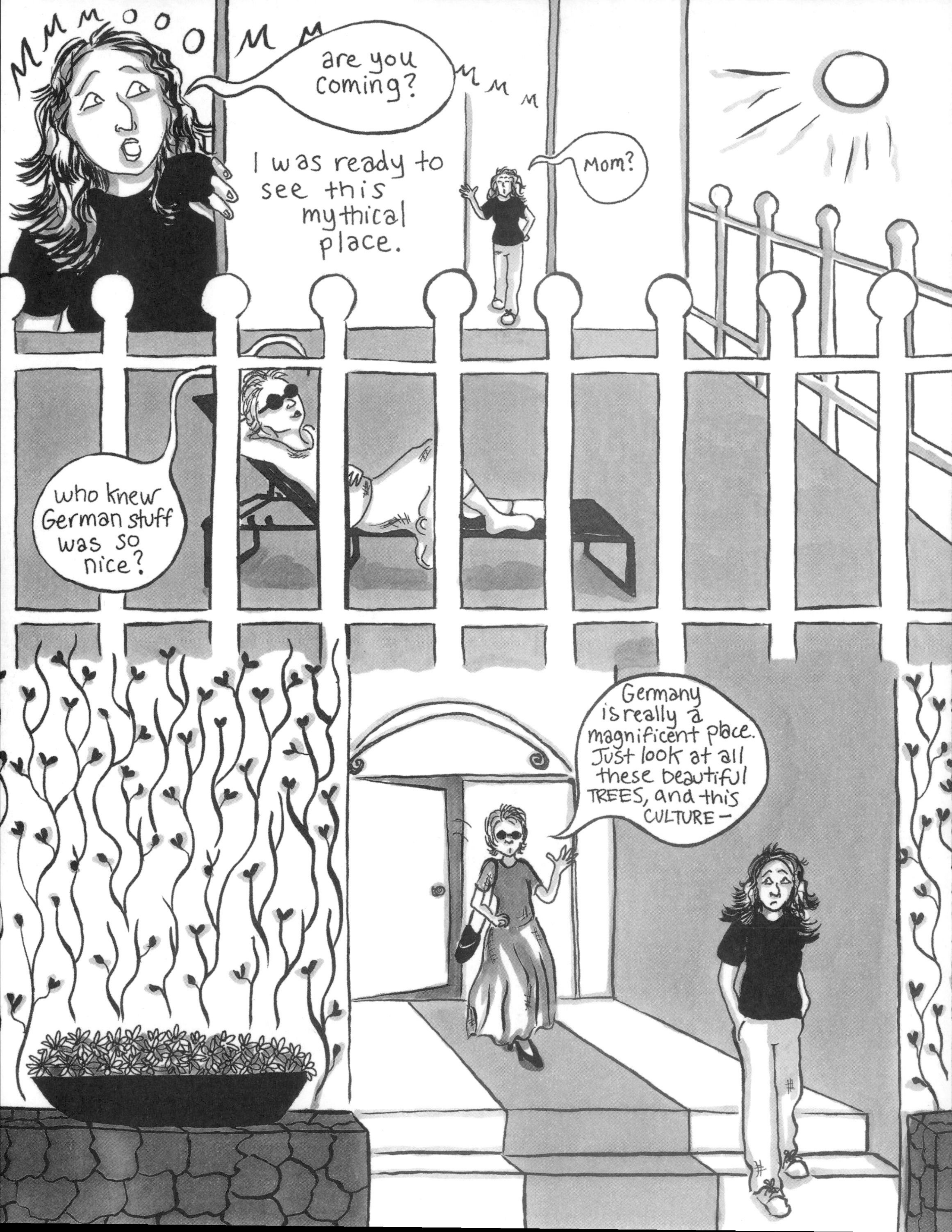
MMMOOOMMMMM
are you coming?
I was ready to see this mythical place.
Mom?
who knew German stuff was so nice?
Germany is really a magnificent place. Just look at all these beautiful TREES, and this CULTURE—

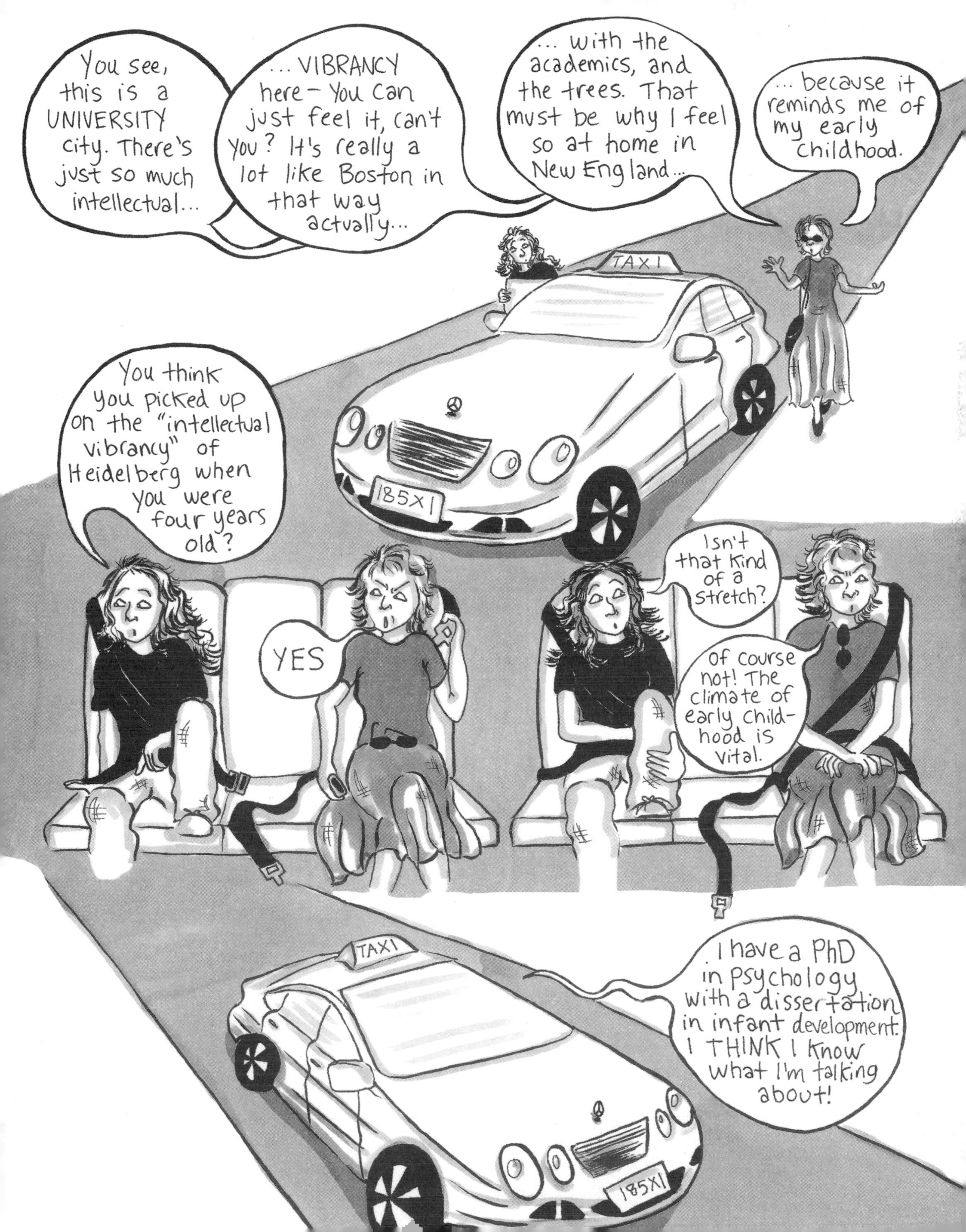
You see, this is a UNIVERSITY city. There's just so much intellectual...
... VIBRANCY here – You can just feel it, can't you? It's really a lot like Boston in that way actually...
... with the academics, and the trees. That must be why I feel so at home in New England...
... because it reminds me of my early childhood.
TAXI
185X1
You think you picked up on the "intellectual vibrancy" of Heidelberg when you were four years old?
YES
Isn't that kind of a stretch?
Of course not! The climate of early child-hood is vital.
TAXI
I have a PhD in psychology with a dissertation in infant development. I THINK I know what I'm talking about!
185X1

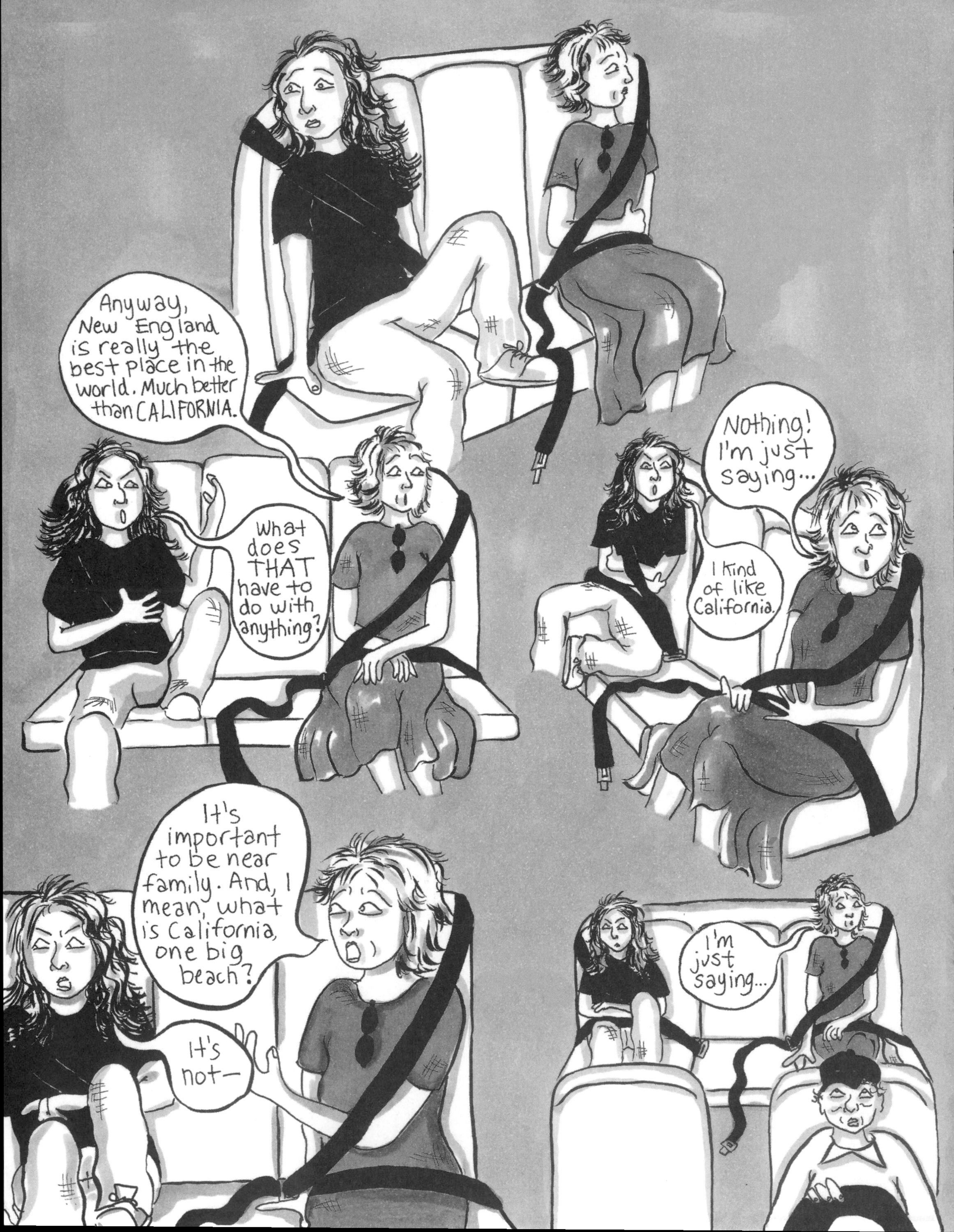
Anyway, New England is really the best place in the world. Much better than CALIFORNIA.
What does THAT have to do with anything?
Nothing! I'm just saying...
I kind of like California.
It's important to be near family. And, I mean, what is California, one big beach?
It's not—
I'm just saying...

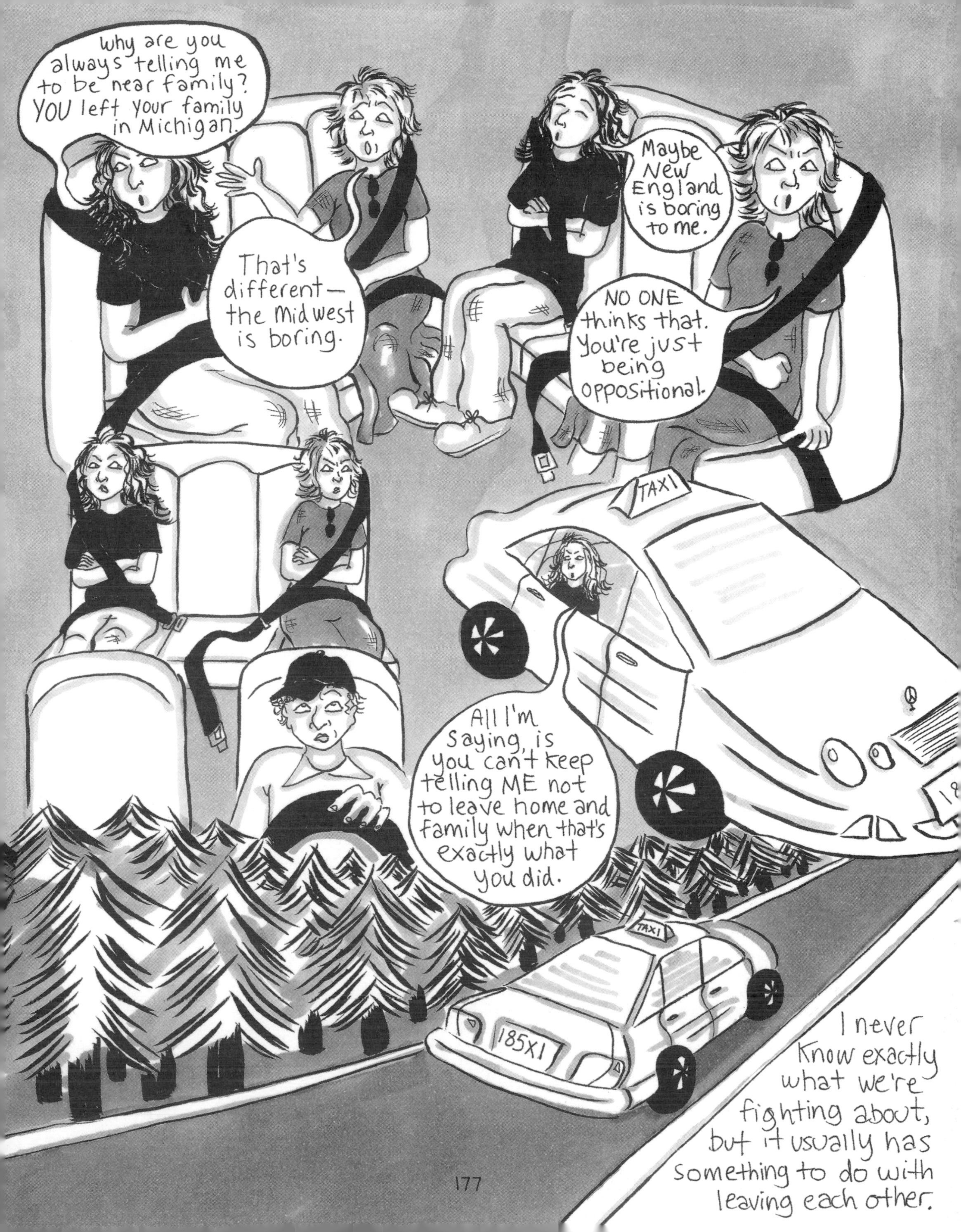
Why are you always telling me to be near family? YOU left your family in Michigan.
That's different— the Midwest is boring.
Maybe New England is boring to me.
NO ONE thinks that. You're just being oppositional.
TAXI
All I'm saying, is you can't keep telling ME not to leave home and family when that's exactly what you did.
TAXI
185XI
I never know exactly what we're fighting about, but it usually has something to do with leaving each other.

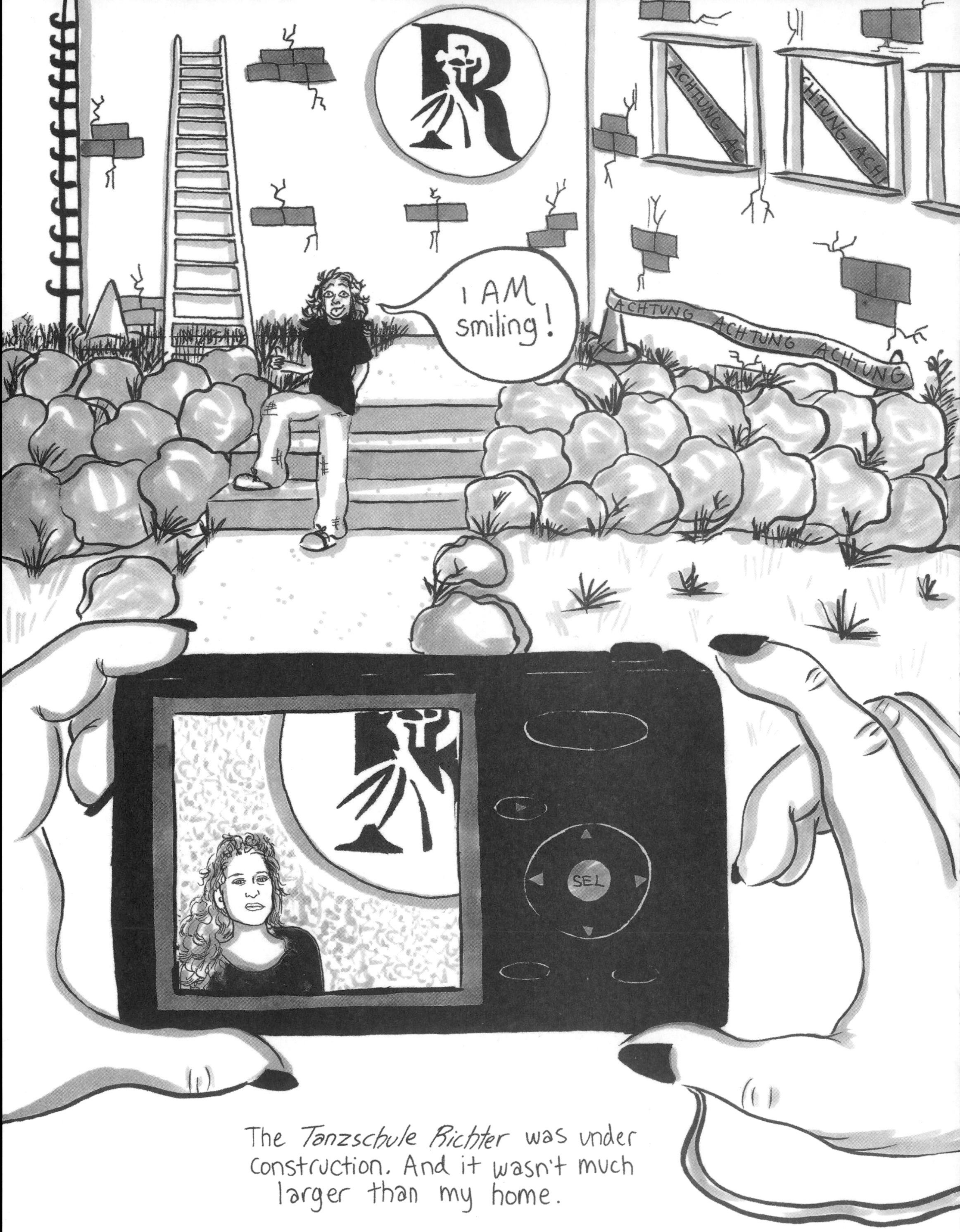
ACHTUNG
I AM smiling!
ACHTUNG ACHTUNG ACHTUNG
SEL
The *Tanzschule Richter* was under construction. And it wasn't much larger than my home.

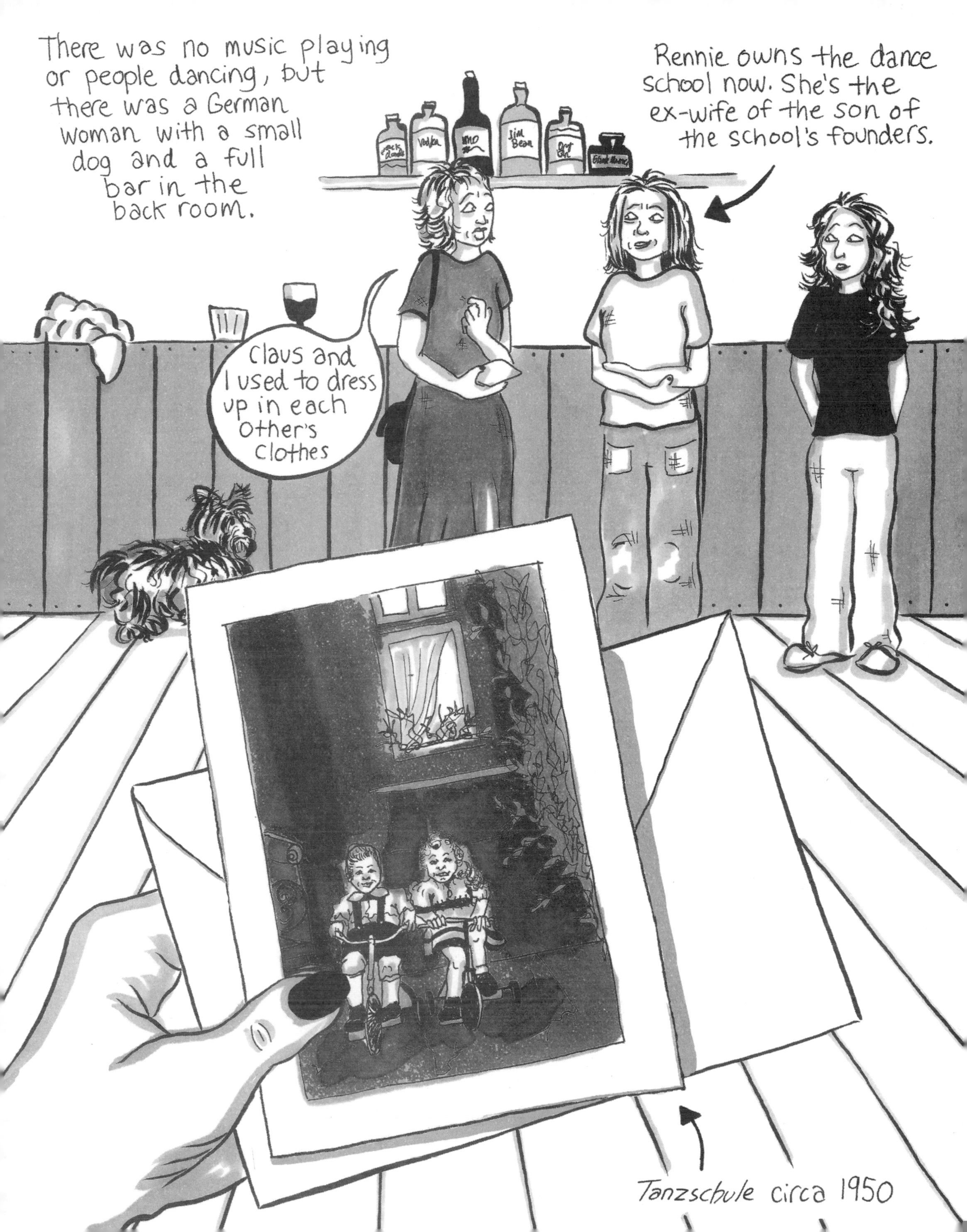
There was no music playing or people dancing, but there was a German woman with a small dog and a full bar in the back room.
Rennie owns the dance school now. She's the ex-wife of the son of the school's founders.
Claus and I used to dress up in each other's clothes
Tanzschule circa 1950

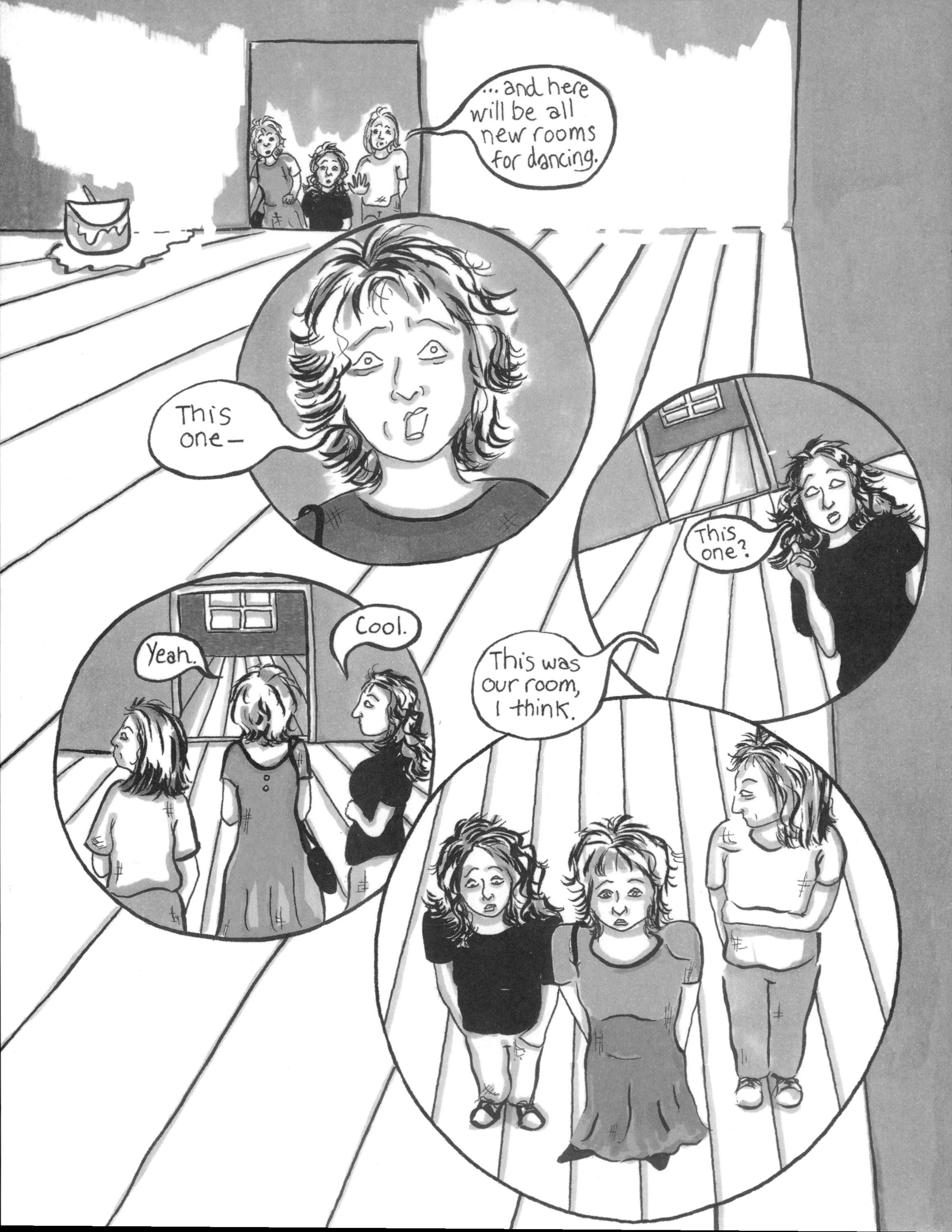
...and here will be all new rooms for dancing.
This one—
This one?
Yeah.
Cool.
This was our room, I think.

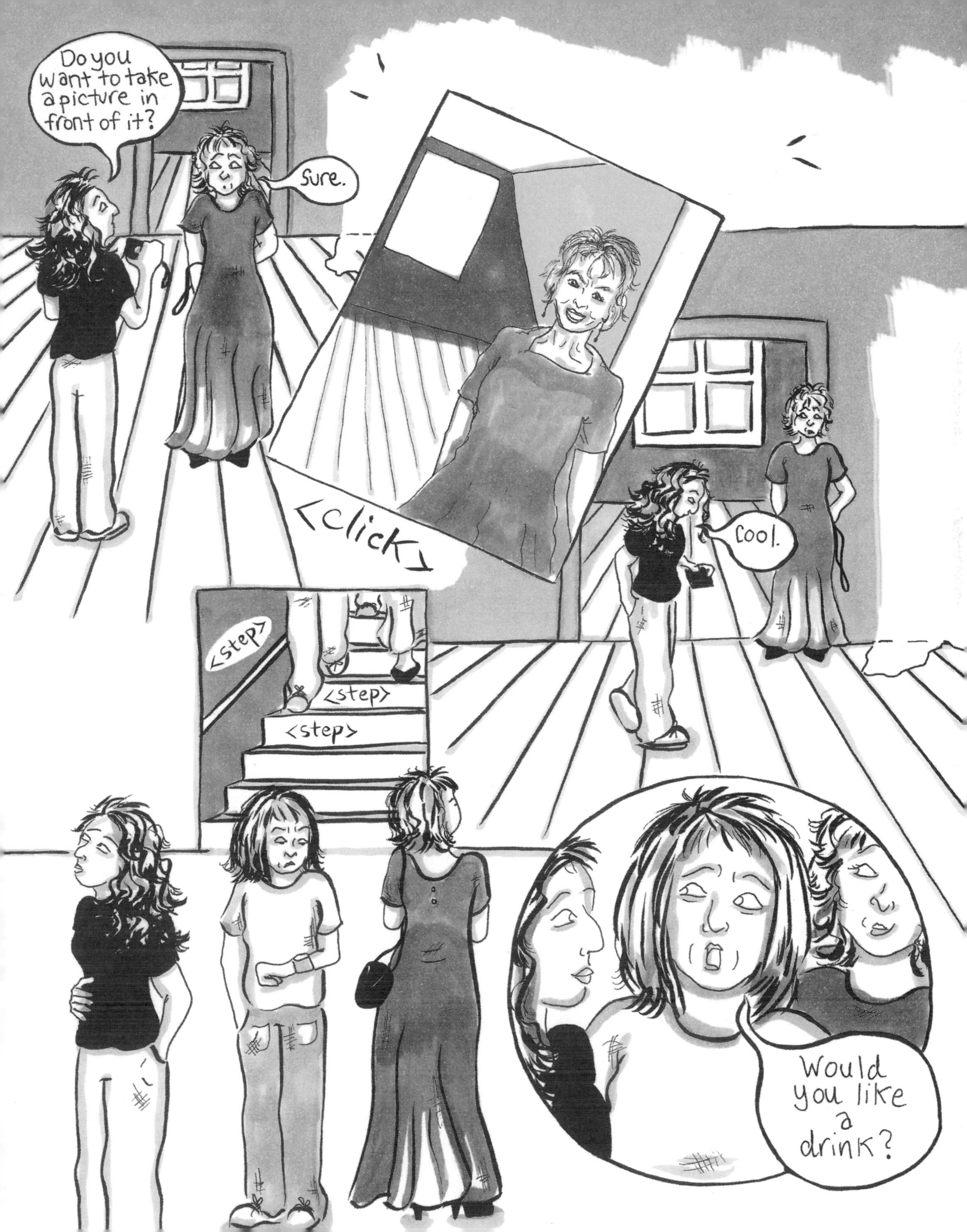
Do you want to take a picture in front of it?
Sure.
<click>
Cool.
<step>
<step>
<step>
Would you like a drink?

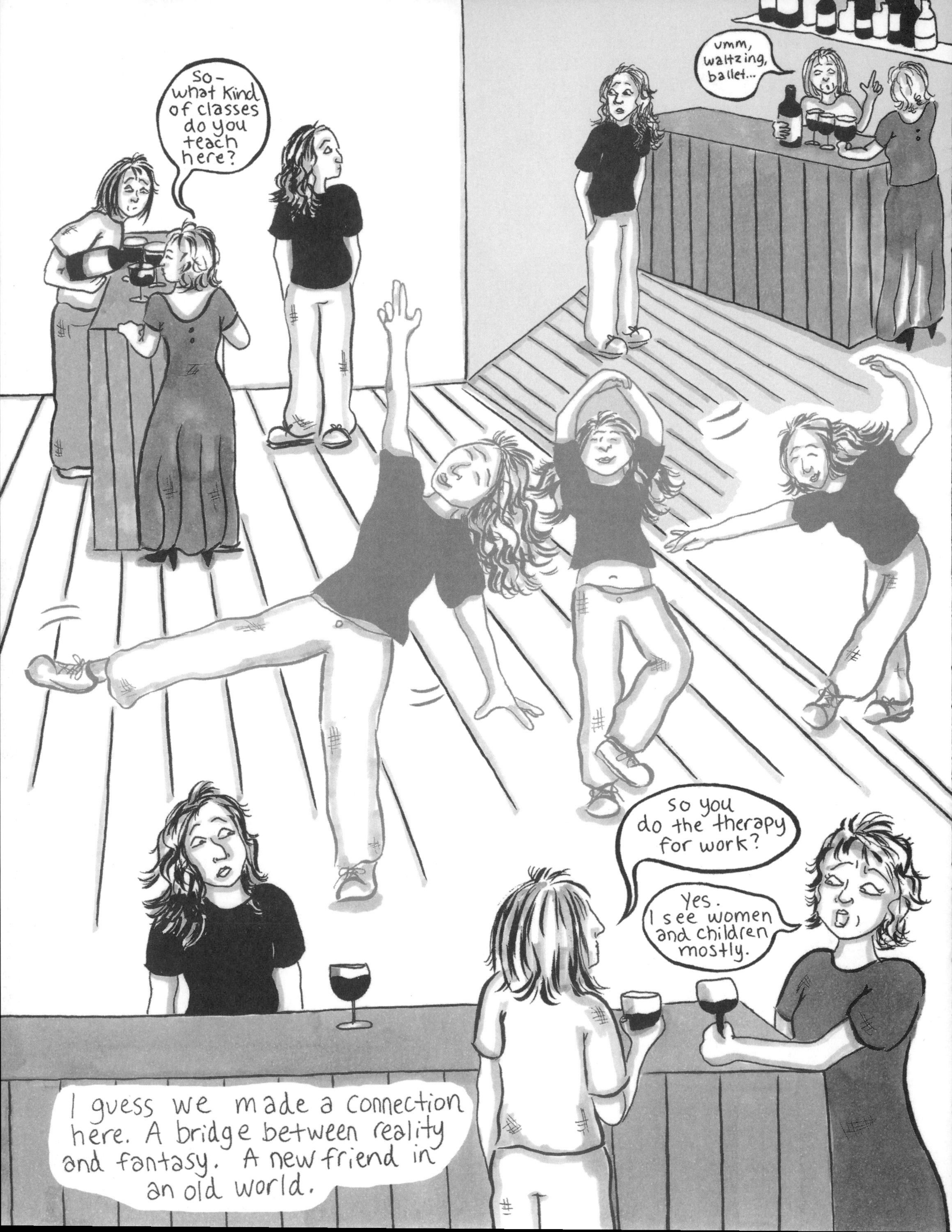
So- what kind of classes do you teach here?
umm, waltzing, ballet...
so you do the therapy for work?
Yes. I see women and children mostly.
I guess we made a connection here. A bridge between reality and fantasy. A new friend in an old world.

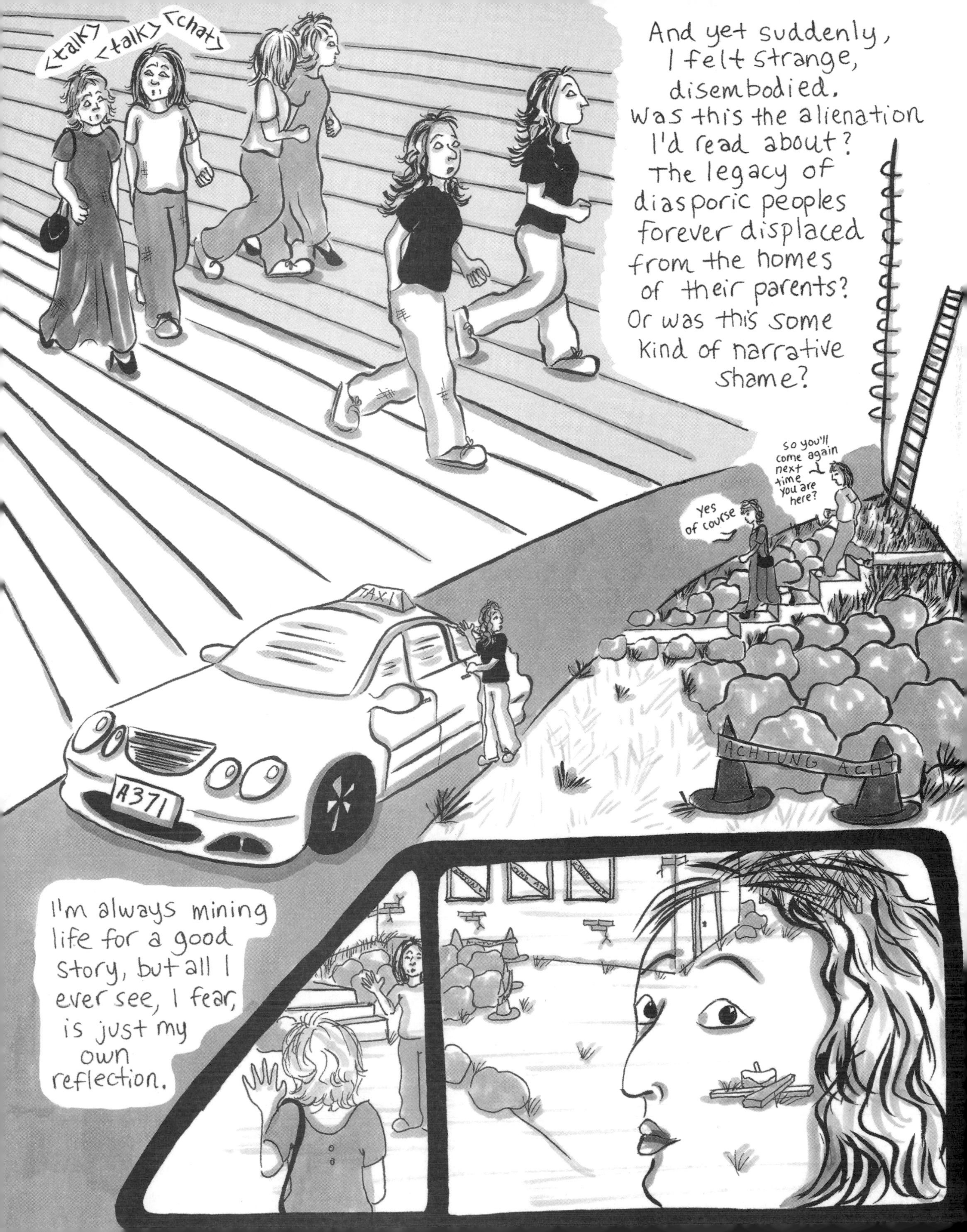
<talk>
<talk>
<chat>
And yet suddenly, I felt strange, disembodied. Was this the alienation I'd read about? The legacy of diasporic peoples forever displaced from the homes of their parents? Or was this some kind of narrative shame?
so you'll come again next time you are here?
Yes of course
TAXI
A371
ACHTUNG ACHT
I'm always mining life for a good story, but all I ever see, I fear, is just my own reflection.

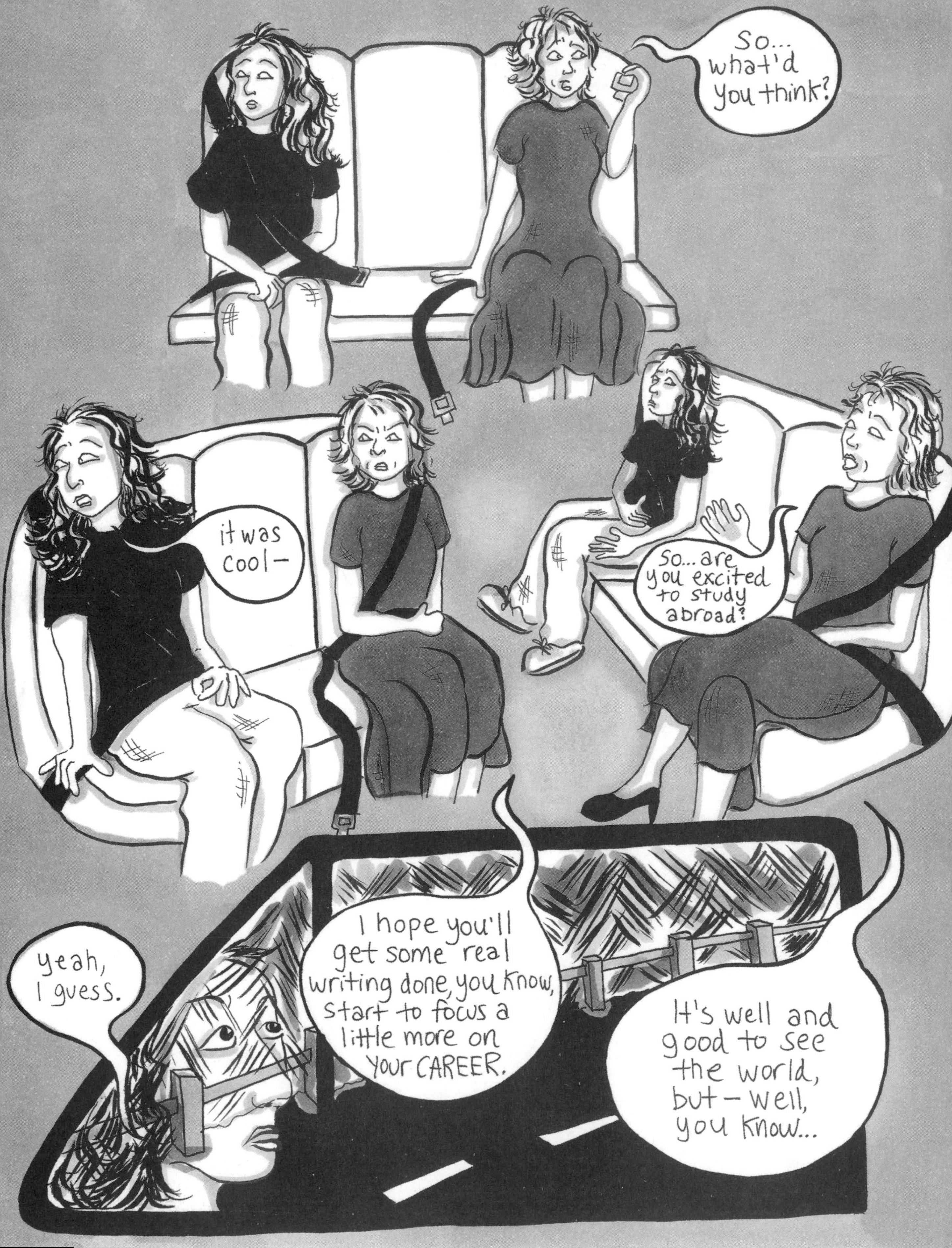
So...
what'd
you think?
it was
cool—
So... are
you excited
to study
abroad?
yeah,
I guess.
I hope you'll
get some real
writing done, you know,
start to focus a
little more on
your CAREER.
It's well and
good to see
the world,
but—well,
you know...

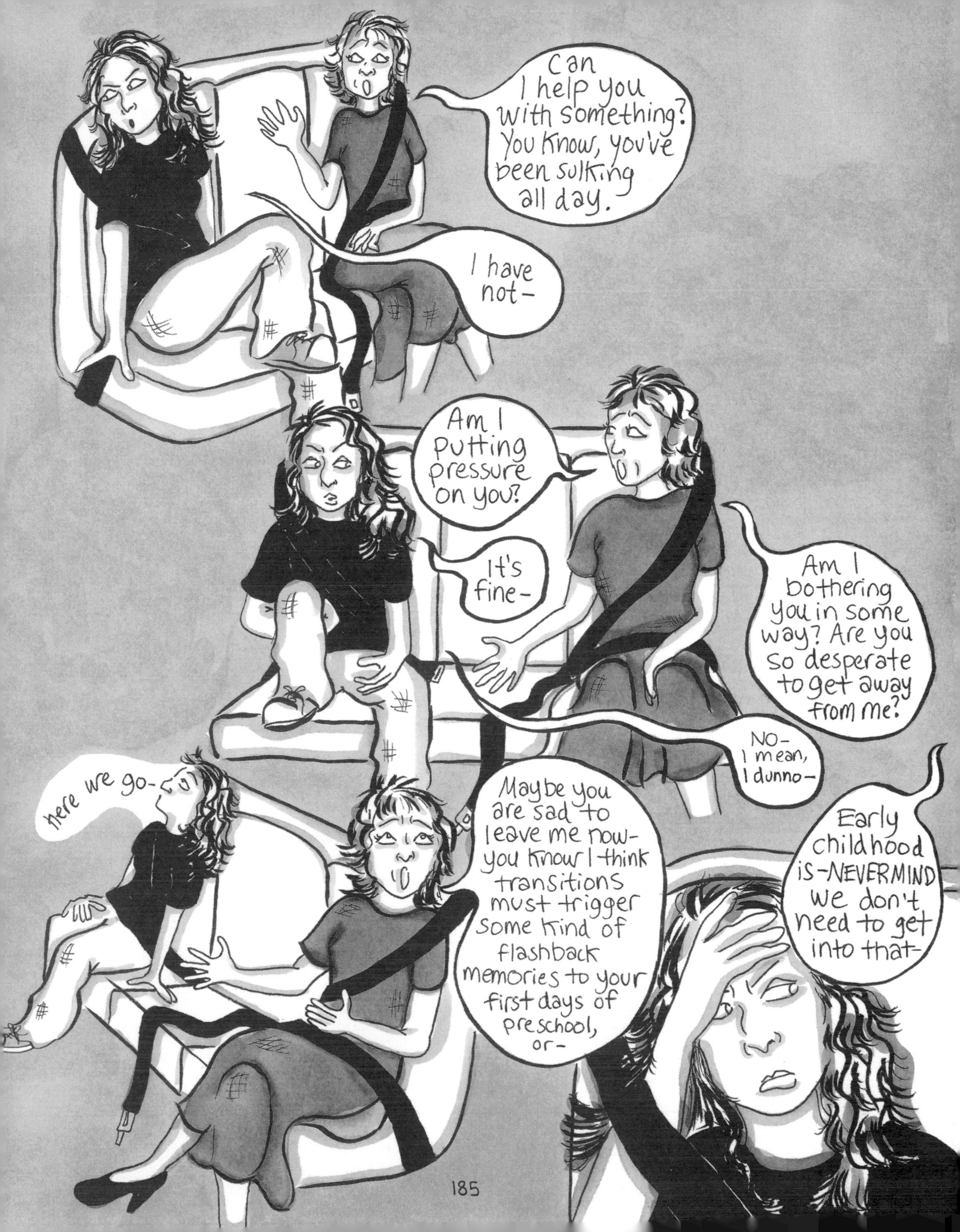
Can I help you with something? You know, you've been sulking all day.
I have not-
Am I putting pressure on you?
It's fine-
Am I bothering you in some way? Are you so desperate to get away from me?
No- I mean, I dunno-
Here we go-
Maybe you are sad to leave me now- you know I think transitions must trigger some kind of flashback memories to your first days of preschool, or-
Early childhood is-NEVERMIND we don't need to get into that-

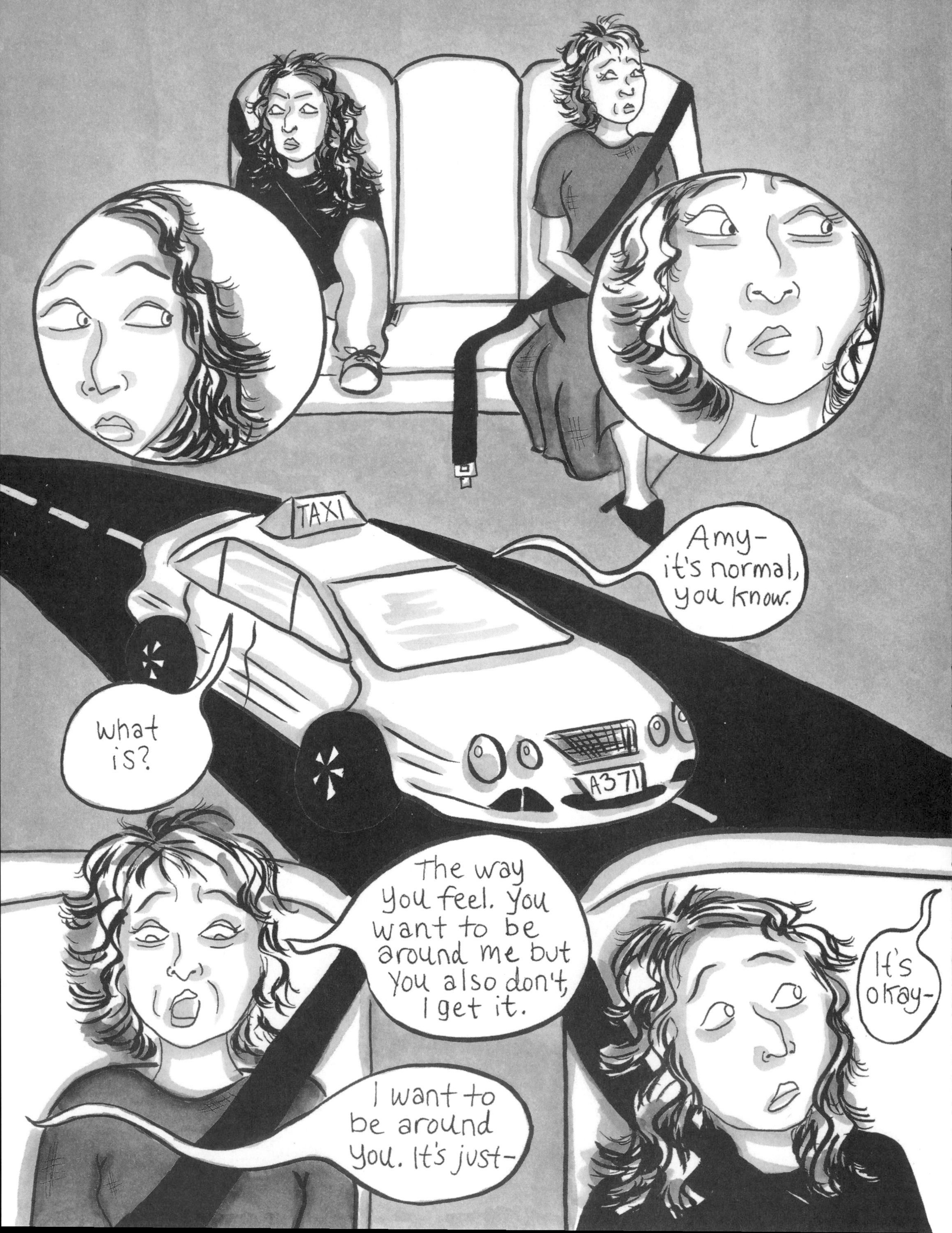
TAXI
Amy- it's normal, you know.
what is?
A371
The way you feel. You want to be around me but you also don't, I get it.
It's okay-
I want to be around you. It's just-

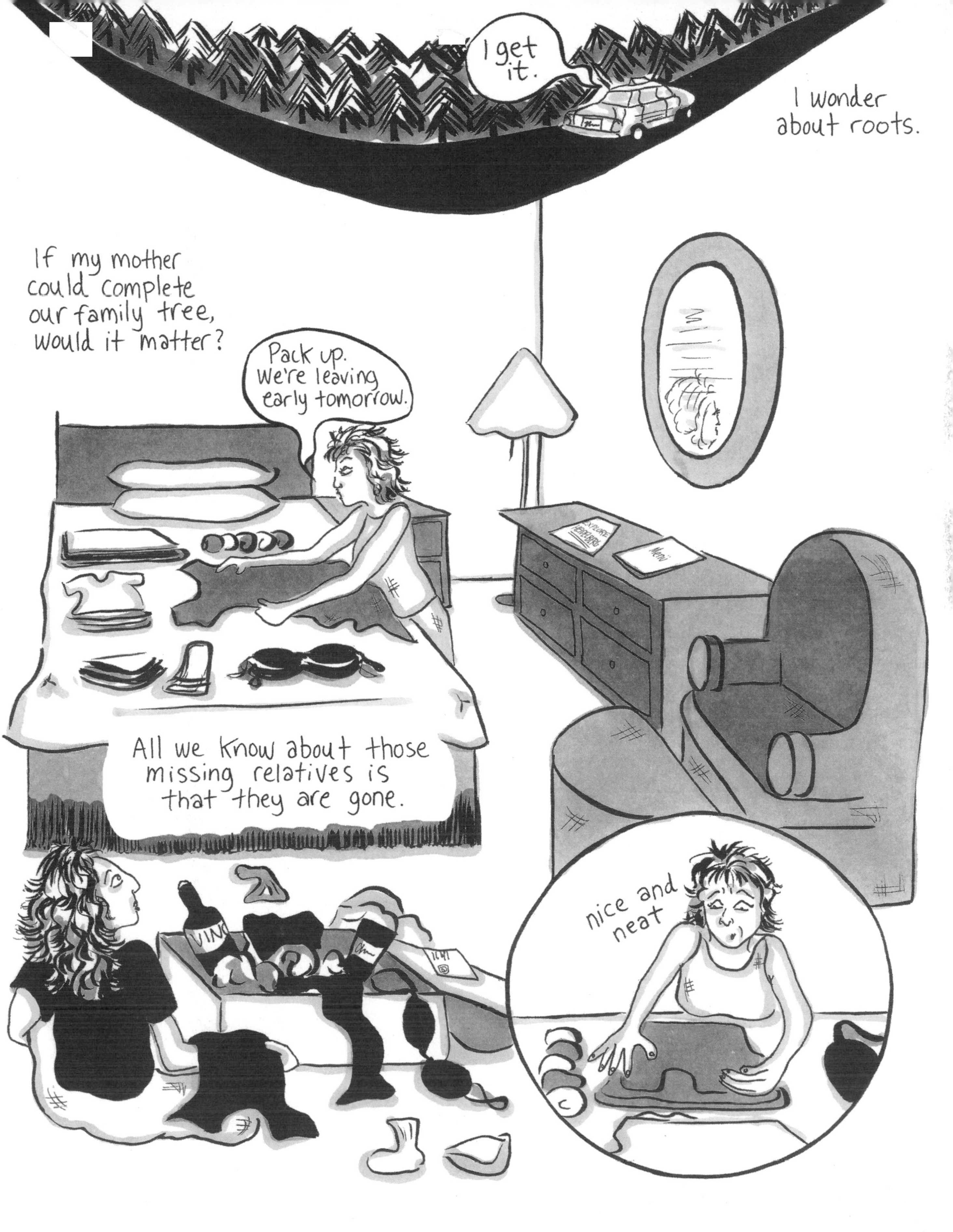
I get it.
I wonder about roots.
If my mother could complete our family tree, would it matter?
Pack up. We're leaving early tomorrow.
All we know about those missing relatives is that they are gone.
nice and neat

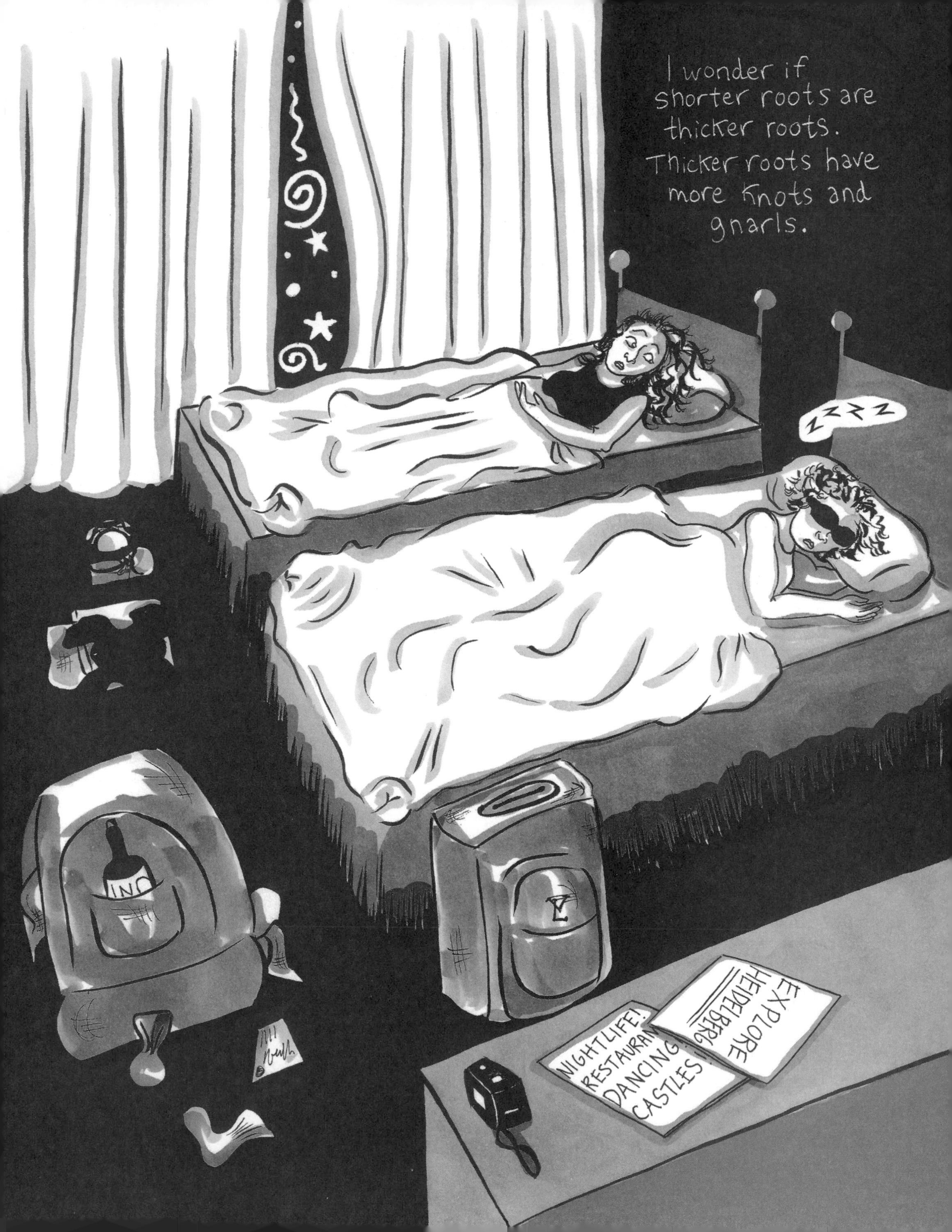
I wonder if shorter roots are thicker roots. Thicker roots have more knots and gnarls.
ZZZZ
EXPLORE HEIDELBERG
NIGHTLIFE!
RESTAURAN
DANCING.
CASTLES!

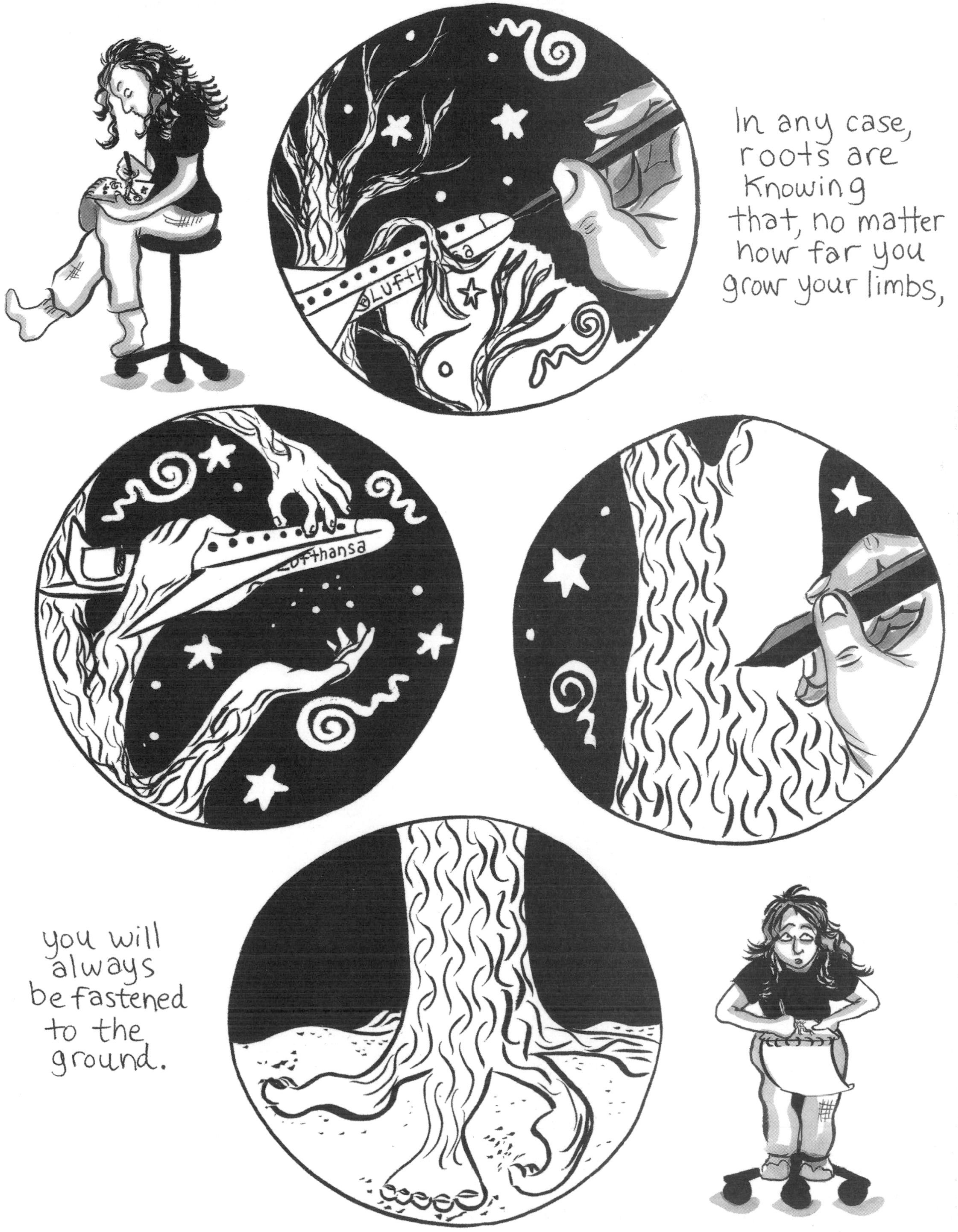
In any case, roots are Knowing that, no matter how far you grow your limbs,
Lufthansa
you will always be fastened to the ground.

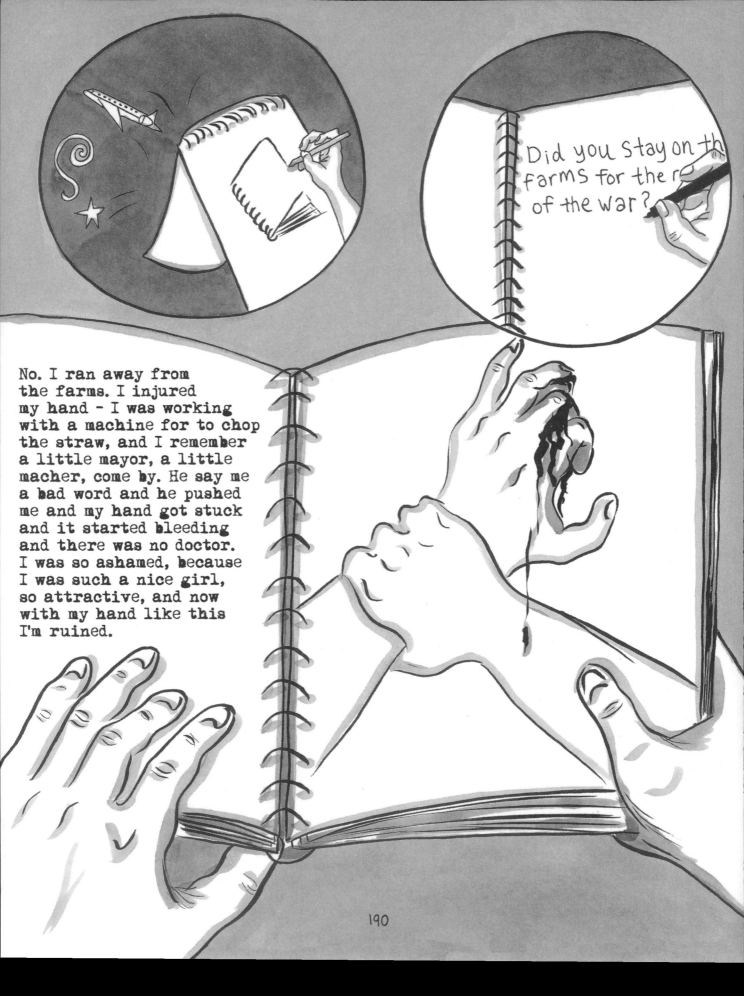

No. I ran away from the farms. I injured my hand - I was working with a machine for to chop the straw, and I remember a little mayor, a little macher, come by. He say me a bad word and he pushed me and my hand got stuck and it started bleeding and there was no doctor. I was so ashamed, because I was such a nice girl, so attractive, and now with my hand like this I'm ruined.

Did you stay on the farms for the r of the war?

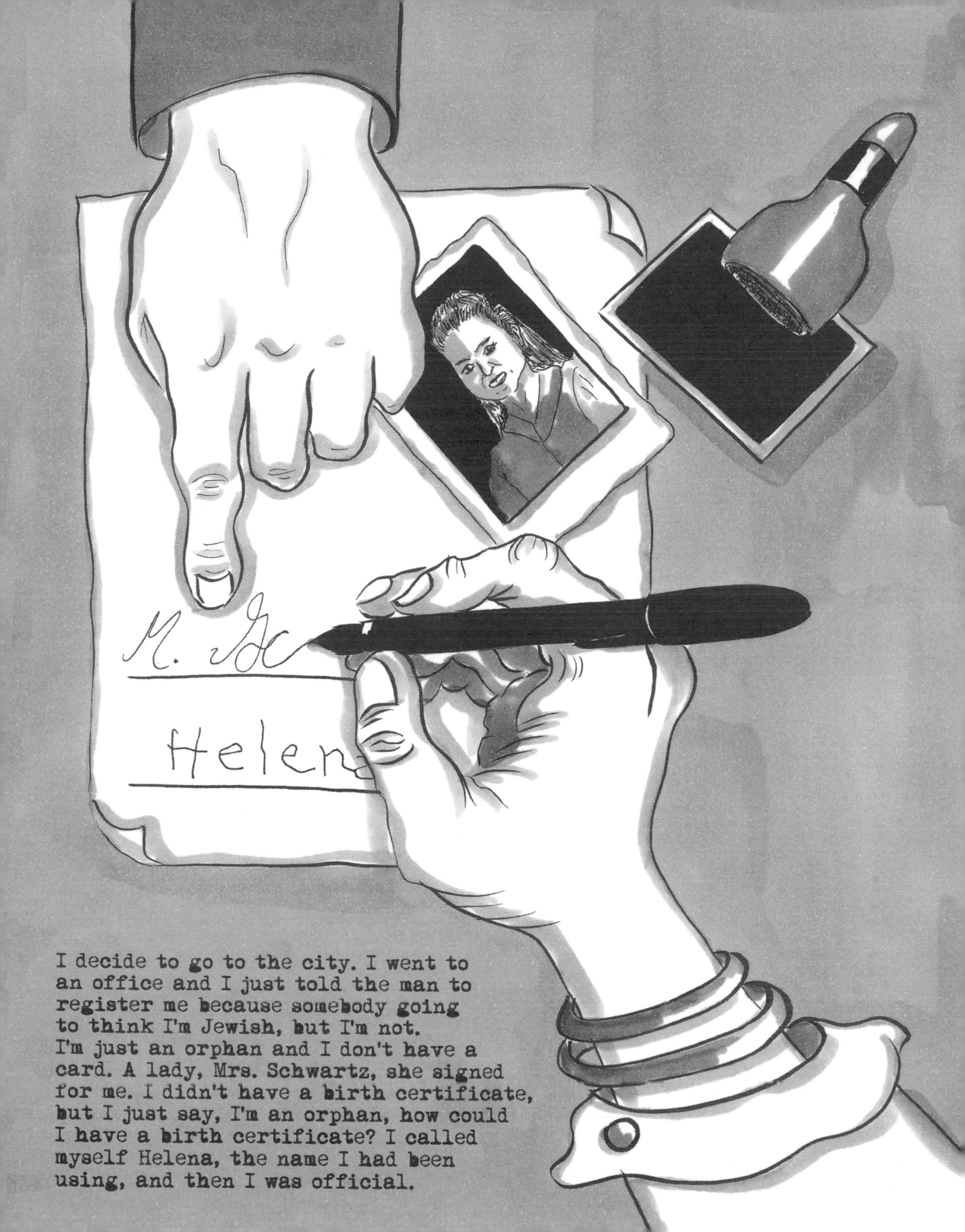
I decide to go to the city. I went to an office and I just told the man to register me because somebody going to think I'm Jewish, but I'm not. I'm just an orphan and I don't have a card. A lady, Mrs. Schwartz, she signed for me. I didn't have a birth certificate, but I just say, I'm an orphan, how could I have a birth certificate? I called myself Helena, the name I had been using, and then I was official.

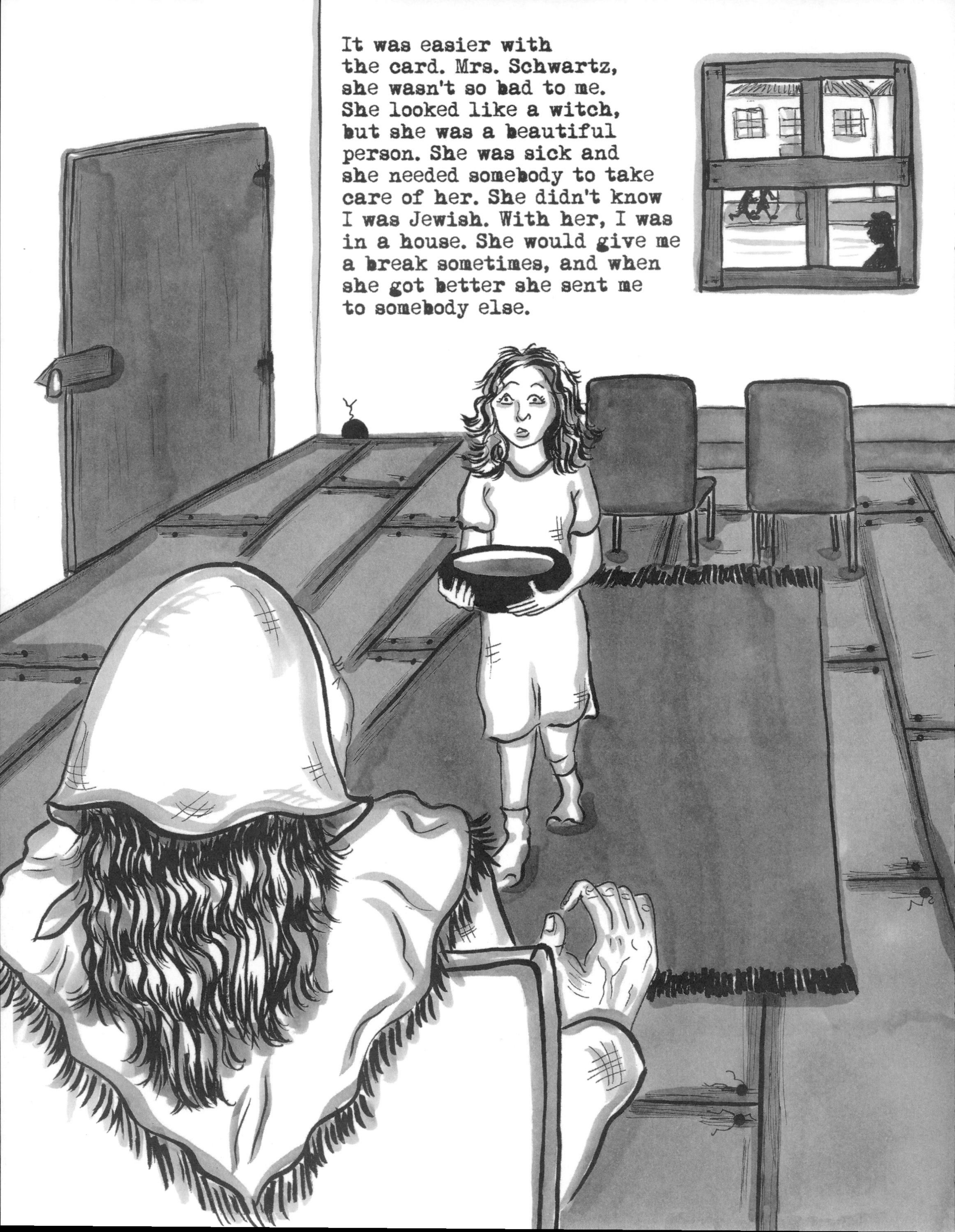
It was easier with the card. Mrs. Schwartz, she wasn't so bad to me. She looked like a witch, but she was a beautiful person. She was sick and she needed somebody to take care of her. She didn't know I was Jewish. With her, I was in a house. She would give me a break sometimes, and when she got better she sent me to somebody else.

Sometimes in the city, I would go to the place
where they kept the woods, the logs for heat,
because they didn't have electricity where I
was then. I would go to this place which was
dark and I'd be alone gathering the woods,
and I'd say to myself, What am I? Do I still
speak Jewish? And I would try to say a little
bit of Yiddish words to myself, but I was so
scared. I couldn't do it. Even all alone like
that, they were locked up inside me.

I didn't think the Jews existed anymore.
I thought, I'm the only one.

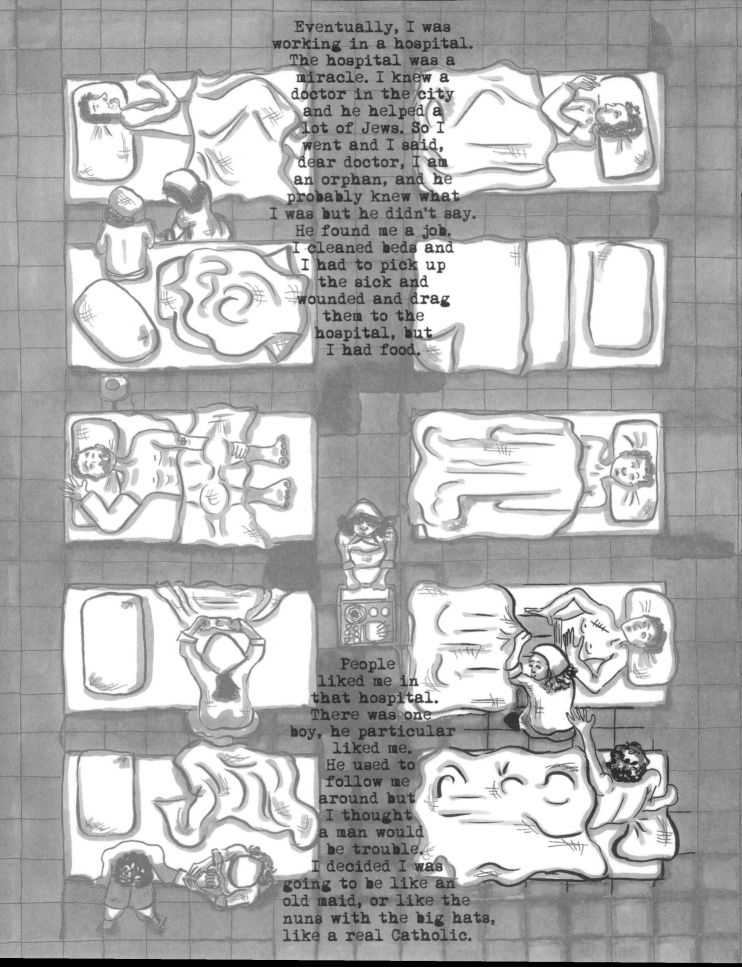

Eventually, I was working in a hospital. The hospital was a miracle. I knew a doctor in the city and he helped a lot of Jews. So I went and I said, dear doctor, I am an orphan, and he probably knew what I was but he didn't say. He found me a job. I cleaned beds and I had to pick up the sick and wounded and drag them to the hospital, but I had food.

People liked me in that hospital. There was one boy, he particular liked me. He used to follow me around but I thought a man would be trouble. I decided I was going to be like an old maid, or like the nuns with the big hats, like a real Catholic.

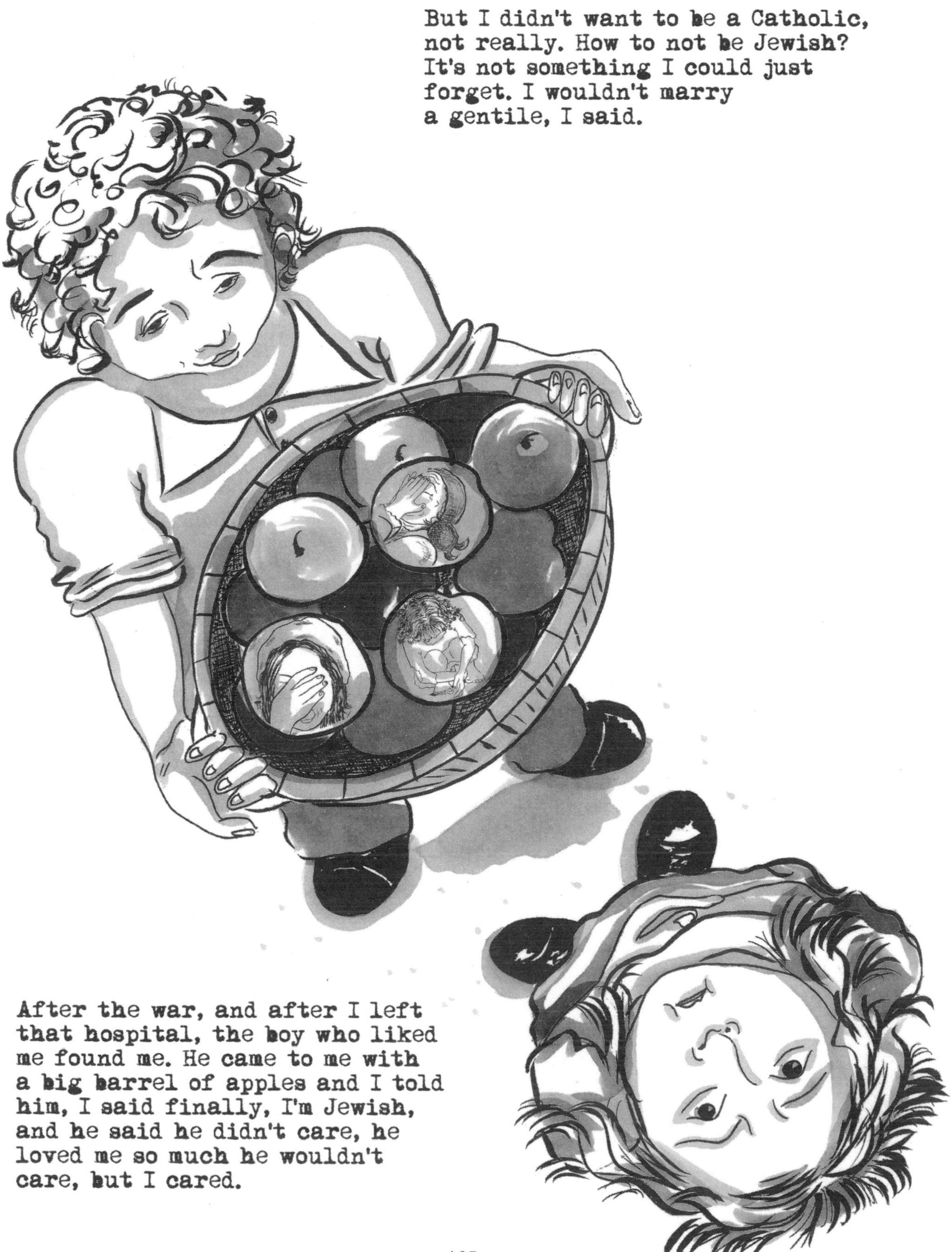
But I didn't want to be a Catholic, not really. How to not be Jewish? It's not something I could just forget. I wouldn't marry a gentile, I said.
After the war, and after I left that hospital, the boy who liked me found me. He came to me with a big barrel of apples and I told him, I said finally, I'm Jewish, and he said he didn't care, he loved me so much he wouldn't care, but I cared.

We didn't have no newspaper, no nothing, but I knew the war
was over when I seen sad German soldiers, German soldiers
walking around with no boots - when the Russians got a hold
of the Germans they say a bad curse word and take their boots.
Imagine, the German soldier used to be big, so powerful, gonna
eat up the whole world they thought. Now they walking around
without boots. It's crazy, but I felt pity for them.

What they did to you, the pain in your heart so deep. They took
away everything, but when you see a person walking around
with no boots, you feel bad, you feel sorry for them.

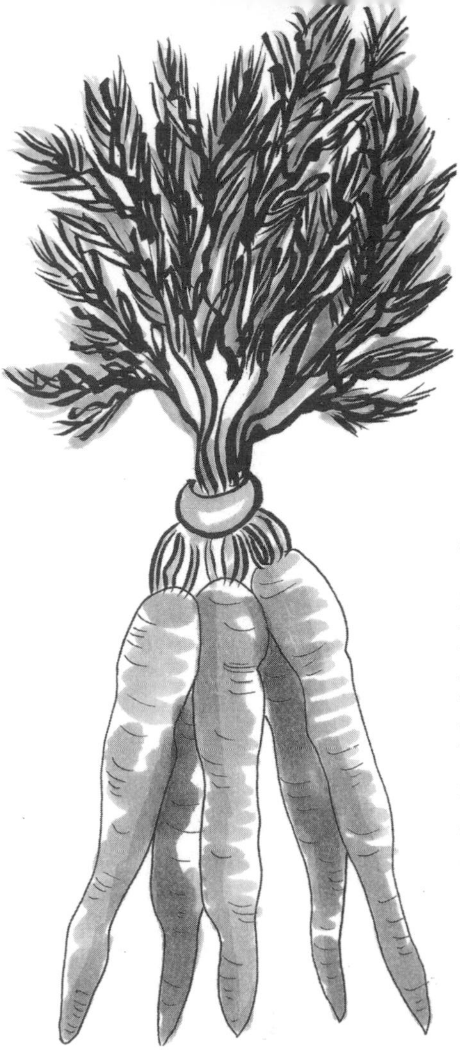

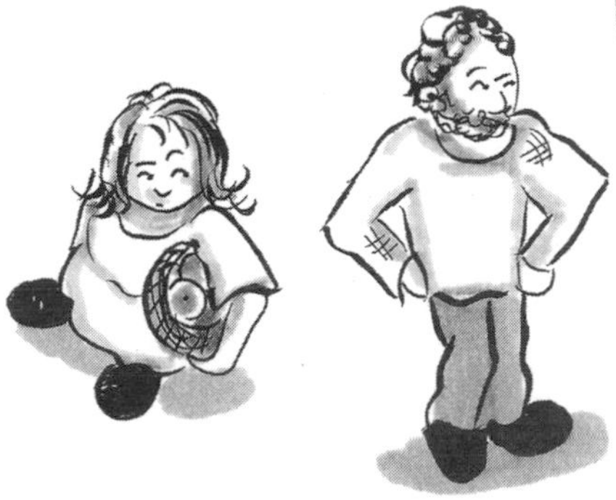

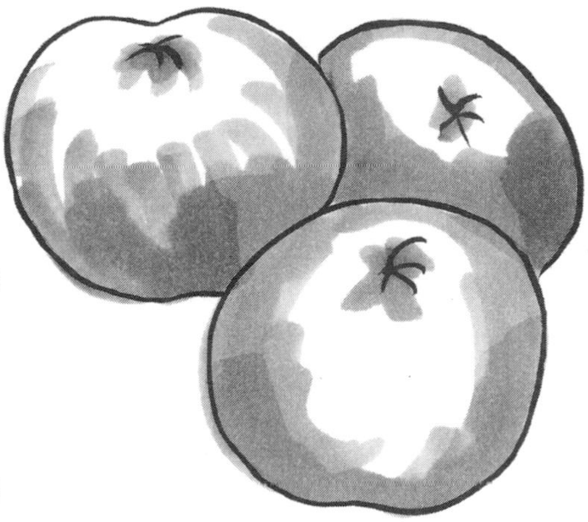

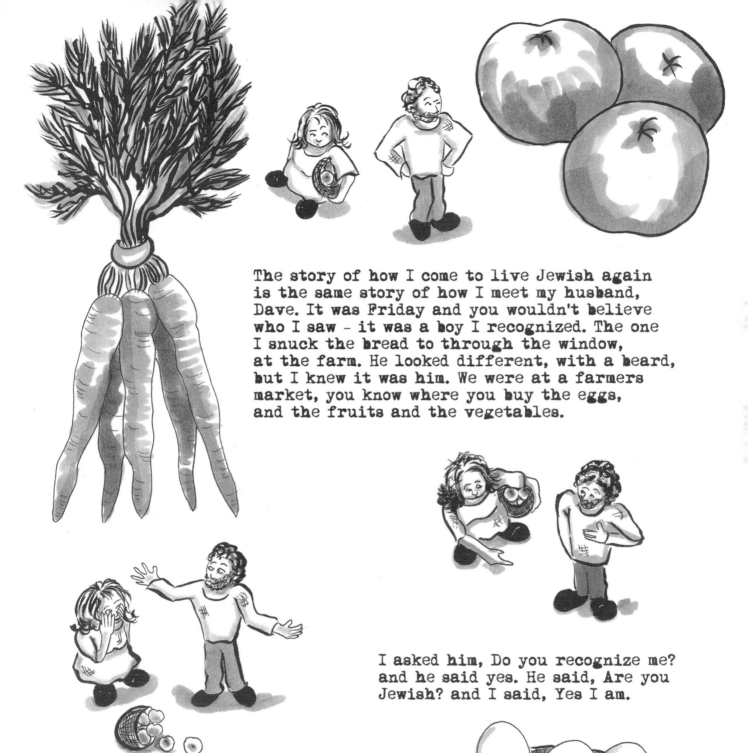

The story of how I come to live Jewish again is the same story of how I meet my husband, Dave. It was Friday and you wouldn't believe who I saw - it was a boy I recognized. The one I snuck the bread to through the window, at the farm. He looked different, with a beard, but I knew it was him. We were at a farmers market, you know where you buy the eggs, and the fruits and the vegetables.

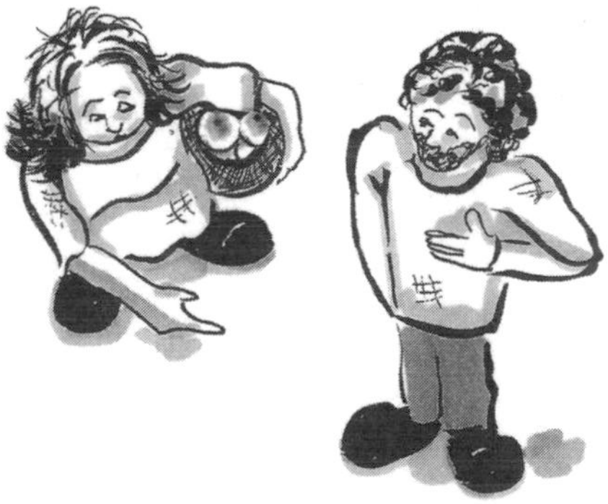

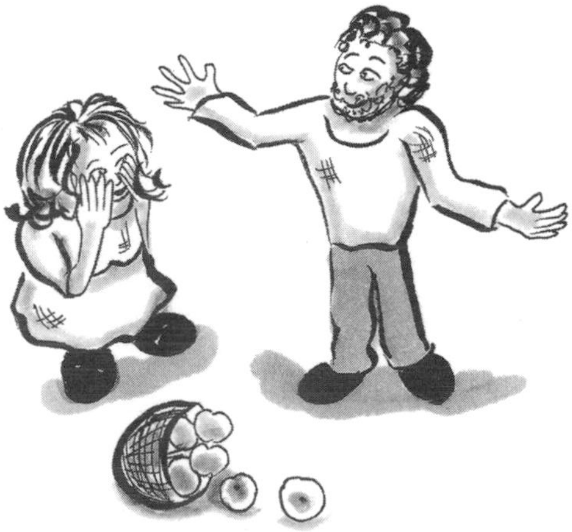

I asked him, Do you recognize me? and he said yes. He said, Are you Jewish? and I said, Yes I am.

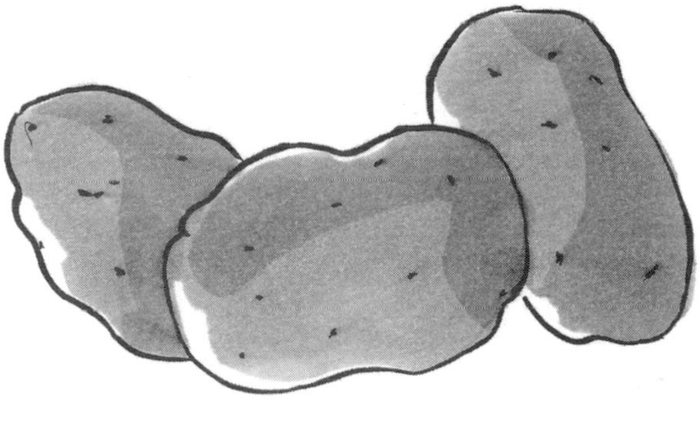

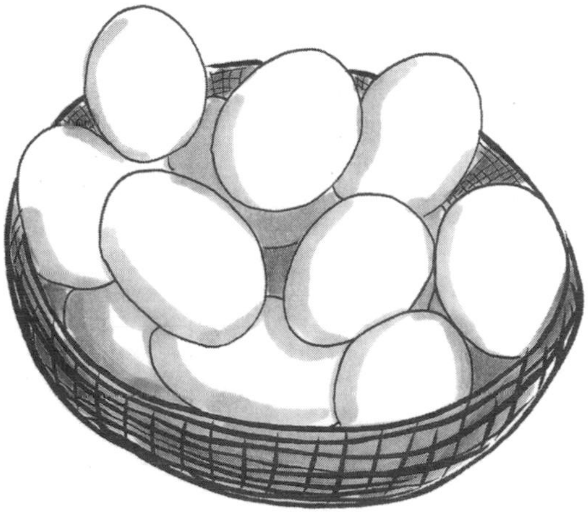

He brought me to a little house. There were eight or nine families there, laying on the straw, single men too, including Dave. There was no furniture and everybody looked yellow. I seen candles and I started crying. My first Shabbat again. I hadn't seen those candles for four years.

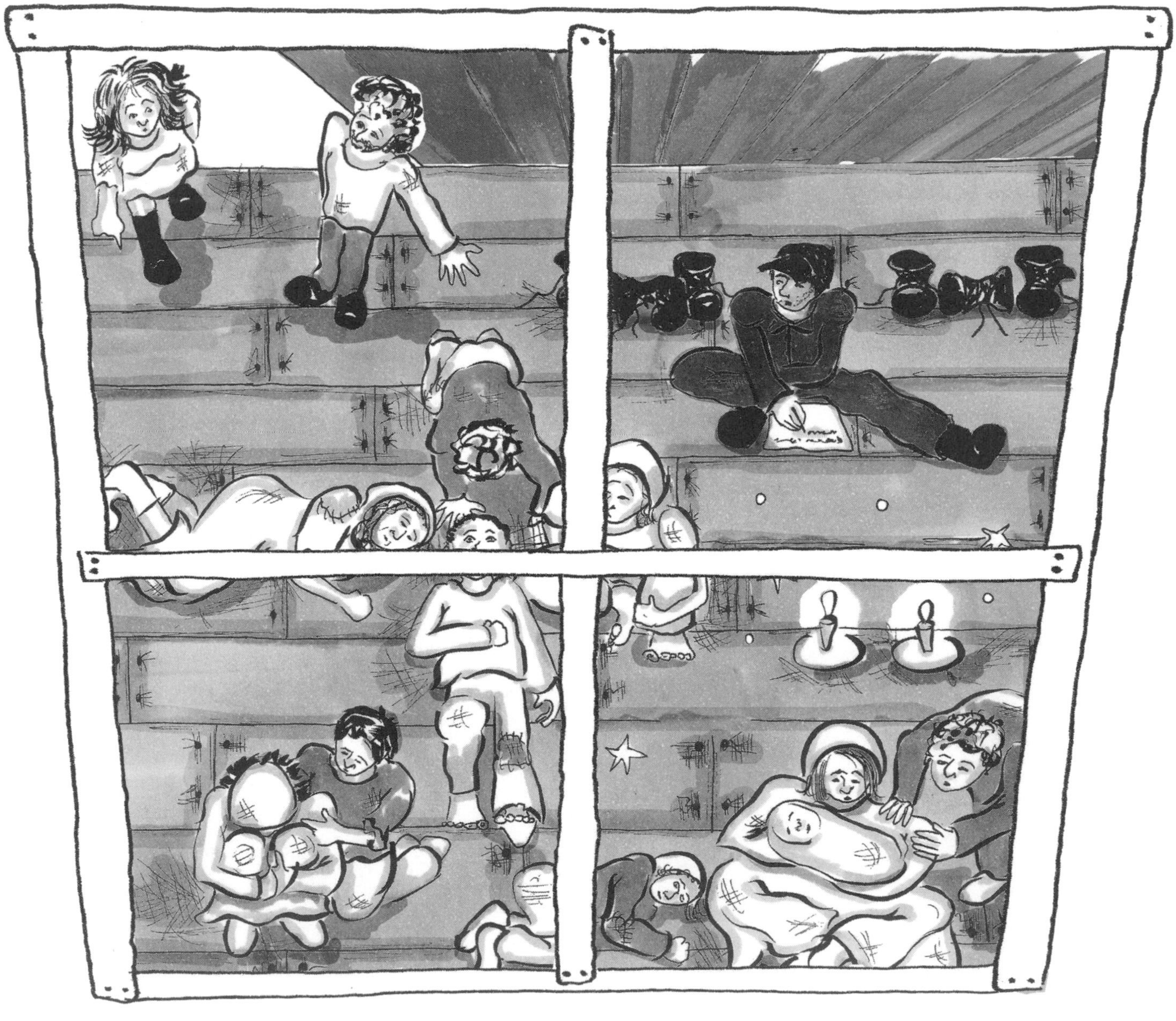

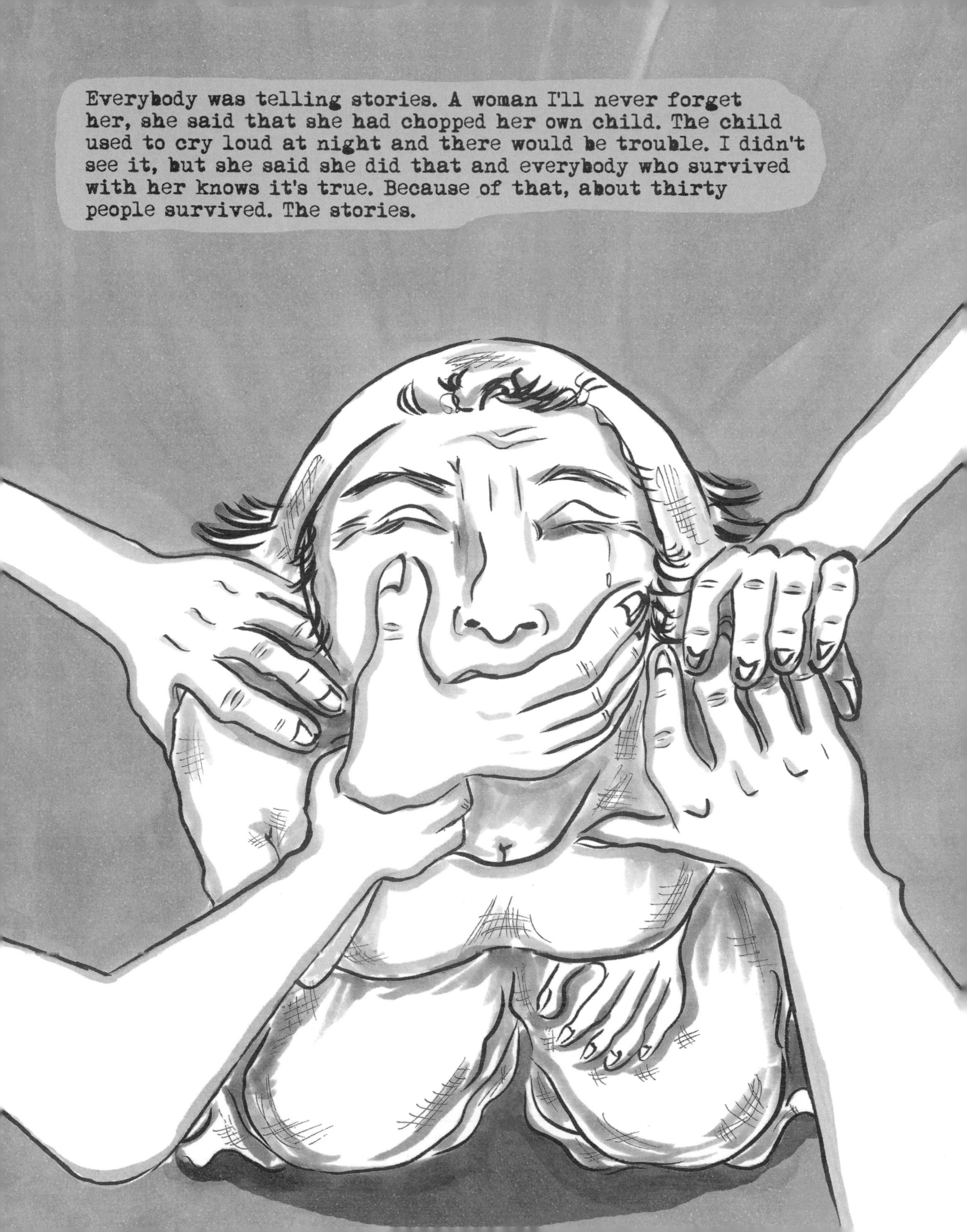
Everybody was telling stories. A woman I'll never forget her, she said that she had chopped her own child. The child used to cry loud at night and there would be trouble. I didn't see it, but she said she did that and everybody who survived with her knows it's true. Because of that, about thirty people survived. The stories.

I thought I wouldn't
touch a man, like I said.
But Dave was a beautiful
man, with a Jewish face,
blue eyes and such a sad
look. He was wearing a
uniform and he had such
nice handwriting.

Szanowa Luba!

Zauważyłem cię dzisiaj smutny

Mam nadzieję, że nie rozpaczysz

Wojna się skończyła, i my odbudujemy

Wiele możemy zrobić, aby zapewni

przetrwanie. Widzę że jesteś silna. Poznaję

że jesteś bardzo miła. Być może będziemy

mogli spędzić więcej czasu razem i

razem spojrzeć w przyszłość.

Twój,
Dawid

I asked the boy from the market
about Dave. He said they survived
together in the woods. And then
they was sent to the Army when
the Russians came. Now they were
in the city bringing people
and organizing.

It was 1945. I was nineteen years old. Six weeks. We got married!

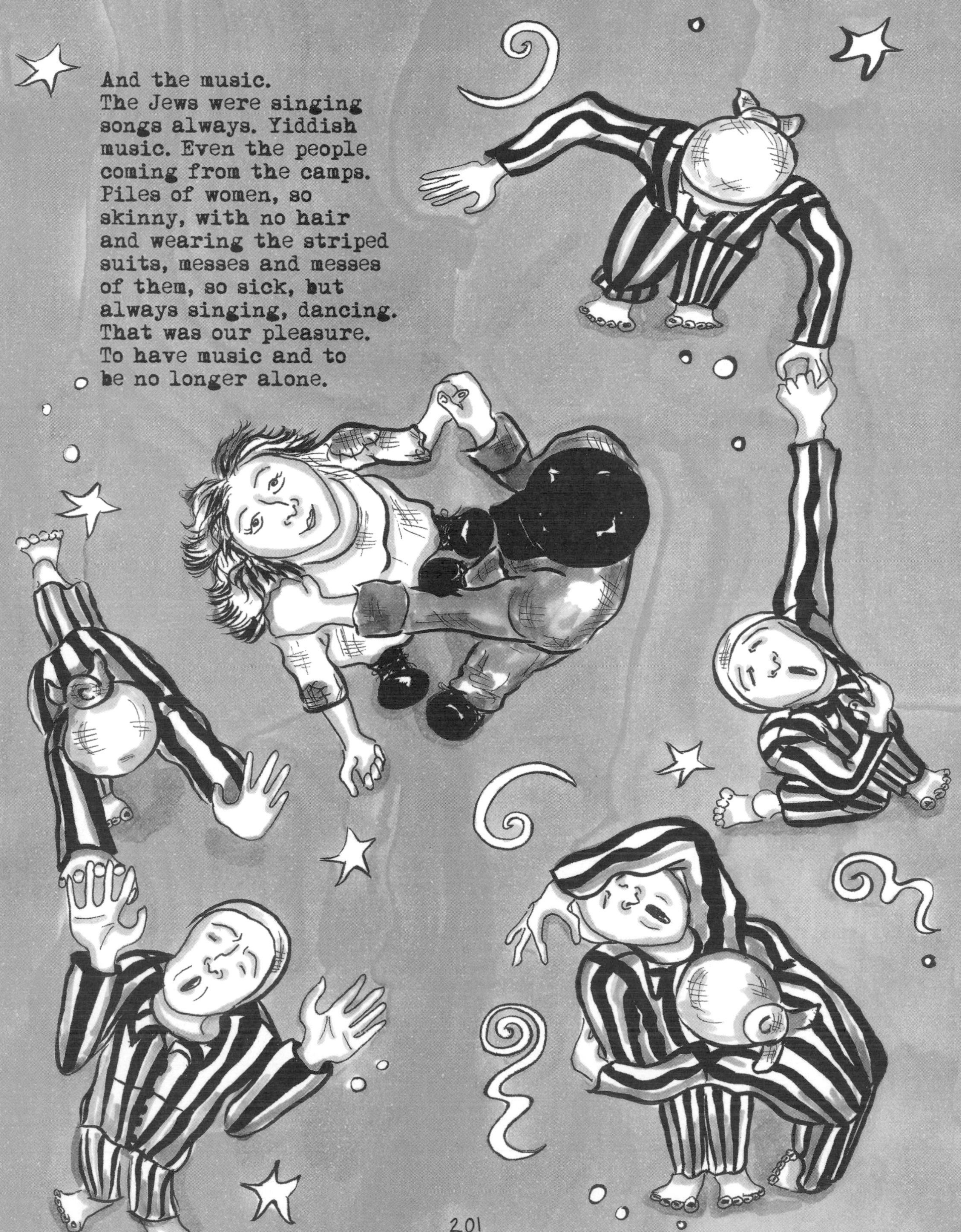
And the music.
The Jews were singing songs always. Yiddish music. Even the people coming from the camps. Piles of women, so skinny, with no hair and wearing the striped suits, messes and messes of them, so sick, but always singing, dancing. That was our pleasure. To have music and to be no longer alone.

chapter six:
Homecoming

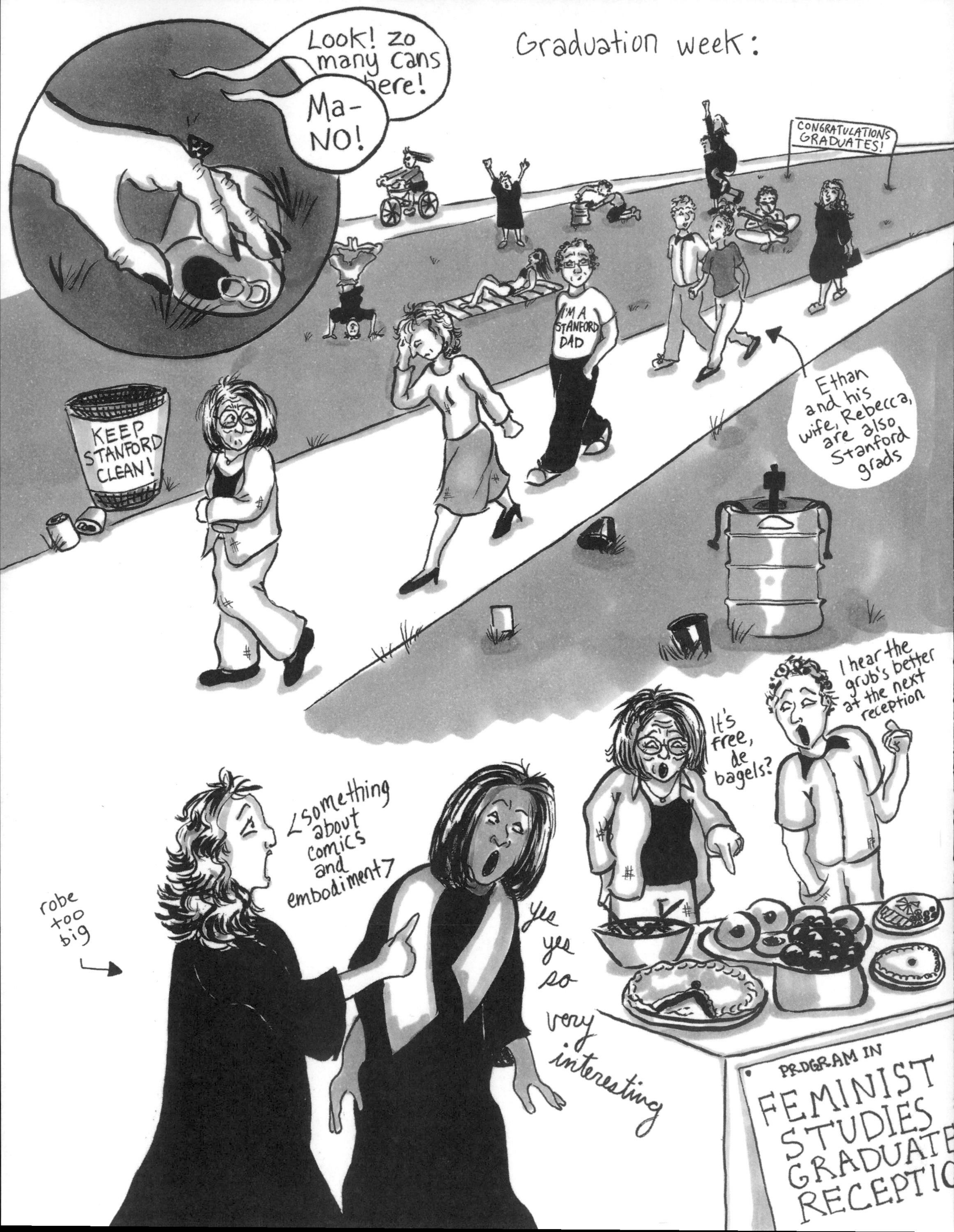
Graduation week:
Look! zo many cans here!
Ma- NO!
CONGRATULATIONS GRADUATES!
I'M A STANFORD DAD
KEEP STANFORD CLEAN!
Ethan and his wife, Rebecca, are also Stanford grads
I hear the grub's better at the next reception
It's free, de bagels?
<something about comics and embodiment>
robe too big
yes yes so very interesting
PROGRAM IN FEMINIST STUDIES GRADUATE RECEPTIO

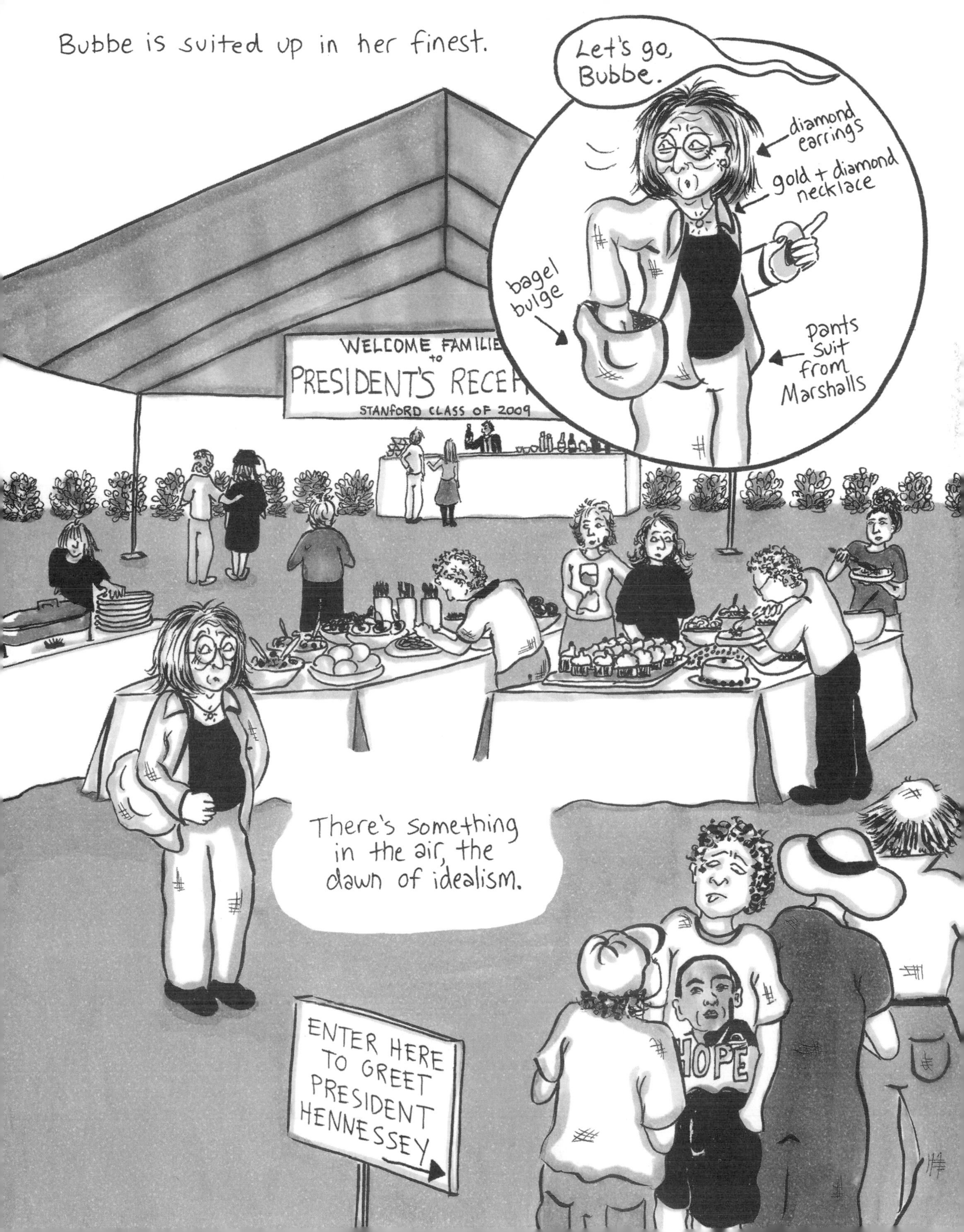
Bubbe is suited up in her finest.
Let's go, Bubbe.
diamond earrings
gold + diamond necklace
bagel bulge
Pants suit from Marshalls
WELCOME FAMILIE to PRESIDENT'S RECEP
STANFORD CLASS OF 2009
There's something in the air, the dawn of idealism.
ENTER HERE TO GREET PRESIDENT HENNESSEY
HOPE

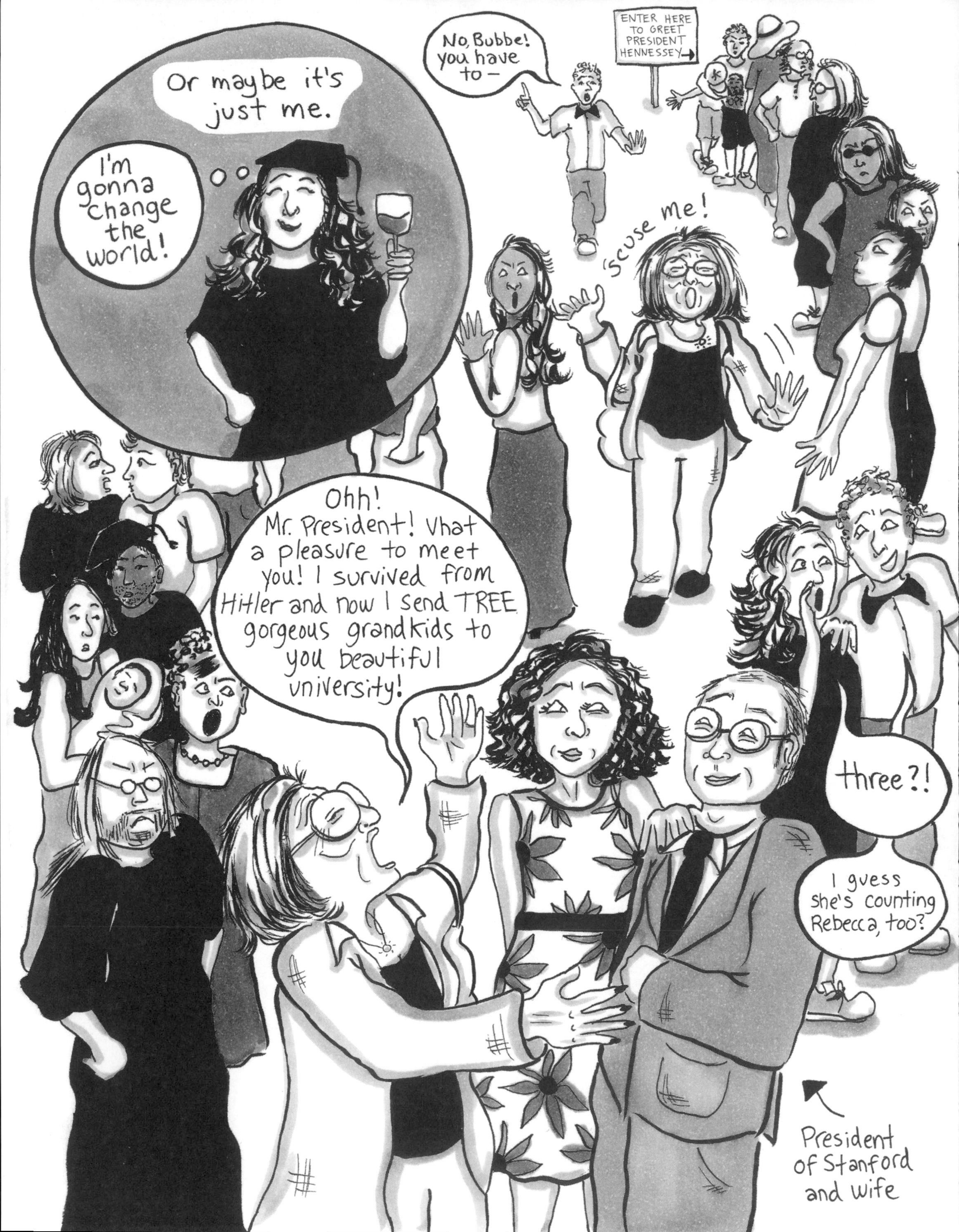

Or maybe it's just me.
I'm gonna change the world!
No, Bubbe! you have to—
ENTER HERE TO GREET PRESIDENT HENNESSEY→
'scuse me!
Ohh! Mr. President! Vhat a pleasure to meet you! I survived from Hitler and now I send TREE gorgeous grandkids to you beautiful university!
three?!
I guess she's counting Rebecca, too?
President of Stanford and wife

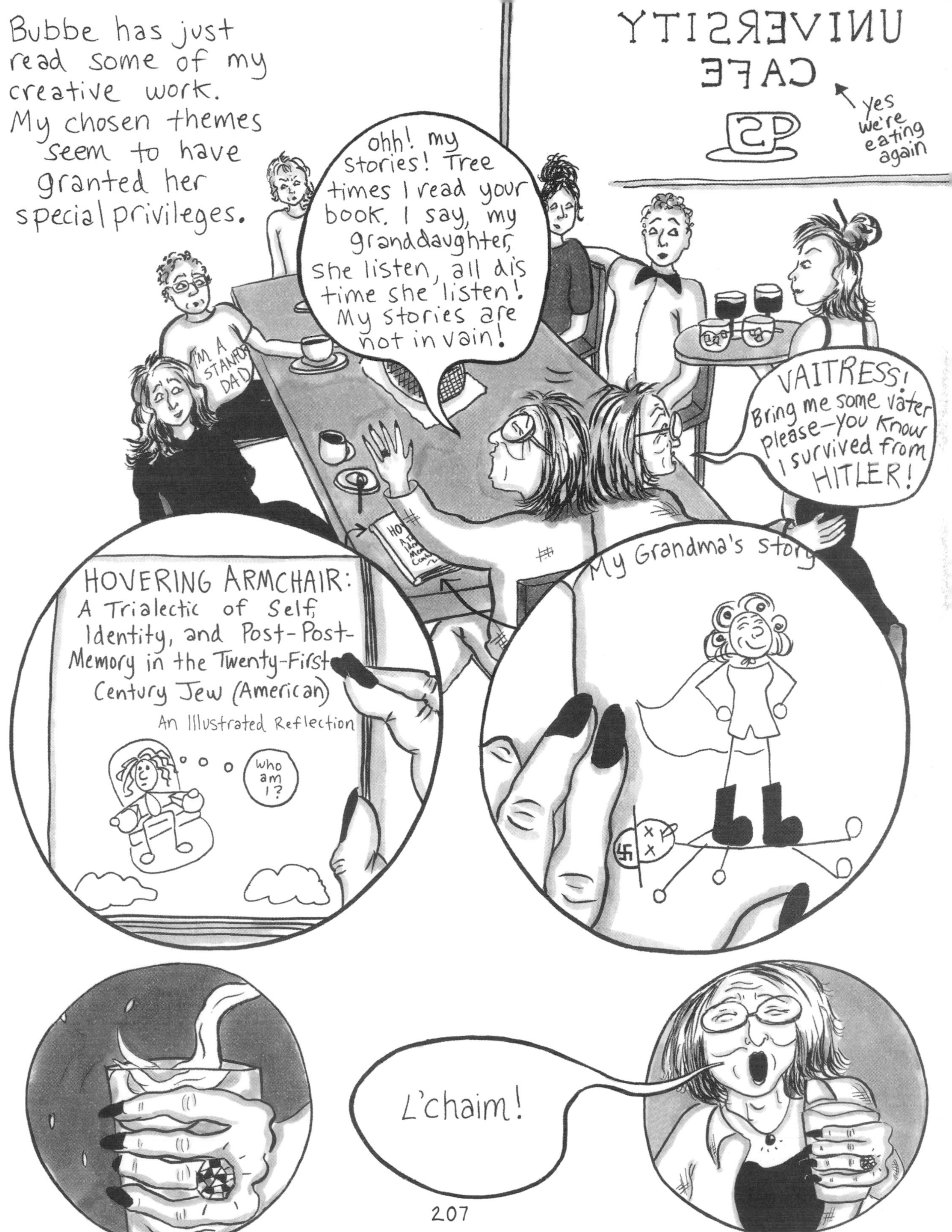

Bubbe has just read some of my creative work. My chosen themes seem to have granted her special privileges.
UNIVERSITY CAFE
yes we're eating again
ohh! my stories! Tree times I read your book. I say, my granddaughter, she listen, all dis time she listen! My stories are not in vain!
I'M A STANFORD DAD
VAITRESS! Bring me some vater please—you know I survived from HITLER!
HOVERING ARMCHAIR: A Trialectic of Self, Identity, and Post-Post-Memory in the Twenty-First Century Jew (American)
An Illustrated Reflection
who am I?
My Grandma's Story
L'chaim!

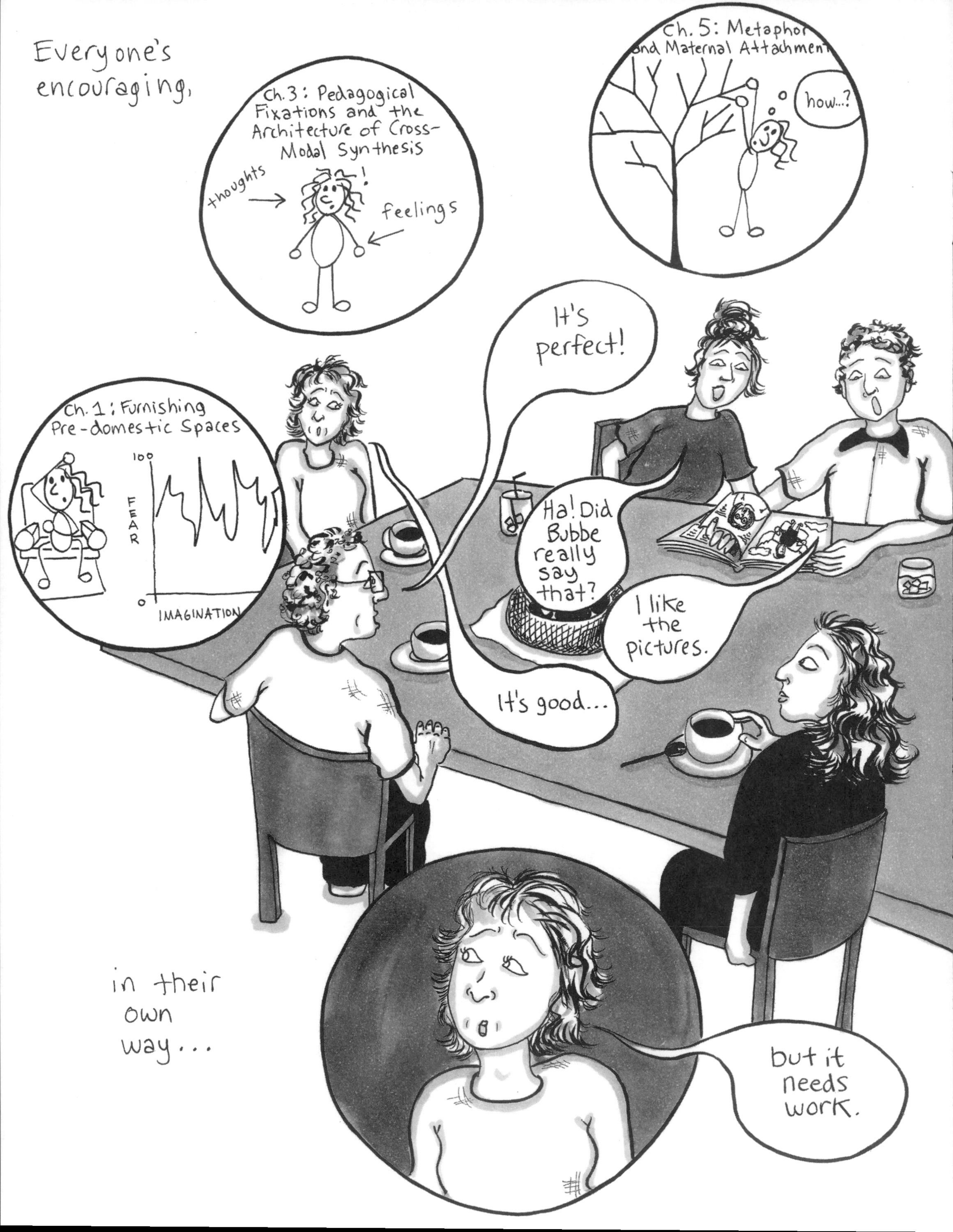
Everyone's encouraging,
Ch. 3: Pedagogical Fixations and the Architecture of Cross-Modal Synthesis
thoughts
feelings
!
Ch. 5: Metaphor and Maternal Attachment
how...?
Ch. 1: Furnishing Pre-domestic Spaces
100
FEAR
0
IMAGINATION
It's perfect!
Ha! Did Bubbe really say that?
I like the pictures.
It's good...
in their own way...
but it needs work.

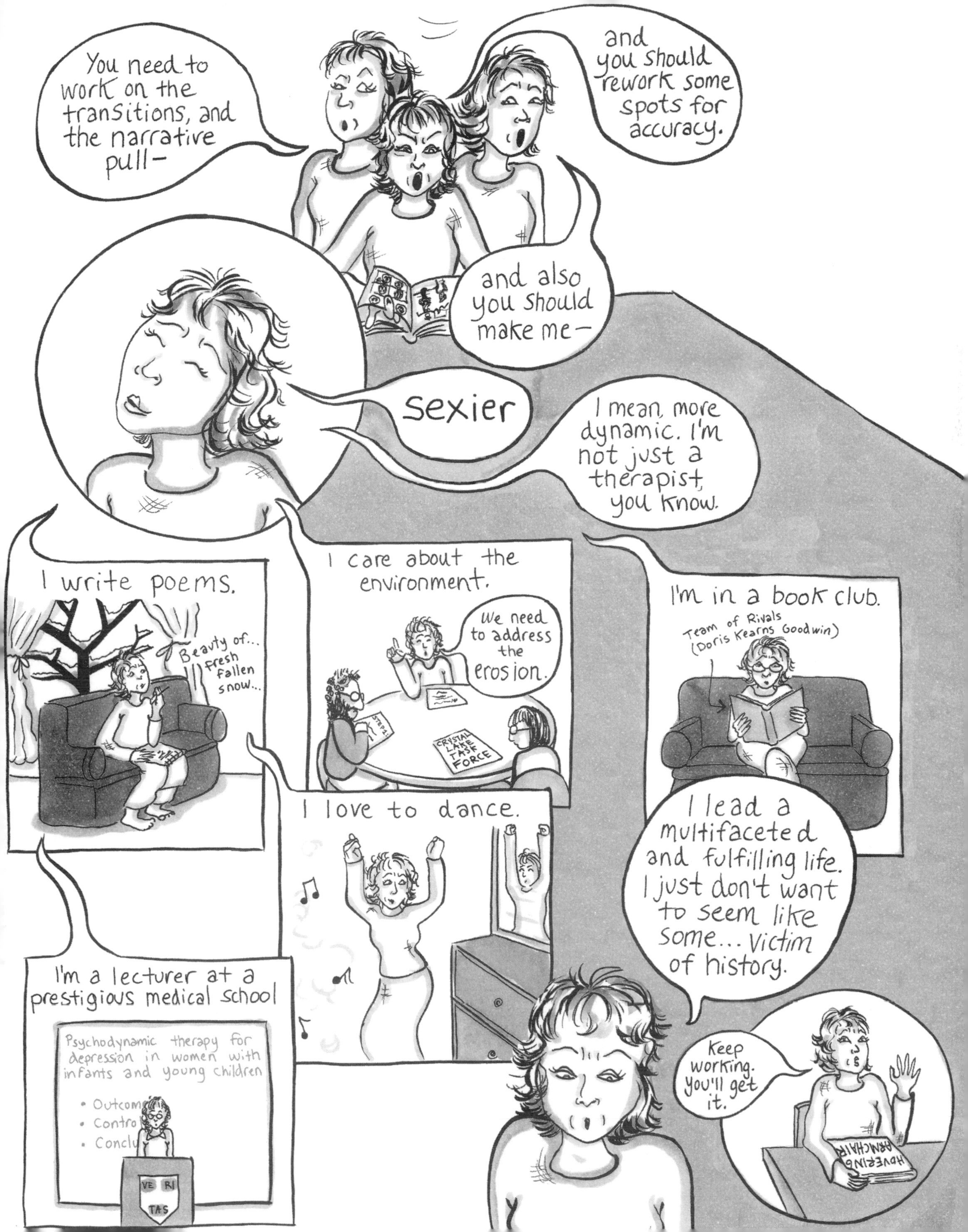

You need to work on the transitions, and the narrative pull-
and you should rework some spots for accuracy.
and also you should make me-
sexier
I mean, more dynamic. I'm not just a therapist, you know.
I write poems.
Beauty of... fresh fallen snow...
I care about the environment.
We need to address the erosion.
STEPS
CRYSTAL LAKE TASK FORCE
I'm in a book club.
Team of Rivals (Doris Kearns Goodwin)
I love to dance.
I'm a lecturer at a prestigious medical school
Psychodynamic therapy for depression in women with infants and young children
• Outcom
• Control
• Conclu
VE RI TAS
I lead a multifaceted and fulfilling life. I just don't want to seem like some... victim of history.
Keep working. You'll get it.
HOVERING ARMCHAIR

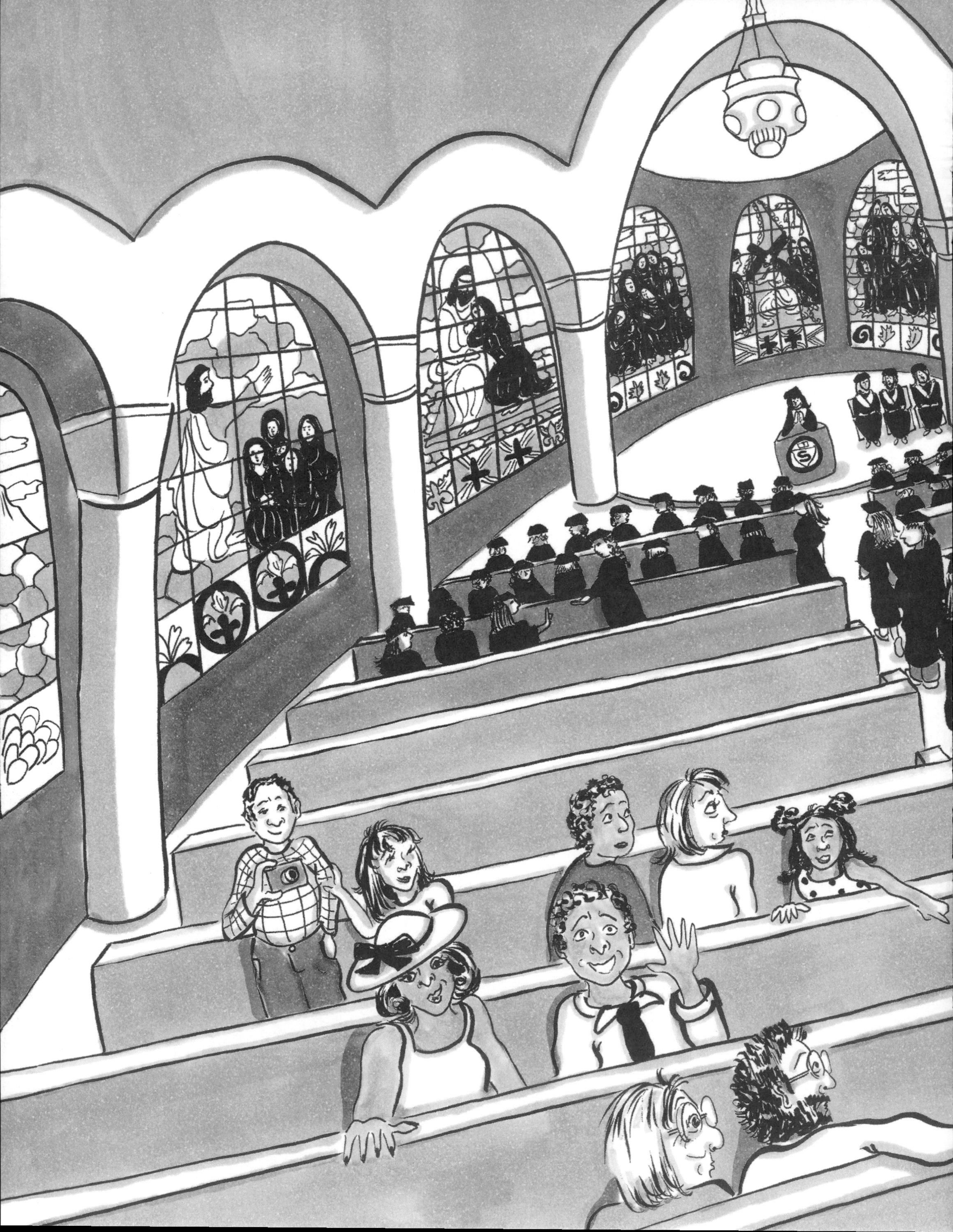

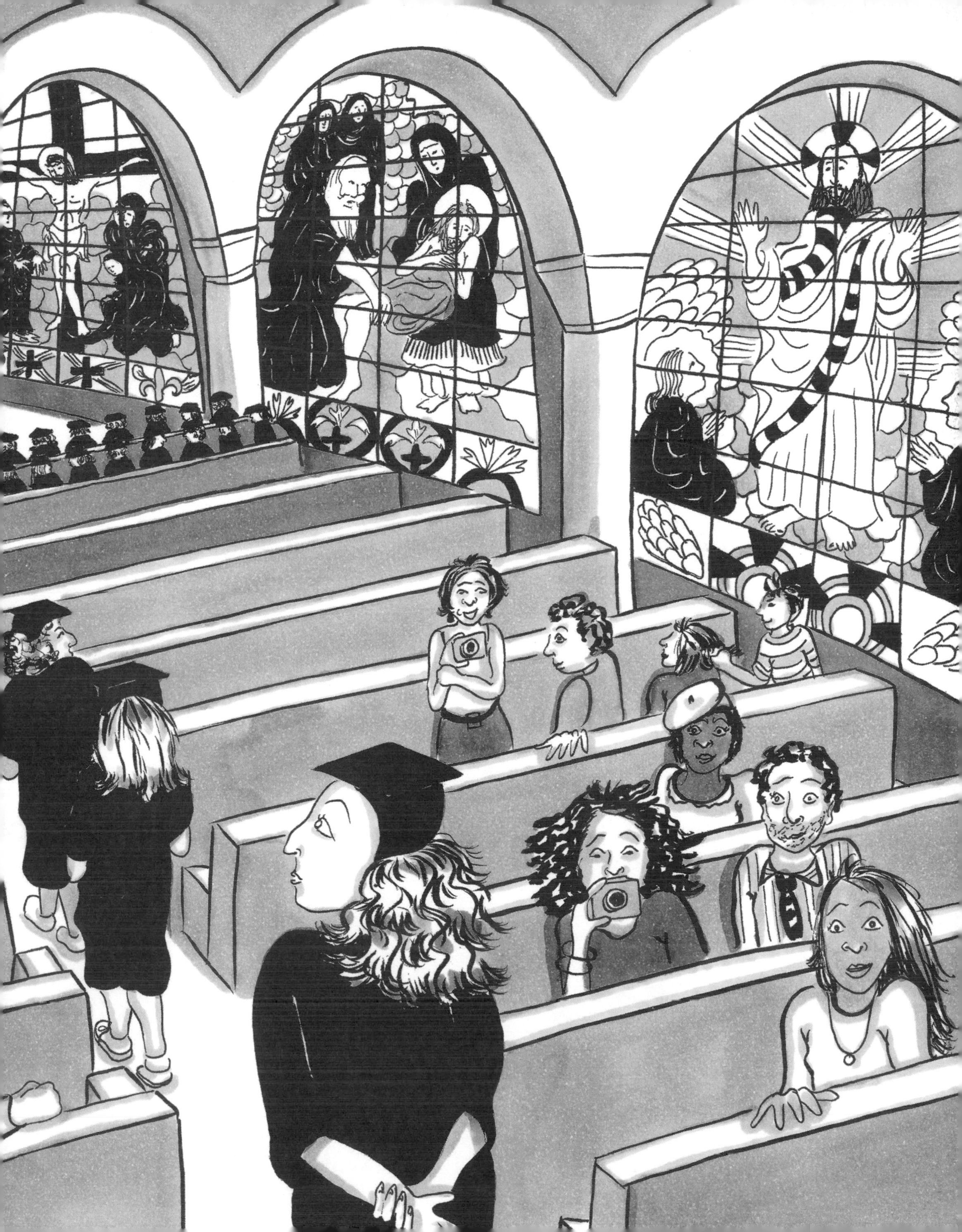

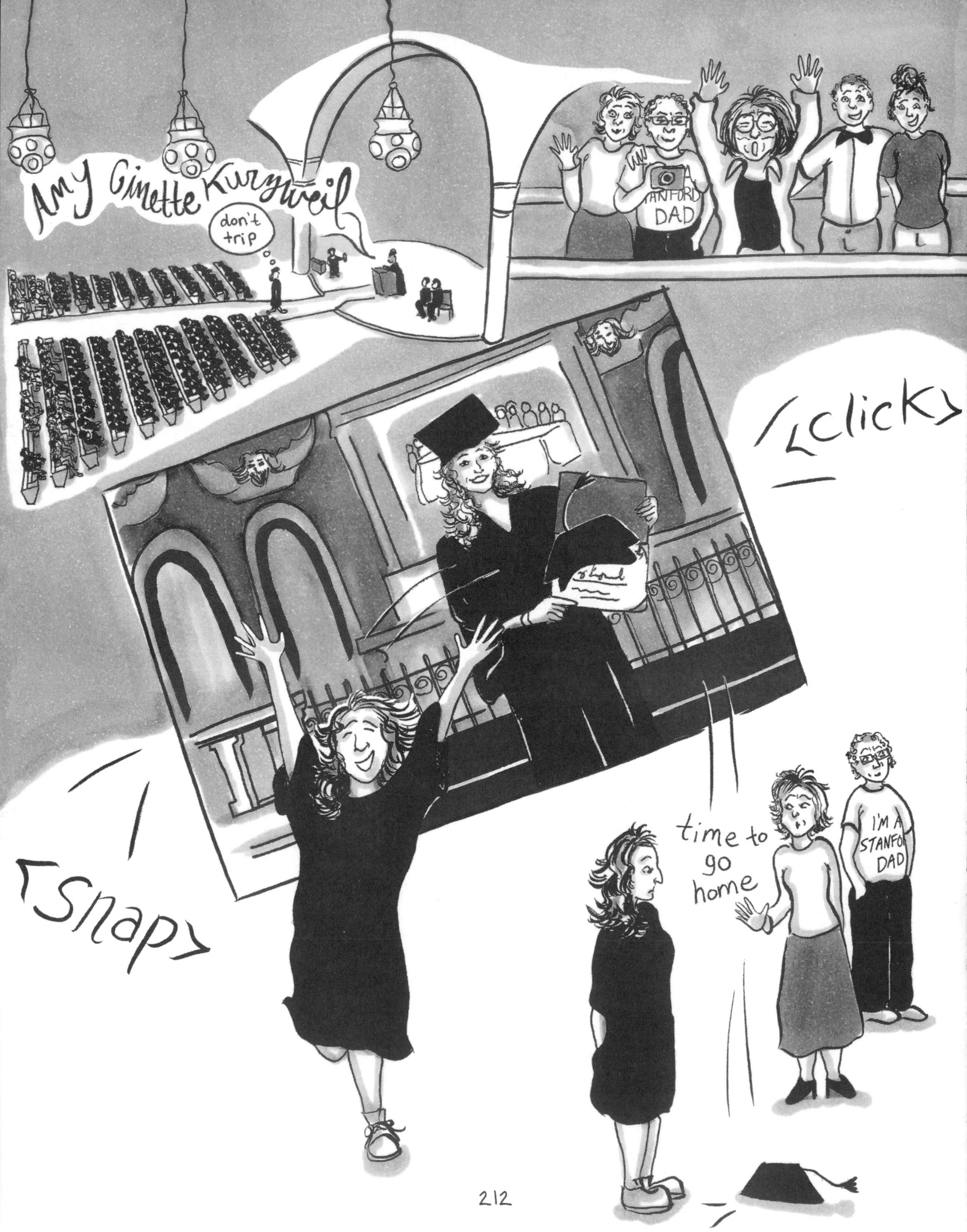
Amy Ginette Kurzweil
don't trip
I'M A STANFORD DAD
<click>
<snap>
time to go home
I'M A STANFORD DAD

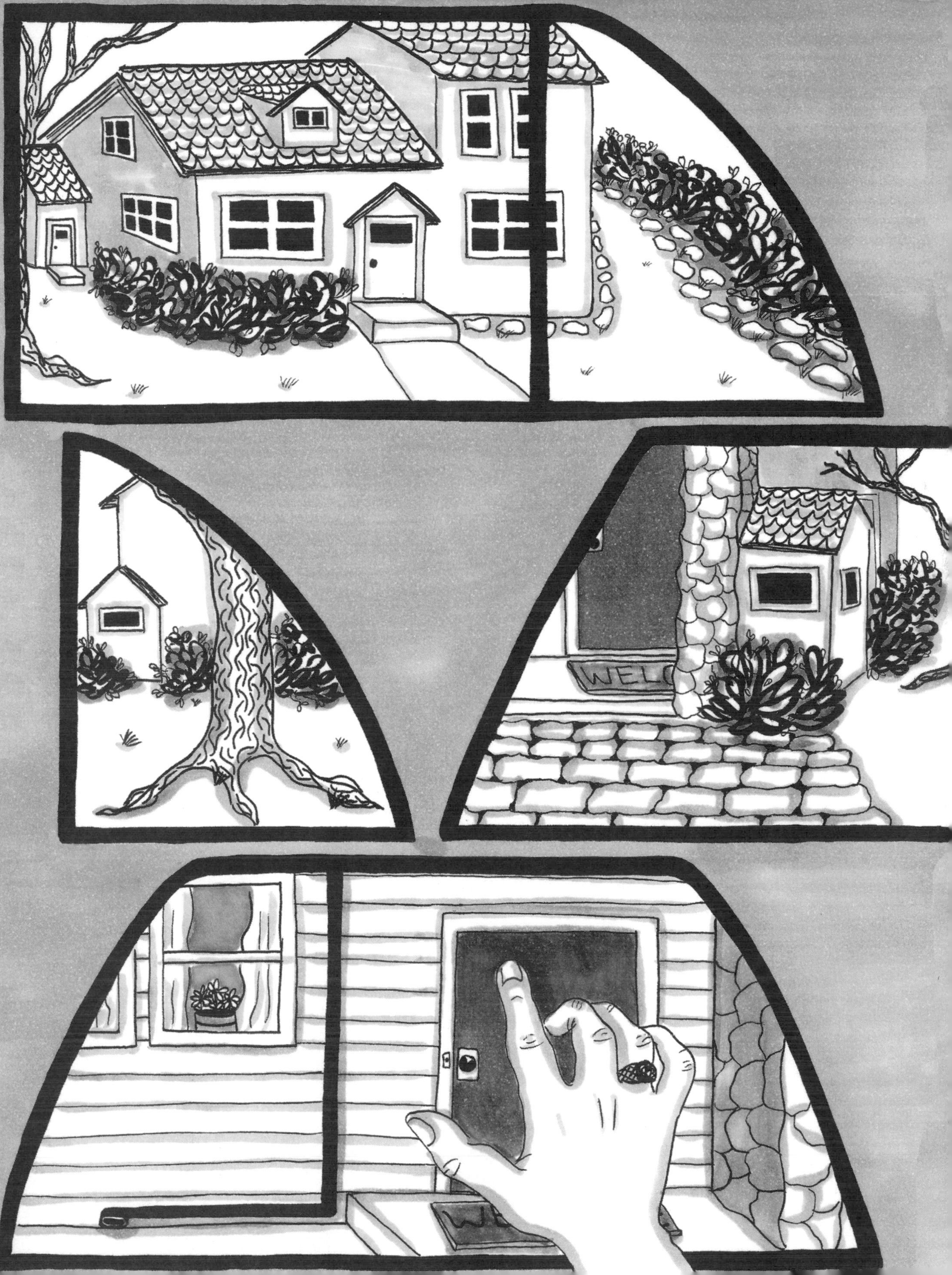
WELC

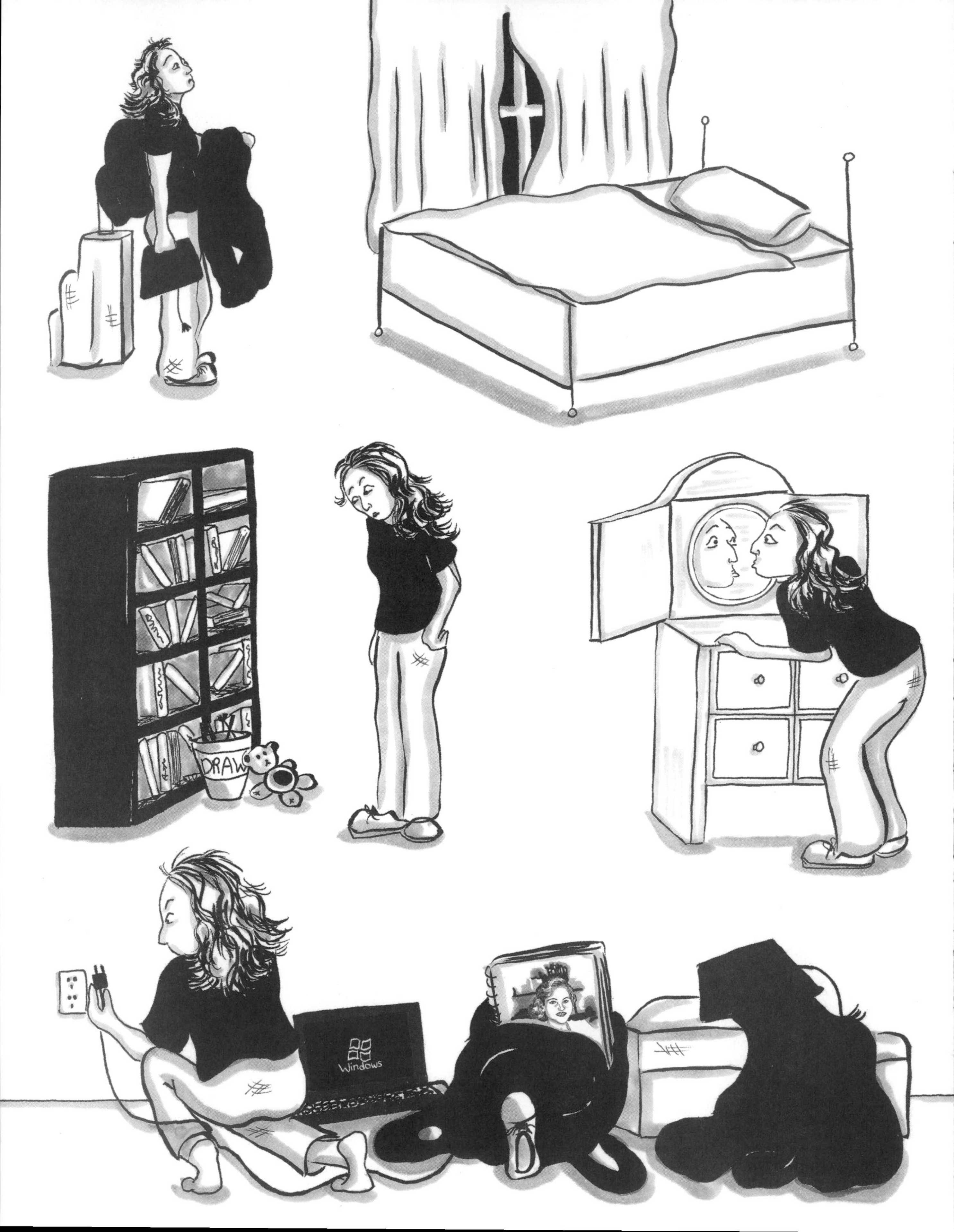
DRAW
Windows

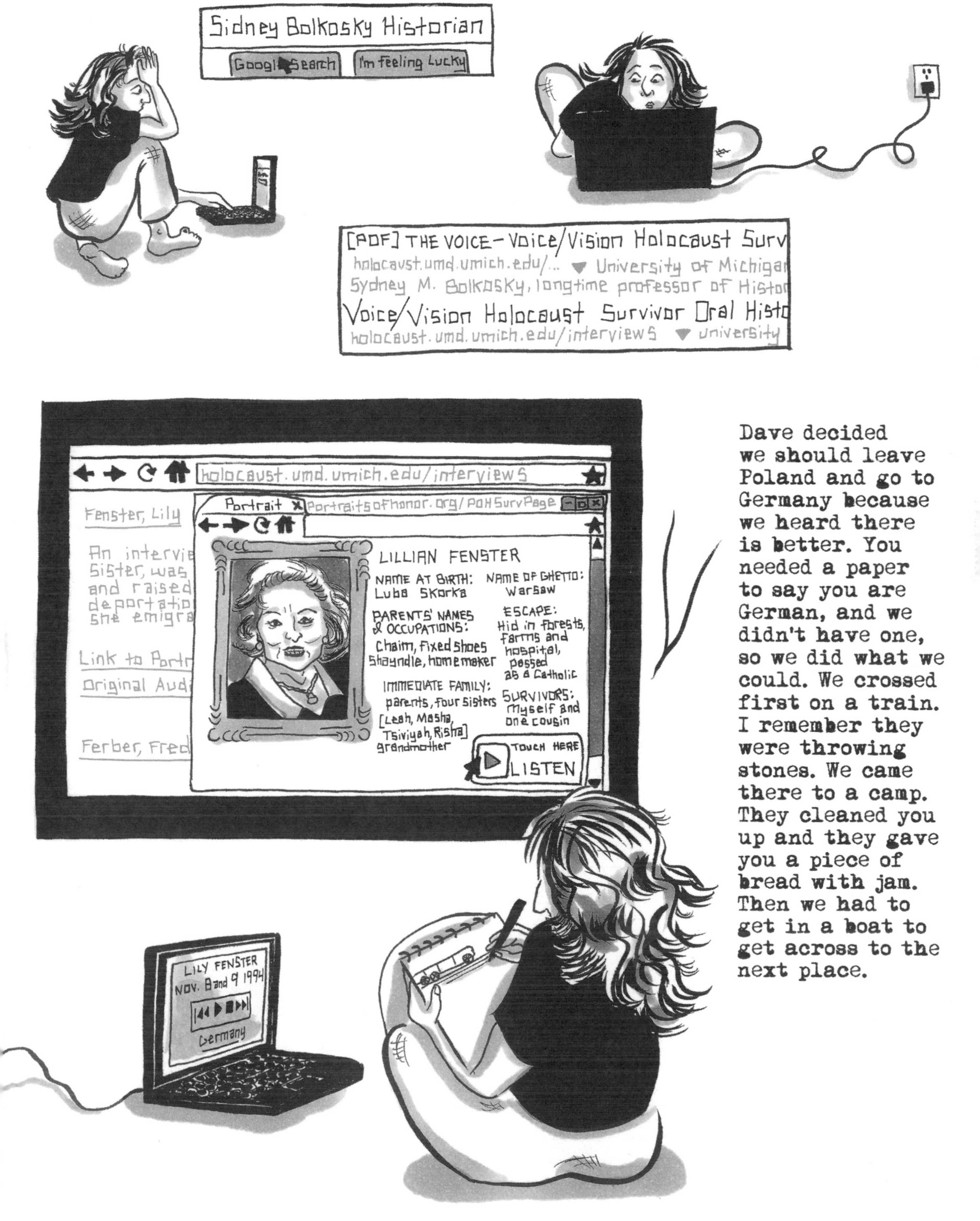

Sidney Bolkosky Historian
Google Search
I'm Feeling Lucky
[PDF] THE VOICE – Voice/Vision Holocaust Surv
holocaust.umd.umich.edu/... University of Michigan
Sydney M. Bolkosky, longtime professor of Histo
Voice/Vision Holocaust Survivor Oral Histo
holocaust.umd.umich.edu/interviews university
holocaust.umd.umich.edu/interviews
Fenster, Lily
Portrait
Portraitsofhonor.org/POHSurvPage
LILLIAN FENSTER
NAME AT BIRTH: Luba Skorka
NAME OF GHETTO: Warsaw
PARENTS' NAMES & OCCUPATIONS: Chaim, fixed shoes Shayndle, homemaker
ESCAPE: Hid in forests, farms and hospital, passed as a Catholic
IMMEDIATE FAMILY: parents, four sisters [Leah, Masha, Tsiviyah, Risha] grandmother
SURVIVORS: myself and one cousin
TOUCH HERE
LISTEN
Ferber, Fred
Dave decided we should leave Poland and go to Germany because we heard there is better. You needed a paper to say you are German, and we didn't have one, so we did what we could. We crossed first on a train. I remember they were throwing stones. We came there to a camp. They cleaned you up and they gave you a piece of bread with jam. Then we had to get in a boat to get across to the next place.
LILY FENSTER
NOV. 8 and 9 1994
Germany

On that boat, Sonya was jumping in my stomach, I thought she was gonna eat me up. It almost caved over, the boat, and I was still so hungry.

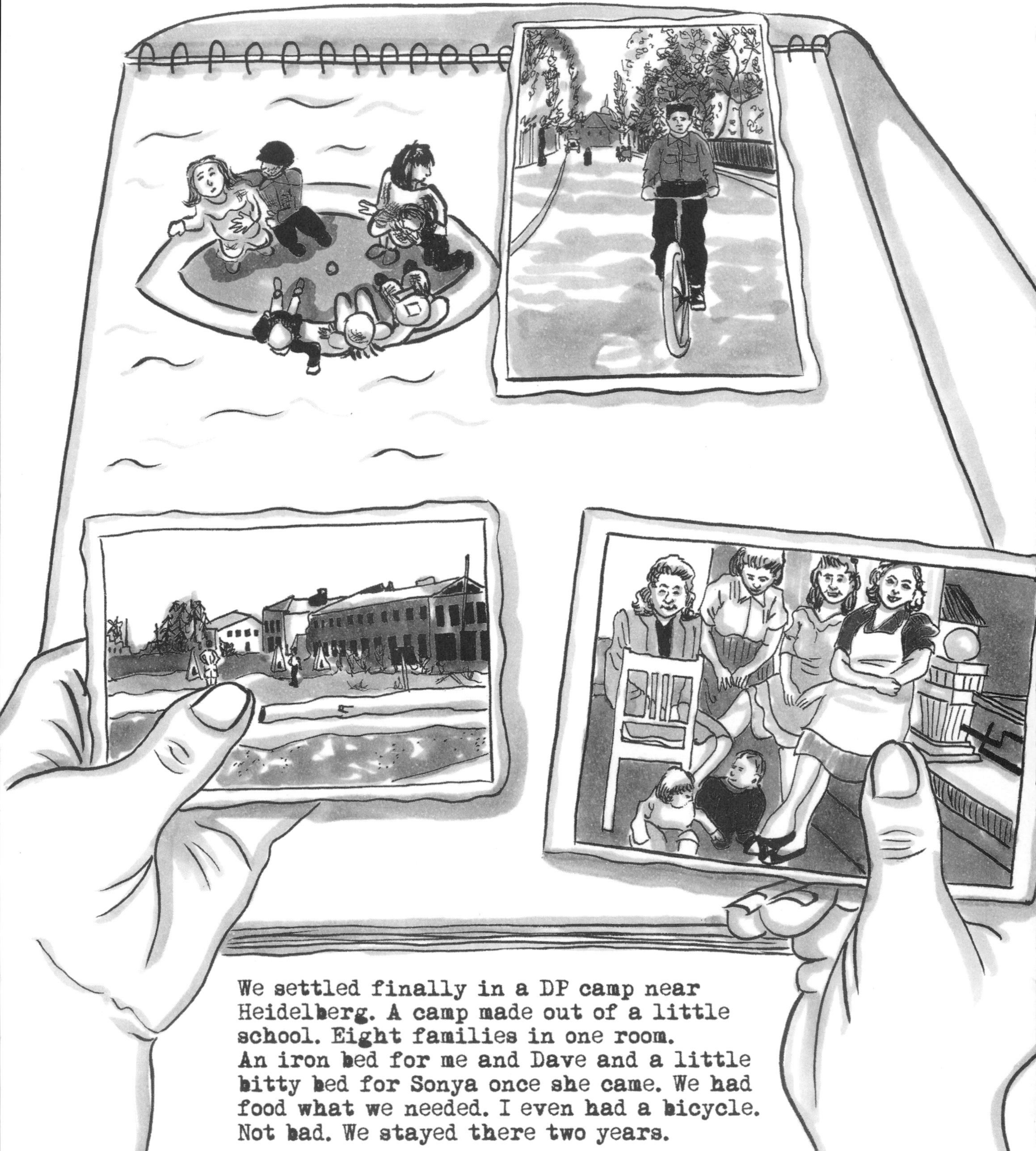

We settled finally in a DP camp near Heidelberg. A camp made out of a little school. Eight families in one room. An iron bed for me and Dave and a little bitty bed for Sonya once she came. We had food what we needed. I even had a bicycle. Not bad. We stayed there two years.

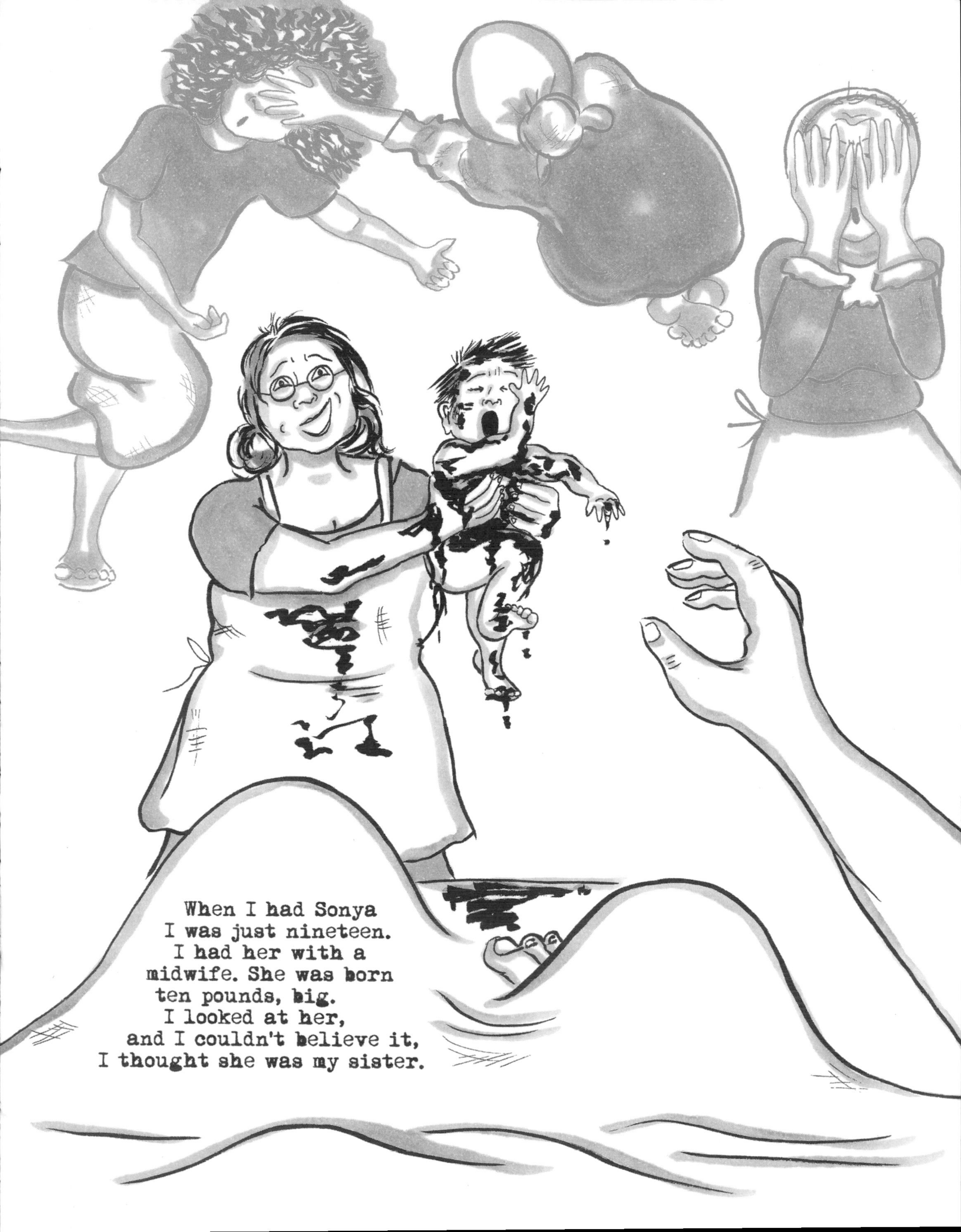
When I had Sonya
I was just nineteen.
I had her with a
midwife. She was born
ten pounds, big.
I looked at her,
and I couldn't believe it,
I thought she was my sister.

Everyone loved my little girl. She was like a little gypsy.
But is that a place to bring up a child?

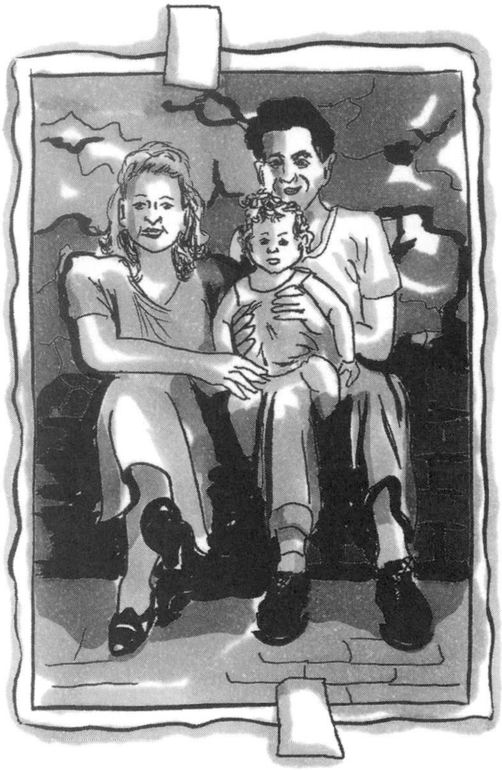

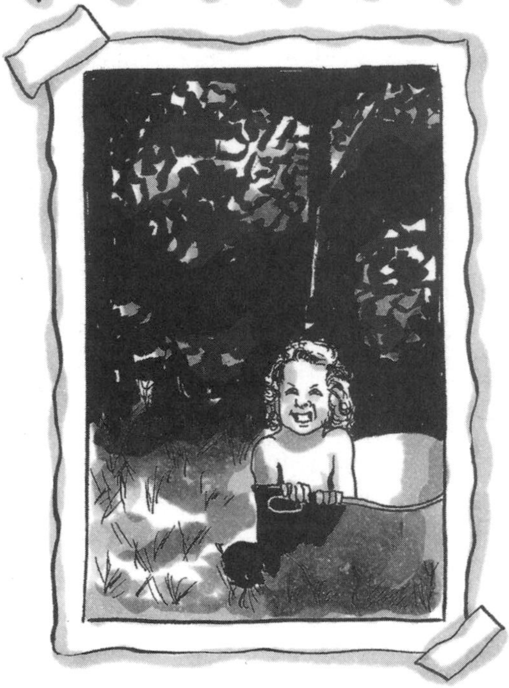

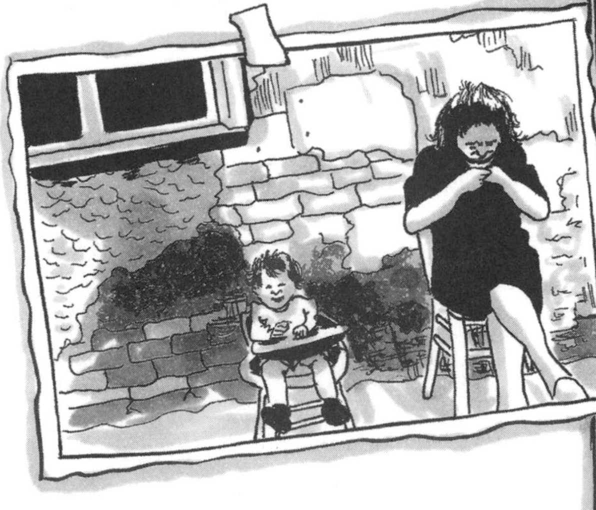

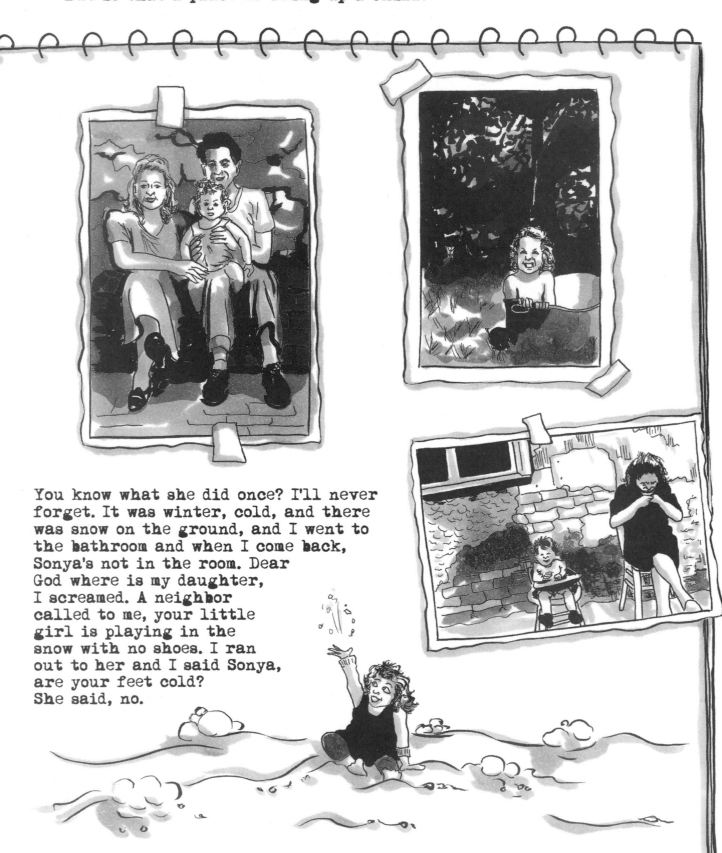

You know what she did once? I'll never forget. It was winter, cold, and there was snow on the ground, and I went to the bathroom and when I come back, Sonya's not in the room. Dear God where is my daughter, I screamed. A neighbor called to me, your little girl is playing in the snow with no shoes. I ran out to her and I said Sonya, are your feet cold? She said, no.

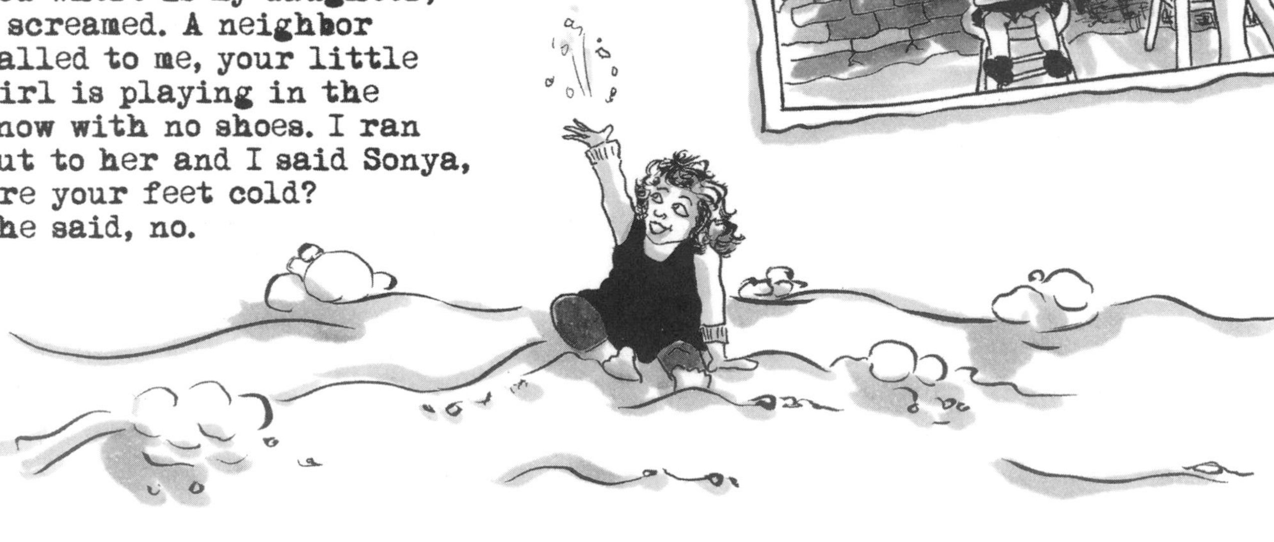

She didn't even know she had cold feet.

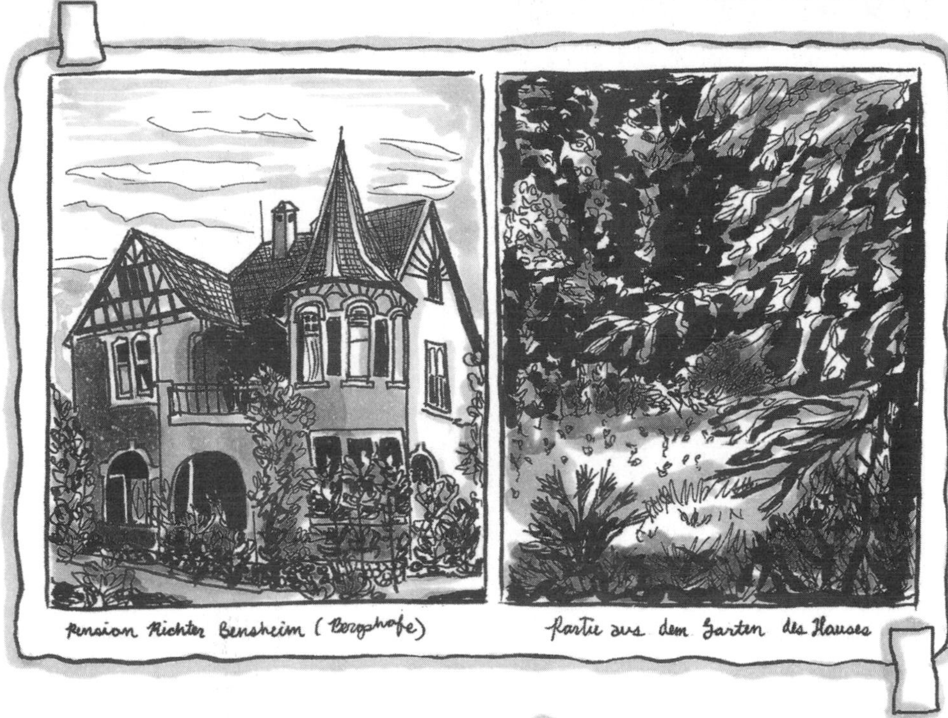
Pension Richter Bensheim (Bergstraße)
Partie aus dem Garten des Hauses

We were living
next in a
little school,
a dancing school,
in the attic.

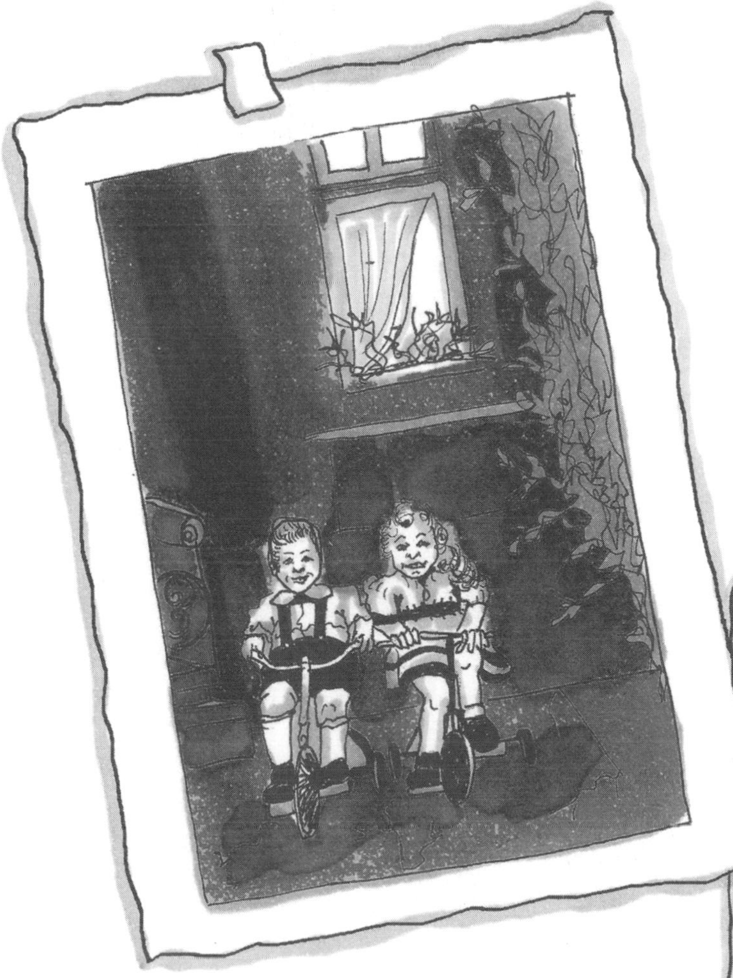

But we always knew we wanted to come to America if Dave should get us the papers. He did it. It was 1951. We went first to New York, to an island, you know, the place where the newcomers come...

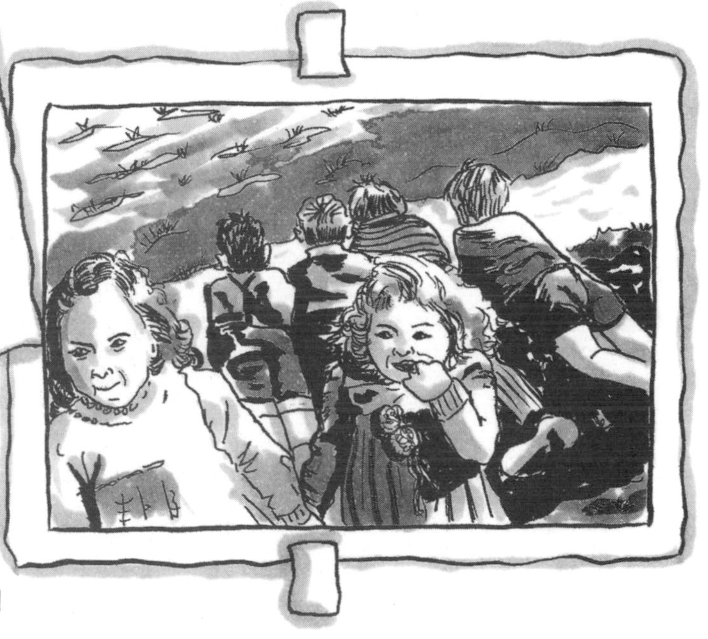

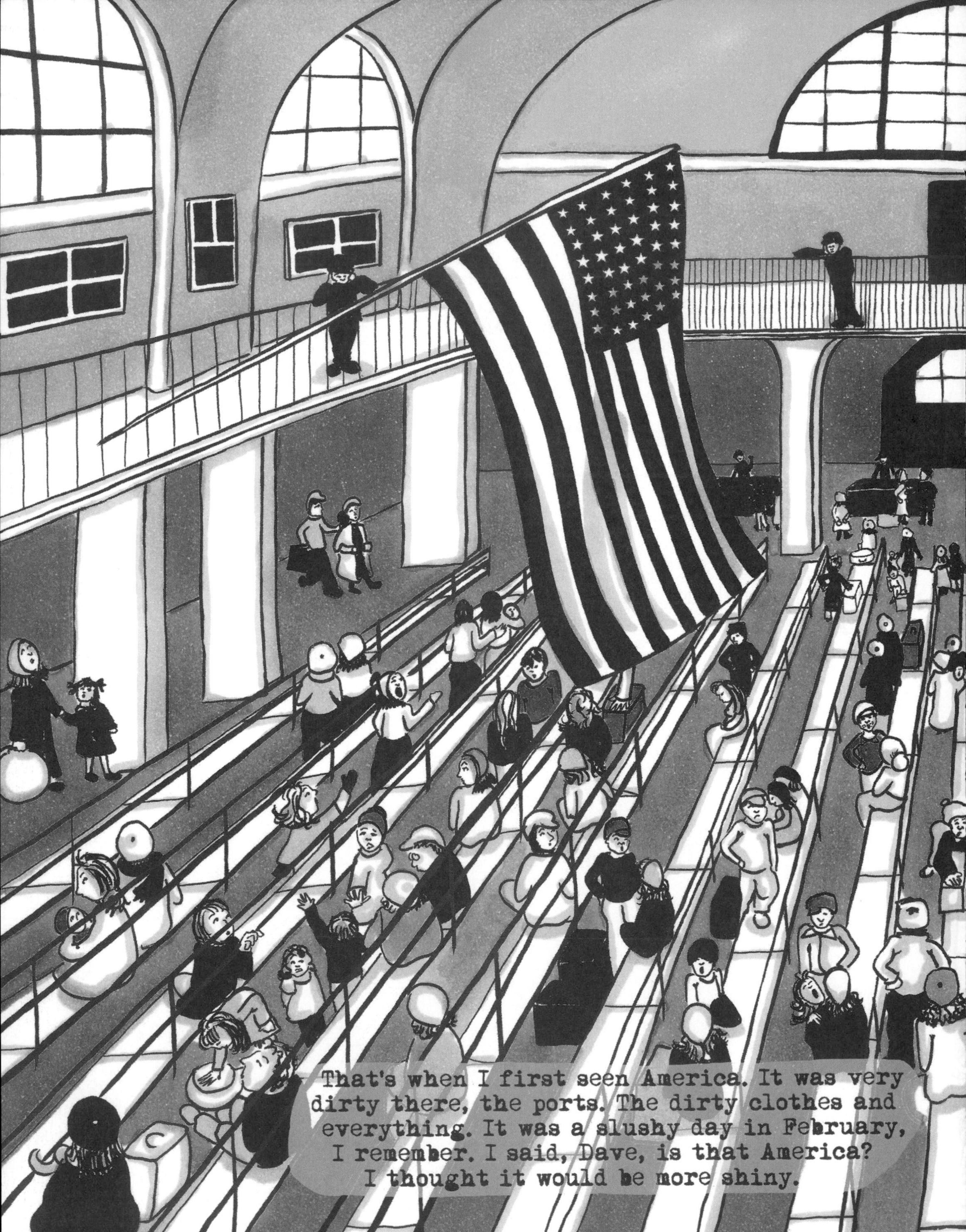
That's when I first seen America. It was very dirty there, the ports. The dirty clothes and everything. It was a slushy day in February, I remember. I said, Dave, is that America? I thought it would be more shiny.

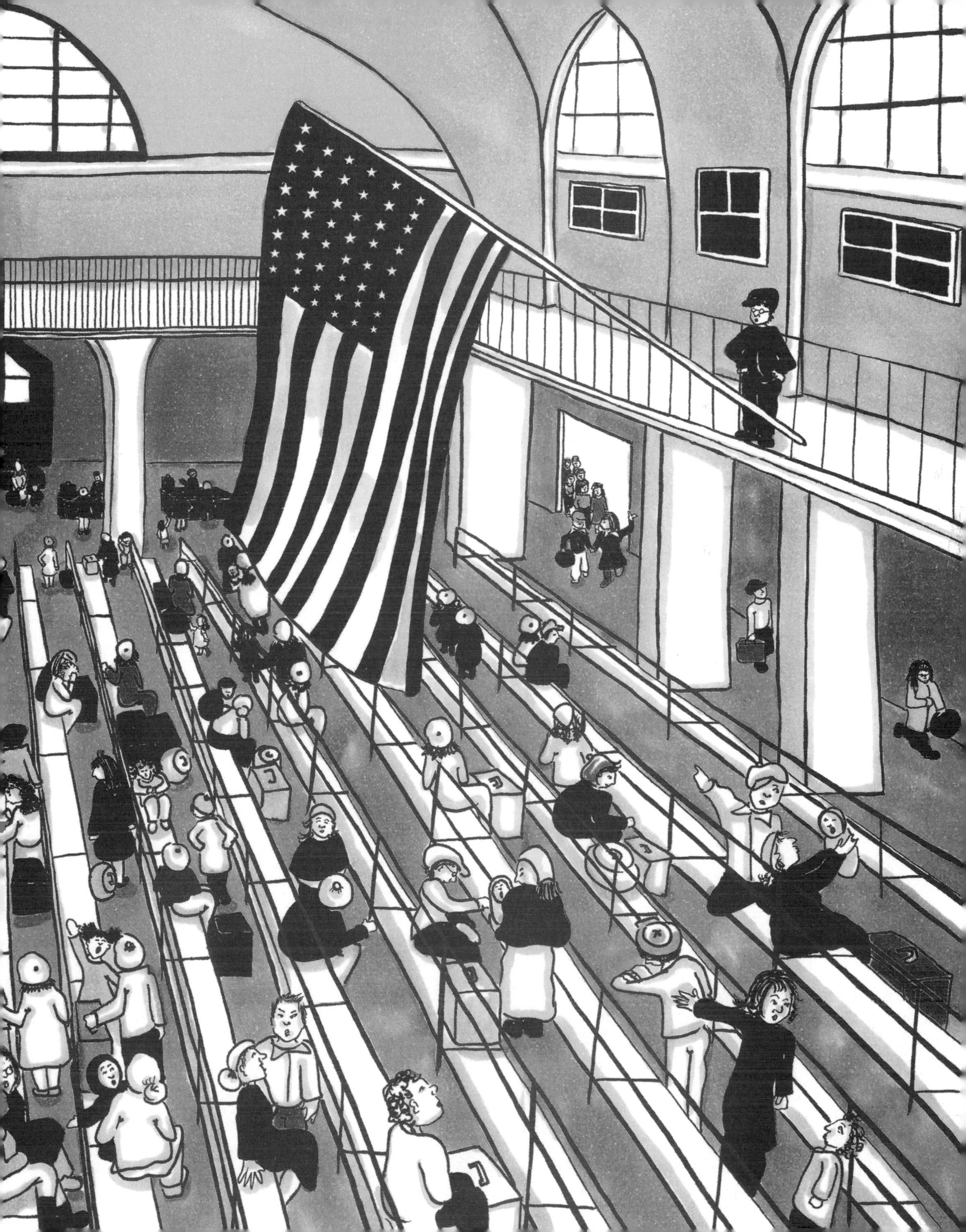

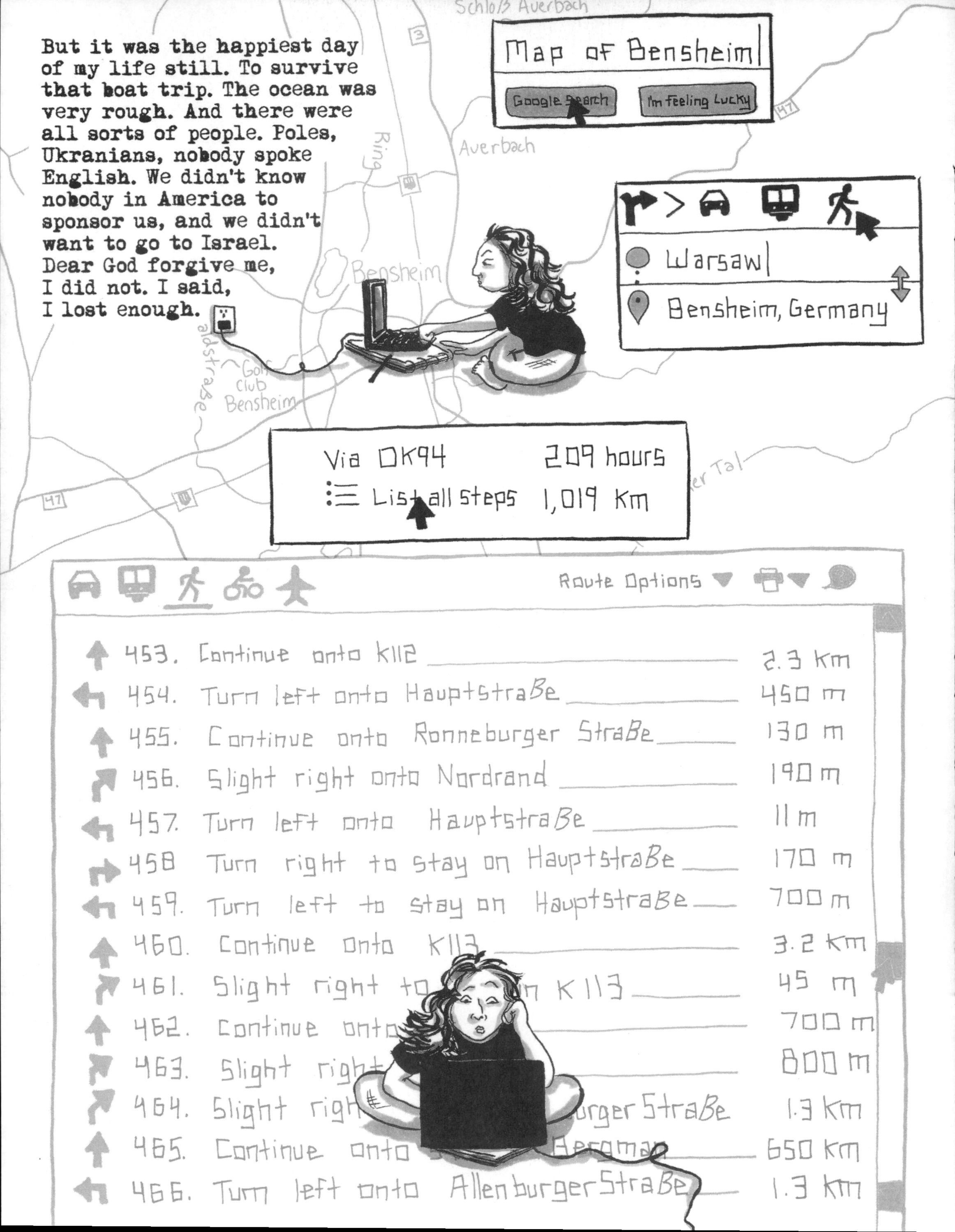
But it was the happiest day of my life still. To survive that boat trip. The ocean was very rough. And there were all sorts of people. Poles, Ukranians, nobody spoke English. We didn't know nobody in America to sponsor us, and we didn't want to go to Israel. Dear God forgive me, I did not. I said, I lost enough.
Schloß Auerbach
Map of Bensheim
Google Search
I'm feeling Lucky
Ring
Auerbach
Bensheim
Warsaw
Bensheim, Germany
Golf Club Bensheim
Via DK94 209 hours
List all steps 1,019 km
47
Route Options
453. Continue onto K112 2.3 km
454. Turn left onto Hauptstraße 450 m
455. Continue onto Ronneburger Straße 130 m
456. Slight right onto Nordrand 190 m
457. Turn left onto Hauptstraße 11 m
458 Turn right to stay on Hauptstraße 170 m
459. Turn left to stay on Hauptstraße 700 m
460. Continue onto K113 3.2 km
461. Slight right to K113 45 m
462. Continue onto 700 m
463. Slight righ 800 m
464. Slight righ urger Straße 1.3 km
465. Continue onto Bergman 650 km
466. Turn left onto Allenburger Straße 1.3 km

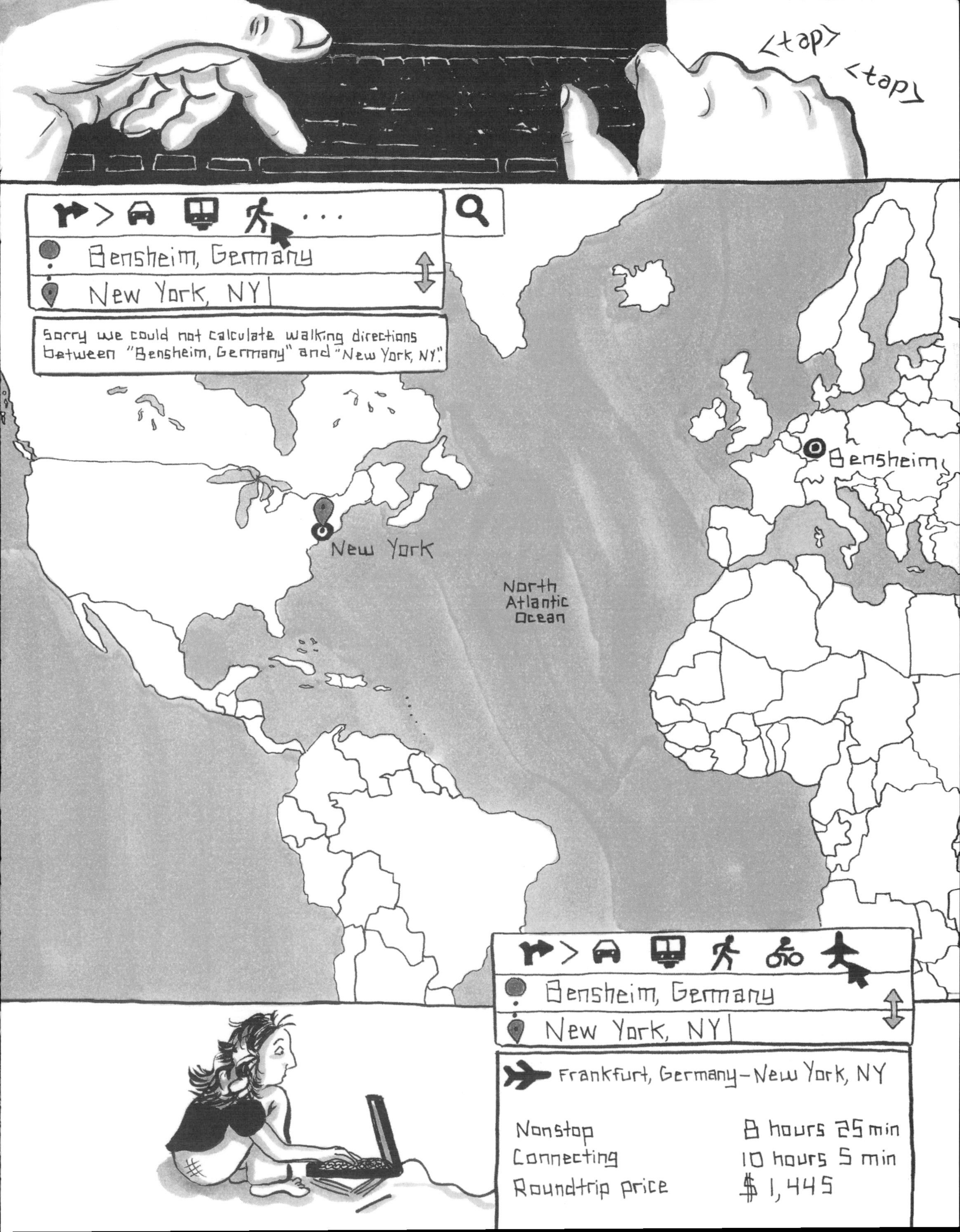
<tap>
<tap>
Bensheim, Germany
New York, NY
Sorry we could not calculate walking directions between "Bensheim, Germany" and "New York, NY."
Bensheim
New York
North Atlantic Ocean
Bensheim, Germany
New York, NY
Frankfurt, Germany–New York, NY
Nonstop 8 hours 25 min
Connecting 10 hours 5 min
Roundtrip price $ 1,445

When we came to New York there was a social worker waiting for us to fill out some application. It asked, What do you do for work? And Dave didn't know what to say, so he just wrote down: mechanic. What's he for a mechanic? So they sent us to Detroit, you know, because of the cars.
We rode on a train, and we were so hungry. The social worker lady gave us twenty dollars, but we didn't speak the language so we didn't know how to order. We went to the dining car and I just point. It turned out to be baked apples, twenty dollars of baked apples!

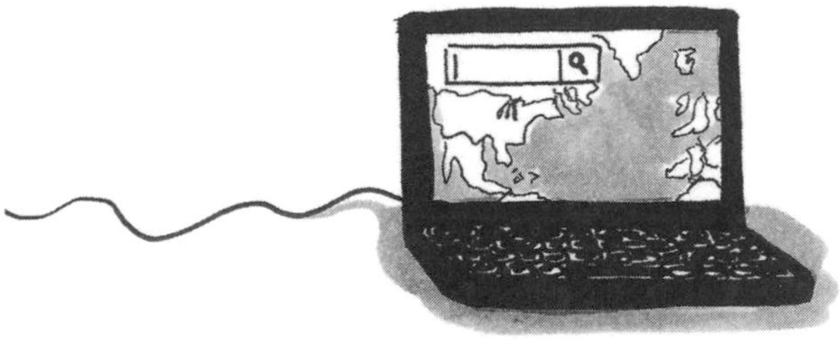

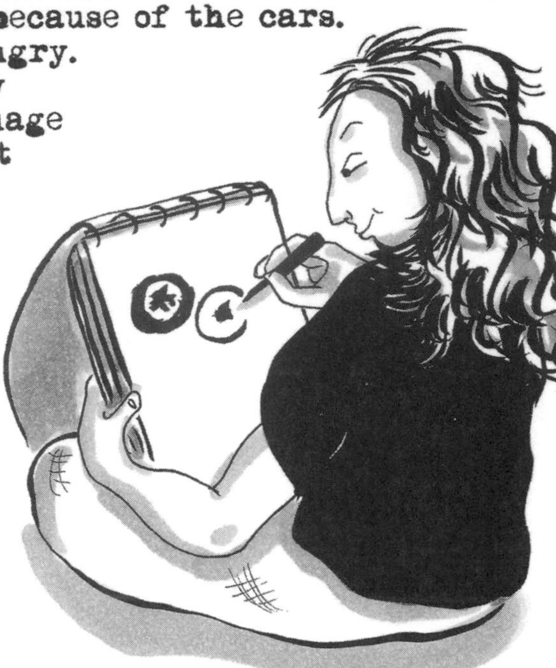

In Detroit, we lived first in a tiny house, one bathroom, six families, but we worked hard. You give me one hundred dollars, I'll save seventy-five. We moved next to a nicer place on Gladstone. A four-family flat. Sonya slept with us in the little room.

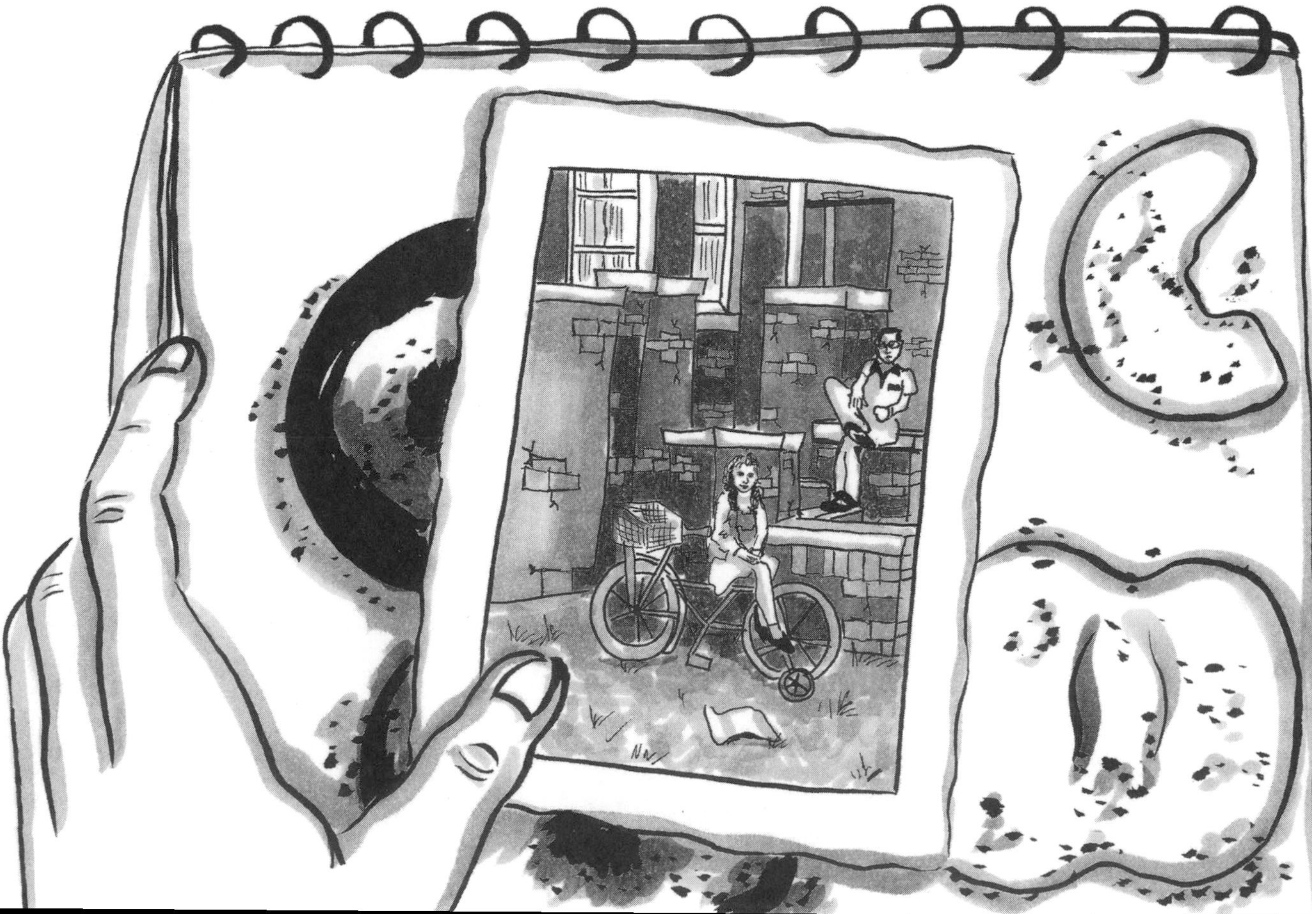

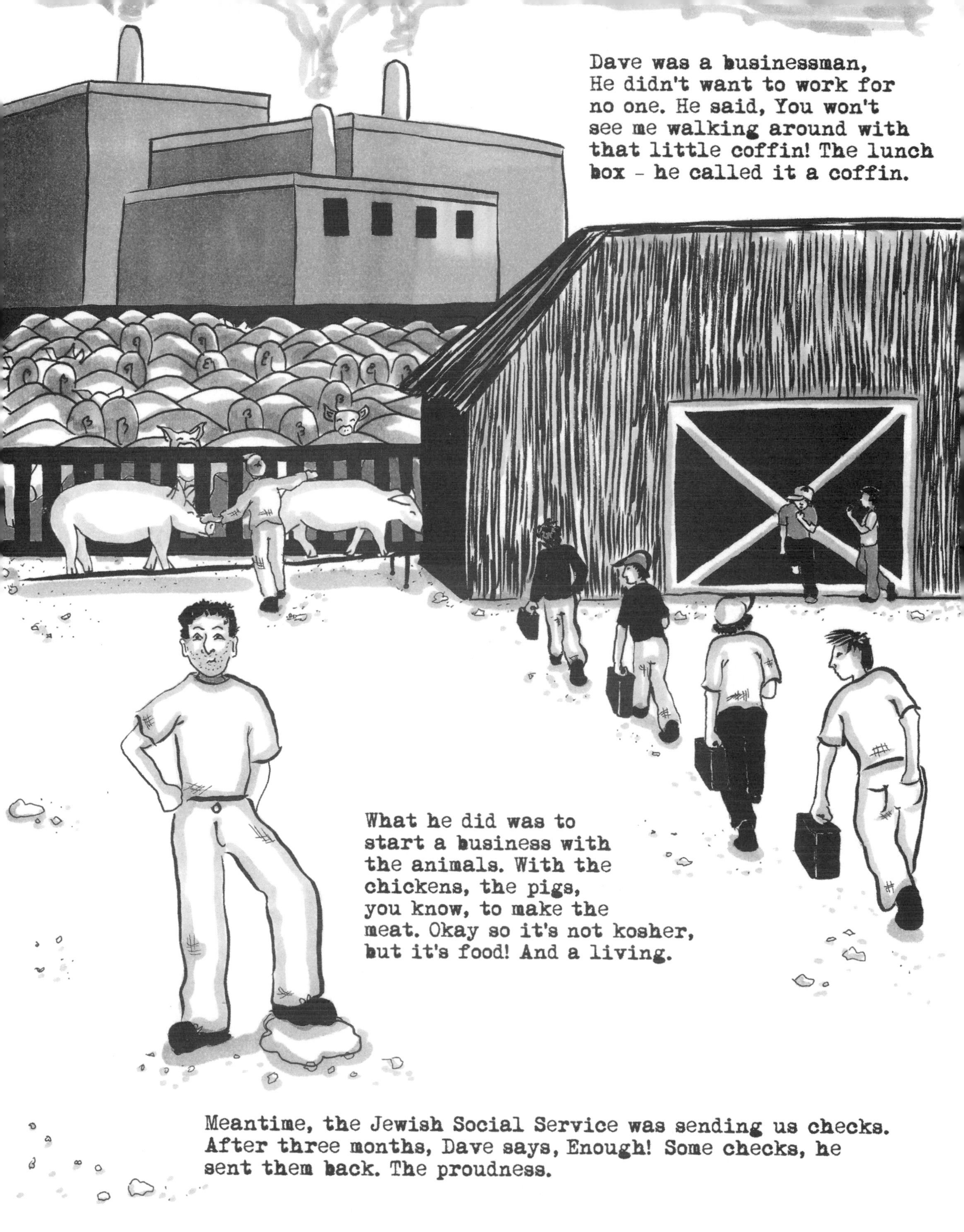
Dave was a businessman, He didn't want to work for no one. He said, You won't see me walking around with that little coffin! The lunch box - he called it a coffin.
What he did was to start a business with the animals. With the chickens, the pigs, you know, to make the meat. Okay so it's not kosher, but it's food! And a living.
Meantime, the Jewish Social Service was sending us checks. After three months, Dave says, Enough! Some checks, he sent them back. The proudness.

I was working too. For an old gentleman who worked in a store on the corner of Linwood. He was in his eighties, working. I cleaned up his house and things. Sometimes cook him some soup. I would speak to him in Yiddish, and he blessed me. He paid me forty-five dollars a week.

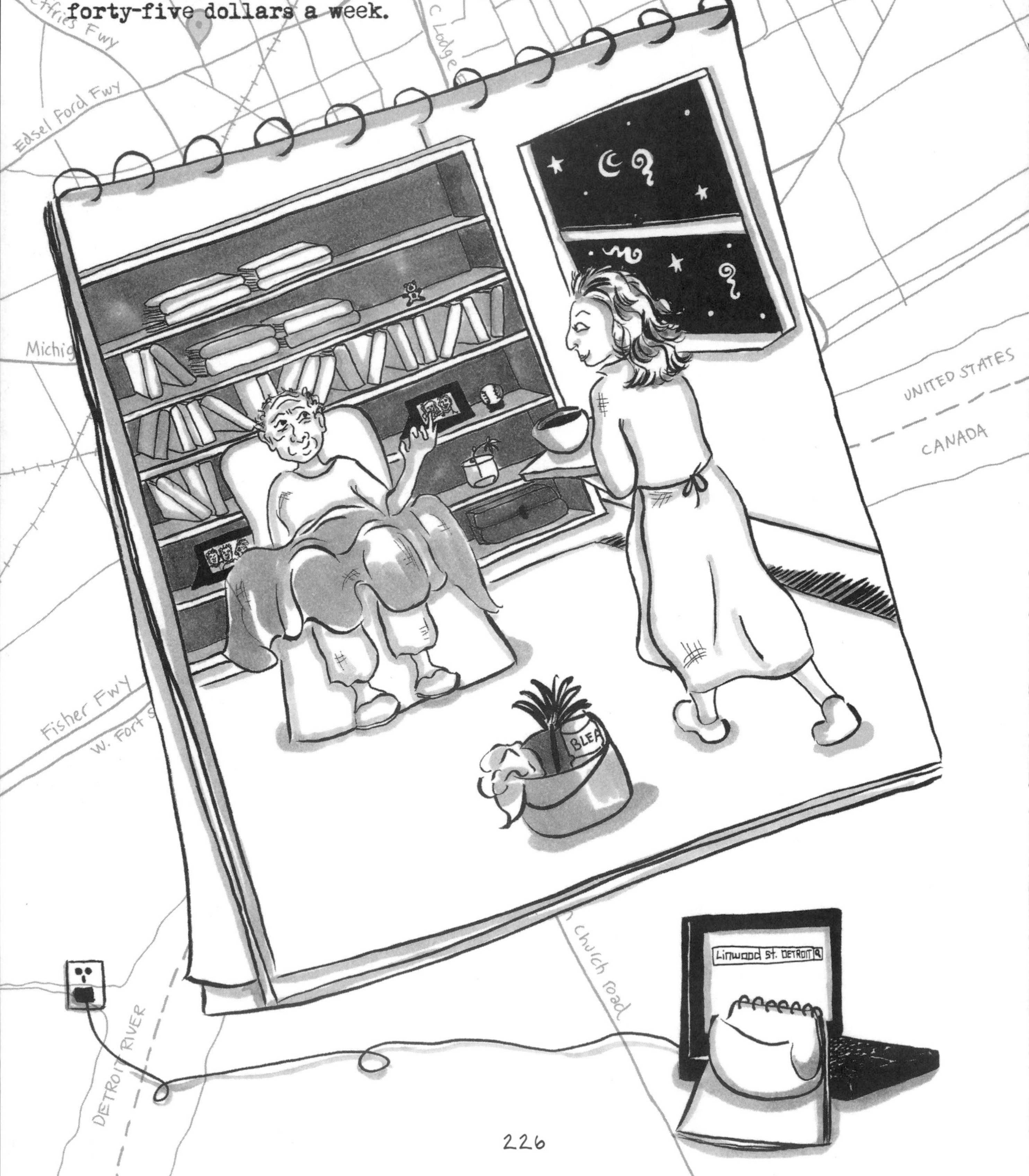

Jeffries Fwy
Edsel Ford Fwy
Michig
UNITED STATES
CANADA
Fisher Fwy
W. Fort S
BLEA
Church road
Linwood St. DETROIT
DETROIT RIVER

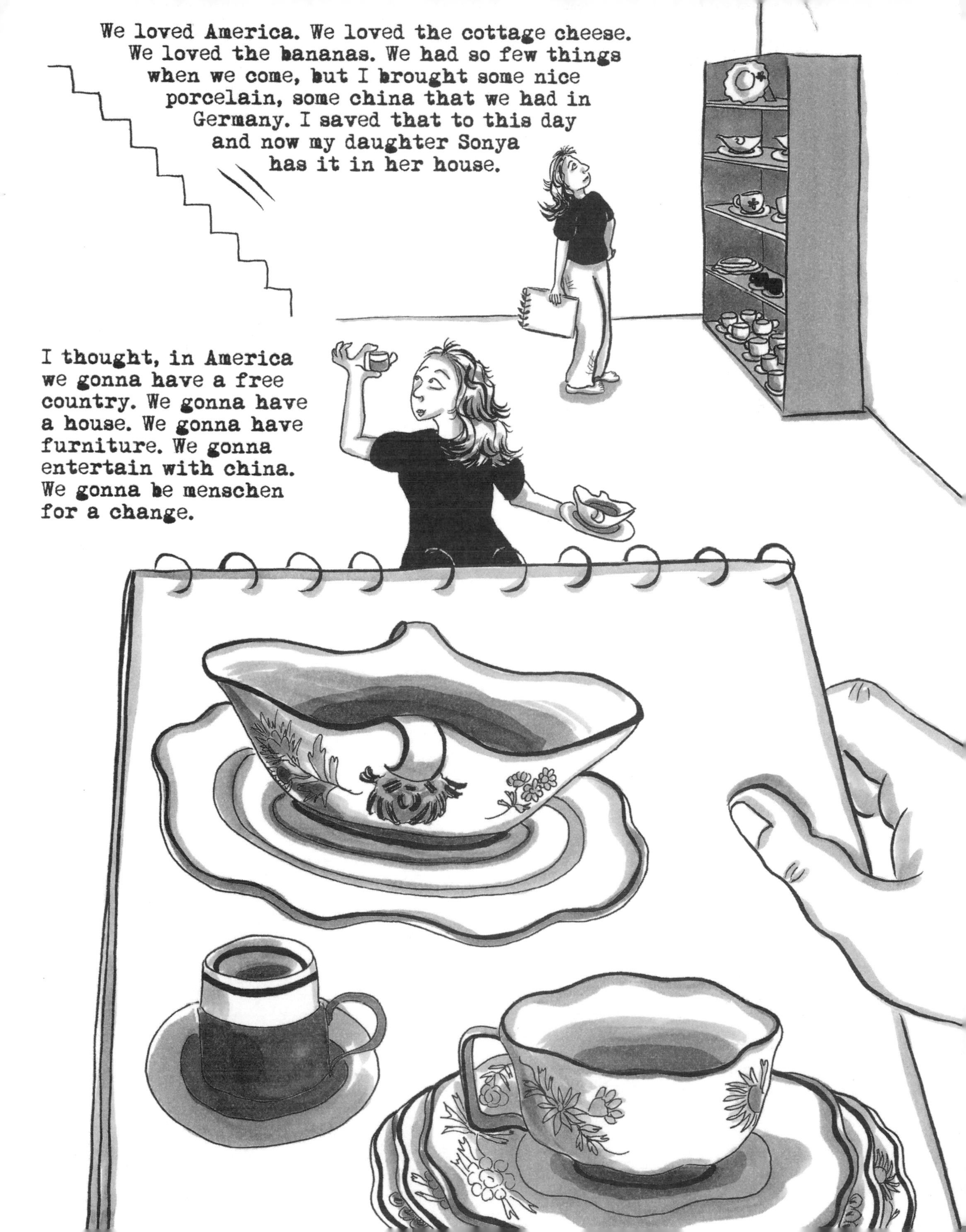
We loved America. We loved the cottage cheese. We loved the bananas. We had so few things when we come, but I brought some nice porcelain, some china that we had in Germany. I saved that to this day and now my daughter Sonya has it in her house.
I thought, in America we gonna have a free country. We gonna have a house. We gonna have furniture. We gonna entertain with china. We gonna be menschen for a change.

When I went back to Europe - in the seventies it was - I looked for family that survived. Everyone was listed, you know how they did it. I was checking names, looking. I was thinking, maybe...but I didn't see nothing.

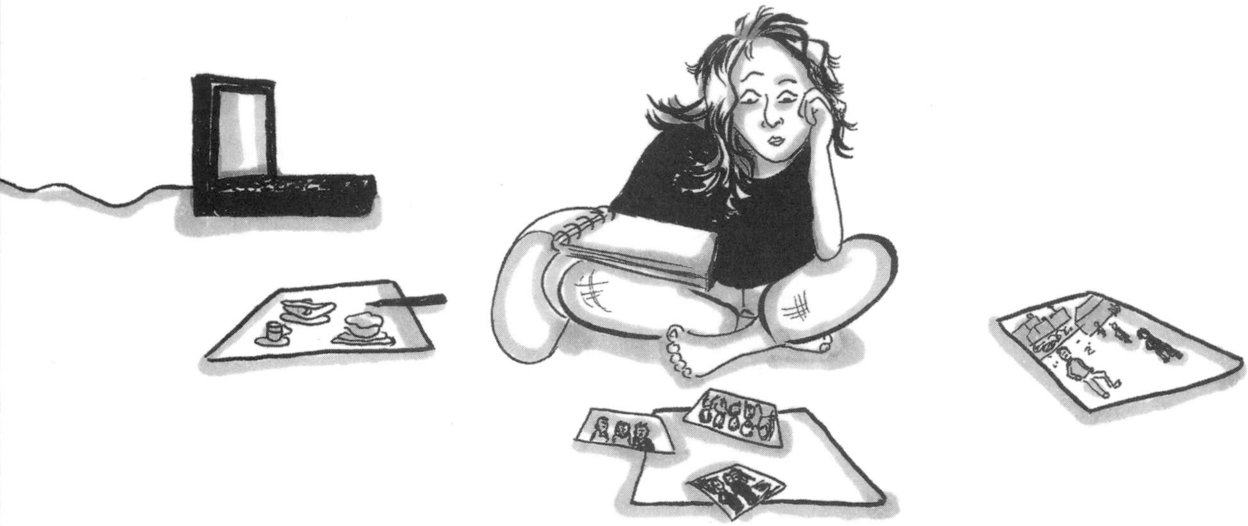

Finally I seen I had one aunt who survived. My daddy's youngest sister. When I met her in Israel, after so many years, I recognize her right away because of the eyes. The greenest eyes, with gorgeous lashes. She was in Russia. She had just one person left, her oldest daughter, Luba. Named Luba like me after our grandma. Luba lived in Israel and had three beautiful children with those same eyes, and now grandchildren still coming.

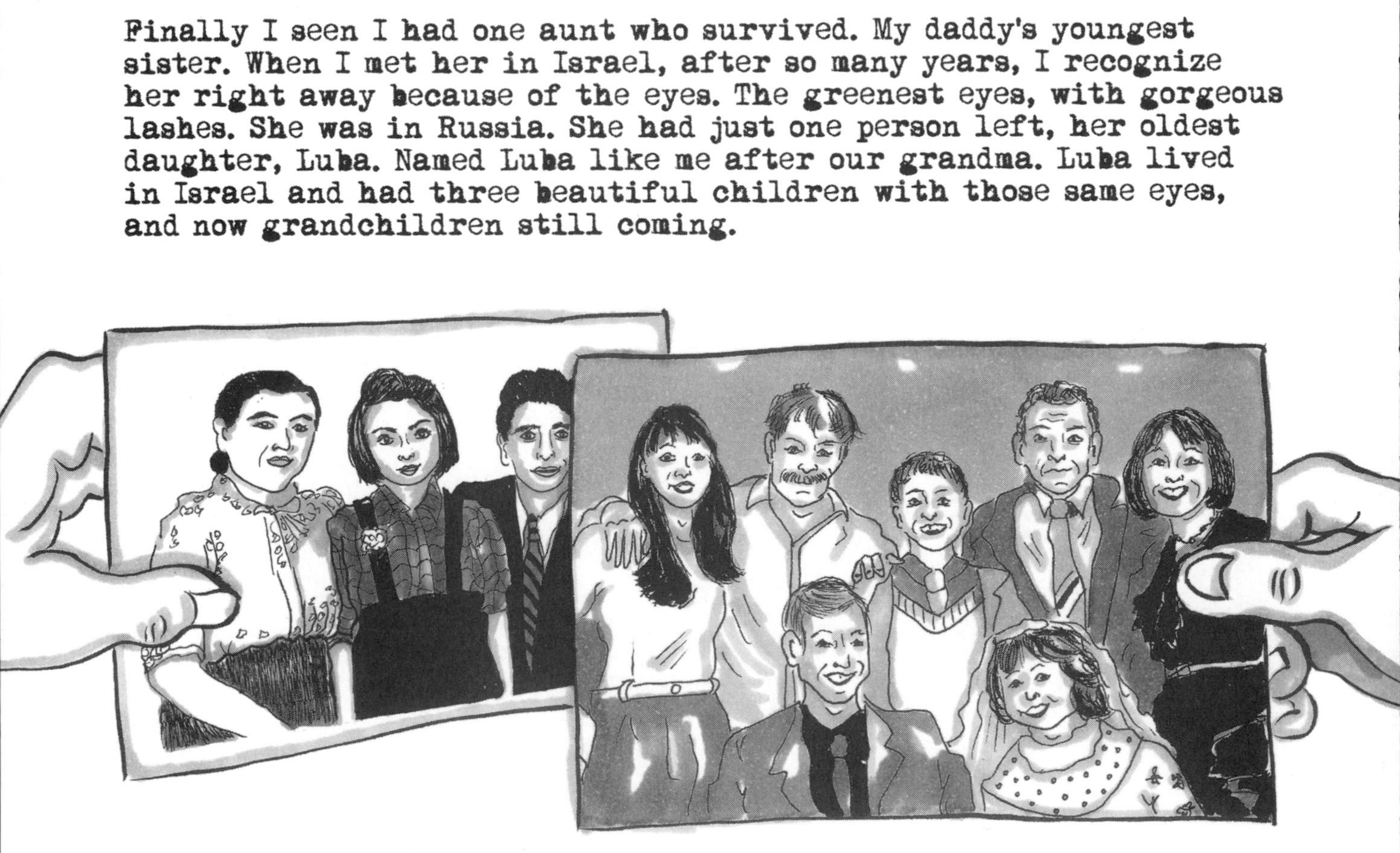

Family. Me and Dave raised each other practically. He was a bright person, and oh did he have stories. But he didn't want to talk. He always wanted to help people, but he never wanted to be honored. Didn't want it to be known if he did something good. He says if you do something good, don't talk about it.

I met other survivors but we didn't really talk about it either. Sometimes little things would come out. They say, How did you survive? I say, I was a shiksa, and they know. But lately now we talk more. Since people began to say never again. Never again. Now we want to talk because we don't want for it to happen again, not to anyone.

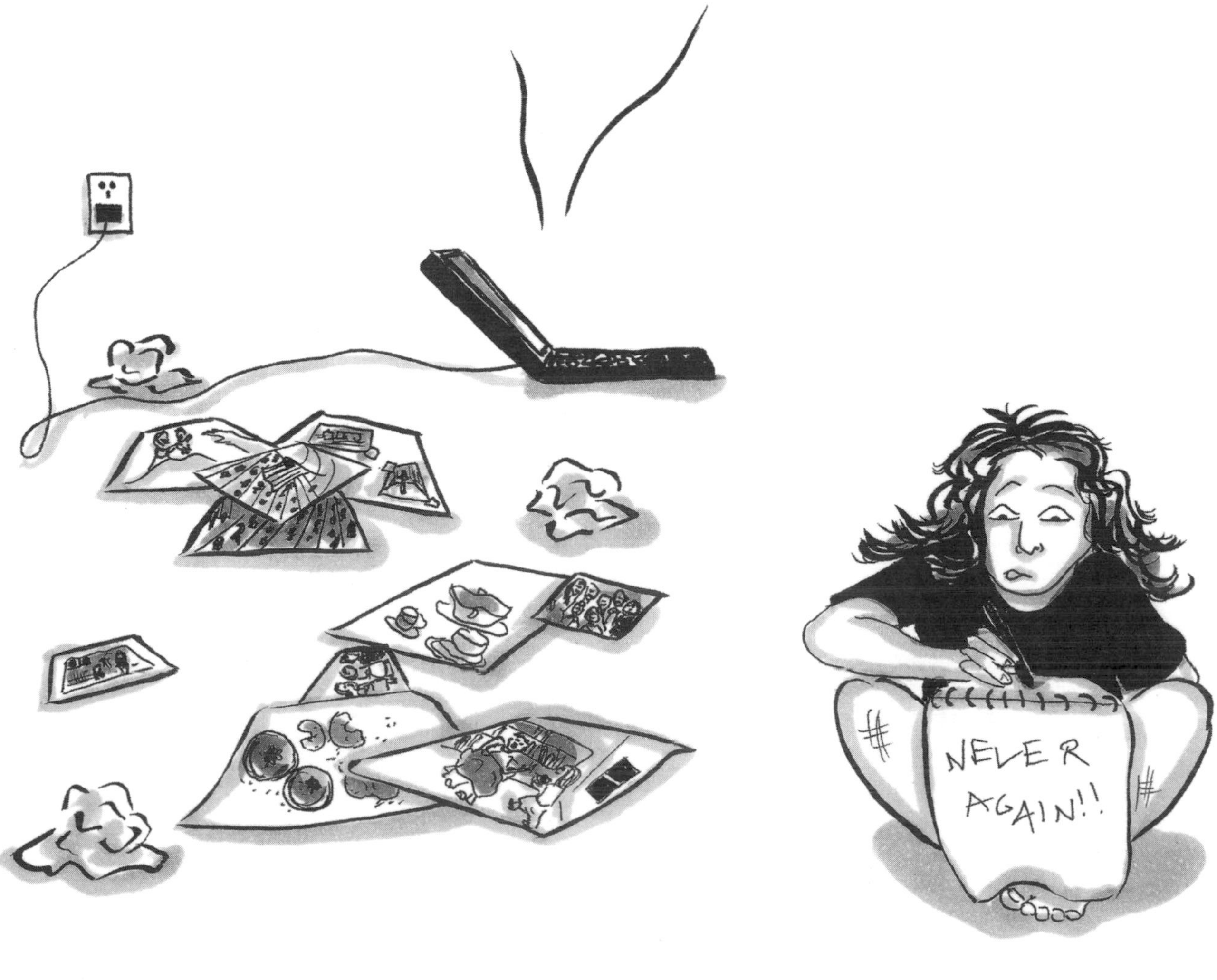
NEVER AGAIN!!

When my children grew up,
they didn't know my stories,
but they were all very sort
of sad. Why don't I have an
uncle, they say. Why don't
I have cousins? Why don't
I have grandparents?
Why? Why? I said, I'm
sorry, if I could buy
you an uncle I would
buy you an uncle!

Now my children, they understand
They ask me, how was your heart
and you never cried? They say,
you never told us. Now they don't
ask so much because they know.
But I love to talk. So much time
I spent alone, in a prison with
myself, holding on to a secret
like a bomb, then keeping inside
more memories and pain like
sinking stones in the stomach.
No more. I want all my children
to hear my stories, for
everybody to hear it.

But my daughter, you see, in the beginning, she didn't really want to know. She was the firstborn, you know. There's problems sometimes with the firstborn that we had to go through that. Even when I was pregnant with her, maybe she felt it, I don't know, the shouting, the running. She was in my stomach. Maybe she was scared the way I was scared.

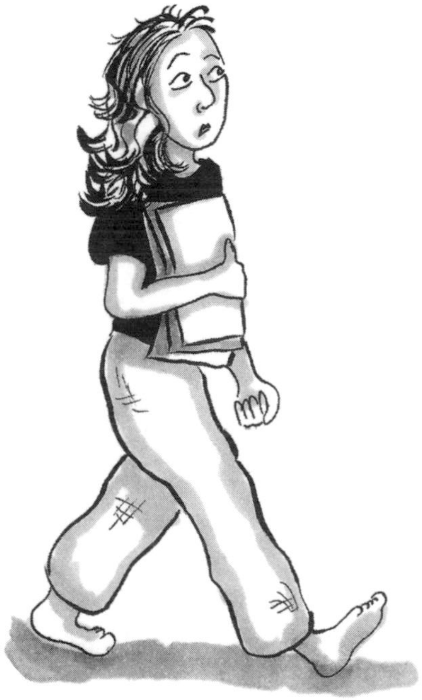

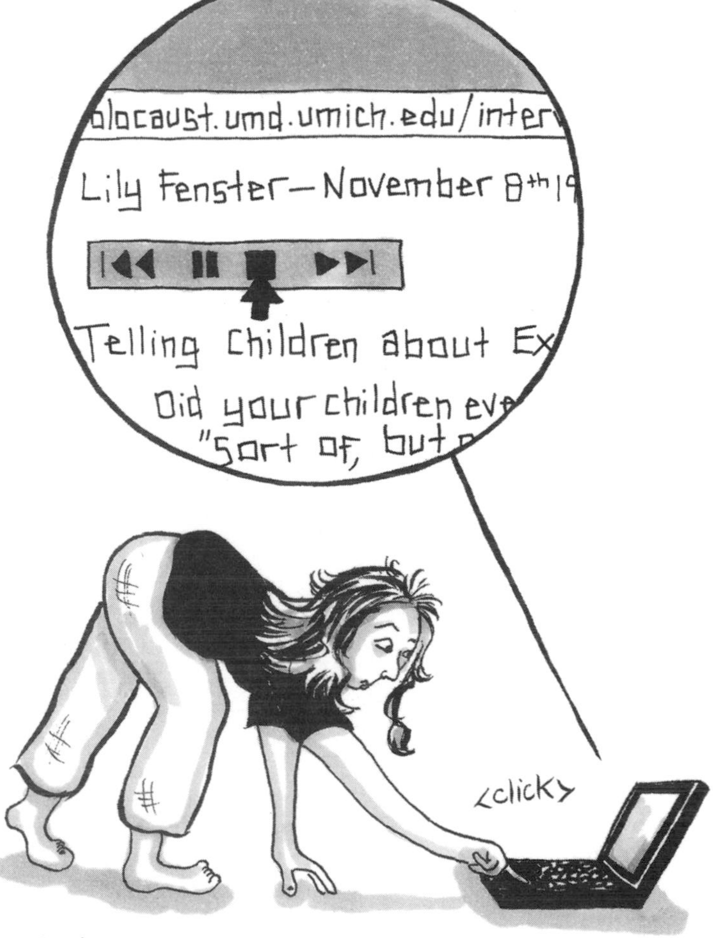
olocaust.umd.umich.edu/inter
Lily Fenster—November 8th 19
Telling Children about Ex
Did your children eve
"Sort of, but
<click>

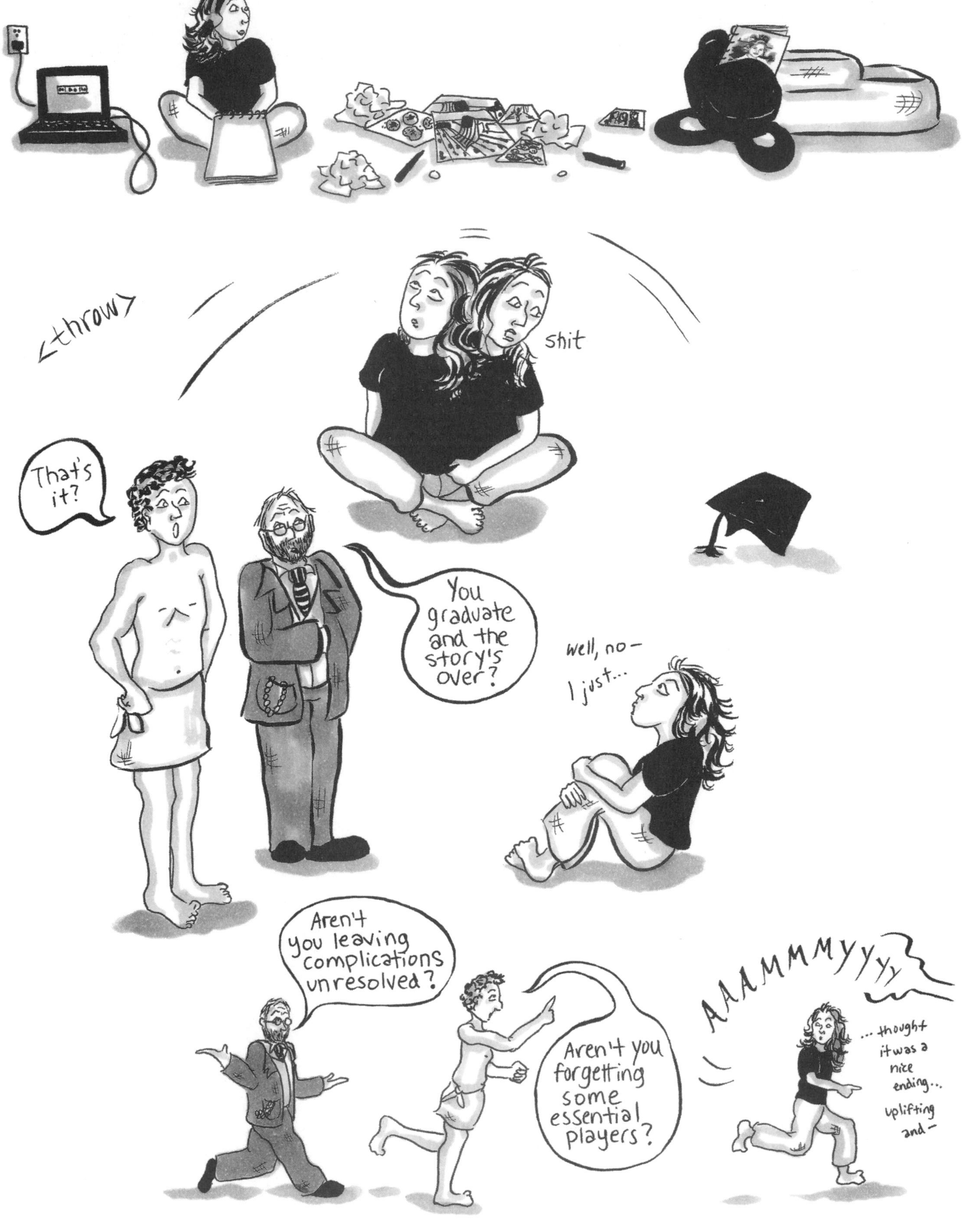
<throw>
shit
That's it?
You graduate and the story's over?
well, no— I just...
Aren't you leaving complications unresolved?
Aren't you forgetting some essential players?
AAAMMMMYyyy
...thought it was a nice ending... uplifting and—

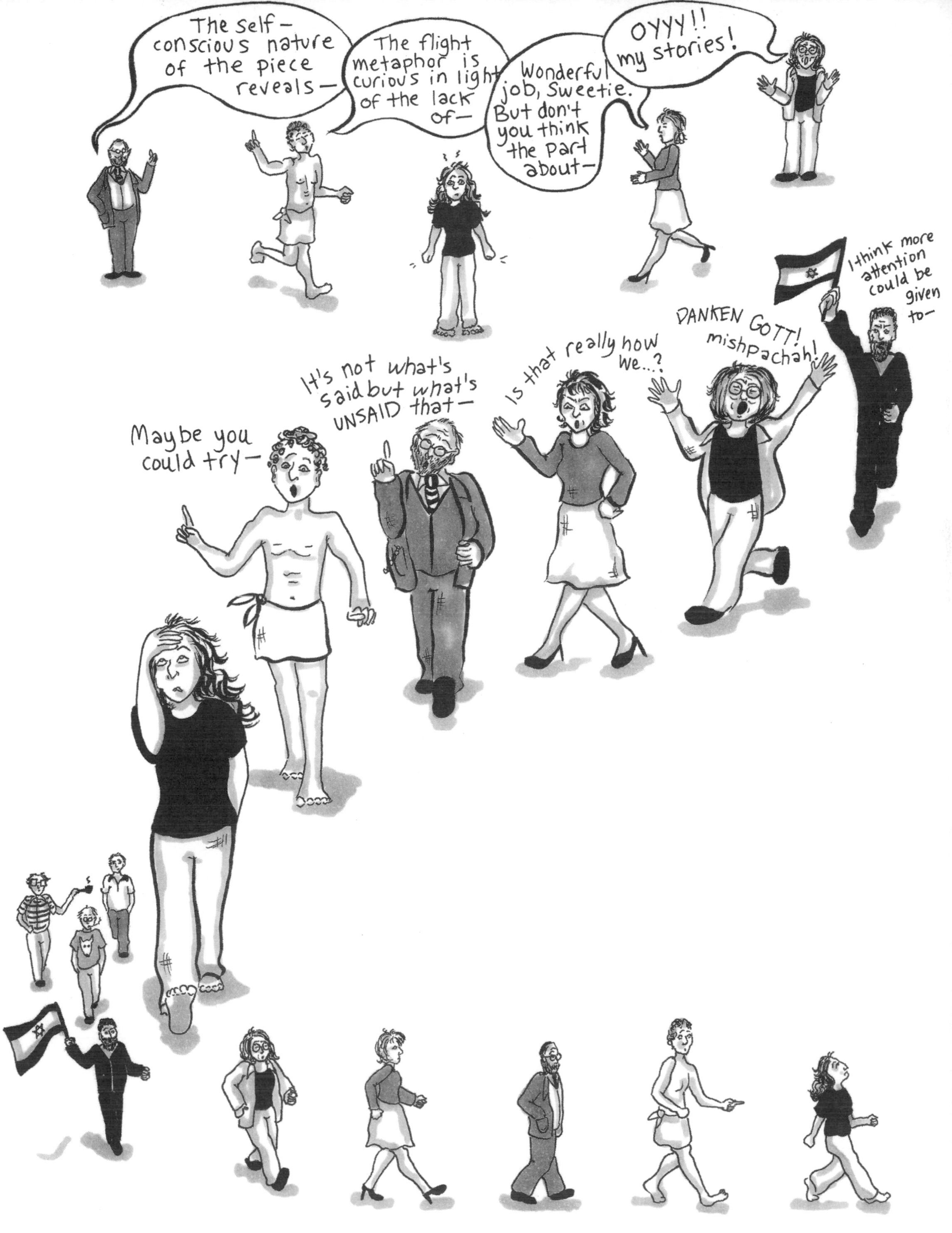

The self-conscious nature of the piece reveals—
The flight metaphor is curious in light of the lack of—
Wonderful job, Sweetie. But don't you think the part about—
OYYY!! my stories!
I think more attention could be given to—
DANKEN GOTT! mishpachah!
Is that really how we...?
It's not what's said but what's UNSAID that—
Maybe you could try—

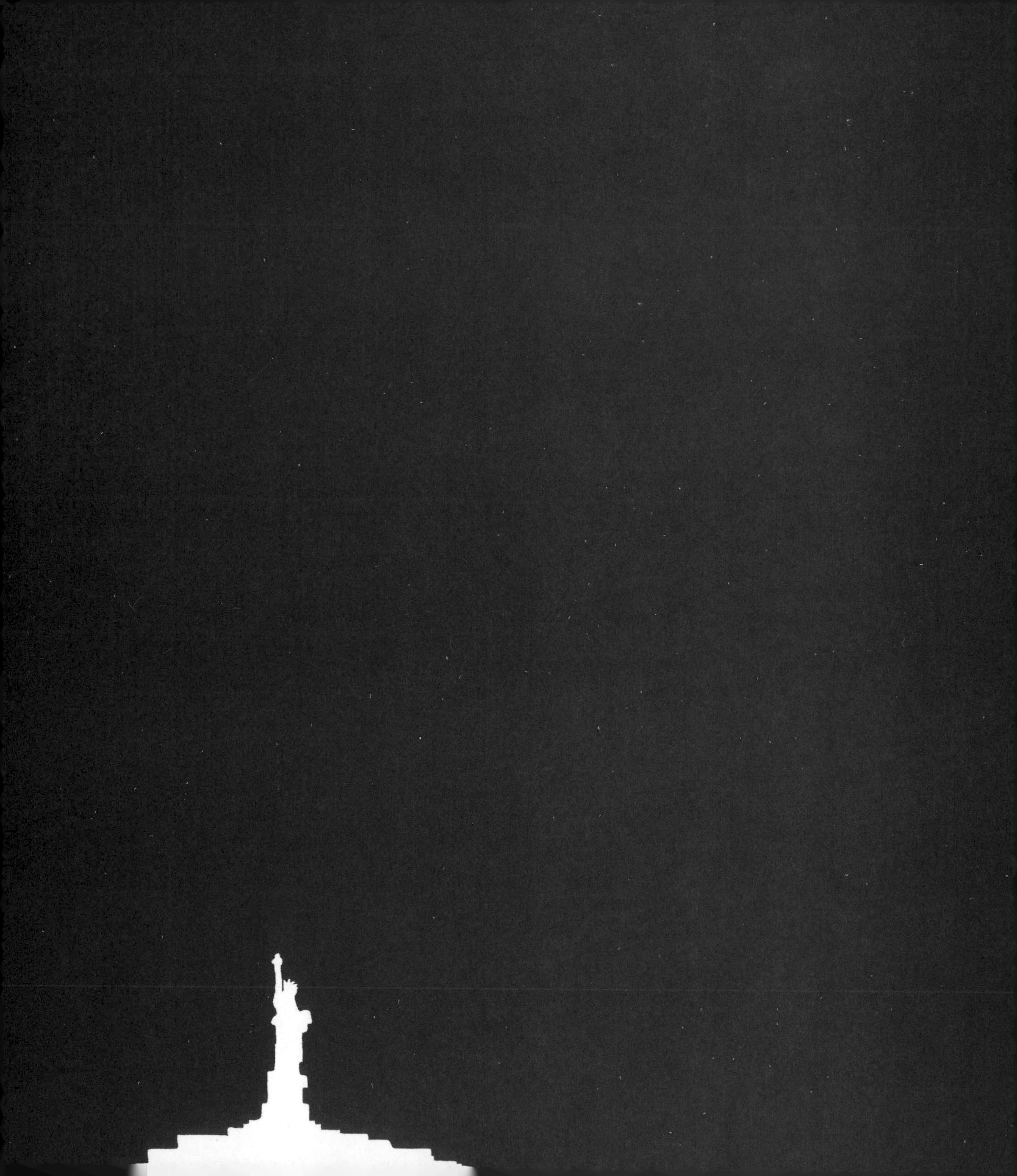

Chapter Seven.
Bedbound

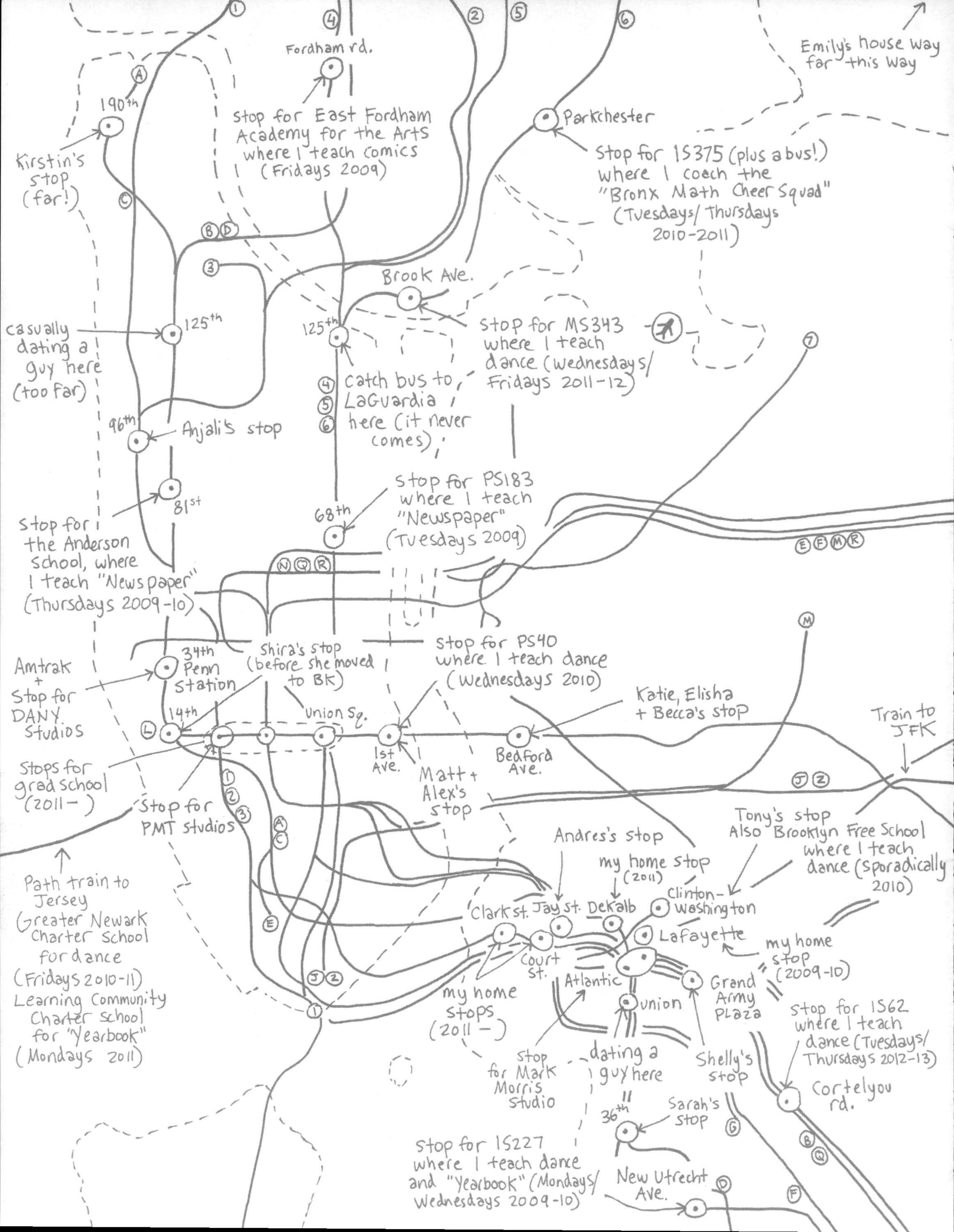

Emily's house way far this way
Fordham rd.
Stop for East Fordham Academy for the Arts where I teach comics (Fridays 2009)
190th
Kirstin's stop (far!)
Parkchester
Stop for IS375 (plus a bus!) where I coach the "Bronx Math Cheer Squad" (Tuesdays/Thursdays 2010-2011)
Brook Ave.
125th
casually dating a guy here (too far)
125th
Stop for MS343 where I teach dance (Wednesdays/Fridays 2011-12)
catch bus to LaGuardia here (it never comes)
96th
Anjali's stop
81st
Stop for the Anderson school, where I teach "Newspaper" (Thursdays 2009-10)
68th
Stop for PS183 where I teach "Newspaper" (Tuesdays 2009)
Amtrak + Stop for DANY Studios
34th Penn Station
Shira's stop (before she moved to BK)
Stop for PS40 where I teach dance (Wednesdays 2010)
Union Sq.
14th
Katie, Elisha + Becca's stop
1st Ave.
Bedford Ave.
Train to JFK
Stops for grad school (2011-)
Stop for PMT studios
Matt + Alex's stop
Tony's stop Also Brooklyn Free School where I teach dance (Sporadically 2010)
Andres's stop
my home stop (2011)
Path train to Jersey (Greater Newark Charter School for dance (Fridays 2010-11) Learning Community Charter School for "Yearbook" (Mondays 2011)
Clark st.
Jay st.
Dekalb
Clinton-Washington
Lafayette
my home stop (2009-10)
Court st.
Atlantic
my home stops (2011 -)
Union
Grand Army Plaza
Stop for IS62 where I teach dance (Tuesdays/Thursdays 2012-13)
Stop for Mark Morris Studio
dating a guy here
Shelly's stop
Cortelyou rd.
36th
Sarah's stop
Stop for IS227 where I teach dance and "Yearbook" (Mondays/Wednesdays 2009-10)
New Utrecht Ave.

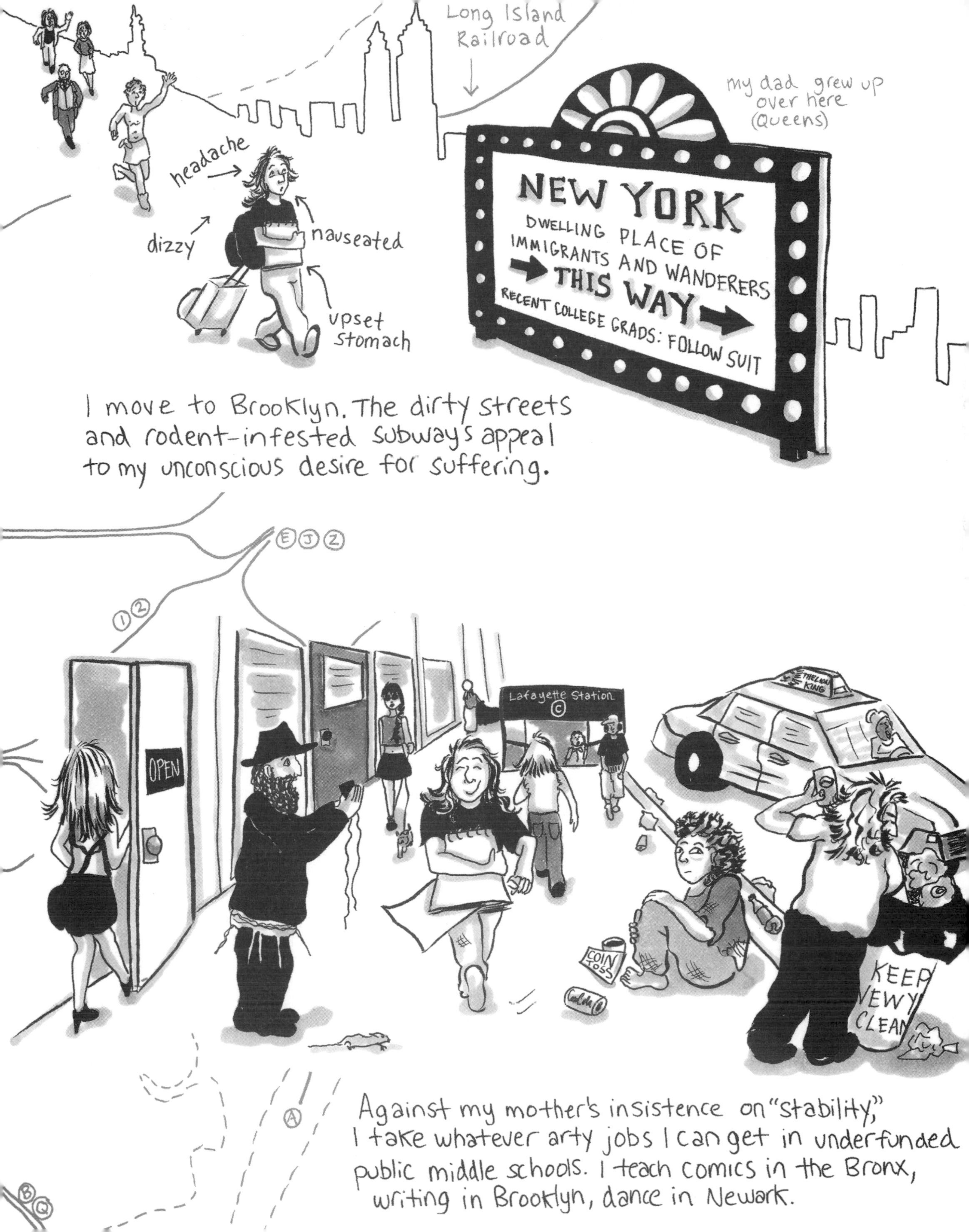
Long Island Railroad
my dad grew up over here (Queens)
headache
dizzy
nauseated
upset stomach
NEW YORK
DWELLING PLACE OF IMMIGRANTS AND WANDERERS
THIS WAY
RECENT COLLEGE GRADS: FOLLOW SUIT
I move to Brooklyn. The dirty streets and rodent-infested subway's appeal to my unconscious desire for suffering.
E J Z
1 2
OPEN
Lafayette Station
C
COIN TOSS
KEEP
EWY
CLEA
Against my mother's insistence on "stability," I take whatever arty jobs I can get in underfunded public middle schools. I teach comics in the Bronx, writing in Brooklyn, dance in Newark.
A
B Q

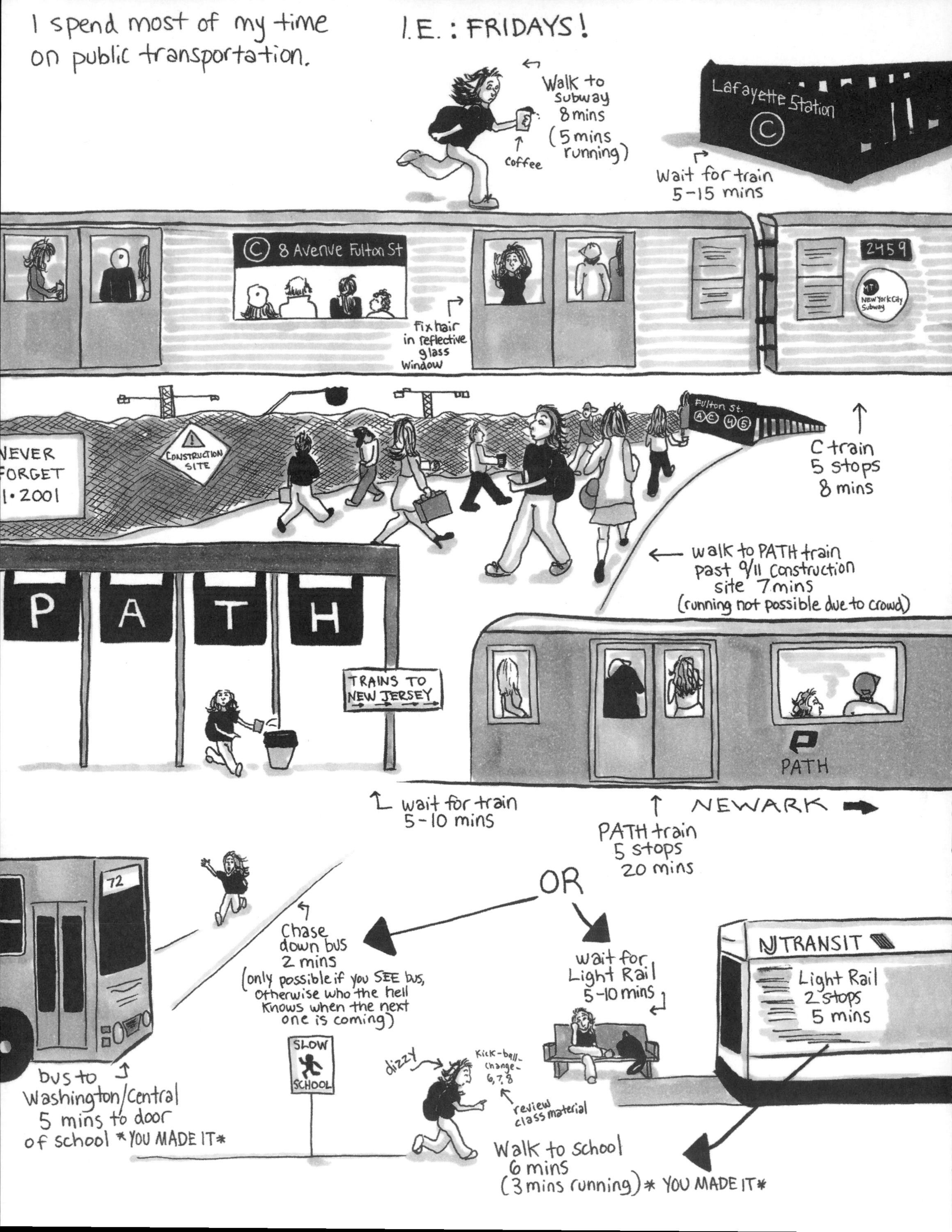
I spend most of my time on public transportation.
I.E.: FRIDAYS!
Walk to subway 8 mins (5 mins running)
coffee
Lafayette Station
Wait for train 5-15 mins
C 8 Avenue Fulton St
fix hair in reflective glass window
2459
New York City Subway
C train 5 stops 8 mins
Fulton St.
NEVER FORGET
1•2001
CONSTRUCTION SITE
walk to PATH train past 9/11 construction site 7 mins (running not possible due to crowd)
PATH
TRAINS TO NEW JERSEY
PATH
wait for train 5-10 mins
PATH train 5 stops 20 mins
NEWARK
OR
72
Chase down bus 2 mins (only possible if you SEE bus, otherwise who the hell knows when the next one is coming)
bus to Washington/Central 5 mins to door of school *YOU MADE IT*
NJ TRANSIT
Light Rail 2 stops 5 mins
wait for Light Rail 5-10 mins
SLOW SCHOOL
dizzy
Kick-ball-change-6,7,8
review class material
Walk to school 6 mins (3 mins running) * YOU MADE IT*

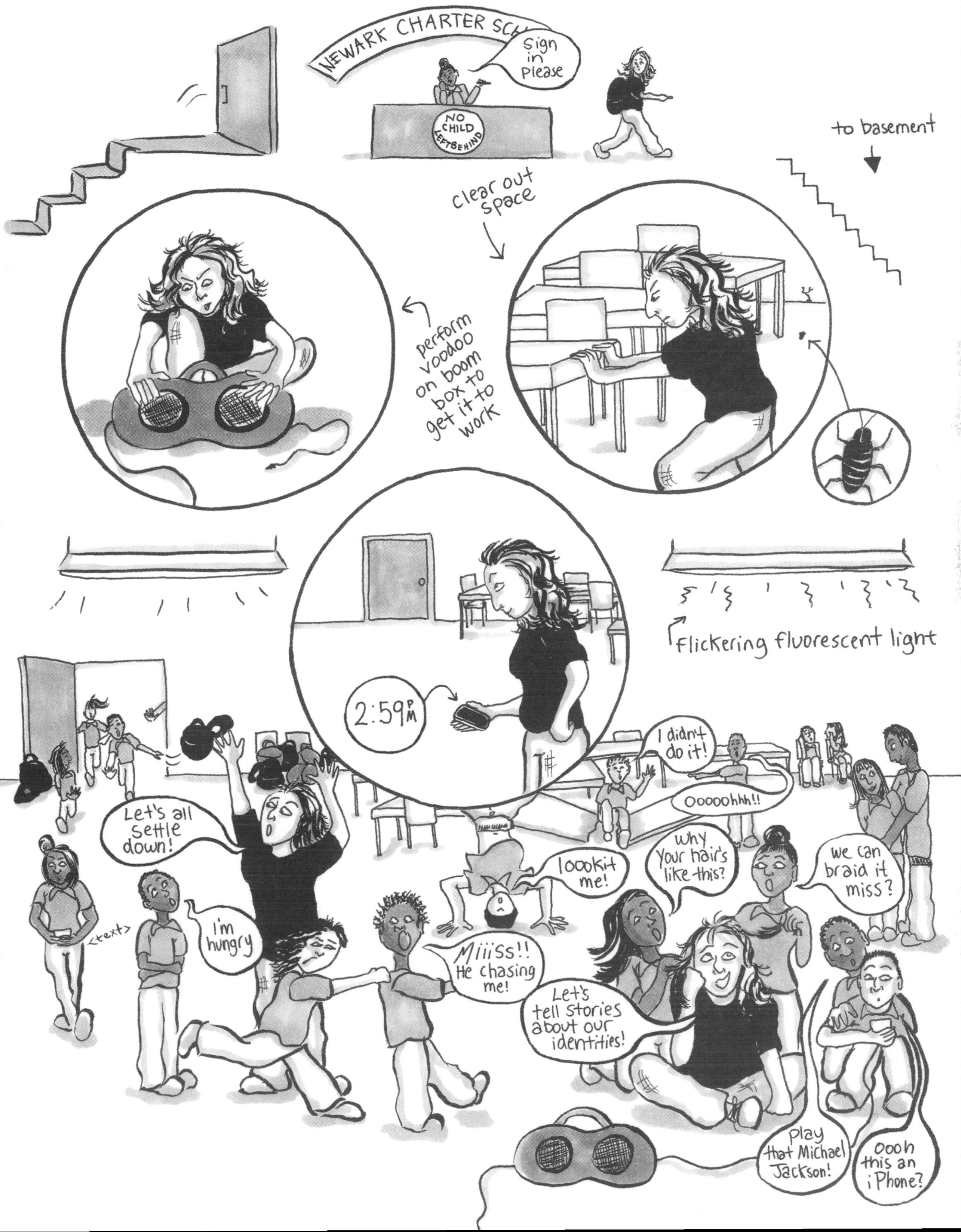

NEWARK CHARTER SCH
Sign in please
NO CHILD LEFT BEHIND
to basement
clear out space
perform voodoo on boom box to get it to work
2:59 PM
Flickering fluorescent light
I didn't do it!
Ooooohhh!!
Let's all settle down!
lookit me!
Why your hair's like this?
We can braid it miss?
<text>
I'm hungry
Miiiss!! He chasing me!
Let's tell stories about our identities!
Play that Michael Jackson!
Oooh this an iPhone?

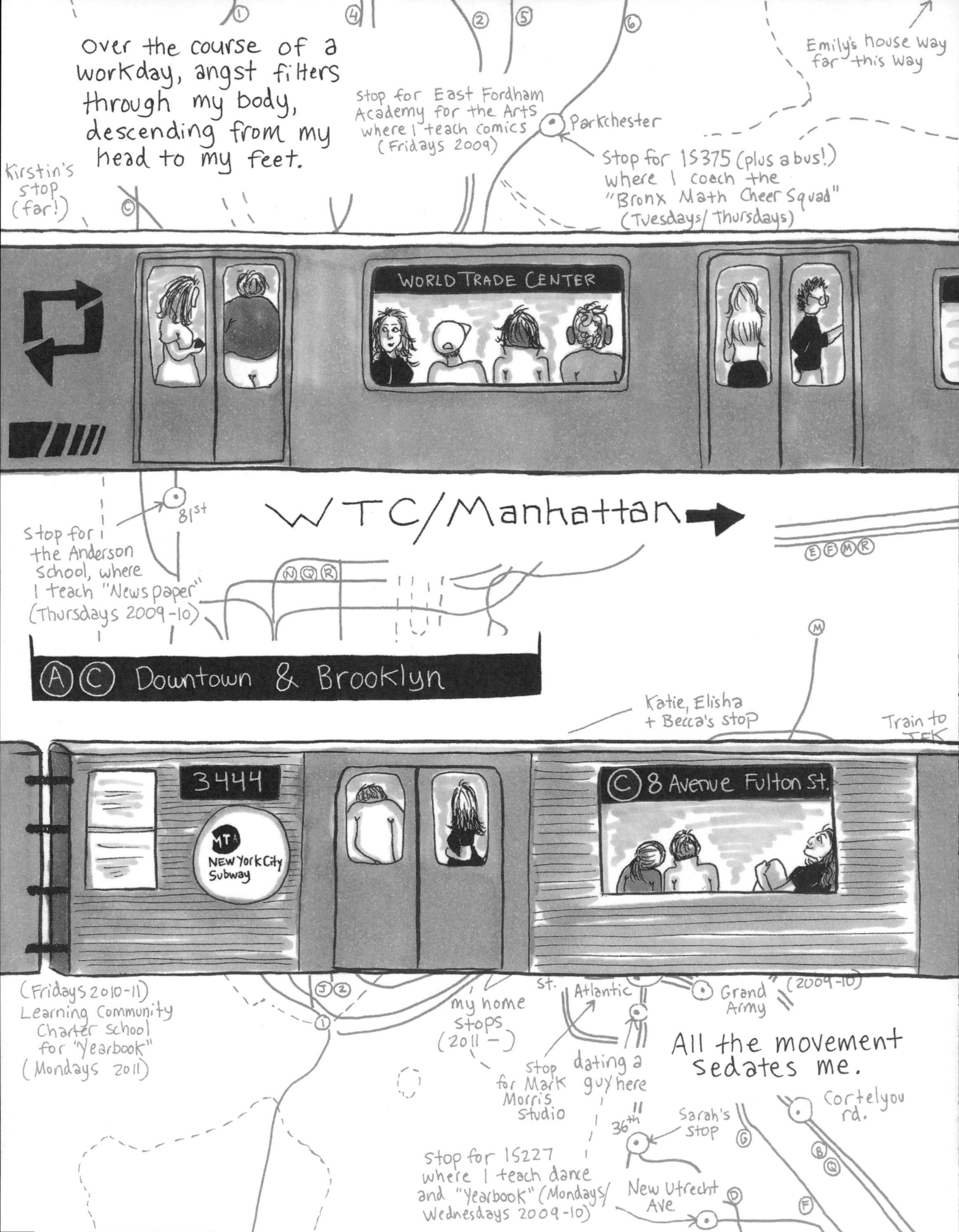
Over the course of a workday, angst filters through my body, descending from my head to my feet.
Emily's house way far this way
Stop for East Fordham Academy for the Arts where I teach comics (Fridays 2009)
Parkchester
Stop for IS375 (plus a bus!) where I coach the "Bronx Math Cheer Squad" (Tuesdays/Thursdays)
Kirstin's stop (far!)
WORLD TRADE CENTER
Stop for the Anderson School, where I teach "Newspaper" (Thursdays 2009-10)
81st
WTC/Manhattan
Ⓐ Ⓒ Downtown & Brooklyn
Katie, Elisha + Becca's stop
Train to
3444
MTA
New York City Subway
Ⓒ 8 Avenue Fulton St.
(Fridays 2010-11) Learning Community Charter School for "Yearbook" (Mondays 2011)
my home stops (2011 –)
St.
Atlantic
Grand Army
(2009-10)
All the movement sedates me.
Stop for Mark Morris Studio
dating a guy here
36th
Sarah's stop
Cortelyou rd.
Stop for IS227 where I teach dance and "Yearbook" (Mondays/Wednesdays 2009-10)
New Utrecht Ave

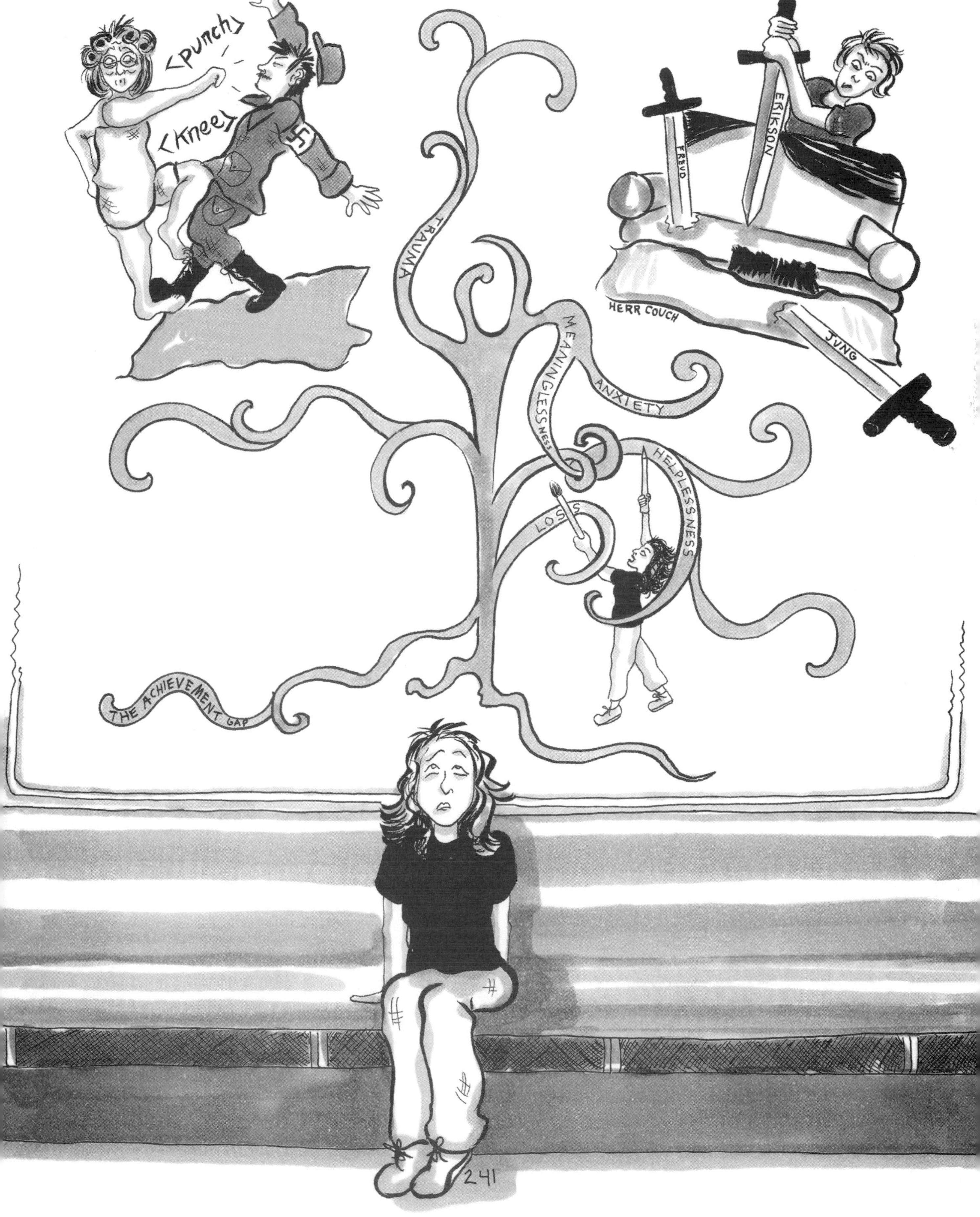
<punch>
<Knee>
FREUD
ERIKSON
JUNG
HERR COUCH
TRAUMA
MEANINGLESSNESS
ANXIETY
HELPLESSNESS
LOSS
THE ACHIEVEMENT GAP

My life doesn't feel like a hero's journey.

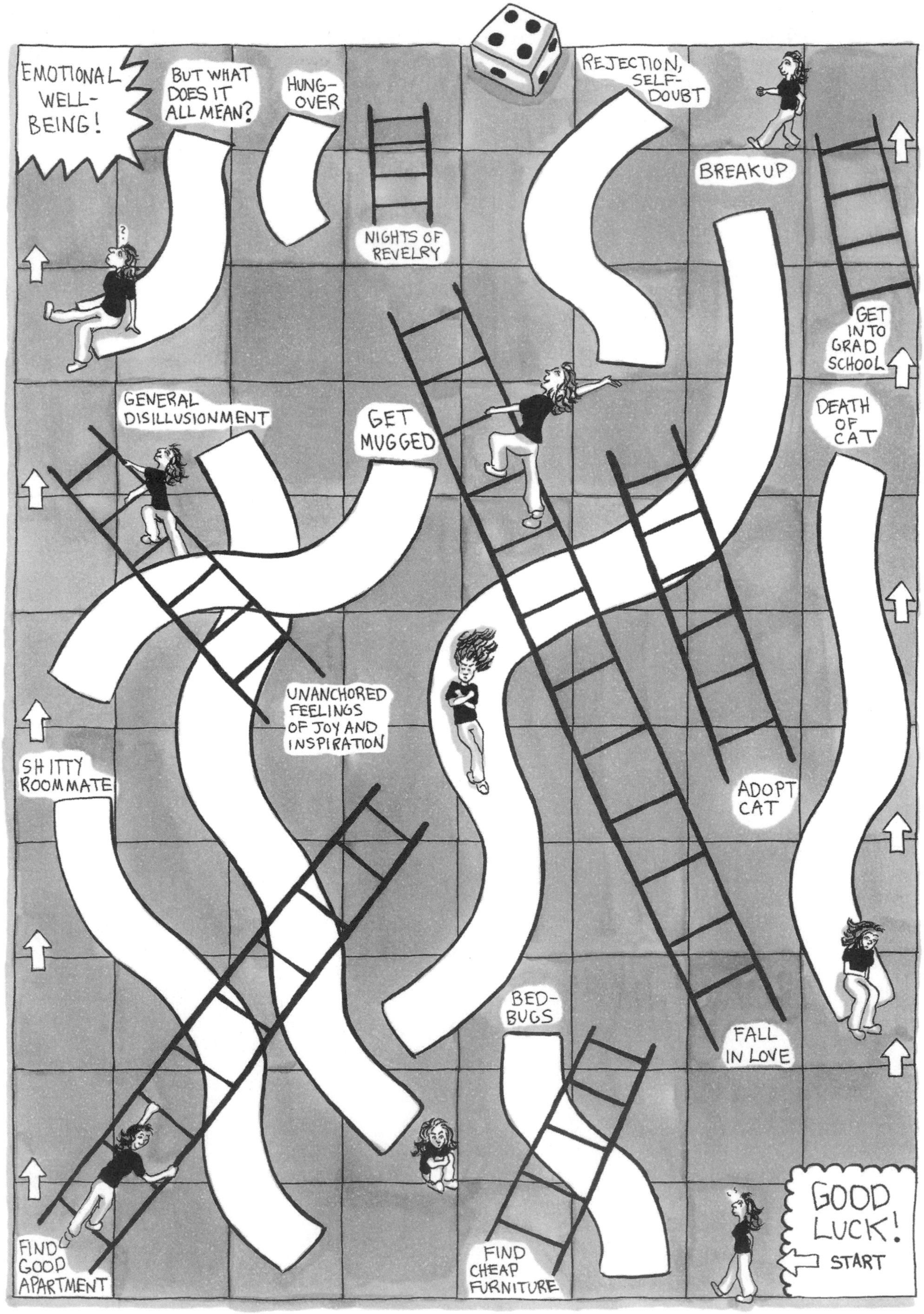
EMOTIONAL WELL-BEING!
BUT WHAT DOES IT ALL MEAN?
HUNG-OVER
REJECTION, SELF-DOUBT
BREAKUP
NIGHTS OF REVELRY
GET INTO GRAD SCHOOL
GENERAL DISILLUSIONMENT
GET MUGGED
DEATH OF CAT
UNANCHORED FEELINGS OF JOY AND INSPIRATION
SHITTY ROOMMATE
ADOPT CAT
BED-BUGS
FALL IN LOVE
GOOD LUCK!
START
FIND GOOD APARTMENT
FIND CHEAP FURNITURE

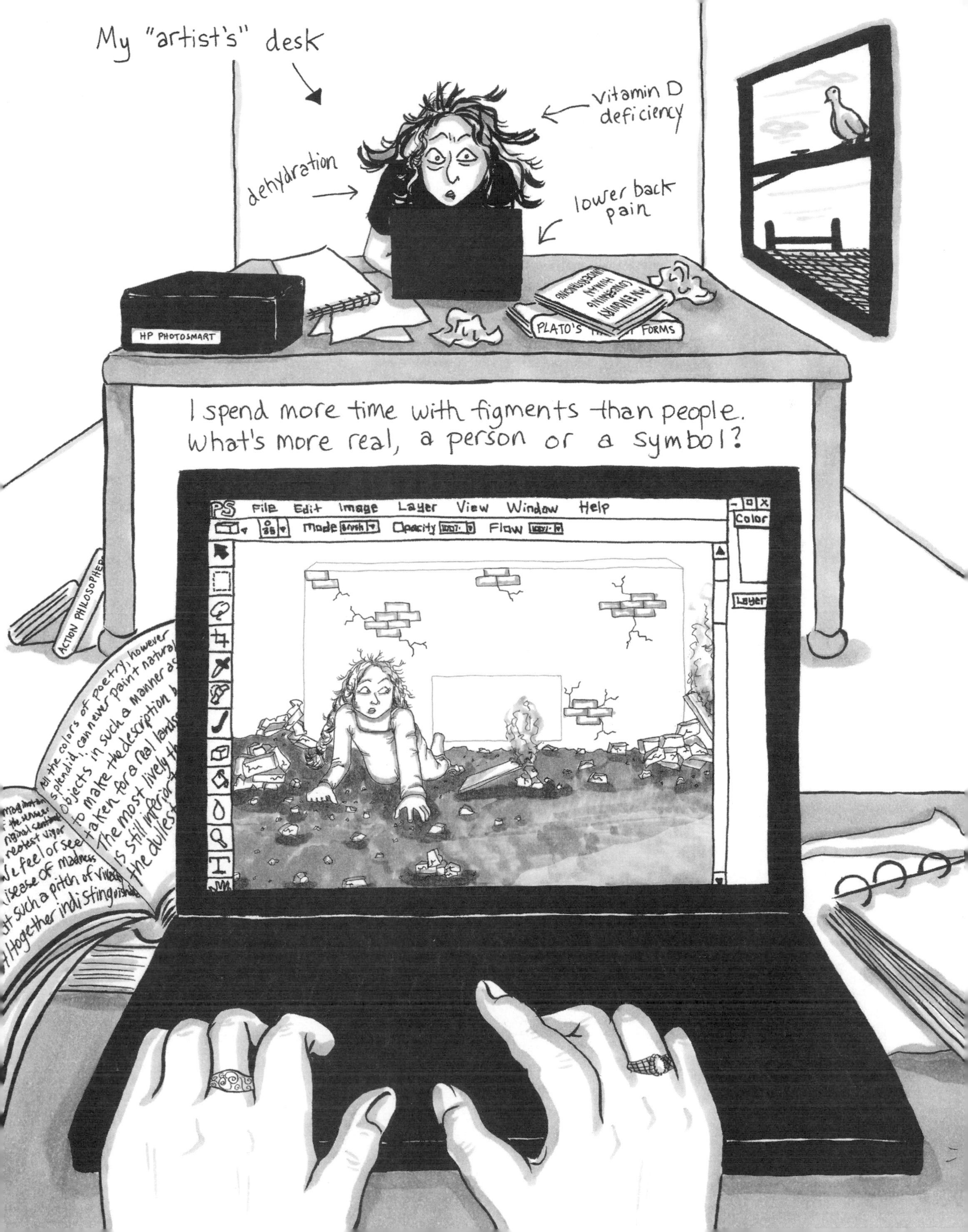

My "artist's" desk
vitamin D deficiency
dehydration
lower back pain
HP PHOTOSMART
AN ENQUIRY CONCERNING HUMAN UNDERSTANDING
PLATO'S
FORMS
I spend more time with figments than people.
What's more real, a person or a symbol?
ACTION PHILOSOPHER
All the colors of poetry, however
splendid, can never paint natural
objects in such a manner as
to make the description be
taken for a real lands
The most lively th
is still inferior
the dullest
reatest vigor
we feel or see
disease of madness
such a pitch of vivacity
altogether indistinguishable
PS File Edit Image Layer View Window Help
Mode
Opacity
Flow
Color
Layer

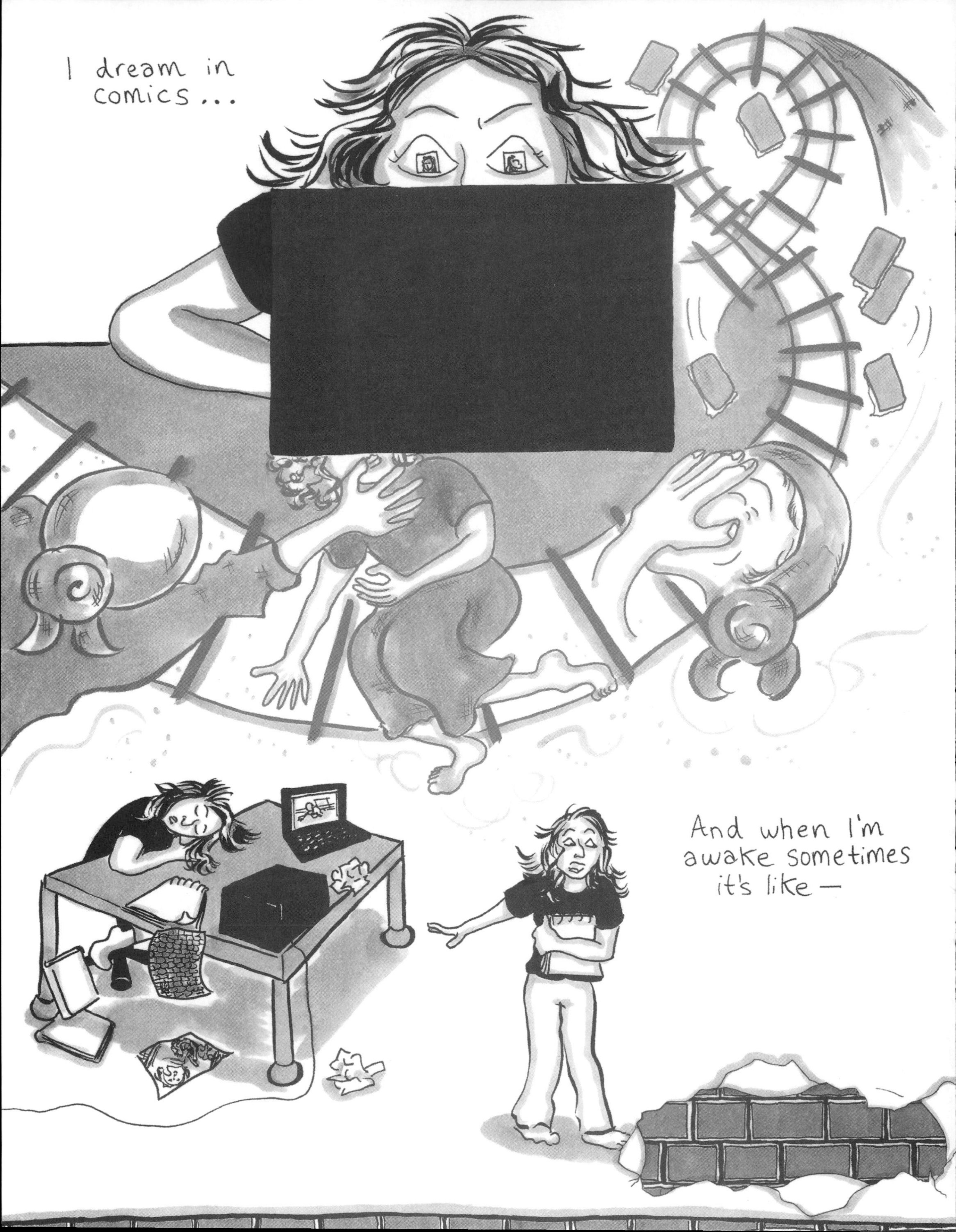
I dream in comics...
And when I'm awake sometimes it's like—

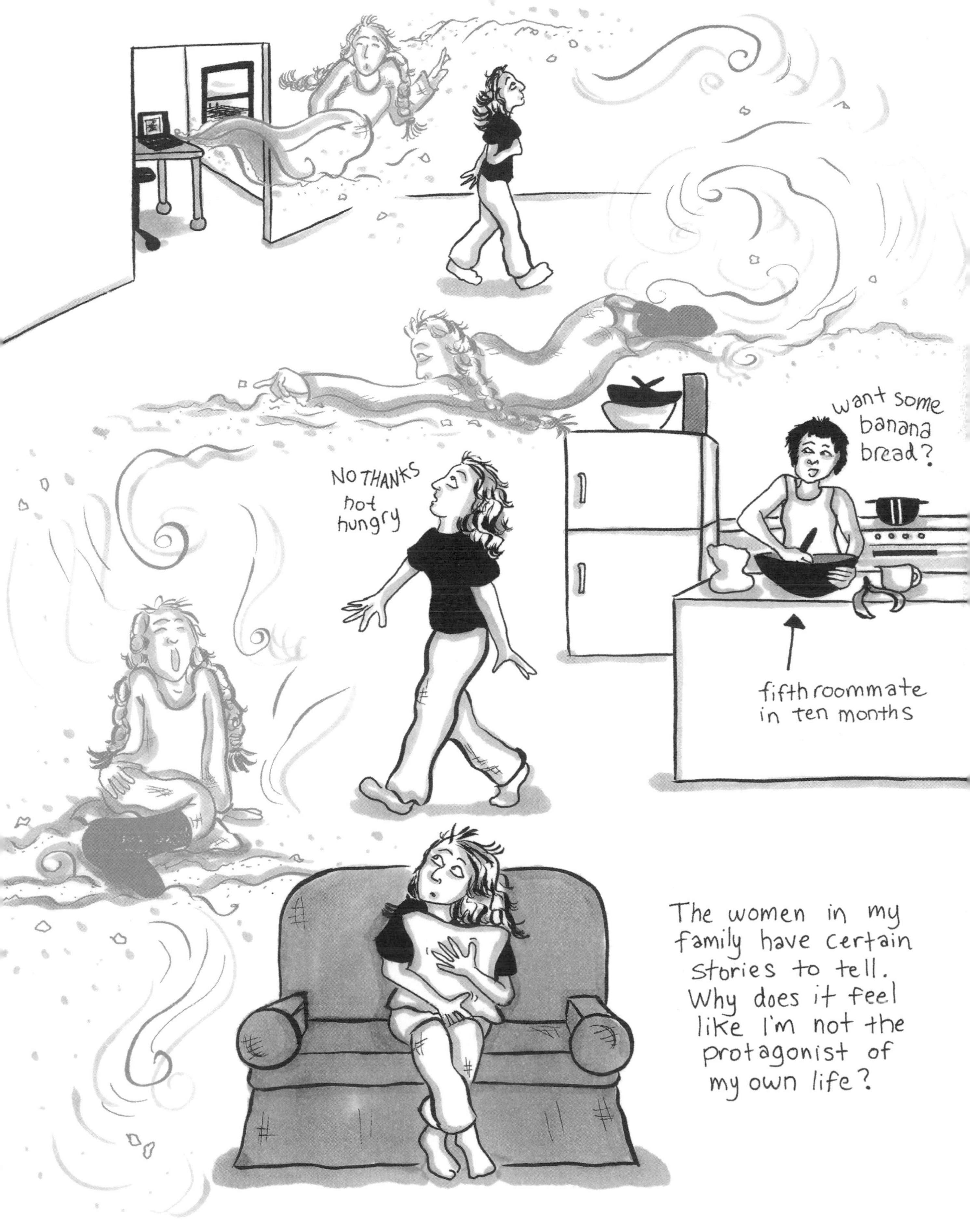
want some banana bread?
NO THANKS
not hungry
fifth roommate in ten months
The women in my family have certain stories to tell. Why does it feel like I'm not the protagonist of my own life?

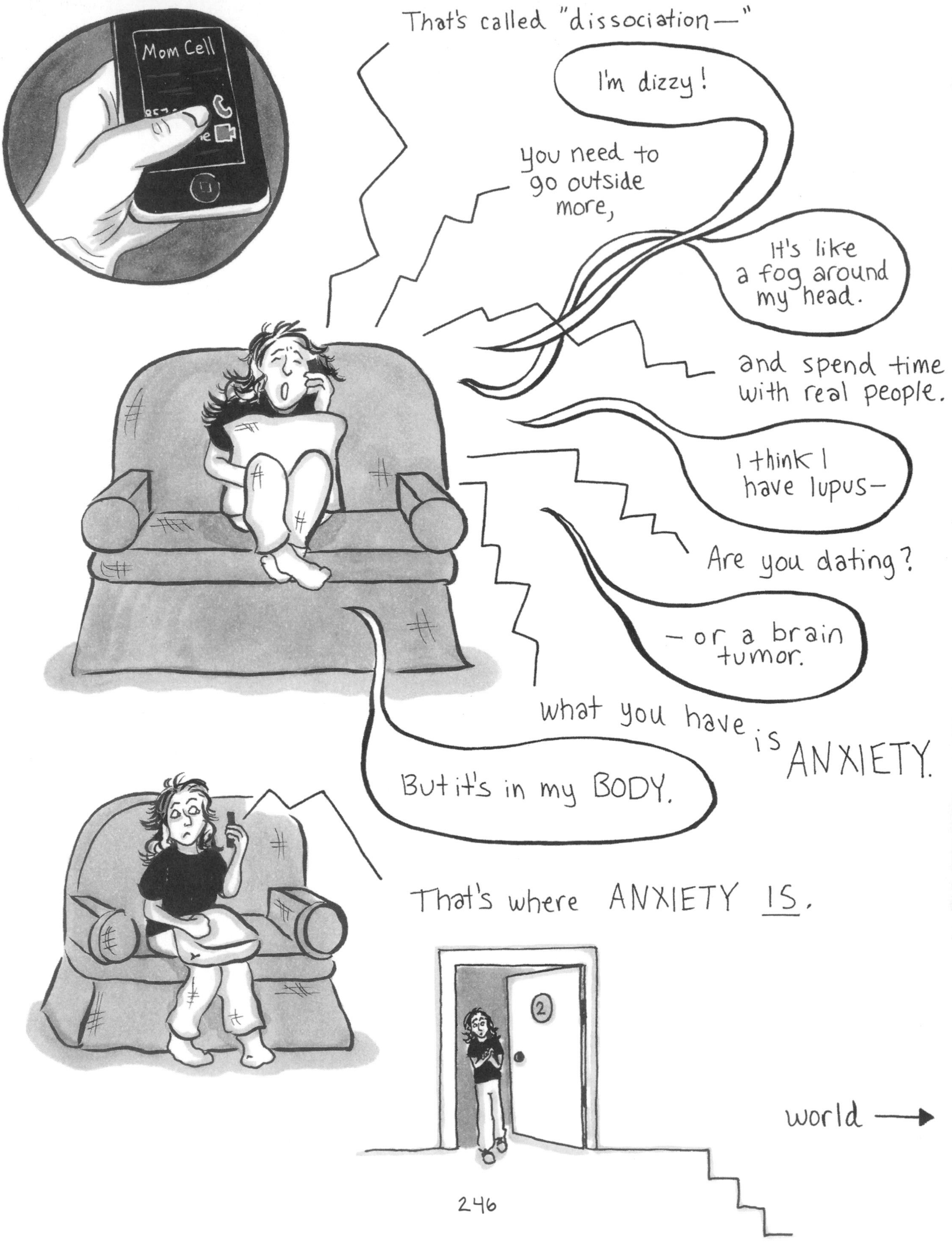
Mom Cell
That's called "dissociation—"
I'm dizzy!
you need to go outside more,
It's like a fog around my head.
and spend time with real people.
I think I have lupus—
Are you dating?
—or a brain tumor.
what you have is ANXIETY.
But it's in my BODY.
That's where ANXIETY IS.
2
world →

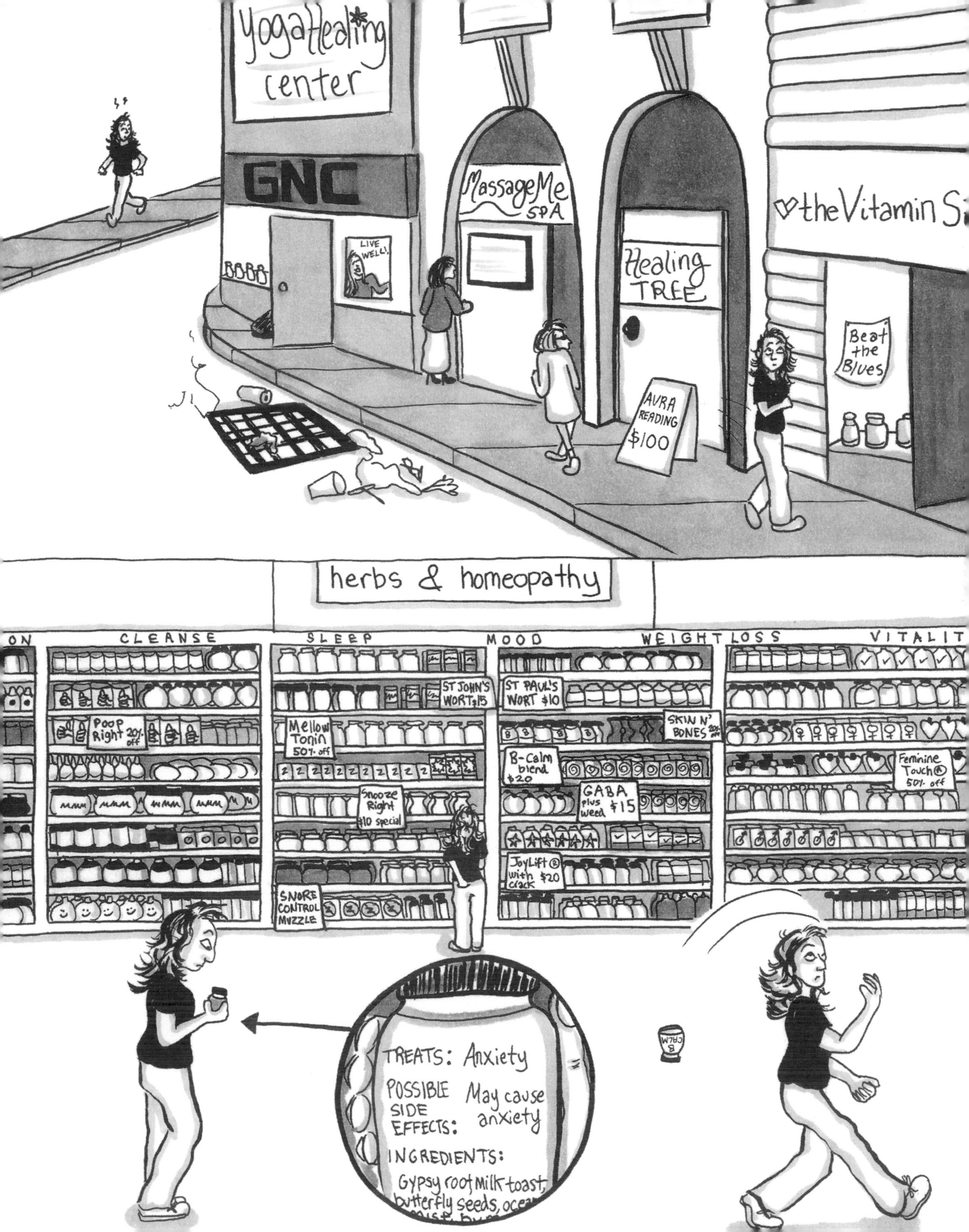

YogaHealing center
GNC
LIVE WELL!
MassageMe SPA
Healing TREE
AURA READING $100
the Vitamin S
Beat the Blues
herbs & homeopathy
CLEANSE
SLEEP
MOOD
WEIGHT LOSS
VITALIT
Poop Right 20% off
Mellow Tonin 50% off
ST JOHN'S WORT $15
ST PAUL'S WORT $10
SKIN N' BONES 20% off
B-Calm blend $20
GABA plus weed $15
Snooze Right $10 special
JoyLift® with crack $20
Feminine Touch® 50% off
SNORE CONTROL MUZZLE
TREATS: Anxiety
POSSIBLE SIDE EFFECTS: May cause anxiety
INGREDIENTS:
Gypsy root, milk toast, butterfly seeds, ocea

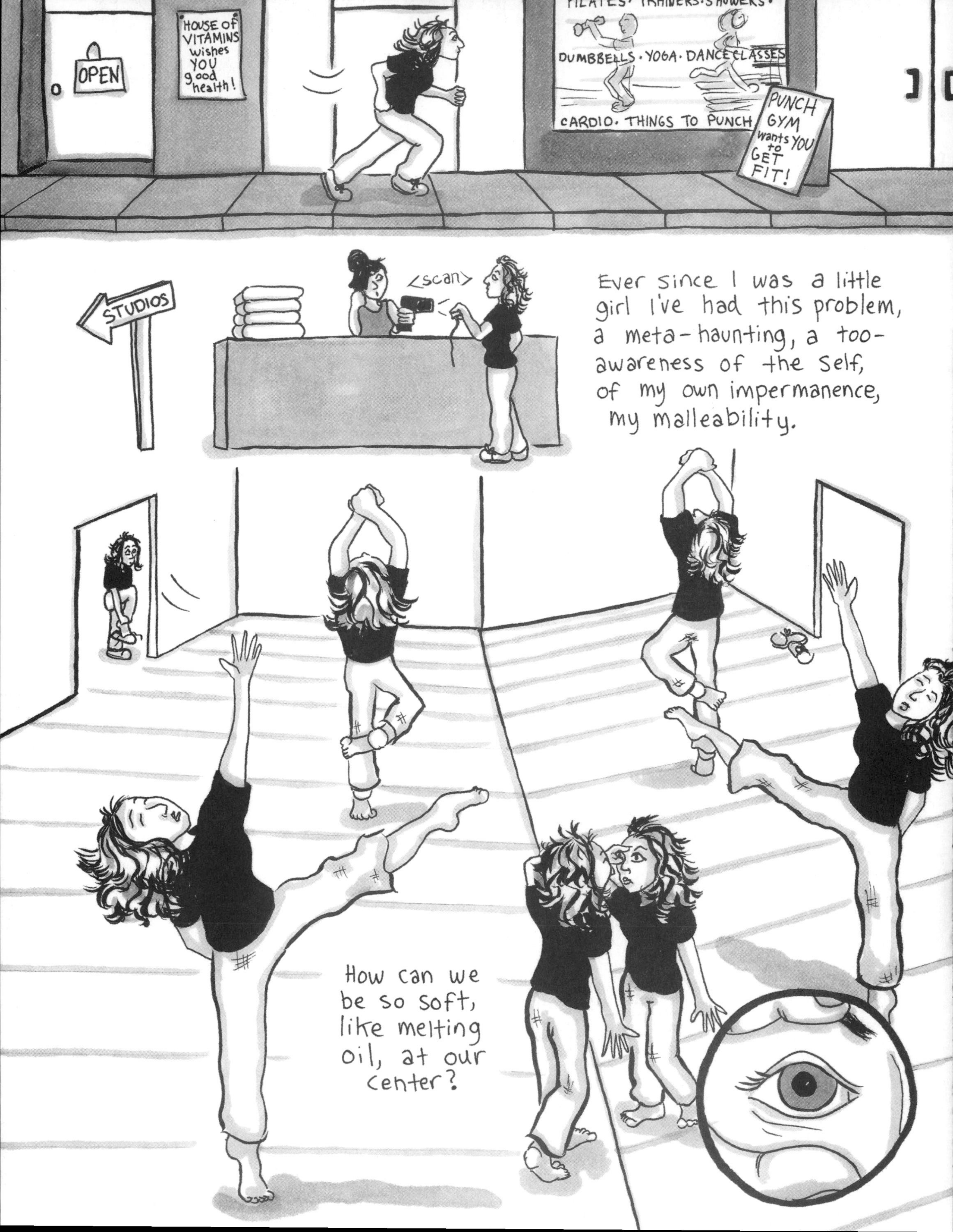
OPEN
HOUSE OF VITAMINS wishes YOU good health!
DUMBBELLS · YOGA · DANCE CLASSES
CARDIO · THINGS TO PUNCH
PUNCH GYM wants YOU to GET FIT!
STUDIOS
<scan>
Ever since I was a little girl I've had this problem, a meta-haunting, a too-awareness of the self, of my own impermanence, my malleability.
How can we be so soft, like melting oil, at our center?

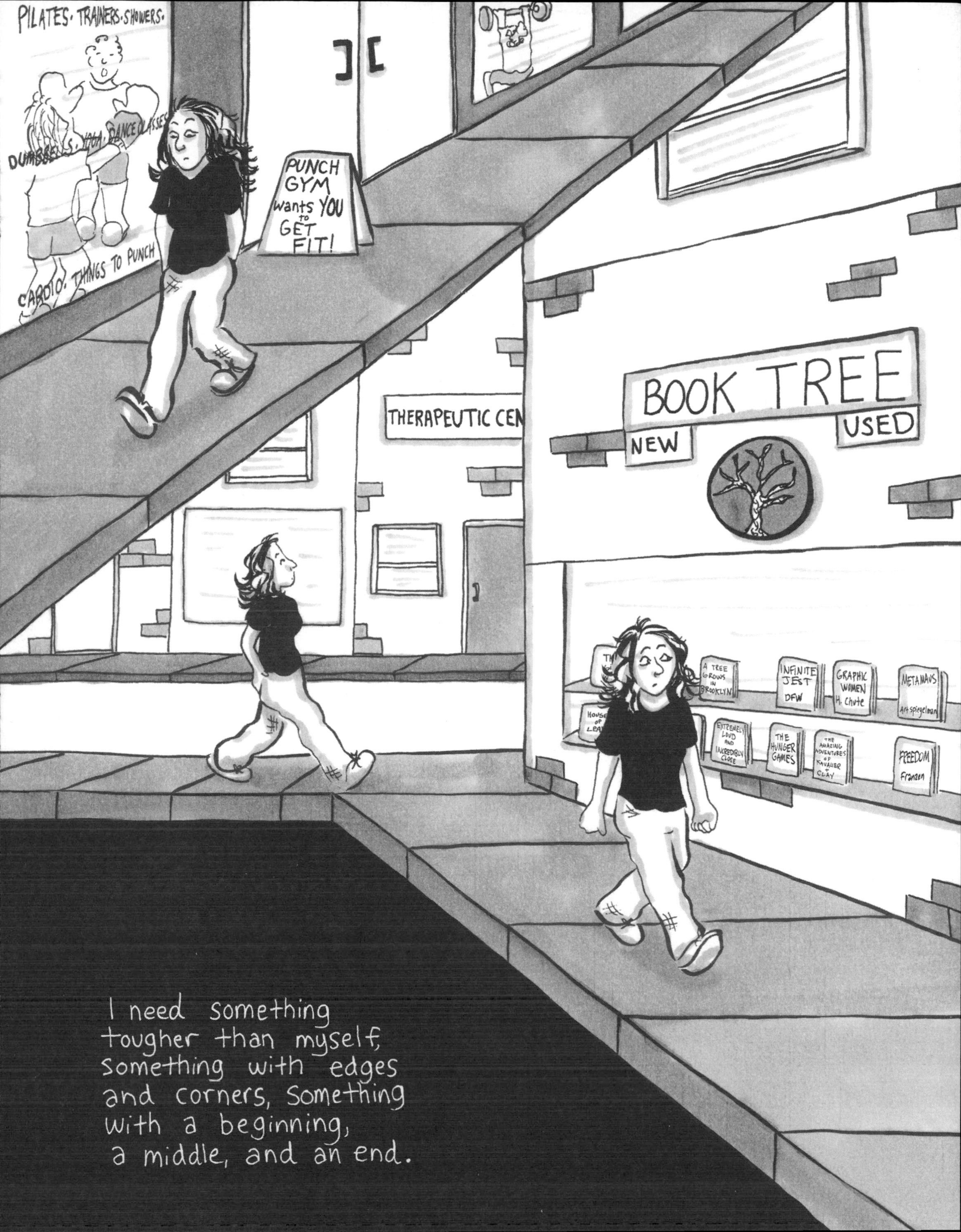

PILATES · TRAINERS · SHOWERS ·
DUMBBELLS · YOGA · DANCE CLASSES
CARDIO · THINGS TO PUNCH
PUNCH GYM wants YOU to GET FIT!
THERAPEUTIC CEN
BOOK TREE
NEW
USED
A TREE GROWS IN BROOKLYN
INFINITE JEST DFW
GRAPHIC WOMEN H. Chute
METAMAUS Art Spiegelman
EXTREMELY LOUD AND INCREDIBLY CLOSE
THE HUNGER GAMES
THE AMAZING ADVENTURES OF KAVALIER & CLAY
FREEDOM Franzen
I need something tougher than myself, something with edges and corners, something with a beginning, a middle, and an end.

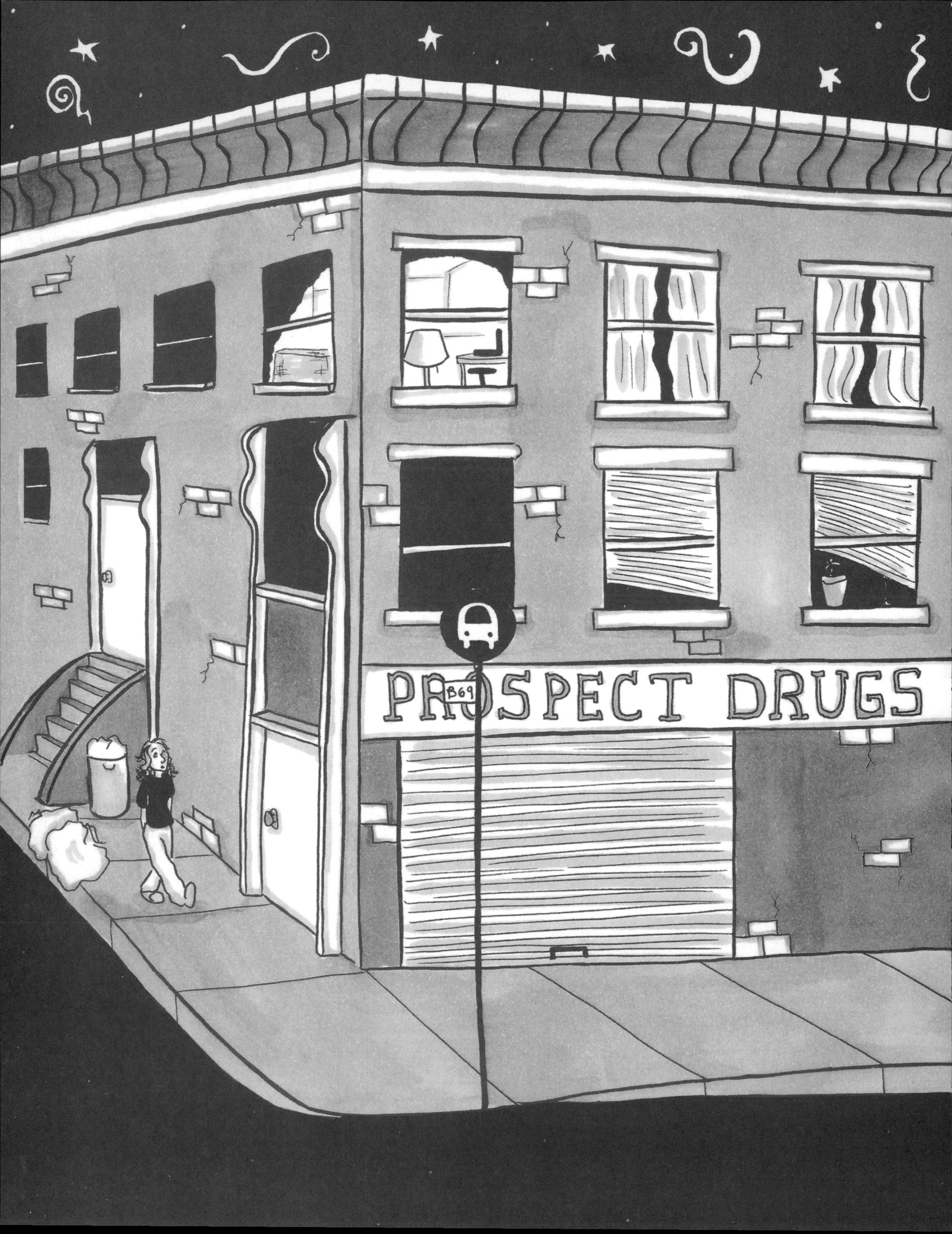
PROSPECT DRUGS
B69

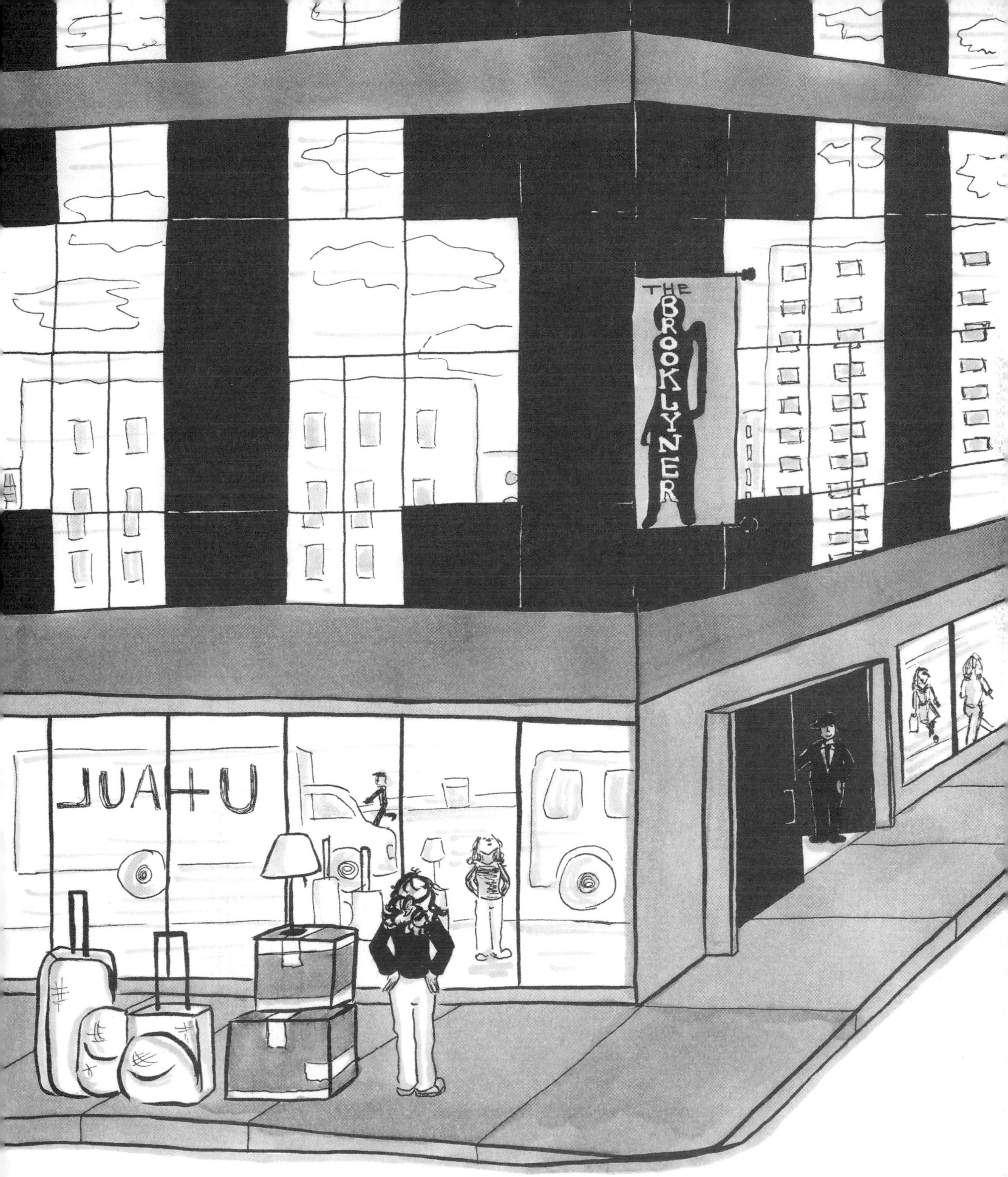
THE
BROOKLYNER

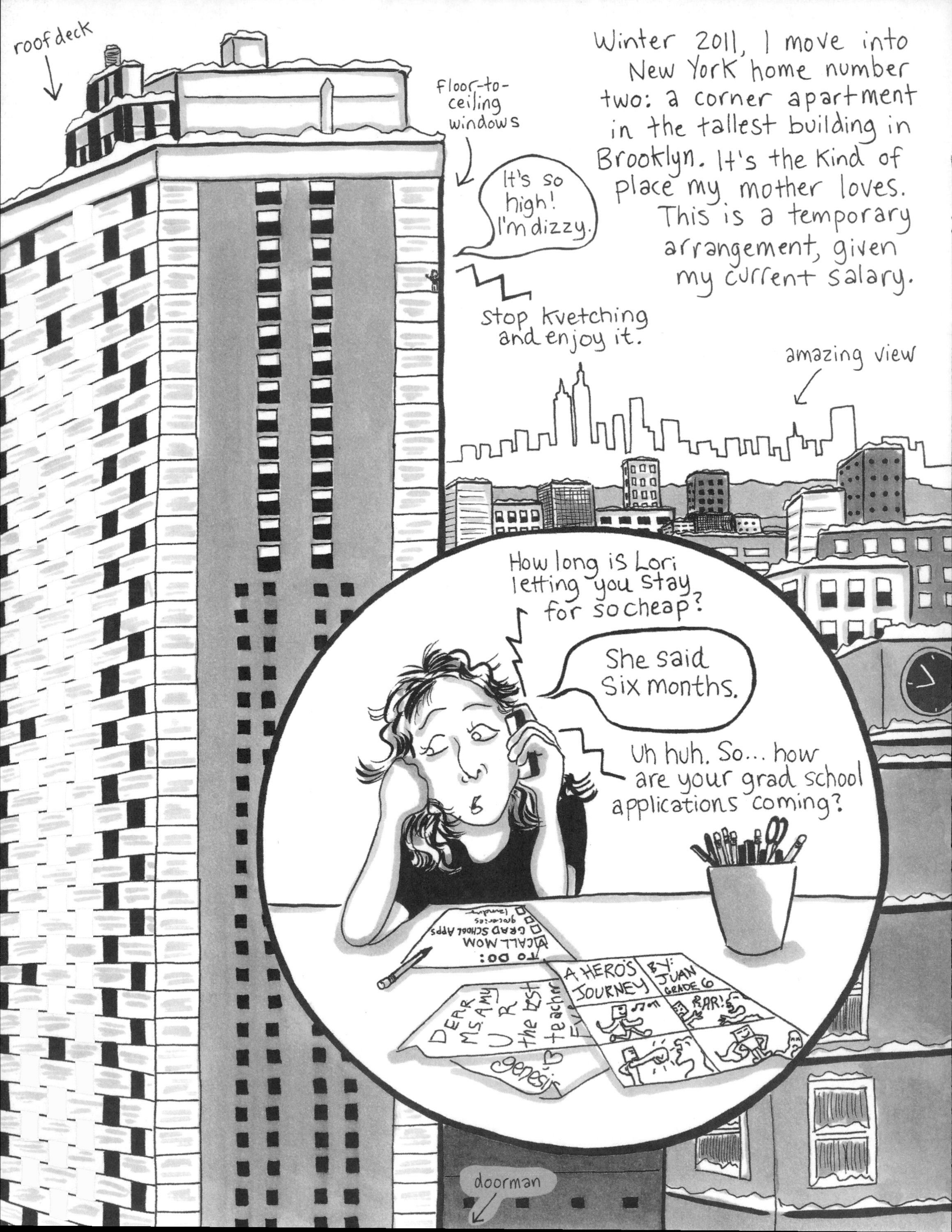
roofdeck
Floor-to-ceiling windows
Winter 2011, I move into New York home number two: a corner apartment in the tallest building in Brooklyn. It's the kind of place my mother loves. This is a temporary arrangement, given my current salary.
It's so high! I'm dizzy.
Stop kvetching and enjoy it.
amazing view
How long is Lori letting you stay for so cheap?
She said six months.
Uh huh. So... how are your grad school applications coming?
TO DO:
CALL MOM
GRAD SCHOOL APPS
groceries
laundry
A HERO'S JOURNEY
BY: JUAN GRADE 6
RAR!
DEAR MS. AMY U R the best teacher
genesis
doorman

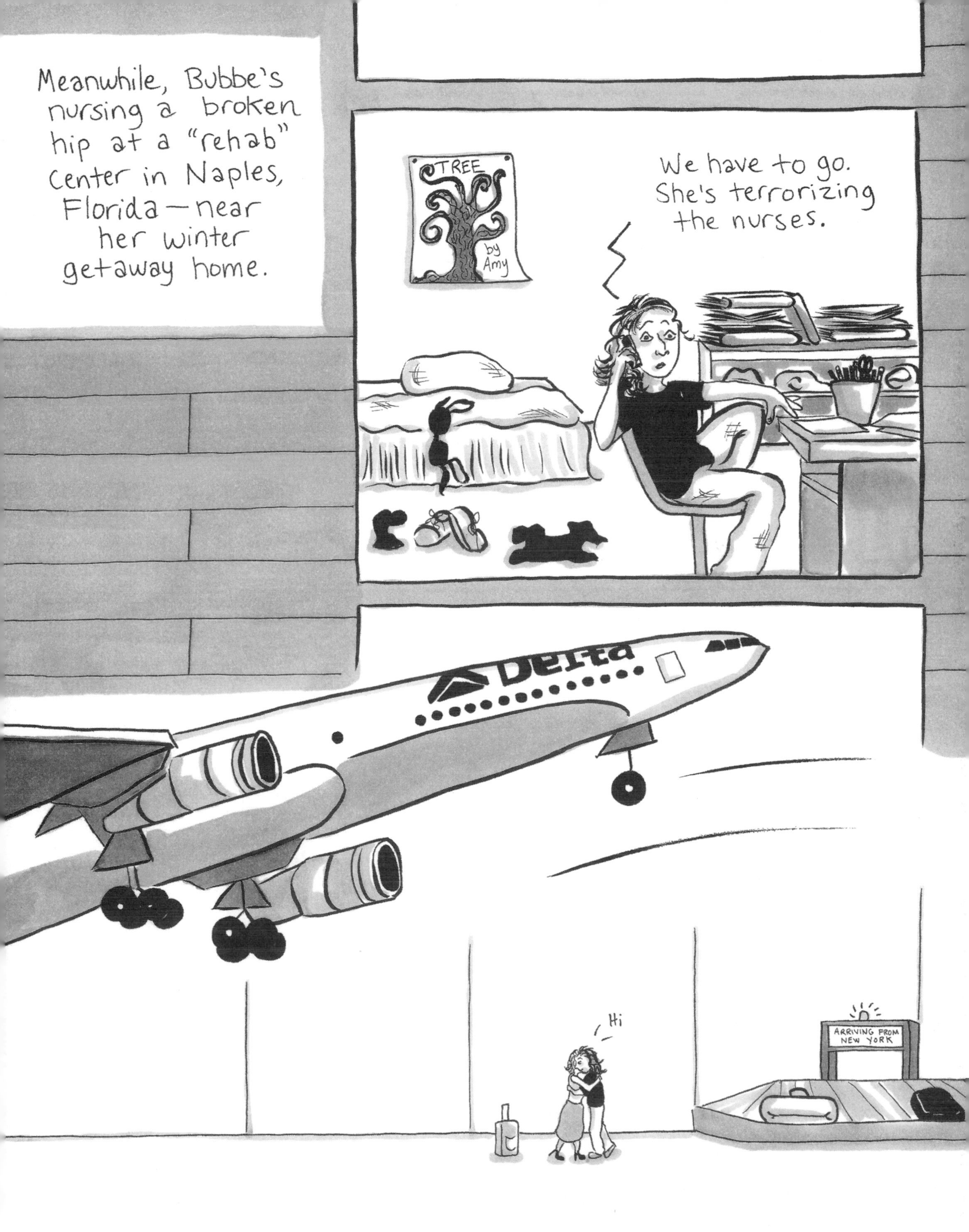
Meanwhile, Bubbe's nursing a broken hip at a "rehab" center in Naples, Florida—near her winter getaway home.
TREE
by Amy
We have to go. She's terrorizing the nurses.
Delta
Hi
ARRIVING FROM NEW YORK

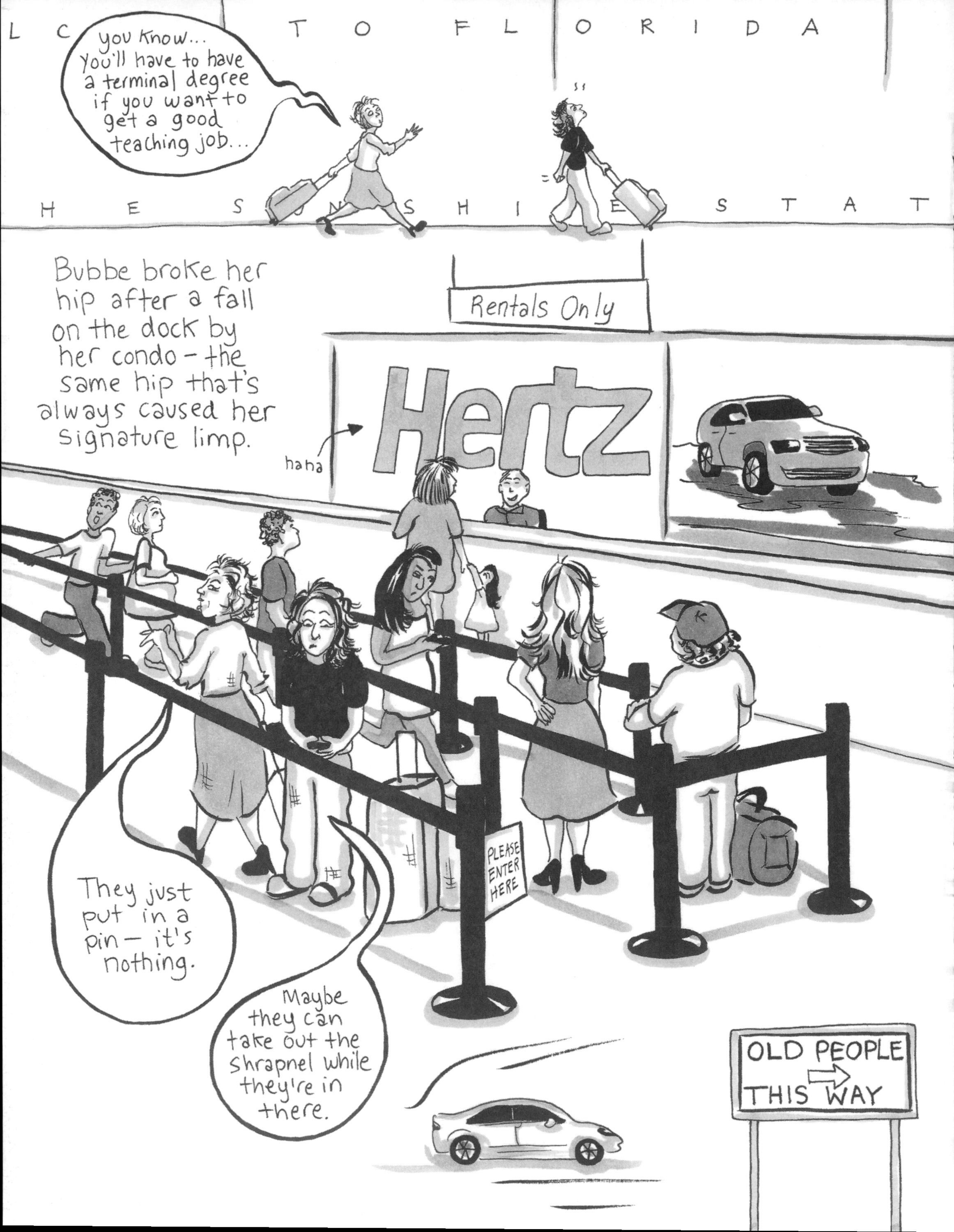

L C T O F L O R I D A
you know... you'll have to have a terminal degree if you want to get a good teaching job...
H E S H I S T A T
Bubbe broke her hip after a fall on the dock by her condo – the same hip that's always caused her signature limp.
Rentals Only
Hertz
haha
PLEASE ENTER HERE
They just put in a pin – it's nothing.
Maybe they can take out the shrapnel while they're in there.
OLD PEOPLE THIS WAY

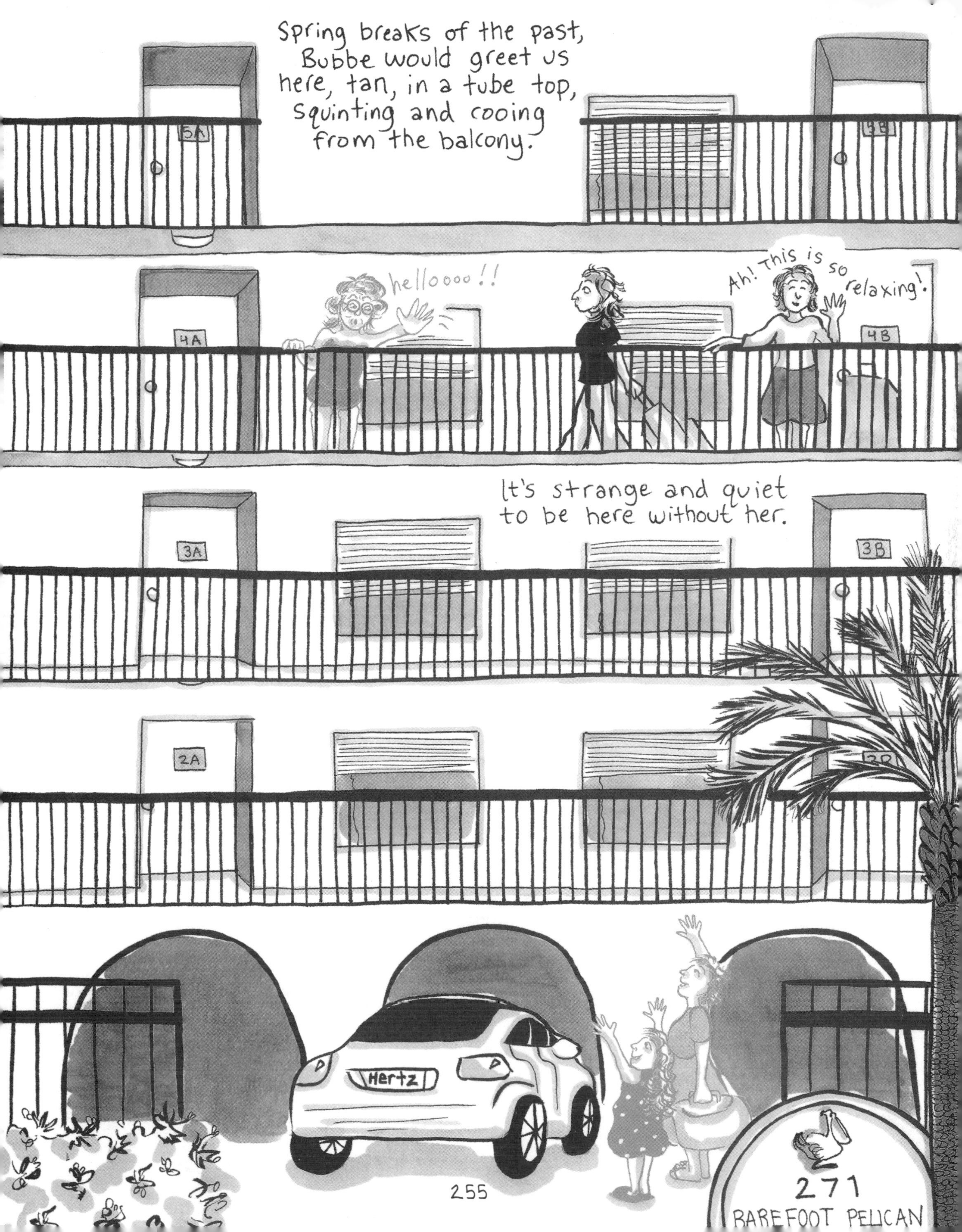
Spring breaks of the past, Bubbe would greet us here, tan, in a tube top, squinting and cooing from the balcony.
5A
hellOOOO!!
Ah! This is so relaxing!
4A
4B
It's strange and quiet to be here without her.
3A
3B
2A
Hertz
271
BAREFOOT PELICAN

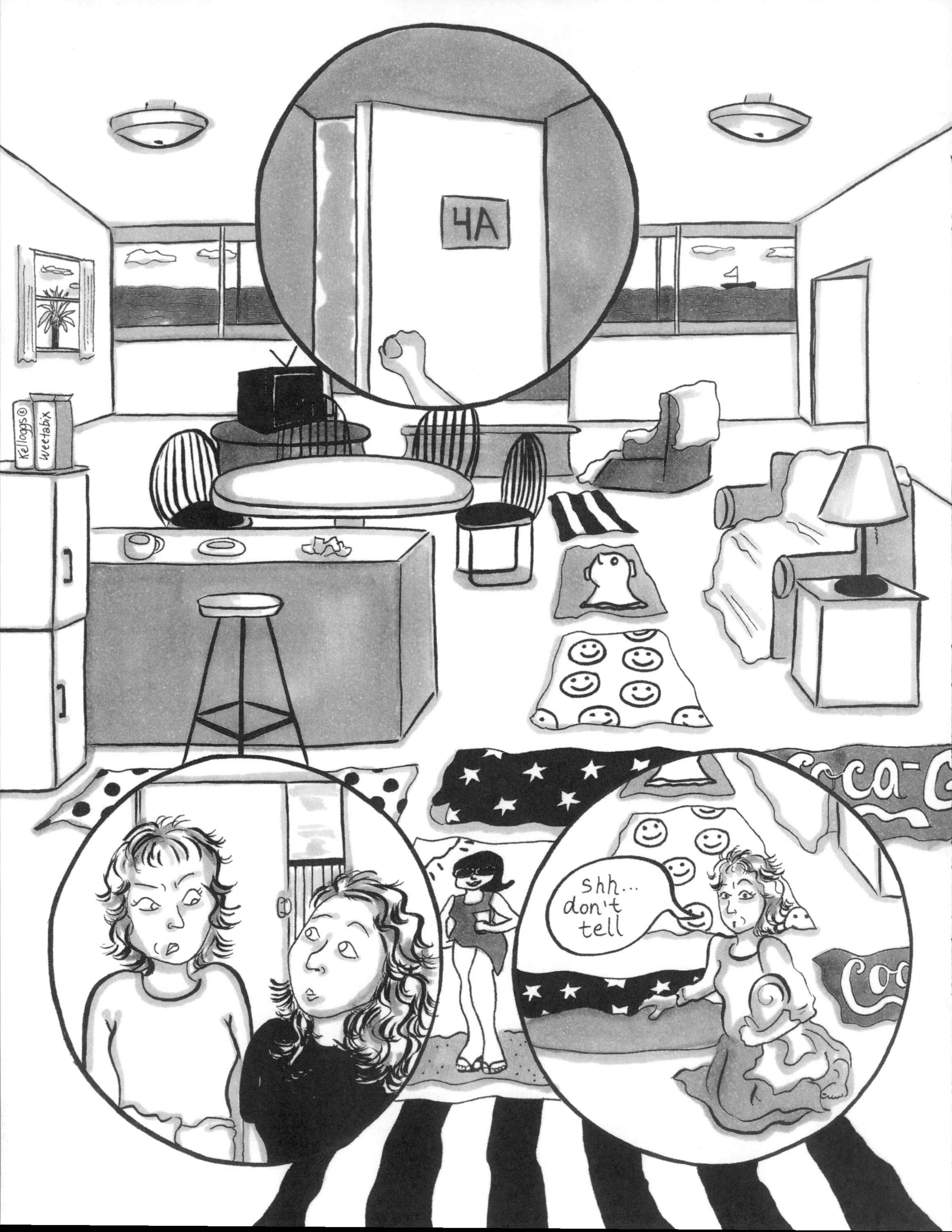
4A
Kelloggs®
Weetabix
Coca-Co
shh... don't tell
Coc

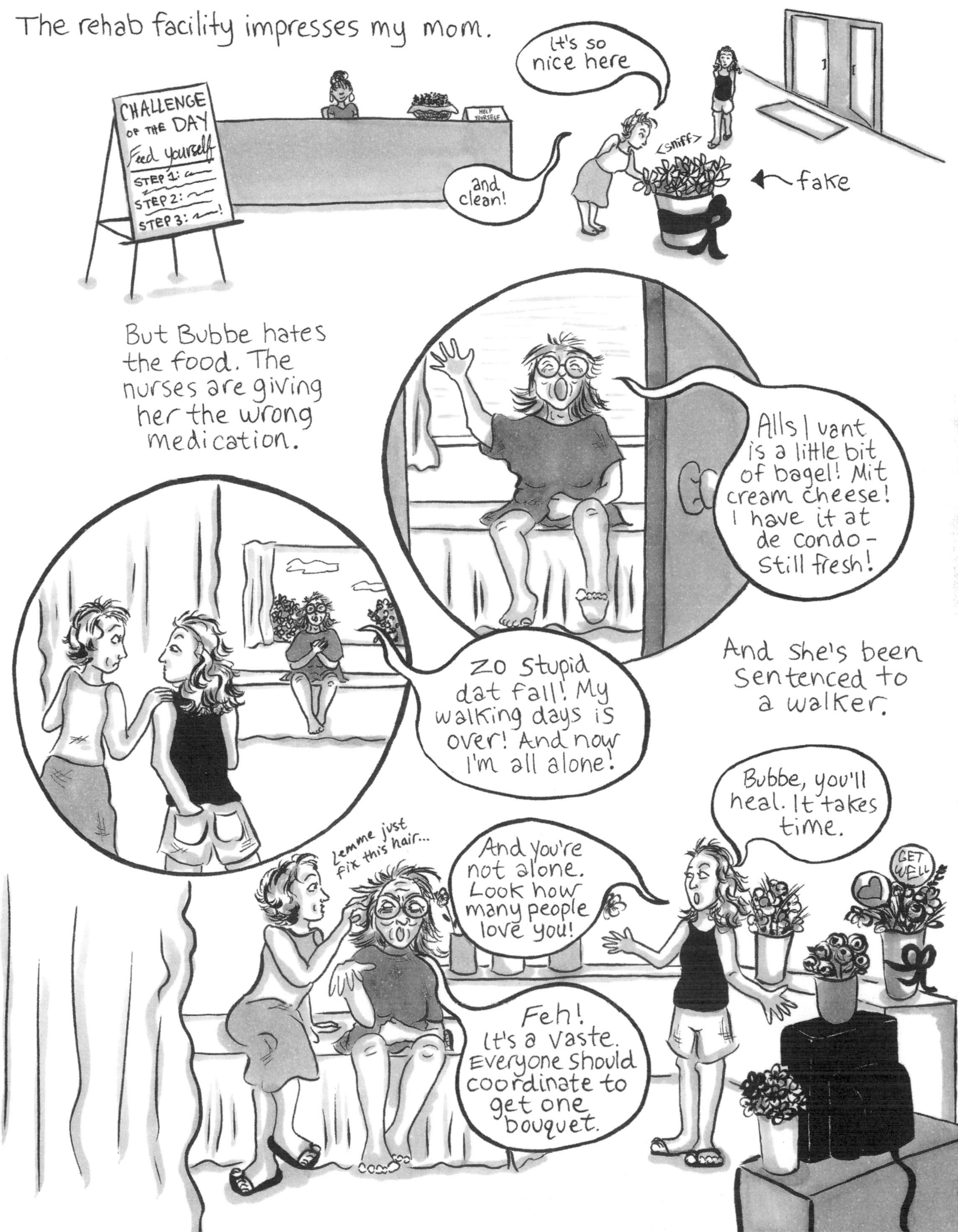
The rehab facility impresses my mom.
CHALLENGE OF THE DAY
Feed yourself
STEP 1:
STEP 2:
STEP 3:
HELP YOURSELF
It's so nice here
and clean!
<sniff>
fake
But Bubbe hates the food. The nurses are giving her the wrong medication.
Alls I vant is a little bit of bagel! Mit cream cheese! I have it at de condo - Still fresh!
And she's been sentenced to a walker.
Zo stupid dat fall! My walking days is over! And now I'm all alone!
Bubbe, you'll heal. It takes time.
Lemme just fix this hair...
And you're not alone. Look how many people love you!
GET WELL
Feh! It's a vaste. Everyone should coordinate to get one bouquet.

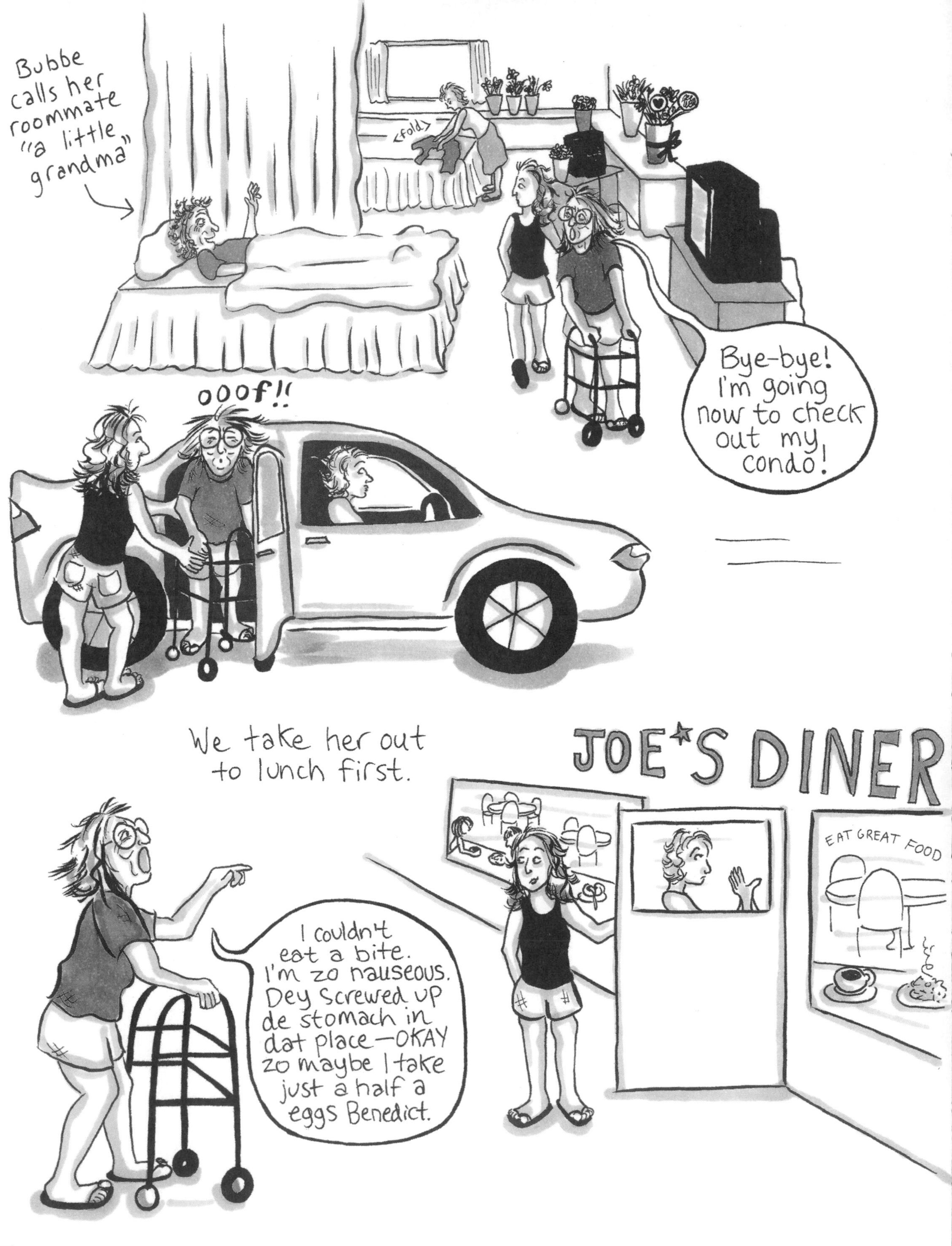
Bubbe calls her roommate "a little grandma"
<fold>
Bye-bye! I'm going now to check out my condo!
ooof!!
We take her out to lunch first.
JOE'S DINER
EAT GREAT FOOD
I couldn't eat a bite. I'm zo nauseous. Dey screwed up de stomach in dat place—OKAY zo maybe I take just a half a eggs Benedict.

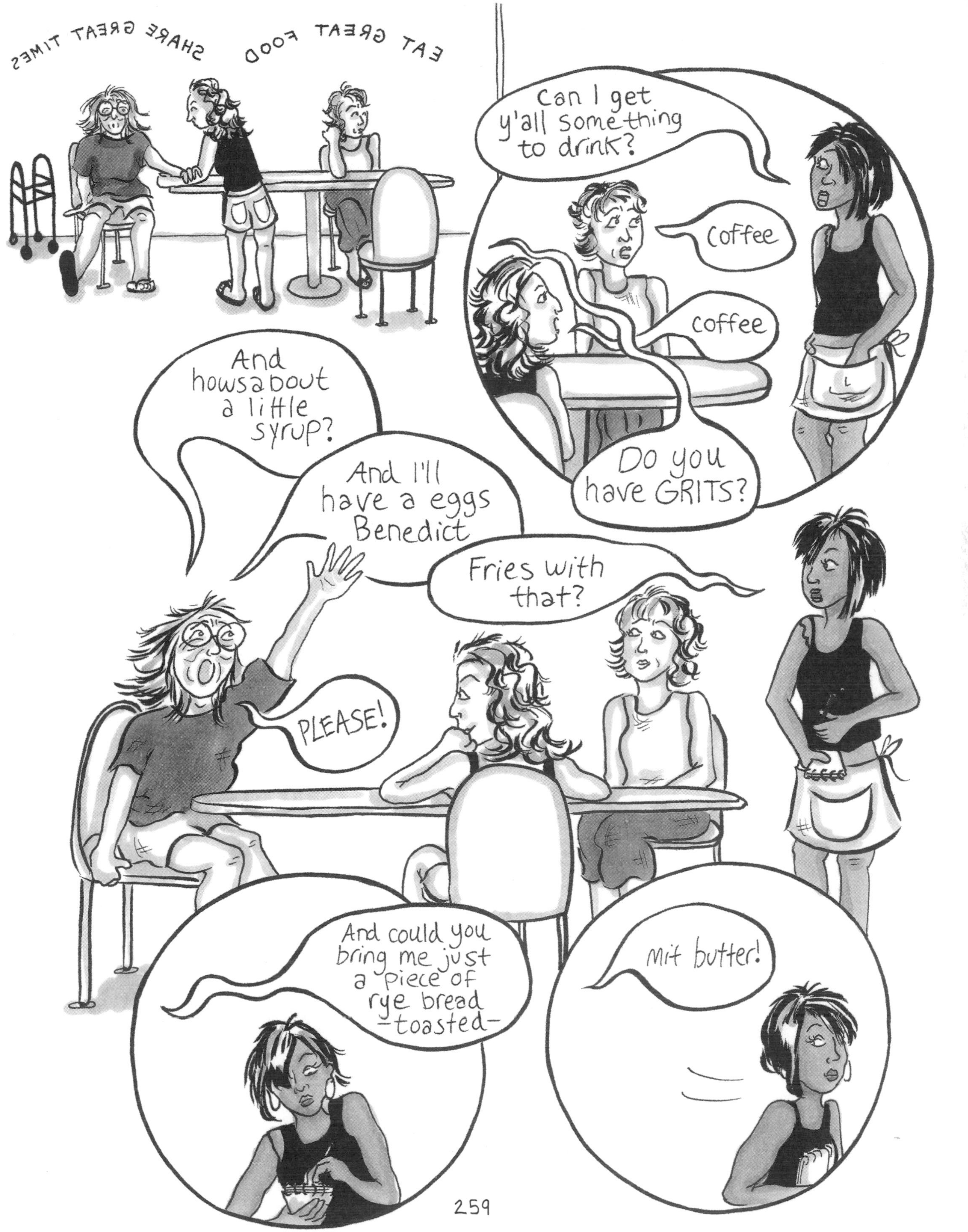
EAT GREAT FOOD
SHARE GREAT TIMES
Can I get y'all something to drink?
Coffee
coffee
Do you have GRITS?
And howsabout a little syrup?
And I'll have a eggs Benedict
Fries with that?
PLEASE!
And could you bring me just a piece of rye bread -toasted-
Mit butter!

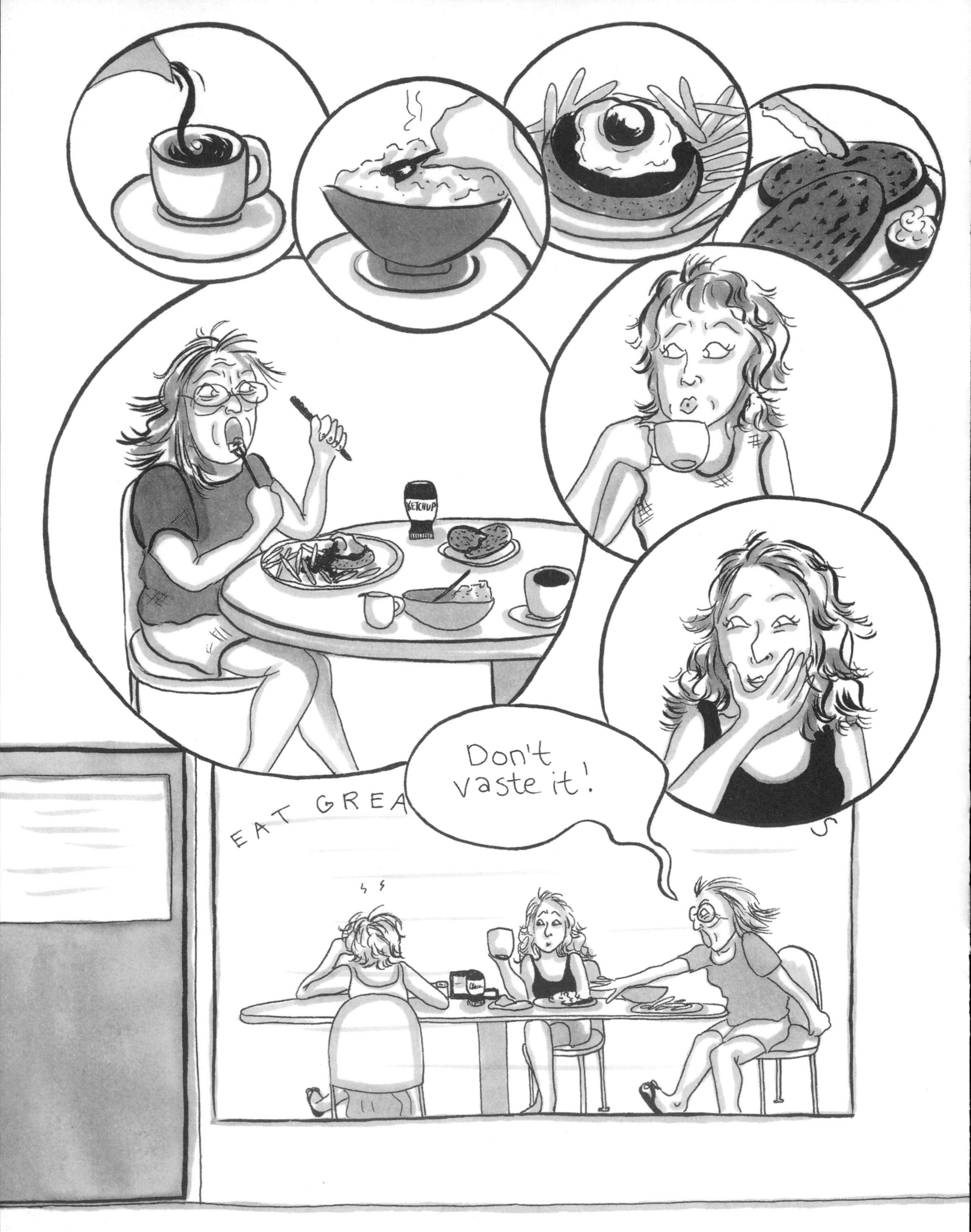
KETCHUP
Don't vaste it!
EAT GREA

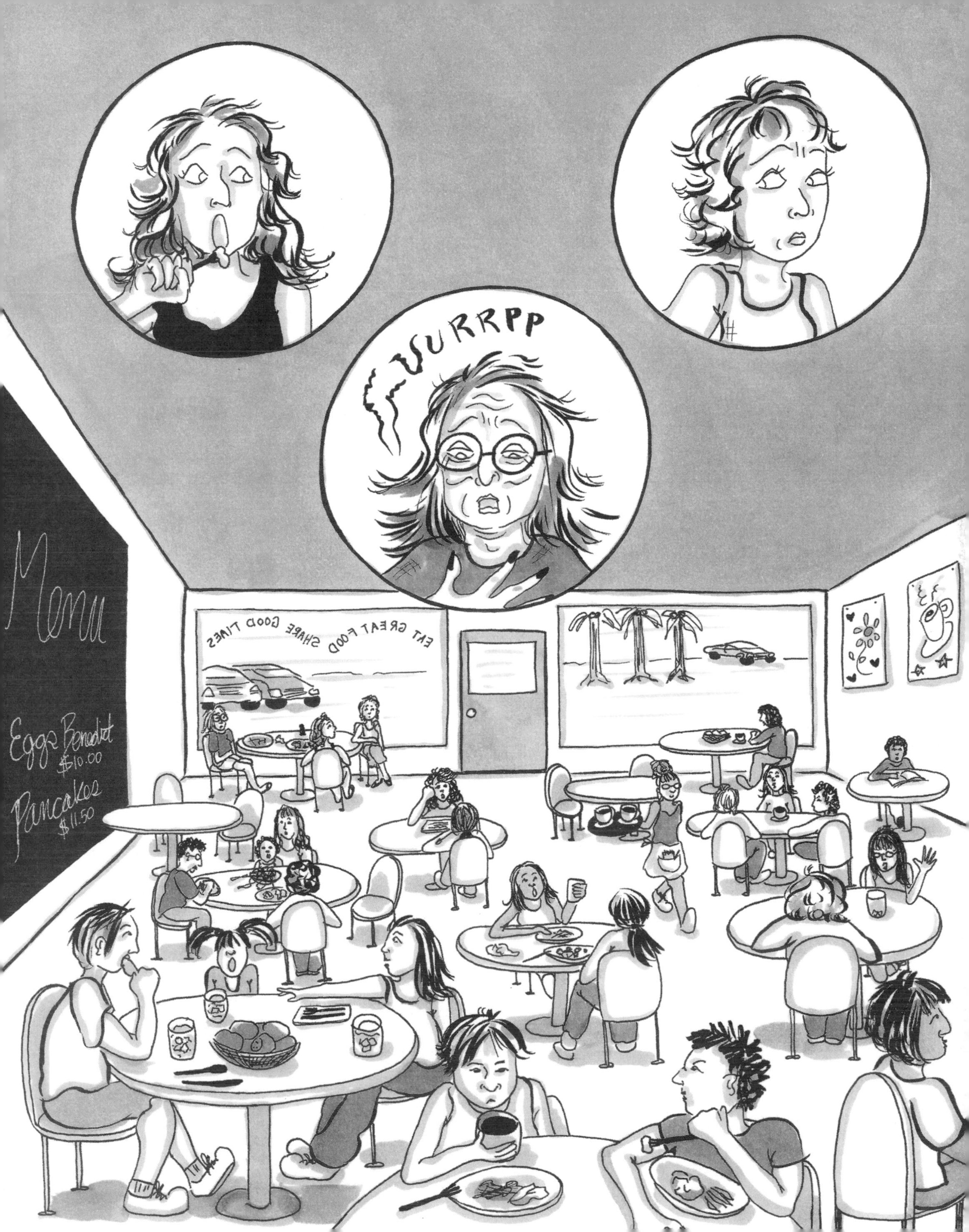
SURRPP
Menu
Eggs Benedict $10.00
Pancakes $11.50
EAT GREAT FOOD SHARE GOOD TIMES

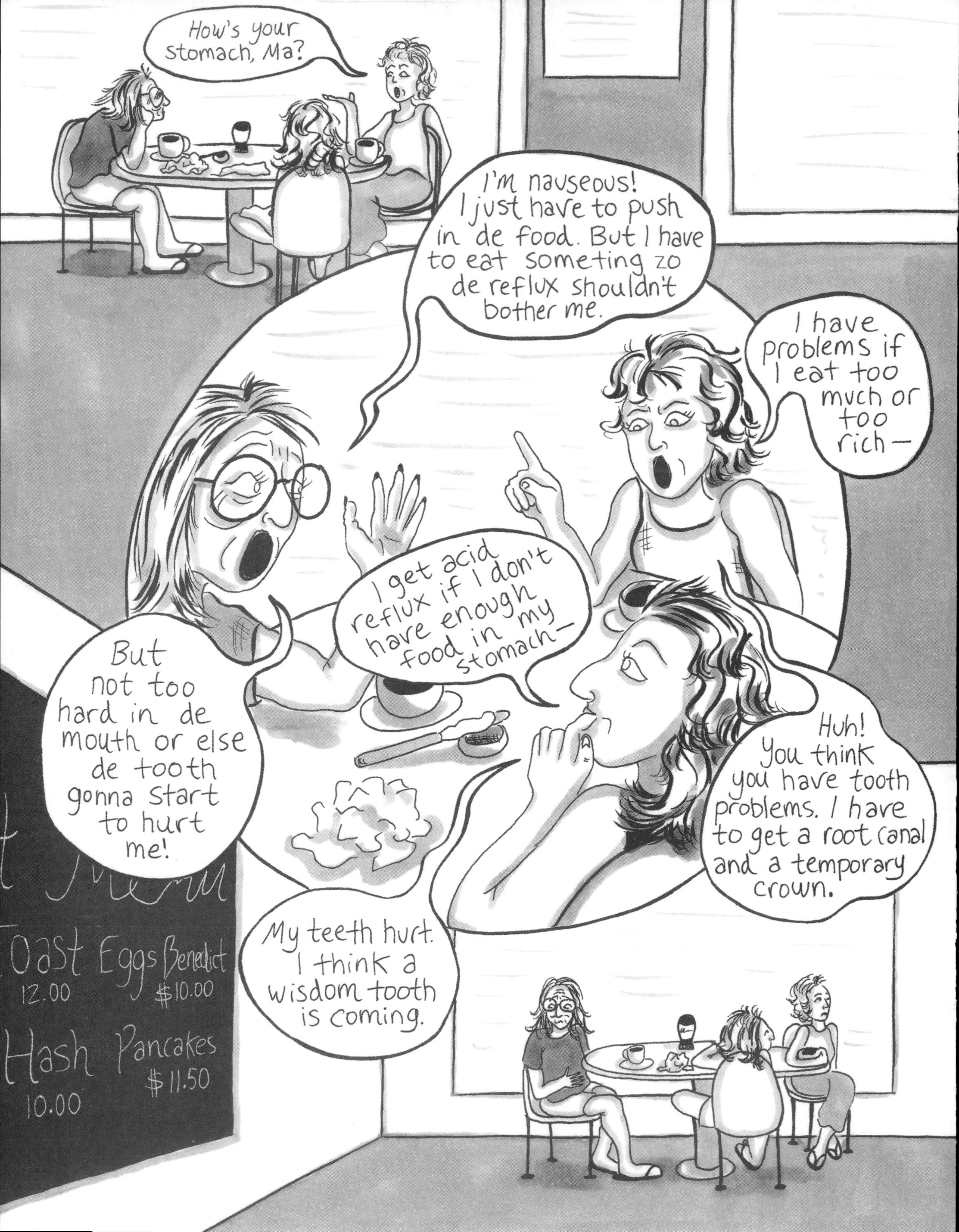
How's your stomach, Ma?
I'm nauseous! I just have to push in de food. But I have to eat someting zo de reflux shouldn't bother me.
I have problems if I eat too much or too rich—
I get acid reflux if I don't have enough food in my stomach—
But not too hard in de mouth or else de tooth gonna start to hurt me!
Huh! You think you have tooth problems. I have to get a root canal and a temporary crown.
My teeth hurt. I think a wisdom tooth is coming.
Eggs Benedict $10.00
12.00
Hash
10.00
Pancakes $11.50

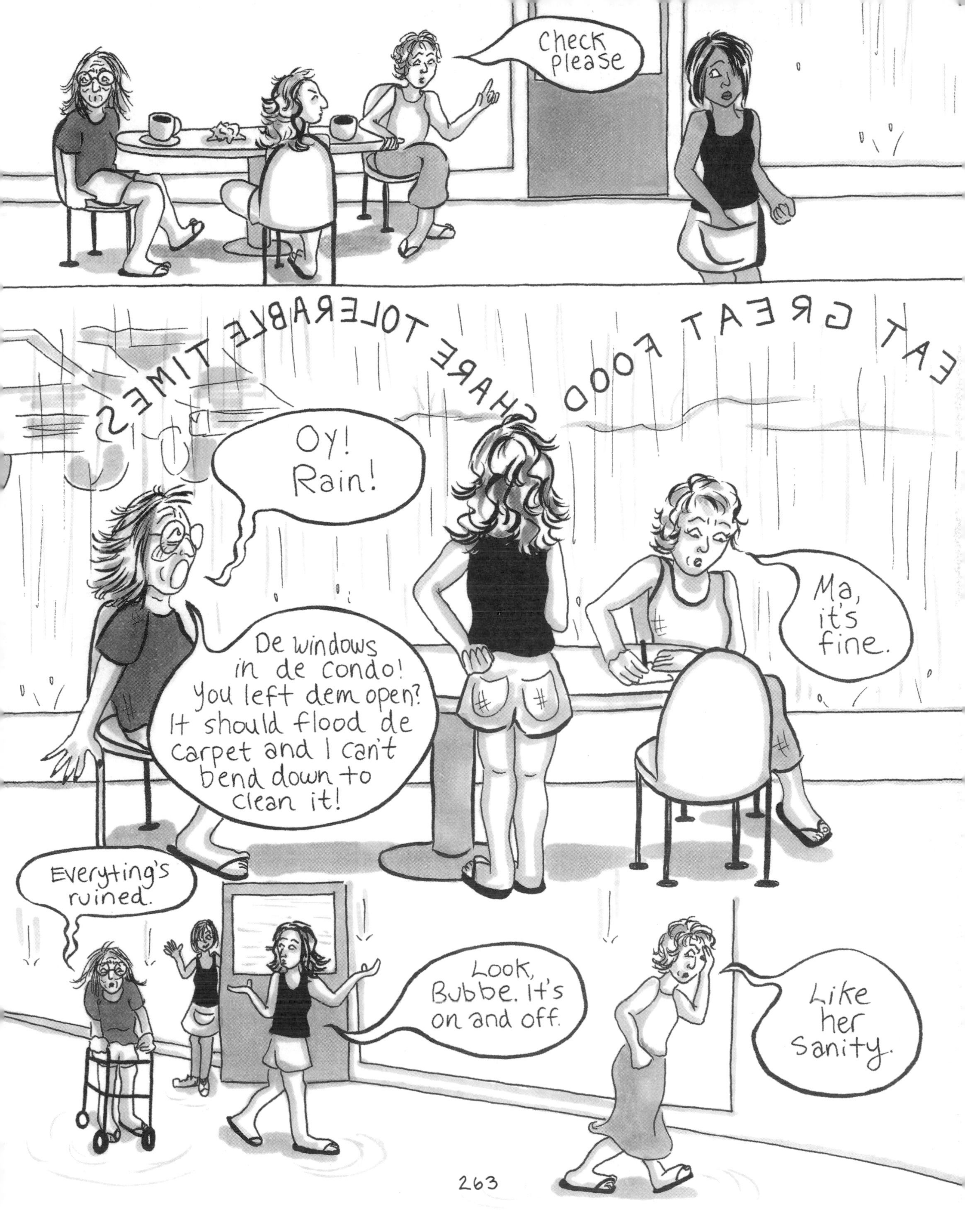
Check please
EAT GREAT FOOD SHARE TOLERABLE TIMES
Oy! Rain!
De windows in de condo! You left dem open? It should flood de carpet and I can't bend down to clean it!
Ma, it's fine.
Everyting's ruined.
Look, Bubbe. It's on and off.
Like her sanity.

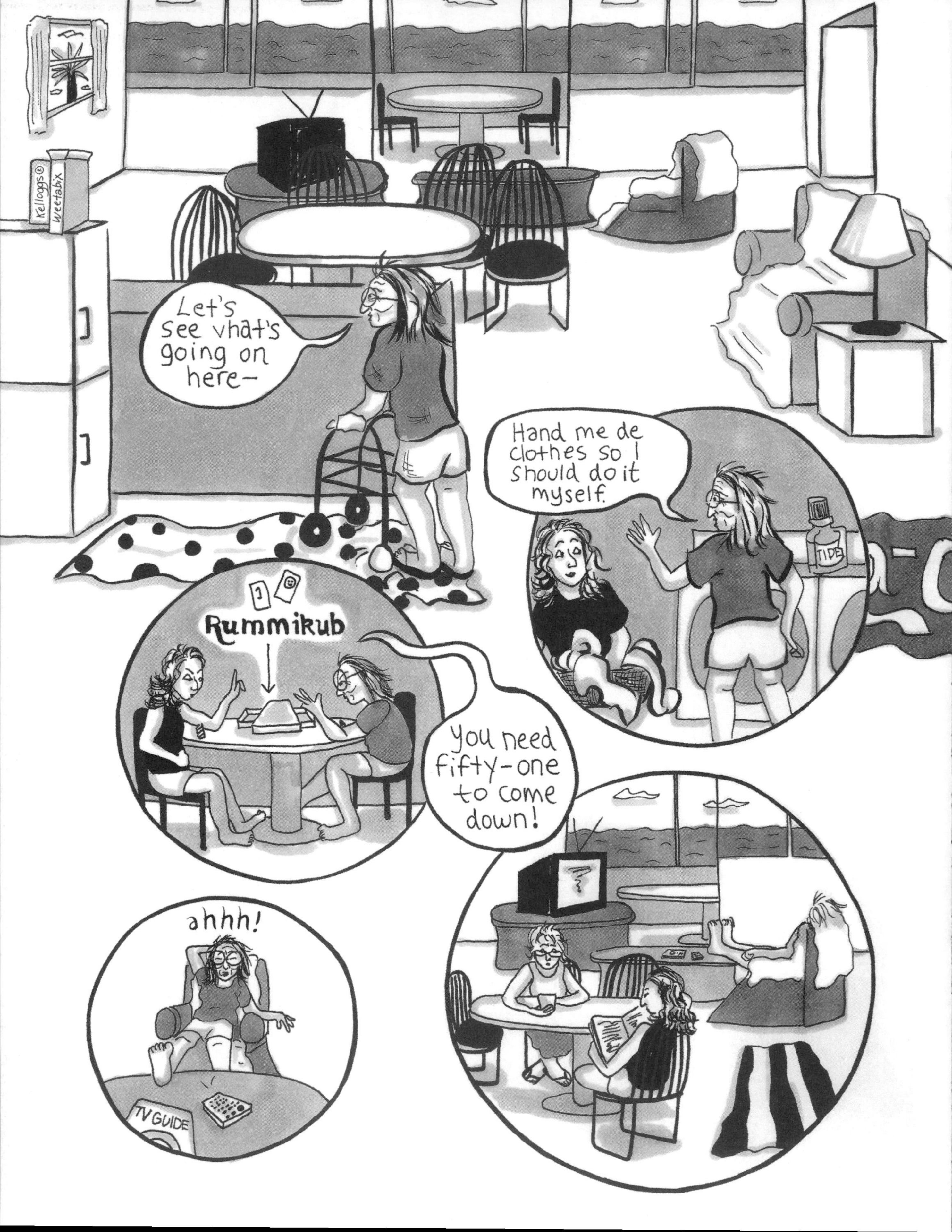
Kelloggs®
Weetabix
Let's see vhat's going on here–
Hand me de clothes so I should do it myself.
TIDE
Rummikub
You need fifty-one to come down!
ahhh!
TV GUIDE

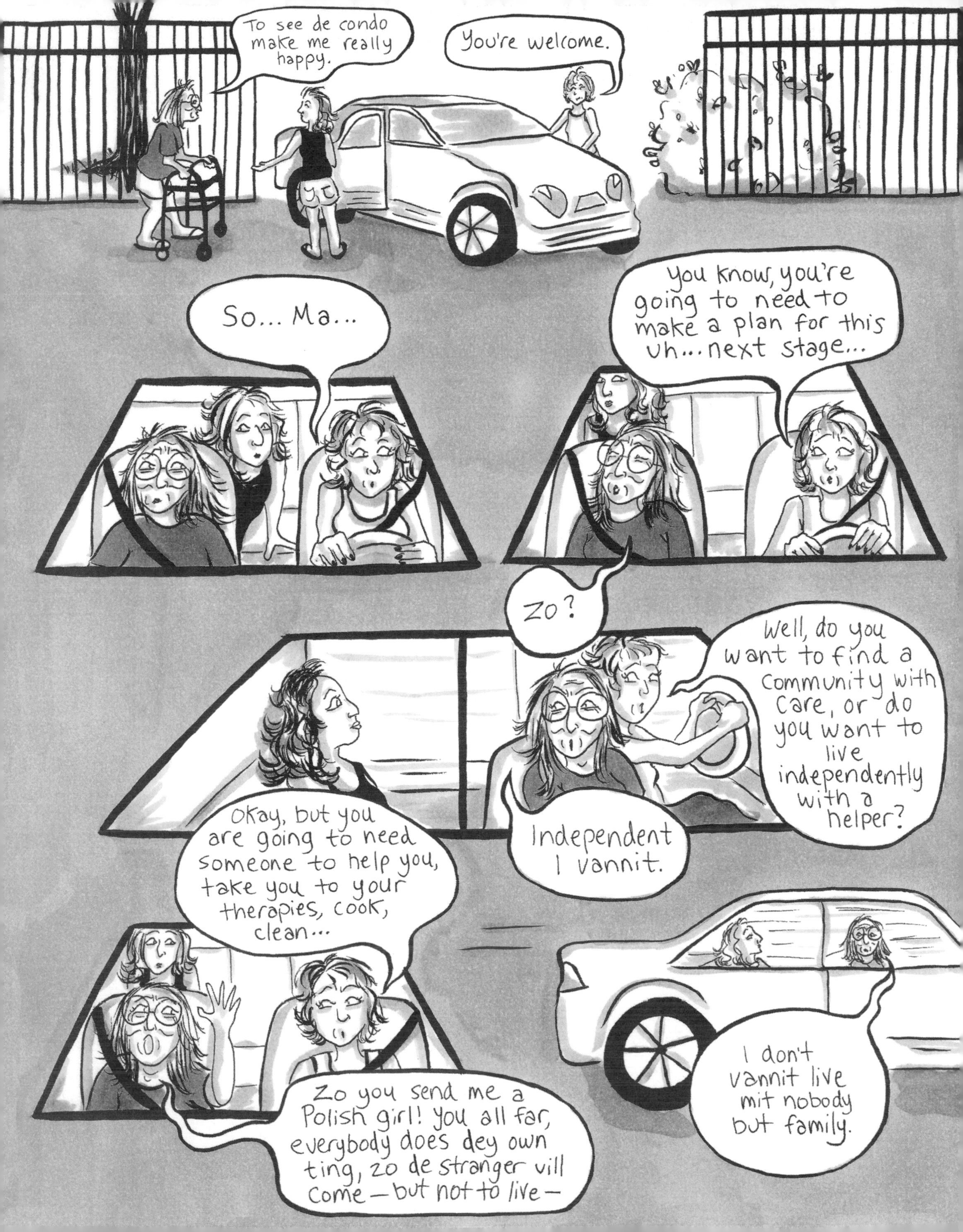
To see de condo make me really happy.
You're welcome.
So... Ma...
You know, you're going to need to make a plan for this uh... next stage...
Zo?
Well, do you want to find a community with care, or do you want to live independently with a helper?
Independent I vannit.
Okay, but you are going to need someone to help you, take you to your therapies, cook, clean...
Zo you send me a Polish girl! You all far, everybody does dey own ting, zo de stranger vill come— but not to live—
I don't vannit live mit nobody but family.

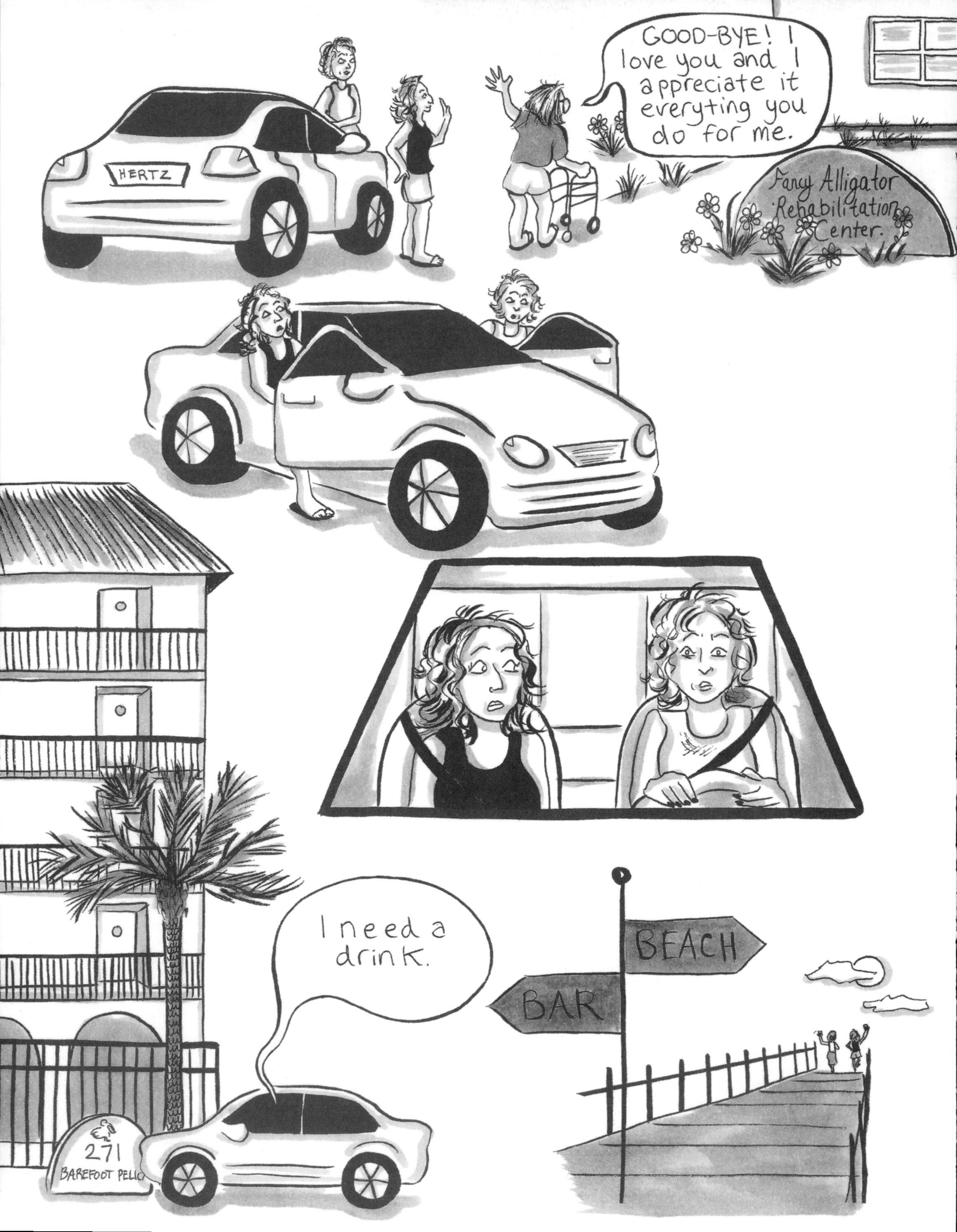
HERTZ
GOOD-BYE! I love you and I appreciate it everyting you do for me.
Fancy Alligator Rehabilitation Center.
I need a drink.
271
BAREFOOT PELIC
BEACH
BAR

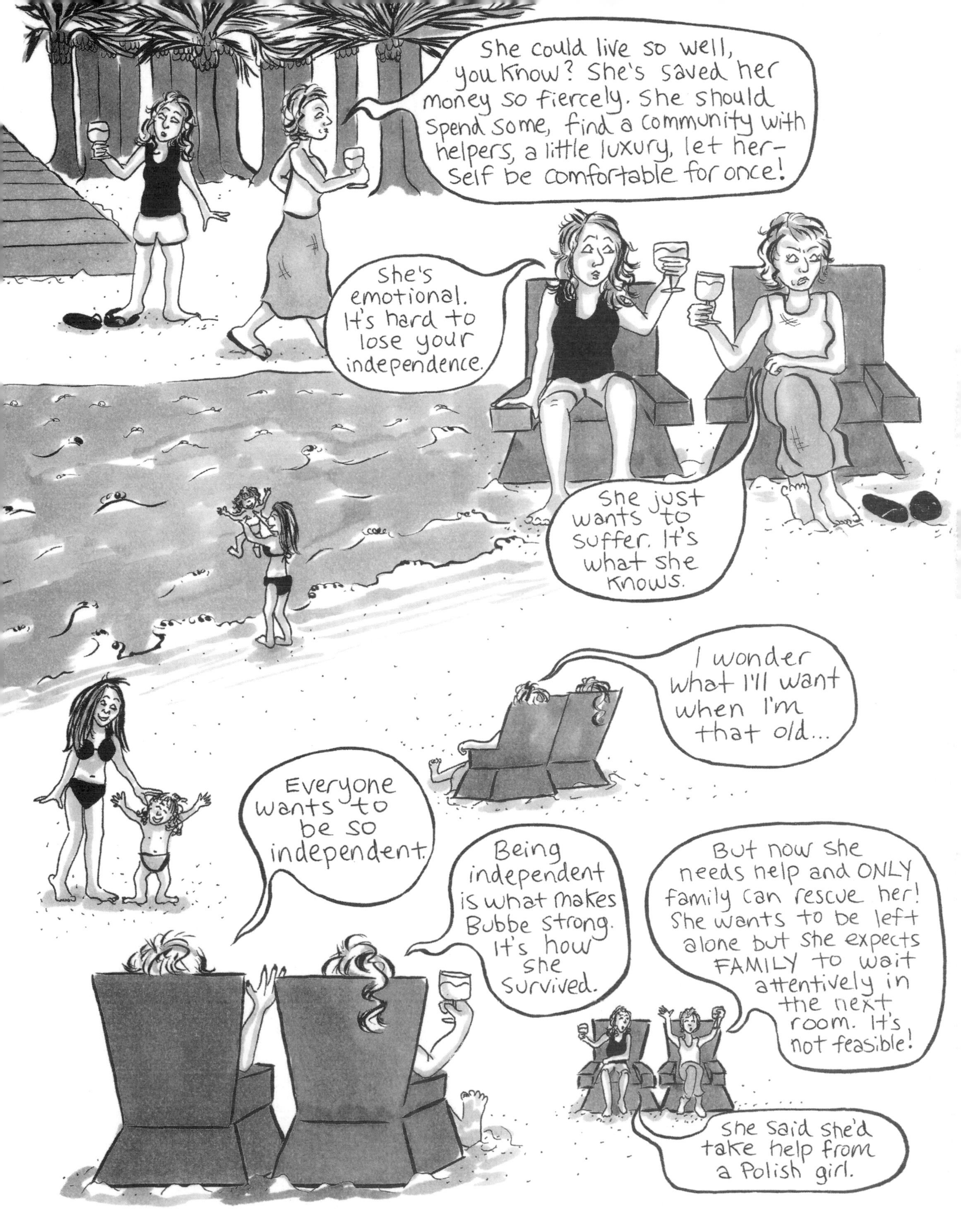

She could live so well, you know? She's saved her money so fiercely. She should spend some, find a community with helpers, a little luxury, let herself be comfortable for once!
She's emotional. It's hard to lose your independence.
She just wants to suffer. It's what she knows.
I wonder what I'll want when I'm that old...
Everyone wants to be so independent.
Being independent is what makes Bubbe strong. It's how she survived.
But now she needs help and ONLY family can rescue her! She wants to be left alone but she expects FAMILY to wait attentively in the next room. It's not feasible!
She said she'd take help from a Polish girl.

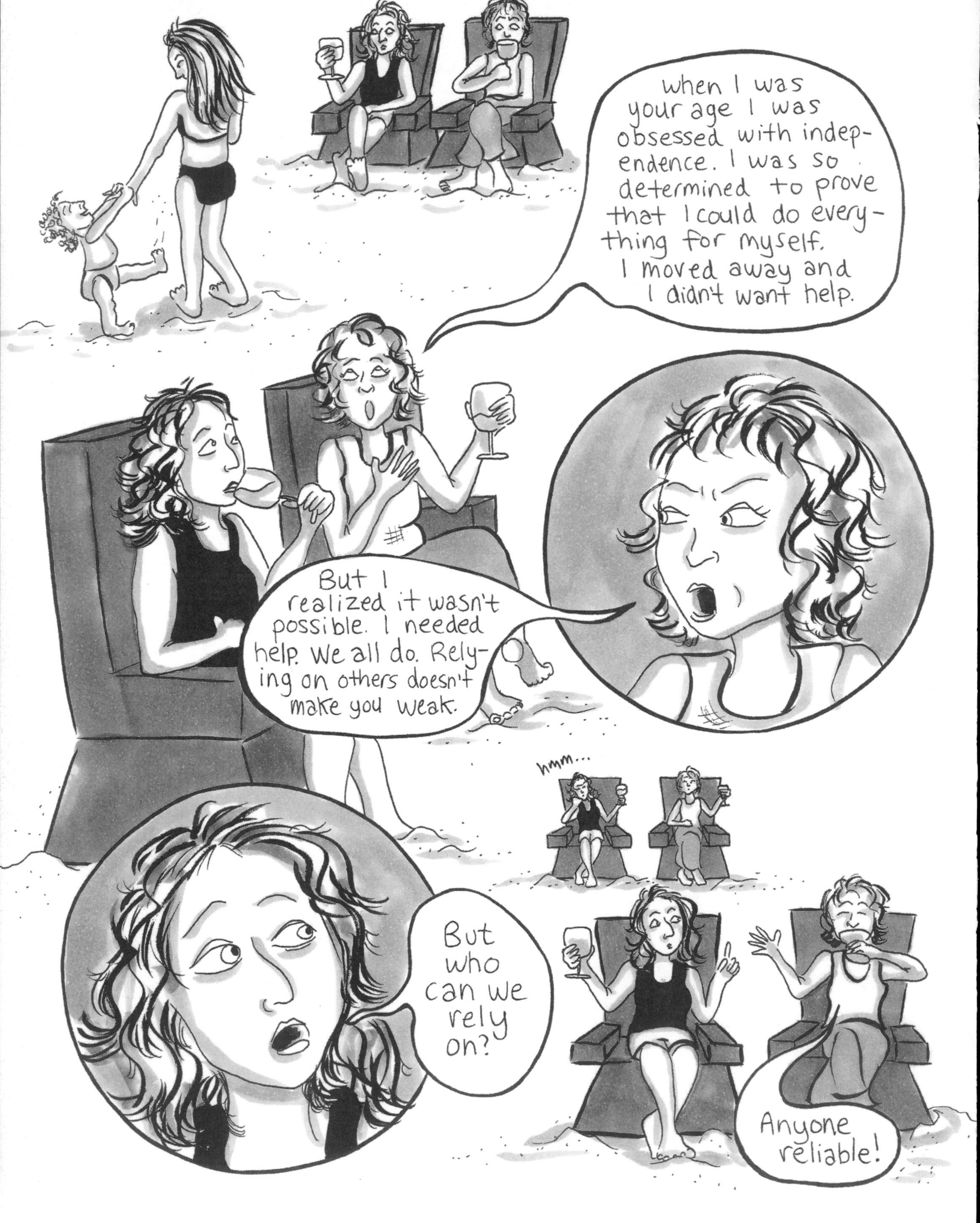
when I was your age I was obsessed with independence. I was so determined to prove that I could do everything for myself. I moved away and I didn't want help.
But I realized it wasn't possible. I needed help. We all do. Relying on others doesn't make you weak.
hmm...
But who can we rely on?
Anyone reliable!

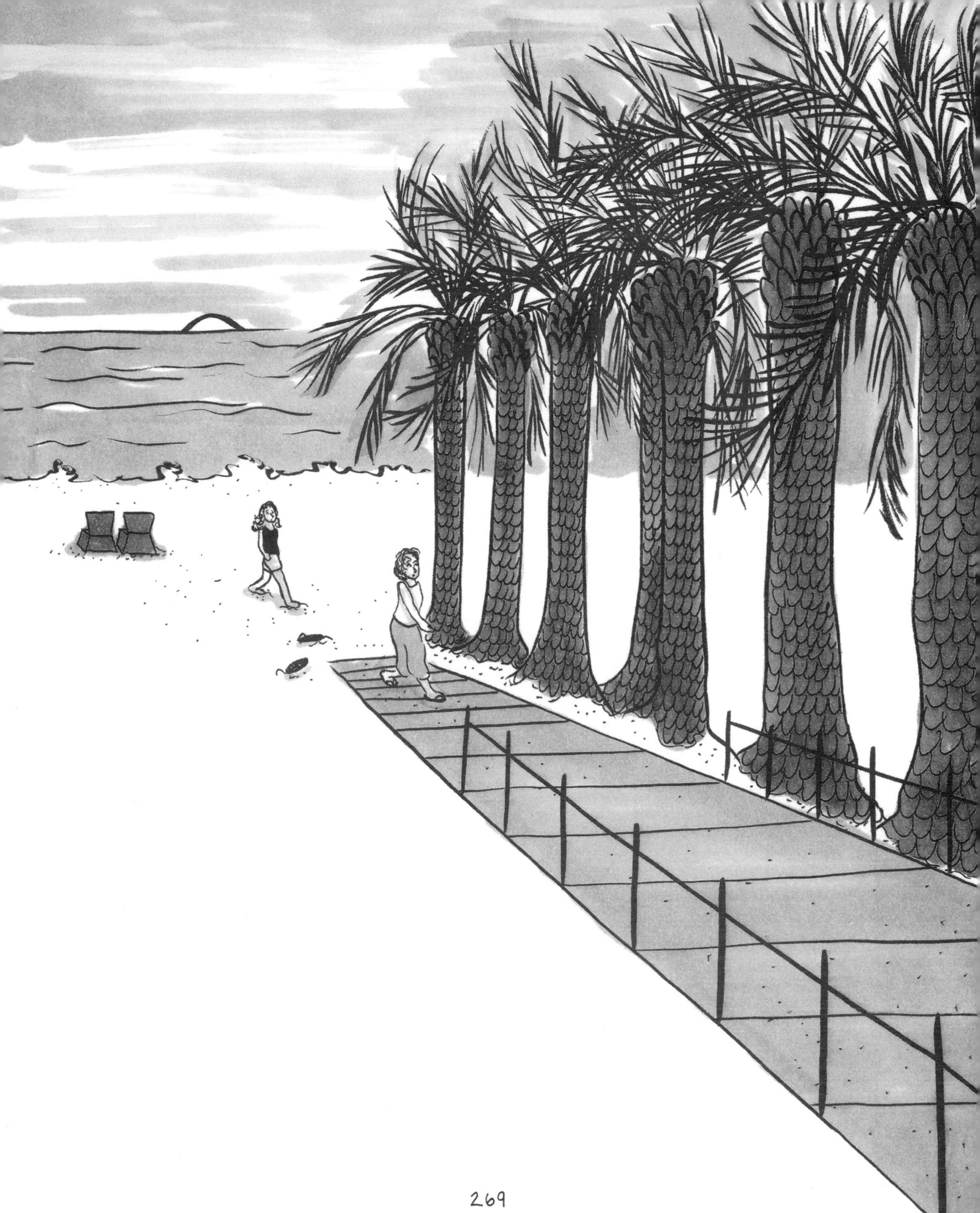

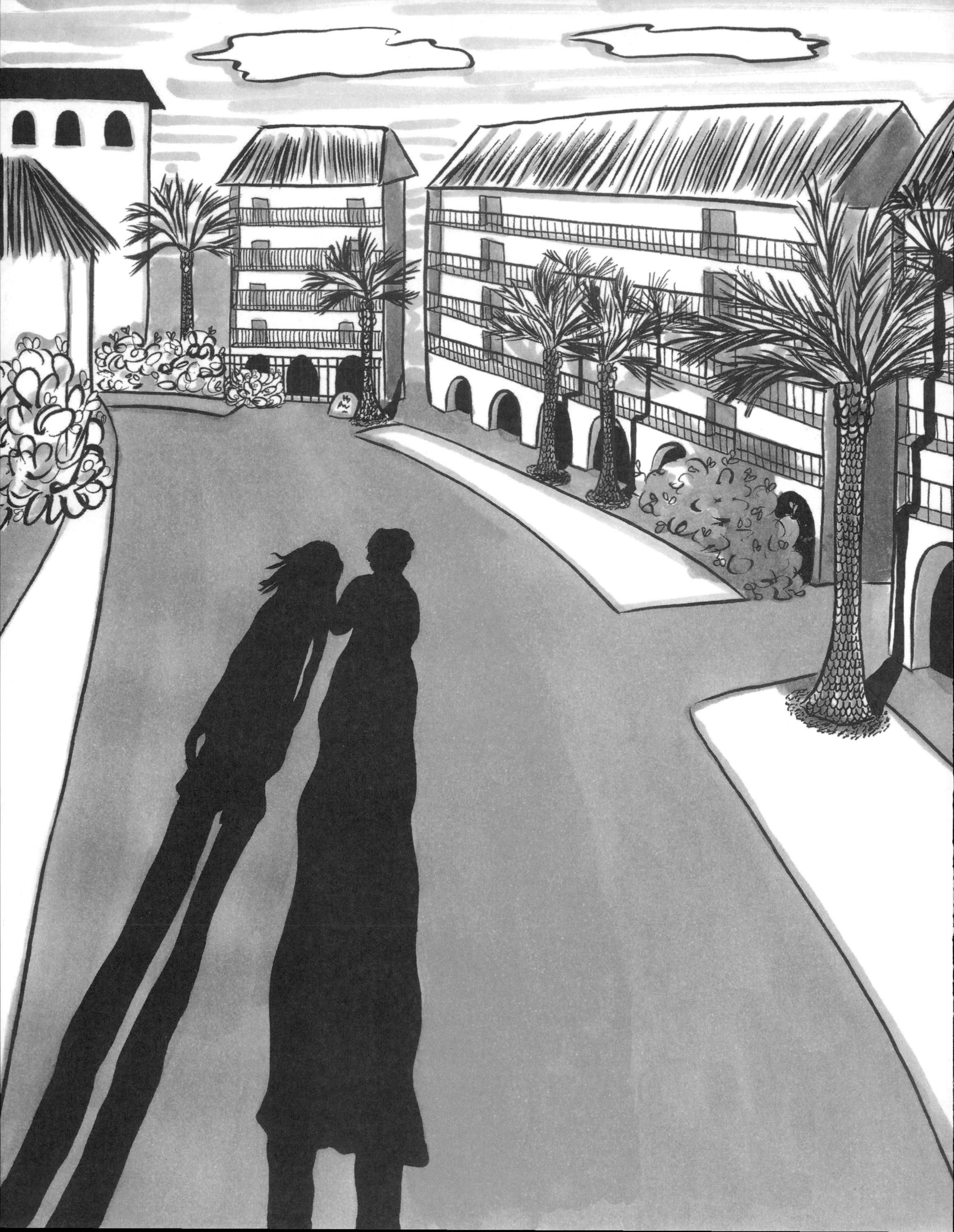

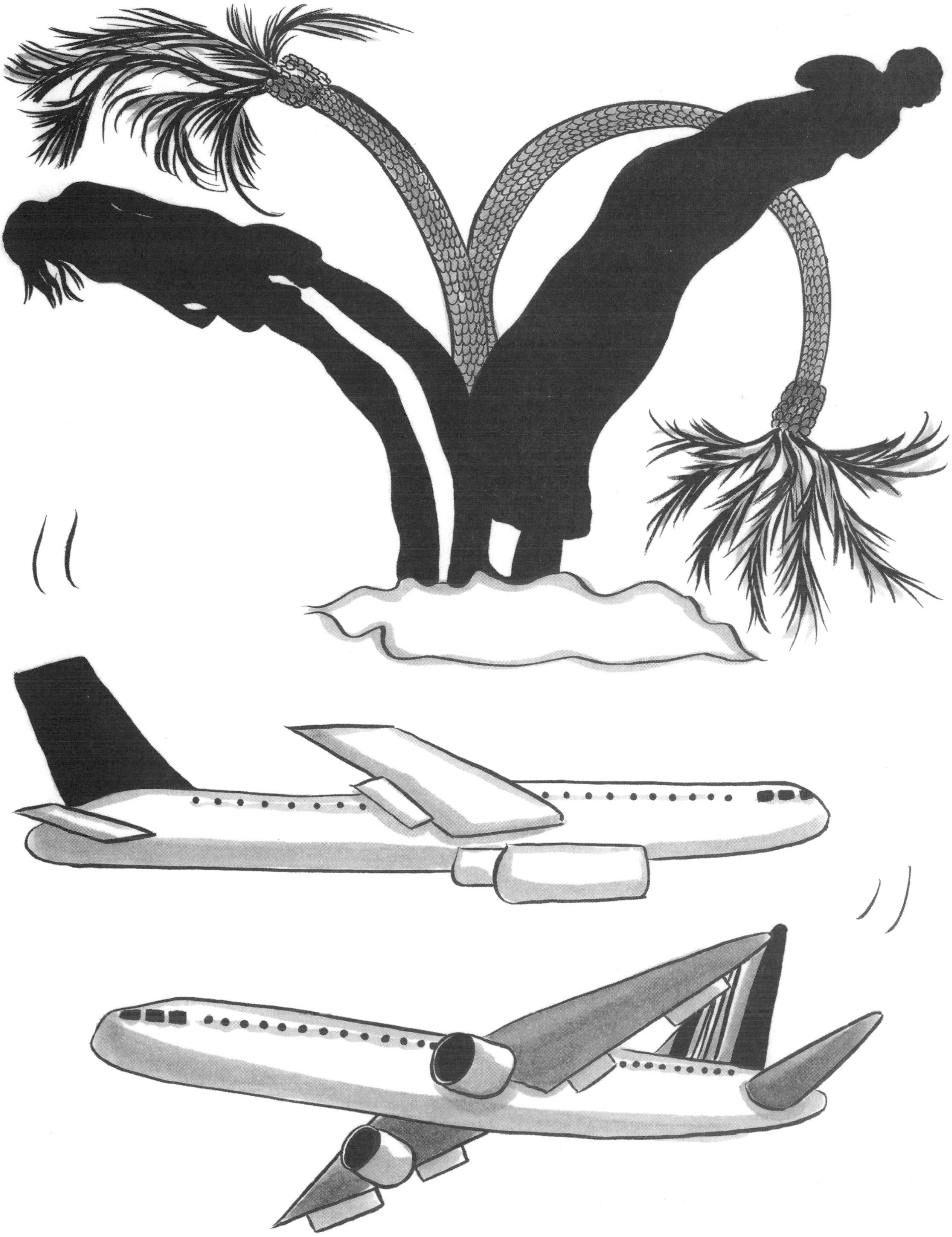

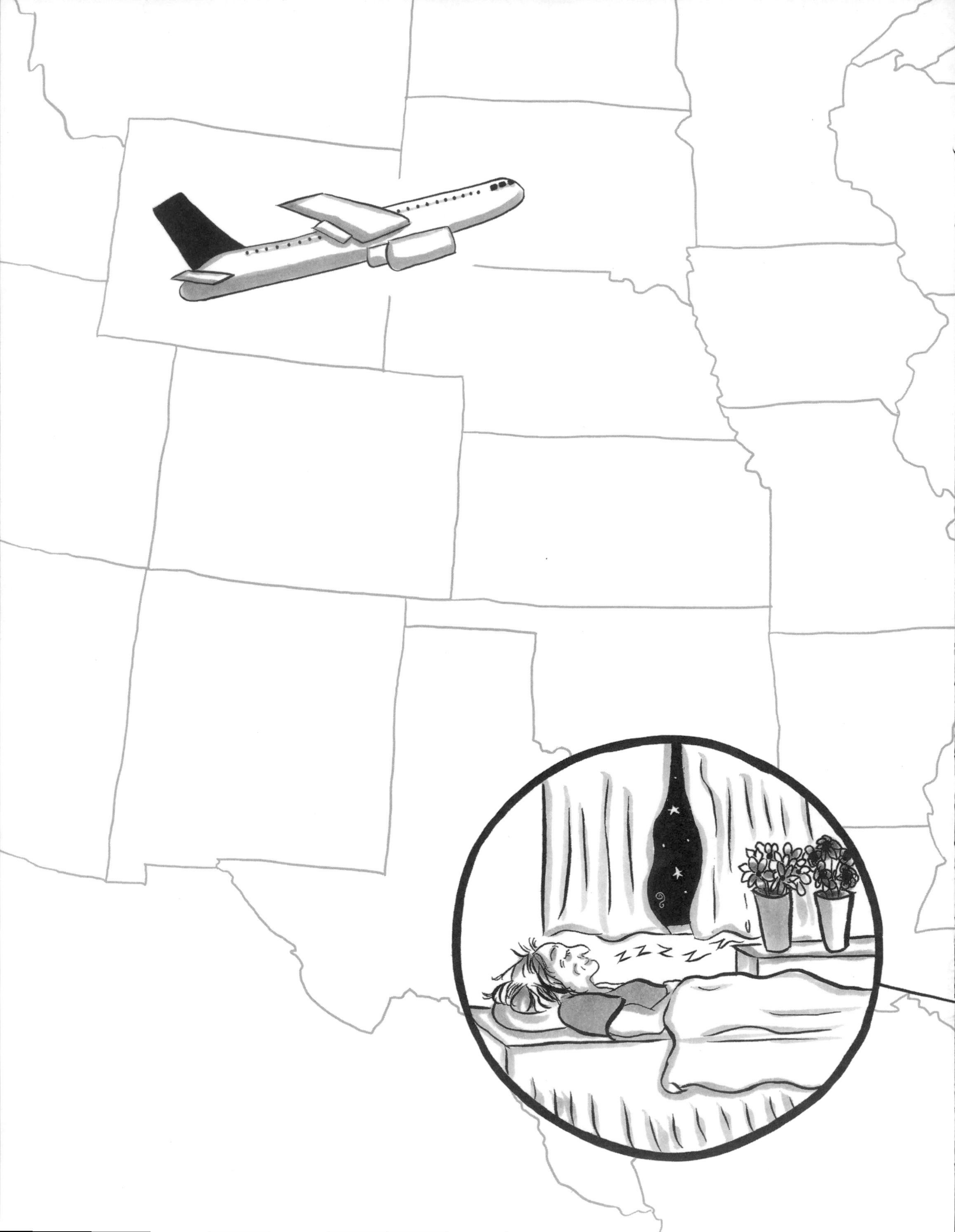

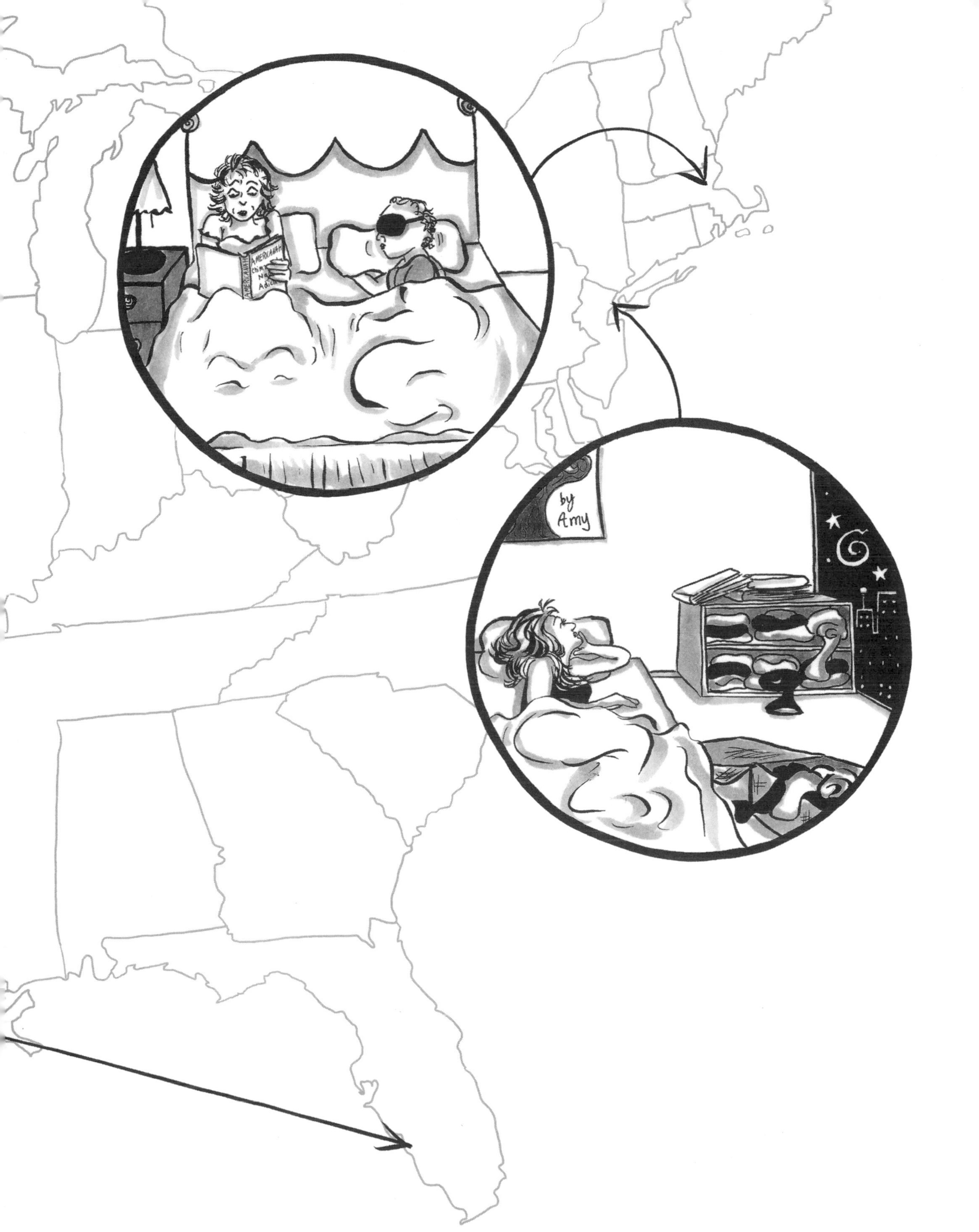
AMERICANAH
by
Amy

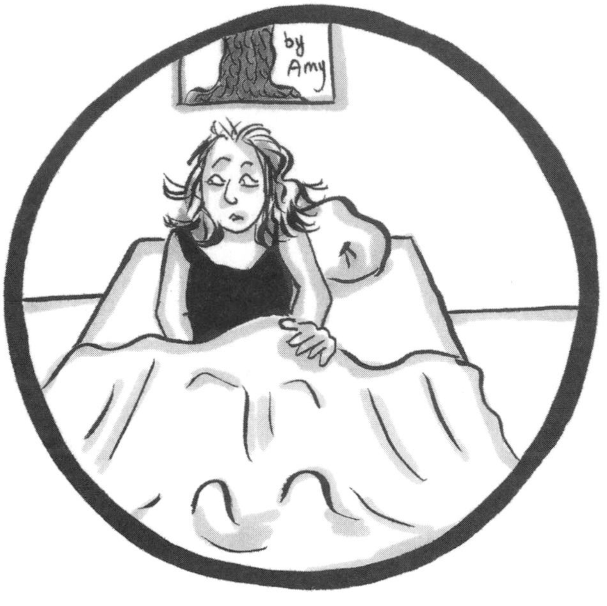
by
Amy

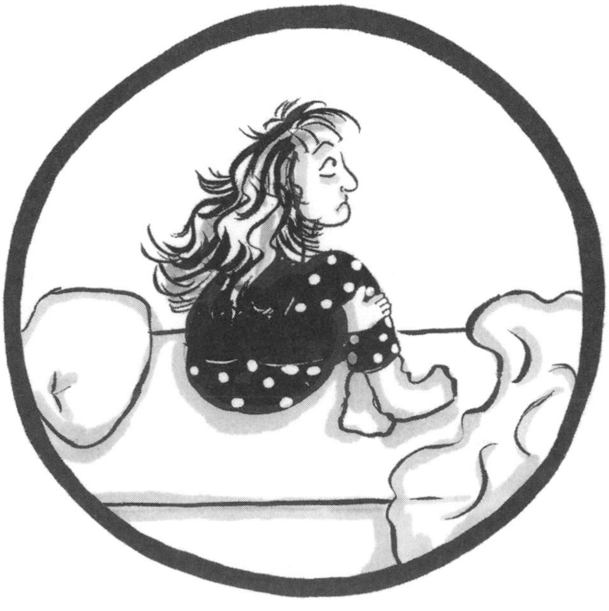

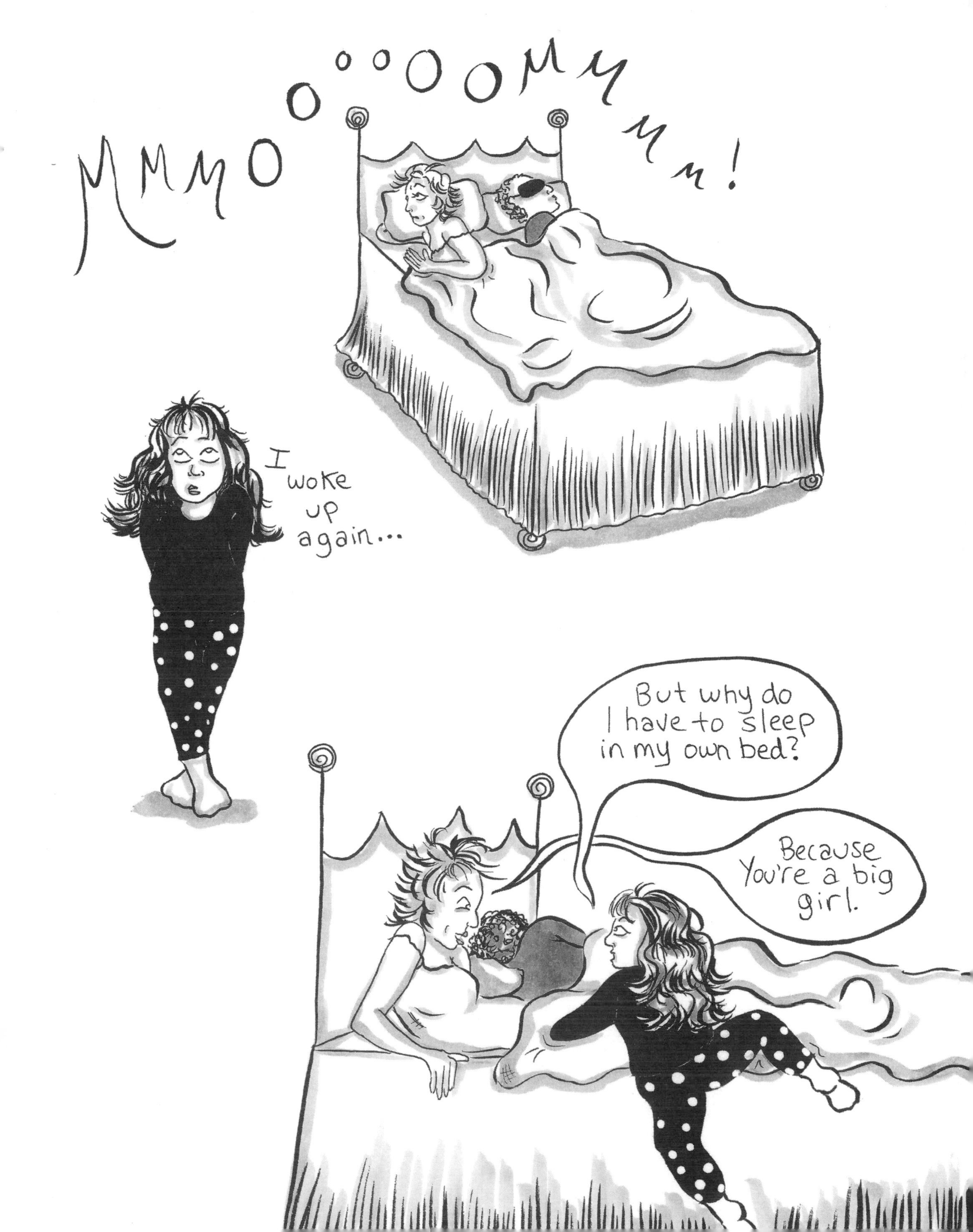
MMMOOOOOOMMMMm!
I woke up again...
But why do I have to sleep in my own bed?
Because You're a big girl.

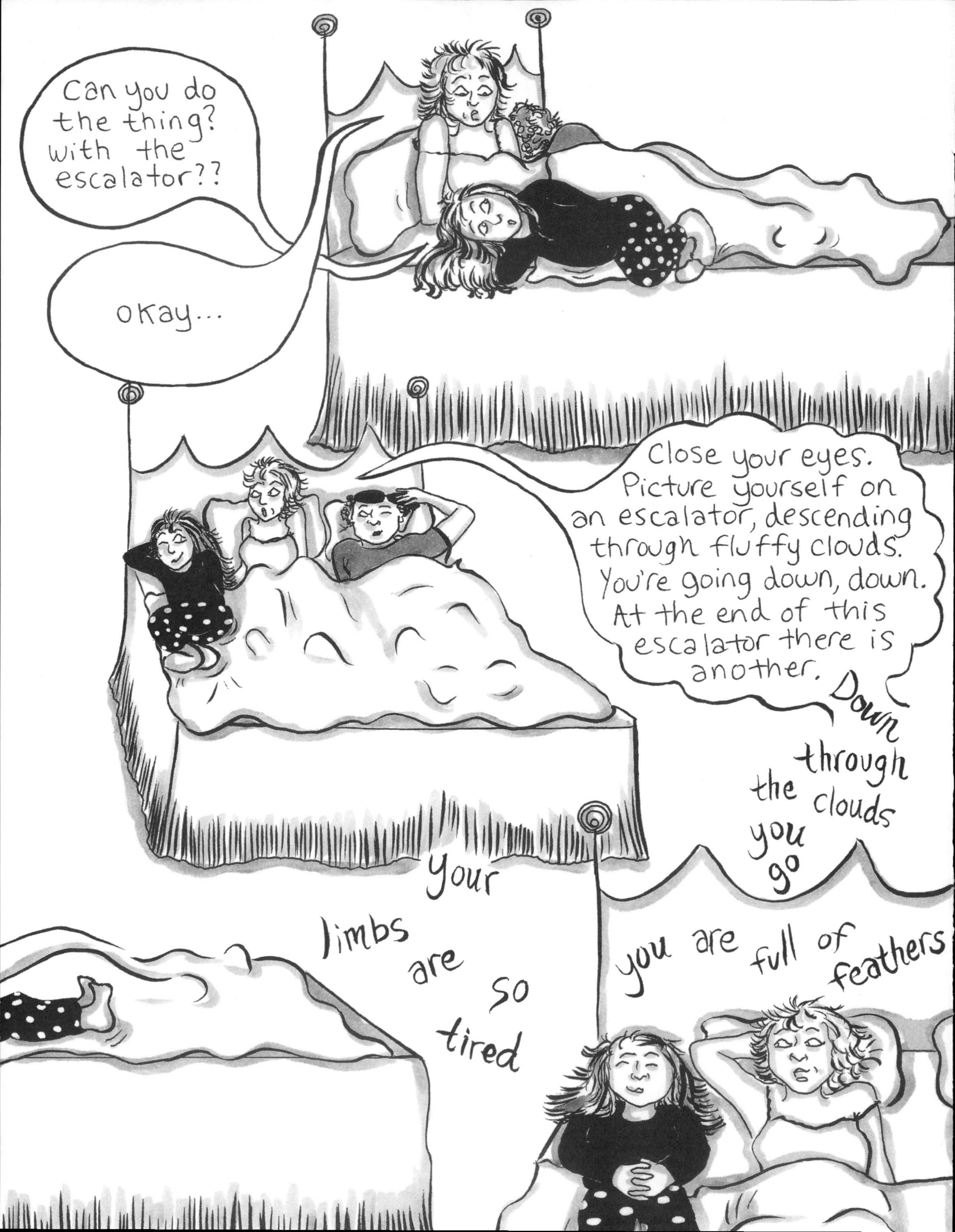
Can you do the thing? with the escalator??
okay...
Close your eyes. Picture yourself on an escalator, descending through fluffy clouds. You're going down, down. At the end of this escalator there is another.
Down through the clouds you go
Your limbs are so tired
you are full of feathers

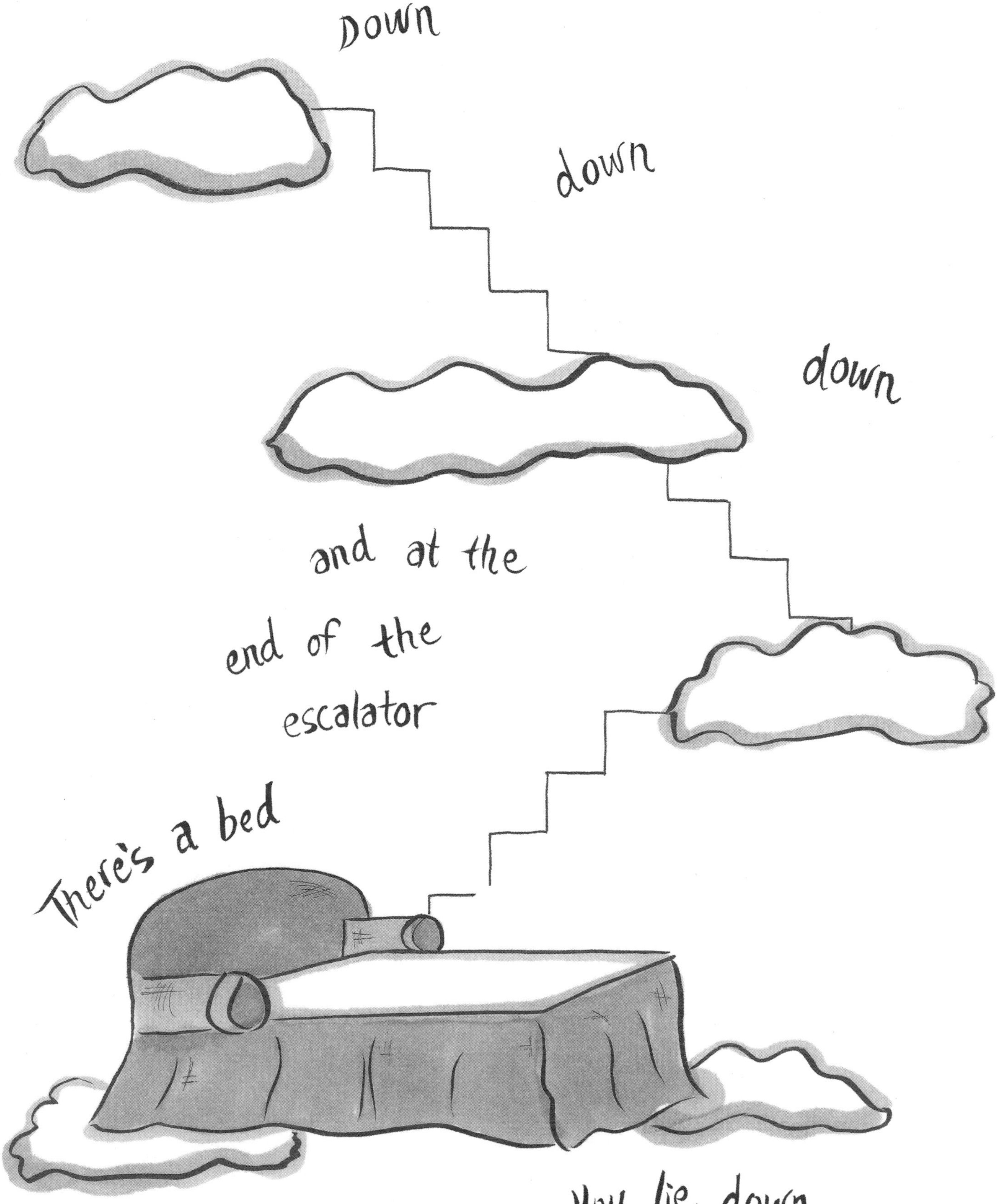
Down
down
down
and at the
end of the
escalator
There's a bed
You lie down

Bubbe heals and goes home, first to her condo, then back to Michigan. A Polish "helper" is engaged, but soon she's dismissed, and Bubbe is back to walking the streets on her own.

She's probably out walking right now.

DeKalb Avenue
B Q R

She does sell her big house, though, moves to a smaller place, easier to clean.

Court St Station
R

Enter ... r buy MetroCard at all ... r see agent at B... h Hall.

⟨pant⟩

I am moving again, too. My third Brooklyn apartment in three years.

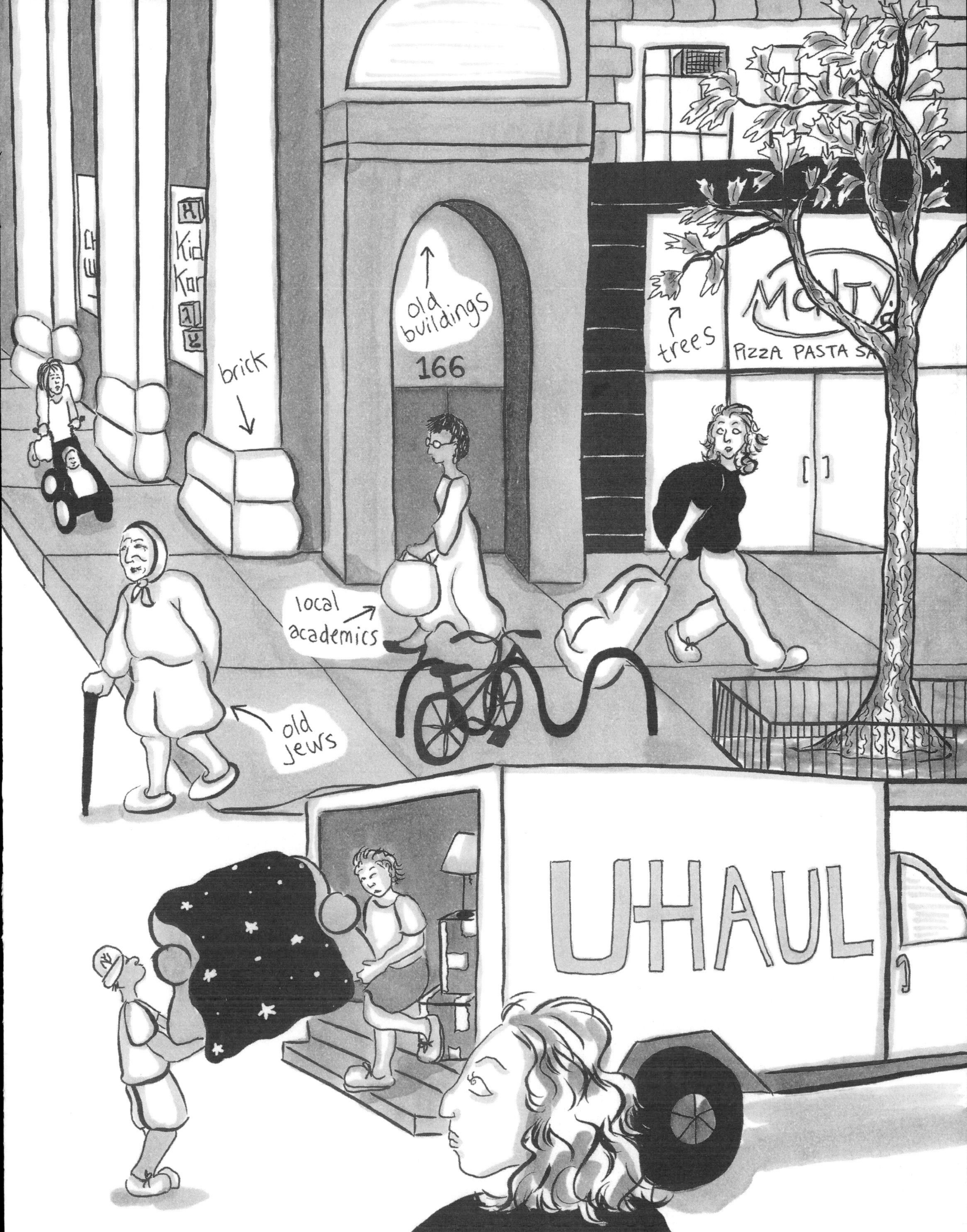
old buildings
166
brick
trees
local academics
old jews
UHAUL

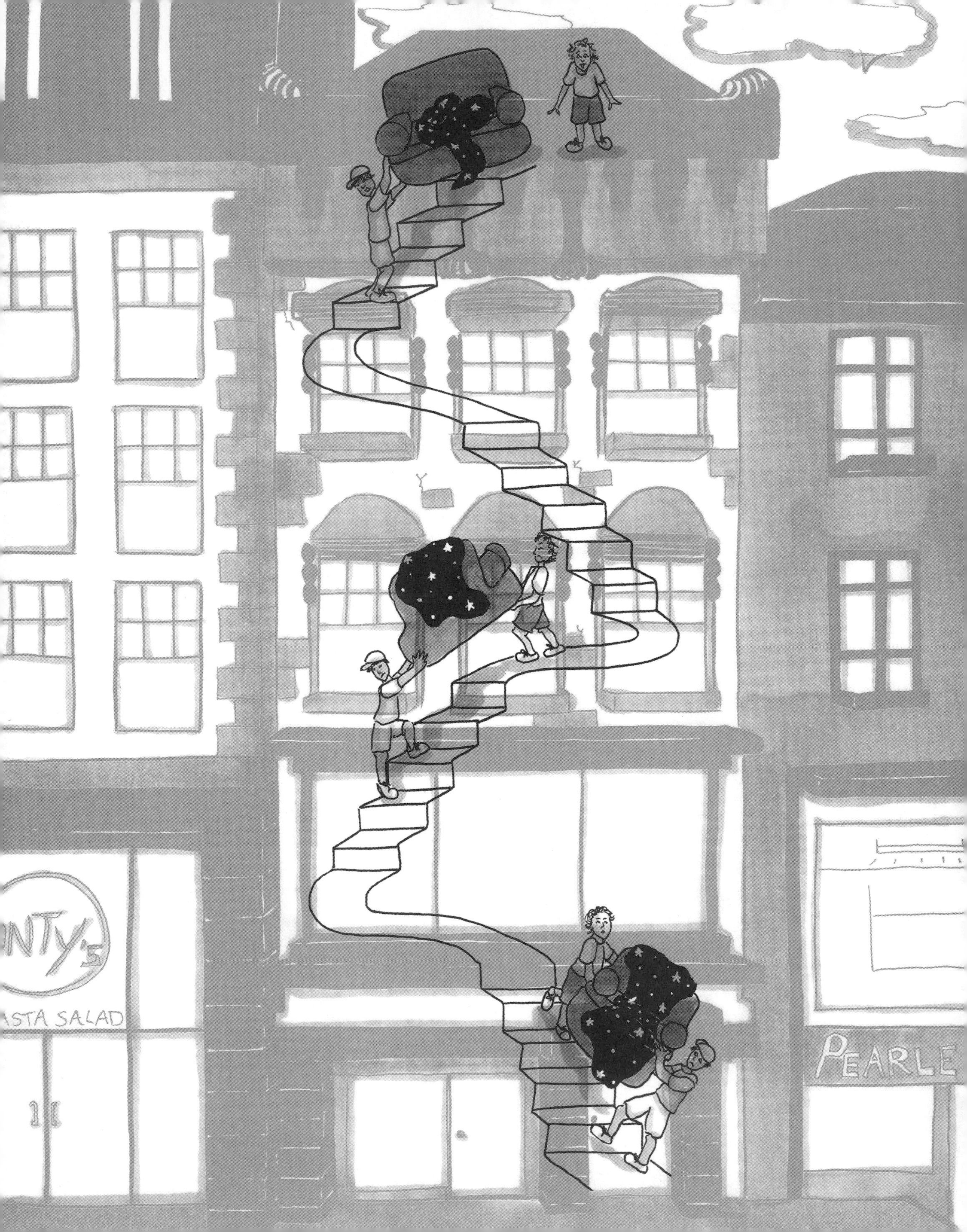
NTY'S
ASTA SALAD
PEARLE

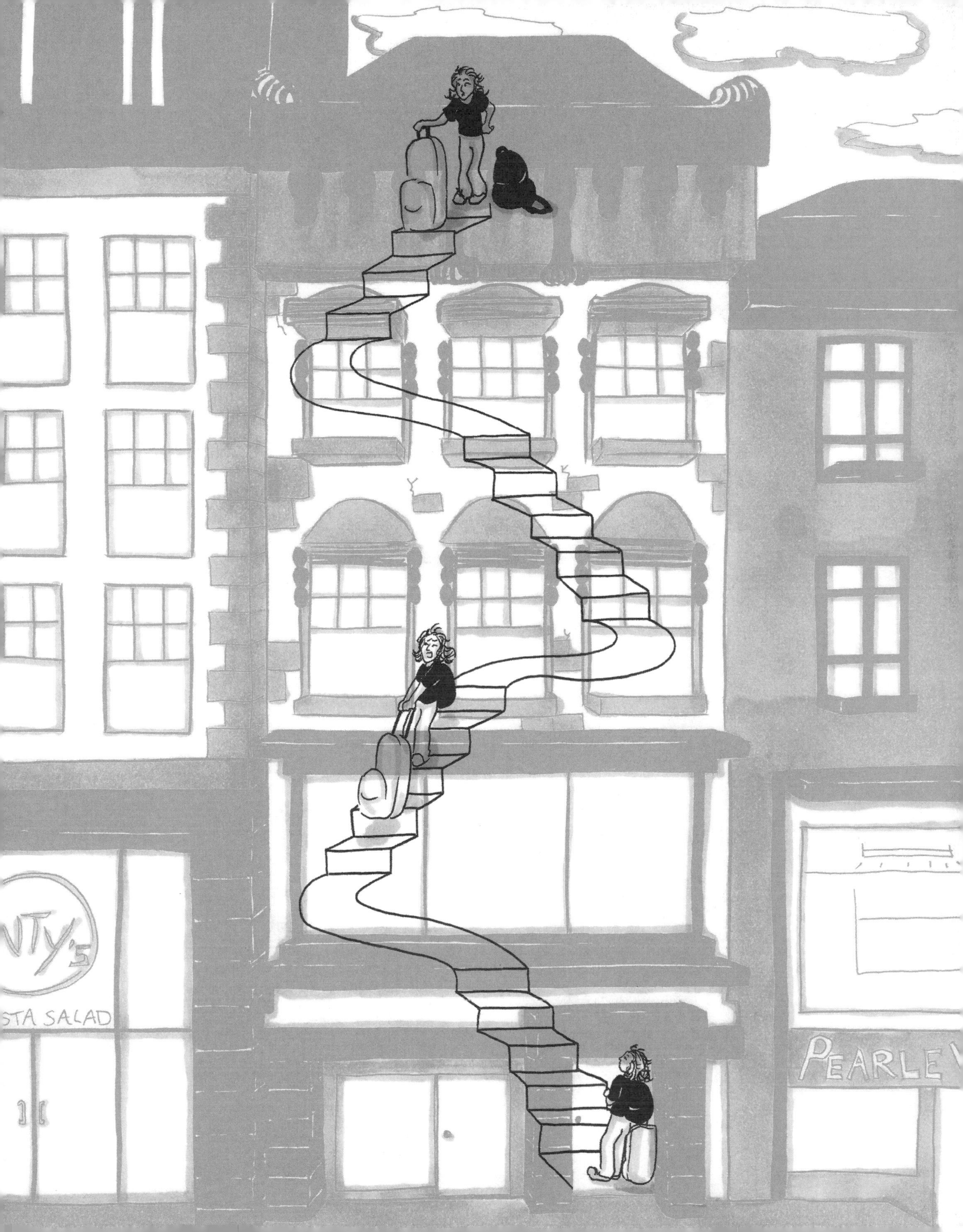
NTY'S
STA SALAD
PEARLE

I am acquiring stuff.

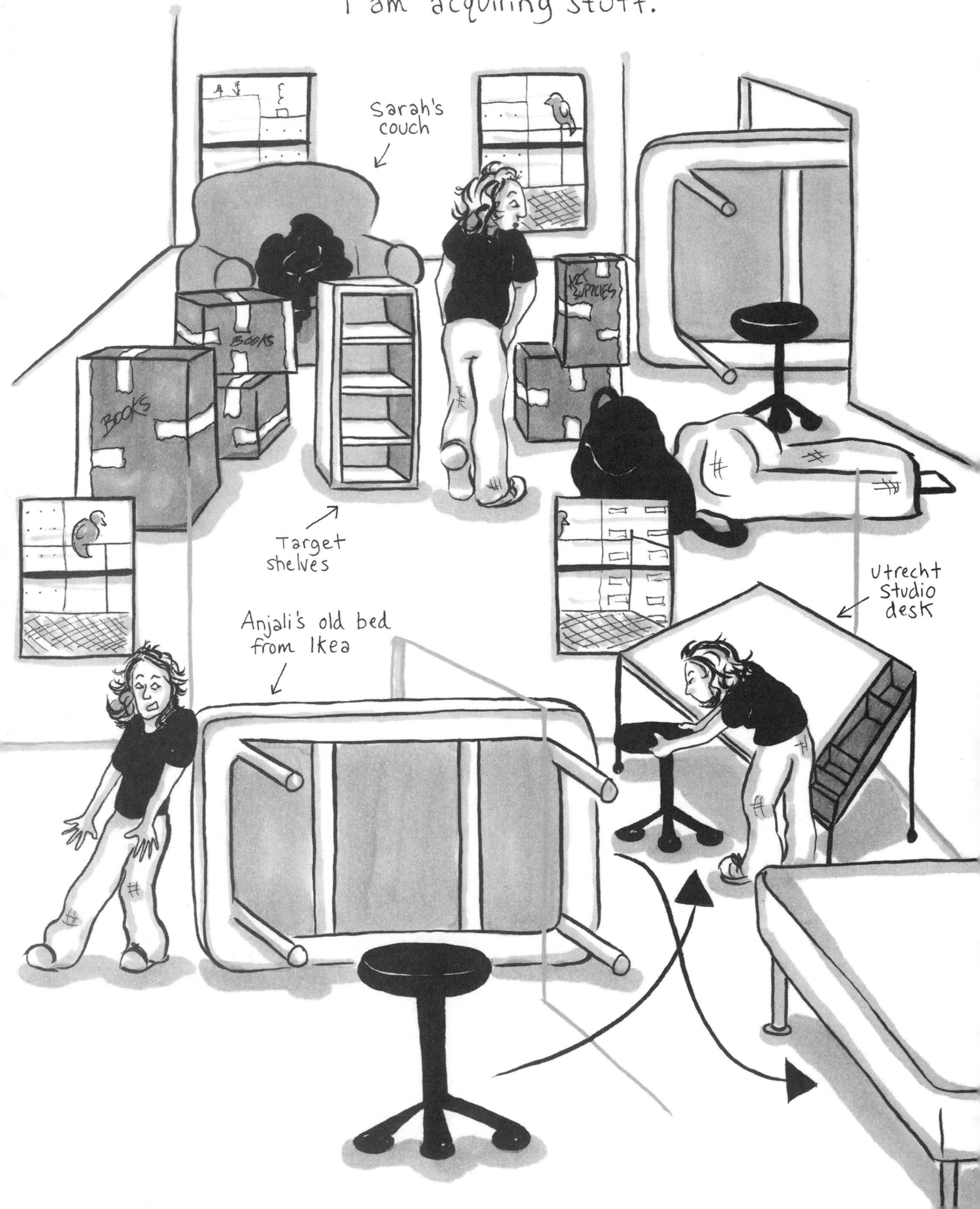
Sarah's couch
BOOKS
BOOKS
ART SUPPLIES
Target shelves
Utrecht studio desk
Anjali's old bed from Ikea

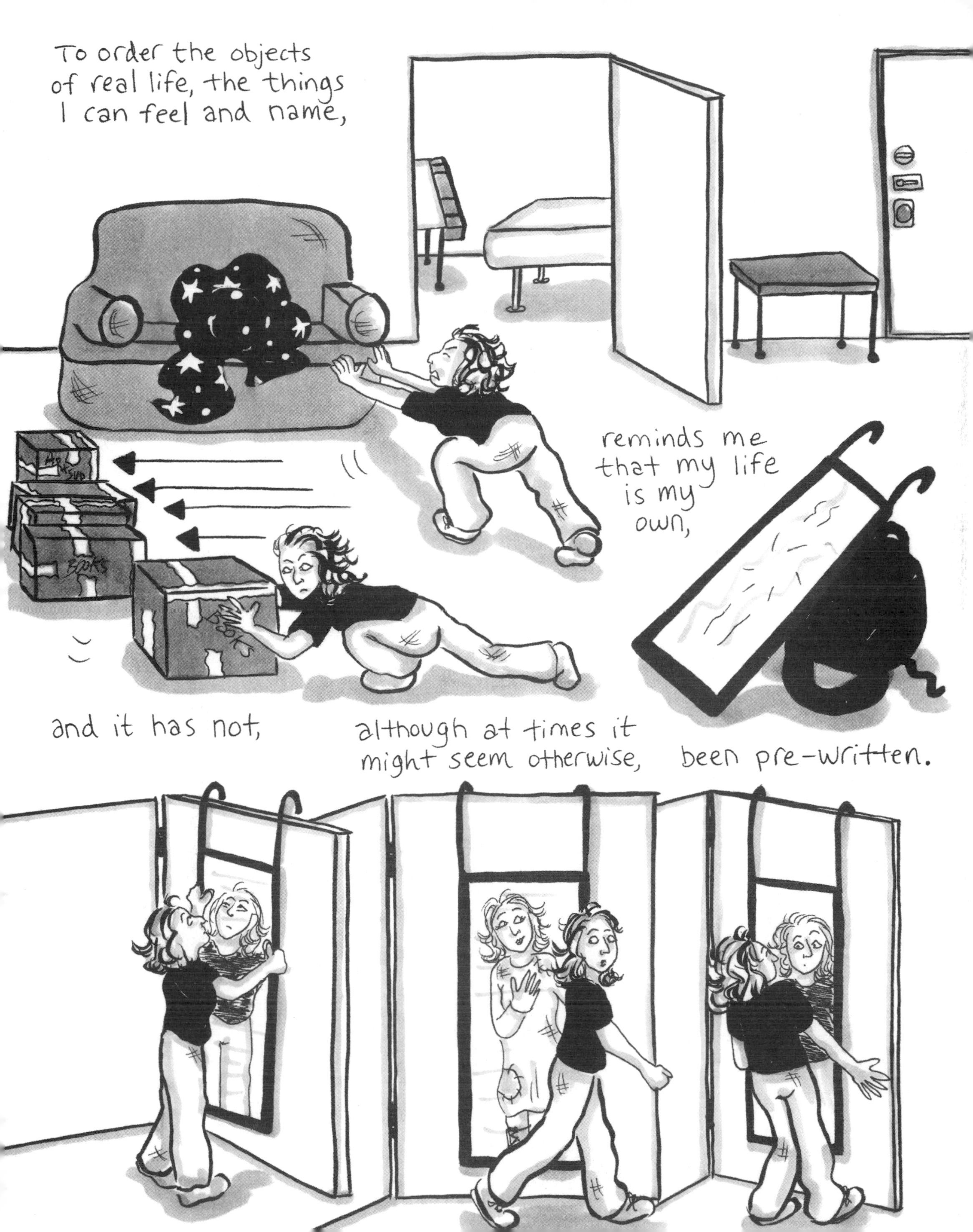
To order the objects of real life, the things I can feel and name,
reminds me that my life is my own,
and it has not,
although at times it might seem otherwise,
been pre-written.

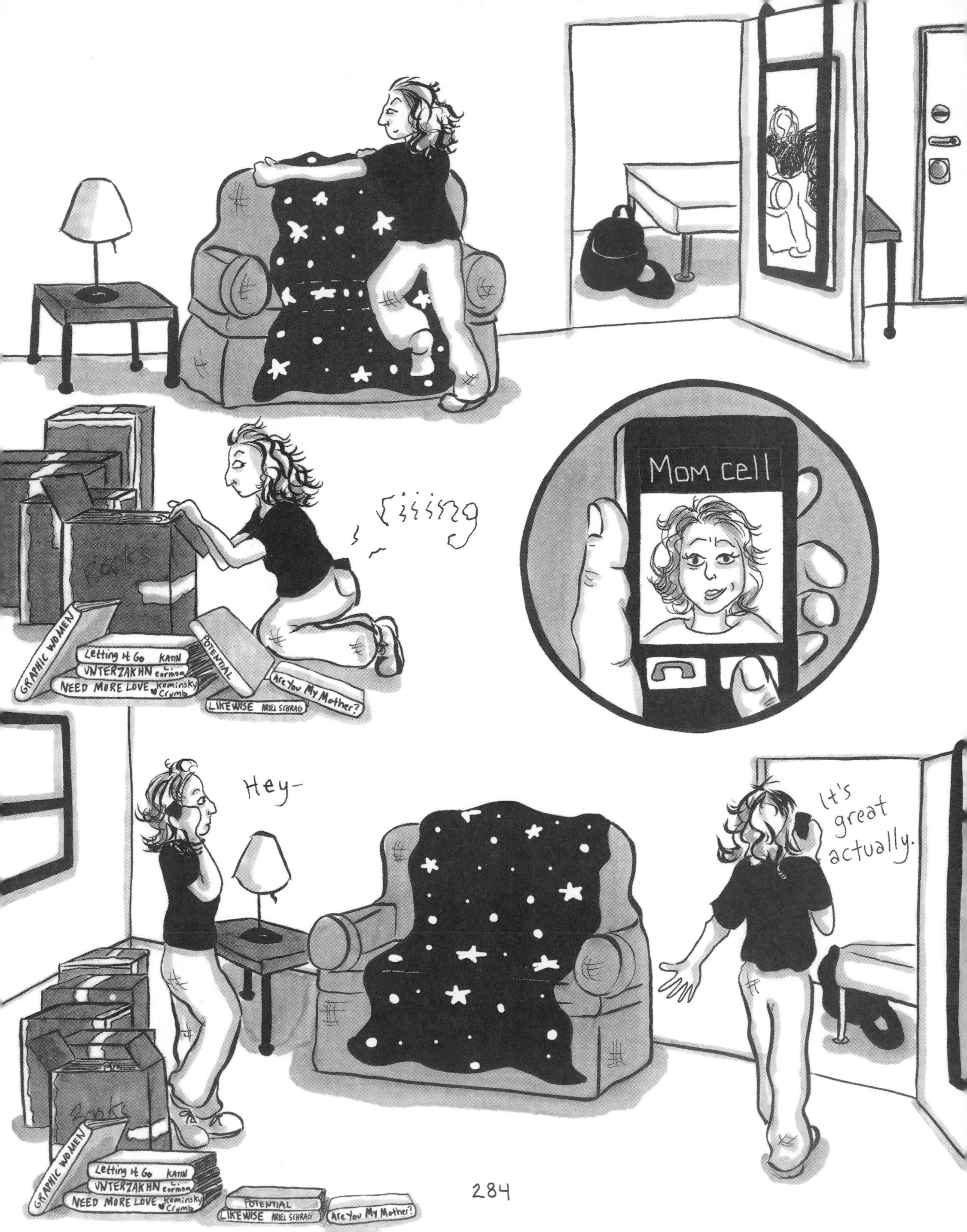
Books
GRAPHIC WOMEN
Letting It Go KATIN
UNTERZAKHN
NEED MORE LOVE Kominsky Crumb
POTENTIAL
Are You My Mother?
LIKEWISE ARIEL SCHRAG
Mom cell
Hey-
It's great actually.

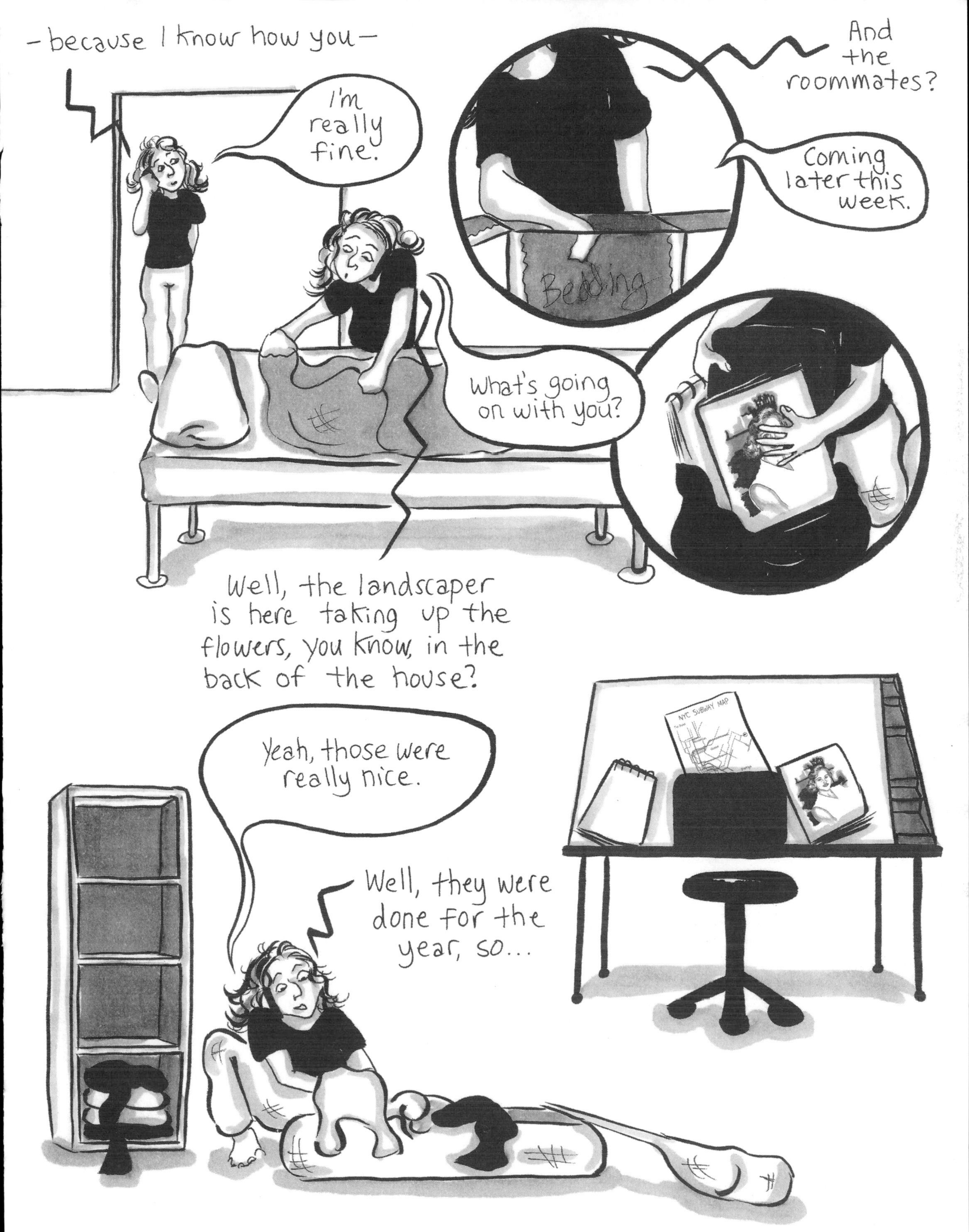
-because I know how you-
I'm really fine.
And the roommates?
Coming later this week.
Bedding
What's going on with you?
Well, the landscaper is here taking up the flowers, you know, in the back of the house?
Yeah, those were really nice.
Well, they were done for the year, so...
NYC SUBWAY MAP

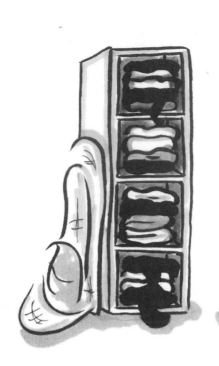

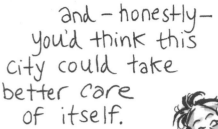

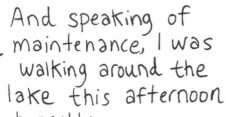
And speaking of maintenance, I was walking around the lake this afternoon and — honestly — you'd think this city could take better care of itself.

I mean, aesthetically — and for safety. The sidewalks are all cracked up, and the amount of potholes — it's just absurd. Plus all the off-leash dogs.

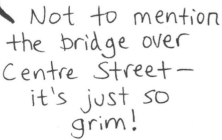

Not to mention the bridge over Centre Street — it's just so grim!

It's like I'm living in the Third World over here!

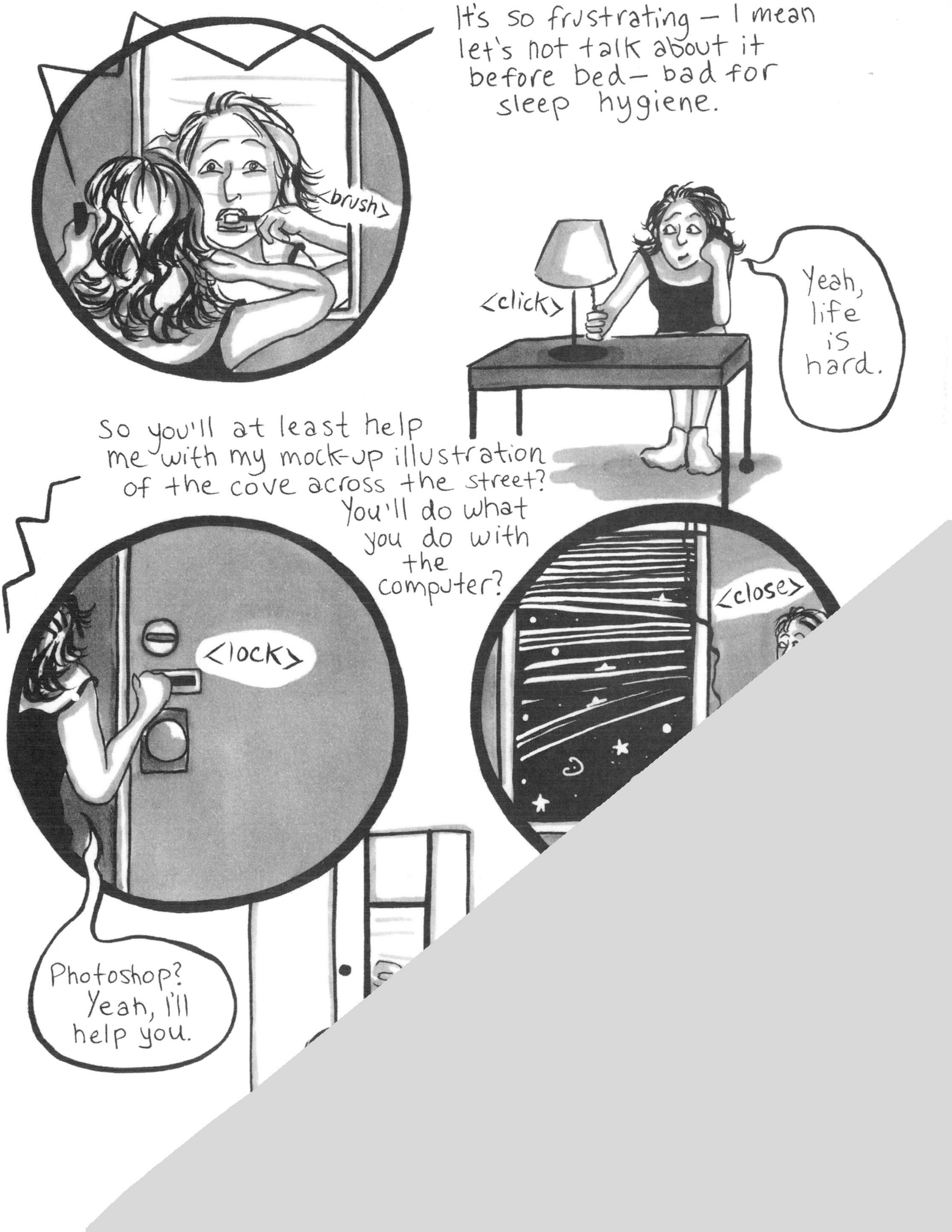
It's so frustrating — I mean let's not talk about it before bed — bad for sleep hygiene.
<brush>
<click>
Yeah, life is hard.
So you'll at least help me with my mock-up illustration of the cove across the street? You'll do what you do with the computer?
<lock>
<close>
Photoshop? Yeah, I'll help you.

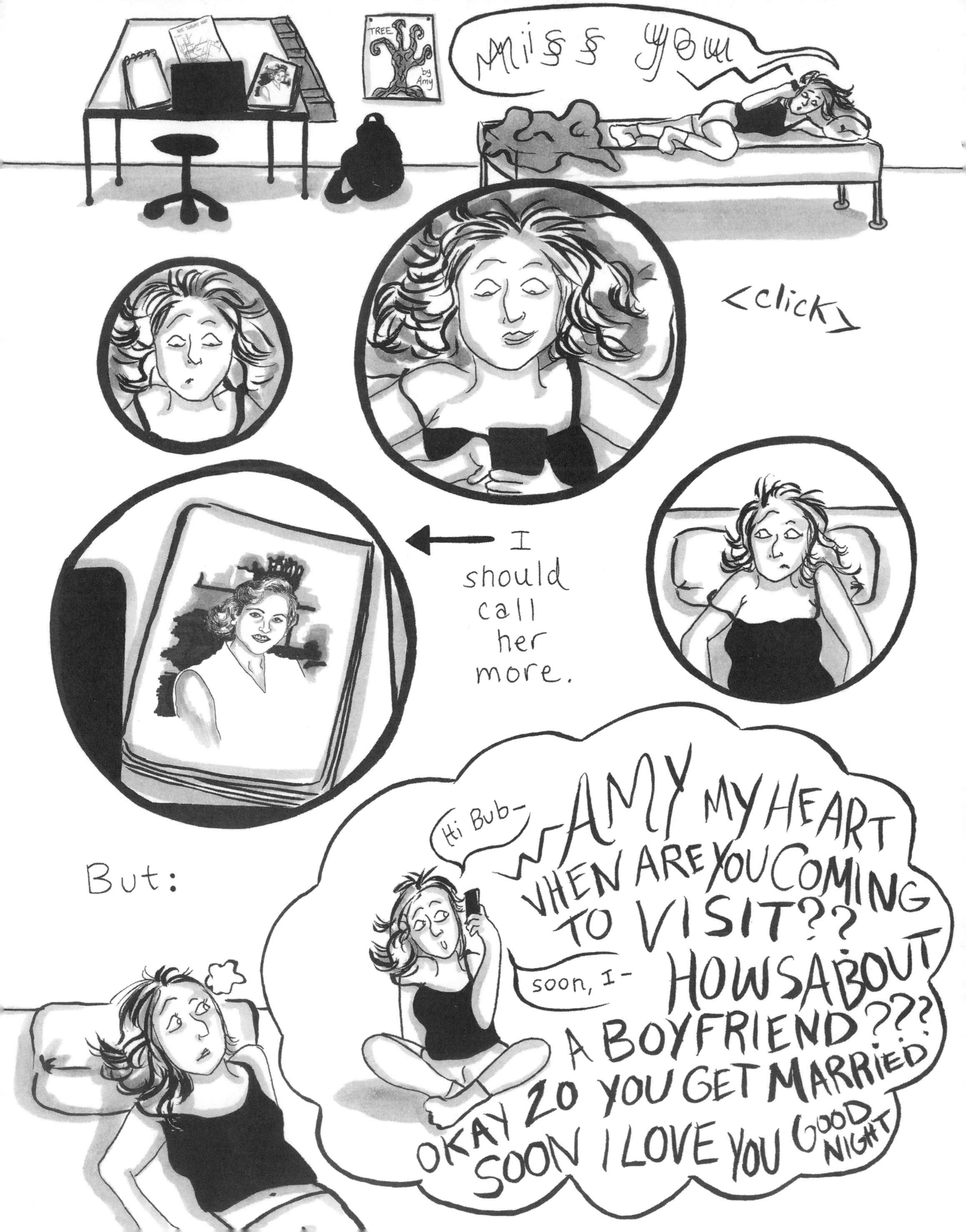
TREE by Amy
Miss you
<click>
I should call her more.
But:
Hi Bub-
AMY MY HEART WHEN ARE YOU COMING TO VISIT??
soon, I-
HOWSABOUT A BOYFRIEND???
OKAY ZO YOU GET MARRIED SOON I LOVE YOU GOOD NIGHT

Our relationship has never involved many words.

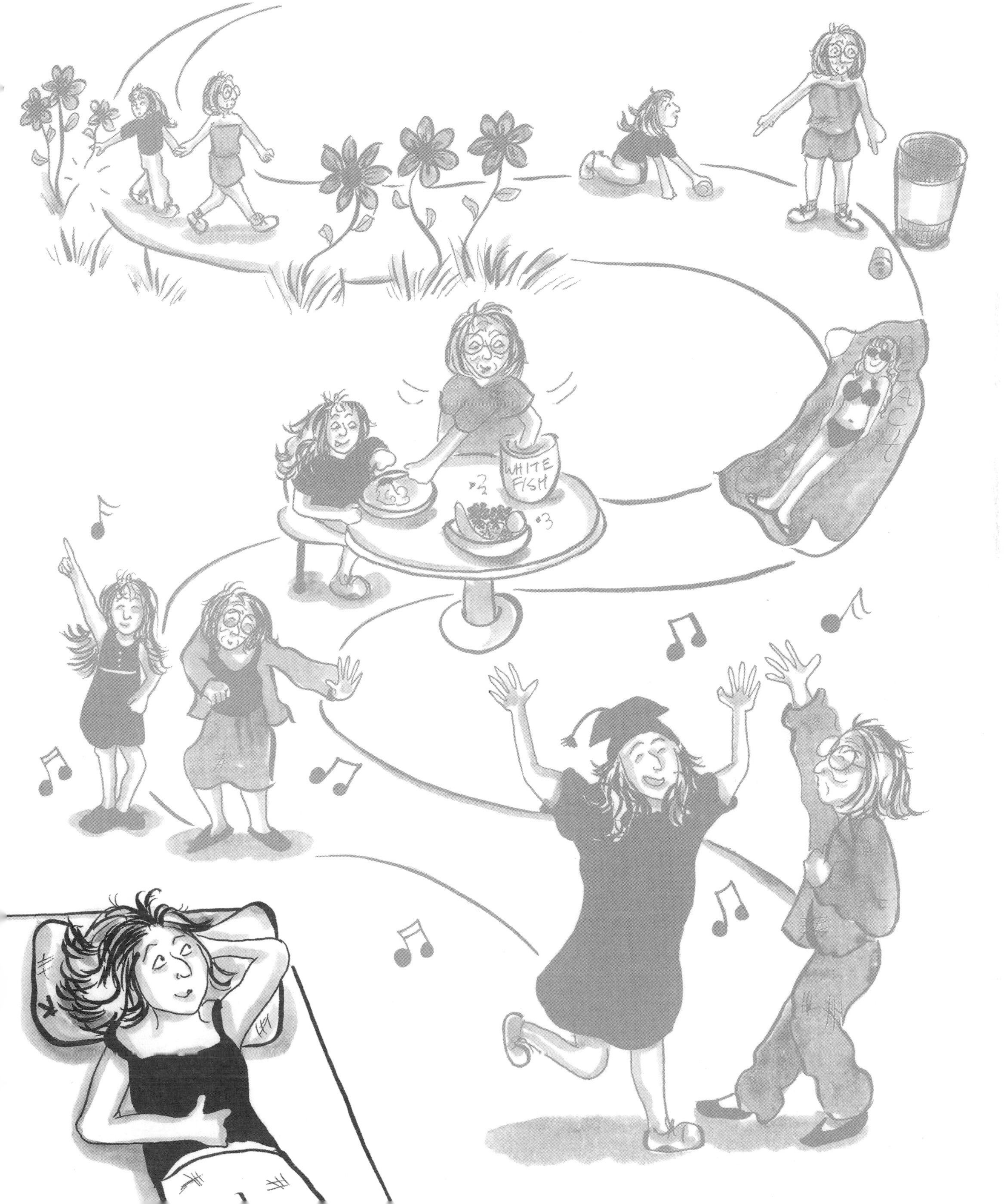
WHITE FISH
#2
#3

TREE by Amy
<click>

Mom?

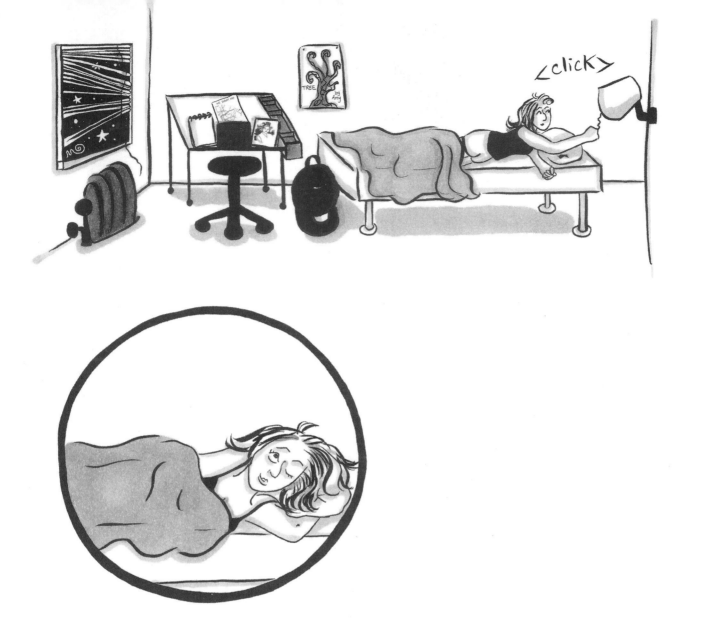

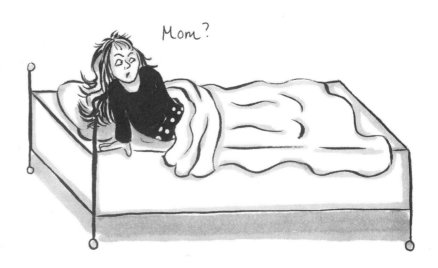

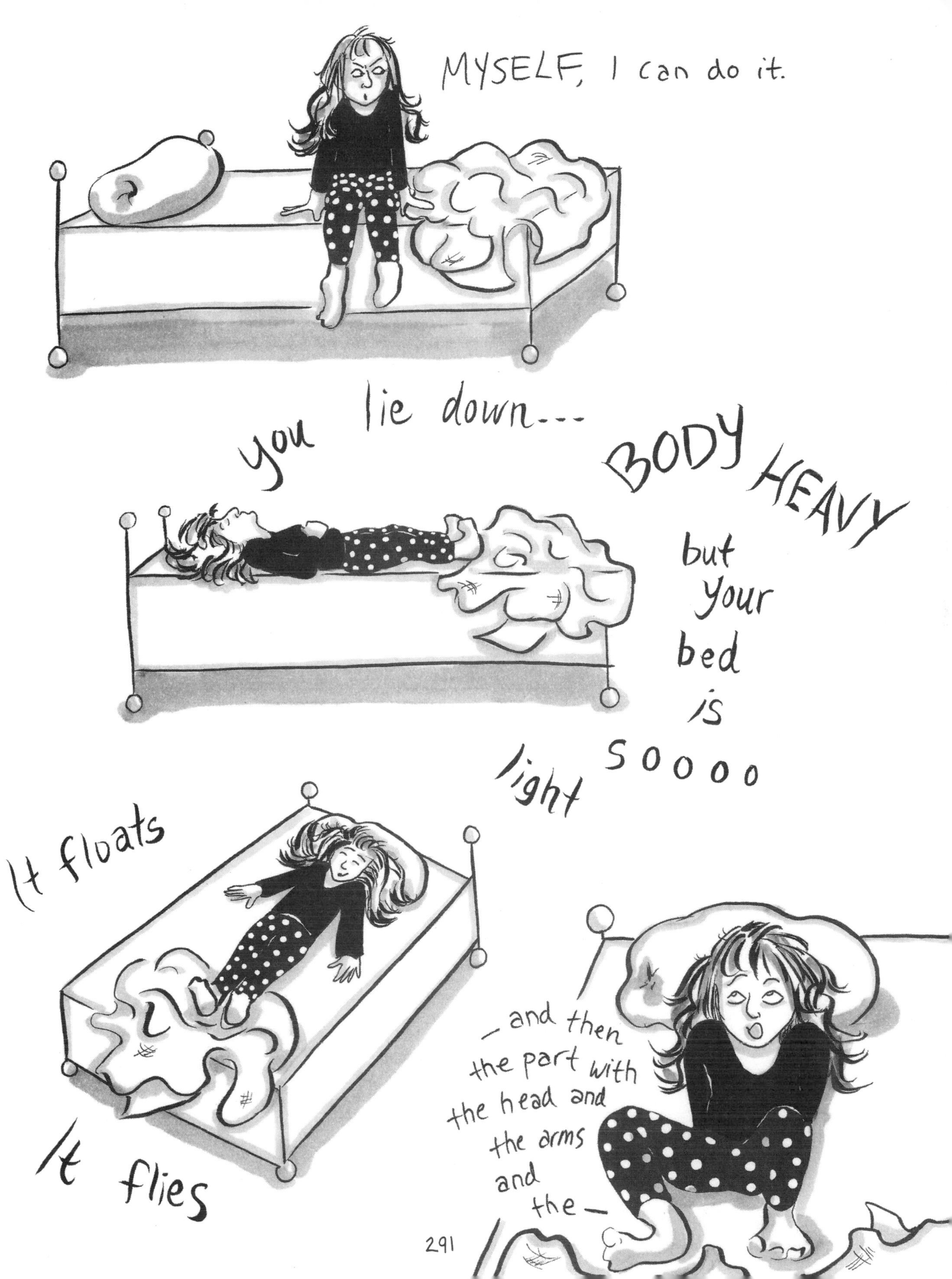
MYSELF, I can do it.
you lie down...
BODY HEAVY
but your bed is soooo light
It floats
It flies
– and then the part with the head and the arms and the –

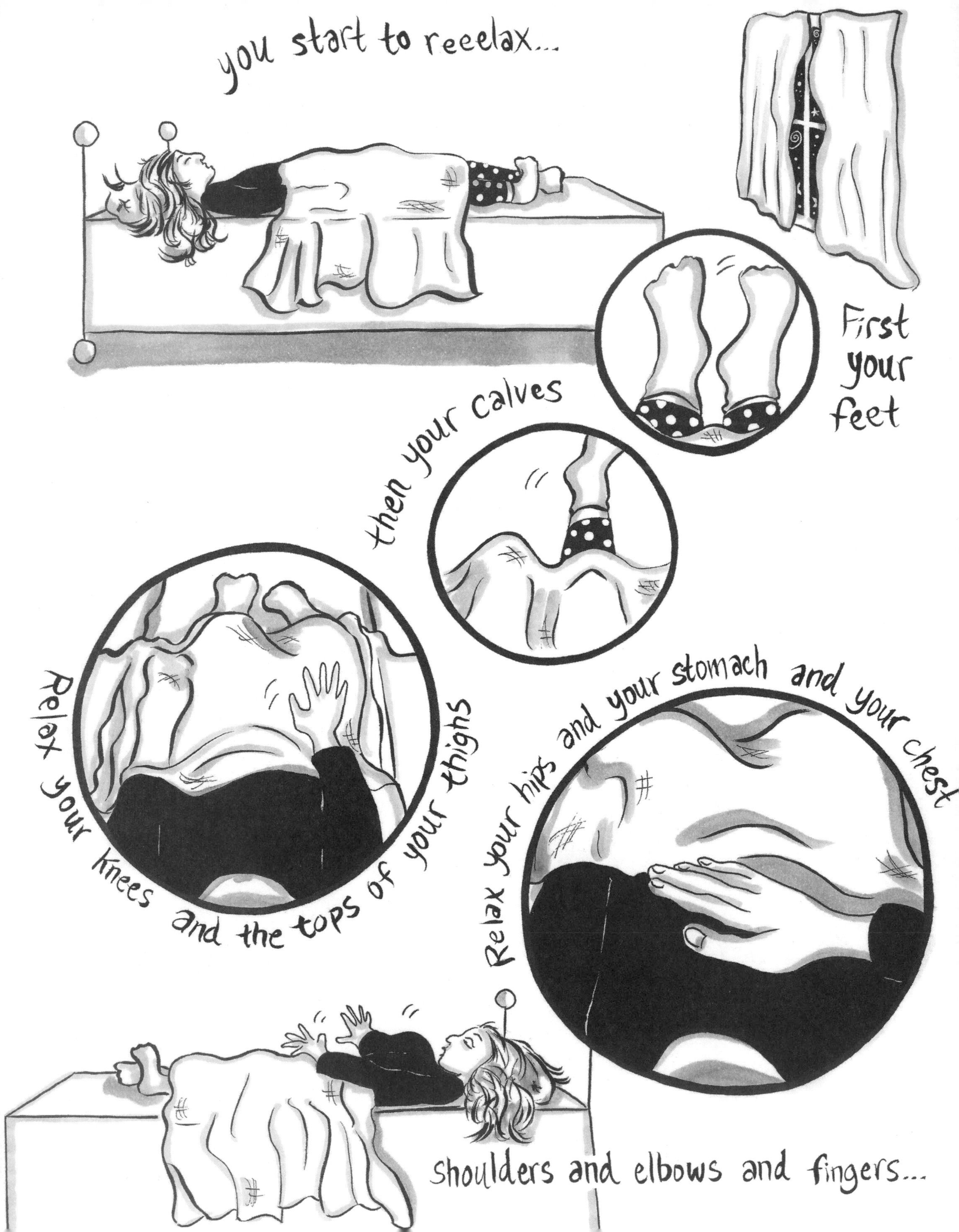

you start to reeelax...
First your feet
then your calves
Relax your knees and the tops of your thighs
Relax your hips and your stomach and your chest
shoulders and elbows and fingers...

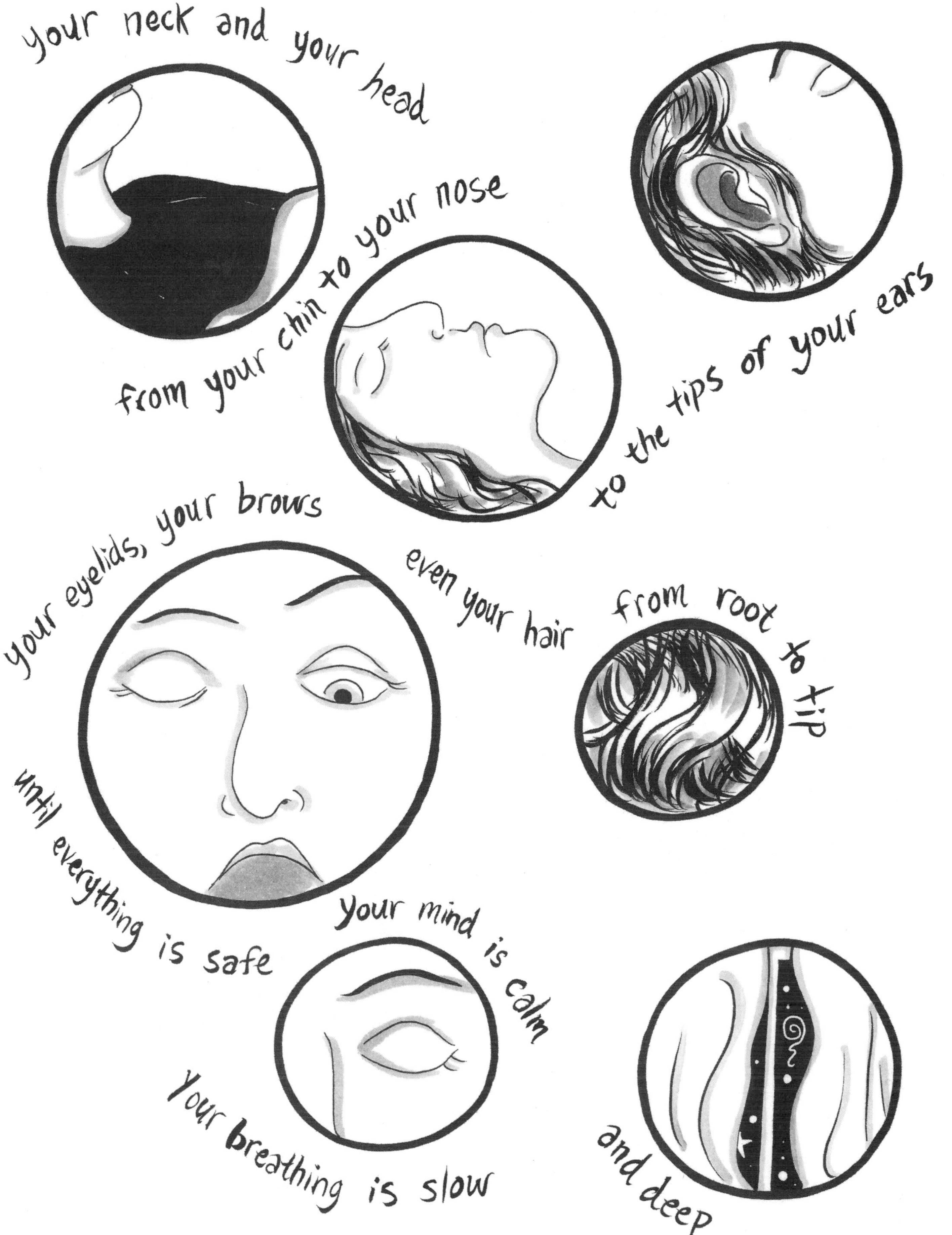
your neck and your head
from your chin to your nose
to the tips of your ears
your eyelids, your brows
even your hair
from root to tip
until everything is safe
your mind is calm
Your breathing is slow
and deep

Thank yous (because it takes a village to write a book)

to Julie Buntin, editor of my starry-eyed dreams

to Jenni Ferrari-Adler, who took a chance on something different

to Casey Gonzalez for her expert graphic eyes

to Charlotte Strick and Claire Williams for help with the perfect cover

to Alyson Sinclair and Jennifer Abel Kovitz for letting the world know

to the production team at Neuwirth, especially Molly

to Elizabeth, Andy, Pat, Leigh and everyone at Catapult/Black Balloon
There's no group I'd rather have launch my couch and keep it afloat

Thank you to The New School Writing Program
for turning me into a real writer

to Ariel Schrag, who is smart and kind

to the members of The Crazy Table →
because every party is better by their sides.

BECCA
ELISHA
SARAH
EMILY
KATIE

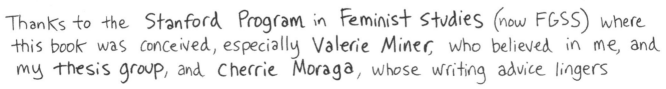

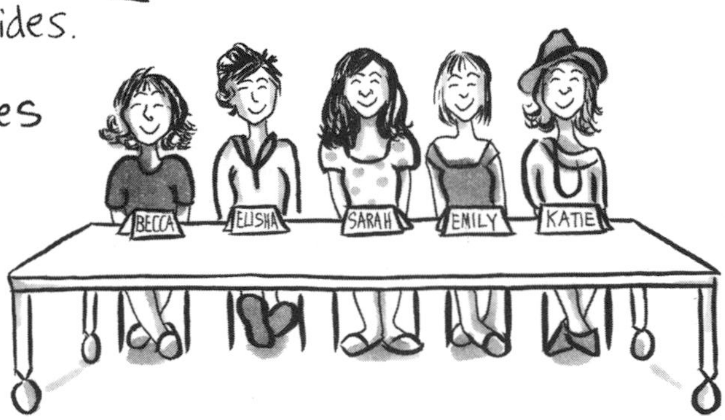

to writing peers down the street, like Andres
and others far, like Hannah, Gregg, JT

to my teachers:
Jeff, Tiphanie, Helen, Jackson,
Bob, Shelley and Honor

Thanks drDOCTOR!

Thanks to the Stanford Program in Feminist Studies (now FGSS) where this book was conceived, especially Valerie Miner, who believed in me, and my thesis group, and Cherrie Moraga, whose writing advice lingers

to many Stanford University affiliated individuals and funds whose investment helped this project find its way

A special thank you to the late Sidney Bolkosky and the Voice/Vision Holocaust Survivor Oral History Archive

Thanks Birthright and Temple Shalom of Newton

Thanks to Michelle Andelman and the late, great Loretta Barrett for their belief in the earliest couch

to Bienfang gridded paper, Pentel brush pen, Copic multiliner .2 (with refillable ink and nib!) and marker toner grey no. 3, Hp Photosmart 5520, Wacom intuos tablet, and MacBook Pro (so glad I switched!)

to the authors of my favorite comics for inspiring me to write with pictures: Art Spiegelman, Marjane Satrapi, Alison Bechdel, Craig Thompson, Chris Ware, Lynda Barry and others

to all my friends, especially my many roommates

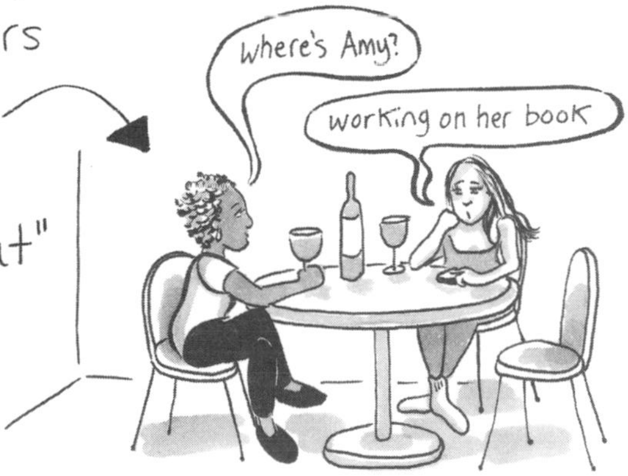
Where's Amy?
working on her book

to Jacob, who reminds me "what it's all about"

to my family

to all the Fensters for letting our history be my inspiration and our family in Israel

Thanks Ethan for your sense of humor and Rebecca for writer talks (and to you both for birthing more Kurzweils)

Thanks Dad for your faith in me, your eternal optimism I owe you more than I can ever repay

Thanks Bubbe for your whole miraculous life, for your voice, which fills us all with joy and gratitude

Thank you Mom for teaching me never to rest until it's right, for your insights, your support, for guiding me toward beauty and grace

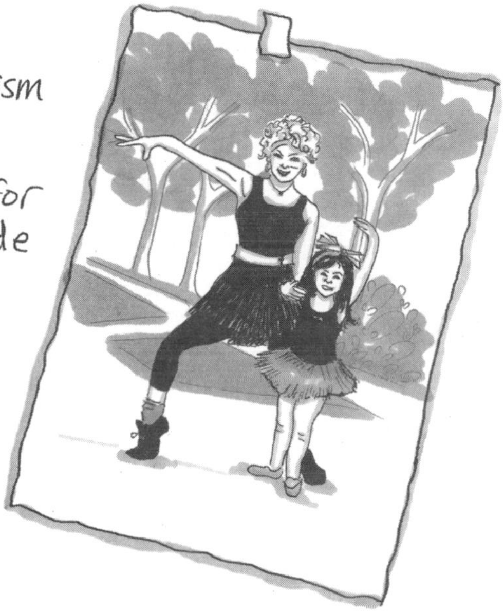

ABOUT THE AUTHOR

Amy Kurzweil's comics appear in *The New Yorker* and other publications. Her series *GutterFACE* is hosted by the literary webcast drDOCTOR, and her short stories have appeared in *The Toast*, *Washington Square Review*, *Hobart*, *Shenandoah*, and elsewhere. She teaches writing and comics at Parsons School of Design and at the Fashion Institute of Technology. Amy lives in Brooklyn.